THE HISTORY
OF THOROUGHBRED RACING
IN AMERICA

THE HISTORY
OF THOROUGHBRED RACING
IN AMERICA

WILLIAM H. P. ROBERTSON

BONANZA BOOKS • NEW YORK

This edition published by Bonanza Books,
a division of Crown Publishers, Inc.
by arrangement with Prentice-Hall, Inc.
c d e f g h

to
Arden, Caroline, Zip and Winter,
Jack
and
Haden

FOREWORD

ORSE RACING HAS GROWN AStoundingly in scope and in popularity since the early settlers brought to these shores a native love for such contests of speed and stamina, and so permanently injected it into our way of life that today racing is America's number one spectator sport. Modern racing is a highly organized, thoroughly controlled and jealously guarded industry of coast-tocoast proportions, and an integral part of the revenue-producing machinery of more than half the United States.

To those of us who have been intimately associated with the thoroughbred horse and have witnessed his exciting exploits on the track and through the field, it is readily understandable why this wonderful and most graceful of animals, with his superb physique, speed and courage, has captured the admiration and affection of sports lovers the world over. Like all sports fans, racing enthusiasts wish to learn as much as possible regarding the personalities, habits and backgrounds of their favorites, and to read accounts of their thrilling exploits in competition. To satisfy this desire for information there has been enough written about horses, owners, trainers, jockeys, handlers and races to provide a great portion of today's sports literature.

Fortunately for those who enjoy such information, the author of this history has provided a veritable treasury of stirring, informative and authoritative facts concerning prominent persons, horses and contests that have illuminated American racing. Mr. Robertson's book pictures racing from its pioneer days in this country, when the gentry matched the speed and endurance of their stock across fields, over obstacles or along the streets of sparsely settled villages, through the trying times of several conflicts and the reconstruction days that followed, on to the revival of a dying sport that brought about an entirely new concept of racing, under rules and regulations which have endured to the present.

The author takes us again to colorful and exciting contests, which he describes in absorbing, factual detail enlivened by amusing anecdotes which help us visualize the settings more clearly.

Readers of these pages are brought into contact with many of the great thoroughbreds of American history as well as with historic personages—grantees of Colonial charters, presidents of the United States and others—who, at one time or another, have been identified with racing. We also meet the more modern giants of the sport whose wisdom and foresight placed racing on such a solid foundation that it has been able to withstand the onslaughts of reformers and oppressive legislation.

After reading this comprehensive and absorbing History of American Racing, one experiences a deep sense of pride in having been privileged to participate, even so remotely, in a great sport that can boast among its devotees such distinguished Americans as William Penn, George Washington, Andrew Jackson and a host of other eminent patrons whose interest in the thoroughbred horse has been such that they gave of their time, effort and fortune to racing, so that it may be enjoyed by the American public.

JAMES E. FITZSIMMONS

INTRODUCTION

THE PROBLEM IN THIS BOOK was not of gathering material, which was all too plentiful, but rather the sifting of the enormous quantity available and deciding what to retain.

Any horse is worth a story, and so are a lot of people. There are literally hundreds of horses and men who played such important and interesting roles on the American turf that each of them could well be the subject of an entire volume, and a number of them have been. Hence, to include mention of every horse, man, race and race track worthy of note is impossible without resorting to what would be at best a giant statistical digest, which, however useful it might be for occasional reference, would be sticky going from the standpoint of readability.

Therefore, it has not been possible to give every player his proper moment upon the stage, and apologies hereby are rendered to those who have been omitted. Rather, in an effort to capture the over-all flavor of this popular sport, certain selected episodes and individuals are dealt with in sufficient detail to provide, it is hoped, an adequate picture not only of the specific subjects, but also of the general era and setting in question.

The selection of these featured performers and performances is arbitrary throughout, and artificial as well so far as the period before the Civil War is concerned. Documentary records of early American racing consist mainly of contemporary accounts (which are sparse), and of subsequent memoirs (which are copious).

As to contemporary accounts, newspapers were relatively late arrivals on the scene: the *Boston News Letter* was first published in 1704, the *New York Gazette* in 1725, the *Maryland Gazette* in 1728, the *Pennsylvania Gazette* in 1729, the *South Carolina Gazette* in 1732, the *Virginia Gazette* in 1736 and the *North Carolina Gazette* in 1755; moreover, there was an eleven-year hiatus in the publication of the Maryland paper as its editor, William Parks, abandoned it to found the Virginia sheet. When they finally did come into being, space was at such a premium and typesetting so laborious that descriptions were kept as brief as possible. This was particularly true of local events, such as races, which virtually everyone was assumed to have seen anyway.

As to memoirs, many of them have something of a George-Washington-slept-here flavor, which a cynical reader might criticize as rendering them less than 100 percent objective; it must be remembered that a person who keeps a diary is not apt to minimize his own significance or that of events with which he personally has been connected. However, in justice to these early chroniclers it should be pointed out that their lives were so circumscribed, and communications so limited, that the instance of several "greatest horses" and "greatest races" appearing on the scene virtually simultaneously is easily explained. With few exceptions, racing in each area was an activity unto itself, and had a history of its own. The Virginian who saw a horse race as far away as Maryland was a rarity, and very few persons' experience included racing throughout the colonies.

The history of American racing might be compared, very roughly, to an hourglass. For a time, it was spread throughout the nation, such as it was; then, there was a period during which the sport was concentrated into a relatively small portion of the country, after which it proliferated again until at the time of writing it is scattered among twenty-five states.

The stem of this hourglass, through which the main stream has continued to flow, has been the area along the northeastern Atlantic seaboard, especially New York—the so-called Big Apple—and for this reason there will be, geographically speaking, perhaps disproportionately frequent reference to New York, but the fact remains that, over the years, a remarkable number of famous horses have run for important prizes in the Empire State.

ACKNOWLEDGMENTS

So wide is the scope of American racing that no one observer can speak with the authority of personal observation on the subject as a whole. Grateful acknowledgment is made to the numerous horsemen who patiently have recounted their own experiences to the author, to tracks whose films provide fresh views of bygone races, and to artists who painted those pictures worth more than a thousand words in description of their particular periods. Most especially, acknowledgment is made to the publications listed below which are the sources of quotations and general material contained herein.

BOOKS

Racing in America, the monumental series published in five volumes by the Jockey Club, and written by John L. Hervey, Walter S. Vosburgh and Robert F. Kelley, in particular the first two volumes by Hervey, was the backbone from which the structure of this history was developed for the period prior to, and some years after, the Civil War.

The American Racing Manual, an annual series published by Triangle Publications, Inc., was the source of statistical data relating to the twentieth century, and was of inestimable value in establishment of a chronological outline of noteworthy events. Official charts compiled by the same publisher's *Daily Racing Form* also were relied upon heavily.

Other books used as references included *Across the Board,* by Tony Betts; *American Race Horses,* an annual series published originally by Sagamore Press and more recently by the American Thoroughbred Owners and Breeders Association; *American Stud Book; American Turf Register; Catalogues* of Elmendorf, Hamburg Place, Idle Hour Farm, Nursery Stud, Rancocas Stud, Rancho del Paso and H. P. Whitney; *Cherry and Black,* by Vosburgh; *Famous Running Horses,* by Colonel John F. Wall; *From Here to the Bugle,* by Frank Jennings; *Giants of the Turf,* by Dan M. Bowmar III; *Goodwin's Official Turf Guide; Krik's Guide to the Turf;* the *Life and Times of Sir Archie,* by Elizabeth Blanchard and Manly Wellman; *Matriarchy of the American Turf,* by Roger L. Gerry; *Spell of the Turf,* by Samuel C. Hildreth and James R. Crowell; *Sport's Golden Age,* selections from several authors, published by Harper and Brothers; *Tales of the Turf,* by Horace Wade; *This Was Racing,* by Joe H. Palmer; *Thoroughbred Racing and Breeding,* published by the Thoroughbred Racing Associations of the United States, Inc.; and *Tod Sloan,* by Himself.

PERIODICALS

The files of *The Thoroughbred Record* have provided the bulk of source material for the period since 1875, and grateful acknowledgment is made to all members of the staff for their assistance and co-operation.

For descriptions of races in the nineteenth century, the author also is indebted to the *Spirit of the Times,* and such other periodicals no longer in existence as *Breeders' Gazette, The Horseman, New York Sportsman, Turf Field and Farm* and *Wallace's Monthly.* References used in connection with modern racing included the *Blood-Horse, The Maryland Horse, The Thoroughbred of California* and *Turf and Sport Digest,* the news bulletins of Lanny Leighninger and notes from Hy Schneider.

OTHER

Gratitude also is expressed for the assistance rendered by Amelia Buckley of the Keeneland Association Library, the staff of the National Museum of Racing, Frances Kane, Mary Jane Gallaher, Arnold Kirkpatrick; Leon Rasmussen, Dick Nash and other of the *Record* correspondents, and the numerous others who have made the going easier.

THE HISTORY
OF THOROUGHBRED RACING
IN AMERICA

PART ONE

COLONIAL DAYS

CHAPTER ONE

IT IS CUSTOMARY AT THE OUTset of an historical treatise to remark upon the startling changes, giant strides and great progress that have taken place over the years. In the case of racing, this evolution has not occurred. An original colonist who happened to have gone Rip Van Winkle one better, and slept for 300 years, undoubtedly would be mystified by the various mechanical gadgets and elaborate procedures should he by chance awaken at a modern American race track, but so far as the basic activity is concerned, he would catch on right away: the horse which gets there first is the winner.

Unlike such other popular sports as baseball and football, which might have been based on similar English games, but today are so essentially American in character as to be indigenous, racing in its pure concept has undergone no such changes. And, it was here to begin with. Whenever two or more men with horses have gathered together, sooner or later there has been the desire to test these horses' speed. It pre-dates the origin of America, or for that matter the origin of recorded history of any country.

Geographically, the center of gravity of American racing has changed only a few miles. Richard Nicolls, who in 1664 received the surrender of New Amsterdam from its Dutch governor, Peter Stuyvesant, became the first governor of the colony under its new name of New York. Less than a year after Nicolls assumed command he laid out what is generally conceded to be America's first formal race course. This track was located on Long Island upon what was then called Salisbury Plain, but later was known as Hempstead Plain, in what is now Nassau County. The site of this first American race course is quite near today's modern symbol of American racing: Aqueduct, the "Big A." In between these two historic centers of the old and the new in American racing, there was the Union Course, which opened in 1821, also on Long Island, just west of Jamaica.

Of course, there were horse races in America long before Governor Nicolls arrived, but these races were of a spontaneous, informal variety. As early as 1610, the London Company, which under a charter from King James I had established the first colony at Jamestown only three years earlier, sent over seven horses. They did not last long, since a terrible famine the following winter caused them to be killed and eaten by the colonists, but replacements followed shortly thereafter (there is on record a shipment of twenty mares "beautiful and full of courage" in 1620) and racing, at least of a sort, was on its way.

These races differed drastically from the sport in England, and as it was later to be conducted on Long Island, for very practical reasons. America in those times was what Longfellow described as the forest primeval. Land was cleared of the dense undergrowth only at terrific expense and back-breaking labor, and as the specter of famine was ever present, every inch of available land was urgently needed for agriculture. To set aside land for the sole purpose of sport was an intolerable thought. As a result, racing took place on whatever short paths in whatever small areas were available.

It was inevitable, as well as logical, that the colonies adopt the obvious expedient. They took to racing down the streets of the settlements. Although it is said that every member of the first King's Council which governed Virginia either had owned or bred race horses at home in England before coming to America, one of the council's first acts was to pass a statute forbidding racing in the streets (the lot of the pedestrian has ever been a hard one). Even among the Pilgrims who landed at Plymouth Rock in 1620, there is circumstantial evidence that horse racing was in vogue. A Plymouth decree of 1674 states that "whatever person shall run a race with a horse kind in any street or common road shall forfeit five shillings in money forthwith to be levied by the Constable or sit in the stocks one hour if it be not paid." Similar evidence was later to turn up in Philadelphia, where citizens were warned that habitual racing of horses on Sassafras Street was dangerous, although the warnings evidently were not altogether effectual, since residents of the city persisted in calling it Race Street, which name finally was formally adopted as the official one.

As civilization crept westward, the problem accompanied it, and in 1793 the authorities of Lexington, Kentucky, enacted what stands as probably the most polite and timidly phrased piece of legislation on record, which, in view of the temper of that particular community, undoubtedly was all they dared pass:

> The Trustees of the Town of Lexington, feeling the dangers and inconveniences which are occasioned by the practice (but too common) of racing through the streets of the inn and out lotts of the town, and convinced that they are not invested with sufficient authority to put a stop to such practices, recommend it to the people of the town, to call a public meeting, to consider of the means which ought to be adopted for applying a remedy to the growing evil.

The peculiar circumstances under which colonial American racing was conducted led to a form of sport still universally recognizable as racing, but distinctly American in character: short, straight dashes in which all the emphasis was on quick starting and fierce speed. America soon produced its own special brand of horses notable for those talents. As the frontier moved outward from the Atlantic, so did this type of racing, and it remained popular among frontiersmen even after they had crossed the Mississippi and entered the wide open spaces of the West, where the artificial restrictions which originally created this type of racing did not apply. Today the great Southwest continues to be the stronghold of the quarter horse, a breed which is American to the core.

In the East, where through a combination of circumstances—cheap slave labor, increase in population, and abandonment of fields which had become "tobacco poor"—the sport gravitated toward the English practice of course racing, although here, too, America imprinted its individual stamp. In England, racing truly was the sport of kings, and the courses had been laid out by noblemen to suit their own particular tastes or whims, with no thought for other spectators. The democratic spirit in America resisted such treatment. The public demanded that contestants in races should be visible from start to finish, rather than disappear over a hill, and for this reason the circular track came into existence.

Although the welfare of the common man was taken into consideration as a spectator in colonial America, racing itself continued to be primarily a sport for the gentry. The court records of York County, Virginia, contain the following entry dated September 10, 1674:

> James Bullocke, a Taylor, having made a race for his mare to runn w'th a horse belonging to Mr. Matthew Slader for twoe thousand pounds of tobacco and caske, it being contrary to Law for a Labourer to make a race, being a sport only for Gentlemen, is fined for the same one hundred pounds of tobacco and caske.
> Whereas Mr. Matthew Slader and James Bullocke, by condition under the hand and seal of the said Slader, that his horse should runn

8

out of the way that Bullocke's mare might win, w'ch is an apparent cheate is ord'ed to be putt in the stocks and there sitt the space of one houre.

Obviously, the standard for gentlemen, though rigidly fixed, was not very high.

Despite the primitive conditions under which colonial American racing was conducted, the over-all gist of the sport was, in some ways, surprisingly modern. Weights carried by horses were adjusted according to age (and also according to height), fillies received an allowance from males, winners were penalized for their victories by having to carry higher weights in subsequent races and foals yet unborn were matched against each other in forerunners of the futurity races of later centuries. Those most modern of all innovations, the supplementary fee and "early bird" nomination fee to stakes races, had their colonial equivalent in the form of sliding scales whereby entry fees varied according to how long before the race the animal concerned was entered. Of course, grass racing, which is still something of a novelty at many American tracks, was the original surface over which racing was conducted in the colonies, and, finally, today's fans who get snowbound on a Bowie race train and marooned overnight had their predecessors. In his book, *Racing in America,* John Hervey tells of an incident in which patrons had so thronged the Hempstead Plains course that the Brooklyn Ferry could not accommodate the huge crowds, and many of the spectators had to remain overnight on Long Island.

The location of America's first true race course was entirely fortuitous. When the enraged Peter Stuyvesant stomped back and forth on his wooden leg considering the impertinent British command to surrender his colony, he ruled over only 1,600 persons, most of them of placid Dutch stock who were not particularly interested in sports. What horses that existed in New Amsterdam were mostly draft animals. The first shipment from Holland did not come over until 1625, fifteen years after the original

shipment to Virginia and five years after the second "undigested" Virginia consignment.

Whatever may have been the sporting proclivities of Governor Nicolls, he was fortunate in finding a ready-made outlet for them. In contrast to the rest of America, which at that time was covered with impenetrable forests, there was in New York an area described by a Jamaica pioneer, Daniel Denton, only six years after the Dutch surrender as follows:

> Toward the middle of Long Island lieth a plain sixteen miles long and four broad, upon which plain grows very fine grass that makes exceeding good hay; where you shall find neither stick nor stone to hinder the horse-heels or endanger them in their races, and once a year the best horses in the Island are brought hither to try their swiftness, and the swiftest rewarded with a silver cup, two being annually provided for the purpose.

Blessed with this natural advantage, the leadership in organized racing was more or less thrust upon New York. There is some doubt as to precisely how long this original course, which was described as 2 miles around and was called New Market, after the famous English racing center, continued in operation. Some authorities insist it was replaced in 1764, after about a century of use, by a 1-mile track near what is now Garden City, and in 1804 either remodeled or again replaced by the Washington Course, but, in any case, all these tracks were in the same general area.

Governor Nicolls' position as father of the American turf does not hinge solely upon the circumstance of his having laid out the first track. He also gave to the sport an undying phrase which has sustained it through the years, and offered the first known trophy to the winner of a horse race. In announcing that he would give a silver cup to be run for each spring and fall over the original race course, Nicolls explained that he was doing so "not so much for the divertisement of youth as for encouraging the bettering of the breed of horses, which through great neglect has been impaired."

This "improvement of the breed" is frequently quoted tongue-in-cheek nowadays by those who take a jaundiced view of the undeniably pronounced commercial and gambling aspects of modern racing, but so long as racing is to remain a sport, improvement of the breed must remain an appreciable element thereof, and in Governor Nicolls's regime this was especially so.

Far from being a mere entertainer, the horse was a vital cog in the nation's economy. Besides his numerous agricultural functions, some of which persist to this day, in colonial America, except in areas fortunate enough to be located near navigable waters, the horse was the sole means of transportation. Doctors visited on horseback, lawyers went to court by the same means, circuit judges rode their rounds on horses, businessmen went to and from work, and the cavalry charger was the bulwark of armies. Mailmen and lovers encountered each other on bridle paths, legislators rode to and from their capitals, scholars to and from school and the horse carried ministers to church as well as members of the congregation.

There was little animosity between the church and racing, and in many cases the exact opposite was true. One of the most prominent turf figures in colonial America was the Reverend James Blair, D.D., who, among other accomplishments, founded the College of William and Mary, achieved such great political influence that he was able to have three Royal Governors of Virginia recalled to England, and for a time was acting governor himself. The Reverend Doctor Blair was instrumental in having the capital of Virginia transferred from Jamestown to Williamsburg, and during his residence there the latter city became the racing capital of America. Doctor Blair's word was accepted as authority in matters of the turf as well as in matters of faith. He once acted as end-man—or placing judge—for William Soane in a match against Robert Napier which, as did many races of the period, wound up in civil court. At the trial, Dr. Blair appeared on the stand as witness of his own testimony; Soane, not surprisingly, won the verdict.

The same harmony seems to have prevailed elsewhere in the colonies. One of the earliest references to racing in Maryland is a resolution that a vestry should meet "on Thursday at the race-grounds near the Bensons," although tolerance toward other viewpoints was apparent, too, in a subsequent act passed by the General Assembly which forbade horse racing "near the yearly meetings of the people called Quakers."

Regardless of certain variations in the attitude toward racing, there could be no disputing the importance of the horse. This importance is impossible to visualize today. Teenagers who nowadays might be found tinkering with hot rods, in that era would have been racing horses in impromptu matches; there being no community baseball or football teams, pride in one's home town was often expressed by matching the fastest local horse against the fastest horse of a nearby community and everyone, even if he did not happen to own one, came into contact with horses in his daily life. As waves of reform swept back and forth across the country from time to time, and attempts were made to suppress racing, Governor Nicolls's words were staunch support for the sport, and often enabled racing to win by a blue nose in the contest for survival.

Although, as has been stated, the offer of silver cups accompanied the original announcement of racing on Long Island in 1665, the oldest existing racing trophy is that dated 1668: a silver porringer which bears the inscription, "1668. wunn att hampsted plaines. march 25." This trophy was discovered by Miss Mary Atterbury Stimson of New York (whose nephew, Henry L. Stimson, served in the cabinets of Presidents Hoover and Franklin D. Roosevelt) in an antique shop on Fifth Avenue in New York. When she later discovered that the trophy had been the property of the Sill family she resold it to Howard Sill of Baltimore. According to the family it was won originally by a horse owned by one of their ancestors, Captain Sylvester Salisbury, commander of the Royal Forces and High Sheriff of Long Island under Governor Nicolls, and the man for whom Salisbury Plain might have been named. This trophy presumably was the last donated by Governor Nicolls, as he returned to England a few months after the inscribed date.

New York maintained its eminence as the center of organized racing (as distinguished from the frontier variety) for some twenty years before the sport went South. Although New York stayed in the running, and from time to time gained attention, it did not regain this undisputed eminence until after the Civil War.

CHAPTER TWO

THER TRACKS BESIDES THE New Market course sprung up in the New York area. In 1725 the New York Subscription Plate at 2-mile heats, best two of three, weight 140 pounds, including saddle and bridle, was run for at the Church Farm Course, which land was later conveyed to Kings College, now Columbia University. At about the same time there was another track on that part of Manhattan Island which now is Greenwich Village. Some years after the inaugural of the New York Subscription Plate, the Church Farm passed into the control of one Francis Child, who advertised in the *New York Gazette,* "All persons coming into the field, subscribers and winning horses only excepted, are to pay six pense each to the owner of the grounds." This is the first recorded instance of admission being charged to a race course, and Mr. Child may well have been the pioneer race-track promoter. Another early racing relic is the Morris Bowl, which appears to have been awarded for the twenty-fifth renewal of the New York Subscription Plate. It is inscribed as follows: "This Plate Won By A Horse Cal'd OLD TENOR Belonging To Lewis Moris, Jun'r, Octob'r ye 11, 1751." Although the race obviously had been contested many times previously, and Morris himself had won it before, Old Tenor is the first stakes winner whose name is included in Northern records. The 1751 renewal, incidentally, was open only to horses bred in America, which indicates that efforts already were being made to encourage home-breds.

Lewis Morris, Jr. (1726-1798) was the original tycoon of the New York turf. The grandson of an earlier Lewis Morris, who was the first governor of New Jersey after it became an independent colony, the younger Morris was quite distinguished apart from his racing activity. He was a member of the Continental Congress and one of the signers of the Declaration of Independence, and a half-brother to the even more famous Gouverneur Morris, the noted financier and statesman who helped frame the Constitution. The family estate, Morrisania, was one of the most opulent in early

Lewis Morris, Jr., a signer of the Declaration of Independence and a founding father of the northern turf.

America, but it was destroyed by the British when they occupied New York during the Revolutionary War.

The last recorded running of the New York Subscription Plate was in 1753, when victory went to a horse named Smoaker, also owned by an historic personage, John Leary, an Irish immigrant who operated a livery stable on Cortlandt Street and who was the first professional jockey mentioned in chronicles of the American turf as well as possibly the first operator of a public training stable. His capability in his profession is demonstrated by the fact that Smoaker was still racing fourteen years after his Plate victory.

Vying with the Morrises as foremost patrons of the turf was the DeLancey family, which was of a vastly different stripe. Founded by a French Huguenot refugee, Steven DeLancey, who married the daughter of Stephen Van Cortlandt, New York's first mayor, the DeLanceys dominated Manhattan politically, financially and socially. Stephen's son, James, also married the daughter of a former New York City mayor, and it was their son, James the younger, born in 1732, who was the most glittering turf figure of his time. Having been educated in England, as were many young men of wealth in that period, upon his return to America he took on many British trappings. After inheriting his father's Bouwerie Farm, he remodeled it extensively and the racing stables, paddocks and a private ½-mile training track were located in what is now the Bowery. James DeLancey imported British bloodstock, including the stallion Wildair and an unnamed mare by Cub; the latter was called "the grandmother of the American turf" by the eminent bloodlines authority, R. L. Gerry, because of her profound influence at stud. Through her daughter by Wildair, Slamerkin, she founded an immense family which includes, among others, the celebrated stallion of the 1950s, Nearco, sire of Nasrullah and Royal Charger.

Unlike the Morrises, who were strongly sympathetic to the American cause, the De-Lancey family was Tory. When in 1774 the uneasiness of the times led to suppression of all public sport, James DeLancey read the handwriting on the wall, and, not wishing to war against his countrymen, he auctioned off his stud the following year and moved to England with his family, where he remained the rest of his life.

As a harbinger of the great North–South races which were to cause such feverish excitement in the future, there was an intersectional match in New York before the Revolution which, quite apart from its significance, provides a fascinating commentary on the climate of the times.

Having been impressed by a Maryland-bred horse named True Briton, and apparently depressed by the then prevailing practice of sending to England for racing stock, A. W. Waters of Long Island formed a partnership with General Nathaniel Heard of New Jersey to purchase True Briton, and soon afterward Waters announced the following challenge: "Since English horses have been imported into New York, it is the opinion of some people that they can outrun the True Briton. This is to satisfy the public, that I will run him with any horse in America; to run on Long Island the four-mile heats, or of one heat, carrying eleven stone [154 pounds], for 300 pounds [£] or more, at any time only to give me one month's notice."

This was simply too much for John Leary, who, after remarking that Mr. Waters' challenge had been phrased in "most illiterate, unsportsmanlike terms," and accusing him of "squinting with great contempt" at British steeds, eagerly reached for the gauntlet. He suggested a match between the recently imported Old England, which he had just acquired, and True Briton at 4-mile heats for £100 a side, carrying 9 stone, to be run at Harlem. Having completed his warm-up, he further proclaimed that Old England was "much better qualified as a stallion, being far superior in shape, strength and action," and suggested a race between the produce of a mare covered by True Briton and one covered by Old England to be contested in April of their four-year-old form, which was to say some six years in the future! (The age of horses was then reckoned from May 1.) He concluded these amenities by stating that, should True Briton's owner decline the issue, "I desire that he will not presume to rank him with any others than the common mongrels of the country, from which he was derived, and that he will be forever silent on the subject of matching and racing." Leary signed his communication "A Lover of the Turf" rather than with his own name, which was to be a common practice for years to come, and in view of the explosiveness with which feelings were expressed, probably was the only prudent one.

In his reply, after getting in his licks about Leary, Waters objected to Harlem as a site for the contest because, as he said, "I will never start a horse when a certain person is Judge of a race or has anything to do with it otherwise than as a Party; for though I do not like the man, I have no objection to his money if he dare sport it." He then countered with an offer for a match in which True Briton would give Old England 50 yards head start in each heat.

Unlike many similar episodes of the period, which produced nothing more than sound waves and hot collars, this one bore fruit. A substitute official must have been found for the "certain person" who had been the subject of Waters' delicate innuendo, for the race took place in Harlem. True Briton (what a name for a horse carrying the hopes of America!) finished so far ahead of Old England in the first heat that the latter was pronounced "distanced" and there was no necessity for further heats.

In heat racing, it ordinarily was necessary to win two heats in order to be adjudged winner. However, a "distance" was measured back from the finish and marked, usually by a red flag, and any horse which had not yet reached this point when an opponent crossed the finish line was eliminated then and there. Sample "distances" were 170 yards for 4-mile heats, 130 yards for 3-mile heats, 90 yards for 2-mile heats and 50 yards for mile heats. These figures, of course, varied among the individual jockey clubs and could be adjusted by agreement among the parties concerned.

The rest period between each heat also varied according to the length of the race. Representative intervals were thirty minutes between 4-mile heats, twenty minutes between 3-mile heats and fifteen minutes between heats of shorter length. Although it obviously was to the advantage of a horse which could do so to "distance" his rival, occasional episodes are encountered in later turf history in which the winner is pulled up and walked across the finish in order to allow an opponent to "save his distance." Such tactics were gestures of sportsmanship on the part of the winning owners, similar to the courtesy game in a set of tennis, or they may have been motivated by more mundane reasons: a desire to get a full race into the winner in preparation for severer tests coming up in the future, a disaffection for losing the starting fee and the opportunity to bet in subsequent heats, or a fear that the winner might be assigned too severe weights in subsequent races if he demonstrated superiority.

CHAPTER THREE

LTHOUGH NEW YORK IS AC-
knowledged to have been the
original center of organized racing, there is little question that,
from the very beginning, so far
as racing in general is concerned, or the degree
of interest manifested therein, Virginia was the
hotbed of the sport. Its early settlers mainly
were of the Cavalier tradition. Its economy was
mostly agrarian and its mores reflected the
outdoor life. As has been noted, early racing
in Virginia was among quarter horses along
narrow, straight paths cut from the forest for
an abbreviated distance. These races were immensely popular with the pioneers and are described by Hervey as follows:

> . . . the race path was a narrow strip of
> ground, about fifteen to twenty feet wide, and
> from a quarter of a mile to 500 yards long, per-
> fectly straight and with room at one end for the
> two opponents to get off and at the other to
> pull up—this being no great space, as one of
> the most indispensable attributes of the quarter-
> horse was his ability to whirl and get off at top
> speed in two strides and to come to a stop from
> full flight with equal facility. . . .
>
> The start of the quarter-race was supposed to
> be a standing one, but the two contenders, rear-
> ing and circling at the scratch, in reality took
> off flying. The "jockeying" for the advantage
> here was one of the great sights of the sport.
> Both horses and riders were trained to ma-
> neuver in the most spectacular way and the out-
> come often depended upon which got the best
> of the break and was able to seize the preferred
> strip of the path. If well matched the two would
> run the entire course closely locked, which led
> to the claims of crossing, jostling and fouling

often brought up in the suits-at-law that were so
frequently the aftermath.

> The firing of a pistol, blast of a trumpet, or
> tap of a drum was the signal to break and the
> exacting and ungrateful office of the starter
> then as now was one only to be entrusted to a
> man thoroughly two-fisted and well able to
> handle the situation. At the coming-out place
> the endman was stationed to decide the
> winner . . .

Quarter horses of exceptional speed, like the
side-show strong man of later centuries, would
travel from settlement to settlement challenging
all comers, and occasionally such a horse of
awesome reputation would be smuggled under
disguise into strange territory for a betting
coup.

Tobacco, which was the mainstay of Virginia's economy and which soon came to be
regarded as legal tender, has the faculty of de-
pleting the soil in which it grows and rendering
the land useless for other crops. As cleared land
thus became available, so-called race fields
made their appearance. These were, as the
name implies, nothing more than abandoned
crop fields, some of which still were furrowed,
their shape and gradient governed by the local
terrain. However, they did foreshadow what
was to become the standard American race
course, an ellipse or circle approximately 1
mile in circumference.

With the coming of such race courses, crude
though they were, the quarter horse pushed on
to the frontier, where his talents were more
appreciated. Virginians, closely allied to the
British by blood and by inclination, took more
and more to distance racing. As early as 1691,

15

Francis Nicholson, Royal Governor under King William and Queen Mary, issued a public notice that he would "give first and second prizes to be run for by Horse on the 22d day of April next St. George's Day being Saturday." Mention of a second prize indicates that the race was not for quarter horses, since that form of racing customarily involved only two contestants (the race paths could not accommodate more). This one apparently was for a field of horses and over a distance.

After Jamestown was burned during Bacon's Rebellion in 1676, Richmond became the focal point of Virginia racing and there were at least five specially constructed quarter racing paths in Henrico County. That Virginians took even this form of racing very seriously is illustrated by the numerous lawsuits of that time which involved racing. One such litigation involved a horse, Young Fire, who was the first named race horse in American records. A pure white (which implies, almost surely, Oriental blood) he was owned by John Gardiner, who offered to race him against all comers for 1,000 pounds of tobacco and 20 shillings. The challenge was accepted by Daniel Sullivant, who borrowed a horse for the purpose from John Baker, and although the race was won by Young Fire on the track, Sullivant got the decision in court. Other suits were based on a jockey's allegedly having flagrantly pulled his horse in a race, and an owner's brother who ran across the track in front of a rival horse, causing him to shy and leave the path. Judging from court records, the prominent racing families of this period were the Ligons (or Liggons), the Cockeses and the Randolphs.

In 1699, when the capital of Virginia was shifted from Jamestown to Williamsburg, the latter city became the racing center as well as the hub of political and social life. It is recorded that during race week in old Williamsburg, the normal population of 2,000 would swell to 6,000, and, as common folk did not travel about except when absolutely necessary, the visitors were mostly figures of fashion.

A notable event of this period was the importation into Virginia in 1730 of a stallion, Bulle Rocke, believed to be the first "bred" horse imported to America from England. In this connection it should be remembered that the term "thoroughbred" had not yet assumed its modern meaning. Although it had been in use for some years previously (as an adjective, not a noun; applied to persons, not horses) it was not to be formally defined until 1755 when, in his historic dictionary, Samuel Johnson listed it as meaning "completely educated; completely taught." England's General Stud Book, which was to become the basis of the thoroughbred breed, was not published until after the Revolution, although the Racing Calendar, an official summary of turf affairs, was begun in 1727.

Nevertheless, there seems to have been a keen appreciation of certain types of horses at this period, and references to "half-bred" animals can be found long before the official origin of the thoroughbred breed.

Among the Virginians, again following British precedent, "colt racing" was considered barbaric. Three-year-olds were just beginning to be allowed to race and four-year-olds were campaigned sparingly. To race a horse younger than five at 4-mile heats was considered unsportsmanlike. And, naturally, the time required to develop campaigners for this type of competition, not to mention the time required to acquire suitable race courses, was a factor in the delayed appearance of distance racing on the American scene.

That course racing over a distance was well established by 1737 is evident from an announcement that year in which it was "proposed that 20 Horses or Mares do run around a three miles course . . . at the Old Field in Hanover County . . . If permitted by the Hon. William Byrd Esquire, Proprietor of said Land." Permission from Byrd was forthcoming, for the race subsequently was run and won by a bay horse belonging to a Mr. Tynes.

With horses they imported and horses they

16

bred—which included such cornerstones of the breed as Monkey, Traveller, Jolly Roger and Lee's Mark Anthony—colonial Virginians earned recognition as founding fathers of the American thoroughbred. Among the numerous stallions imported into Virginia before the Revolution, two stand out as having exercised particular influence on the breed: Janus, imported as a ten-year-old in 1756 by Mordecai Booth, and Fearnought, brought over as a nine-year-old in 1764 by John Baylor.

Janus, who probably is the subject of more turf lore than any animal of the period, became a legend in his time. A small (14 hands ¾ inch) chestnut, he was distinguished by his remarkable strength and the tremendous power of his hindquarters; also, he stamped his get so reliably that even casual observers were able instantly to pick out his offspring. Though he was himself a proved 4-mile horse, he imparted such intense speed to his get that he became highly sought after as a sire of quarter horses, and he established the pattern of the sprinting type for generations to come. To capture his fantastic speed, it became common practice to mate Janus with his own daughters and subsequently to mate him again with fillies thus produced. For exact reasons not known, Janus stood in the fashionable Tidewater area only four seasons, when, before his get had the opportunity to prove themselves one way or another on the race course, he went south across the James River into the area where quarter-horse racing was still popular and where he was hailed as a Messiah. He died at the ripe age of thirty-four in North Carolina.

Fearnought was the subject of much negotiation before he crossed the ocean. Baylor specified in a letter to his English agent that he particularly wanted "a most beautiful strong bay at least 14.3i high, as much higher as possible, provided he has beauty, strength and spi't with it, and one that had won some Kings plates with a pedigree at full length and cert. of age under a noblemen's hand as most of the list belong to noble'n." He even added, "As I expect one of the above I think it advisable to send a groom with him either by the trip to deliver him here to me or to agree with him for a years wages, for I must confess I am not fond of such troublesome impertinent fellows on my plan'n."

A list of twenty prospective horses had accompanied the letter and Baylor's English representative, after two years of pondering, finally settled on prospect No. 9, with the result that Fearnought crossed the Atlantic. He more than met the qualification as to size, for he stood 15 hands 3 inches and immediately became the most popular stallion in the country. His stud fee was £8, or £10 to insure a live foal, at the same time Janus was standing at a fee of £4 to insure.

Fearnought, after the death of his owner, also went south across the James River, but he died at age twenty-one after standing only three seasons there. Despite his immense success as a sire he did not found an enduring male line; one reason being that because of their size, strength and speed his offspring were very popular with Virginia patriots as mounts during the Revolution, and many of them were lost. However, in other than the top line the blood of Fearnought still abounds in modern pedigrees.

In 1770, when feeling in the colonies against England was running high because of the Stamp Act and other restrictive measures, the Non-Importation Acts were passed in retaliation, and no other stallions were imported into Virginia until after the Revolution.

The most significant turf family of the period immediately preceding and following the Revolutionary War were the Tayloes of Mount Airy in Virginia. John Tayloe II owned the renowned stallion, Yorick, who after six seasons at stud was put back in training in the 1770s to accept a challenge to run a single 5-mile heat against Dr. William Flood's "breed horse" for £500 a side.

At the age of thirteen, Yorick covered the distance in 12 minutes 27 seconds, to win

Mount Airy, built in 1747 by John Tayloe II, a member of one of colonial Virginia's leading turf families.

easily, "in hand the whole way," while carrying 180 pounds.

Tayloe's son, John III, later owned another formidable weight carrier over great distances, the gelding Leviathan, America's first unsexed champion. Racing for Edmund Brooke, and then for Tayloe, Leviathan won twenty-three successive races, and after his string was snapped, he came back in 1802 to win a 5-mile "dash" under 180 pounds conceding 70 pounds to his opponent, Brimmer.

The Tayloes maintained a town house in Washington, and when the British set fire to public buildings in the capital during the War of 1812, President Madison used the Tayloe home (Octagon House) as his executive mansion.

CHAPTER FOUR

THE EARLY HISTORY OF MARY-land closely parallels that of her next door neighbor, although because of its smaller size there was more community life in Maryland. This was reflected especially by Annapolis, which succeeded St. Mary's as capital in 1695, where life was equally splendid but more cosmopolitan than in Williamsburg. Annapolis in colonial times was the Paris of the New World.

Historians list more than twenty racing centers in Maryland before the Revolution. That course racing was well established in Maryland comparatively early is indicated by records at Annapolis which authorized the making of "12 silver spoons of the value of 10 pounds current money" to be run for on September 29, 1721, with the understanding that "the best horse according to the former rules of racing have eight spoons and the second horse four." Mention of rules of racing, the first such reference in colonial history, suggests that the sport was then already well-organized and, .of course, the provision for a second prize rules out quarter racing. One of these silver spoons came into the possession of the late Walter M. Jeffords, first president of the modern-day National Museum of Racing at Saratoga Springs.

Another early Maryland trophy is a silver bowl bearing the inscription "Annapolis Subscription Plate 4 May 1743." This cup was won by Dungannon, owned by Dr. George Steuart and the distance of the race was 3 miles.

Baltimore seems to have anticipated the future with remarkable accuracy, for in 1745, there was advertised a three-day race meeting in which winners on the first or second day were barred from competition thereafter. (A similar practice was instituted in modern times by Santa Anita in its racing program for two-year-olds. In order to provide competitive education for as many youngsters as possible, once a horse has won one of the 3-furlong dashes, it is not allowed to race again during the meeting.)

In another progressive note, the colonial Baltimore advertisement offered "A hat and Ribbon of Twenty-five Shillings Value to be cudgelled for on the second day and a Pair of London Pumps to be wrestled for on the third Day." Arbitrator of any dispute that might arise was Charles Ridgely, a large landowner whose family was to remain prominent on the turf for years to come.

Two of Maryland's foremost turf families were merged in 1741 when Governor Samuel Ogle, after having remained a bachelor until he was forty-seven, married the daughter of Benjamin Tasker. Governor Ogle made a significant contribution to the breed by importing the stallion Spark and the filly Queen Mab, and he founded famous Belair Stud, a magnificent establishment which set a record for continuous operation. In the nineteenth century a later governor of Maryland, Oden Bowie, acquired part of Belair (but not the mansion) and in the twentieth century, under the ownership of William Woodward, Belair reached the zenith of its fame when such horses as Gallant Fox, Omaha, Flares, Granville, Fenelon and Nashua wore its colors.

Colonel Benjamin Tasker, Jr., who took possession of Belair after Governor Ogle's death,

Belair, built in 1750 by Samuel Ogle, a Royal Governor of colonial Maryland, and maintained by successive owners for more than two centuries.

imported the noted stallion, Othello, and a great mare, Selima, who achieved undying fame on the race course in December 1752 by winning a $10,000 inter-colonial race against four rivals owned by Virginia turf magnates William Byrd III, Francis Thornton and John Tayloe II.

Selima achieved even greater fame at stud. She was dam of ten foals (three by Othello), of which nine became celebrities. After the death of Colonel Tasker, she was purchased by John Tayloe II, who took her to his Mount Airy Stud in Virginia and there she spent the rest of her life. However, her name remains identified with Maryland racing through the Selima Stakes run at Laurel each year.

Another famous horse of the period was Nancy Bywell, imported by Henry Mitchell of Fredricksburg, who subsequently sold her to Edward Lloyd IV of Wye, on Maryland's Eastern Shore; this mare won the Maryland Jockey Club purse three years in succession.

Dove and Figure both were imported by Dr. Thomas Hamilton of Schoolfield, and both were successful stallions. Dove lost an unusual race against the crack Selim during the French and Indian War, when affairs were so confused that the Annapolis Course was given up and the race staged on the public road to Baltimore. The horses were required to run 2 miles out of the city limits and back.

Maryland racing reached its pinnacle just before the Revolution under the administration of Sir Robert Eden, a Royal Governor, who was a brother-in-law of the last Lord Baltimore. A generous patron of the turf, he was made a

20

steward of the Jockey Club and imported several good horses. Sir Robert, an ancestor of Lord Avon (Sir Anthony Eden), enjoys a unique distinction. So popular was he that when he left for England in 1776 after the war had broken out, he carried with him a resolution from the state convention expressing the hope that he would return and resume office "when the unhappy disputes which at present prevail are constitutionally accommodated."

CHAPTER FIVE

ROBABLY NO CITY IN AMERICA takes more pride in its antiquity than Charleston, and few areas boast more "firsts" than Carolina. Although they were for a time treated separately, and, on occasion, even had different governors, the boundary between North and South Carolina was not officially established until after the Revolution, and, as South Carolina was to be the first state to secede before the Civil War, North Carolina declared its independence from Great Britain more than a year before the rest of the colonies in the Mecklenburg Declaration.

Charleston also claims to have organized the first Jockey Club, established in 1734, a date some time prior to the founding of the British Jockey Club, upon which most similar American organizations were patterned. There is no denying that Charleston, where the Dock Street Theatre was built in 1736, was a great cultural center of the colonial period. Membership in the Library Society was a mark of extreme social distinction, and as a result of this interest in books, the early history of Charleston is more thoroughly documented than that of other cities. From these early records it is evident that by 1734 racing had at least progressed beyond the quarter-horse stage, although it appears to have been something of an amateur sport, since horses frequently were ridden by their owners and conditions for some races stipulated white riders only. These records also indicate races for "Chickasaw horses," probably descendants of animals brought to America by early Spanish explorers. Although they were described as being extremely beautiful, they were smaller than horses which raced farther north, being as a rule less than 14 hands.

Charleston went its splendid, isolated, sophisticated way for years until in 1755 Edward Fenwick began importing stock profusely. A member of one of England's foremost racing families (Sir John Fenwick had been stud master to King Charles I, and William Fenwick owned Matchem, head of one of the three great thoroughbred male lines), Edward Fenwick inherited from his father the whole of John's Island, the largest of the group outside of Charleston, 30 miles in circumference. He imported to John's Island at least nine stallions and six mares, but eight of the stallions and two of the mares were all from the same line as Matchem. The most famous of these stallions was Brutus, who dominated the scene for several years, particularly as he was a roan and imparted his coat color to most of his get.

Another South Carolina Jockey Club was founded in 1758 by Edward Fenwick with John Drayton, John Mayrant, John Izard, William Moultrie, Samuel Elliott, Daniel Horry and William Williamson, which held its meetings over a track also identified as the "Newmarket Course." Formal course racing was by then in full swing, and in 1769 the report of a race includes the statement, "by several stop watches it appeared they did not exceed eight minutes and a half in running four miles," which indicates that the American preoccupation with running time already was making itself evident.

The dignity of their demeanor notwithstanding, Charlestonians obviously took their racing just as seriously as their less restrained neighbors to the north, as is attested to by an incident which followed a race in 1769, in which a local hero named Noble was distanced by a supposedly inferior opponent. One Fenwick Bull, Esquire, a gentleman of impressive credentials, which included being "one of his Majesty's Justices of the Peace, Register of Mesne Conveyances, Notary Public, Agent to the contractors for victualling His Majesty's troops in this province, Clerk to the Board of Commissions of the Pilotage &c, &c.," was found to have bribed Noble's jockey. "After receiving the usual and proper discipline of the horsewhip, his worship was carried into a room by the gentleman of the turf to protect him from the mob . . ."

Noble had stood a season at stud before returning to the races; this was not unusual in colonial times, either for stallions or mares.

Some of the conditions for Charleston races included the clause, "No less than three reputed running horses to start for the purse, or no race," so apparently the problem of short fields, which racing secretaries struggle over in the mid-twentieth century, has been in existence a long time.

Racing in North Carolina during this period was mostly of the quarter-horse variety, although occasional forays were made into Virginia, with which state North Carolina was more closely identified than with its neighbor to the south.

CHAPTER SIX

HROUGHOUT THIS PERIOD there was racing of one kind or another all over the colonies, even in staid New England, as has been noted in connection with legislation, and among the Quakers in Pennsylvania. William Penn personally imported in 1699 the stallion Tamerlane and two mares, and in 1760 a Jockey Club was formed. Penn's plans for the City of Brotherly Love included a group of vacant squares intended as public recreation grounds, and one of these areas, Centre Square, was frequently used for racing, accounts of which include descriptions of horses "dodging in and out among the trees." (The trees might have been somewhat preferable, at that, to the Square's later accoutrements; Hervey reports that when it was cleared and converted into a common, the Square was utilized for public hangings, and the horses raced around a gallows which stood in the infield.)

The first Philadelphia Jockey Club having experienced difficulty getting on its feet, another one was formed in 1766 by seventy-one gentlemen who subscribed £257 "To encourage the Breeding good Horses" and "to promote the Pleasures of the Turf." Richard Penn, last Royal Governor of the state, was chosen president and the famous financial genius, Robert Morris, also was a member. This was the fanciest such organization yet formed, and its register includes a record of the racing colors of various historical figures: James DeLancey, blue; Lewis Morris, Jr., yellow; Jacob Hiltzheimer, red; Richard Samuel, blue; Andrew Orr, green; Nathaniel Heard, crimson; Horatio

Sharpe, yellow; Governor Eden of Maryland, green; Colonel Lloyd, dark blue; Israel Waters, red, etc. In a note of elegance not elsewhere found, the rules specified that jockeys "appear in a neat Waistcoat, Cap and Half Boots." The Philadelphia meetings were the first (and for a time the only) American version of the sport to rate mention in the haughty British *Racing Calendar*—and even so, they were put under the heading "New England."

The Maryland champion Selim appeared in Philadelphia in 1767 to defeat three rivals in straight 4-mile heats while carrying 140 pounds. His time, 8:02, was said to be the fastest in America up to that time, although the Centre Course was later found to be 144 yards short of its supposed distance of 2 miles. (This was a problem that recurred often in early American racing, since tracks were laid out by only approximate measurements.)

Racing and breeding in colonial Pennsylvania was closely intermingled with that in New Jersey and New York. The track at Paulus (or Powlas) Hook, located in what is now part of Jersey City, was directly across the Hudson River from the Church Farm track on Manhattan Island. It was more easily accessible from New York via the Cortlandt Street Ferry than were the tracks on Long Island, and horses and people went back and forth across the river much as they do today. Racing in New Jersey "for lucre or gain" was outlawed by the legislature in 1748 except at fairs and on certain specified days, but this ruling was repealed in 1761, at which time the sport was made permissible anywhere except within 2 miles of a place of public worship.

The fair grounds were at Perth Amboy, which became known as "The Race Grounds," during the time of repressive legislation. There were other tracks at Elizabethtown and Morristown.

Lewis Morris, Jr.'s sister married Michael Kearney, who became the leading turfman of New Jersey, and their child, General Stephen Kearney, won fame in the War of 1812. Their grandson was General Phil Kearney.

New Hampshire got into the act with yet another race course named Newmarket. Advertisements of race meetings appeared in the Boston *News Letter* in the early 1700s and there was racing of some sort in Connecticut and Rhode Island.

Any proper account of pre-Revolutionary American turf history should include the following announcement, which appeared in the Maryland *Gazette* for April 23, 1761, in which mention is made of a man who as a young boy had helped survey the town of Alexandria, Virginia, and who was to play a major role in the great conflict to come:

To be run for on Thursday, the 28th of May, on the usual race ground at Alexandria, a purse of fifty pounds, three times around the ground (being near three miles) the best in three heats, by any horse, mare or gelding, 14 hands to carry 10 stone, below that measure weight for inches. . . .

The horses to be entered on the Monday before the race with the managers, Mr. George Washington, Mr. John Carlyle and Mr. Charles Digges . . . each horse to pay fifty shillings entrance on the first day and twenty-five shillings on the second day;

All differences that may arise, will be decided by the managers.

CHAPTER SEVEN

EORGE WASHINGTON WAS born near Fredericksburg, Virginia, and spent his boyhood there. None of the many facets of his remarkable life is more characteristic of him than that of the wealthy Virginia planter and, as such, horses and racing inevitably played a significant role in his life. A neighbor, and one of his closest friends, was William Fitzhugh, owner of Chatham, one of the largest studs in America, to whom Washington wrote: "I have put my legs oftener under your mahogany at Chatham, and have enjoyed your good dinners, good wine and good company more than any other." Washington's adopted son, G. W. P. Custis, later married Fitzhugh's daughter, Mary; and another neighbor and friend, Alexander Spotswood of Newpost, married the daughter of Washington's half-brother, Augustine. The Spotswood family also was related to that of Martha Dandridge Custis, Washington's wife.

His connection with meetings in Alexandria indicates that George Washington was far more than a mere spectator in racing. He also subscribed to the purses given by the Williamsburg Jockey Club and his frequent visits to that city almost invariably coincided with race week. Washington was a well-known figure at out-of-state meetings in Annapolis and Philadelphia, and his diary includes a number of entries pertaining to racing and/or to the lavish balls which were an accompaniment of the sport.

One entry in 1772 tersely observes that he lost £1/6 in bets at Annapolis—even those so cynical as to question the cherry-tree story must admit that he was a gentleman of surpassing forthrightness.

George Washington also is credited with having exerted considerable influence on the breed through his connection with the stallion Lindsey's Arabian. During his New York campaign, General Washington was struck by the uniformly handsome gray mounts of a troop of Connecticut rangers, and he sent "Light Horse Harry" Lee to inquire about their origin, which, it turned out, was romantic to say the least. These horses were all sired by a white Oriental stallion known as Ranger, who had been recovered from a shipwreck and was standing at Windham, Connecticut, as a popu-

George Washington, an official at the Alexandria, Virginia, race meetings during the colonial period.

lar sire of saddle stock. General Lee sent a Captain Lindsey to Connecticut, and the Captain purchased the stallion for 125 hogsheads of tobacco, equivalent to about $3,000. The horse was sent to Virginia, where he was known both by his former name of Ranger and as Lindsey's Arabian, and his blood persists in thoroughbred pedigrees to this day.

In the first crop of foals got by the Arabian in Virginia was Magnolia (or, as Washington himself spelled the name, Magnolio) owned by George Washington and foaled at Mt. Vernon in 1780. This horse raced for General Washington and remained in his possession until December 9, 1788, when, according to his diary, he sold Magnolia "to Colonel Henry Lee for 5,000 acres of Kentucke land." Henry Lee, of course, was Washington's old cohort of the battlefield, "Light Horse Harry," and the father of Robert E. Lee.

Many years later, in 1830, Thomas Peter wrote in the *American Turf Register* of having seen Magnolia defeated about 1790 at the Alexandria Jockey Club races by a colt owned by Thomas Jefferson, which would be the only time a President of the United States and a future President opposed each other on the race track. Because this story was so long in coming to light, it is regarded with suspicion in some quarters, but Peter, who married Martha Park Custis, the daughter of Washington's stepson, obviously had more than a nodding acquaintance with the first President, and he is mentioned in Washington's diary.

CHAPTER EIGHT

NY WAR MAY BE EXPECTED TO cause more or less of an upheaval in existing customs, but the Revolutionary War, particularly as it affected racing and breeding, was virtually a complete demolition job.

Horses ranked along with guns, ammunition and food as the most strategic of war materials, and much of America's finest stock was lost in military action. Moreover, besides these outright losses, many animals, through theft, abandonment or flight, were shifted around in a helter-skelter turmoil which resulted in loss of their identity, or, worse, coming to be known by other names. There are numerous tales of daring raids in which the objective was a prominent horse.

During the British occupation of New York, racing continued as a source of amusement for the English cavalry officers, along with such Americans as James DeLancey, a cousin of the one previously mentioned, who because of his Tory persuasion still was sitting high in the saddle. (Justin Morgan, founder of the light horse breed of that name, is said to be a son of a horse stolen from this second James DeLancey during the Revolution.)

Adding insult to injury, the British, besides requiring that "God Save the King" be played every hour, took over the Flatland Plains race course—in Brooklyn, of all places—and renamed it Ascot Heath. The racing programs were interspersed with bull baiting and other typical English pastimes, and there were races for women jockeys. By and large the crack runners of this period were owned by British cavalry officers, who took them home with them after the Revolution.

As for the native stock, especially since Virginia, the bailiwick of the horse, also was the scene of some of the war's most fierce fighting, it was devastated. Running through the stud books which survived is the pathetically monotonous entry, "last record."

Farther south in Carolina and Georgia, which areas also included a number of Tory sympathizers, there was frequent raiding back and forth as the British commander, Colonel Banastre Tarleton, seemed particularly interested in horses. He was opposed by "Light Horse Harry" Lee, Marion, Morgan, Sumter and Pickens. Possibly as a result of this squeeze—horses fleeing south from the Virginia Tidewater and north from the Charleston area—after the Revolution North Carolina was to assume more importance as a breeding center and, although other parts of Virginia continued to play vital roles, the Tidewater never again regained the unquestioned supremacy it had enjoyed during colonial days.

However, the argument whether Virginia or Kentucky is more rightfully described as the cradle of the American thoroughbred is somewhat futile, when it is considered that until 1792 Kentucky was a part of Virginia.

PART TWO

FROM THE REVOLUTION

TO THE CIVIL WAR

CHAPTER NINE

HE REVOLUTION WROUGHT changes, not only in America's status, but also in the general climate of feeling among its citizens. A natural reaction against things English ensued. The typical American no longer was willing to stand with his hat in his hand and gaze enviously and respectfully at his "betters." He wore his hat on his head, tilted at a rakish angle if he liked, and acknowledged no betters. Racing, as a sport associated with the nobility and gentry, felt the impact of this new feeling. As the Church of England was toppled from its position as the state religion, its traditional "sporting parson" took a tumble, too. Evangelists and ministers of more severe sects, who deplored sports of all kinds as being frivolous and sinful, took over the reins; a noted Virginia breeder, John Broaddus, was subjected to such harsh "discipline" by his church for selling a mare, knowing she was to be used for racing, that he refused to sell his other horses. Men with an ear to the ground and an eye on the ballot box took cognizance of this feeling, until eventually the tradition was established that a President of the United States would never appear at a race track while in office.

Along more concrete lines, repressive legislation quickly made its debut. The new Constitution had not been fully ratified a year before the North Carolina General Assembly enacted a law designed to hamper racing. In 1792 the Virginia Assembly prohibited all bets of more than $7 at "any horse race, cock fighting, or any other sport or pastime." New York, Pennsylvania and New Jersey put onto their books measures intended to prevent racing. Similar legislation has been in existence on and off in various states ever since.

Another practical effect of this turning away from English custom was the change in the laws of inheritance. Instead of passing on intact from oldest son to oldest son, vast estates were divided among several heirs and some of the large studs thus broken up.

These were but slight aberrations on an otherwise perfect running surface, however. For, until another great war intervened, the United States was to enjoy unprecedented growth, of which racing received a generous share.

The Industrial Revolution was to begin, but not yet was the reign of the horse to be threatened. In the great westward push which was to reach the Pacific Ocean, the horse continued to be the key figure. Racing and breeding flourished throughout the vast new land. Kentucky, Tennessee, Alabama, Georgia, Ohio made their presence felt as breeding centers, and tracks sprung up in Chicago, St. Louis, Mississippi, Louisiana—all the way to California.

In at least one instance, racing acted as catalyst for development of a new area. Near the end of the eighteenth century, when western New York still was virgin forest, Sir William Pulteney, nephew of the Earl of Bath, purchased more than a million acres of land in that district and hired a Virginian, General Charles Williamson, to establish a town there. After laying out the town, which he named Bath, Williamson immediately constructed a race course to attract population; owners of

31

competing horses and their families were offered free room and board during the race meeting, at Forest Manor, built expressly for that purpose.

More than 2,000 accepted the invitation, a number of them Southerners, who brought along slaves, and when William Dunn's Silk Stocking defeated George Chichester's Virginia Nell in an historic match in 1796, some of the slaves changed ownership in the betting, and remained in New York.

It was during this period that American racing acquired a distinctive flavor all its own and the American thoroughbred achieved a stature in his own right not equaled before or since.

Compounding the general disaffection for English ways, as a prelude to, and aftermath of, the War of 1812, embargoes against commerce with England reduced importation of thoroughbreds from that country to a trickle. The inaugural of England's most famous classic, The Epsom Derby, was in 1780. Spread Eagle, winner of this race in 1795, was so enthusiastically received after being imported to America by John Hoomes, that 234 mares were booked to him in 1801. Within a few years, though, the American attitude was to change, and from 1806 to 1830 the trans-Atlantic equine traffic was nil.

Far from seeking to imitate England, America regarded the new-style British racing with disdain or outright contempt. The Derby and its companion classics, the Two Thousand Guineas and the St. Leger, and the Oaks and One Thousand Guineas for fillies, were restricted to three-year-olds and were decided by a single dash—in sharp contrast to the accepted American standard of excellence, races among mature horses over the heroic distance of 4 miles, in which to establish superiority it was necessary to win two heats or else distance all opponents.

According to the modern scale of weights, a thoroughbred does not become fully mature until March of his four-year-old season, i.e., at that time he ceases to receive weight con-cessions from his elders; and according to veterinary studies of a horse's bone structure, full maturity actually is not reached until much later than that. Nevertheless, the majority of the richest races in the twentieth century have been dashes for two-year-olds, and such youngsters, roughly the equivalent of high-school athletes, are offered huge purses far out of proportion to their relative population. There are a variety of reasons for this, not the least of which is a desire by owners to get a quick return on the enormous investment which a modern race horse represents, and the concomitant consideration that, the attrition rate being what it is, the careers of many horses have ended before they reach full maturity.

These considerations did not apply before the Civil War. The horse was such an integral part of the over-all economy that his upkeep was not very expensive. Moreover, if an intended race horse did not pan out, it was not a total loss, since there were an infinite number of other uses to which he could be put. Such events as there were for two-year-olds were run at the Southern meetings from January through April, and, since the universal birthday of the thoroughbred at that time was May 1, the animals concerned were nearing their third birthday.

The American preoccupation with precise clocking manifested itself during this period. The report of a 4-mile race at Maiden Head Course on Bowery Lane in New York in 1785, won by Sloven, in three heats, includes notation of the time: 9:07, 9:09 and 8:47. Track after track began to claim records for various distances—and various indeed were the distances because many of the tracks were found to be short of their supposed length—and as word began to spread of the fantastic speed shown by horses in the upstart region around Lexington, the expression "Kentucky watches" came into being. French chronometers capable of registering to the nearest sixtieth of a second became the vogue, and the fetish for fast time reached its crescendo in New Orleans, where the course was sprinkled to provide speedier footing and poetic license was invoked at least once: Henry Perritt, a bad actor at the post, after dawdling at the start until the field was well under way, caught up with the pace setter at the end of a mile in 1:47½; but because he was deemed to have started 5 seconds late, he was credited with having run the distance in 1:42½, and, accordingly, a record was claimed!

The Union Course on Long Island was opened in 1821 and its "skinned" surface became the model of tracks for the future. The eminent turf historian Cadwallader R. Colden was quick to note in the *American Turf Register* that "the same horses take from 3 to 5 seconds more time to run a mile over the New Market turf than over the naked soil of the Union Course."

The grandstand not yet having come into custom, ladies rode out to the course in carriages and young gentlemen on horseback paraded back and forth showing off their riding skills and sartorial splendor at the same time. As one result of this social facet, the tiny stands provided for officials became symbols of prestige to which visiting dignitaries were invited, often to act as honorary stewards or judges. This practice, too, reached an apotheosis of a sort in New Orleans, where Henry Clay and Daniel Webster were invited to officiate at the same meeting (although actually not on the same date).

As even the regular officials often were chosen on the basis of general community prominence rather than their familiarity with racing, the rules of the sport, which were somewhat elastic to begin with, frequently were interpreted with whimsy, if not downright caprice. But it all seemed to come out in the wash. The transgressor who ran into a Draco one day stood a good chance of catching a Louis XV next time around.

A literature of the turf, beyond those accounts which appeared in regular newspapers, was developed during this heroic age of American racing. In 1829 John Stuart Skinner of Baltimore published the first volume of the *American Turf Register and Sporting Magazine*. (Mr. Skinner was no stranger to the publishing business, as ten years before he had founded *The American Farmer,* and shortly after the bombardment of Fort McHenry during the War of 1812, he had become impressed by some verses written by his friend, Francis Scott Key. Skinner had them published, and the "Star Spangled Banner" thus was brought to public attention.)

The *Turf Register* was a monthly. In 1831 William T. Porter began publication of the popular weekly, *Spirit of the Times,* which later was taken over by George Wilkes.

Another publication, famous as much for its omissions as its content, was *The American Stud Book,* compiled by Patrick Nisbet Edgar, the first volume of which appeared in 1833. A promised second book was scratched, Mr. Edgar having become piqued by criticisms which greeted his first work and having refused to publish Volume II until sufficient advance sales were guaranteed to ensure recovery of expenses.

The new American spirit showed itself in other ways. Whereas former custom had been to hold but one 4-mile race (consisting of as many heats as were necessary) a day, additional events were added to the program by a dovetailing procedure whereby, while the horses from one race were cooling out between heats, a heat of another race was contested. Professional management of race tracks became more the rule, and in 1808 Banks Moody, proprietor of the New Market Course in Petersburg, advertised as follows:

> The subscriber who keeps the New Market Course has proved from long experience that to serve the public attentively and moderately are the most certain means of being remunerated for his labor, that he is therefore determined that every exertion shall be made on his part to promote the convenience and add to the amusements of those who may visit the races.

An elegant stand 100 feet in length is already built on the field in which sumptuous dinners will be served up each day of the races. The advantages of being protected from inclement weather or the hot sun, feasting on the fat of our land and quaffing the choicest liquors all in full view of the contending coursers must greatly add to the gratification of the gentlemen . . .

The chain track operator also appeared on the scene, best exemplified by Yelverton N. Oliver, who regarded publicity as something to be sought rather than avoided. He was game for anything, from the staging of a single match race at someone else's track, to the complete construction of a new race course; he would start a meeting with as few as twenty horses on the grounds (not so small a number as it seems, when it is considered that the same animals ran over and over) and in his heyday once reckoned one day's gate receipts as "nearly three barrels of dollars."

Finally, American pride and American gregariousness combined to produce an impossible situation. Certain bloodlines became so popular that it was difficult to breed a mare other than to one of her own close relatives, and it then was necessary to turn again to England for fresh blood.

On the race track, betting, which formerly had consisted mainly of the stakes put up by contending owners and side bets among friends, assumed more and more importance. Public selling pools, similar in operation to the Calcutta auction pools sold in golf tournaments today, made their appearance. Since wagering on heat races was based more on the final outcome than on the results of individual heats, they did not provide as much action as dash races, and public participation in betting caused a trend away from heat racing.

Although the heroic age continued until the Civil War, the handwriting on the wall began to appear some time before then.

It was, nevertheless, a great age while it lasted, populated by heroic figures, a few of whom will be touched on, although it is impossible to cover the ground thoroughly.

CHAPTER TEN

 HORTLY AFTER THE REVOLU-
tion, there came to the United
States four stallions who, almost among themselves, sustained American racing through
its heroic age. They were in order of their
arrival, Medley, Shark, Messenger and Diomed.

Medley was imported in 1784 by the firm of
Hart & McDonald of Louisa, Virginia, as part
of a draft of six stallions brought over for the
express purpose of being resold. A then eight-
year-old son of Gimcrack out of Arminda, by
Snap, in four seasons he had won nine races,
two matches and had received forfeit in another. He was purchased from Richard Tatter-
sall (which name has continued as the foremost among British bloodstock dealers) for
about $500. Having been acquired essentially
as a business proposition, Medley stood at a
different location every year until he died at
age sixteen after eight stud seasons in this
country, although shortly before his death a
half-interest in him had been sold for 29,000
pounds of inspected tobacco, the equivalent of
more than $7,000 and an unprecedented val-
uation.

Medley was a gray, rather small, but of elegant physique, who imparted his coat color to
a number of his get. In his time, he was noted
principally as sire of a famous quartet—Bell-
air, Calypso, Grey Diomed and Quicksilver—
which formed the bulwark of a fantastically
successful stable owned by the previously mentioned John Tayloe III.

Tayloe kept a diary which showed that his
stable won 113 races in 141 starts during the
period 1791-1806, not counting the 1802 sea-

Colonel John Tayloe III who carried on his family's
colonial Virginia turf empire after the Revolutionary War.

35

Stud poster of Messenger, who became a foundation sire both of thoroughbreds and standardbreds.

son which was "one of great success," but concerning which the list had been lost.

Medley's later fame rests on his descendants Hanover and Domino, both of whom trace to him in numerous lines of their pedigrees.

Shark, a brown son of Marske out of the Pigott mare, by Snap, was imported in 1786 by Benjamin Hyde of Fredericksburg, Virginia, who acquired him via the Tattersalls auction. On the track Shark had won more than any horse in England at that time; his official earnings were listed as G.16,057 in cash, plus the Clermont Cup (valued at G.120), eleven hogsheads of claret, and The Whip, the latter being the Newmarket challenge whip which was emblematic of the British turf championship. Shark also moved about in his new country, standing at three different locations, all in Virginia. Although he was an accomplished 4-mile horse, he also was noted for extreme speed and his best-known offspring included Virago, Annette, the elder Black Maria, Black-Eyed Susan, Betsey Lewis, Betsey Baker and Narcissa. Evidently, he was one of those mathematical or genetic oddities, "a filly sire."

How Messenger arrived is something of a mystery, but once here he left an unmistakable impression as a patriarch of two breeds, a successful thoroughbred stallion and the founding father of the harness breed. A gray son of Mambrino out of an unnamed mare by Turf, Messenger had won ten of sixteen races in England, chiefly as a "match horse," in races for which the side bets exceeded the purse in importance, and never at a greater distance than about 2¼ miles. Without any prelude, he was advertised in a Philadelphia newspaper in 1788 as just imported, with inquiries to be made "at Alexander Clay's at the sign of the Black Horse in Market Street . . ." Presumably he had been imported by a Thomas Benger who left Philadelphia in a hurry during an epidemic of yellow fever, but in 1793 Messenger was sold in New York to Henry Astor. Eventually Cornelius W. Van Ranst acquired ownership of the stallion. Messenger stood in various locations

Diomed winner of inaugural Epsom Derby in 1780, who later came to America where he left numerous sons and daughters.

around New York and New Jersey, which area at the time did not offer a very select group of mares, but despite these limitations he was a huge success. He sired numerous successful running horses, and his son, Rysdyk's Hambletonian (Messenger had another son named Hambletonian) became the cornerstone of the Standardbred breed.

If the story of Diomed were submitted as a plot for a work of fiction, it would be rejected as too implausible. The chestnut son of Florizel out of Pastorella's Dam (also known as Sister to Juno), by Spectator, had won ten consecutive races, including the inaugural of the Epsom Derby, and was for a time considered the best colt seen in Britain since undefeated Eclipse. However, after laying up for a rest period, he re-emerged as something of an in and outer, and although he did manage to win a King's Plate at 4-mile heats while carrying 168 pounds, that was his last victory, and when he subsequently retired to stud it was at a fee of G.5 ($25), a modest one considering his early brilliance.

This was merely the beginning of ignominy for Diomed, though, for by the time he was twenty-one years old his stud fee had dropped to G.2 with very few takers at that price, and at an age when most stallions have ended their careers, Diomed's owner, Sir Charles Bunbury, put him up for sale. He was bought by Colonel John Hoomes of Bowling Green for $250 in the spring of 1798, and shipped to Virginia, where he began stud service immediately (perhaps the poor horse thus achieved some distinction by covering mares in England and in the United States the same season).

Although Colonel Hoomes was among the most active importers of the period, and, like all horsemen, he bought and sold a few now and then, he was not exclusively a bloodstock speculator, for he maintained a large stud and racing stable. Diomed stood his first season in America under the management of Hoomes, apparently with his good friend John Tayloe III as a partner. Incidentally, James Weatherby, who acted as English agent for both Tayloe and Hoomes, wrote the former a letter

37

warning that Diomed was a "tried and proved bad foal-getter" and recommending that Tayloe "avoid putting any mares to him!" The appearance of the old horse, who stood nearly 16 hands, was enough to reassure Tayloe (and one of his stallions had had an accident, leaving his book unfilled), but in any case he patronized Diomed.

The stallion who supposedly was over the hill before he ever came to America climbed to unprecedented heights in his new home. Following the custom for celebrated horses of that time, he moved about from one stud to another, and lived until age thirty-one, active to the last. Among his last foals, begotten when Diomed was thirty, was Haynie's Maria, the only creature, equine or human, that ever successfully thwarted Andrew Jackson. In the last decade of his long life, the old stallion's stud fee had increased tenfold, and Colonel Hoomes sold him (or a majority interest in him) for six times his purchase price shortly after his arrival.

Colonel Hoomes, who operated the stagecoach line between Alexandria and Richmond, and who served in the Virginia Assembly both as delegate and senator, imported numerous other memorable animals (Spread Eagle, Buzzard, Stirling, etc.) but Diomed was, of course, his chief contribution to the American turf. His battalion of noted offspring included undefeated Ball's Florizel, plus Potomac, Stump-the-Dealer, Duroc and the son who took up where his sire left off, and went far, far beyond —Sir Archie.

If there can be such a thing as a stallion being too good for his own good, Diomed is an example. Years later, when it became necessary to go again to England for fresh blood, Benjamin Ogle Tayloe expressed it this way: " . . . A few years ago the prominent stallions of our country were all of *one blood*. If a man wished to raise a blood colt what was the fact? Why, he had only to determine whether his mare, she, too, of the Archy stock, should be put to Henry, Sir Charles, or Eclipse!" If the produce was a filly, as soon as her time came for breeding the choice again was to be made of a stallion from that identical trio.

(Henry and Sir Charles were both by Sir Archie himself, and Eclipse was a son of Duroc—all were grandsons of Diomed.)

CHAPTER ELEVEN

N O INDIVIDUAL, BEFORE OR since, was so prominent upon the American turf as William Ransom Johnson, born in 1782 in Warrenton, North Carolina, in the "Halifax District," just across the border from Virginia and closely allied with that state in its preoccupation with the horse. Although the typical North Carolinian of that era was a trifle uncouth for polished Virginians, the Johnsons were accepted in the highest of circles of their neighbor state, and William's father, Marmaduke Johnson, had married a Virginia girl.

When Marmaduke Johnson's carriage driver on the sly unhitched a mare and put her into a local race—which she won—instead of punishing the servant, Johnson became interested in racing. As his son grew up, the father tried all the usual methods to divert him into a business career, even to rigging a match between a specially trained horse of his own and one trained by William while the latter was still a boy. The object lesson backfired when the son's horse soundly whipped the father's, and having been shown the error of his ways, Marmaduke Johnson gave William a free hand with the family stable and stud.

The man who was to be known as "The Napoleon of the Turf" was an accomplished horseman before his twentieth birthday and active in other fields as well. He served in the North Carolina legislature when he was twenty-five, and later, after moving to Virginia where he settled down at Oaklands, near Petersburg, he was elected to that state's legislature. On his lavish estate which overlooked the Appomattox there was a 2-mile training track, not circular, but straight, so Colonel Johnson and his guests could observe the horses throughout their works. At the main entrance to Oaklands hung a sign which read, "There is nothing so good for the inside of a man as the outside of a horse."

A striking figure with a springy shock of hair which turned white at a premature age (the girls called him "Irish Beauty") Johnson earned his Napoleon nickname in the two seasons of 1807-1808 when he started horses in sixty-three races and won sixty-one of them. Later, he won seven of the eight races contested during a four-day meeting of the Union Course. Whenever any question concerning any phase of racing or breeding arose, his answer was accepted as word from an oracle, and, as suggested by stallion advertisements of that period, stud fees often were based on W. R. Johnson's opinion of the animal concerned. To his credit, his opinions as quoted did not vary with the tide of fashion or personal convenience. He expressed them succinctly, clearly, and stuck by them. Sir Archie, for example, might have been a source of embarrassment to a lesser man, because Johnson had let him get away, but even when Sir Archie was standing at stud under other management, Johnson steadfastly maintained he was the best horse to have raced in America with, later, the possible exception of Boston. (He was unwavering in his pronouncement of Reality as the best filly.)

His character was such that even his rivals would turn over special horses to him for training or management, and his stature was

William Ransom Johnson, the "Napoleon of the Turf."

such that in any group undertaking, the great North–South races which were to come, the establishment of a new jockey club, or the construction of a new track, he was automatically the leader.

He was of steel, rather than iron, and could sway a little when necessary. He did not allow his determination to degenerate into pure stubbornness. When another horse defeated one of his, if he considered the race truly run, Johnson often would buy the rival, and it was said he was never more dangerous than in defeat.

Of the countless historic horses with whom Johnson was associated, one of the earlier ones was Maria, who, through a highly unusual chain of circumstances, had to run 20 miles to win one race.

Paradoxical as it may be, dead heats were a comparative rarity before the invention of the photo finish camera, but the Fairfield Jockey Club Purse, $500, at Richmond on October 3, 1810, resulted in two such rarities in a row. And, although three of the five contestants were eliminated for one reason or another, it was necessary to run five heats to decide the outcome.

When the judges could not separate Sir Alfred and Duroc after the first heat, the excitement was intense. When the second heat was pronounced dead—between the same two horses—the excitement was prodigious. However, Sir Alfred emerged with his hind legs bleeding which, according to his jockey, had been caused by Duroc's jumping on them, and Duroc's owner was so enraged by this accusation that he withdrew his colt from the next heat. Lady Teazle, having been distanced in the second heat, was ineligible for further competition, and that left three runners. Sir Alfred won the the third heat, and the race appeared at his mercy.

However, Maria, who had been conceded little chance before the event, chose this moment to pull an upset, and a runoff became necessary. The exhausted Sir Alfred—who had run 12 miles without being defeated—was withdrawn, and Maria beat her only remaining opponent in the fifth heat. The race is summarized as follows:

	Finish Position by Heats				
	1st	2nd	3rd	4th	5th
W. R. Johnson's bay filly, Maria, 4, 98 lbs.	4	3	3	1	1
Wm. Wynn's bay mare, Malvina, 5, 108 lbs.	5	4	2	3	2
John Minge's bay colt, Sir Alfred, 4, 100 lbs.	0	0	1	2	drawn
Wade Mosby's chestnut colt, Duroc, 4, 100 lbs.	0	0	drawn		
Gen. Chamberlane's bay filly, Lady Teazle, 4, 98 lbs.	3	dist.			
Time (track muddy)	8:14	8:16	8:52	8:37	8:49

The winner of this race, a daughter of Bay Yankee, sometimes is referred to as "Bay Maria" or "Johnson's Maria," to distinguish her from a subsequent winner of another 20-mile race named Black Maria. The name was an inordinately popular one.

CHAPTER TWELVE

HE EMERGENCE OF TENNESSEE into the racing picture was virtually simultaneous with that of Kentucky, which will be described later. The neighbor states also had in common certain bluegrass areas on belts of limestone soil, centered around Nashville in Tennessee and Lexington in Kentucky; which proved to be exceptionally suitable for raising horses. The dominant figure in early Tennessee racing was Andrew Jackson.

Born in the border area before there was a definite boundary between North and South Carolina, he saw action as a mounted orderly in the Revolution at the age of thirteen. At fifteen he was recognized as an expert judge of horseflesh, and legend has it that when he received a $1,500 legacy from the estate of his grandfather as a sixteen-year-old, Jackson spent it at the Charleston races. He reached official manhood and Tennessee at just about the same time, having crossed the Blue Ridge Mountains shortly after his twenty-first birthday to settle eventually in Nashville.

One of Jackson's closest friends was the prominent horseman, William Donelson, who owned a farm near Nashville which Jackson frequently visited, and where he courted his host's sister, Rachel Donelson Robards, who became Mrs. Jackson. Grey Medley, believed by some authorities to have been the first purebred stallion introduced into Tennessee, made his first season west of the mountains at William Donelson's farm, and very likely Jackson had something to do with locating the horse there.

The future President was among those who established Nashville's original race course,

Clover Bottom, which vied with the nearby track at Gallatin for the most important turf events. Shortly after arriving in Tennessee, Jackson had purchased a plantation near Natchez, Mississippi, but soon abandoned that project and concentrated his activity at the Hermitage near Nashville.

In the spring of 1805, Major John Verell had brought the distinguished Virginia race horse Truxton into Tennessee, presumably with the idea of making a killing in the backwoods. In this case, however, the pigeon turned out to be an eagle, for Truxton was defeated by Lazarus Cotton's Greyhound. Jackson, however, thought Truxton had not been in condition, and after the race he bought the horse and challenged the owner of Greyhound to a rematch. After being subjected to a severe training regimen by Jackson (some authorities maintain that Major Verell stayed on as trainer) Truxton won in straight heats.

Cash was relatively scarce, so besides all his available money, Jackson had bet considerable wearing apparel. After the race, describing himself as "eased in finances and replenished in my wardrobe," Jackson also purchased the loser, and Greyhound quickly won himself out.

One of Old Hickory's friends, Patton Anderson, had supported Truxton with even greater enthusiasm. He had wagered all his money, plus fifteen fine horses standing on the grounds, and only after Truxton had won did anybody notice that most of the horses had ladies' saddles on their backs and didn't belong to Anderson in the first place.

Unorthodox wagers apparently were a weakness with Anderson. In his later days at the

41

Andrew Jackson on Sam Patch.

White House, Jackson told of another incident at Clover Bottom. As he was watching a horse cool out about dusk, Anderson ran up, pursued by a crowd of excited men. Jackson, who explained, "I was bound to make common cause with Patton," reached into his coat pocket and pulled out a tin tobacco box which he clicked shut with a sound very like that of cocking a pistol. In the darkness, Anderson's irate pursuers decided not to pursue this matter any

further. (Other historians represent this incident as having occurred in the daytime, but Colonel Balie Peyton, according to the *Spirit of the Times,* vouched for the foregoing version.)

Later Jackson actually did fight a duel with Charles Dickinson, in which Jackson was severely wounded and his opponent killed. The immediate cause of the affair was a remark Dickinson made about Mrs. Jackson, but there was bad blood between the two men because of earlier arguments growing out of races between Truxton and Ploughboy, the latter owned by Dickinson's father-in-law. The pair was originally matched in 1805 but Ploughboy became lame and his owner had to pay forfeit, although another race was agreed upon for the following spring. Between races, the following stud advertisement appeared:

> The present engagement with this horse is such that he cannot be put to mares any sooner than the above-stated time—He is now engaged in a match of $3,000, half forfeit, against Gen. A. Jackson's celebrated Truxton . . . In a few days after the race he will be ready to receive mares . . . Gentlemen who wish to breed fine horses would do well not to put their mares to horses until after the race, as at that time it will be seen (barring accidents) whether or not he be the true bred racer.

As it turned out, Jackson almost had to pay forfeit because Truxton wrenched a thigh in his last trial before the race, but the indomitable Old Hickory replied to friends who urged him to concede with the dramatic statement: "Gentlemen, Truxton will run."

The indomitable Truxton backed him up, winning in straight heats.

When he later became President it was no secret that Jackson maintained a racing stable in Washington, although technically the horses were listed as belonging to Major A. J. Donelson, his private secretary. And, the Chief Executive often actively participated in the horses' training.

Jackson was notoriously paternal toward his hand-picked successor, Vice-President Martin

Van Buren, and newspaper cartoonists had a field day with an incident that took place on the National Course when the two men were watching a trial by Busiris, an immense horse of tremendous power. As Busiris became unmanageable and began "kerlaraping," according to Colonel Peyton, Jackson shouted, "Get behind me, Mr. Van Buren! They will run over you, Sir!"

HAYNIE'S MARIA, 1808
(Diomed—Mare by Tayloe's Bellair)

The saying, "All men are equal on the turf and under it," was never better illustrated than by the experience of Andrew Jackson. The successful Congressman, U. S. Senator, justice of the supreme court of Tennessee, general and President of the United States was balked in his fondest ambition.

When the noted trainer Green Berry Williams came to Tennessee around 1806, the first horse he saddled for a race in his own account was beaten by one owned by General Jackson, which turned out to be the most expensive victory of Jackson's career. "Uncle Berry" Williams served under Jackson in the Creek War, but friend and admirer of the general though he was, thereafter he made it a point to beat Old Hickory on the race track, which he did— thirteen times in succession—and Haynie's Maria was his principal instrument of torture.

This filly, owned by Captain Jesse Haynie, in her debut at Nashville in 1811 distanced five of her six opponents at 2-mile heats, among them a colt owned by Jackson.

He vowed vengeance. The next fall he purchased an interest in another colt and trained it himself for a race with Maria, but she again galloped away, this time at 4-mile heats.

Although Jackson had to give up training shortly thereafter, due to his involvement with the War of 1812, he didn't forget Haynie's Maria. Even while masterminding his Natchez campaign, he commissioned W. R. Johnson to acquire for him "the best four-mile horse in Virginia without regard to price." Johnson filled

the bill with Pacolet, whom Jackson matched against Haynie's Maria for the Nashville Fall Meeting of 1813. The irrepressible general suffered probably the sharpest sting of all when Pacolet wrenched an ankle and Jackson had to pay $500 forfeit. He purchased three more horses: one of them also fell prey to injury and the other two were soundly trounced by Maria. News of these developments was sent down the river to Jackson while he was directing the New Orleans campaign.

Maria having proved invincible in conventional racing, the great strategist tried a new tactic. As one of his mares was noted for early speed, Jackson backed her against Maria in a half-mile dash, $1,500 a side, $500 payable at the first quarter-pole, $500 at the 600-yard mark and $500 at the wire. Haynie's Maria led all the way and won by more than ten lengths!

A week later Jackson borrowed a horse from his friend, Colonel Edward Ward, and challenged his nemesis again, and again she led all the way. Finally a 2-mile dash was arranged in which Maria conceded Jackson's mare 120 yards—a "distance" under the rules in effect. A celebrated Negro jockey, Dick, was imported from Virginia to carry Jackson's colors, but Maria, after toying with her rival for slightly more than a mile, was touched once with the spurs and went on to win by 180 yards.

Old Hickory surrendered.

When Captain Haynie later sent his mare to Virginia and offered to match her for $5,000 a side against all comers, Jackson said to him, "Make the race for $50,000 and consider me in with you. She can beat anything in God's whole creation."

In later years, when Jackson was asked whether he ever in his life had failed in any undertaking, he replied, "Nothing that I can remember except Haynie's Maria; I could not beat her."

As was her trainer, Maria's jockey was a celebrated figure of the time: "Monkey" Simon, a 4-foot 6-inch hunchback who was said to have been a prince in his native Africa. Exceptionally intelligent and a gifted musician, he was as much in demand as an entertainer at parties as he was in the saddle, but he nevertheless retained some of the superstition acquired during his youth. On one occasion a rival jockey, who figured he could beat Maria with a quick burst in a 2-mile race if his mount weren't worn out in the early running, told Simon, in strictest confidence, that he had received an occult communication warning him that if Maria took the lead before the half-mile pole, she would fall under an evil spell and trip. The sensitive jockey brooded about this for some time, and in the race was hard put to restrain Maria from her front-running habit, as the crowd roared its disapproval. The instant his rival passed the half-mile pole, though, Simon urged the mare forward and she won out of sight. (Simon's rival had miscalculated; he should have located the voodoo at the finish line.)

Haynie's Maria raced on through Kentucky, Tennessee and Georgia without defeat, until, in her last start, at the age of nine, after she had been sold and was no longer trained by Williams or ridden by Simon, she suffered her only loss.

Sharing honors with Haynie's Maria as the best of the numerous horses trained by Williams was the popular old gelding, Walk-in-the-Water, a son of Sir Archie whose ancestry on his dam's side was in dispute, but whose racing class was unquestioned. He never made any of the various pedigree catalogues, but his actions spoke louder than print. Williams brought him to Tennessee from the east coast, and the old campaigner ranged as far afield as Natchez, traveling on foot from meeting to meeting, winning race after race, and conceding weight to rival after rival. Older horses were required to carry more pounds than their juniors—but "Walk" was one of the few who lasted until his "second childhood," when the process was reversed. At the age of fifteen and beyond he got the weight concessions.

He was finally retired at eighteen, and turned over to Thomas Foxhall, who promised to provide him with a comfortable home. The temptation of just one more race was too great, however, and Foxhall entered "Walk" in a purse at Nashville on October 10, 1831. Williams protested, but he no longer was the official owner. Although Walk-in-the-Water was defeated, he ran creditably enough, but Williams had turned his back and sat deliberately facing away from the track throughout the race.

Another famous horse of the period was Dr. R. B. Sappington's Tennessee Oscar, who never paid a forfeit or lost a heat, nor, it was said, was he ever forced to top speed by a competitor. Although he was limited to local competition, he was so formidable that he walked over in his second start. He was described as the perfect racing machine: 15 hands 3 inches, ". . . his head was all mouth and nostrils and he could stand with all his feet in a washtub."

Tennessee Oscar was bred by the Reverend Hubbard Saunders, and sport in the Volunteer State seems not to have been lacking for divine guidance, for the Reverend Hardy M. Cryer, a founding father of the Tennessee turf and one-time manager of Andrew Jackson's stable, owned the most famous brood mare in that region. This was Madame Tonson, who produced, by Pacolet, four sons who collectively earned renown not only for their racing performances, but for their great beauty as well.

Most impressive of this remarkable quartet of full brothers was Monsieur Tonson, who, after losing his debut when green and unfit, won all his remaining starts in a career which took him through Tennessee, Alabama, North Carolina and Virginia against the best horses of the day. Owned in his later years by Henry M. Clay, Monsieur Tonson once traveled 1,200 miles through wilderness and over mountains, having to swim or wade across rivers in the process, without interrupting his string of victories. He beat the sizzling fillies Sally Walker and Ariel more than once, and his versatility was astounding: this successful 4-mile horse twice beat the noted quarter horse, Camel, at the latter's specialty, 2-furlong dashes. Monsieur Tonson later was the leading American stallion for the 1834 season.

In over-all impact upon American racing, however, Andrew was not the biggest Jackson in Tennessee. That honor goes to James Jackson (1782–1840), no relation to Old Hickory, who was about fifteen years younger. Although the two were friends, and at one time owned horses in partnership, in later years they were not on speaking terms.

Having himself crossed the Atlantic from Ireland as a young man, James Jackson became the most successful importer of thoroughbreds in the nation. He arrived in Nashville with substantial working capital and quickly became one of the city's leading businessmen, expanding his interests until he established headquarters as far away as New Orleans. His breeding activity was concentrated at Forks of Cypress, a large stud farm in Northern Alabama, just over the Tennessee line near Florence. He became a citizen of that state, and after serving in the Alabama legislature, moved on up to become president of the state senate. Another of the most active importers of thoroughbred stock during this period was Elijah H. Boardman of Huntsville, Alabama.

Among Jackson's early importations was Leviathan, who was brought over in 1830 at the age of seven. So named because of his size —he was a full 16 hands and heavily framed —the horse was considered too big, so Jackson did not keep him at Forks of Cypress, but sent him to stand in Nashville under the management of Colonel George Elliott. The big horse was a huge success at stud, heading the sire list five times, and in 1838 he became the first stallion in American history to sire the winners of more than $100,000 in a single season as his get that year won ninety-two races.

When he imported Glencoe in 1836, Jackson made his deepest impression. This son of Sultan had been highly successful in England; at three he won the Two Thousand Guineas and became the first three-year-old in history to win the 2½-mile Goodwood Cup, a victory

so easy that he won another race the next day; and, as a four-year-old, he walked over for The Whip.

His breeding career was phenomenal. After his first season, when he was mated with only a few mares and got but two foals, he was active at stud for twenty-one years. James Jackson died before Glencoe reached the peak of of his fame, and the stallion later moved north to Tennessee and after that into Kentucky, where at the age of twenty-four he had a crop of fifty known foals. He was leading sire in America eight seasons, a record which was to be surpassed only by Lexington, and, as a number of breeders point out, Lexington benefited greatly by being mated to Glencoe's daughters.

In 1957 a later James Jackson, of Memphis, Tennessee, a great grandson of Glencoe's owner, wrote the author asking whether any descendants of the famous stallion still remained prominent; specifically, were any of them entered in that year's Kentucky Derby. The Jackson clan was having a reunion in Florence, and it was thought this information might make an interesting sidelight.

The answer was easy. Iron Liege, the winner of that year's Derby, descended from Glencoe, as did every other horse in the race, and the same is true of any great race of any country any year.

Since ancestors multiply so quickly as one traces a pedigree, horsemen have adopted the artificial device of emphasizing only the top and bottom lines, although, genetically speaking, it cannot logically be assumed that the tail-male or tail-female lines exert any more influence than the others. Glencoe's direct male line today is sparse, but in collateral lines he appears as ancestor of Domino, Hanover and numerous other "foundation" stallions. Moreover, before he left England he begot Pocahontas, the greatest producing mare in the history of the thoroughbred breed, dam of fifteen foals, including Stockwell (the "Emperor of Stallions"), Rataplan and King Tom, so it would be difficult, if not impossible, to find a modern thoroughbred which does not trace to Glencoe at least once—the majority trace to him several times.

Glencoe was a "filly sire" nonpareil; one of the most unusual aspects of his unusual career is that, of the 481 foals by him in the *American Stud Book,* 317 were fillies and only 144 were colts (sex was not specified on the other 20). Not surprisingly, his daughters achieved more fame on the race course than his sons.

One of his American daughters is of particular interest. When Glencoe was mated to Giantess, by Jackson's previous notable importation, Leviathan, the result was a filly 16-hands 2¾-inches tall and correspondingly robust in general physique. Originally named Glumdalclitch, after the giantess in *Gulliver's Travels,* with her new name of Peytona she was to become, literally, the biggest money winner on the American turf and southern representative in the last of the epic North–South races.

CHAPTER THIRTEEN

THE HERO OF HEROES IN AMERica's heroic age was a four-legged one: Sir Archie, a bay colt foaled in 1805 by Diomed out of the blind mare Castianira, whom John Tayloe III had imported from England and turned over to his friend, Captain Archibald Randolph, to breed on shares. Originally named Robert Burns, this colt must have been the cause of severe second guessing in later years, because he changed hands three times before his true quality became appreciated.

When Robert Burns was a two-year-old, Randolph sold his half-interest in him to Ralph Wormeley IV, who subsequently acquired Tayloe's interest in exchange for a filly and $400 boot. Meanwhile Tayloe had changed the colt's name to Sir Archie in honor of his co-breeder (although Captain Randolph was called "Archie," in some publications his namesake is spelled "Sir Archy").

Before Sir Archie made his first start his owner decided to quit the turf and offered him for sale, and, although he was described as "a fraction over sixteen hands high, vigorous, clean limbed, and swift, of ideal proportions," there were no takers. While awaiting his first engagement, the Washington sweepstakes in the autumn of his three-year-old year, Sir Archie caught distemper, but he was sent into the race without having fully recovered because of his owner's desire to save forfeit. The future colossus of the American turf was distanced by Bright Phoebus in his first outing. Still not fully recovered, he was entered in the sweepstakes at the Fairfield Course in Richmond in

Broadside of 1817 announcing the stud services of Sir Archie in North Carolina.

October against six rivals. The best he could do was save his distance in the first two heats and finish third in the next one, as the race was won by True Blue, who, as it happened, was owned by none other than William Ransom Johnson.

The Napoleon of the Turf could appreciate class in friend or foe, and after the race he bought Sir Archie for $1,500 on the spot. Under the guidance of Johnson and his trainer, Arthur Taylor, Archie was given time to recover and prepared for the major competition of that day, 4-mile heat racing. The following spring he was returned to the scene of his

47

earlier humiliation, the Fairfield track, where he won the annual Post Stakes from Wrangler, who on the previous day had won the Jockey Club Purse. This decision was reversed in a return meeting at the New Market Course in Petersburg the following week, although the second heat was so close that Colonel Johnson did not think Wrangler actually had won. He challenged that horse's owner to a further 4-mile match for a substantial side bet, but Wrangler's owner, Colonel Miles Selden, declined. That fall the two sons of Diomed met again in the Jockey Club Purse at Fairfield, when Sir Archie distanced Wrangler and his three other opponents. A week later Sir Archie distanced his field again in the Jockey Club Purse in Petersburg. His last start was in a match with General Stephen Carney's crack Blank at the Scotland Neck Course in Halifax, North Carolina. Archie won in straight heats and so impressed one of the spectators, General William R. Davie, that he offered Johnson $5,000 for the colt, which was accepted.

On the bare record, Sir Archie's racing performance—four wins in seven starts—scarcely seems earth-shaking, but, before the race against Blank, Johnson had expressed willingness to match his horse for $5,000 or $10,000 a side at 4-mile heats against all comers, adding that "Sir Archie is the best horse I ever saw, and I well know that I have never had anything to do with one that was at all his equal and this I will back, for if any horse in the world will run against him at any halfway ground, four-mile heats, according to the rules of racing, you may consider me $5,000 with you on him."

The history of American racing is filled with similar sweeping challenges, some of which were more audacious in wording and more valuable in purse, but a careful examination suggests that a lot of them were timed and placed with suspicious care; they sound like a man offering to lick anyone in the house—during a convention of midgets.

In the case of Sir Archie, however, the challenge was legitimate, and it came from a giant.

With such a citation from the Napoleon of the Turf it is unlikely Sir Archie could have found competitors had he remained in training, and he was immediately retired to stud. (Why Johnson sold him is not known, but successful racetrackers all through the years have operated on the well-recommended theory that $5,000 never bowed a tendon.)

Sir Archie stood at various locations, for a time under lease by Johnson—who was not nicknamed "Napoleon" without reason—and eventually the horse came to rest at the Mowfield Plantation (also called Moorfield) of William Amis in North Carolina. Sir Archie stood his last season at stud in 1831 at the age of twenty-six, and two years later died as a pensioner. John Amis, who inherited the stallion from his father, computed that, just during the period from 1818 onward when he had stood at Mowfield, Archie had cleared $76,000 in stud fees.

His success at stud was fantastic, not only from the standpoint of the numerous outstanding offspring he sired (Timoleon, Sir Charles, Henry, Marion, Bertrand, Walk-in-the-Water, Lady Lightfoot, Vanity, Reality, Flirtilla, Sally Hope and numerous others) but in the way it withstood the intense inbreeding to which he was subjected. As had been the case with Janus in colonial days, Sir Archie was bred to his own daughters and daughters of his sire, Diomed; and, in his case, some of the results were excellent, notably Henry, Beggar Girl, Duchess of Marlborough, Janet, and Virginia Taylor.

This intense inbreeding carried on in subsequent generations produced such fine get as Wagner, Grey Eagle and Bonnets o' Blue.

The Colonial turf leaders of Maryland and northern Virginia must have spun in their graves with humiliation when, in 1827, the Washington, D. C., Jockey Club announced a race meeting open only to "any horse, mare or gelding, *bona fide* owned and trained for six months previous to the races, North of the York or Pamunkey Rivers." And, picking up the cue, the Maryland Association announced that only the first half of the Baltimore meeting would be open to all comers; the second half (which usually was the richer) would be limited to entries owned in Maryland or the District of Columbia, and the glorious final day would be restricted to animals actually raised in Maryland or D. C.

In reply to outraged criticism from the South, the *National Intelligencer* published a frank explanation:

> We are afraid that our friends in North Carolina are *displeased* at our Jockey Clubs having excluded the Roanoke Racers, but surely without reason. Do they not perceive that in so doing, our Clubs pay them the compliment of considering them invincible? Our breeders acknowledge themselves beaten to their heart's content—they give up: What more would our friends in the South ask of them? Whenever we can produce animals that are able to compete, with any chance of success, with those South of the Pamunkey, our friends may be assured that they will be welcome. Of late, the associations here and at Baltimore have had all the pleasure of making up purses, for the Roanokers to come and take for asking. This was not only an expensive amusement, but it also defeated the object of these "trials of speed," as our friends at Boston call them, which is, to hold out inducements to emulations in the improvement of the breed of horses.

And what were the horses which caused these restrictions? The sons and daughters and grandchildren of Sir Archie.

On May 24, 1830, the great National Colt Stake was run far to the north at the Union Course on Long Island. Similar to the Futurity of later years, stakes had been posted three years before. Of the fifteen original nominees, seven faced the starter, and six of them were descendants of Sir Archie, who at the time still was active at stud. The sole exception was an animal named Hermaphrodite, by Duroc, he by Sir Archie's sire, Diomed. (There was some argument concerning whether this oddly named creature should carry the 90 pounds specified for a colt or the 87 pounds required of a filly, but the judges ordered full weight.)

Winner of the race was Bonnets o' Blue, Sir Archie's double granddaughter—by his son, Sir Charles, out of his daughter, Reality.

Probably best of Archie's daughters was Lady Lightfoot, foaled in 1812, in her sire's first crop. At Marlboro, Maryland, in 1817, she and Hermaphrodite (not the same animal as the one mentioned above) staged a thrilling contest, he winning the first heat and she the next two, in 7:52, 7:53, 7:52. Although it was Lady Lightfoot's first attempt at the full 4 miles, they were the fastest heats run in Maryland up to that time.

Incomplete records show that this great mare won 23 races, of which 15 were at 4-mile heats, but according to legend she won all told somewhere between thirty and forty races. More remarkable still, she refuted the theory that strenuously campaigned fillies don't make good brood mares by racing until the age of eleven and, after retirement, producing eight foals in nine years, several of whom achieved fame, and one of whom, *the* Black Maria, was rated even greater than her dam.

Bred by John Tayloe III and foaled at Belair Stud, Lady Lightfoot had several owners, but she was trained and managed mostly by General William Wynn. In the 1817 winter meeting in Charleston, Wynn swept five of the six races with Lady Lightfoot and her kinsman, Timoleon, also by Sir Archie.

Today Wynn might be compared with William Hal Bishop, judging from the number of horses which passed through his hands. He was so ubiquitous as to seem almost two persons, which, indeed, in a sense he was, for he had a nephew, Colonel William Wynn, who also was an extremely active horseman, and who was whom is not often made clear in the records.

The senior Wynn was referred to as "Racing Billy," but the nickname, too, sometimes spilled over onto his nephew.

CHAPTER FOURTEEN

ECLIPSE FIRST—THE REST NO-where." That immortal phrase was inspired by the undefeated English horse, Eclipse, whose male line is the most prominent one in the thoroughbred breed today. His name was derived from the fact that he was foaled in 1764 during an eclipse of the sun, and he lived up to it by putting every horse he met in the shade. Since his time, the name has sprung up again and again whenever a breeder thought he had a likely looking foal, and while a few of the horses thus hopefully named justified it, the majority did not.

American Eclipse was the brilliant exception.

Product of an auspicious mating, by Duroc, out of Miller's Damsel, by Messenger, who in her racing days had been known as the Queen of the Northern Turf, American Eclipse attracted attention from the very beginning, and his early life is the most thoroughly documented of any old-time champion.

Bred by General Nathaniel Coles, American Eclipse was, according to *Wallace's Monthly,* foaled

> . . . in the gray of the morning of May 25, 1814 . . . Just before the son of Miller's Damsel was weaned, he gave his owner such an exhibition of his stride, strength and speed that he named him American Eclipse, believing he would render that name as illustrious on this side of the ocean, as English Eclipse had on the other side. He was weaned 10th of November and was allowed a generous supply of shorts and dampened clover-hay during the winter. The next summer he was on grass with no grain in any shape till the 10th of November again,

when he was put on the same food as the first winter, with the amount increased to ten quarts daily. The third summer he was again turned to grass, with four quarts of shorts per day. On the 1st of September, commenced handling and breaking, and then, for the first time, he was allowed oats, at the rate of eight quarts daily. That winter he had ground corn and oats, equal to eleven quarts of oats, and all the hay he wanted.

On the 1st of March following he was shod, and commenced training, which was continued nine weeks when, in a two-mile trial, he showed himself a very superior colt. He was now three-years-old, and he was again turned to grass, with the equivalent of nine quarts of oats daily, till the 1st of March, 1818, when he was taken in hand in earnest, being then four years old. Late in May of that year he ran at Newmarket, Long Island, three-mile heats, beating with ease Black-Eyed Susan and Seagull. In June he was again turned to grass, with six quarts of oats a day, and through the winter the same allowance of grain, with all the hay he would eat . . . he was allowed to run out of his stable every pleasant day in winter.

As a five-year-old American Eclipse was sold to Cornelius W. Van Ranst for a reported price of $3,000 and he raced twice that season for his new owner, at 4-mile heats, over the Bath Course near Gravesend, Long Island, and won both times. The state legislature having passed a law which in effect prohibited racing, Eclipse was retired to stud undefeated and as a six-year-old in 1820 he was bred to eighty-seven mares at the low stud fee of $12.50.

The repeal of the above-mentioned legislation, and the opening of the famous Union

Course the following year in a great drive to rehabilitate the sport in New York, led Van Ranst to put his champion back in training. This renowned sportsman, naturally, was subjected to considerable second guessing for this gesture, but on opening day at the new track October 15, 1821, American Eclipse won the featured 4-mile race against three rivals in straight heats. In the first he defeated the vaunted daughter of Sir Archie, Lady Lightfoot, by two lengths, and in the second heat he distanced her, time 8:04 and 8:02.

American Eclipse, undefeated champion of the "Heroic Age" and winner of the epic match against Henry.

CHAPTER FIFTEEN

IN 1822, AMERICAN ECLIPSE continued his undefeated streak. Now eight years old, he beat Bela Badger's well regarded Sir Walter in straight heats at the Union Course in May, and in October beat him again in a race which also included the noted mares Duchess of Marlborough and Slow and Easy.

At that time Sir Charles was the lion of the Virginia turf and his owner, James J. Harrison, challenged Eclipse to a match. Van Ranst accepted and the race was set for November 20, in Washington, D. C., 4-mile heats, $5,000 a side, Eclipse to carry 126 pounds and the six-year-old Sir Charles 120. Although a great crowd came out to watch this match, it fizzled when Sir Charles struck a tendon in a workout and his owner paid a forfeit. A substitute match—just a single heat for $1,500 a side—was arranged, but, after running creditably for 3 miles, Sir Charles broke down as Eclipse cantered home.

Prior to this race Sir Charles had boasted a record of 20 wins and four seconds in 24 starts, and his debacle brought Southern pride to a boil. The evening of the race W. R. Johnson issued a challenge in which he offered to run a horse against Eclipse over the Union Course on the last Tuesday in May, 1823, $20,000 a side, $3,000 forfeit. Thus the most famous race of the nineteenth century was born. John C. Stevens, a close friend of Van Ranst, immediately posted the forfeit and subscribed $6,000 of the backing money. The other $14,000 was raised by a syndicate of

prominent New Yorkers, and a similar Southern group was organized.

In addition to Stevens and Van Ranst, the New York group included Michael Burnham, publisher of the *Evening Post*, William Niblo, proprietor of Niblo's Garden, a favorite hangout of the gay blades; Stephen Price, manager of the Park Theatre; John Livingston of the distinguished family closely associated with the Stevenses, and numerous other well-known figures of the sporting world.

There can be no denying that the New Yorkers were sports—perhaps more so than they realized.

A century later, Colonel E. R. Bradley, a professional gambler, would give 4-to-1 odds in the winter against any specific three-year-old making it to the post for the Kentucky Derby the following May, such are the hazards of getting a horse ready for a certain race at a certain time and place several months in the future. The Van Ranst-Stevens syndicate had blithely agreed to have Eclipse, who would be nine years old at the time, ready to go six months hence, while the Southern group did not have to name its representative until post time, and Johnson had the full resources of his area to choose from.

Having come into the game with loaded dice, the Napoleon of the Turf proceeded immediately to blow on them. After canvassing the Southern owners, who hastened to place their horses at his disposal, he decided to prepare no less than five prospective candidates: the veteran 4-milers, Childers and Betsey Richards; and the three-year-olds Henry, John Richards

52

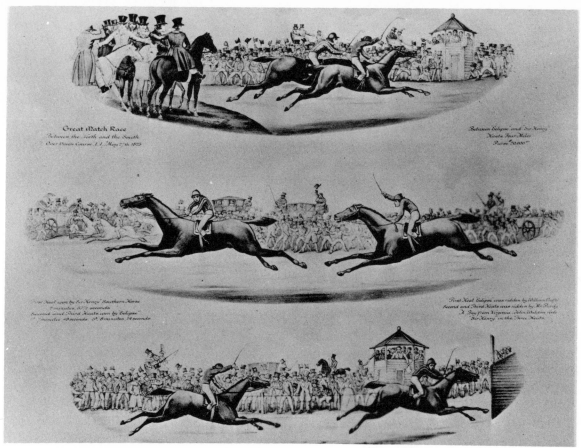

American Eclipse vs. Henry, first of the great North-South matches.

and Washington, as yet untried over the heroic distance. The plan was to test them in Virginia racing early the next year, then move up to Bela Badger's Fairview Course in Bristol, Pennsylvania, for final preparation.

At Petersburg the next spring Henry proved himself quite competent in his debut at 4 miles by beating Betsey Richards in straight heats, 7:54 and 7:58, track record time for two heats. The others also having run well in conditioning races, the caravan moved up to Pennsylvania, making almost the entire journey by water. Here, John Richards, considered by Johnson to be his best bet, grabbed a quarter in a trial, and Washington tailed off in his training, so only three survivors were sent the remaining 90 miles to the Union Course. Henry, who as a four-year-old would be required to carry only 108 pounds against the 126 on Eclipse, was the logical candidate, but no definite commitment was necessary until the bugle.

Because the population of New York City at that time was only 150,000, the contemporary report that 60,000 persons attended the great match has been questioned. On the other hand,

this was the period when the horse was king, and fully 20,000 were said to have traveled up from the South to witness the great joust.

The city was in an uproar with high festivities scheduled to precede the race. William Niblo had a rider posted at the track to signal the results of the race so he could run up a white flag from the top of his coffee house if Eclipse won (or a black one, of course, if he should lose). Michael Burnham arranged to publish a special edition of his newspaper at 4:30 the afternoon of the race.

The road to the Union Course was thronged long before the scheduled post time of 1:00 P.M. as spectators had begun gathering around the scene the evening before, and more came flooding in at the beginning of the day.

Andrew Jackson, serving briefly as the first American governor of Florida, was present, as were Vice-President Daniel Tompkins and the U. S. Representative (later Senator) from Virginia, John Randolph, and Aaron Burr, who had finished in a dead heat with Jefferson for the Presidency and later killed Alexander Hamilton in a duel.

53

When Henry was led forth at saddling time it was no surprise, and Southern enthusiasm, plus the fact that Eclipse had not raced since the previous November, made the younger horse a hot favorite for the first heat.

In accordance with his custom, the famed turf historian Cadwallader R. Colden ("An Old Turfman") covered the race mounted on a fast horse, so he could gallop along with the contestants and obtain close-up impressions as they ran through the stretch each time around. Assisting him was the noted ex-jockey and trainer, John Buckley, and Colden's thorough step-by-step account of the race as published in the *American Turf Register* is a classic of its kind. The start was described as follows:

> At length the appointed hour arrived, and word was given to saddle, and immediately afterward to mount. Eclipse was ridden by William Crafts . . . and Henry by a Virginia boy, of the name of John Walden . . . Eclipse, by lot, had the left or inside station at the start. Henry took his ground, about twenty-five feet wide of him, to the right, with the evident intention of making a run in a straight line for the lead. All was now breathless anxiety. The horses came up evenly; the drum tapped; and away they went. Henry, apparently the quickest, made play from the score, obtained the lead, and was then taken in hand. By the time they had gone the first quarter of a mile . . . he was full three lengths ahead . . .

Henry maintained his lead, under a hard pull although the pace was "a killing one," for 3¾ miles, until turning for home on the final circuit, Eclipse's rider challenged. The description continues, in part:

> . . . Crafts was making every exertion with both spur and whip to get Eclipse forward, and scored him sorely both before and behind the girths. At this moment Eclipse threw his tail into the air, flirted it up and down, after the manner of a tired horse, or one in distress or great pain . . . the rider of Henry turned his head around to take a view of his adversary. Walden used neither whip nor spur, but maintained a steady pull, under which his horse appeared accustomed to run. Crafts continued to make free use of the whip; his right hand, in so doing, was necessarily disengaged from the bridle, his arm often raised high in the air, his body thrown abroad, and his seat loose and unsteady, not having strength to hold and gather his horse in one hand, and at the same time keep his proper position. In order to acquire a greater purchase, he had thrown his body quite back to the cantle of the saddle, stuck his feet forward by way of bracing himself with the aid of the stirrup, and in this style he was rocking to and fro, belaboring the horse, from right to left, girth and flank . . .

Crafts's urging was to no avail as, still under a pull, Henry calmly passed the finish post a length in the clear. The time was 7:37½, the fastest ever recorded in America.

There was jubilation among the Henry supporters, particularly since it was said that "the Virginians took time by the forelock" and bet heavily on the outcome of the first heat. (In his book, *The New Encyclopedia of Sports,* the late Frank G. Menke describes the entire race as a betting coup by the Southern group, indicating that it had been planned all along to sacrifice Henry as necessary to win the first heat, but that the over-all result was of little interest to his party. However, this interpretation doesn't agree with contemporary accounts which state that 6-to-4 was offered on Henry for the second heat, with no takers. John Randolph, for one, reportedly rose up and piped, "I will bet a year's crop of slaves on Henry.")

Certainly, the second heat appeared to be at the Southern horse's mercy. Having run 4 miles in record-shattering time, Henry, according to Colden, "was less distressed than I expected to find him." Eclipse came out of the contest considerably the worse for wear. "Crafts, in using his whip wildly, had struck him too far back and had cut him not only upon his sheath, but had made a deep incision upon his testicles," stated the reporter. "The blood flowed profusely from one or both these foul cuts . . . and gave a more doleful appearance to the discouraging scene of a lost heat."

However, the old horse made a remarkable recovery, and Northern hopes were revived further when it was announced that Crafts—a slender boy weighing only 100 pounds—would be replaced by Samuel Purdy in the second heat. This noted jockey had ridden Eclipse in the horse's youth, but since had retired from the saddle at age thirty-eight. Of the numerous stories concerning the episode, some assert that Purdy and Van Ranst had fallen out, and, when offered the mount on Eclipse the ex-jockey accepted it reluctantly. Other stories indicate Purdy had come to the track dressed in riding clothes under his overcoat, and after the first heat approached Van Ranst with tears in his eyes, begging to be allowed to ride.

Ride he did, and in the second heat Henry was not allowed to coast along in front unmolested until the very end. After pressing the pace more closely in the early rounds, Purdy moved up at the end of the third mile until Eclipse was breathing on the leader's flank, and they entered the final round lapped on. Going round the first turn, Purdy gambled all by easing Eclipse and slipping him through on the inside, risking being cut off in the process, but when they straightened away for the run down the backstretch, the Northern horse was in the lead for the first time that day. He continued to draw away "with the help of the persuaders, which were freely bestowed" and won the heat by about two lengths. ". . . the shouting, clapping of hands, waving of handkerchiefs, long and loud applause sent forth by the Eclipse party exceeded all description," wrote Colden. "It seemed to roll along the track, as the horses advanced, resembling the loud and reiterated shout of contending armies."

Time for the second heat was 7:49, and it was time also for a jockey change on Henry. Arthur Taylor, the trainer, who, besides being 2 pounds overweight, had not ridden competitively in years, was substituted, but only through the persuasiveness of Randolph.

The diary of Josiah Quincy (a Puritan from Boston who took care to explain that a college friend had just happened to procure a ticket to the race for him) describes the second heat and interval before the third heat as follows:

Directly before me sat John Randolph, the great orator of Virginia . . . Apart from his great sectional pride . . . he had bet heavily on the contest, and it was said, proposed to sail for Europe upon clearing enough to pay his expenses . . .

. . . Sir Henry took the inside track, and kept the lead for more than two miles and a half. Eclipse followed close on his heels and, at short intervals, attempted to pass. At every spurt he made to get ahead, Randolph's high pitched and penetrating voice was heard, each time shriller than before:

"You can't do it, Mr. Purdy! You can't do it, Mr. Purdy! You can't do it, Mr. Purdy!"

But Mr. Purdy *did* do it . . . and although I had not a cent depending I lost my breath, and felt as if a sword had passed through me . . .

. . .The confidence on the part of the Southern gentlemen was abated. The manager of Sir Henry rode up to the front of our box and, calling to a gentleman, said: "You must ride the next heat; there are hundreds of thousands of Southern money depending on it. That boy don't know how to ride; he don't keep his horse's mouth open!"

The gentleman positively refused, saying he had not been in the saddle for months. The manager begged him to come down, and John Randolph was summoned to use his eloquent persuasions. When the horses were next brought to the stand, behold the gentleman appeared, with a jacket on his back, and a jockey cap on his head . . .

It was no use. Both horses were by this time exhausted, but the more seasoned Eclipse, under constant urging by Purdy, won the third and deciding heat in 8:24; Henry, after a gallant but futile effort which got his nose up to his rival's flank, finished three lengths astern.

Besides the basic purse of $20,000, it was estimated that ten times that sum had changed hands in the wagering.

55

John C. Stevens, famed yachtsman, steamboat and railroad pioneer, and leader of the New York forces in the North-South match races.

The Southern manager referred to by Quincy was Otway P. Hare—and where was the redoubtable William R. Johnson during all this frenzied activity?

The Napoleon of the Turf was in bed at his hotel, attended by doctors and nurses, as a result of severe indigestion from a banquet the night before. Some said a plate of oysters had done him in, but the acerbic Randolph attributed it to lobsters and champagne. In any case, the shrewd country boy who had put one over on the city slickers lost the main event.

A brass band struck up "See the Conquering Hero Comes" as Eclipse was led in. The *Eve-*

ning Post came out with what is believed to be the first sports extra in American journalism. And the white flag went up over Niblo's tavern.

The next day W. R. Johnson was up and about, writhing with chagrin. He addressed a note to John C. Stevens proposing another match the next fall on terms both more opulent and less one-sided, as follows:

Sir—

I will run the horse Henry against the horse Eclipse in Washington City, next fall, the day before the Jockey Club Purse is run for, for any sum from twenty to fifty thousand dollars; forfeit $10,000. The forfeit and stake to be deposited in the Branch Bank of the United States at Washington, at any nameable time, to be appointed by you.

Although this is addressed to you individually, it is intended for all the bettors on Eclipse, and if agreeable to you and them, you may have the liberty of substituting for Eclipse, any horse, mare or gelding foaled and owned on the northern and eastern side of the North River; provided, I have the liberty of substituting in the place of Henry any horse, mare or gelding foaled on the South side of the Potomac . . .

(The leopard hadn't changed his spots radically, however, for these terms matched the entire Southern horse country against what, for practical purposes, amounted only to part of Long Island.)

Stevens' reply was a classic piece of correspondence—the epitome of graciousness, with the deft twist of a stiletto neatly incorporated:

Dear Sir—

The bet just decided was made under circumstances of excitement, which might in some measure apologize for its rashness but would scarcely justify it as an example, and I trust that the part I took in it will not be considered as proof of my intention to become a patron of sporting on so extensive a scale. For myself, then, I must decline the offer. For the gentlemen who with me backed Eclipse, their confidence in his superiority, I may safely say, is not the least impaired. But even they do not hesitate to believe that old age and hard service may one day accomplish what strength and fleetness, directed by consummate skill, has hitherto failed to accomplish.

For Mr. Van Ranst I answer, that he owes it to the association who have so constantly supported him, to the State at large, who have felt and expressed so much interest in his success, and to himself as a man, not totally divested of feeling, never, on any consideration, to risk the life or reputation of the noble animal whose generous and almost incredible exertions have gained for the North so signal a victory, and for himself such well-earned and never-failing renown.

I remain, Sir, your most obedient servant,

John C. Stevens.

Napoleon's opposite number was one of the few men who had the distinction of having ridden in a steamboat before Robert Fulton. John C. Stevens and his brother, Robert, had accompanied their father, John Stevens, famed inventor and steamship and railroad pioneer, on a trial run in a steam-propelled boat three years before Fulton made his celebrated voyage up the Hudson in *The Claremont*. Stevens also was part owner of *America,* the yacht which won an international match against England in 1851.

Both the brothers maintained elaborate training stables and John C. followed the practice still employed in South America today of weighing his horses before and after every trial.

As to the John Randolph who figured so prominently in the great match race, he, too, was famous apart from his association with racing. A United States Senator and once Minister to Russia, and a great expert on pedigrees, he vied with W. R. Johnson as an oracle of the turf, although Randolph did not achieve nearly so much success, primarily because he was so infatuated with Janus blood that it became an obsession with him. A controversial figure, and in many ways eccentric, he was considered one of the master orators of his time, despite his

John Randolph of Roanoke: senator, foreign minister and oracle of the turf.

high-pitched voice. He had a penchant for becoming involved in quarrels, and once, just making conversation at the Virginia Hot Springs, he called Sir Archie's ancestry into dispute. He later retracted what he had said but the affair became quite a *cause célèbre.*

An accomplished horseman, Randolph, who always appended "of Roanoke" to his name to distinguish himself from his numerous relatives, was one of the first described as riding "like a monkey." His contentious personality is probably best conveyed by the comment of the famous trainer, Green Berry Williams who, when offered employment by Randolph at an unprecedented salary, politely declined and explained to a friend: "Man, I would as soon have been shut up alone in his stall with Ball's Florizel as down on his plantation with John Randolph." Williams (whose first name sometimes was spelled Greenberry) had trained this undefeated, but notoriously bad-tempered horse.

When Randolph died, his estate included more than 130 horses.

In the National Museum of Racing at Saratoga Springs, there may be seen a colored kerchief printed with scenes from the Eclipse–Henry match, presented to the museum by H. M. Jackson, a sixth-generation descendant of its original owner, Smith Barrett—who had to walk home from the race. (The kerchief, incidentally, does not record Arthur Taylor as rider of Henry in the final heat.) There also may be seen the whip used on Eclipse by Samuel Purdy, a thin, cruel-looking cattail not at all like the bats with flat poppers used by modern jockeys. Eclipse's rider, Purdy, was later a successful businessman, an alderman of New York City, and the father of John F. Purdy, a steward and the first handicapper for the American Jockey Club.

Having emulated, with distinction, the horse for whom he had been so hopefully named, American Eclipse retired undefeated with earnings of $56,700, an American record. A 15-2 chestnut "of great power and vast substance . . . His form throughout denoted uncommon strength and was much after the model of his grandsire, Messenger," according to C. R. Colden. Eclipse was immensely successful at stud and eventually he was purchased by W. R. Johnson.

The racing career of American Eclipse, it will be remembered, was interrupted by a year at stud, and in his first crop of foals there was a filly of such delicate grace and daintiness that she was named Ariel after the sprite in Shakespeare's The Tempest. She ran to her looks, too, winning her first six starts in a row, although most of them were at a mile or less.

Speed she had, but what about bottom? Her owner, Henry Lynch of New York, certainly was confident because although Ariel was only three, at a dinner after her sixth victory he offered to run her in 4-mile heats for $1,000 each turn of the course, plus $10,000 a side on the final result, against any named opponent. Ariel's intense early speed, of course, would have been a tremendous advantage under such conditions, and this challenge went unaccepted. However, a second offer for a conventional 4-mile heat race, $10,000 a side, was snapped up and another North–South match was born, the opponent chosen being Racing Billy Wynn's five-year-old mare Flirtilla. In view of Ariel's age, it later was agreed to reduce the distance to 3 miles, and with various friends coming in on both sides, the purse eventually reached $60,000. Flirtilla was immediately turned over to William R. Johnson for preparation and management.

Flirtilla sulked in the first heat, and though she came again, Ariel won by three and a half lengths in 5:59. In the second heat Flirtilla was 100 yards ahead in the homestretch when she again sulked, but Ariel's jockey, having given up hope and put her into a canter, could not quite make up the lost ground and missed by 6 inches. The time was 5:54½.

In the third heat Flirtilla ran steadily to win by 100 yards in 5:54.

In a gesture typical of both Johnson and Wynn, they were so favorably impressed by Ariel that she was purchased by the Southerners and went home with them. Precisely who became her new owner cannot be established because she raced under various names. The custom followed by local jockey clubs was

58

to permit only members to run for the jockey club purses, but on the other hand the member did not necessarily have to own the horse he nominated, and Ariel frequently was "borrowed" in this manner. Despite her daintiness and "fairy stride," the little mare raced on through the age of eight, winning 42 of her 57 starts, never failing to finish and never paying a forfeit. Twenty-eight of her victories were at 4-mile heats, and it was computed that she raced approximately 345 miles besides being roaded about 3,000 miles going from one track to another.

The second Black Maria was the result of mating between those former rivals American Eclipse and Lady Lightfoot. Bred by Charles Henry Hall, she raced for John C. Stevens and, as are a number of exceptional fillies, she was a big one: 15 hands 3 inches, extremely long-bodied and entirely black except for a small fleck of white on her withers. She is remembered chiefly for her victory as a six-year-old in the Jockey Club Purse at the Union Course on October 13, 1832, which went five 4-mile heats.

Like the previously described five-heat race, this one was run over a deep, muddy track. Trifle, who had defeated Black Maria in their previous meeting, was a slight favorite, but the black mare won the first heat easily, and in the second heat appeared to have ended the whole contest when Trifle caught up in the last stride to dead-heat. Then, after Trifle won the third heat cleverly, it was almost any price on her. However, in the fourth heat Lady Relief came into the picture and beat Maria a neck, as Trifle, youngest of the survivors, finished in obvious distress. In the final heat Black Maria let the other two set the pace for 3 miles, then came forward to win by as many lengths as her jockey desired while Trifle failed to beat the flag.

Black Maria dropped from 900 to 800 pounds during this grueling contest, but she didn't miss a feed afterward, and eleven days later was back in action at Baltimore finishing

second to Andrew in a field of four runners at 4-mile heats.

Trifle, so-named because of her tiny size, recovered from her harrowing experience so well that she never lost another race. She ended her career with 19 victories and five seconds in 25 races, her only unplaced effort having been in the race described above. She won her last twelve races in succession, ten of them at 4-mile heats. The *Turf Register* described her as ". . . the best race nag of her size we have ever had, and for both speed and bottom, surpassed by no nag that has run in America in the last fifteen years . . . In the opinion of some judges she ought never to have been beaten . . . she is of perfect symmetry and her action is surpassingly beautiful." The term "nag" at that time, obviously, did not have a disrespectful connotation.

Another North–South match, or Stevens–Johnson contest, was arranged for the spring meeting of 1836 at the Union Course. For the North, Stevens selected the five-year-old Post Boy owned by Robert Tillotson, and Johnson's candidate was John Bascombe, also five, owned by Colonel John Crowell of Alabama. Post Boy, combining the blood of the famous 1823 match race since he was a son of Henry out of a close relative of American Eclipse, was a duly recognized Northern champion, but John Bascombe (who was named for a well-known revivalist) was a comparatively late arrival as a celebrity. After a modest success at small Alabama meetings, he had achieved overnight acclaim by beating Wade Hampton's Argyle at the Lafayette Course at Augusta, Georgia, for a purse— actually, "pot" is a better word—of $32,000. The unusual conditions of this race called for Argyle's owner to put up $17,000 against $15,000 for any horse in Colonel Crowell's stable; John Bascombe was selected as the challenger and he distanced the favored Argyle in the first heat, 7:44.

Having already walked more than 525 miles in his Southern travels, Bascombe was roaded from Augusta to Petersburg, where he joined

Boston, winner of 40 races and sire of Lexington.

the Johnson Stable and traveled most of the remaining distance to New York by boat. Since both were five-year-olds, the weights were level, 114 pounds. Post Boy was ridden by Gilbert Patrick (better known as Gilpatrick) and Bascombe by the colored rider Willis, first jockey to the Johnson Stable, who proceeded to white-wash his rival.

Post Boy had drawn the pole, but at the tap of the drum Willis sprinted Bascombe to the front and took the rail going around the first turn, skillfully keeping Post Boy on the outside thereafter and making him lose ground. Abandoning all hope, Gilpatrick pulled up Post Boy as soon as he passed the distance pole and walked him in as Bascombe waltzed past the finish in 7:49 to the delight not only of those who had wagered on him, but also of those who had made bets based on time, 2-to-1 having been offered that the heat would not be run in less than 7:50 because of a high wind.

After this exhibition, the bulk of the betting on the second heat concerned not who would win, but whether Post Boy could save his distance, which he did, with emphasis. It was a grueling struggle in which Bascombe barely managed to win by a length in 7:51½.

In a gesture of true sportsmanship Cornelius Van Ranst, who had won for the North with American Eclipse thirteen years earlier, presented Willis with the saddle, bridle, jacket, cap and spur used by Purdy on that occasion. Challenges and counter-challenges for a re-match between the two horses came to naught.

The report of this race carried fractional times, by miles, for each heat as follows: first heat 2:02, 1:56, 1:54, 1:57; second heat 2:00, 1:56, 1:56, 1:59½.

BOSTON, 1833

(Timoleon–Sister to Tuckahoe, by Florizel)

By coincidence, America's outstanding horse, Lexington, and his sire, Boston, both were named (albeit in a roundabout way) for cities in Massachusetts, which in early history was one of the areas most opposed to racing.

Lexington was named for the Kentucky town which in turn, had been named for the site of the first battle for American independence.

Boston was so called because he was won in a card game of that name. John Wickham, a distinguished Virginia attorney who had been counsel for Aaron Burr in the latter's trial for treason, came out loser in a session of card playing with his friend Nathaniel Rives one evening in 1835. To settle the account, Rives agreed to take an unbroken two-year-old colt by Sir Archie's distinguished son Timoleon out of a not otherwise named sister to the brilliant horse Tuckahoe (she raced as "Sister to Tuckahoe").

For a time it appeared that Rives had been finessed, for the colt, duly named Boston, was incorrigible. He was broken by John Alston, in the stable of John Belcher, and as a three-year-old Boston was sent to L. White for finishing touches to his training. His new exercise boy couldn't stay aboard, so Boston was returned to Belcher with the recommendation that he be "either castrated or shot—preferably the latter."

Belcher did neither, and after a number of lessons with the whip, Boston was entered in a match at the Broad Rock Course in Richmond against a colt from the stable of his rejector, Colonel White. After gaining a long lead, he stopped dead and sulked, whereupon Belcher turned him over to a heavy exercise boy named Ned, with instructions that Boston be converted into a common hack until he acquired enough manners to race. It was quite a performance, much of it taking place on the streets of Richmond, but by autumn Ned had succeeded in exacting from his pupil a sort of grudging obedience.

Although his vicious temper was still evident (he bit horses who tried to pass him), he was a drastically different race horse. He won fifteen races in succession and received forfeit twice before tasting defeat again, in his first start as a six-year-old, and raced on until ten, winning 40 of his 45 starts. Thirty of his victories were at 4-mile heats.

Reminiscing on the old warrior in the *Spirit of the Times,* William T. Porter said:

This wonderful horse went on winning race after race at four-mile heats, beating almost every horse of any pretensions, from Georgia to New York, whether he met them single handed or in a crowd. If the course chanced to be knee deep in mud, so much the better for him; if it happened to be light and well adapted for time, the circumstance was equally in his favor. He was equally a leviathan in "soft" or "tight" places; the owners of horses everywhere "fought shy" of him, and it is not much wonder he went blind in his old days, for there was many an imprecation against his eyes when he showed his white nose on the track. Proprietors of courses were almost ready to league against his paying them a visit on any terms. Several times they actually paid him five hundred dollars to clear himself, as otherwise he would have cleared the course of horses and spectators . . .

(What a far cry from modern times, when star horses are so assiduously wooed by the operators of race tracks.)

Boston—"damn his eyes"—was considered to have been beaten only once on his merit, by Fashion at the Union Course on Long Island on May 10, 1842. This was another in the series of great North–South contests.

Fashion was a daughter of two distinguished parents. Her sire, Trustee, was shuffled about from place to place and owner to owner, but at the age of nearly twenty, when some question arose concerning how good he had been in his racing days, he was put back in training long enough to run a 4-mile heat in 8 minutes flat. Fashion's dam, Bonnets o' Blue, was the previously mentioned good mare trained by W. R. Johnson, who also had trained the next dam, Reality. "The Old Nap," as he was coming to be known, had sold Bonnets o' Blue, however, and William Gibbons of New Jersey was

Fashion's breeder, while Johnson, despite having been intimately associated with Fashion's first three dams, was to assume his customary role of leader of the Southern forces and manager of the filly's opponent.

On October 28, 1841, Boston, not having fully recovered from a hard victory in Baltimore a week earlier, had been distanced in the first heat of a race in Camden, New Jersey. It was the first, and only, such humiliation he suffered in his entire career, discounting his debut when he had sulked, and the ultimate winner of the race was Fashion, so here came another challenge:

> To the Friends of the distinguished Race Nag, Fashion
>
> In the four-mile race recently run over the Camden and Philadelphia Course, Boston was distanced by John Blount and Fashion in the first heat—Blount winning the heat in 7:42. The second heat was won by Fashion in 7:48 —Blount breaking down.
>
> We, the undersigned, now propose to run Boston against Fashion, a match, four-mile heats, over the Union Course, Long Island, agreeably to the rules of said Course, in Spring, 1842, or any day during the month of May, for $20,000 a side—one half or one fourth forfeit, as may be most agreeable to the friends of Fashion. The forfeit to be deposited (in New York money, in any bank in the city), and the day of the race to be named, when the match shall be closed. The challenge shall remain open during the month of November.
>
> (Signed) William R. Johnson
> James Long
> New York, Astor House, Nov. 5, 1841

Although Gibbons deplored such ostentation (a conservative man, he raced only horses he bred himself, and never bet), the public demand for the match was irresistible, and on November 30, the last day before the challenge would lapse, one-fourth forfeit money was deposited. The forthcoming clash provided conversational fodder throughout that winter and spring, and the sporting press luxuriated in this windfall during the intervening months.

On race day a crowd estimated at 70,000

Fashion, champion four-mile mare, who set a record of 7:32½ for that distance.

Edward Troye, Jockey Club

attended, including, it was claimed, 40 U. S. Senators and Congressmen who came up from Washington especially for the contest. A capacity 8,000 persons willingly paid the $10 admission fee to the grandstand. Train service from New York broke down, and a mob ran amuck, tearing down the ticket office. One trainload reached the course after the first heat, and rushed the fence until repelled by a group headed by the prize fighters Yankee Sullivan, Isaiah Rynders and Jeroloman. A daily newspaper had set up a press on the grounds which issued extras after each heat, and carrier pigeons flew latest developments to other newspapers in the city.

Fashion, five-years-old, was ridden by Joe Laird and carried 111 pounds. Boston, nine, was assigned 126 pounds and ridden by the veteran Gilpatrick.

In the first heat, Boston struck his hip against the rail and received a long, jagged cut, and both horses were bothered by the crowd surging out onto the track and leaving them only a narrow lane, yet the distance was run in the unprecedented time of 7:32½, Fashion the winner by slightly more than a length.

Both cooled out well, Boston blowing like a locomotive, but that was his habit, and there was a slight delay while the track was cleared of spectators for the second heat. Although Boston was leading after 3 miles had been run, Fashion overtook him and sailed away to win by about 60 yards, Gilpatrick having pulled Boston up after passing the distance stand when he saw the cause was hopeless. Time was 7:45 with fractions for each mile as follows: first heat 1:53, 1:50½, 1:54, 1:55; second heat 1:59, 1:57, 1:51½, 1:57½.

From a public relations standpoint, the race had been a fiasco, and it later was learned that the two distinguished judges, Alexander Barrow of New Orleans and John M. Botts of Virginia, after journeying all the way to New York to preside, had been forced to pay $10 to get into the track. The Long Island Railway Company, as well as operators of the track, were severely criticized for inefficiency and avarice. Henry K. Toler, secretary of the New York Jockey Club, issued a card announcing his resignation and disavowing responsibility for the confusion. Efforts to arrange a rematch failed and both horses went their separate ways, but it was not long before a bandwagon began rolling in the South for a new challenger, Peytona, who, in a comparatively brief career, had amassed more earnings than Fashion.

Different people react to crises in different ways. Just as a housewife who finds herself overdrawn in her bank account might seek relief by going out and charging a new hat, when the financial Panic of 1837 was in full swing, Andrew Jackson's young friend, Colonel Balie Peyton, conceived of a strange antidote. He decided to stage the richest race in world history.

So-called produce races, the equivalent of modern futurities in which nominations are made far in advance and the purse swelled meanwhile by various installment payments, had been in vogue for some time, but none on the scale envisioned by Peyton. In 1838 he announced a race for yet unborn foals of '39, to be run at Nashville as four-year-olds in 1843, $5,000 to subscribe and $1,000 in forfeit payments, with an estimated value at maturity of $150,000.

The calculated shock value of this announcement had its effect in that it created a sensation, but when entries closed it was Colonel Peyton's turn to be shocked. There were only thirty subscribers, but as time went on and the depression grew worse, some of the owners reneged on their forfeit money, and when race day finally arrived only four runners responded to the bugle.

Alexander Barrow won the first heat with an unnamed colt, and Wade Hampton II of South Carolina took the second with Herald. The previously described Glumdalclitch, cleverly maneuvered over the atrociously muddy track with only the "Southern weight" of 97 pounds burdening her mammoth frame, won the next two. (Balie Peyton's own entry, Great Western, finished two-three-distanced.)

Despite the various financial jolts the race had suffered, value to the winner still amounted to about $35,000 and Glumdalclitch became the leading money winner of her sex in America. Her name was changed to Peytona in honor of her great victory.

Owned by Thomas Kirkman and trained by Isaac Van Leer, the huge filly, said to stride 27 feet, had won all four of her previous races. Peytona remained undefeated after moving down to New Orleans, and she thereupon was chosen to challenge Fashion for national honors.

A match was accordingly arranged, with $10,000 a side, $2,000 forfeit, to be run on May 15, 1845, at the Union Course. Peytona, managed by her own trainer (W. R. Johnson acted as a consultant on this occasion), made a leisurely journey up from Mobile in company with four other horses and a big baggage wagon, as crowds turned out to cheer the cavalcade at every city along the way.

In the North, Fashion received similar adulation. Various articles of merchandise were named in her honor, from ladies' gloves to men's cigars, not to mention more permanent tributes such as steamboats and hotels.

This, which was to be the last of the epic matches at the Union Course, far exceeded all the earlier ones in interest. The lowest estimate of the crowd was 70,000 and the top was somewhere around 100,000. Toler having become treasurer, the secretary of the New York Jockey Club was none other than William T. Porter, a turf writer turned target for the criticism he formerly had administered. Although local sentiment made Fashion a slight favorite, there was little to choose between the contestants, and much of the betting concerned merely whether the race would be run in time slower or faster than 7:40.

On the morning of the race there were reports that Fashion was showing evidence of being under the influence of her estrous cycle, but the race went off as scheduled. Fashion, this time the senior competitor, carried 123 pounds with her regular jockey Laird, while Peytona, at 116, was ridden by Francis "Barney" Palmer, the rider in her previous victories. Peytona won in straight heats, both of them hard fought, in time as follows: first heat 1:54, 1:53, 1:57, 1:55¾, final time, 7:39¾; second heat 1:58, 1:54, 1:55, 1:58¼, final time, 7:45¼.

As this made the score 3-2 their favor in the intersectional matches, all was gleeful among the Southerners, although Northerners consoled themselves that Peytona was both trained and ridden by Yankees (as, on previous occasions, Southerners had consoled *themselves* by pointing out the Virginia blood in the Northern winners).

In any case, the triumph had to be enjoyed while it lasted, because Fashion emerged from this race in good condition while the bulky Peytona, who had been shod with very light plates, came out with feverish front feet and ankles. Although both mares had been entered for a Jockey Club Purse four days later, Peytona could not start and Fashion won it easily, pulled up to a trot.

She met Peytona again at Camden on May 28, and again Fashion won pulled up, as Laird took care not to embarrass his erstwhile conqueror by leaving her outside the distance pole.

Further challenges were made—both on behalf of Peytona and also Boston (who had been at stud for three seasons)—but nothing came of them. After a two-year layoff because of injuries, Peytona made one unsuccessful attempt to return to racing, then retired with earnings of $62,400, a record at that time for either sex.

Fashion went on and on, ending her career in 1848 at the age of eleven. Widely hailed as the greatest racer, if not the top money winner, of her sex ever to appear on the American turf, she won 32 of her 36 starts and was second in the other four.

At stud neither Peytona nor Fashion matched the brilliance they had shown on the race course. The former, having been acquired by A. Keene Richards, who was experimenting at the time with Arabian stallions, was bred mostly to them and had only four foals by thoroughbred sires; Fashion had a creditable record but not a remarkable one.

Despite his hard use Boston became America's leading sire for three successive seasons, 1851-1853, as well as a noted sire of trotters. He had begun stud duty before his match with Fashion. In 1841 he was bred to forty-two mares in the spring, then raced five times in September and October; and in 1842, after the North–South match and two other races in May, he did some stud service before returning to the track in October.

Completely blind in later years, and pitifully emaciated, he retained his fierce spirit to the very end. On the morning of January 31, 1850, he was found dead in his stall, the sides of which were covered with blood where Boston repeatedly had struck his head and legs in his final furious struggle. Not even the grim reaper could distance him, however, for Boston's last crop, foaled after his death, included Lexington and Lecomte.

CHAPTER SIXTEEN

THERE ARE EXCEPTIONS, OF course, but as a general rule an extremely high class thoroughbred doesn't just happen. Somewhere in his background there are numerous little details, perhaps unnoticed and each in itself inconsequential, which, when added together, culminate in a champion. In this sense it was especially appropriate that Lexington become the greatest horse foaled in America, since he represented the crowning achievement of several notable persons—and an entire state.

The passion of early Kentuckians for racing of any sort already has been commented upon, and the area quickly became known for its good stock (the Army was advertising to buy Kentucky horses in 1792). Despite the intense popularity of quarter racing among the first settlers, there is evidence that course racing was in progress as early as 1789, three years before Kentucky was admitted to the Union, in the form of the following notice which appeared that year in the Kentucky *Gazette:*

> A purse race at Lexington on the 2nd Thursday in October next, free for any horse, mare or gelding, weight for age, agreeable to the rules of New Market, (three mile heats) the best two in three; one quarter of an hour allowed between heats for rubbing. Each subscriber to pay one guinea, and every person that enters a horse to pay two guineas, including his subscription.
>
> One guinea for every horse starting to be considered as entrance money for the second best horse.
>
> Judges to be appointed by a majority of the Starters on the day of running, the horses to be entered the day before running with Mr. John Fowler, who will attend at Mr. Collins' Tavern on that day. The age of the horses to be ascertained to the satisfaction of the judges appointed before they can be admitted to start, even although they have paid the entrance money &c., and the money paid remain for the good of the purse. But the starter may be admitted to start his horse at the age adjudged by the judges agreeable to the rules of New Market. The horses to start precisely at one o'clock: Any horse not starting agreeable to the appointment, to be adjudged a distanced horse. All disputes arising to be left to the decision of the judges. Subscriptions taken in by Nicholas Lafon, Lexington.

There is mention of 4-mile heat racing in Lexington in 1795, and in 1797 the Lexington Jockey Club was organized at Postlethwait's Tavern on the site of today's Phoenix Hotel. That same year, Blaze was advertised as the first authentic English horse to stand in Kentucky.

Before 1800 there was racing at Equiria in Woodford County, at Georgetown, Danville, Bardstown and Shelbyville—with Versailles, Winchester and Maysville soon joining in.

Louisville was a relatively late arrival on the scene, but the most talked-about races in Kentucky before the Civil War were held there in 1839.

Miles Dickey's Grey Eagle as a three-year-old had won a 2-mile race in straight heats, 3:41, 3:43½, the fastest time yet in America, so much so that a demand was made that the track be measured. This was done, and it was found to be more than 12 feet longer than a mile. When Grey Eagle followed this up with another victory a week later in 3:48, 3:44, he was hailed as the greatest horse in Kentucky.

Farther South there developed dissenting opinion as James Garrison was campaigning a horse named Wagner (owned by John Campbell) who had defeated practically everything in sight at Mobile, New Orleans, and Natchez. This was a situation tailor-made for the impresario in Yelverton N. Oliver, who at that time was operating the Oakland Course in Louisville. Immediately after Grey Eagle's second sensational race, he announced a great sweepstakes for all ages to be run at the 1839 fall meeting, at 4-mile heats under provocative conditions: $2,000 to enter, half forfeit, with the stands receipts to be added to the purse.

This strange fit of generosity was more easily understood when Oliver promptly purchased a half-interest in Grey Eagle and made him the first entry in the stake. The race attracted ten subscriptions, including Wagner, but by post time, on Monday, September 30, there were but four survivors.

Wagner, a five-year-old seasoned 4-mile horse, ridden by the popular colored jockey, Cato, won the first heat easily from his year younger rival, who was making his first start over the heroic distance. The only excitement provided was the time, 7:48, which was the fastest yet seen in Kentucky. It was a harder task in the next heat, however, as Grey Eagle whirled the distance faster than the still fresh record; after a seesaw battle, he was in front 100 yards from home, but Wagner (or rather, Cato, who was riding literally for honor and freedom, as he had been promised his liberty should he win) refused to quit. He won by a neck in 7:44.

The victorious Wagner was paraded up and down before the stands, which included such notables as Henry Clay and the journalist William Porter, who had come all the way from New York to cover the race, while Cato jubilantly waved aloft the stake money, which amounted to $14,000 with the gate receipts yet to come.

Oliver had no reason to regret his action, however, because even without the stands fees he cleared about $15,000 on general admission and concessions, and there was an immediate clamor for a return match. This came about on Saturday when an even bigger throng turned out, and this time Oliver had not bargained away part of his gate.

Willa Viley started the filly Emily Johnson, against the two principals, and she surprised the crowd by splitting the rivals in the first heat, won by Grey Eagle in 7:51. The second heat was strictly a match, as, after a stubborn fight, Wagner beat Grey Eagle a neck in 7:43, Emily Johnson distanced. In the third heat Grey Eagle broke down during the second mile and came to a dead stop, so no time was taken.

Ironically, Grey Eagle was saved for stud and became a very popular stallion while Wagner, except for a walkover, never won another race and began his stud career under a cloud, although he later did achieve an excellent reputation.

Wagner was by Sir Charles (son of Sir Archie) out of a granddaughter of Sir Archie. Grey Eagle was by Woodpecker (grandson of Sir Archie) and also out of a granddaughter of Sir Archie.

It was through breeding more than racing that Kentucky gained its fame, however, and the foremost expert in this field was Elisha Warfield, Jr. (1781–1859). A native of Maryland, who came west with his family at the age of nine, Warfield later attended Transylvania College, the first institution of higher learning to be established beyond the Alleghenies. After taking his medical degree, he entered practice, and also was Professor of Surgery and Obstetrics at Transylvania, until poor health forced him to retire at forty. Advised to live as much as possible in the open, and having been keenly interested in livestock all along (he had starters at the Lexington race meetings while still in his twenties) Dr. Warfield thenceforth made horses his specialty. Combining the practical lore of a Bluegrass resident with the penchant for research and scientific analysis derived from his medical training, he became the acknowledged final authority in his horse-wise region.

He was a practical man, too, as is illustrated by an advertisement he had published in 1806 which offered the services of his horse, Tup, for $22 cash, or bricks at $4 per 100; beef on foot at /15 per hundredweight; whiskey at £2 per gallon and numerous other alternatives.

Adding a theatrical touch to his distinguished career, Dr. Warfield's greatest success came shortly before the final curtain. He was nearly seventy years old when Alice Carneal, a mare he had bred himself, in 1850 foaled a bay colt by Boston, which later was to be known as Lexington.

LEXINGTON, 1850

(Boston—Alice Carneal, by Sarpedon)

Under the name of Darley, the colt won his first two races in the colors of his breeder, but actually he was running for a partnership. Dr. Warfield, at seventy-two, did not feel he could do justice to the son of Boston, and he had leased his racing qualities to "Burbridge's Harry," a former slave and well known local trainer. Since Harry was not permitted to enter a horse in his own right, "Darley" carried Dr. Warfield's racing silks, but the two men had shared the $100 entry fee for the horse's debut in competition. His first start was the Association Stakes for three-year-olds, mile heats, at Lexington on May 23, 1853. On a muddy track, "Darley" won in straight heats, 1:55½, 1:57, distancing eight of his eleven rivals in the first heat and another one in the next.

Four days later, again under the name of Darley and carrying Dr. Warfield's colors, he came out for the Citizens' Stakes at 2-mile heats, although Harry, not yet having collected his half of the purse from the first race, borrowed the post fee from Dr. Warfield's son and politely informed his erstwhile partner that in this race he "didn't know nothing about no

Lexington, superior racehorse and incomparable sire of the 19th century.

Edward Troye, Jockey Club

halves." After finishing second in the first heat, won in 3:42½, Darley won the next two, easily distancing four of his six opponents in 3:41½, 3:49.

Among the spectators that day was Richard Ten Broeck, who approached Dr. Warfield and asked him to name his price on the colt. This was done, and the next day Ten Broeck wrote the editor of *The Spirit of the Times* announcing that he had purchased Dr. Warfield's Boston colt and renamed it "Lexington." Appended to a certification of Lexington's pedigree was the following signed statement by his elderly breeder: "The colt was bred by me, as was also his dam, which I now, and will ever, own . . . E. Warfield."

Considering his age, it was understandable that Dr. Warfield should sell his prize, but why literally "down the river," because assuredly Ten Broeck was expected to take the colt to New Orleans for the Great State Post Stake, a much-publicized race scheduled for the following year? The explanation might be that Ten Broeck assuaged local pride by taking in as partners three of the most popular Kentuckians of the time: Captain Willa Viley, General Abe Buford II, and Junius R. Ward. Moreover, Lexington would represent Kentucky in the great race coming up.

This sale was remarkable in other ways. Presumably, Ten Broeck had purchased Lexington either between heats or before the running of the Citizens' Stake, and he attempted to collect Dr. Warfield's share of the $1,300 purse money. However, what Dr. Warfield had sold him was "his interest" in the colt, which was nil in that particular event, financially speaking, since Old Harry had put up the entire post fee, and he steadfastly maintained that he was entitled to the full purse. The buyers then tried to deduct the share of the purse to which they felt themselves entitled from the agreed-upon purchase price—having contracted to buy the greatest horse in America for only $2,500, they sought a $650 rebate—but Dr. Warfield held out for the original amount.

Richard Ten Broeck, a man of mystery who cast a long shadow in turf affairs.

Added to a more than sufficient quantity of adventure, there is an element of mystery in the life of Richard Ten Broeck (1811–1892), the man who played an important part in the lives of both Lexington and his arch rival, Lecomte.

In profile, Ten Broeck looks innocuous enough, but the head-on view in the portait of him which hangs in the National Museum of Racing at Saratoga shows a handsome, intense, bearded face, with icy blue eyes that could make Bat Masterson throw in his hand

69

without drawing a card. Ten Broeck looked the perfect prototype of the old Mississippi riverboat gambler. In fact, during one phase of his provocative career, he was.

Born into an old distinguished family in Albany, New York, Richard Ten Broeck entered the U. S. Military Academy at West Point in 1829, from which he resigned the next February under circumstances which never have been clear. (One rumor is that he considered himself insulted by one of his instructors, and resigned in order to challenge the offender to a duel; another version indicates he did assault the officer and was allowed to resign in lieu of expulsion.) He severed connections with his family and disappeared from view for ten years, apparently spending most of this time on the pleasure boats which plied the Mississippi River. His name began showing up in turf records about 1840, and by 1844 he was well known in what was then the turf capital of America, New Orleans. Along the way, he had acquired friendships with a number of important figures, including W. R. Johnson, who trained some horses for him, and by 1847 Ten Broeck had become a powerful influence in his own right. He managed the Bascombe Course at Mobile, the Bingaman Course in New Orleans, and also had an interest in the Metairie Course in the latter city.

Adam L. Bingaman, Duncan F. Kenner, William J. Minor and Thomas J. Wells, at that time were the Big Four in the Deep South. Bingaman was so successful an owner that his opponents at times turned their horses over to his stable, which was trained by J. B. Pryor, reminiscent of the stature enjoyed by W. R. Johnson. Bingaman sometimes was referred to as "The Napoleon of the South."

Duncan F. Kenner, president of the Louisiana Jockey Club, owned a powerful stable trained by George Graves, and maintained a large breeding farm up the river from New Orleans. He also owned the noted colored jockey, Abe Hawkins. William J. Minor, who was related to Kenner, and a neighbor of Bing-

aman, was one of the leading planters in the Natchez area, and he and Bingaman founded the Pharsalia Course in that city. Thomas J. Wells owned Wellswood Plantation, the largest stud in the Deep South, located near Alexandria, Louisiana, and the trainer of his racing stable was a slave named Hark.

Ten Broeck, although he arrived at his eminence via a vastly different path, was to join these men at the head of the Southern turf.

New Orleans, by 1830, had exceeded 100,000 in population, which placed it in a virtual dead heat with Baltimore for third rank among American cities. As an entertainment capital, however, the Crescent City was without rival, and despite her relatively late start in racing, before the Civil War at one time or another there were at least seven different tracks in operation: Eclipse, Metairie, Bingaman, Louisiana, Union, Algiers and Jackson.

As the horses from Tennessee and Kentucky poured into New Orleans, the running times became faster and faster until cynical Easterners began to question the distance of the tracks, but the moist ground of the Crescent City was responsible, with an assist from the Southern scale of weights which was 4 pounds lighter than that then prevailing in the North.

Although sports of all kinds found favor with the city's numerous transients or newcomers —disdainfully referred to as "les Américains" by the entrenched citizens—racing did not attain the social éclat it enjoyed in other cities until the appearance on the scene of Yelverton N. Oliver, who organized a New Orleans Jockey Club which included the most prominent figures of the community. He opened the Eclipse Course, which was known not only for its running surface (Oliver had loads of sand hauled in to blend with the track's natural soil) but for its opulent appointments and the way it catered to ladies.

Racing became fashionable overnight, and having seen Oliver's success, another jockey

70

Race Day at Metairie.
Louisiana State Museum

club was formed to build an even more luxurious racing plant on Metairie Ridge, the highest ground in the vicinity of the city (although barely above sea level at that, as New Orleans itself is below that mark). The new track was built by the Canal and Banking Company, which leased it to another New Orleans Jockey Club organized by Richard Adams and James Garrison, both of whom owned tracks in Virginia. To insure prestige, Alexander Barrow was installed as president, and Balie Peyton, T. J. Wells and Thomas W. Chinn were vice-presidents.

Yet another track followed Metairie, and the promoters of this one outdid their predecessors by securing as a partner Bernard Xavier de Marigny de Mandeville, a high-spirited local playboy who enjoyed entrée among the city's noblest families. (New Orleans historian, Grace King, likened him to the final bouquet of a pyrotechnical display. He once lit a $5 bill to look for a coin a lady had dropped, and eventually he completely dissipated his family's fortune.)

In the end, it was the Metairie Course which was to outstrip its rivals. As the Panic of 1837 began to make itself felt, one by one the other tracks faded, leaving Metairie as the heir to all the grandeur. The track was purchased outright by Richard Ten Broeck in 1851, and became the undisputed temple of American racing, not only by reason of its lavish physical appointments, but because it also was the scene of historic performances by historic horses.

At the 1840 spring meeting Beeswing won a 4-mile heat in 7:38, although the effort broke her down and she had to be withdrawn from the second heat. A year later Grey Medoc and Altorf ran a dead heat in 7:35.

Metairie was the scene of a match in 1842 between two renowned mares, Reel and Miss Foote, which the former won in straight heats. Reel was to become dam of Lecomte and Prioress. Miss Foote, a dainty filly not over

71

14 hands 2 inches, was the scourge of males throughout the Midwest; she won a "free-for-all" at a mile which went seven heats.

Revenue won two Jockey Club Purses in Metairie, and apart from his formidable record he is remembered as the last winner trained by W. R. Johnson. Indeed, the Napoleon of the Turf was down to just the one horse at the end. After Revenue's victory at Metairie on December 11, 1848, Johnson moved on to Mobile where on February 10, 1849, he died at the age of sixty-seven.

T. B. Patterson's great mare Charmer, winner of 27 races, including a famous victory over Louis d'Or in five heats of 4 miles each, appeared at Metairie, as did the filly Prioress, later to gain fame in England. As a two-year-old in New Orleans she ran successive mile heats in 1:46¼, 1:45 to set a record. Other stars were W. J. Minor's La Vraie Reine, who won eleven races in a row without losing a single heat; T. B. Goldsby's Brown Dick, the phenomenal 3-miler; and the peripatetic Maid of Orleans. But the most remarkable horses to appear at Metairie, or any other track, were Lexington and Lecomte.

After his sale to Ten Broeck and partners, Lexington was shipped to A. L. Bingaman's trainer, J. B. Pryor, at Natchez, and let up in training to await the great Post Stake the next April. However, J. L. Pool of Mobile had a four-year-old filly named Sally Waters who had scorched the Metairie Course in a 2-mile race against another of Ten Broeck's horses, the heats having been run in 3:40, 3:37½ and 3:39. A fellow Alabaman, Louis Smith, (who was no friend of Ten Broeck's to begin with) then challenged Lexington to a match with Sally Waters at Metairie, 3-mile heats, offering to post $5,000 against only $3,500 by the owners of Lexington. Although Lexington never had been tried at 3 miles, had not raced since May and had been taking it easy on everything but the feed bag (while Sally Waters had won as recently as November 21), Ten Broeck couldn't resist the odds, and he

accepted a December 2 match. Lexington won in straight heats, 6:23½, 6:24½, track muddy, as his older rival failed to beat the distance flag in the second heat.

The Great State Post Stake of April 3, 1854 had been envisioned as the richest horse race ever contested, with every racing state expected to subscribe to this unusual event which was designed to settle regional supremacy. The conditions provided in part: ". . . Subscriptions at $5,000 each; $1,000 to each starter, if not distanced, the remainder to the winner. Each state subscribing to be represented by the signatures of three responsible gentlemen, residents of said State, the majority of whom shall name the horse to start . . . Four-mile heats."

Only four states mustered candidates deemed worthy to represent them. It was a beautiful day, although the track was muddy from earlier rain, and downtown New Orleans was practically deserted since many businesses declared a holiday. Former President Millard Fillmore was an official judge, along with General Wade Hampton III of North Carolina (serving for Alabama in this race, however), Robert Evans serving for Kentucky, Colonel J. J. Hughes serving for Louisiana and Judge Pinckney Smith for Mississippi. Results were as follows:

GREAT STATE POST STAKE

New Orleans, La., April 1, 1854

	Finish by Heats	
	1st	2nd
Representing Kentucky: Lexington, b.c., 3, 86 lbs. (Henry Meichon)	1	1
Representing Mississippi: Lecomte, ch.c., 3, 86 lbs. (John)	2	2
Representing Alabama: Highlander, ch.c., 4, 100 lbs. (Gilpatrick)	3	dist.
Representing Louisiana: Arrow, ch.g., 4, 97 lbs. (Abe)	dist.	
Time (track muddy):	8:08¾	8:04

It was a glorious day for Boston (the stallion) and for Kentucky (the state) as three of the four starters were sons of the white-nosed old curmudgeon, bred in Kentucky, the sole exception in each case being Highlander. Pride of ownership must have been quite mixed, however, for Mississippi's representative was owned by Louisiana subscriber T. J. Wells, while Louisiana's candidate was owned by Ten Broeck, who also was part owner of Lexington.

It was a dark day for the brilliant Lecomte, who had been undefeated in previous outings, but his camp was not too depressed because there was a jockey club purse coming up the next Saturday in which he would have an opportunity to avenge his defeat, and they were confident that he would.

Had not three of Lexington's four victories been won on muddy tracks in slow time and, moreover, had not he lost a heat to John Harper's filly, Midway, in the Citizens' Stake, the only occasion he had caught a fast track? So far, Lexington had proved himself in competition to be a superior mudder, nothing else.

That Lexington was considerably more versatile his owners well knew. In a trial before the Post Stake he had been worked against four different horses who took turns running at him, one mile each. One of these horses was the mightiest atom in American racing history, Little Flea, a gelding who stood only 14 hands but set several time records carrying his official weight; he was reserved for the fourth mile of the trial, but Lexington flicked him off as casually as he had the others.

Following this trial, and the victory in the Post Stake, Captain Willa Viley had Lexington's shoes pulled off, but Ten Broeck insisted that he run again the next Saturday. A conflict of interests between Viley, an essentially racing man, and Ten Broeck, a track owner who was sensitive to gate receipts, and a betting man as well, led to a stalemate which was only resolved when Ten Broeck bought out his Kentucky partners for an undisclosed sum. Lexington was entered in the Saturday race.

The excitement was intense and the wagering heavy. Lexington was 4-to-5 in the field, or 3-to-5 with respect to Lecomte only, and in the wagering among the fair sex, "who risked many gloves, handkerchiefs and pretty trifles," Lexington also was favored although precise quotation of the odds is not available.

Only one opponent, John Hunter's aged gelding Reube, 124 pounds, came out to face the awesome pair, but he was no significant factor in the wagering nor the race that followed. It was Lecomte's shining hour, as the Wells colt fully justified the optimism of his connections.

Carrying 89 pounds, and this time ridden by Abe Hawkins, Lecomte took the lead at the start of the first heat and was never headed. The equally weighted Lexington, Henry Meichon up, followed within good striking distance for the first 3 miles, but each time he attempted to pass his kinsman he was thwarted. In the fourth mile, Meichon resorted to whip and spurs in a last ditch effort, but Lecomte—untouched by either—drew away to win easily by six lengths.

The result was no more startling than the time. The winner had covered the 4 miles in 1:53, 1:54, 1:49½ and 1:49½ for a final clocking of 7:26, a new record, 6½ seconds faster than the former mark that had been set by Fashion in her match against Boston twelve years earlier. Moreover, Lecomte appeared "bright and gay" after his feat, while Lexington seemed "much distressed, with drooping head, heaving flanks, distended nostrils and every sympton of exhaustion." Lecomte became a 2-to-5 favorite to win in straight heats.

Ten Broeck's colt made a remarkable recovery during the rest period, however, and at the start of the second heat it was he who took the lead. Hawkins was content to follow Lexington's pace through the first 2 miles, run in 2:02 and 1:58, but in the third mile he called on Lecomte; the result was the fastest such segment ever recorded in a 4-mile race—1:46—by the end of which Lecomte had taken the lead. He increased it during the final mile, run in

1:52¾, to cross the finish four lengths clear of Lexington, as Reube failed to beat the distance flag. The 7:38¾ for the second heat, coupled with the unprecedented time of the first, was a new record for 8 miles of 15:04¾.

In the light of subsequent knowledge, historians are inclined to make excuses for their heroes. It has been pointed out that Lexington was fed indulgently for a couple of days after the Great Post Stake, before it was decided to run him again; but on the other hand, even though he lost the first heat by six lengths, he, too, had bettered the former record by about 5 seconds. It also was claimed that during the second heat one of Lecomte's supporters had run onto the course at the end of the third mile and shouted to Meichon to pull up, which Lexington's jockey, thinking the race was over, did, causing his mount to lose considerably more ground than the ultimate margin of defeat. That even a novice jockey would be so naive as to take instructions from a spectator is difficult to believe.

The fallout from this race exceeded anything of its kind before or since. Ten Broeck immediately challenged General Wells to another match, $10,000 a side, but was curtly turned down. Desperate with frustration, Ten Broeck then inserted the following notice in the *Spirit of the Times*:

> Although the mistake made by the rider of Lexington in pulling up at the end of the three miles in the recent fast four-mile race at New Orleans, was witnessed by thousands of persons, I believe it has not been referred to in print except in the last number of your paper. As Lexington will probably follow the fashion in making a foreign tour, I propose the following as his valedictory: I will run him a single four miles over the Metairie Course at New Orleans (under the rules of the Club) against the fastest time at four miles that has been run in America, for the sum of TEN THOUSAND DOLLARS—one-fourth forfeit. Two trials to be allowed, and the race to be run between the 1st and 15th of April next, Arrow to be substituted if Lexington is amiss.

> Or, I will run Lexington over the same course, four-mile heats, on the Thursday previous to the next Metairie April meeting, *against any named horse!* at the rate expressed in the proposition subjoined.

> Or, I will run him over the Union Course, at New York, the same distance, on the third Tuesday in October. The party accepting the last race to receive *Twenty-Five Thousand Dollars* to Twenty Thousand Dollars or to bet the same odds if Lexington travels to run at New Orleans. The forfeit to be FIVE THOUSAND DOLLARS, and to be deposited with Messrs. COLEMAN & STETSON, of the Astor House, when either race is accepted. If the amounts of the last proposition are too large, they may be reduced one-half, with forfeit in the same proportion. The first acceptance coming to hand will be valid—subsequent ones declined; and none received after the commencement of the races at the National Course in New York, the 26th of next month.

> R. TEN BROECK.

The notice was dated May 30, 1854, nearly a year in advance of the proposed races.

It was the custom among the old sports to use the pages of the *Spirit* as a clearing house for challenges, opinions and accusations (frequently without consulting the other parties concerned beforehand) often signed with didactic, if not pompous, pseudonyms. Some of these pen names, backed up by truly competent turf experts such as "Observer" (Benjamin Ogle Tayloe) became famous in their own right, but there was no way of knowing when they were misappropriated by less-qualified authors. Ten Broeck seems to have had influence with the editors of the *Spirit,* since he enjoyed apparently complete access to its pages, perhaps because he doubled as correspondent of a sort, sending in accounts of races in the faraway spots he visited.

An epidemic of challenges, comments, counter-challenges and rebuttals followed Ten Broeck's letter, during which General Wells announced that he would run Lecomte against "any horse in the world, any day, any distance, for any amount of money," with a reasonable leeway as to track, too: Metairie, Mobile or Natchez. (In another, more specific communication, he offered to pay $500 expense money to any challenger not a resident of Louisiana, which eliminated Ten Broeck.)

Two weeks after Ten Broeck's challenge appeared Calvin Green and John Belcher of Virginia, disdaining any flesh-and-blood candidate to send against Lexington, announced acceptance of the first proposition, backing "Time." Later on, Belcher, who owned the formidable Red Eye, yet another son of Boston, who was sulky and something of an in-and-outer, but in often enough to win 33 races, had second thoughts and expressed interests in matching him against Lexington with certain changes in the conditions, but it was declined.

Meanwhile Lexington went on up to New York, and Lecomte was returned to his owner's Wellswood Farm in central Louisiana. The campaign through the Atlantic states planned for Lexington never did materialize, as his bridle broke during a workout and he veered off into a field of corn, injuring his leg to an extent that his owners struck him from his autumn engagements (and there were a lot of insinuations about that).

Back down the river he went, stopping off at Natchez, while Lecomte, after winning a 2-mile race on opening day of the Metairie fall meeting, was returned to Wellswood, from whence his owner isued an announcement that the colt would run on the 4-mile day at the Metairie Spring Meeting, and he was willing to participate in an inside stake with the owner of any other horse.

Lexington, however, had his previous commitment, and preparation for his race against the 7:26 record was made. The track was specially prepared, and, after considerable discussion among the judges, it was agreed that he might have a flying start and be assisted by pacemakers.

The afternoon of April 2, 1855, was selected for the assault against time (which allowed Lexington thirteen days in which to make a second attempt should he fail), and there was no other racing on the program. At about 3 o'clock Lexington, ridden by Gilpatrick, strode onto the track accompanied by his pacemakers, Arrow and Joe Blackburn. The latter might as well have stayed in the barn.

Lexington walked down to the distance stand, turned and built up speed coming to the wire. He hit the official start running so fast that Joe Blackburn was left behind while Lexington went on to run the first mile in 1:47¼. This was regarded as much too fast, and instructions were shouted to Gilpatrick to take back. Arrow came on as pacesetter at this point and they went the second mile in 1:52¼, both horses continuing on through a third mile in 1:51½, when Arrow dropped out and Joe Blackburn came in again, but again so far astern as to be useless. Gilpatrick ceased rating his horse near the end and Lexington ran the final mile in 1:48¾ for a 4-mile clocking of 7:19¾ —to defeat his opponent, Time, by 6¼ seconds.

Historian John Hervey even found an excuse for his hero's performance in this race. He states "there were two deterrents to fast time. There was a high wind blowing which Lexington had to face a good part of the way in each round of the course. In addition, the removal of the top dressing next the rail had left a surface almost as hard as concrete, and as he was kept in there all the way, and was shod with the lightest of plates, Lexington's feet began to sting him so keenly that he made repeated efforts to swerve out into the softer going all through the homestretch of the final mile and Gilpatrick had great difficulty to keep him from doing so . . ."

(Presumably, that wind which was against Lexington "a good part of the way," was in his favor an equal part of the way, and hugging the rail on a hard track is hardly a deterrent to fast time.)

Having cleared the first hurdle, Ten Broeck called General Wells' hand on his challenge for an inside stake on 4-mile day, and the agreement to post $2,500 each merely served to increase the regular purse since no other horses were entered against the two sons of Boston when they jousted for the final time.

This race took place twelve days after Lexington's successful contest against time. Although he had stung his feet a bit, this was quickly alleviated by tubbing, and it was Lecomte who had troubles. Early in the week before the race he reportedly had an attack of colic for which he was given drastic treatment, and although he resumed galloping, he did not seem to have his usual vitality. For days in advance, racing fans from all over the country had been converging on New Orleans, and although post time was not until 3 o'clock, the infield was filled during the morning.

At the appointed time, on Saturday, April 14, 1855, the arch rivals lined up for the start, Lexington having drawn the pole. At the tap of the drum both horses went off as though the race were to last only a mile, which for all practical purposes might as well have been true, since after the first half in 53 seconds, during which Lecomte was under constant pressure and Lexington highballing easily, it was all over but the technicalities. By the last mile Lecomte was in obvious distress, and although Gilpatrick had Lexington in hand, an outburst of shouting as he entered the stretch caused the horse to take off and he went under the wire in 7:23¾, with Lecomte barely saving his distance.

That, too, proved to be academic, for General Wells withdrew him from the second heat and Lexington walked over. It was his last race.

Although he was at the height of form, sound of wind and limb, a magnificent-looking blood bay, standing 15 hands 3 inches, Lexington had been suffering increasing loss of vision in one eye for some time. Now the other eye was beginning to go (his sire, Boston, had gone blind), so Lexington was shipped immediately to W. F. Harper at Midway, Kentucky, entering stud that same year, 1855, at a $100 fee.

Lecomte was rested until the fall, when he beat Arrow at Natchez, and then in December was beaten by that same horse at Metairie in a 3-mile race. Three days later Lecomte walked over for the 4-mile race, and his American record was closed the following spring with two successive defeats by Pryor. Arrow and Pryor were both owned by Ten Broeck, who up to that point was the only man to get Lecomte's number.

He also got Lecomte himself, for General Wells decided to call it quits and sold the horse to Ten Broeck for $10,000, along with Lecomte's three-year-old half-sister, Prioress, for $2,500. The next year, Ten Broeck took his stable to England, but Lecomte, who had acquired "a leg" before leaving America, and had been put to stud briefly, was so unsatisfactory in training that he did not run until September, 1857, and in this start he pulled up lame, beaten by twenty lengths. In October of that same year he had another attack of colic and died.

Prioress salvaged something for the stable by finishing among the first three in the famous triple dead heat for the 1857 Cesarewitch Handicap, and then—her American background of heat racing obviously standing her in good stead—winning the run-off.

If the sale of Lecomte to Richard Ten Broeck by his bitter enemy, General T. J. Wells, was odd, stranger still was the circumstance that General Wells became president of the Metairie track after Ten Broeck left for England, and under his regime it was improved even beyond its former grandeur with a wholly new brick and iron grandstand added, said to be the first such "permanent" structure in America.

In England, at the same time as Ten Broeck, was R. A. Alexander, who was then assembling stock for his Woodburn Farm, near Midway, Kentucky, and had gone abroad in search of a suitable stallion to head his stud. Ten Broeck sold him Lexington for $15,000, the highest price ever paid for an American-bred horse, and as a result of this trans-Atlantic transaction, after the 1856 breeding season Lexington was moved the few miles to his new home, which he was to make famous. "The Blind Hero of Woodburn" became the most successful stallion in history, leader of the American sire list sixteen seasons, fourteen of them in succession.

Ten Broeck remained abroad for many years, and after nearly three decades of relative obscurity, he enjoyed some success as manager of the stable James R. Keene sent to England.

However, the legend which accompanies his portrait in the National Museum of Racing states, ". . . the balance of his life had best be forgotten." He finally did return to America and lived alone in straitened circumstances near San Mateo, California; after death in 1892 his body was brought to Louisville for the funeral, at which Henry Watterson and Basil Duke were among the pallbearers.

Despite his reputation as a bon vivant, Benjamin Franklin is one of the few outstanding leaders of colonial America not known to have been closely identified with horses or racing. Nevertheless, he had a connection with the sport which, though indirect, was profound.

When Franklin was Minister to France, he formed a friendship with a Scottish merchant and banker, William Alexander, a former Lord Provost of Edinburgh, who had married a French woman. Their son, Robert, while still in his teens, had been Franklin's private secretary, although he returned to school in England when Franklin was recalled from Paris.

After the Revolution, William Alexander came to America, and, at Franklin's urging, his son soon followed. In 1790, the year of Franklin's death, Robert Alexander purchased a vast tract of land along Elkhorn Creek in Kentucky, and there established Woodburn Stud Farm. His parents later moved west to join him.

Alexander married relatively late in life, but had four children, of whom the eldest was christened Robert Spreull Crawford Aitcheson

Jean Lacretelle

Robert A. Alexander (1819-1867), a pioneer in the adaptation of businesslike efficiency to farm procedures, who developed Woodburn Stud into America's foremost breeding establishment, famed equally for cattle and horses.

Alexander, but the son customarily signed his name "R. Aitcheson Alexander." After a boyhood in Kentucky, R. A. Alexander returned to Scotland to live with a bachelor uncle. He was graduated from Trinity College, Cambridge, and remained overseas until he was thirty years old, when he resolved to return to Kentucky. Woodburn Farm, meanwhile, had been bequeathed by the senior Robert Alexander to his four children jointly, and R. A. bought out the interest of his brother and sisters and settled down to develop it into a model stock farm. He began with cattle and sheep but within two years thoroughbreds were added.

History seems to have taken special recognition of America's greatest horse. She arranged what amounted to a changing of the guard ceremony between Lexington's breeder and the man who was to manage the horse during his stud career. Dr. Elisha Warfield won his last race at the Lexington spring meeting in 1856; R. A. Alexander won his first race at the fall meeting of the same track that same year.

CHAPTER SEVENTEEN

LTHOUGH THE FOREGOING AC-count of racing between the Revolutionary and Civil Wars emphasizes certain areas, the sport was spreading throughout the young nation. Shortly after the Revolution, Richmond, Virginia, enjoyed a tenure as a racing capital of America with at least three formal race courses—Fairfield, Tree Hill and Broad Rock—and meetings of one Jockey Club sometimes were held at the track of another, yet another practice which became common in modern times. The Newmarket track at nearby Petersburg completed a concentration of sport of the highest order in this area.

Baltimore, which replaced Annapolis as the center of Maryland racing, boasted two tracks within walking distance of the city after damages of the War of 1812 had been repaired, and not many miles away in Washington, the new nation's capital also had a race track. The colorful General Charles Ridgely, Governor of Maryland and master of the majestic manor, Hampton, which was modeled after an English castle, succeeded John Tayloe III as the racing monarch of the middle Atlantic seaboard. Among the many horses owned by Ridgely were Post Boy, Tuckahoe and Maid of the Oaks.

Up in Massachusetts a race course was opened at Medford in 1811, and racing in the Boston style went on for some six years before dying out. Leaving the results of the races to speak for themselves, one reporter in a description of a day's racing said: ". . . the genteel company expressed the highest satisfaction in the regularity that attended the proceedings of the Institution and their good wishes for its

utmost improvement and perpetuation." Apparently bolstered by such assurance, even the stiffest of the Back Bay element approved, for future governor John Brooks was president of the local jockey club and the vice-presidents were Colonel Blake and Samuel Appleton.

Barefoot, winner in England of the celebrated 1823 St. Leger, in which twenty-three of the horses ran the 1¾-mile course, only to be called back because of a false start and required to re-run the event, stood at Brighton for a few years, but the chilly reception he received caused him to be sent to locales where horse breeding was more popular.

In many areas racing was an off-and-on proposition, as repressive legislation flowed back and forth, causing shutdowns, some temporary and some permanent.

In 1854 efforts were made to establish one national track which would serve as the focal point of American racing, and the National Jockey Club was formed in New York. There was great enthusiasm for the general idea but disagreement concerning particulars. Washington, D. C., as capital of the Union, was submitted as the logical location for such a track, but the Southerners felt it should be located farther south. Even this degree of harmony evaporated when it came to specific points. Virginians thought it was a wonderful idea, and Richmond would be the perfect place—whereas Kentuckians spoke up for Louisville, Tennesseeans for Nashville and the Deep South for New Orleans.

The New York group went ahead under its own steam and built an elaborate racing plant at Newton, Long Island, 65 acres of which were enclosed by a 9-foot brick wall. The National Course grandstand was 1,200 feet long and could accommodate 25,000 patrons under roof and a further 12,000 on top. Two meetings in 1854 were unsuccessful, and the white elephant was put to pasture the next year (P. T. Barnum offered to take over, but was refused). In 1856 it was revived, but not very vigorously; eventually, the great new track was renamed the Fashion Course, and it became the home more of trotters than of thoroughbreds.

Spade work for international racing proved equally futile. In 1838, when pride in the American horse was at its peak, a pair of matches between British and American horses on a home-and-home basis was proposed, but as England no longer emphasized 4-mile heat racing, the plan was ignored.

In the winter of 1842–1843 a meeting at Havana, Cuba, in which such stalwarts as James Garrison, founder of Metairie, and Richard Ten Broeck were involved, aborted because spectators were too demonstrative when dissatisfied with the results of the races. (Garrison and Ten Broeck should have known better, because Y. N. Oliver had explored the ground first and had come home "shaking his head.")

There were race courses in Cincinnati and St. Louis which attracted some of the best horses in the period, and in 1840, Chicago, which had not yet acquired its big shoulders, but already was manifesting its characteristic attribute of big thinking, began to flex what it did have. "A knot of good fellows" wrote *The Spirit of the Times* requesting a copy of the by-laws of New York's Union Course and announced: ". . . We propose making three days play, commencing on the first Wednesday in September next. We have not a string of fast crabs in our capacious stables, but hold one or two that keep sound skins when the prairie is on fire, and shortly expect one that 'will be heard of.' We have some trotting nags, not 'Ned Forrests' 'tis true, but they can get close into the neighborhood of the 'thirties,' which is doing the clean thing in a new country."

Within four years Chicago had more than doubled its population and a jockey club was formed with W. B. Ogden, Chicago's first mayor, as president. The club built not one, but two race tracks, one 4 miles in circumference and the other a conventional mile track in the infield of the first. This monster didn't survive because, after an inaugural three-day race meeting in which only eight individual horses started (the first winner was W. G. Ellis's Snag) the next year racing was held on a new 1-mile course on the lake shore, owned by Dr. William Tichenor. Mixed programs of running and harness racing were conducted, and a correspondent who signed himself "Sucker" waxed enthusiastic in his report to the *Spirit:* "We had some sport here and no mistake. I reckon you, and other old sportsmen, may ridicule it all as mere children's play, as you probably will when you look in vain for your Fashions, Peytonas, and others of that like, among our performers: notwithstanding, I shall stick to it that we had first-rate sport . . . permit me to observe, that we out here are beginning just about these days to entertain considerable tall notions about ourselves . . ."

The tide of civilization which, during the nineteenth century, swept westward over the prairies and mountains until it eventually touched the Pacific was, as has been noted, borne largely by the horse. Moreover, when the settlers finally reached California, they found there a culture which was superior to that which many of them had known before, and horsemanship in a correspondingly high state of development.

In the June, 1962 Silver Anniversary edition of *The Thoroughbred of California,* Barry Whitehead traced the influence of the Spanish horse in America in an article which is summarized roughly herewith.

A century before the first Spanish settlers arrived in California, the Duke of Newcastle had described the horses of Spain as follows:

. . . of all the horses in the world, of whatsoever nation they be, Spanish horses are the

Thoroughbred of California

Spanish horse in sling for shipment to America, 15th century.

wisest, and strangely wise, beyond any man's imagination—I assure you, he is the noblest horse in the world—He is the most beautiful that can be, for he is not so thin and ladylike as the Barb, nor so gross as the Neapolitan, but between both. He is of great courage, and docile: Has the proudest walk, the proudest trot, and best action in his trot; the loftiest gallop, the swiftest careers; and is the lovingest and gentlest horse in the world . . ."

Although by tradition, caballeros of Spain disdained mares and geldings as mounts, and by law, officers of the King's cavalry rode only stallions, a royal decree specified that five of the twenty cavaliers who accompanied Columbus on his second voyage to Hispaniola in 1494 take two mares each instead of a horse. Six years later the crown reportedly had a ranch on the island "that boasted sixty brood-mares," so it is likely that Spain was establishing breeding farms in other parts of the New World. In 1769, when Captain Rivera y Moncado advanced from Lower California toward San Diego for a rendezvous with Gaspar de Portola, he was accompanied by 140 horses, and racing of a sort probably began shortly after the expedition settled down at San Diego Bay in May 1769.

Unlike the forests of the East, California offered open land suitable for races, most notably the beaches. A French visitor in 1827 took note of the fondness of Californians for racing, and Richard Henry Dana, who came around Cape Horn in 1835, also described the beach at Santa Barbara as "a favorite place for running horses." His writings indicate an advanced form of the sport, on grounds especially set aside for the purpose, with judges, rules and stakes, involving horses that were "not so sleek and combed as our Boston stable horses but with fine limbs and spirited eyes."

Reminiscent of similar episodes in the East, in 1834 Governor Figueroa prohibited the running of stray horses in Monterey, San Jose and San Francisco, and litigation concerning the outcome of California races also is included in court records of the period. Hubert Howe

81

Bancroft tells of a race at Los Angeles in 1839 for "a barrel of brandy, two broken horses and five dollars," in which one Avila protested that his rival Duarte struck his (Avila's) horse on the head during the race. The judge, a Solomon reincarnate if ever there was one, fined both men $10 and ordered them to run the race over twenty days later.

Ironically, California, which today is characterized by its most reasonable attitude toward taxation of racing—an attitude which has enabled the sport in that state to achieve an enviably well-balanced structure—as early as 1841 explored the possibilities of obtaining revenue from racing. In Los Angeles that year, a new law provided that the winner of each race pay a tax of 20 reales for every $25 bet, $5 for every $50 and 6 percent of all sums of $100 or more. This law was abolished in 1846.

Walter Colton, a navy chaplain who with Robert Semple founded *The Californian,* first newspaper in the state, stated that "the dance and a dashing horse are the two objects which overpower all others in interest with the Californians." He also observed that "a Californian is most at home in his saddle—His horse with his long flowing mane, arching neck, broad chest, full flanks, and slender legs is full of fire. He seldom trots and will gallop all day without seeming to be weary . . ."

In 1848 an advertisement for sale of the horse, El Canelo, was published in the San Francisco *Californian:* ". . . Terms coin or gold dust at $10 per ounce."

El Canelo, so-called because of his cinnamon coat color, had been ridden by Colonel John C. Frémont on a round trip from Los Angeles to Monterey in which 840 miles over virgin terrain had been covered in 76 hours riding time, spread out over eight days. Spare mounts were used on this historic jaunt, the loose horses galloping on ahead, but El Canelo in one day had carried Frémont at least 90 miles and galloped a further 30 miles without a rider.

Another item in that newspaper on March 15 the same year told of a Captain Sutter having found gold in the raceway of a sawmill recently erected on the American Fork. This item, widely reprinted in the eastern papers, opened the gates for the California Gold Rush. A great need for horses materialized and Eastern dealers began rounding them up in large groups for shipment to the west coast, whereupon the gap, such as it was, between Western and Eastern racing was quickly bridged.

Whitehead tells of a race course in Los Angeles, 4 miles long, alongside what is now Pico Street; a similar course in San Francisco near the Mission Dolores, and others on the beach at Santa Barbara and along the banks of the San Diego River.

California's first formal race track, of the Eastern variety, was San Francisco's Pioneer Course, opened in March, 1851, which operated under the rules of the Union Jockey Club of New York. Samuel Brannan, who brought the first gold from the Sierras to San Francisco, was a steward and Tom K. Battelle, leader of the first vigilante committee, was the judge, as well as owner of the winner of the first race, a colt named Boston.

About the same time, Alderman Alfred E. Green built a half-mile track called the Pavillion Course, which advertised "finest brands of Wines, Liquors, and Segars," but where racing apparently was of less impressive quality, because it soon was converted into a mile track, shaped somewhat like the future "goose egg" course at Jamaica, and renamed the Union Course. Tracks sprang up in quick succession until it now is estimated that there are no fewer than eight old race courses buried beneath the streets of present-day San Francisco.

In 1851, the same year the Pioneer Jockey Club opened, the Brighton Course near Sacramento held its inaugural meeting, and the generosity of purse distribution which distinguishes California racing to this day immediately became apparent. The mare Black Swan, imported from Australia and known as the first thoroughbred to be introduced into California, met the gelding Ito, another importation from Down Under, in a $10,000 match, won by the latter. The next year, Black Swan's owner, Don Andreas Sepulveda, challenged his good friend Governor Pio Pico to run his native-bred champion Sarco, a horse of pure Spanish blood, against the mare under any conditions Pico might care to impose. A match was arranged over 9 miles, cross-country, for 5,000 pesos and 1,000 head of cattle a side, which Black Swan won by only 75 yards, in 19 minutes 20 seconds.

Ito got his comeuppance in June, 1852, in a match against Fred Coy on which "horses, saddles, bridles, hats, boots, and everything of any value" were staked, and the plaintive query "Does your horse carry double?" which had been voiced by disillusioned fans walking home from races in Virginia, Tennessee and Kentucky was sounded west of the Sierra Nevadas.

Californians, who were to depend upon the Pony Express for mail service, obviously had a keen appreciation of distance racing. On May 2, 1858, over the Pioneer Course in San Francisco, John Powers rode 150 miles in 6 hours, 43 minutes and 31 seconds to win a $5,000 bet. He weighed in at 153 pounds, not counting his heavy Spanish saddle; his mounts were different horses "of the wild mustang breed, grass fed, ungroomed and had never seen the inside of a stable." A couple of months later, at the Union track, Thomas MacNab rode 200 miles in 9:58:30, using forty-two horses, to win a wager of $2,500.

The first mentions of heat racing in California begin in 1853. The next year there was a celebrated encounter between two Kentucky geldings, Atilla and Wake-Up Jake, at 2-mile heats for a $6,000 purse, which Atilla won.

The first race at 4-mile heats took place at the Centerville Course in Sacramento on May 10, 1859, in which Nathan Coombs's Ashland defeated W. M. Williamson's Owen Dale in straight heats, 7:56, 7:49½.

Commodore Robert F. Stockton, commander of the American forces which won California's independence from Mexico, was very active in turf affairs of his native New Jersey (among his several importations had been Trustee, sire of Fashion) and he also played a role in bringing the thoroughbred to the Far West. In 1841 Stockton had shipped a group of horses from his stud in Princeton, New Jersey, to Franklin, Ohio. In the group was American Boy, who, after arrival in Ohio, sired Belmont.

Bred by Garrett Williamson, and often referred to as "Williamson's Belmont," this rather fantastic animal had not been broken to bridle as a six-year-old, and he never raced, but he nevertheless headed a great dynasty. Included in a draft of horses taken west by Williamson's sons, Belmont arrived in California in 1854, when racing's popularity was at its height, and he became the foundation sire of the Pacific Coast, both of thoroughbreds and of trotters.

It was one of Belmont's sons, Langford, who knocked the above-mentioned Ashland off his pedestal, defeating him at 2 miles in their first encounter, and at 4 miles in a re-match for $5,000 a side, both times in straight heats. Langford, owned by Leland Stanford's brother-in-law, E. S. Lathrop, was undefeated during the 1860 season.

Five years later, as the Civil War was coming to a close in the East, a son of Langford was foaled who was destined to spread the fame of the California thoroughbred throughout the nation: Thad Stevens, whose exploits will be recounted in a later chapter.

The history of racing in Charleston is recounted separately because in truth it seems to have been a sport unto itself, conducted on the highest plane. There was inevitably some communication back and forth between Charleston and other racing areas, but practically speaking that proud city went its own way.

Although Charleston had been among the

Wade Hampton I, founder of a South Carolina turf dynasty.

towns most seriously damaged by the Revolution, it was one of the first to recover, and by 1783 a jockey club was back in operation. Such organizations were chartered for a stated period, rather than indefinitely, and five years later a new jockey club was organized, of which the chairman was General William Washington, a distant cousin (but close friend) of George Washington, and a distinguished war hero in his own right.

In 1792 the Washington Course was opened under the ownership of a subsequent South Carolina Jockey Club of which the president was Charles Cotesworth Pinckney, a father of the Constitution and Minister to France, who originated the historic quotation: "Millions for defense but not one cent for tribute." The other members of the jockey club included all the important families of that time, and the charter of this organization was renewed and renewed until, after 108 years of existence, it deeded its property to the Charleston Library Society in 1899—the largest gift of its kind in the city's history. The piers from the old Washington Course later were installed at the entrance to Belmont Park.

Other towering figures in South Carolina included the dynasty of Wade Hampton, father, son and grandson, all of the same name, and each of them prominent on the turf. One of the richest planters in the area, Wade Hampton I achieved an economic landmark in 1799 when he sold 600 bales of cotton for $90,000; later he was a pioneer in development of sugar plantations in Louisiana. He established Millwood at the state capital, Columbia, where Wade II was born, and under the son's ownership it was expanded into the most luxurious stud in the South. The stables at Millwood were 120 feet long, exceeded in size only by those of the Stevens Brothers on Long Island.

General Wade Hampton I in 1800 won every race at the four-day Charleston meet. In general turf stature, his son carried on where he left off, as did Wade Hampton III.

Next to the Hamptons, Colonel Richard Singleton, owner of High Hills of Santee, was probably the most active South Carolinian in racing, while Colonel James B. Richardson of Sumter County and his son-in-law, Colonel J. R. Spann, were a formidable team.

On Christmas day, 1830, the locomotive "Best Friend of Charleston" pulled the first train of cars ever drawn by a steam engine on an American railroad, and in February, 1838, Charleston chalked up another first when a trainload of horses en route from Augusta (one horse to a freight car) had a wreck, and Wade Hampton's Monarch became the first horse ever injured in a railway accident.

PLANET, 1855

(Revenue–Nina, by Boston)

That the insularity of its attitude did not detract from the quality of Charleston racing is illustrated by the experience of Planet, the last great star of the ante-bellum period.

Bred by Major Thomas W. Doswell, to whom *The Spirit of the Times* awarded the niche, "First position as an American turfman," Planet was foaled in 1855 at his owner's Bullfield Stud in Virginia, a majestic layout that included three different training tracks. A son of Nina, a famous mare who had raced for Major Doswell, Planet maintained this all-in-the-family motif, by winning his first start as a three-year-old, the Doswell Stakes.

The colt's subsequent racing career cannot be associated with any particular area as he ran—and won—at Petersburg, Richmond, Savannah, Charleston, New Orleans, Mobile, Ashland and Augusta, appearing several times in most of these places.

One of his more notable victories was over Sue Washington, La Variete and others in the Great Post Stake at Metairie, on which the betting pools reached $27,290. As a result of his performance, the Planet Post Stake the following year was named in his honor, and he returned to win that one, too.

The Doswell horse also made a shambles of an attempt in 1860 to stage another "epic encounter" at the Fashion Course on Long Island by distancing the only rival that came out to face him in the first heat. Like many other noted horses, Planet was binary, in that he could trot as well as he could run. Said to be capable of a mile in three minutes without exertion, he seemed to prefer the former gait in his exercise, and, seeing him at work one morning, the track superintendent of the Fash-

Planet, 1855, the last great star before racing was disrupted by the Civil War.

ion Course called Planet's rider over and ordered him to "take that trotter off the track."

His career interrupted by the outbreak of the Civil War, he retired absolutely sound, having won 27 of his 31 starts and finished second in the other four. With earnings of $69,700 he displaced Peytona as leading American money winner. But lion that he was elsewhere, Planet did not awe the Charleston horses, as he was defeated there twice, by Sock as a four-year-old and by the mare, Albine, at six.

The all-orange silks borne by Planet have continued very much in action through modern times. A protegé of Major Doswell was Captain R. J. Hancock, who became Doswell's partner after the Civil War and subsequently acquired control of the entire stud, which was moved to Ellerslie, Virginia. His son, A. B. Hancock, later transferred to Kentucky and established Claiborne Farm, the most successful American breeding farm of the mid-twentieth century, and the Claiborne horses fly the old Doswell colors.

Throughout the period of peace, racing in Charleston maintained an aura of social acceptability that was the envy of other cities. The Jockey Club Ball was the major event of the year for high society, and the menu for the 1860 dinner shows, after the soup course, four varieties of fish, nine different kinds of broiled meat or seafood, ten kinds of roasted meat, fourteen varieties of game, six vegetables, nine choices of dessert, plus four "ornaments."

All this magnificence was doomed to crumble, for in the early morning of April 12, 1861, just outside Charleston, the Confederate troops at Fort Johnson trained their guns on nearby Fort Sumter, and the heroic age of the American thoroughbred ended.

86

CHAPTER EIGHTEEN

THERE HAD BEEN INDICATIONS of changes in the broad aspect of American racing for quite some time prior to the Civil War, beginning with the renewed enthusiasm for foreign blood in the 1830s. This reached a climax of a sort shortly before the clash, when, as though to lay up a supply for the lean times ahead, in three successive years there were imported stallions which were to help sustain the American thoroughbred through the future. In order of arrival, they were Bonnie Scotland, imported as a four-year-old in 1857 and sold to the firm of Reber and Kutz of Lancaster, Ohio; Australian, imported in 1858 as a suckling alongside his dam by A. Keene Richards of Georgetown, Kentucky; and Eclipse, shipped from England as a four-year-old in 1859 by Richard Ten Broeck, to stand first at the Fashion Course on Long Island and then in Lexington, Kentucky, under the management of Major B. G. Thomas.

In addition to horses, English styles were being adopted. For a number of years, the northern United States had shown more of an affinity for England than for the South. The North had become industrialized, which created a common bond with England, and a great deal of the nation's wealth was concentrated in the North. Wealthy Northern boys attended school abroad and brought home British ideas; as dash racing was the vogue in that country, it became increasingly popular in America.

The Spirit of the Times published its first set of organized statistics covering the 1836 American racing season, when there were 62 races at 4-mile heats and 247 at 1 mile. By 1860, the last complete season before the war, the number of 4-mile races had dropped to 24 and the number of mile races had increased to 313. Races for three- and two-year-olds also had become more common during this period. The American ideal of running mature horses over an appreciable distance had begun to slip, and the Civil War was for all practical purposes the *coup de grâce*.

In this last armed conflict to take place on United States soil, as had happened before, the theater of war coincided by and large with the race horse regions. Most of the great Southern racing and breeding centers were completely devastated, and the horse himself again became a tool of war. General T. J. Wells of Louisiana equipped a troop of Confederate cavalry (although his own brother refused to espouse seccession) as did A. Keene Richards of Kentucky, although the latter was not obligated to either side.

Sanders Bruce, later to found *Turf, Field and Farm* and the *American Stud Book,* rose to the rank of colonel in the Federal army, while his brother Benjamin (who helped Sanders with the above-named publications and later established the magazine which became the *Thoroughbred Record*) accompanied Richards to New Orleans. To add to the confusion, their brother-in-law was the legendary Confederate raider, John Hunt Morgan, whose operations were designed to discomfit the North, but were of such scope and conducted in such haste as to undoubtedly pinch the South a bit, too. (He robbed a bank and set fire to the Association Track stables in Lexington, but today his statue is on the Court House lawn in that city, and his home is a shrine.)

Regardless of its officially neutral position, Kentucky was the scene of considerable raiding. Since R. A. Alexander was a British subject, and thus a sort of "double neutral," his Woodburn Farm was thought to be an ideal refuge, but that was by no means the case. It was raided several times, and Alexander was forced to send his stock north into Ohio, Illinois and Canada for safety. (Hervey relates the saga of Napoleon Belland, who took two carloads of horses to Canada for Alexander and was left completely on his own for three and a half years, unable to communicate with his employer; at the end of the war, Belland turned over the fruits of his astute management: $300,000.)

War's destruction was not confined to homes, barns, stables and the horses themselves, but paintings, records and trophies also were lost. The Woodlawn Vase, for example, which now is awarded to the winner of the Preakness each year, originally was a challenge trophy run for at Louisville, and after the famous mares Mollie Jackson and Idlewild had earned two legs on it for Captain T. G. Moore in 1861 and 1862, the huge, ornate trophy had to be buried for the remainder of the war. Many portraits by Edward Troye, the country's most prominent painter of horses, were lost.

Raids notwithstanding, Kentucky emerged from the upheaval in better shape than the states which actually had joined the Confederacy, and it quickly became the undisputed capital of breeding, if not of racing.

Racing continued in several cities of the defiant South while hostilities still were in progress, but on a catch-as-catch-can basis. After Lee's surrender, the depleted South plodded on for a while with vain attempts to revive its ante-bellum glory, but this, too, was a lost cause.

The requiem for Southern leadership came on April 11, 1872, when the last meeting at Metairie closed. Faced with competition from the new Fair Grounds, the old queen of American tracks couldn't meet its mortgage payments. Charles T. Howard, who previously had been blackballed when he sought membership in the Metairie Jockey Club and had vowed to turn the track into a graveyard, bought the mortgage and carried out his threat. The cemetery may be seen today.

Control of the sport had long since passed to the victorious North, and by this time, it became apparent that a new era of American racing was underway.

PART THREE

FROM THE CIVIL WAR

TO WORLD WAR I

CHAPTER NINETEEN

WHEN THE CIVIL WAR ENDED, A complete revision of American racing was in progress, during which the public was to assume the dominant role.

Dash racing, which had been making inroads, was to supplant heat racing as the standard American form. (Along with the change to English styles in racing, the North followed the British example in changing the universal birthday of thoroughbreds to January 1. For many years the South clung stubbornly to the old May 1 birthday, which was something of a paradox, since the earlier birthday was advantageous to warmer climates.

To support these stepped-up programs, which required more and bigger purses, it became necessary to depend on public patronage. The pure concept of sport for sport's sake had to be tempered with the realities of economic necessity, and gambling exchanged its stool in the corner for a seat at the main table.

In what must have been a painful experience for those proud gentlemen composing the American Jockey Club, which operated the nation's most high-toned track, Jerome Park, they were forced in 1877 to acknowledge this state of affairs formally. In a petition to the New York Senate, requesting that body not approve a measure abolishing pool-selling which had passed the lower house, it was stated, in part:

1. That the American Jockey Club was formed . . . for the purpose of improving the breed of horses . . . and for other purposes duly set forth in the act of incorporation . . .

2. That in pursuance of these purposes, the American Jockey Club has . . . annually offered . . . prizes and rewards to be competed for by the owners of horses . . .

3. That, in order to obtain the necessary means for offering such prizes and rewards, it has been found absolutely necessary, in the case of the American Jockey Club, as in all other cases of the same kind throughout the world, to secure the attendance of the general public at these exhibitions of skill and endurance, and to stimulate the interest of the general public in the development and improvement of the breed of horses.

4. That to this end nothing has been, or can be, found so effective as a well-ordered and well-conducted system, under which all persons who attend these exhibitions, and take an intelligent interest in them, may safely and fairly stake such sums of money as they think proper upon the accuracy of their judgment in regard to the qualities and merits of the animals which contend for the prizes and rewards, above described . . .

The plea went unheeded, for the Senate passed the bill and the pool sellers went across the river to New Jersey, but not long thereafter they were outlawed in that state, too.

This was but one in a long series of skirmishes between race tracks and legislators, and the history of American racing during this period is dotted with similar episodes. The sport expanded and contracted like a giant bellows according to the tide of legislative whim.

Not only did gambling become a big issue, but the very nature of thoroughbred racing was called into question. As the heavily populated northeastern sector of the United States became more urban, the horse became less a part of everyday life, and running races were regarded by some sophisticated citizens as too primitive. Although he published news concerning both forms of sport, John H. Wallace, editor of *Wallace's Monthly,* did not bother to conceal his preference for the trotting horse over the thoroughbred. Harness racing with carts, or trotting horses under saddle, were lovingly described in great detail, while often as not thoroughbred races were given short shrift. Mr. Wallace, and a number of others, looked upon running races much as a lover of ballet might regard an amateur square dance. To them, the development of a horse for performance at precise gaits was a demanding task that required skill, but they disdained the thoroughbred as a primitive animal which required relatively little training since he ran in his natural gait.

There were, of course, two sides to this argument and the *Nashville American,* for example, deplored the trend away from riding horseback and criticized the growing practice of young boys driving fancy buggies instead of riding astride. "The whole business of buggy riding . . . is expensive, extravagant, and demoralizing," said one editorial. "If we could return to the fashion of riding more on horseback, we would save millions to the farmers, and the boys and girls would develop better forms, and have better health. Any lazy lout can ride in a buggy, but to be a graceful rider on horseback, one must have some energy and get-up in his nature . . . The country is full of road horses that some man or boy loves to pull the strings on. They are usually poor saddle horses, slow walkers and rough. We need a reform . . ."

Although the running horse eventually was to win the battle for popularity, and the two sports co-exist amicably today, it was nip and tuck for quite a while. Many famous old thoroughbred tracks were turned over to trotters and pacers, and, as the buggy supplanted the

saddle in the nation's over-all economy, harness racing was treated more leniently by the various state legislatures.

It was rough going, politically, but thoroughbred racing survived.

Through an interlocking cause and effect process, the changes in the broad concept of the sport brought about changes in the details of the individual events. In addition to providing a suitable entertainment spectacle, it was necessary that a race also provide an attractive medium for betting.

What had been the *pièce de résistance* of the old meetings, the jockey club purse, which was open to members only, was replaced in importance by the proprietor's purse, open to all. The more horses eligible, the more potential betting.

There were adjustments elsewhere on the program, too. While spectators might admire a runner that was obviously superior to his opposition, such a stalwart was a poor business proposition—the odds were too short to bet on him, and it was foolhardy to bet against him. Moreover, other owners tended to avoid crack rivals, which reduced the size of the field. To counteract this aspect, various artificial devices were introduced to manipulate a horse's natural form.

The conditions for a typical race, other than sweepstakes, before the Civil War consisted of a few simple words: "Purse $300, for all ages. Two mile heats."

Weights were carried according to the age and sex of the individual animal, although there were occasional exceptions for special events.

After the Civil War exceptions became the rule. Handicap races, wherein weights were assigned according to assessed ability, in an attempt to give every contestant a theoretically equal chance of winning, became increasingly popular. In other races, various allowances and penalties were imposed, based on previous performance.

For example, Hamburg carried weights as a two-year-old in 1897 which would cause a modern five-year-old to be retired. For the Prospect and Rising Generation Stakes, he packed 127 pounds; for the Double Event, Flash and Autumn Stakes his load was 129 pounds; and for the Congress Hall Stakes he carried 134. Those were "allowance" events, and although Hamburg made formidable concessions, some of his better opponents had to haul the same weight or almost as much. As to handicap races, Hamburg was assigned 132 for the Electric Handicap and 135 for the Great Eastern. He won all the races mentioned, conceding 24 pounds to the runner-up and 40 to the light-weight in the Great Eastern, not only during the race, but during a half-hour delay at the post as well.

The most effective of all devices for encouraging large fields, and promoting heavy betting, was the selling race, which concept, like dash racing and bookmakers, was imported from England. (This type of race had been used before the Civil War, but very rarely.)

By forcing owners to classify their own horses, selling races, at least in theory, made for evenly matched contests. Certainly the conditions were such that practically everyone was able to concoct some excuse for betting on some horse, as the following example illustrates:

> For three-year-olds and upwards. Selling. By subscription of $10 each, with $600 added; of which $100 to the 2d and $50 to the 3d. The winner to be sold at auction for $2,500. If entered to be sold for less, 1 lb. allowed for each $100 down to $500. Winners during this meeting 10 lbs extra . . .

With a possible 30-pound spread, on top of that provided by differences in age and sex, the opportunities for finding a good betting spot in such a race were limitless, or so it seemed, at any rate.

After the race, the winner was sold at auction, with his listed price as the opening bid. Although the winning owner could bid on his own property, rival owners could run the price up, forcing him either to lose the horse or buy it back again at a higher sum. The difference between entering price and ultimate auction price sometimes was allotted to the owner of the runner-up as compensation for having been defeated by a horse presumably running below his true class; sometimes this difference was taken over by the racing association and applied to purse money for subsequent races, and sometimes it was divided between the owner of the runner-up and the racing association.

There were various permutations of the selling race. In some of them, only owners who started a horse in that particular race were allowed to bid; in others, any owner who had started a horse at the meeting was eligible and in still others the bidding was open to all. (Tod Sloan, the high-spirited jockey, used to run up the bidding against owners who had incurred his disfavor.)

There were other races in which only the winner could be claimed, for the stated price, with priority of claim according to the order of finish, except that the winning owner had last choice. There were races in which any runner could be claimed, the order of preference as above.

All these races had in common the purpose of keeping owners "honest" in placement of their horses. An owner who ran a horse for too small a price ran the risk of losing him; on the other hand, to run the horse over his head was futile, so the only alternative was to run him where he belonged, which provided a good contest from the standpoint of the racing association and the public. Gradually, these races evolved into the modern claiming race, which is the backbone of today's racing programs.

The auction pool method of wagering had become quite common before the Civil War. As has been explained, its operation was identical to "Calcutta" pools which are popular in golf tournaments today. Each contestant was "sold" to the highest bidder and the money thus collected went to the "buyer" of the winner. In the race-track pool, the auctioneer deducted a percentage as his fee and in turn paid the racing association a flat sum for the privilege of operating on its premises. Even when conducted honestly (which was not invariably done), this method of betting had obvious disadvantages. For one thing, the odds against an individual horse were not known until all the horses had been sold. For another, the bettor with the greatest amount of capital to start with could monopolize the most logical choice ("them what has, gits") although in so doing he knocked down his own odds.

The increased public interest in racing led to a demand for a method whereby the small investor could participate, and the bookmakers moved in to fill this demand. Not only could they accommodate punters of all shapes, sizes and economic standing, but they offered fixed odds in advance. The heavy plunger could make a large bet at odds that would stick (the bookmaker, naturally, could shorten his odds after such a bet, but the payoff on each bet was made according to the odds which prevailed at the instant that particular bet was made).

Precisely when bookmaking began is moot. Many sources indicate it started in England during the reign of George IV, but according to other references there was a form of public wagering, suspiciously similar to bookmaking, on the chariot races in ancient Rome, and it would not be at all surprising if some researcher turns up the information that Ham quoted a line to Shem and Japheth on whether the dove was going to land on the port or starboard side of Noah's Ark.

The first bookmaking in America, according to the New York *Herald,* was performed around 1866 by the Philadelphia firm of Sanford, Sykes & Eaves, whose business was based primarily on cricket games, regattas and trotting races, but who would try their hand at anything. The *American Racing Manual* lists

James E. Kelley of New York, who opened a winter book on the 1871 Belmont Stakes, as the pioneer specialist in horse racing.

In an article on the subject published in 1894, the *Herald* estimated that the bookies at Brighton Beach handled an average of $3,000 each per race. As there were about sixty bookmakers in action, and six races a day, the gross handle was in excess of a million dollars on a typical afternoon. The bookmaker usually paid $100 a day to metropolitan tracks for his franchise. (Assuming sixty bookies, the track's revenue was only $6,000, whereas today, a New York City track receives $50,000 and the State gets $100,000 as revenue from a million-dollar handle.)

In a fascinating discussion of the subject, the *Herald* article continued:

> Bookmaking has been almost revolutionized during the past ten years. The public has become educated and wise in its bets. In former times, before the study of "form" became a science . . . making a "round book" was an easy affair . . . in those halcyon days of bookmaking, before the newspapers published an index of a horse's ability, the well-known "Pittsburgh Phil" [George Smith] kept an index of his own . . .
>
> He was ten years in advance of his time, but "Pittsburgh Phil's" glory has departed. Go to any bookmaker and he will tell you that there are a hundred frequenters of the race track who bet quite as heavily as "Phil" . . . every betting man at a race track nowadays carries what is known as a "dope book" . . .
>
> In the average race nowadays, in a field of, say, ten horses, the bookmaker will take in nine-tenths of his money on three or four horses at the outside, and the chances are that he will not get in a dollar on the others. You can readily see the difficulty of keeping on the right side of the ledger under such circumstances. The modern bettor is very smart, and he will have nothing to do with "long shots."
>
> Most of the books of the present day are what are known as "gambling books". That is, in the dearth of opportunities to make a percentage book they will "hold out" the horses

94

they think will win and raise the odds against the others. In this way, with their favorite out, they stand to win or lose any sum of money they may decide upon . . .

So fine has the system of form betting become that it happens almost every day that the first choice in a race will win, the second choice will run second, and the third choice third . . .

In addition to the public, bookmakers have each other to look out for. The "piking" or smaller bookmakers sometimes resort to a system of "shaving" that is very unpopular with the bigger fish. Suppose, for instance, you are laying even money against a favorite. A rival bookmaker from across the ring strolls up and takes $500 worth of the good thing. Then he goes back to his own stand and lays four to five against the same horse. Thus he takes in $500 of the public's money for which he only pays out $400 . . . he is therefore $100 ahead. If the horse loses he breaks even.

It is surprising the way bookmakers watch each other. A cat and a mouse are no comparison. Every one of them carries big glasses with which he is constantly sweeping the bookmaking horizon. In this way they catch the fluctuation of odds just as a Wall Street broker reads the tape. A very important feature of modern bookmaking is the "outside man" whose duties are multifarious. In the first place, he must know everybody, particularly the big bettors. The little plungers always take care of themselves. He must notify his book of what is going on in different parts of the ring, out of range of the bookies' keen vision. For instance, if the bookmaker is laying even money against Armitage on one side of the ring, and his "outside man" rushes up with the information that "Mike" Dwyer's commissioners have knocked the price to four to five on the opposite side, the bookie would be obviously foolish to lay anything higher. A good "outside man" can save his book a great many dollars through the medium of keen eyes and prompt action.

All the big plungers are personally known to the bookmakers, and the latter invariably reserve the privilege of accepting or rejecting the bets of these big fish. Young Riley Grannon and Billy Mackin are two of the most prominent gambling bookmakers in the ring. Time and again, they have taken Mr. Dwyer's heavy commissions single handed, but while Mackin is contented to take the risk at the prevailing odds, Grannon doubles his risk by taking the money and spending it out on another horse. He either wins or loses double. Although Grannon has been exceedingly lucky so far, old conservative bookmakers are of the opinion that sooner or later he will be landed high and dry by some of the big plungers. It is well known that Mr. Mike Dwyer's commissioners are "gunning" for him at every opportunity. Mackin is just as cool and daring as Grannon, but he has a far more conservative disposition. Orlando Jones, with his peaked whiskers and shrewd eyes, is another gambling bookmaker who is well-known for his occasional heavy plunges against favorites.

The sources of Jones' information are many and varied, and it is said that he not only employs an "outside man," but that he has a "track man," who is on the inside of almost every stable on the tracks. It is the same with that grizzly-haired, stubbly mustached veteran, Ike Thompson. There is no bookmaker around the ring more closely watched than Thompson. He is on the inside of a great many good things, and when the gang sees him marking up the price against the favorite, or "killing" it, as the term goes, and holding out a longshot, the most of them follow suit through a sort of blind instinct. They know very well that something is in the wind. Thompson is an English importation, and he shows his spectacular instincts by hoisting flags over his betting cage. He makes the largest and most comprehensible figures in the ring, and he does it with a three-card monte flourish that is fascinating to look at. Mackin's figures are those of a bank clerk.

"Virginia" Carroll is one of the queerest characters in the ring. He comes of an old Presbyterian family, but at the present writing there is very little Presbyterian in his nature. While making books he keeps up a continual running fire of comment. "Are you sure this money is good? All right; four to one. Longbrook." Then he varies the monotony by tearing a ten-dollar bill in pieces and throwing it at

95

his cashier. Next he puts a bill in his mouth and chews it up. Altogether, he is a Punch and Judy show all by himself.

One of the best liked among all the bookmakers is Ed Burke. He is quiet, courteous, cool, and he makes a legitimate book for all there is in it. George Kunhsman is another man with whom it is a pleasure to invest money.

Unlike Billy Mackin and Riley Grannon, both of the above men know when to stop taking money.

Ten years ago John Duffy was a poor man . . . when he started in the business one of his first customers was Denman Thompson, of "Old Homestead" fame. He won about $25,000 from the actor on a street book—a handbook, as they are now called.

Over in the corner of the ring—and there are always corners to a betting ring—you will find John Hill . . . ten years ago he was a huckster. He became sporty and sold his wagon and horse for $110 and started bookmaking. It was not much of a book, and took bets as low as 25 cents. He was very shrewd, however, and soon won enough to start bookmaking at the track . . . it is probable that he can still lay his hands on a quarter of a million . . .

One of the keenest pencilers in the business is Ike Hakelburg. His judgment is respected by everybody in the profession. He does not make book only when he thinks it is a winning game. He seems to be one of the few who can beat horse racing either making book or betting on the outside.

Everybody knows big, burly, Saul Lichtenstein. You can see him at Jerome Park any day, with rumpled hair and chalky hands, making figures and taking bets that would bewilder an ordinary man . . .

The whole art of bookmaking lies first in judgment, and second in the mental ability to quickly calculate the percentages . . . when you can do all that without difficulty you can gather your capital together in a valise . . . and begin business with the utmost certainty that every man's hand will be against you, and your hand will be against all men. Big plungers will bulldoze you. Little plungers will make your life a burden with their puzzling dollar bets, and all that is crooked in the turf will militate against you. Speaking of little plungers, you will be surprised at their number.

. . . There are great, big fellows with small bankrolls, and little bits of chaps who carry weight for age in the matter of money. Probably the smallest plunger on the tracks, both physically and in age, is little George Shannon. He is only fifteen years of age, yet he does not look it. He handles millionaire Pulsifer's money in the ring and he handles it well. Some times he gets hold of $200 or $300 of his own, which he bets with the sang-froid of a veteran. When he first went into the ring, he absolutely flabbergasted the talent with his combination of extreme youth and nerve. Finally, however, they became used to him, and now George can walk around the ring with a $2,000 commission without exciting undue suspicion.

Altogether the betting ring at the modern race track is a wonderful educator.

In view of its ultimate significance, by far the most important development during the period between the Civil War and World War I was the advent of the pari-mutuels. Unlike most features of American racing, which were copied from England, this one came from France, and it was a long time being accepted.

Pari-mutuel wagering was introduced by Pierre Oller, owner of a perfume shop in Paris. Actually, the system is merely a refinement of the auction pool, the only difference being that it is unnecessary to have enough money to outbid others in order to wager on one's choice.

While the South was losing the Civil War, across the Atlantic Oller was losing his shirt to French bookmakers. Disenchanted by the odds they had been offering him, he hit upon a scheme whereby the betting public could, in effect, lay its own odds. In his perfume shop he sold tickets at a standard price on the different horses in each race. From the money thus collected Oller deducted 5 percent as commission for his services, then distributed the remainder among holders of winning tickets in proportion to the number of such tickets that had been sold. Oller's business caught on so well that the owners of Parisian tracks introduced it within their grounds, and it soon replaced bookmaking entirely, becoming the only legal form of wagering at French tracks (the "take" was increased from 5 to 8 percent).

Literally translated, pari-mutuel means "mutual bet," and when this method of wagering first appeared in America, it was referred to as the "mutuals," although the French spelling later became the accepted form.

Despite its obvious advantage over the old-fashioned selling pool, the pari-mutuels did not catch on at American tracks. Bookmakers, naturally, were violently opposed to the system. The really big bettors didn't like it because large bets would depress the odds, and the small bettor also seemed to prefer his friendly, local bookmaker who would take a wager of any size, whereas the "mutuals" would accept bets only in $5 units.

Even so, in retrospect it is difficult to understand the apathy which greeted the pari-mutuel system. In the 1870s and 1880s it received numerous tryouts in various places—New York, New Jersey, Kentucky, Maryland, Chicago, Washington, D.C.—and the system received considerable favorable publicity on October 12, 1872, when a four-year-old gelding named Nickajack, carrying 75 pounds, won a race at Jerome Park and paid $1,178. With the bookmakers and in the selling pools he was lumped with several other horses at odds varying between 5-to-1 and 20-to-1, but the mutuel payoff was at 234-to-1. The tryouts of the pari-mutuels were on a here-and-there, off-and-on basis, however, and perhaps this is the reason it failed for many years to become popular. As Pierre Lorillard, who had seen the system in operation in France and favored its universal adoption in the United States, later observed, if a large group of American tracks had given pari-mutuels an extended trial, the public probably would have adopted it.

In at least one instance, the public did indicate a distinct preference for pari-mutuel wagering, but was overruled by the track. When the Kentucky State Racing Commission in 1908 issued its "mutuel betting only" edict, in the middle of the Latonia spring meeting, Louis A. Cella complained that he could not afford to continue operations without books. The Cincinnati *Post* thereupon published a detailed survey, accounting for the $100 fee from each bookmaker every day of the previous year's meeting, which showed a legitimate income to the track of only $53,700, compared to the $74,632.80 income from the corresponding thirty days of the pari-mutuel meeting then in progress. Nevertheless, Cella, who controlled the books as well as the track, issued his immortal pronouncement, "If bookmaking don't go the track will be closed," and closed it was ten days before the scheduled end of the meet. (As a member of the Cella–Tilles–Adler syndicate, which controlled three tracks in St. Louis, and possessor of interests in several other tracks in various parts of the country, Cella had plenty of fish to fry.)

Latonia re-opened that fall, with books; the racing commission revoked its license; the track filed suit against the commission, and finished out the meeting while litigation was in progress. In 1909 the books were on again, but did not survive long.

On the other hand, one never knows whether the public of its own volition ever would have embraced the mutuels wholeheartedly. There was an understandable preference for doing business with a bookmaker, many of whom were very well liked, rather than with an impartial machine. How the pari-mutuel system finally achieved official sanction belongs to a later chapter, but it might be mentioned here that even the machines were not impervious to American ingenuity. Comedian Joe Frisco used to stutter through an hilarious routine describing his experience with the "iron men" at a bush track (the location of which varied according to where Joe was playing at the time). After betting on a 10-to-1 shot, he watched in horror as the odds dropped to 5-to-1 when his horse went to the lead after a half-mile, skidded again to 3-to-1 as the horse still was on top entering the stretch, slipped to 2-to-1 at the sixteenth pole, and, after he crossed the finish line, the infield board would black out, then flash the dismaying tidings: $2.60, $2.40, $2.20.

Electronic refinements and state racing commissions have relieved Frisco's plight, but nevertheless there remain today many people who hate and distrust the mutuel machines.

Again getting ahead of history somewhat, the big plungers found a cure for their principal objection to pari-mutuel betting. Selecting a sure thing at some small track, where a little money went a long way in the pari-mutuel machines, they would bet "around the favorite," i.e., pour in money on every horse except their choice, which would increase its odds. Meanwhile, a much larger sum had been bet on the horse with a bookmaker, who paid off at track odds. Thus, the crumbs of bread cast upon the waters at the track were repaid many times over in bookmakers' dough. The smart bookies soon caught on to this trick and refused bets on races at bush meetings; the dumb ones went out of business.

CHAPTER TWENTY

IN 1861, THE YEAR THE CIVIL War began, Lexington commenced his long reign as America's leading stallion, and his crop of foals that year included the three best colts in the country, all of them out of mares by Glencoe.

Two of these colts, Norfolk and Asteroid, were undefeated, while the third colt, Kentucky, lost only one race—and that to Norfolk.

The occasion of his defeat was the Jersey Derby run at Paterson on June 7, 1864, while the war still was in progress although fighting had gone south with Grant's Wilderness Campaign. Patterned after the English race of that name, conditions for the Jersey Derby were as follows:

> Sweepstake premium of $1,000 for three-year-olds, $50 entrance, play or pay, one and one-half mile dash, colts to carry 100 pounds, fillies and geldings allowed three pounds; ten or more nominations to fill.

Norfolk was the most celebrated member of the field for two reasons. In his debut at the Laclede Course in St. Louis about three weeks earlier, he had defeated the good colt Tipperary in straight heats, and thereupon was sold to Theodore Winters of California for $15,001. The odd dollar was the result of a vow made by R. A. Alexander eight years before, at the time he bought Lexington. When a friend chided him for paying $15,000 for the stallion Alexander retorted that some day he expected to sell one of Lexington's colts for an even greater sum. Norfolk made good that vow.

Of the thirty-two original nominees to America's first Derby, twelve showed up to face the starter. This was a larger field than had contested the original Epsom Derby eighty-four years previously, a fact which was noted with some pride by the unnamed correspondent for *The Spirit of the Times* who described the epochal event. Portions of that description follow:

> For many weeks the interest felt in the coming event had been widening and deepening . . . there was no end of the excitement created in this vicinity. Where men met for business by day and assembled for amusement at night, the Derby, next to the war and the state of the country, was the prevailing topic. In the saloons and drawing-rooms of the fashionable avenues and squares, the ladies exhibited laudable and natural curiosity touching the coming race . . . Costly carriages and stately equipages, four-in-hand, swept along after fast-trotting horses . . . The Erie Railroad carried vast numbers of people in immense trains of cars, and from every direction visitors tended toward the course, until some 10,000 had met to witness the event of the first Derby Day . . .

We first inspected Norfolk, a colt exactly calculated to fill the eye of a lover of the race-horse. A bright bay with three white feet and a crooked blaze, good length and size, and first-rate moving machinery, he walked with a regal port of a prince among horses and a Derby winner. His bright eye . . . wiry neck, deep but narrow chest and springy pasterns, indicated a speedy one at the first glance, and a second was sufficient to show that the gray old trainer Ansell, who trudged patiently and lovingly after him with a blanket on his arm, had got him fit to run for a man's life. Tipperary, another colt of great note, is a big-

Norfolk, 1861, undefeated champion from coast to coast and winner of America's first Derby.

ger horse than Norfolk, who is himself about 15-3. Tip. is more than sixteen hands, somewhat gaunt and angular, but with the points good though plain. When this colt fills out his great bony frame, and acquires the additional stamina which a big youngster is sure to get, he will make a very fine racehorse. Indeed, he would be regarded as an immensely fine colt now, if he had not had the luck to encounter such a flyer as Norfolk at St. Louis and Paterson. Kentucky was much admired, and with perfect justice, for he is a splendid colt. But there was an apparent lack of hard polish about him, which is fully accounted for by the fact that his work was stopped twice towards the close of his preparation . . . Now, they were all mounted. Gilpatrick bestrode Kentucky, the dark and solemn face of Abe bent over the lofty crest of "Tip." The fat and sooty countenance of Bill Bay, with a broad grin on it, loomed large over Eagle . . . Sewell, another of the dark division, and looking ominously out of his one eye, leapt into the saddle of Brother to Jack Malone . . . And now, with some serpentine twisting of the neck and impatient pawing of the hoof, Norfolk is mounted by John Lewis . . .

. . . A start was soon effected, but it was not a good one. The favorite had the advantage, and being able to go like a bullet from the jump, he was lengths away, while the others were all tangled up, Tip among them. The last to get off was the black Eclipse colt and Brother to Jack Malone. Their heads were the other way when the start was made. Kentucky was the first that showed clean of the ruck after the favorite, who came away at a splitting pace, and literally parted company with his pursuers. It was like a stag running away before a pack of hounds . . . It was now a terrible tailing race. They were strung out about a quarter of a mile, and Norfolk had a victory of the easiest kind in hand when he was back at the starting-place. This mile was run in 1 m. 47 s. The pace was now sensibly abated. Norfolk came on at an easy gallop, ten lengths ahead of Tip, who had a large gap between himself and Kentucky. Half-way up the pickets young Lewis raised his whip hand over the winner, and the colt made a forward bound, as if he was just then beginning to run. At the distance, Eagle, who ran very true and honest, came out from the middle string, challenged Kentucky for the third place and won it in gallant style by a head. Kentucky was fourth, and no more were placed . . . Time 2:46¼.

Kentucky's defeat by Norfolk brought about a clamor for a match between the winner and Lexington's other undefeated son, Asteroid.

John Hunter, one of the founders of Saratoga, and first chairman of the Jockey Club.

The relative merits of these two colts was the subject of considerable debate, but that was as far as it went because Norfolk's new owner took him home to California after the Jersey Derby. However, R. A. Alexander, who had bred both colts, stated unequivocally that he considered Asteroid "the best race horse in the U. S. by long odds."

Efforts then were made to stage a match between Asteroid and Kentucky, and Alexander was gleeful at the prospect of a killing. In a letter to his brother, he described a trial by Asteroid—4 miles in 7:23½ while carrying 11 pounds overweight over a so-so track—and instructed his brother to burn the letter after reading it.

On the other hand, Kentucky's owner, John Hunter, was equally confident, replying to those who hailed Asteroid as the greatest horse in America with the comment, "He leads Kentucky alphabetically—in no other respect."

Since the owners of both horses insisted that the match take place in home territory, it finally was agreed to run two races, $10,000 a side, one in New York and the other in Louisville or Cincinnati. Asteroid was shipped up to meet his rival in the feature race on opening day at Jerome Park in 1866 but, on the Sunday before the race, he pulled up lame after a workout and was retired.

CHAPTER TWENTY-ONE

THE SMOKE FROM THE BATTLE of Gettysburg scarcely had evaporated when America's oldest existing race track began operations. Precisely one month after Pickett's charge against Cemetery Ridge, horse hooves began pounding against the turf at Saratoga, senior citizen and *grande dame* among American racing centers.

Saratoga Springs, in upstate New York, for years had been a popular summer resort health center and playground, a great deal of the play in this case consisting of gambling. There had been several harness meetings of the country fair variety in Saratoga, and, on August 3, 1863, an experimental four-day running meeting commenced on the Horse Haven track in the cool piney woods. It proved to be so successful that Horse Haven was diverted to a training ground and a new track built across the road where racing was resumed the following year on a permanent basis.

The official version credits John Hunter and W. R. Travers with having inspired Saratoga's original race meeting, but the unofficial version, which is considerably more colorful, casts John Morrissey in that role. An ex-bouncer, bare-knuckle prizefighter, bartender, ward heeler—ex- quite a number of occupations except gambler, for he remained that all of his life—Morrissey was an ambitious street urchin from Troy who had to travel a long road to make it to Saratoga Springs, only 25 miles away. The basis of his fortune was a string of gambling houses, which required a certain amount of political activity, that in his case led to a term in the Congress of the United States. Although his legislative impact was negligible, Morrissey did achieve immortality of a sort through a speech that under ordinary circumstances would have been trite, but in that particular setting was a milestone: he once offered to lick any man in the House.

John Morrissey, the bare-knuckle champion, gambler and U.S. Congressman, who brought racing to Saratoga.

Saratoga Springs City Museum

102

Although he discreetly withheld his name from formal documents, according to the more generally accepted belief it was Morrissey who put up the money to launch racing at Saratoga and induced Travers and Hunter to lend the prestige of their names to the undertaking. Certainly this version is more in keeping with the tradition of the place, which over the years was noted as a meeting ground of extreme types bound together by a common interest in sport and gaming, where dignified captains of industry rubbed elbows with high-rolling adventurers and painted ladies of the stage.

Whoever started racing at Saratoga started something. The regulation meeting of 1864 attracted a large number of fashionable spectators, and the inaugural of the United States' oldest stake race was run with rather poetic results. It was named for Travers and won by Kentucky, owned at the time by Hunter and Travers in partnership with George Osgood. (Later, a stake race was named for Morrissey.)

The next year the meeting was extended to six days and in 1867 the program was increased from two to three races per day. The Saratoga meetings already had come to be looked upon as something special where sport for sport's sake was emphasized and where the leading horses from various areas gathered each August to settle differences of regional opinion on the race track.

After a few years this happy state of affairs began to degenerate when the bigger stables showed a tendency to use Saratoga as a resting ground for their horses rather than a racing center. The track then was purchased by a vigorous new group, of which W. C. Whitney was president, and a program of vast improvements to the physical facilities and emphasis on stakes races was instituted until Saratoga again became the symbol of American racing at its best.

In 1865, the last year of the Civil War, Leonard W. Jerome decided that, in keeping with its status as the nation's largest city, New York needed a race course patterned after the elaborate European model, and he purchased the old Bathgate Estate in Fordham, upon which he built the fanciest racing plant in America. Among the features of Jerome Park, which opened in 1866, was a clubhouse on the order of a luxury hotel. Besides spacious dining rooms and a magnificent ball room, there were facilities for sleighing, trap shooting, skating and, later, polo. Overnight accommodations also were available, and it was quite the fashion for an owner to entertain his friends at a lavish ball, after which they could spend the night in the clubhouse and watch the morning gallops the next day.

This clubhouse, which was open all year around, was exclusive in location as well as clientele, for it was on a high bluff overlooking the backstretch of the track, while the double-tiered grandstand was in its customary position on the front side, near the stewards' and judges' stands and opposite the finish. Walter S. Vosburgh described the scene at old Jerome Park:

> Coaching was in great vogue at the time, and on race days the stately four-in-hands rode gracefully through the members' gate to the level below the club-house, where the drags were "parked," the horses unhitched, and refreshments served, while Manhattan's fairest daughters viewed the racing in a display of costume that caused old-fashioned people to stare at this exhibit of the "wealth of nations," visiting, as at the opera, among the boxes. Then, for the great race of the day, the ladies and their escorts would descend the hill to the members' stand, and all was eminently gentle and well bred.

The race track itself had to detour to get around the clubhouse hill, which gave it an odd shape, like an inverted pair of aviator's goggles, but there was a special chute for 6-furlong races and later a straightaway course was added. Another special facility worthy of note was an area set aside as a betting enclosure.

The track was administered by a jockey club that included 1,300 of the nation's most prominent figures, socially, politically and fi-

Leonard W. Jerome, pioneer American race track entrepreneur, and grandfather of Sir Winston Churchill.

nancially; the club maintained headquarters in downtown Manhattan where members could gather to discuss racing news and make bets. All bets were pay or play unless specified otherwise, and the penalty for non-payment within twenty-four hours was expulsion from the club. August Belmont was president, and therein lies a tale.

Leonard Jerome (1818–1891), the man who conceived the idea and built America's glamor track, was one of New York's most distinguished figures, a successful lawyer, publisher, financier and patron of the arts. His daughter, whom he named for the noted singer, Jenny Lind, later became the mother of Sir Winston Churchill.

In selecting his chief partner in the venture, Jerome virtually extinguished his own light, for it was said of Belmont, "If he cannot have a thing his own way, he won't touch it at all." As John Collins, of the New York *Sun* explained it, "When Leonard Jerome got up his park and started the Jockey Club, he was looking for a president. The name of Mr. Belmont suggested itself quite naturally. Jerome is a man of too broad intelligence to have wished to see a mere figurehead presiding over the club, or to have ever supposed that Belmont was a person of whom a figurehead could be made under any circumstances. But he must naturally enough have expected that he would preserve a kind of complimentary influence over the management of an institution upon which he had spent a half-million dollars. Not a bit of it. By the close of the very first season of his presidency, Belmont was the autocratic ruler of the club, while Jerome, like the ghost of Don Quixote, stood powerless by his side as one of the vice presidents."

The portrait of August Belmont (1816–1890) which hangs in the National Museum of Racing suggests that, bereft of his whiskers, he would have made an excellent double for movie actor Charles Boyer—but Belmont was a hard man to shave. A native of Hesse-Darmstadt, Germany, he had become associated with

August Belmont I, dashing leader in society and turf affairs.

Nevertheless, after his marriage to Carolyn Slidell Perry (a daughter of Commodore Matthew C. Perry, a niece of Oliver Hazard Perry and also of statesman John Slidell) August Belmont became the leader of New York society.

He seems even to have had his way with horses: the twelfth Earl of Derby established and gave his name to the race which was to become England's championship event for three-year-olds in 1780. It was 1787 before the Earl could win the race he created, and although successive holders of the title supported the event lavishly, it was nearly a century and a half later, in 1924, before the family won another Derby.

The equivalent American race, the Belmont Stakes, was inaugurated in 1867, and two years later August Belmont took first and second in it with Fenian and Glenelg, following which the family won four more renewals—with Hastings in 1896, Masterman in 1902, Friar Rock in 1916 and Hourless in 1917—before their racing stable was disbanded.

Public acceptance of racing at Saratoga and Jerome Park was so enthusiastic that a demand arose for more. Since Long Branch, New Jersey, was a popular seashore resort catering to the theatrical and political crowds, a track was built there and racing began in July, 1870.

No race track ever began more auspiciously, for on the first day of racing the program was loaded with stars: General Abe Buford's Enquirer beat the famed mare Maggie B. B. in one event, and Helmbold defeated Glenelg in the inaugural Monmouth Stakes. This was but a sample of what was ahead, for Monmouth became the mecca of stakes horses.

Senator Amos Robins was the first president of the track, but it was sold in 1878 to George Lorillard, D. D. Withers, G. P. Wetmore and James Gordon Bennett. With Lorillard as president, the track put on the best and richest races of the period. Monmouth Park was the perennial leader in daily average purse distribution (in the neighborhood of $9,500) and its

the Rothschild banking firm at the age of fourteen, and by the time he was twenty he had achieved a position of responsibility. He came to the United States as a representative of the Rothschild firm during the financial Panic of 1837, and quickly became one of New York's most talked-about men.

On the one hand, his polished manner, his knowledge of art and the ability to speak several languages which he had acquired during his travels through Europe, made him something of a social plum. But on the other hand, his disdain for convention and the fact that he participated in a duel with Edward Heyward cast him in another light.

105

version of a Derby, the Lorillard Stakes, was at one time the richest race in the nation. Later, this distinction passed to the same track's Junior Champion Stakes for two-year-olds, until the Futurity in New York was inaugurated. Other of old Monmouth Park's fixtures, some of which were bequeathed to modern racing associations, were the Omnibus, Select, Hopeful and Champion Stakes, Monmouth Oaks (one of the pioneer stake events exclusively for fillies) and Monmouth Cup.

Another innovation at the Jersey track was a long race meeting. In contrast to the brief meetings typical of the period, Monmouth opened on July 4 and ran through the end of August.

Besides a track to run on, in order to have a race meeting obviously there must be horses to run on it, and the majority of men who led the revival of the sport were wearing two hats: they built the tracks and also furnished the competing stables. Some of them wore three hats, for they maintained the studs where the horses were produced, as well.

John Hunter and W. R. Travers, founders of Saratoga, were owners of race horses, as was John Morrissey, who also founded Saratoga. Hunter and Travers were partners in many historic horses including Kentucky, Olipita, Sultana (who became the dam of Salvator) and Alarm, an invincible colt at a mile or less, undefeated as a three-year-old, who was to be grandsire of Domino.

Leonard Jerome, whose principal contribution to the sport was as an organizer (in addition to the track which bore his name, he later was to help establish Sheepshead Bay and Morris Park) kept a large stable, although in this venture he was not correspondingly successful. He, too, owned Kentucky at one time, paying $40,000 to install him as head of his stud. Jerome's racing stars included Fleetwing and De Courcy.

August Belmont's successes in the race named for him have been mentioned. Actually, Glenelg, runner-up in the 1869 Belmont Stakes, was considerably better than the win-

ner, but Belmont had bred Fenian and preferred to win with him, so, as Vosburgh wrote, "Glenelg's jockey almost had to pull his head off to let Fenian finish first." Imported *in utero* by R. W. Cameron, and foaled at his estate on Staten Island, Glenelg got better as he grew older, and after retiring the horse, Belmont (who by this time had Kentucky at his stud) sold Glenelg to Milton H. Sanford to stand at the latter's Preakness Stud. Subsequently, Glenelg led the American sire list four times in five seasons. Belmont's effect as a breeder was profound, and he also imported some significant thoroughbreds. A proper accounting of the famous horses he either bred or owned is a subject unto itself—but they included besides those already mentioned, Woodbine, Wade Hampton, The Ill-Used (so named because his own stablemate knocked him down in a race), Silk Stocking, Raceland, Potomac (winner of the richest race in the nineteenth century, the 1890 Futurity) and Fides.

Belmont's influence was exercised not only through tracks and horses, but also by way of people, for he was associated along the way with such noted trainers as Jacob Pincus and James Rowe, and most important of all, he imparted to his own son a tradition which carried on to even greater heights, eventually culminating in the production of America's greatest race horse, Man o' War.

Francis Morris was a three-hat man of impressive proportions. No relation to the previously mentioned Morris family, Francis Morris later owned an imported stallion, named Eclipse. He had himself immigrated to America as a boy, operated mail steamers and was allied with Samuel F. B. Morse in the first telegraph line in this country. The all-scarlet colors of the Morris stable led the parade for years, principally worn by home-breds. The mating of Eclipse to the mare Barbarity produced Ruthless, winner of the inaugural Nursery Stakes in 1866 and the inaugural Belmont Stakes the following year. This same mating also produced Relentless, Remorseless, Regardless and Merciless, all of them stakes winners and, remarkably, all fillies, while the colts resulting from this same mating were of no consequence. This gang of ferocious females was known as the "Barbarous Battalion." (Ruthless, incidentally, died probably the strangest death of any prominent thoroughbred on record. A hunter wandering by Morris' farm in Westchester shot her by mistake.)

In later years, when Leonard Jerome provided the impetus for establishment of a palatial new race track, Francis Morris' son provided the funds, and the track was named for him.

David D. Withers, apart from the role he played in the advancement of Monmouth Park, brought racing jurisprudence to a position of respect it never had held before. In contrast to officials who were perhaps first-class citizens, but of questionable qualifications for adjudication of a complex sport, Withers was an eminent authority, whose experience encompassed residence in New Orleans when Lexington and Lecomte were ruling the roost, and a tenure in France. He first ran horses in partnership with John F. Purdy, another racing official, who was the son of Samuel Purdy, rider of American Eclipse, and their Vespucius boasted a victory over Glenelg. Withers went on his own later, and his cosmopolitan background was reflected in his stable, for he was a lavish importer of foreign animals, without, it might be added, any great measure of success. Withers later became a breeder, with headquarters at Brookdale Farm in Red Bank, New Jersey, which area was to become more famous later through the agency of James R. Keene and W. C. Whitney. Ironically, in view of his admiration for foreign blood, the best horse Withers owned was Laggard, bred by himself. (Withers, who was the symbol of rectitude, along with the equally distinguished sportsman, A. J. Cassatt, once was arrested on a complaint of bookmakers, who charged them with cutting off their wire service from the track.)

One of the largest and most effective racing strings of the immediate postwar period was that of Colonel David McDaniel, who won three Belmont Stakes in a row with Harry Bassett, Joe Daniels and Springbok—a trio which was even more possessive with respect to the Saratoga Cup. The colonel would be classified as more of a professional racing man than a hobbyist; he had little taste for folderol and cared not for creating an image of himself as a big sport. Jockey Frank McCabe stated that after he won the 1872 Dixie Stakes with Hubbard, McDaniel added the munificent sum of $2 to his regular fee. (It was a realistic evaluation of the performance at that, for McCabe had a rocking chair ride in the course of which Hubbard won by six lengths from a stablemate.) The "McDaniel Confederacy" was a strong current in the tide of racing affairs, and the colonel's son, "Uncle Henry" McDaniel, as well as another protege, James Rowe, also became powerful forces in their own rights.

They were not all New Yorkers or residents of that general region, these men who revived the corpse of racing after the Civil War and put more life into it than it had possessed in the first place. Price McGrath, Major Thomas Doswell, John Harper, J. A. Grinstead, Daniel Swigert, Duncan Kenner and others too numerous to list—they came from all over the country (the Alabama Stakes at Saratoga was named in honor of William Cottrell of Mobile, who modestly objected to a race being named for him personally).

The biggest popular idol during the decade after the Civil War was John Harper's Longfellow, a son of Leamington—Nantura, by Brawner's Eclipse. The colt's name derived from his size; he stood 17 hands and was said to stride 26 feet.

Because he was a long time growing, Longfellow didn't start at two, and in his first race at three he was distanced by another son of Leamington, Enquirer, who was in the process of racking up an undefeated season.

By autumn of his sophomore year Longfellow had come around—he won five races—and as a four-year-old he was terrific. He beat Preakness and Helmbold in the 2½-mile Monmouth Cup and frightened off every opponent but Kingfisher for the Saratoga Cup. At the start of that race, Longfellow was facing the wrong way, but he immediately turned around, gathered himself for a spring and literally bounded into the lead. He won this one easily —but in his next start Helmbold beat him at 4 miles in the mud, Longfellow's great size being a disadvantage in that type of footing.

That same season Harry Bassett went undefeated as a three-year-old, and the next year, 1872, Colonel McDaniel challenged Harper to match Longfellow against him. Harper merely replied that anyone wishing to test his horse's mettle was free to do so in the Monmouth Cup. Bassett was entered and the race became the object of intense advance interest, reminiscent of the Boston–Fashion match years before.

After winning two races at the Lexington spring meeting, Longfellow headed east in a special car which bore a sign, "Longfellow on his way to Long Branch to meet his friend Harry Bassett." Cup day, July 2, dawned bright and clear, and as all ten of the other nominees were withdrawn, a match it was to be. Fully 30,000 spectators jammed the course to see the great contest. Some of them rode out on the tops of cars, traffic was so heavy and accommodations so strained. What they saw was a farce.

Bassett, a heavy favorite in the betting, was too friendly, and refused to dispute the issue. Longfellow "won in a canter by 100 yards," said the chart of the race. "Harry Bassett sulked after going a mile and a half, and the race was over. Longfellow galloped in alone."

Two weeks later the rivals met again in the 2¼-mile Saratoga Cup, with John Morrissey's Defender joining the field. Harry Bassett took the lead and ran the first 2 miles in 3:30 (5¾ seconds faster than his own track record set the year before) at which point Longfellow changed legs and his jockey stood up in his stirrups and began flogging. The big locomotive responded, but Harry Bassett went under the wire a length clear in 3:59, breaking the track record for the full distance by 2½ seconds.

Longfellow, it turned out, had lost half of a front plate, and the pain to his foot when it bent had caused him to falter. He was never able to race again, but became a great sire.

CHAPTER TWENTY-TWO

BALTIMORE WAS QUICK TO FOL-
low New York in the rehabilitation of racing after the Civil
War, and, by what seems an
odd chain of circumstances
today, Bowie founded Pimlico and helped con-
ceive the Preakness while at Saratoga.

A group of sportsmen at a dinner party in
Saratoga one evening in 1868 agreed to run a
sweepstakes in Baltimore two years later. Originally there were only seven subscribers, but the
idea caught on so well that the Dinner Party
Stakes, as it was known, had attracted thirty
nominations by the time it closed in October.
In fact, so intrigued were the participants that
betting was opened on the race a week later,
slightly more than two years before post time.

The Maryland Jockey Club, of which Governor Oden Bowie was president, opened Pimlico
Race Course on October 25, 1870, and the
Dinner Party Stakes was duly run. Preakness,
owned by M. H. Sanford, one of the original
subscribers, was the winner, and the colt's
name is commemorated by the classic for three-
year-olds at the Pimlico spring meet.

Maryland racing expanded further when the
Benning track in Washington, D. C., came
along in 1876, and Timonium in 1878.

The main stops on what in modern times is
known as the Midwest Circuit of racing—i.e.,
up and down the Mississippi Valley—were in
existence at the time of the Civil War although the circuit was not as yet integrated.

On the southern end, the Fair Grounds had
opened in New Orleans in 1872, before Metairie closed.

In Kentucky, racing in Lexington had continued through the Civil War, and, although
interrupted in Louisville, it was resumed there
before the war ended. However, the meeting at
the Greenland Course was abandoned after
1869, and Woodlawn, the only remaining
track, closed the next year. Colonel M. Lewis
Clark then organized a group to revive racing,
and in 1875 the Louisville Jockey Club held
its inaugural meeting at what later was to be
named Churchill Downs. One of the feature
races that year was a modestly endowed 1½-
mile dash for three-year-olds which drew fifteen starters. H. P. McGrath's Aristides won
this race, collecting $2,850 for his effort, and
the Kentucky Derby has been renewed every
year since.

The third member of Kentucky's "Three L"
circuit was added in 1883 when Latonia
opened at Covington, just across the river from
Cincinnati, Ohio.

The top of the midwest circuit is Chicago.
There were brief meetings at various tracks
there and elsewhere in Illinois beginning in
1864, but full development was not achieved
until 1884 when Washington Park was opened
with General Phil Sheridan as president. A
beautiful racing plant, comparable to the best
in the East, it featured a 1⅛-mile course (at
that time equal to the largest in America) with
a concentric track of conventional size in the
infield. The American Derby, more than double
the Kentucky Derby in value, was inaugurated,
and the day it was run was practically a public
holiday in Chicago. In 1893, the year of the
World's Fair, it was the richest race in the
nation.

American Derby day at old Washington Park.

Washington Park rolled smoothly along a path of great popularity and social acceptance equivalent to that of the swank New York tracks for about ten years.

After Hawthorne, Garfield Park and a track at Harlem were added in the early nineties, the overabundance of racing led to public antipathy, and Washington Park stopped its meet. Racing later was resumed for a brief period, but the fierce competition among local tracks,

fed by political intrigue, continued, and it was not long until the situation had become so bad that the sport was suppressed.

During the period between the Civil War and World War I, at one time or another there were many tracks in Ohio, principally Cincinnati, none of which survive today. Missouri, too, was a center of the sport and the old Laclede Course in St. Louis was the scene of numerous good races during the period 1863-

110

1869. Later, the St. Louis Fair Association took over the management of racing and in 1904, as an attraction at the Louisiana Purchase Exposition, the $50,000 World's Fair Handicap was run.

C. E. Rowe's Colonial Girl, the winner, was ridden by A. W. Booker, who some 27 years later, when he had become a trainer, was to become associated with another historic race. He saddled a horse named Eagle Bird for a claiming race at Caliente, and gave a leg up to an aspiring young jockey named George Edward Arcaro, then watched them both win their first race.

As was true of other parts of America, racing in Canada was born with the nation; as soon as horses were available, some form of the sport began. Shortly after she ascended the English throne, Queen Victoria, in keeping with the improvement-of-the-breed tradition, offered a prize of G.100 for a race run in Montreal; this event subsequently was abandoned, but it became the basis of North America's oldest stake race, known as the Queen's Plate or King's Plate, depending upon the reigning monarch.

In 1859 the Toronto Turf Club petitioned the Queen to grant a prize for racing, and royal assent was forthcoming in the form of a gift of G.50, which was won by James White's five-year-old Don Juan on June 27, 1860, in the inaugural of the Plate as it continued to exist. For about twenty years the race was contested in various locations under a variety of conditions until it found a permanent home at Woodbine, in Toronto.

The Woodbine track—or, rather a Woodbine track—had been in existence for some years previously, but the Ontario Jockey Club, which was to conduct racing on a really organized basis, was not formed until 1881. Under the management and patronage of the wealthy Hendrie and Seagram families (which have continued prominent in Canadian racing through the time of writing) Woodbine took its place among the foremost racing plants in America. The Plate itself has been largely a provincial affair (but nonetheless a valuable

The clubhouse at St. Louis on World's Fair Handicap day in 1904.

one) limited in one way or another to Canadian horses, under conditions of eligibility which have changed over the years, finally crystallizing into the equivalent of a Derby, i.e., an event for three-year-olds. Over-all, however, racing in Ontario was on a par with the best on the continent.

In San Francisco, far from the scene of the conflict which was raging in the East, racing continued to expand during the Civil War. In 1863 Senator George Hearst, father of William Randolph Hearst, spearheaded construction of Bay View Park, built at a cost of more than $200,000. Bay View was one of the fastest tracks in the country, a distinction which later was to pass on to Golden Gate Fields in the same area, and at one time the track could boast records at either extreme of the distance scale. In 1867 Amanda Fortune set a record of 51½ seconds for a half-mile, and the next year jockey Neel Mowrey achieved a world record of 14 hours and 9 minutes for 300 miles, using thirty horses in the process. Mowrey covered the first 200 miles in 8 hours flat, thus clipping 42 minutes from the previous world record for that distance which had been set at Newmarket, England, in 1831, by Squire Osbaldeston who used twenty-eight different horses during his feat.

Within two years after Bay View opened, the fast-growing city had engulfed the Pioneer and Union tracks and was already threatening Bay View. Theodore Winters, Nathan Coombs and A. J. Bryant organized the Pacific Jockey Club, and chose a well-isolated spot on the edge of the ocean for construction of another race course.

Ocean View Park (also called Ocean House Park) launched its inaugural meeting in May, 1865, and the first race was a match between Winters's four-year-old colt, Norfolk, winner of the previous season's Jersey Derby, and C. H. Byran's five-year-old Lodi. Ridden by Gilpatrick, Lodi made a dead heat in the first trial, run in 3:43⅕, then Norfolk beat him in the next two heats, 3:42⅗ and 3:51⅘. They met again twice at Sacramento in September, with a new set of jockeys, but Norfolk won both races in straight heats—2 miles in 3:37⅗ and 3:38¼, and 3 miles in 5:27½ and 5:29½.

Of the numerous tracks in San Francisco, the one destined to remain in operation longest was the Bay District Course, built at the base of Lone Mountain by Senator Leland Stanford. A few years after it opened, Elias J. "Lucky" Baldwin joined Stanford to form the Pacific Coast Blood Horse Association, which became a sort of governing body for turf affairs on the West Coast, analogous to the Board of Control which later was to be set up in the East.

When the Bay District Course was completed, Ocean View Park was closed, and its principal events transferred to the new track. Incorporated in this legacy were the last of the epic intersectional 4-mile heat races in this country.

CHAPTER TWENTY-THREE

A<small>S MEN HAD DONE BEFORE</small> them, horses began to pour across the Rocky Mountains in quest of California gold after the Civil War. This tide was given added impetus in 1873 when the Pacific Jockey Club announced a race at 4-mile heats for a purse of $20,000 *in gold*. One of the nation's numerous financial panics was in progress that year, and considering the various species of specie in circulation, it is difficult for the modern reader to appreciate fully the impact of this announcement.

The tempting prize was not just lying around waiting to be picked up casually, however, for standing guard over it was George Treat's mighty California-bred champion, Thad Stevens.

He was the most popular champion of his day. By this time eight years old, the son of Langford—Mary Chilton, by Glencoe, did not waltz through his races with supercilious ease. He had to scramble, and the crowds loved him for it. Devastating at any distance from 1 to 4 miles, Thad Stevens usually was favorite for any race in which he started, but the results were not a foregone conclusion. It generally required a couple of heats for his ancient bones to warm up, and the possibility that he might be distanced in the first heat added a touch of excitement to his races.

In 1873, for example, Stevens opened the season with three races at mile heats, in which Nettie Brown beat him once and he beat her twice. Moving up to 2 miles, he won an easy match against Ben Wade at Oakland in June. Then, he went into his pattern.

At Sacramento in July, in a best three-out-of-five race against four opponents, Thad finished third to William Pierce's colt, Thorn Hill, in the first two heats, then won the next three in succession. On September 16 at Union Park, Thad won a conventional (repeat) heat race by finishing 4-2-1-1. Two days later the chestnut (listed as sorrel in those days) son of Langford won a three-out-of-five event, running 4-3-1-1-1.

Because of this characteristic cold start and hot finish, the betting odds on Thad Stevens occasionally would perform weird gymnastics. After he lost a heat, his price would shrink while the odds on the horse which beat him would get bigger; so long as Thad could save his distance in the first heat, his admirers were confident he would get the job done eventually.

Among the horses which had come west to challenge for the pot of gold was the previous season's three-year-old champion, Joe Daniels. Racing for Colonel David McDaniel, the son of Australian—Dolly Carter, by Glencoe, had won the Belmont Stakes, Jerome, Travers, Annual and Kenner Stakes. Now the property of G. A. Johnson, Joe Daniels got his first taste of what was to come when he met Thad Stevens in a 4-mile heat race on October 18, at the Oakland trotting park. Daniels won the first heat in 7:42 as Thad finished next to last. But the old pro came back to win the next two heats in 7:30 (a record for a second heat) and 7:43, to expand his championship status to transcontinental proportions.

The run for gold was at Ocean View Park in San Francisco on November 15. Entering the lists against Thad Stevens and Joe Daniels was another Eastern colt, J. F. Chamberlin's four-year-old True Blue, winner of four races that season in the last of which, on July 30 at Saratoga, he had set a 2-mile record of 3:32½ (Joe Daniels fourth). At 111 pounds Thad Stevens was the favorite in all pools sold before the day of the race, with True Blue second choice and Joe Daniels third, each at 108 pounds. The only other starter was a mare named Mamie Hall. The much publicized extravaganza was described by *Turf, Field and Farm,* in part, as follows:

San Francisco, Cal., November 15, 1873— An immense assemblage, variously estimated at from ten to fifteen thousand persons, were present at the Ocean View Park Course to-day, to witness the great $20,000 four-mile heat contest. The occasion evoked the greatest enthusiasm, and it is estimated that previous to and during the race at least $100,000 changed hands. Never before was so much excitement evinced at a race meeting by all classes of people, even by the straight-laced, long-faced Jeremiahs, with whom nothing at the present is equal to what they had seen in the past. The managers were particularly favored by fine weather, the day being one of the most delightful of the season. The turnout of aristocratic equipages was numerically larger than at any previous gathering in the State, while the number and styles of other vehicles were simply legion. Less pretentious pedestrians came in platoons from all quarters, and at 1½ P.M. the scene and the countless objects that vivified it with bustling animation were strongly suggestive of Derby day at Epsom Downs . . .

First Heat—Promptly at the call Thad Stevens, Joe Daniels, True Blue and Mamie Hall went to the post, with Thad on the inside and Joe Daniels on the outside. At the signal Mamie Hall jumped off with the lead and held on for the first mile, with Thad Stevens running second, True Blue third, and Joe Daniels fourth. In the second mile True Blue took the lead and held it to the fourth mile, when Joe Daniels, who had been trailing, made play for the lead, and after a fine brush

with True Blue, took it, winning the heat by two lengths in 7:45, True Blue second, Thad Stevens third, and Mamie Hall distanced.

The result of this heat was almost entirely unexpected, and gave a different turn to the betting. The excitement around the pool-sellers was tremendous, and high figures were the order. The friends of Thad Stevens rallied promptly to his support, and backed their opinion in the handsomest manner. In one of the first pools sold after the first heat, Thad Stevens was made first choice for $2,100, Joe Daniels bringing $1,500, and True Blue $800. Before the call for the second heat several large pools were sold, averaging in amounts from $1,500 to $3,000.

Second Heat—The horses were called for the second heat at a quarter to four, and the preliminary rubbing down and saddling having been accomplished, at five minutes to four another excellent start was made, the three horses passing the score even . . .

The remainder of the race was typical. True Blue won the second heat by five lengths in 8:08 from Joe Daniels, as Thad Stevens finished another seven lengths away third. In the third heat old Thad came to life; he won by ten lengths in 7:57 from Daniels, leaving True Blue outside the distance flag. (There was tremendous conjecture as to the cause of True Blue quitting, various reporters stating that the colt had broken his leg, or fallen, or stepped into a gopher hole; Barbee, his jockey, was quoted as accusing Palmer, on Joe Daniels, of cutting True Blue down.)

That left Thad Stevens and Joe Daniels to contest the deciding heat, which was not started until it was nearly dark. ". . . as they disappeared in the gloom the old horse was leading by fully five lengths, an advantage he held all through the heat," and Thad won the one that counted in 7:46, remarkable time for a final heat, especially since it was noted that the track was "some seconds slower" than the Oakland surface.

Elsewhere in the account of the affair, the Pacific Jockey Club is soundly criticized for having suddenly changed the scale of weights so as to require an additional 5 pounds on the young Eastern colt and 4 pounds less on Thad Stevens. "This discrimination," said the reporter from *Turf, Field and Farm*, ". . . does not reflect any great credit upon the Pacific Jockey Club, and has not a parallel in the history of the American turf. Had the Club in their original advertisement announced the change, it is more than possible Mr. Chamberlin would not have entered True Blue . . ."

On the other hand, it should be mentioned that the foregoing account of the race was written for an Eastern audience, since *Turf, Field and Farm* was published in New York, and in any case, in their October meeting Thad Stevens had beaten Joe Daniels, carrying 115 pounds to the younger horse's 103.

No such sectional criticism could be leveled at the following year's renewal of this race—certainly not on the ground of provincialism. The purse was increased to $25,000 and, for the first time, the fourth horse to finish was allotted a share. A compromise was reached regarding the scale of weights, whereby aged horses carried 114 pounds against 110 for five-year-olds and 104 pounds for four-year-olds. There was no allowance made for sex, but as it turned out, none was needed.

Among the horses in the large stable of Colonel McDaniel, former owner of Joe Daniels, was a filly named Katy Pease, a daughter of Planet out of Minnie Mansfield, by Glencoe. McDaniel had bought the mare while she was carrying Katy, and had the colt, Hubbard, at foot, for only $325, which developed into one of horse history's great bargains.

Katy (often also spelled "Katie") began the 1874 season with three straight victories at Jerome Park in June, following which she won two out of three at Utica. Moving on to Saratoga she won her first start and then was beaten four times in succession, the last occasion being a 4-mile dash won by Fellowcraft in 7:19½, which broke the record of 7:19¾ set by Lexington in his famous race against time nineteen

years earlier. It was Katy's only experience at the distance before her big score. A. S. Gage had leased the filly for this race and thereafter she campaigned in his name.

Katy Pease next swept through the Buffalo meeting like a whirlwind. On opening day, September 8, she distanced two opponents in the first heat of a mile race, came back again the very next day to win a 2-mile dash, although she was disqualified for a foul; and on September 10, in her third race in three days, she won a 2½-mile dash in 4:28½ to set a new record.

Thad Stevens, meanwhile, had not started since his great victory the previous year, but despite this long layoff, he was favorite in the advance betting on the 1874 contest up until a week or so before the running. Then, little Katy Pease, who began to attract a following the instant she arrived on the Coast, ousted him in most of the pools sold. "How easily she moves," wrote J. C. Simpson in a description of one of her workouts. "When the blue and the brindle (greyhounds) were in full career after the flying hare, their loins appeared to be continually rounded, so rapid were they in recovering their strokes. There is a good deal of the same action in Katy although she appears to do her work more easily . . ."

The display of hospitality toward Katy was somewhat less than unanimous, however. No less an authority than the groom of True Blue warned his opposite number in the Katy Pease contingent concerning the temper of the Californians. After True Blue had won the second heat of the 1873 race, he said, he had become carried away and began singing and waving his hat while rubbing the horse during the rest period. One of Thad Stevens' admirers cracked him behind the ear, knocking him down, and the hat had not since been recovered. Katy Pease's rubber digested this information carefully, then remarked, "Katy beats him, I'se never holler till I gets back in the States, then I makes more noise than a . . . camp meeting."

When the great day finally arrived, in all pools recorded, Thad Stevens had resumed the status of favorite for the country's richest race. Describing the scene for *Turf, Field, and Farm,* "Rolyat Mot" wrote:

> . . . from the richest men in the State, in their four-in-hands, down to the licensed vendor, dog carts, tandems, express wagons, mountain coaches—everything on wheels were out, and those who couldn't go on wheels footed it. The day was such as only California can get up, and if put up to order couldn't have been better. The atmosphere was as clear as a bell, not a cloud in the sky, no wind, and warm and comfortable as a May day at home in the East. The track was everything that could be desired, and the horses in good condition. What more could one ask? By 8 o'clock A.M. the stream of carriages commenced, and until half-past two o'clock there was almost an unbroken line to the course. It was estimated that there were 1,200 vehicles *inside* the course and half that number outside, while there were 16,000 tickets sold, and that 30,000 people viewed the race from the stands and surrounding hills . . .

There was little to the telling of the race. After trailing the field for a while, Katy Pease moved up when it pleased her jockey, Hennessy, to win easily in straight heats (the times were 7:43¼, 7:36¼) without once being touched by the whip. Thad Stevens was fourth in both heats, and Joe Daniels and Hock Hocking were distanced in the second heat.

In the opinion of one reporter, Joe Daniels could have made a contest out of it, but he had his mind on romance, and each time he approached Katy he showed no inclination to proceed beyond her. This was an expensive bit of gallantry, so it is refreshing to record that a few years later, in a more appropriate setting, the affair was consummated, to use the legal term; the result was a chestnut filly.

It is a harsh fact of life that gallant old gladiators frequently are undone by fresh, young females, so the downfall of Thad Stevens scarcely can be considered unique. It is also a harsh fact of life that champions seldom come back, but then what makes life

Billy Lakeland, rider of Foster, and later the trainer of Domino.

interesting is that the so-called facts thereof are not immutable. Although Thad Stevens was not himself involved in it, there was a sequel to his downfall, in which another nine-year-old horse turned back the clock and reversed the plot.

One of the horses nominated for the Pacific Jockey Club Purse won by Katy Pease was Foster, a then seven-year-old son of Lexington out of Verona, by Yorkshire. During an Eastern racing career, in the stable of Captain T. G. Moore, he had reached his peak at the age of four, but had to be retired because of troublesome feet and was sent to stud in Oregon. The huge purse at San Francisco lured him out of the woods, but while training for the 1874 race he went lame and was again retired.

Moore, meanwhile, in partnership with M. A. Littell, had taken dead aim on the next

116

bag of gold with Wildidle, a son of the top mare, Idlewild, who in her racing days had set a distaff record of 7:26¼ in a 4-mile dash. The son was no slowpoke either, having won in 7:25½, a sequence of performance unmatched by any other mother-son combination.

Then Wildidle broke down. Casting about for a replacement, Moore remembered Foster tucked away up there in Oregon. Forlorn as it was, Foster was the partners' only hope, so he was shipped to California by boat and put through a training program designed either to kill him or make him fit.

The rehabilitation of Foster is a story in itself, but suffice it to say that it was another illustration of the saying, "There's nothing new under the sun." In the mid-twentieth century there was dramatic improvement among human runners—far more so than among horses—and the four-minute mile, which not very long before had been considered impossible, became commonplace. Much of the two-legged athletes' improvement was attributed to "repeat" and "interval" training.

A description of Foster's training regimen includes references to "three-mile gallops, then two miles and repeat," which suggests that a version of this ultramodern technique was in use eighty years earlier.

After two bad breaks, Moore and Littell received a good one, when through a concatenation of flubs (nominations were delayed in closing and there was a question concerning the lease of the Bay District Fair Grounds by the Pacific Jockey Club) the race went through a series of postponements. What was to have been the 1875 renewal, when finally contested, was on Washington's Birthday, 1876. By this time the purse had been raised to $30,000, with $15,000 to the winner, $6,000 to second, $5,000 to third and $4,000 to fourth. Also— and this was important—the conditions included a clause which stipulated "no horse to get more than one money, and no horse distanced to get a prize."

The breathing spell notwithstanding, life was not boringly serene in the Foster camp. Those who watched the old horse take shape before their very eyes while undergoing preparation at Sacramento were just beginning to regard him seriously when, ten days before the race, he pulled up limping after a workout and his shoes were removed.

When pool selling began five days before the race, "Lucky" Baldwin's Rutherford was favorite, with Katy Pease, now a mature six-year-old, and Hock Hocking also well regarded. Although no one seemed to notice it at the time, in the light of future events it was significant that Billy Lakeland, who was to ride Foster, bet $500 and two gold watches on his mount, in spite of the presumed injury to the horse in his training.

By post time—and this, too, was to assume significance later—Foster was second choice to Rutherford in the betting at the track. (Downtown, Katy Pease was favorite, with Rutherford second choice and Foster third.)

Correspondent "Lem" of *Turf, Field and Farm* described the great race as follows:

The oft post-poned and much-talked-of four-mile-and-repeat race has come off at last, with as fine a day and track as the most fastidious could ask or most patriotic of '49ers brag over as the usual climate of their chosen country.

Mr. A. J. Bryant, the president of the Pacific Jockey Club, who is also Mayor of San Francisco, was most courteous . . . interspersing information with some good brandy.

The horses were rung out a little after half-past one, and, without much delay, the gong sounded the start, and then the recall, to the surprise of everyone . . . as all the horses got off even, with the exception of Hock Hocking, who had about a length and a half advantage, and as no one expected him to win and the start seemed so fair, there were various comments made, until the gong started them again, at least, all of them but Chance, who was some thirty yards behind, when they were recalled from the most straggling attempt to start I ever witnessed. The third time they went off well together with Chance cutting out the running, which he did well, holding the lead until the end of the first mile, which was run in two minutes, and the horses came by the stand all well up but Revenue, Jr., while Foster was lapping the leader with his head at his girth and Lakeland holding him so serenely in hand that I could not help remarking to my next neighbor: "Foster wins," and to his look of incredulity, adding, "Mark Littell enters to win when he can, and that horse is going as if he could do it." The second time they came around Rutherford had taken the lead, but Foster was still second, and going at ease, and he held the position through the third mile and to the turn on the fourth, where he came gradually up, and rushing down the quarter-stretch side by side with Rutherford, came under the string winner by a handsome head and neck, amid a hearty greeting, though the knowing ones had been badly sold in their investments.

After a little consultation, the rest were declared distanced, though many of the outsiders claimed that Hock Hocking had saved his distance. Time, 7:38½.

The rush to hedge on the part of disappointed pool-holders made Foster the favorite, though many of Rutherford's friends claimed still that he was all right, and would show it in the next heat. The bell rung the horses up for the second heat, and they started promptly without the bell sounding "go," and only when they had nearly finished the mile did the bell sound for them to stop. This created some excitement, and Lucky Baldwin, the owner of Rutherford, was more emphatic than polite in his loud expressions of dissatisfaction at the judges, and relieved the minds of his hearers of any doubt they might have of his being the proper representative hoodlum to send to the Philadelphia Centennial.

The second trial they got off with Foster half a length in the lead; but the next few jumps showed that Lakeland intended he should stay there, and I said, "Foster will hold his lead to the end," which proved correct, as only once, at the end of the second mile, when Rutherford made a rush, Lakeland let him get head and head with him and then letting

out a length resumed his place of half a length lead, turning his face to the judges with a smile as he passed. The positions were unchanged, until coming down the home stretch Lakeland shook Foster out a little, and came home winner of the heat and race by two lengths. Time, 7:53.

The riding of Lakeland was simply perfect, and showed him equal to a waiting or a leading race, and was well worth a long trip to see . . .

All hell broke loose after this race. Six horses from supposedly the best field yet assembled in the West distanced in the first heat—not to mention the convenient delays which resulted in the race being run on a profitable holiday—was too much for the local press to swallow, the "good brandy" dispensed by the president of the Pacific Jockey Club notwithstanding. The San Francisco *Chronicle* asserted that a number of prominent turfmen, including some who had "emerged from the ordeal financially ahead," protested that Hock Hocking was fully five lengths inside the distance stand, with Katy Pease and Golden Gate not much behind him. It was theorized that the "distancing idiocy" was a scheme by the association to avoid payment of third and fourth money. The affair was referred to as a "put-up job" and "$30,000 fraud," and "a prominent member" of the Bay District Association was quoted to the effect that never again would the track be lent to the Pacific Jockey Club for such extravaganzas.

The *Post* dredged up the previous renewals of the race, charging that the whole idea had been "to fleece the public rather than to promote legitimate sport" all along. Taking the long range view, an editorial in *Turf, Field and Farm*, published 3,000 miles away, finally came out with the observation: "Horse owners who value their reputations in the future certainly will fight shy of the Pacific Jockey Club. Its name has an unsavory smell."

When the race was renewed a year later, the purse had been cut drastically, to $5,000, but it remained at the heroic distance and was won by an heroic animal. This time, California provided its own representative.

A bay filly foaled in 1873, by Eclipse, Jr. or Monday, out of Hennie Farrow, by Shamrock, bred by Adolph Mallard, Mollie McCarty was one of an appalling number of fillies by that name (frequently spelled with an "h"), and some historians disagree concerning her origin. As her dam had been owned for years by Californian J. B. Chase, and Mollie raced exclusively in California in the colors of Theodore Winters through age four, the evidence is overwhelming that she was a native daughter of the Golden State.

There was no argument concerning her quality. After winning her only start at two, Mollie McCarty swept through six races as a three-year-old without defeat, including two victories the same day at Agricultural Park in Sacramento on September 18; she completed the season by defeating an all-age field of fillies and mares for a $10,000 purse at San Francisco. This event also included the clause, "no horse to win more than one money, and no horse distanced to get a prize;" Mollie distanced all but one of her rivals in the first heat, so the track saved the $2,500 that had been allocated as third and fourth money.

The 4-mile heat race was her deubt as a four-year-old. Mollie McCarty reduced the purse even further by distancing all her opponents but Bazar, and the minor awards again reverted to the track. She won four more races that year and the next February 22 the big race was postponed because of bad weather. In a substitute event, Mollie was matched over 2 miles against H. Schwartz's Jake at Sacramento March 2, under conditions which required her to concede 14 pounds, although they were of the same age. Jake's rider couldn't make the weight, but Mollie beat him in straight heats, while giving away 11 pounds.

Through this point, Mollie McCarty was undefeated in thirteen starts under the ownership of Winters. Having run herself out of competition in her home state, Mollie was acquired by "Lucky" Baldwin, who sent her to Kentucky. Entered by Budd Doble in a 4-mile match at Louisville July 4, for $5,000 a side, she was distanced by Ten Broeck. Her first defeat—in fact it was the first heat she ever had lost—was ironic, for, in his book *Famous Running Horses,* Colonel John F. Wall records that had Mollie been able merely to save her distance she ultimately must have won because Ten Broeck would not have been able to go around again. Apparently under the influence of an opiate, "he did not perspire, his pupils were contracted, his muscular strength and activity were reduced, and he was languorous and drowsy. To keep the horse awake, it was necessary to fan, whip and keep him moving . . ."

Mollie McCarty was defeated again in the Minneapolis Cup later that year (racing in Baldwin's name), but the following season she came back with victories in a purse race at San Francisco and the Garden City Cup in Chicago before retirement.

The horse which snapped Mollie McCarty's winning streak was no flash in the pan. That race in Louisville had been the last start of a sensational career during which Ten Broeck was generally considered the yardstick of class, whether in dash racing or heats. In fact, as will be related, such was his reputation that on one occasion the Congress of the United States adjourned early so that members could see a race for which Ten Broeck was favorite.

CHAPTER TWENTY-FOUR

THE MAN WHO BROUGHT NOR-folk to California and started Mollie McCarty on the road to fame was associated with numerous other historic horses. Theodore Winters (1823-1894), nicknamed "Black T" because of his luxuriant moustache which resembled the cross tie on a telegraph pole, was born in Fort Dearborn, near Chicago, but went west with the popular tide. He became a prosperous Sacramento businessman with lucrative holdings in gold mining stock. Using Norfolk as foundation sire, he established a highly successful stud in Yolo County where the city of Winters now is located, but he later moved west across the Sacramento River and named his place Rancho del Rio. In the belief that high altitude would benefit lung capacity, Winters also maintained Rancho del Sierra in Nevada.

When Joseph Cairn Simpson, who was to found California's first all-sports newspaper, *Breeder and Sportsman,* came west in the 1870s, he brought with him several horses, including the filly Marian. In need of capital for his newspaper, Simpson sold Marian to Winters and the owner of the Pacific Coast's top stallion thus acquired the West's greatest brood mare. An Illinois-bred daughter of Malcom, Marian produced a veritable galaxy of stars. Mated to Norfolk, she foaled Emperor of Norfolk, Duchess of Norfolk, Prince of Norfolk, The Czar, El Rio Rey and Rey Del Rey. The *Thoroughbred of California* computed that Marian's offspring won, all told, no fewer than 71 stakes events.

Imitating their sire, El Rio Rey and The Czar were undefeated, but Emperor of Norfolk achieved a greater national reputation. In one year and two days of competition, he won 21 races in 29 starts, being unplaced but twice. His reputation literally spanned the continent, for his victories included the Brooklyn Derby in New York, the American Derby in Chicago, plus races at Nashville, Monmouth, Kansas City and Washington, D. C.—although he never competed in his native state.

Marian proved her versatility when, after her succession of auspicious matings to Norfolk, she produced the great mare Yo Tambien, by another stallion, Joe Hooker. In 73 starts, Yo Tambien won 44, was 11 times second and nine times third to earn $89,480 and her victories also were spread all over the country.

Neither Yo Tambien nor Emperor of Norfolk raced for Winters. The former carried the colors of the Kendall Stable and Emperor of Norfolk was sold as a yearling for $2,525 to "Lucky" Baldwin.

Although his horse deals with Winters certainly would have qualified him for his nickname, Elias Jackson Baldwin (1828-1909) had come to be known as "Lucky" years before.

Born in Butler County, Ohio, and raised in Indiana, as a young man Baldwin was a boatman on the Illinois and Michigan Canal. After saving enough capital for the venture, he loaded a covered wagon with sugar and coffee and joined the Gold Rush to California. He sold his merchandise en route for $2,500 at Salt Lake City, and arrived in San Francisco with that amount of cash and the horse he was rid-

Theodore Winters, the California turfman who paid $15,001 for undefeated Norfolk.

Baldwin opened a full-scale race track on the property. The old Santa Anita lasted just two seasons, 1908 and 1909, before it was caught in the tide of repressive legislation, but it was one of the fastest tracks in the nation and, despite its brief tenure, boasted six American records when it closed. Relics of the old Baldwin estate still may be seen at modern Santa Anita Race Course.

The black-and-red Maltese cross which identified Baldwin's racing silks became a familiar sight in winner's circles all over the country. In addition to Emperor of Norfolk, he had three other American Derby winners, which he bred himself: Volante, Silver Cloud and Rey El Santa Anita.

A small, solemn-faced, rather stingy looking version of Mark Twain, Baldwin's actions belied his appearance in every way. He didn't spare the purse strings, either on his ranch or in his stable, buying lavishly as the occasion

Elias Jackson "Lucky" Baldwin, owner of the fabulous Rancho Santa Anita.

ing. He was operating a livery stable in the early 1870s when, in lieu of cash from a customer who owed him a modest debt, Baldwin accepted a block of stock in the Consolidated Virginia, a Nevada mining project. He stuck it in a safe and forgot about it. When the mine hit paydirt, according to the popular story, Baldwin was away on a trip and could not be found, as the stock meanwhile climbed upward and upward. When Baldwin finally returned, he was $2,700,000 richer. He thereupon branched out into numerous other activities which included operations on the Comstock Lode, opening of the Baldwin Hotel in San Francisco, real estate dealings at Lake Tahoe, and ultimately the establishment of fabulous Rancho Santa Anita, named for one of his two daughters.

This vast paradise, unlike most of the other large stud farms of the period which were in the northern part of the state, was located in the Los Angeles area, and shortly before he died

arose until he had a nucleus of fifty-four brood mares. Among the many other historic horses he bred was Rey Del Carreras. This horse, described by Henry McDaniel as the fastest he had ever seen, was a winner both in America and England. He later was sold to Richard "Boss" Croker for $40,000 and his name changed to "Americus." The horse's English daughter, Americus Girl, founded an eminently successful female family which many years later served as a wedge for gaining recognition of America's bloodlines by the English *General Stud Book*.

When he was eighty-one years old and still lively as a cricket, Baldwin was asked the secret of his youthful outlook. He replied that he associated with young people as much as possible, which of course was very true; he had quite a reputation for such companionships, particularly with young people of feminine persuasion.

Another Pacific turf mogul of this period was Governor (later U. S. Senator) Leland Stanford (1824-1893), founder and benefactor of the university named for his son, which now occupies part of old Palo Alto Stud, a splendid ranch of 11,000 acres. Although Stanford was more interested in harness horses than in runners, much of this interest took the form of improving the trotters with infusions of thoroughbred blood.

A meticulous student of every subject with which he became involved, Stanford financed an experiment which ended for all time the argument concerning the running gait of a horse.

As can be seen from an examination of old illustrations, many of which depict a running horse in a physically impossible position, for many years it was believed that a horse at full speed operated two legs at a time in a sort of "rocking horse" action, and at no time was he completely airborne. At the instigation of Stanford, Edward James Muggeridge (also known as Eadweard Muybridge) in 1872 set up a series of fast-shuttered cameras and attached threads to them. As horses ran past, breaking the threads in sequence, a series of photographs were obtained which proved that at full stride a running horse puts his entire weight, in a series of shifting phases, on each leg in turn, and, moreover, that there is an instant when all four feet are off the ground. Muggeridge's work was a significant step in the development of motion pictures.

The foregoing are only a few of the numerous men who provided the impetus which brought turf affairs in the West to a pinnacle before the end of the nineteenth century. Among others (some of whom will be sketched later) were James Ben Ali Haggin, Nathan Coombs, John Halt, William O'Brien Macdonough, the partnership of Dan Burns and Clarence Waterhouse, William and Charles Boots, Marcus Daly of Montana, Senator George Hearst and L. F. Rose.

Tanforan, oldest major California track still in existence, opened in 1889 after a somewhat implausible origin for that rough-and-ready locale. Dan "White Hat" McCarty, induced his friend Lord Talbot Clifton to encourage the project, and the British nobleman in turn brought in a Polish prince, Andre Poniatowski, who obtained financial backing of William H. Crocker. After a glittering beginning— it ran seventy-eight days the first year—the track underwent a variety of woes, but survived them all.

In 1895 Adolph Spreckels and Henry J. Crocker began a track at Ingleside under sponsorship of the Pacific Coast Jockey Club. The next year the California Jockey Club abandoned the Bay District course, after twenty-two years of operation, and transferred across the bay to a new track at Emeryville. Later the two organizations merged as the New California Jockey Club, and meetings were alternated between the Ingleside and Emeryville courses. As it happened, the meeting was at the latter track in 1906 when the San Francisco earthquake hit, and racing never did return to Ingleside.

122

In Los Angeles several tracks preceded "Lucky" Baldwin's short-lived old Santa Anita. Agricultural Park had been built in the seventies, on the spot where the Coliseum now stands, although the track operated in conjunction with the county fair and was used more for trotters than runners. Another track, Ascot Park, came on the scene in 1904. It was built for $20,000, which, as California turf historian Kent Cochran has pointed out, is about what a rest room at modern Hollywood Park or Santa Anita would cost.

The complete roster of California cities which had race meetings between the Civil War and World War I reads like a census list.

In 1894 *Goodwin's Guide* listed meetings in the state: Angels Camp, Arcata, Baker City, Bakersfield, Burlingame, Chico, Concord, Ferndale, Gilroy, Greenville, Hollister, Hueneme, Ione, Lompoc, Los Angeles, Los Gatos, Modesto, Monterey, Napa, Red Bluff, Riverside, Sacramento, Salinas, San Andreas, San Diego, San Francisco, San Jose, San Luis Obispo, San Luis Rey, Santa Ana, Santa Barbera, Smith River, Stockton, Susanville, Ukiah, Vacaville, Vallejo, Willows, Woodland and Yreka. That was just for the 1894 season. Fresno, Marysville, Oakland, Rhoneville and Tulare had failed to renew meetings from the previous year.

CHAPTER TWENTY-FIVE

HERE WERE INTENSE RIVAL-ries, sectional and otherwise, on the eastern side of the Rockies, too, during the 1870s, and one of them developed into an encounter among three of the best horses of that period. The great race at Pimlico, October 24, 1877, was the inspiration for the Baltimore track's trademark which still is in use today. The participants were Ten Broeck (whose race against Mollie McCarty was described in an earlier chapter), Tom Ochiltree and Parole.

A son of Phaeton—Fanny Holton, by Lexington, owned and bred by F. B. Harper of Kentucky, Ten Broeck was foaled in 1872 and did not race as a two-year-old. At three, he won five of eight starts, and at four he won seven races, beating every horse he faced except H. P. McGrath's Aristides. His last race that year was a special event against time in which Ten Broeck ran 4 miles in 7:15¾, to better Fellowcraft's record by 3¾ seconds. (Ten Broeck was the epitome of versatility. At the time he retired, besides his 4-mile record, he held three other American records over a wide range of distances: 1 mile in 1:39¾, 2 miles in 3:27½ and 2⅝ miles in 4:58½.)

As a five-year-old the Harper horse was the terror of the Midwest; he began the season by winning eight in a row, including one walkover and two races against time because no flesh-and-blood opponents could be found. This was in 1877, when, on the East Coast, Tom Ochiltree and Parole were sweeping all before them, including each other.

An enormous colt, 16 hands 2½ inches, 76 inches in girth, 23 inches at the swell of the forearm and 10 inches below the knee, Tom Ochiltree was a familiar figure at Pimlico. The five-year-old son of Lexington out of Katona, by Voucher, had won several races at that track, including the Preakness at three.

Junior citizen of this trio was the gelding Parole, a year younger than his two rivals. In July he had upset Tom Ochiltree in the Saratoga Cup but early in October Ochiltree came back and beat him twice, in the Grand National Handicap and the All-Aged Stakes at Jerome Park, conceding 9 pounds on each occasion. Adding spice to the rivalry, Tom Ochiltree was owned by G. L. Lorillard, whose brother, Pierre, owned Parole.

Suggestive of the modern television technique, the *Kentucky Livestock Record* had two correspondents covering the great race at Pimlico, one to provide color and one to furnish the running description.

A more beautiful and delightful day could not have been devised than was ushered in Wednesday morning for the great race between the King of the Western Turf and his opponents. The sun was bright and warm, and the roads leading to the course were in good condition. By 10 o'clock vast crowds of carriages were wending their way through Druid Hill Park to Pimlico. The attendance at Pimlico today was fully 18,000 to 20,000 persons. Not only was every available place in the Grand Stand filled, but the steps, the cheaper stands, and a line of vehicles extended from the stand, solidly packed, past the three-quarter pole . . . The city of Baltimore and

124

Maryland herself was represented with her beauty, wealth, and intelligent people, while New York, Philadelphia and the West had numerous representative persons present . . .

At a quarter past three o'clock the three horses assembled at the post and when the flag fell Ten Broeck took the lead, with Tom Ochiltree second, and Parole third. At the three-quarter pole, Ten Broeck led a length, Tom Ochiltree second, Parole three lengths off, third. No change occurred at the stand or at the quarter pole. Down the backstretch Tom Ochiltree made play for the lead, and before reaching the half-mile pole he and Ten Broeck were head and head, Ten Broeck shaking him off on the turn. During the stretch Tom Ochiltree again made play for the lead, and before reaching the stand was a length in front of Ten Broeck, with Parole, who had been laying off some four lengths, a good third, and within a length of Ten Broeck. This order was maintained around the turn, and to the quarter. Straightened in the backstretch, Ten Broeck joined Tom Ochiltree, and the pair raced head and head to the half-mile pole, when Ten Broeck showed a length in front of Ochiltree, with Parole lapped on the latter. By the time the homestretch was reached Parole was second and coming with a rush. Before running half way down he was in front and came away and won by four lengths, Ten Broeck second, ten lengths in front of Tom Ochiltree, third. The following was the time of each quarter in the race: First quarter 30½, half 59½, three-quarters 1:28½, mile 1:55½, mile and a quarter 2:20¼, mile and a half 2:47¾, mile and three-quarters 3:15, two miles 3:42, two miles and a quarter 4:09½, two miles and a half 4:37¾.

Ten Broeck sold in the betting pools for $1200 against $400 for Tom Ochiltree and $335 for Parole.

The defeat of their pride and joy caused consternation among the Midwesterners. "When the flag fell Ten Broeck was beaten," wrote one reporter, "for although he went to the front, when he passed the stand in 59½ seconds he was running and driving, with ears pinned back and mouth closed. His rider struck him with the spur as he passed the stand, and he did not respond, but purged freely and labored in his action. He had none of that dash and vim about him; he did not reach for the bit or swing his head from side to side. True, he beat Tom Ochiltree, but he was coughing . . . we alluded to the condition of Ten Broeck at Louisville, and said he was coughing and was too low in flesh . . . to put the best and most charitable face on the defeat of Ten Broeck we will say as Mr. Harper does, that his horse was tied up and full of cold . . . He had no life about him, no dash, no speed, and scoured during the entire progress of the race . . ."

Subsequently it was reported that Tom Ochiltree had been coughing on the morning of the race. In fact, his trainer, Wyndham Walden, was quoted to the effect that he had telegraphed this news to Lorillard and the owner instructed him to let Ochiltree run so as to "not spoil the race," but to bet $500 for him on Parole.

Ten Broeck and Tom Ochiltree were soon retired to stud, but as a gelding Parole raced on and on. After winning several more races in this country, the son of Leamington out of Maiden, by Lexington, was sent to England, primarily as a trial horse for his stablemate Duke of Magenta. However, the latter caught influenza and Parole had to carry the load. As a six-year-old in 1879 he defeated the famous Isonomy in the Newmarket Handicap on April 16. Six days later he won the City and Suburban Handicap and the day after that the Great Metropolitan Handicap. The British were agog over this performance, but it apparently was duck soup for an American horse with his heritage of heat racing. Parole won several more races in England, then went into a long losing streak; but when he returned to America, he won four straight races right off the boat. As an eight-year-old he won twelve of twenty-four starts and at nine he won eight of twenty-one. Racing on through the age of eleven he compiled a lifetime record of 59 victories in 127 races for earnings of $82,184, which made him America's leading money-winning thoroughbred. (Various sources disagree slightly as to Parole's lifetime record, the differences presumably having resulted from converting his English earnings into American money. The foregoing recapitulation was compiled race by race from summaries in the *American Turf Register and Racing Calendar* and *Krik's Guide to the Turf,* the latter having included reports of English racing.)

CHAPTER TWENTY-SIX

THAT PAROLE AND TOM OCHIL-tree, owned by two brothers, should oppose each other on the race course is not in the least surprising. On the contrary, considering whose these brothers were, it would have been nothing short of fantastic if, even had they wanted to, they could have managed to avoid crossing swords. Each campaigned one of the largest and most powerful stables in the country, and there was scarcely a stakes event of importance in the East in which the cherry-and-black of Pierre Lorillard or the blue-and-orange of his brother George—or both—was not seen. As individuals they were redoubtable; combined, they would have been devastating. (Just as a sample, in 1880 Pierre had eighteen yearlings nominated to the next season's Breeders' Stakes, and George was keeping ten two-year-olds eligible to the 1881 Withers Stakes. In 1891, when Monmouth Park went on a stakes splurge, Pierre Lorillard made 173 nominations to the various events.)

Their father, Peter, had immigrated from France and amassed a fortune in the tobacco and snuff business, which Pierre, the business man among the sons, later took control of and expanded greatly. Not only in the operation of their racing enterprises, but in other activities as well, neither brother spared the horses.

Racing was by no means the only sport with which they were identified, as both Lorillards were also renowned yachtsmen, road drivers and trap shooters. Pierre acquired 7,000 acres in Orange County, New York, 5,000 acres of which he had enclosed with an 8-foot wire fence for a shooting and fishing club—the fabled Tuxedo Park.

Ten years older than his brother, Pierre (1833-1901) also survived him by fifteen years, and his career on the turf was correspondingly longer. Very much the internationalist, Pierre cut a wide swath on both sides of the Atlantic, and the most famous horse he owned, Iroquois, earned that distinction by becoming the first American-bred to win the Epsom Derby, which he did in 1881, following up with a victory in the St. Leger. Not until 1954 was this feat to be duplicated, by Robert S. Clark's Never Say Die. Lorillard was well known in France, too, and was awarded the Legion of Honor for financing Charnay's archeological expedition to Central America.

Pierre Lorillard's turf headquarters were at Rancocas Stud in Jobstown, New Jersey, one of the largest breeding farms in America, which reflected in every detail its owner's disposition for first-class facilities. (Lorillard was among the first to consider replacing the heavy old steel horseshoes with aluminum plates. Since they were not yet mass produced, he ordered a set from Tiffany's.) Although he bred his own horses, like W. R. Johnson in his day, Lorillard always was ready to buy a horse he thought was good, regardless of origin. For example, when Drake Carter beat Pizarro in the Omnibus Stakes, Lorillard bought the winner for $17,500.

There also were times when Lorillard reacted in the opposite manner. After E. A. Clabaugh's Cloverbrook won the 1877 Belmont Stakes over a large field in deep mud, Lorillard did not think his colt, Basil, who finished far out of the money, had run his true race. He challenged to a re-match, $5,000 a side, 1¼ miles, which Basil won by ten lengths.

Pierre Lorillard, whose turf operations spanned the Atlantic.

Lorillard won a Belmont Stakes with Saxon, and a Preakness with the gelding, Shirley.

Some years later, when his brother kidded him about Saxon's qualifications as a sire, Pierre offered to match one of the stallion's get against anything in George's stable. Result: Saxon's daughter, Hiawasse, won by four lengths, and she was undefeated as a three-year-old.

The home-bred Wanda also was a champion filly, although Lorillard himself considered Katrine her superior. The list of top horses of either sex could go on and on.

To illustrate the scope and quality of the Rancocas operation, in 1886, when Lorillard decided to disperse his holdings because of the press of other business, he had twenty-seven horses in training, of which twenty-one were either two- or three-year-olds. They brought $149,050 at auction, for an American record average of $5,520.37; the filly Dewdrop, champion two-year-old of the previous season and winner over colts, topped the bidding at $29,000.

In separate sales later that year, thirty-four yearlings brought $23,685; and eighty-three head of breeding stock, led by the stallion Iroquois ($20,000) were sold for $142,895. The over-all gross of these sales was $315,630, back when money was money.

Pierre Lorillard's dispersal was announced about a week before his brother's death, although the events were unrelated. Pierre got back in the business, however, and in an interview only seven years later—when he again was talking about retiring—he estimated he had about 100 mares at Rancocas, in addition to the stallions Sensation and Sailor Prince.

Lorillard's racing activity in the latter part of his life was concentrated in England, where for a time he was a partner with Lord William Beresford in a very successful stable, which included Sibola, winner of the 1,000 Guineas in 1899.

In 1901, returning from a trip to England, Pierre Lorillard was taken off the ship by ambulance, and shortly thereafter died of Bright's disease in a Fifth Avenue hotel. His enormous fortune was distributed among his relatives, but Rancocas Stud was willed to a friend, Mrs. Lillian Allien. The legatee also inherited some of the Lorillard luck, for in 1905 she owned Gold Braid, a 100-to-1 shot which finished second at Brighton, and Mrs. Lillian Allien Barnes, as she was then named, was reported to have won $20,000 in place and show bets.

Whether by design or happenstance, George Lorillard's (1843-1886) racing colors were subdued versions of his older brother's, but there was nothing pale about his racing stable. He did not enjoy the success abroad that came Pierre's way, but on home territory he was second to none. The tremendous record of both Lorillard stables in America is the more impressive in view of the relatively small geographical area they chose to exploit. Unlike other large stables, which sent horses far and wide in search of valuable races, the Lorillards more or less confined their American efforts to New York, New Jersey and Maryland.

A graduate of the Yale Scientific School, George was a qualified physician, but he chose not to practice medicine, devoting himself instead to management of his own and his brother's yachting and other sporting enterprises. While Pierre was known as a generous friend, but an implacable foe, young "Prince George"—unburdened by the cares of business—was geniality personified. The 6-foot, 200-pounder was a crack marksman, winner of the Grand Prize trap shoot at Monaco; he also defeated New York *Herald* editor James Gordon Bennett (the younger) who fancied himself a hot shot of several dimensions, in a $10,000 contest.

George Lorillard first entered racing in partnership with J. G. K. Lawrence, and among their runners were Hyder Ali and Shylock. Lorillard tried his own wings in 1876, and Tom Ochiltree was among his first horses. The colt was four at the time, and already had won

the Preakness, but whatever designs Lorillard had on the Maryland classic were thoroughly fulfilled in short order. He practically owned that particular event: he won the Preakness five years in succession, beginning in 1878, with Duke of Magenta, Harold (a full brother to Iroquois), Grenada, Saunterer and Vanguard.

Lorillard, whose horses were based at Westbrook Stable in Islip, Long Island, and trained by Wyndham Walden, also won Monmouth Park's Hopeful Stakes four times straight, beginning in 1878, with Idler, Rosalie, Spinaway and Memento. Spinaway, champion two-year-old filly of her year, won seven of nine outings. She had been acquired when the Lorillard brothers purchased the yearlings of Aristides Welch's Erdenheim Farm; Pierre chose Iroquois and George got Spinaway, so neither was a loser on the division.

The George Lorillard stable also won the Dixie Stakes three times in a row, and his nonconsecutive monopolies included five victories in the Vernal Stakes and four each in the Juvenile Stakes and Baltimore Cup.

Often the orange-and-blue obliterated the opposition. Harold, Monitor and Idler ran one-two-three in the 1878 July Stakes, and the next year Sensation, Grenada and Rosalie did it again. Then Sensation, Grenada and Rosalie took all the money in the Flash Stakes; and Anne Augusta, Ferida and Idler swept the Maryland Stakes. The number of occasions the Lorillard horses finished one-two were similarly frequent.

Sensation could not have been more aptly named. A brown son of Leamington out of Susan Beane, by Lexington, foaled in 1877, he was tried as a yearling against the two-year-old Monitor and beat him. When he reached racing age the next season Sensation breezed through eight races, all sweepstakes, without defeat and without another horse ever extending him. Unfortunately, he picked up a stone and was lamed between seasons, so did not race again.

Monitor was no mere trial horse. A gelding,

like Parole, he rolled on and on, until he had won 42 races and $62,100. Ferida, mentioned above as a runner-up, also was considerably more than that, as she won the Monmouth Oaks and Alabama Stakes among other races.

In 1878, when George Lorillard led all owners with stable earnings of $67,875, it was feared that he would break up racing, and a group of New Yorkers began scouting around for someone to buy Kentuckian Dan Swigert's colt, Spendthrift, an undefeated two-year-old of that year, and bring him east to challenge Lorillard's runners. James R. Keene finally agreed to provide the necessary $15,000—and thus it was that another historic figure was introduced to racing.

George Lorillard, having been in ill health for some years, had abandoned his racing activity by the time he died of rheumatic complications in the south of France in 1880, one month before he would have been forty-three years old.

The reign of Pierre Lorillard's Parole as financial champion was short-lived, for during the decade after his retirement the money-winning crown changed hands often. There was a certain amount of continuity, however, in that the next three leading American money winners in succession all came from the same stable—a sequence unmatched in turf history.

This stable belonged to a partnership of two brothers from the other side of the tracks, and from across the river as well. In contrast to most leading owners of the period, who were associated with Wall Street, the owners of this fabulous stable came from Bergen Street in Brooklyn; they were Philip J. and Michael F. Dwyer, better known to all elements of racing as Phil and Mike.

Their father owned a butcher shop on Pacific Street which the boys inherited and expanded to a highly successful wholesale meat business. A contemporary writer said of them:

> It would not be strictly accurate to say that the Dwyer Brothers dominated racing in their

time, but they came near it. For thirty years and more there was hardly a great race run in which one of their horses did not figure conspicuously. They were a city-bred pair, but they possessed an instinctive knowledge of horses and a talent for management that made them formidable from the beginning of their career. Philip Dwyer did the buying for the stable and he bought with shrewd judgment and rare luck. Michael Dwyer placed the runners of the stable and did the betting. And the betting operations of stables were of greater importance in the 1870's and 80's when the purses were smaller than those offered in the 90's . . .

Philip J. Dwyer, president of the Brooklyn Jockey Club.

One of the Dwyer brothers' customers was August Belmont, who became friendly with them and sold them their first good horse, Rhadamanthus. This was the beginning of a long procession of top-class runners sporting their red jacket and blue cap.

The Dwyers were great ones for the "try before you buy" theory, and most of their best horses began their careers running for someone else. Bramble (1875) raced first for Johnson & Co., then for Crawford & Co. as a two-year-old. After he upset George Lorillard's highly regarded Duke of Magenta in the Saratoga Stakes, it was announced that he wasn't for sale at any price, but his owner later was wiped out in the betting ring and Phil Dwyer bought the colt for $2,250. Although Duke of Magenta dominated the three-year-old division the next year, Bramble clearly was second best, and when Pierre Lorillard bought the Duke from his brother and sent him to England, Bramble had the field to himself and won fifteen races as a four-year-old. Bramble's earnings were responsible for keeping the stable going during its formative years.

LUKE BLACKBURN, 1877

(Bonnie Scotland—Nevada, by Lexington)

Luke Blackburn was bred in Tennessee by Captain James Franklin, and as a two-year-old he won only two of thirteen starts racing for W. L. Waitzfelder. After the Dwyer brothers bought him, he blossomed.

In his three-year-old debut, the colt was beaten by Fonso (who won the Kentucky Derby in his next start) but thereafter Luke Blackburn swept along like a tornado. In 24 starts at three he won 22 races, the other loss being the result of a fall. Described as the most muscular horse ever seen in America, Blackburn defeated five-year-old Glenmore in the Grand Union Prize, giving him 20 pounds according to the scale of weights, yet jockey Jimmy McLaughlin was so tired from trying to hold back the winner that

he had difficulty returning to scale for weighing in. This immensely powerful horse was injured in his final start that year, and ran only twice at four, after which he retired to stud in his native state, at General William Hicks Jackson's famed Belle Meade. (General Jackson's solid maroon silks are still in action, having been passed along to his grandnephew, Howell E. Jackson.)

HINDOO, 1878

(Virgil—Florence, by Lexington)

In lockstep right behind Luke Blackburn in the parade of Dwyer champions was Hindoo, who, although he did not himself get there, started the stable on its march toward the succession of financial championships.

As a two-year-old, Hindoo raced for his breeder, Daniel Swigert. He won his first seven starts—at Lexington, Louisville, St. Louis, and the West Side Park in Chicago—before meeting defeat at Saratoga, whereupon he was bought by the Dwyer brothers for $15,000.

As a three-year-old he won 18 races in succession, including the Kentucky Derby, Coney Island Derby, Blue Ribbon, Clark, Tidal, Ocean, Lorillard, Travers, Sequel, United States Hotel, Kenner, and Champion Stakes, Jersey St. Leger and a walkover for another sweepstakes at Monmouth Park.

Whereas Hindoo's winning streak undoubtedly was a source of great satisfaction to his new owners, it probably was frustrating as well. The Dwyers (especially Mike) were notorious bettors, and in every one of these races Hindoo was less than even money—in fact, the 1-to-2 against him in his first start of the season was the most generous price offered all year.

To aggravate the irony, the 1881 season was an unusual one during which it often was possible to bet in three dimensions: the selling pools, books and mutuels. For example, here's how the wagering went on three of Hindoo's races during his streak.

OCEAN STAKES
(MONMOUTH PARK, JULY 2)

Order of Finish	Price in Selling Pool (Equivalent Odds)	Book-maker's Odds	Mutuel Payoff $5 unit (Equivalent Odds)
Hindoo	$500 (1-4.63)	1-5	$6.45 (1-3.45)
Monitor	100 (5.08-1)	4-1	
Glidelia	(	15-1	
	(40 (14.2-1)		
Valentine	(	40-1	
Take-out	Est. 5%	12%	5%

TRAVERS STAKES
(SARATOGA, JULY 16)

Hindoo	Not Sold	1-10	$5.70 (1-7.15)
Catoctin	$290 (2.9-1)	30-1	
Getaway	400 (1.83-1)	15-1	
Eole	240 (3.7-1)	15-1	
Compensation	54 (20-1)	25-1	
Duke of Montalban	100 (10.3-1)	20-1	
Baltic	110 (9.3-1)	25-1	
Take-out	Est. 5%	19%	5%

UNITED STATES HOTEL STAKES
(SARATOGA, AUGUST 4)

Hindoo	$700 (1-5)	1-8	$6 (1-5)
Crickmore	11.5 (6.3-1)	6-1	
Bonfire	20 (41-1)	15-1	
Gladiola	50 (15.8-1)	8-1	
Take-out	Est. 5%	20½%	5%

Note: Exact percentage of take-out in various selling pools was not reported; "equivalent odds" in the above table are based on an assumed 5%, i.e., same as the mutuels.

The foregoing races are typical examples, and in each of them the mutuels offered better odds than the books; but, of course, if any large sum had been wagered the mutuel odds would have shortened drastically, and the same applies to selling pools. Judging from their high percentage, it would appear that the bookmakers were taking no chances on Hindoo, but this, too, is misleading; it was so hard to find anyone to bet against the colt, it was impossible to keep the books "round," so the bookmakers ran a risk of losing money, while the selling pools and mutuels took no risk at all.

The generous-looking odds offered by bookmakers on Hindoo's rivals in the Travers, compared to the odds prevailing in the selling pool, resulted from the fact that Hindoo wasn't considered in the pool, whereas the bookmakers included him in their calculations and, obviously, were quite confident he'd win—which he did.

Mike Dwyer was an insatiable chalk-eater. When he thought he was right, which was usually, he'd bet any sum at any odds. At those prices, though, Hindoo was an awfully strong ration of calcium, even for him.

There were several occasions besides the Travers when Hindoo was excluded from selling pools, and in the Jersey St. Leger no betting whatsoever was conducted.

Hindoo won five of his six races as a four-year-old to retire with $72,340 from 31 victories, three seconds and two thirds in 36 starts, never having finished out of the money. Trainer Jimmy Rowe considered him the best race horse of all the Dwyer stars, but jockey McLaughlin held out for Luke Blackburn.

Hindoo's last start had been in the Coney Island Cup at Sheepshead Bay, June 17, 1882, in which he won the easiest sort of victory by four lengths from Fred Gebhart's Eole—"When McLaughlin gave the magnificent son of Virgil and Florence free rein, he cut Eole down as lightly as the clover blossom falls before the scythe . . ." Nevertheless, Gebhart, whom Vosburgh described as "aspiring," was dissatisfied with this result and he haughtily said to the Dwyer brothers, "If you will come to the Union

Miss Woodford, first American thoroughbred to win more than $100,000.

Ezekiel F. Clay, co-breeder of several of the Dwyer brothers' stars, and a chairman of the Kentucky State Racing Commission.

Club I will match Eole against Hindoo for $5,000 a side to run the race over."

"If you will come to our butcher shop," replied Phil Dwyer, "we will match Hindoo against Eole for $10,000 a side."

Nothing ever came of this needle work and Hindoo never raced again. As operators of a betting stable the Dwyer brothers were frequently criticized for running their horses too often, but they did not believe in running them over great distances. In their opinion the 2¼-mile Coney Island Cup ruined Hindoo and the Dwyers thereafter refused to start horses in

cup races. Since they owned so many of the best runners, Vosburgh attributes the general falling off in American cup racing to the Dwyers' boycott.

MISS WOODFORD, 1880

(Billet—Fancy Jane, by Neil Robinson)

Being city boys interested primarily in fast action, the Dwyers had no particular inclination to breed horses, and when Hindoo retired

133

they gave him, along with a couple of fillies, to the Kentuckians Ezekiel F. Clay and Catesby Woodford in exchange for $9,000 cash and the two-year-old filly Miss Woodford.

The Dwyers already owned George Kinney, best colt in this crop, and Miss Woodford turned out to be the best filly. She became the first American thoroughbred of either sex to win $100,000.

By the end of her five-year-old season when she ordinarily would have been retired, Miss Woodford already was America's leading money winner with earnings of $98,170. However, her owners' relative lack of interest in breeding, plus the fact that Miss Woodford was such a big tomboy that she looked too masculine to make much of a brood mare, led the Dwyers to continue her in training, and as a six-year-old she won six races within less than two months. After winning the Harlem Stakes at Jerome Park on May 31, she was shipped to St. Louis for the rich Eclipse Stake at the Fair Grounds there. With the first two winners of the American Derby, Modesty and Volante, among the opposition, Miss Woodford won with little difficulty, and the $10,000 first money pushed her beyond $100,000. By the end of the season she had run this sum up to $118,270 with 37 victories in 48 starts. Besides her unparalled gross income Miss Woodford was a model of efficiency. As long as she was making the trip anyway, she pulled a cart from Kentucky to a race meeting in Chicago. (The Dwyers apparently were correct in their evaluation of Miss Woodford as a brood mare prospect since at stud she produced nothing approaching her own class.)

HANOVER, 1884

(Hindoo—Bourbon Belle, by Bonnie Scotland)

Hanover was an unusual horse in several respects. It is not very often that sentiment pays off on the race track, but in his case it did, with interest. When Phil Dwyer was shown the

1885 crop of yearlings at Colonel Clay's Runnymede Farm, he could not believe Hanover was a son of Hindoo, he was so unlike his sire in appearance. But having been reassured that the colt was by Hindoo, he went ahead and bought him, for $1,250. Hanover was further remarkable in that, although he was undefeated as a two-year-old, he wasn't even the best colt in his own stable. The Dwyers had acquired another colt from Dan Swigert named Tremont.

TREMONT, 1884

(Virgil—Ann Fief, by Alarm)

Tremont was of such phenomenal speed that in a yearling trial he had run a quarter mile in :22½. Hanover, on the other hand, was so lazy and easy-going as to appear sluggish.

The next spring, before either horse had entered competition as a two-year-old, Hanover did beat Tremont in a workout, but trainer Frank McCabe figured only that Tremont was sick that day.

Both colts went through the 1886 season without defeat, Tremont carrying the brunt of the stable duties. The son of Virgil started thirteen times within a space of ten weeks and not only did he win them all, but no horse ever headed him. Vosburgh described him as "the quickest starter ever seen on an American race course . . . he was so quick on his feet that he won his races in the first furlong, carrying his fields so fast they never fell into their stride."

Hanover, held in reserve, started only three times that year, but he won the Hopeful, July and Sapling Stakes, although McLaughlin had to coax him or whip him every step of the way.

Speed takes its toll on a race horse more than any other single factor, and the next year Tremont could not stand training, so Hanover became the stable's first stringer. He proved more than equal to the task by winning fourteen races in a row within a ten-week period, before Laggard upset him in the Raritan Stakes, in which Hanover had to carry a 10-pound penalty and Laggard was allowed 7 pounds off. In a thoroughly remarkable three-year-old campaign, Hanover won 20 races in 27 starts between May 17 and October 31, including the Belmont, Withers, Brooklyn Derby, Swift, Lorillard Stakes and the other important events of the time.

Although he won as a four-year-old, he fell lame and was retired early and "nerved" to deaden the feeling in his bad foot; he nevertheless raced on ("as a commercial proposition," according to Colonel Wall's history) through the age of five, and finally retired to stud having won 32 of his 50 races and finished out of the money only twice. His earnings of $118,872 placed him slightly ahead of Miss Woodford, but the horse destined to supplant Hanover himself already was in the same stable.

KINGSTON, 1884

(Spendthrift—Kapanga, by Victorious)

The Brooklyn butcher boys obviously didn't believe in the expression "embarrassment of riches." Having owned the two best colts from the 1884 crop of foals, they went out and bought another, Kingston. As a two-year-old, Kingston raced in the name of his trainer, E. V. Snedeker, and both Hanover and Tremont beat him. Hanover defeated him again at three the next season, but in July, when Hanover lost his first race, the Dwyers thought he might be getting stale and they purchased Kingston for $12,500 believing it best "to get him out of Hanover's way." Kingston thereupon began a fantastic winning streak which reached its peak when as a six-year-old he won

Kingston, 1884, winner of 89 races, more than any horse in authenticated American history.

nine out of ten starts. By the time he retired at the age of ten he had won eighty-nine races, more than any other horse in the history of the American turf.

The complete racing record of this thoroughly remarkable horse was as follows:

Age	Starts	Won	2nd	3rd	Un-placed	Earnings
2	6	2	4	–	–	$ 11,350
3	18	13	2	2	1	17,644
4	14	10	3	1	–	16,845
5	15	14	1	–	–	22,652
6	10	9	1	–	–	15,820
7	21	15	5	1	–	26,955
8	20	13	6	1	–	17,140
9	25	9	8	5	3	7,885
10	9	4	3	2	–	2,600
	138	89	33	12	4	$138,891

Kingston's record is all the more impressive in that he was not a gelding, and entire horses supposedly become sour if campaigned too long. That it didn't hurt Kingston is illustrated by the fact that he was the leading sire two seasons after he went to stud. (His ex-stablemate Hanover led the sire list four years in a row, although his stud career was cut short by death at the age of fifteen, under weird circumstances. When his feed was cut back following an illness, Hanover developed the habit of stamping his feet to demand more to eat. Unable to feel pain in the forefoot that had been nerved, he broke the coffin bone, and before the injury was noticed, blood poisoning had set in and spread through his system until it became necessary to put him down.)

Others of the Dwyer brothers' many stars were similarly rigorously campaigned. They bought Raceland as a five-year-old at the dispersal of August Belmont's stable and ran him four more seasons until the son of Billet completed his career with 70 victories and $116,931 in 130 starts. As he ranked third on the American earnings list, this gave the Dwyers the distinction of having owned the top four money winners, including the leader of each category: Kingston and Hanover

(colts), Miss Woodford (filly) and Raceland (gelding).

Three of the four had been acquired from Clay and Woodford at Runnymede Farm, but because of their preference for ready-made horses over untried yearlings, the Dwyers let a good one get away in 1886, although they did get him back—at a price.

Runnymede put Sir Dixon, also by Billet, up for auction that year but the Dwyers ignored the colt, who was knocked down to Green B. Morris. When Sir Dixon turned out to be a flashy two-year-old, the Dwyers tried to buy him, but Morris refused to sell until one day, as he described it, "Mike Dwyer came to me in the paddock and said: 'Green, let me have that colt; you don't bet as heavy as we do and he is worth more to us than he'll be to you,' and he put a piece of paper in my hand; it was a check for $20,000. I didn't want to sell, but the Dwyers had been good friends to me and I didn't feel like refusing them. I always regretted selling him as I knew he wouldn't do for their style of racing. He was a bit delicate and couldn't stand hard races close together..."

Although he didn't last very long Sir Dixon was good while he lasted. He won the Withers and Belmont Stakes, among other races, for the Dwyers, and upon retirement to stud at his birthplace, he, too, became a champion sire.

In the 1890s the partnership between the Dwyer brothers split up when Mike took a stable to England over Phil's objections. Their forty-one horses were sold at auction for $94,225, with Phil taking Kingston for $30,000, although the next year he sold the horse to his younger brother. The brothers' racing colors were passed on to the partnership of Price McKinney and James Corrigan.

BEN BRUSH, 1893

(Bramble—Roseville, by Reform)

Mike Dwyer subsequently campaigned Ben Brush, a son of their old bread-and-butter

Ed "Brown Dick" Brown, developer of Ben Brush and other stars.

horse, Bramble. This colt, who was criticized as an "overrated little goat," showed up his critics as a two-year-old when he won several stakes and beat older horses in a handicap while conceding them 11 pounds actual weight. In the following seasons he won more top races including the Kentucky Derby, Latonia Derby and Suburban. (As a four-year-old, Ben Brush was himself beaten by two-year-old Plaudit, but the younger horse was carrying 36 pounds less weight.) After retirement, Ben Brush was a leading sire and founder of an enduring line.

The biggest star owned by Phil Dwyer in his own name was Handspring, a son of Hanover, who in 1896 won the Brooklyn Derby and swapped decisions with mighty Hastings in the Belmont Stakes and Withers.

Mike Dwyer's exuberance soon caught up with him. In 1895 he was flying high: he purchased fourteen yearlings from Milton Young by telegraph, sight unseen, and paid $18,000 for Ben Brush. Three years later he was reported broke, and his health went along with his money. He became a familiar sight at the New York tracks, in his invalid's chair, protesting to the last in a voice so feeble that it scarcely could be understood, that he'd get another good one yet. He died in 1906 at the age of sixty.

Phil Dwyer, who was a millionaire by the turn of the century, continued his prosperous way until he was seventy-three. He caught cold on opening day at Belmont Park in 1917, and was under the care of a nurse at his hotel the afternoon the 31st Suburban Handicap was run. At 4:29⅕ P.M., A. K. Macomber's Boots went under the wire a winner from Borrow and The Finn, and at exactly 4:30 the nurse reported to relatives in attendance that Mr. Dwyer was dead. It was the first renewal of the Suburban he had missed.

CHAPTER TWENTY-SEVEN

The most talked-about, and considered by many the best horse in the latter half of the nineteenth century was James Ben Ali Haggin's Salvator, 1886 (Prince Charlie–Salina, by Lexington) whose relationship with two other members of his generation was rather unusual: despite the great stature he achieved, Salvator never could beat Sam Bryant's Proctor Knott, and on the other hand, he exercised the same sort of Indian sign on the very good colt Tenny. However, Salvator's reputation was at its height when it counted, at the end.

His first meeting with Proctor Knott came in the Junior Champion Stakes in August of his two-year-old season when Salvator was making his debut and Proctor Knott was a seasoned colt, having started six times previously and won three races. Proctor Knott won this one, too, as Salvator finished third. They met again about three weeks later in the inaugural running of the rich new Futurity at Coney Island and Proctor Knott won again, although this time Salvator was runner-up by half a length. He then went on to win his next four starts in succession, but Proctor Knott had retired for the season after the Futurity with the championship of his division in his pocket.

Designed as a breeding contest, with a horse race at the end to settle it, the Futurity was by far the richest race in America. Like the "produce races" of old, it worked on the principle of a poker game—after the original ante, owners were required to make further payments at various stages along the way in order to stay in. However, the produce races ordinarily permitted an owner who kept up his payments to enter any horse he chose when the time came for the race, but for the Futurity the individual animal had to be specified at the outset. Mares were nominated the year they were bred (before the foals concerned were even born) and forfeit payments were required when the resulting offspring became yearlings. From 752 original nominees in 1885, 14 made it to the post in 1888; the fees picked up in the meanwhile, plus $10,000 added by the Coney Island Jockey Club, went into the purse, and for this one effort alone Proctor Knott collected $40,900, more than any other horse earned all season—indeed, more than many very good horses earned during their entire lifetimes. The colt's winnings for the whole season amounted to $69,780.

Salvator and Proctor Knott met only once as three-year-olds, in the Omnibus Stakes, a race which neither won, as Longstreet was first, Proctor Knott second, and Salvator third, although the Haggin colt was conceding 7 pounds to the winner and 5 pounds to the runner-up. Salvator undeniably was the best that season as he won all seven of his other races while Proctor Knott managed to win only twice again in nine starts.

Salvator's nearest rival for three-year-old honors was Tenny, winner of ten races in eighteen starts. The only time they met that year was in the Realization Stakes which Salvator won, Tenny second. The next season, as four-year-olds, their rivalry reached white heat. Tenny won four races in succession in the beginning of 1890 as Salvator stayed on the sidelines until the Suburban Handicap on June 17. Carrying 127 pounds, Salvator won by a neck from the lightly weighted Cassius (107), as

Tenny, under 126 pounds, finished third. His owner, D. T. Pulsifer, was dissatisfied with this result and challenged Haggin to a match, $5,000 a side, half forfeit, over the Suburban distance, 1¼ miles, under the same weights. Haggin balked at the last condition, so it was agreed to use level weights; as it turned out, the seemingly insignificant 1 pound made quite a difference.

The big race was run at Sheepshead Bay June 25, 1890, and the *Spirit of the Times* screamed the result in the largest headlines (not counting advertisements) it ever had used.

SALVATOR!

TENNY!

———————

GLORY FOR

VICTOR AND VANQUISHED

———————

2:05!

———————

Match $5,000 each, h.f.; $5,000 added by Coney Island Jockey Club; one mile and a quarter.

D. T. Pulsifer names b c Tenny, by Rayon d'Or—Belle of Maywood.

J. B. Haggin names ch c Salvator, by Prince Charlie—Salina.

———————

Presiding Judge Simmons' verdict:

"SALVATOR WINS BY HALF A HEAD."

———————

The Luckiest Colt Alive
Winning the Realization from Tenny by eighteen inches; the Suburban by half a head

from Cassius, and the match from Tenny by half a head.

———————

For an unbounded, uproarious manifestation of enthusiasm we never expect to see a parallel to that displayed at Sheepshead by the mass of people who gathered to see the race between the crack four-year-olds, Salvator and Tenny. It is useless to tell people that the only reason people go to see races is to make money . . . no amounts of money could have induced the cheering, yelling, waving of handkerchiefs, clapping of hands and irresistible outbursts which infected even the most decorous, and ladies as much as any. It was an occasion worthy of such a manifestation, a race such as but very few if any of us had seen before and none of us may ever see again . . .

In the paddock Salvator naturally was the observed of all observers, and were he anything but the sweet-dispositioned animal he is, he might have done unlimited damage with his heels.

As the imperturbable Isaac Murphy, sitting well down in his saddle and straight as a dart, cantered the chestnut down past the stand to the starting post, the pair looked the idealization of horse and jockey. The crowd seemed to recognize the fact, and round after round of applause came from the masses of people in the stand, on the lawn, and, in fact, every place where any sight of the race could be gained. Then up the stretch, from where his owner and trainer stood watches in hand, came Tenny. For appearance between the two horses and jockeys, there was no comparison; but evidently Tenny was the bigger favorite of the two with the mob, for thundering salvos of applause greeted him. We think the public thoroughly appreciated what true sporting blood Mr. Pulsifer had displayed in making the match.

A word of admonition from Mr. Caldwell, and the cracks were off, head for head. As they swept by the stand, it was evident that if nature could stand it the record would be lowered and lowered materially. The staunch game head of Salvator had already showed in front, and he was leading by about a neck. Murphy was sitting steady as a rock, so im-

Salvator, ridden by Isaac Murphy, beating Tenny ("The Swayback"), ridden by Snapper Garrison, in the match race at Sheepshead Bay in 1890.

movable that he might have been a figure of wood, but the grand sweeping stride of Salvator was taking him a little bit ahead all the time. The first quarter was run in 25 seconds, and round the lower turn Tenny seemed to manifest a shade of temper. Small wonder for the pace was improving instead of getting slower, as the half mile was run in 49¾ seconds. So it was that at this point the chestnut was some length and a half or two lengths in the lead, he crossing and going on to the rail as they entered the backstretch . . . the five furlongs were run in 1:02½, and the leader was a very good two lengths ahead, and here he stayed till in 1:14¾ six furlongs had been traversed, and Garrison had begun to display some excitement and had gone to work on Tenny with the whalebone. At this point it really looked as if the race was "all over," bar the shouting, and Tenny, instead of drawing

up, was losing inch by inch. Ten Broeck's record for the mile, 1:39¾, was equaled, if not beaten, many watches making it a quarter of a second less. It must be remembered, too, that this old record was made not only on a specially prepared track but in a race against time . . . with only 110 lbs. up. No wonder, then, that as Tenny drew near the quarters which he is accustomed to associate with rest and oats he made as if he would have lingered awhile, only to rouse Garrison to more desperate efforts with whip and spur, changing his whip to the left hand. At the mile and one furlong Salvator was still two lengths ahead, the time being 1:52¾, a quarter of a second faster than Terra Cotta's record . . . Garrison redoubled his work, and never have we seen a man ride with such cyclonic fury . . . the tension of excitement was painful, but as Tenny began to come

140

along with his terrific, frantic rush, which seemed almost irresistible, the excitement of the former moment was as nothing. Murphy looked back and saw what his opponent in the blue and white jacket was doing, and his immovability was gone but not his presence of mind. No thought of gallery finishes crossed his mind, and he went to work in dead earnest on the gallant colt. But Tenny's burst of speed was bound to tell; the hooded head was gaining little by little, but surely, at every jump. The way Tenny came up with his flying rival in the last 100 yards was a miracle, perfectly stupendous. Yet the chestnut held him, just held him, and that's all, and as the pair passed before the judges he still had the advantage of "a short head"—a few inches indeed to decide the disposition of such vast sums of money.

Garrison rode the race of his life. If Tenny had run perfectly true, or had he had the advantage of the one pound difference as in the Suburban weights, the verdict might have been reversed. Human energy—and Garrison's was more like that of a demon—could not have done more. Murphy as usual rode with superb coolness and judgment of pace. "Had Murphy done more with Salvator he would have done worse," was the opinion expressed . . .

Murphy had no chance in the Suburban or the match to make his grandstand finishes. No man with a touch of heart disease should ever back his mounts . . .

Both the winner and the loser had covered themselves with glory, and the race became the subject of a stirring poem "How Salvator Won," by Ella Wheeler Wilcox, which hung in many a parlor for many a year.

> . . . One more mighty plunge, and with knee, limb and hand
> I lift my horse first by a nose past the stand.
> We are under the string now—the great race is done—
> And Salvator, Salvator, Salvator won! . . .

In the same issue (July 12, 1890) that included Miss Wilcox's poem, *The Spirit of the Times* published some sketches of close finishes at Sheepshead Bay, including that between Salvator and Tenny, made from "instantaneous photographs" taken by J. C. Hemment. Four years earlier the publication had made a "strenuous appeal in favor of the adoption by racing associations of the aid afforded by photography in registering an immutable record of the positions of horses in a close finish."

Salvator's four-year old season was the year gigantic new Monmouth Park opened. The older track had proved so popular it could not accommodate the demands made upon it, and in 1890 the biggest racing plant in America was unveiled. The grounds covered 660 acres, the track was 1¾ miles around with a 1⅜-mile straightaway, and the grandstand—entirely of iron—was 700 feet long. Another feature was that racing was offered in a clockwise direction, similar to the European style.

The mammoth course was opened on July 4 and eight days later Salvator put in an appearance for the Monmouth Cup. No horse dared face him and he walked over for the $1,800 prize. Only Tenny came out against him in the Champion Stakes at the same track August 12, and this time Salvator won easily by four lengths. That was the end.

With no live opponent left, a race was arranged for Salvator against time, in this case the record of 1:39¼ for a mile which had been set by Raveloe. The race took place on Monmouth Park's fancy new straightaway August 28, 1890, and even against this inexorable antagonist Salvator was a 2-to-5 favorite. Carrying 110 pounds, he was ridden by Martin Bergen, a substitute for regular jockey Isaac Murphy, who had been suspended. Against two pace makers who ran in relays, half a mile each, Salvator shattered the old record, covering the first quarter mile in :23¾, the half in :47½, six furlongs in 1:11½ and the mile in 1:35½.

Nonetheless, trainer Matt Byrnes criticized Bergen for having sent the horse along so fast in the early running, and he opined that Salvator would have run the distance in 1:33 if Murphy had been the jockey.

"Why," exclaimed Byrnes, "I had warmed him up before the race in 1:50!"

That was Salvator's last race, but the weird consistency of his relationship with Tenny had not yet ended. Reminiscing upon the eerie connection between these two horses, the late Frank Butzow wrote for the *Thoroughbred Record:*

> Tenny raced two seasons longer than the great son of Prince Charlie . . . then followed Salvator to the stud. There they came close to being equal. Each was a failure! But even here, a slight advantage still remained in favor of Salvator. He got Savable who won the 1902 Futurity, something Salvator himself had failed to do . . .

Years passed. It appeared Tenny was destined always to follow behind Salvator, never to be first in anything concerning both, and so it remained until 1909, when each was twenty-three years old.

In that year Tenny looked out across the fields for the last time. He was about to answer the final bugle call. He would finally beat Salvator this time, beat him to the grave, so it seemed. But, as the old swayback's life ebbed away, word came that Salvator was dead. Again, it was close, but again Salvator was first in the last mile.

CHAPTER TWENTY-EIGHT

SALVATOR WAS THE BEST HORSE owned by the biggest operator in the history of American racing, James Ben Ali Haggin (1821–1914). A native of Harrodsburg, Kentucky, he derived his unusual name from his grandfather, Ibraham Ben Ali, a Turkish army officer. As a young man Haggin went down the river to Natchez and New Orleans in search of his fortune without notable success. However, in his late twenties he joined the California gold rush and soon became one of the wealthiest men in America. A lawyer by profession, he had vast holdings in gold, silver and copper mining, not to mention an enormous amount of real estate. Haggin and his law partner, Lloyd Tevis, owned 400,000 acres of grazing land in Southern California and 1,000,000 acres of range in New Mexico and Arizona. His headquarters, Rancho del Paso, near Sacramento in northern California, occupied an additional 44,800 acres. Although he originally was interested more in trotting horses, Haggin eventually established there the largest thoroughbred stud in world history. The private catalogue for 1903 listed 30 stallions, 562 brood mares, plus numerous yearlings, sucklings and miscellaneous stock for a grand total of approximately 2,000 thoroughbreds.

The scope of Haggin's operation defies description. He purchased horses from virtually every breeding state in this country—California, Virginia, Kentucky, New Jersey, Maryland, Pennsylvania, New York, Montana and Tennessee—and imported from England, Ireland and Australia. For the 1900 Futurity he made 196 nominations.

Both Salvator and Haggin's 1886 Kentucky Derby winner, Ben Ali, were bought from breeder Dan Swigert. However, Haggin bred a number of good ones on his own, including Tyrant who was the medium of an ingenious coup. Having been highly tried in California, Tyrant was sent East in quest of the Withers Stakes, preceded by a fair amount of California betting money. To the easterners, however, he was an unknown quantity, and they were inclined to disdain California form anyway, so they paid no attention, even when jockey Patsy Duffy got off the train in Chicago long enough to tell a few friends that this colt was "good enough to win a dozen Withers or Belmonts." The eastern trainers watched Tyrant in his work but were unable to time him because he always pulled up before the finish pole, and not until after he had won the Withers at good odds did they realize what had happened: Tyrant's trainer had not been using the quarter poles in his training, but had been working the colt from marks on the rail beyond those poles. Tyrant went on to prove his victory was no fluke by winning the Belmont Stakes.

FIRENZI, 1884
(Glenelg–Florida, by Virgil)

The greatest runner bred by Haggin was a mare, Firenzi, winner of the Nursery Stakes at two and invincible among members of her own sex at three, after which she was required by the unchivalrous conditions of the day to make her way as best she could in masculine company. It didn't bother her a bit.

She carried her owner's orange jacket and blue sleeves into many battles, and although the Haggin colors were sometimes dipped, seldom were they lowered. The tough little mare raced on through the age of seven, and in 82 starts she was unplaced only five times. She won 47 races, ran second in 21 and third in nine, for earnings of $112,586; her victories included two Monmouth Cups, two Freehold Handicaps, the Omnium, Champion Stakes, Monmouth Handicap and a number of other important stakes.

A contemporary of Kingston and Hanover— the Class of 1884 was a distinguished one—she numbered both these great horses among her victims, plus such other good ones as Raceland and the "young upstart," Riley, winner of the 1890 Kentucky Derby.

Toward the turn of the century, Haggin began to cut back his racing stable and concentrate on breeding for the market, which in his case required that he ship trainloads in-

James Ben Ali Haggin (foreground), owner of the world's biggest turf empire, relaxing in the shedrow.

144

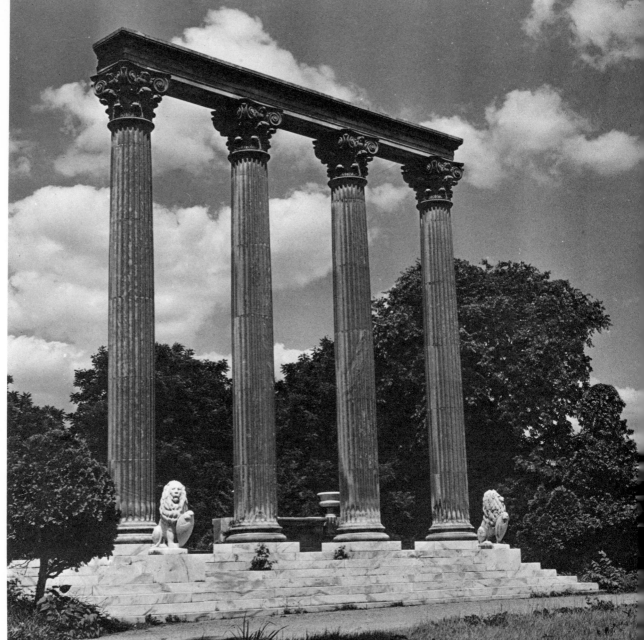

Remnants of "Green Hills," the mansion built by James B. A. Haggin at Elmendorf Farm, Lexington, Kentucky.

stead of carloads of yearlings to the East every summer. The difficulties were such that, encouraged by his wife, who also was a native Kentuckian, he transferred his stud to Kentucky. He purchased Elmendorf Farm from C. J. Enright (who had acquired it from Swigert) and developed it into a showplace comprising 8,700 acres of choice bluegrass land. Many of today's leading thoroughbred nurseries —among them the modern Elmendorf Farm, Greentree Stud, C. V. Whitney Farm, Normandy Farm and parts of Spendthrift Farm— were carved from the land which comprised Haggin's Elmendorf Stud.

The orange jacket and blue sleeves also are part of the Haggin heritage; the colors which were flown by Salvator and Firenzi in modern times have identified the runners of Louis Lee Haggin II.

Although there was nothing to compare in scope with the huge Haggin establishment, a number of other stud farms had comparable success in the production of thoroughbreds for the market. In addition to Dixiana, the previously mentioned Runnymede Farm and Tennessee's Belle Meade Stud, among the foremost was McGrathiana Stud in Lexington, Kentucky. Established by H. Price McGrath, a tailor who made his fortune as a bookmaker (and who was reputed never to have had a bank account), it was one of the most lavish nurseries in the country, and the scene of opulent parties, numbering up to 500 guests, when race meetings were in progress. McGrath was quite successful in his operations there—among other good ones, his horses included the first Kentucky Derby winner, Aristides, also known as the thorn in the side of the great Ten Broeck—but the place reached peak development under its second owner, Milton Young (1851–1918), who purchased McGrathiana after the death of its founder and added to it, including an "auxiliary farm" on the other side of town, until there were some 2,000 acres devoted to horse production.

The man who achieved such a reputation for integrity that Mike Dwyer telegraphed him a *carte blanche* order for fourteen yearlings was a native of Union County, Kentucky, and only thirty-one when he acquired his famous farm. Young had become fascinated with horses during his former profession as hardware merchant; he already owned a sizable stable that had included the noted runners Bancroft and Boatman. Off and on, he would disperse his racing string to apply himself more fully to breeding, and it was in the latter occupation that he was particularly prominent.

He stood up to 10 stallions at a time, the broodmare population of McGrathiana was well in excess of 100, and Young once had 67 foals nominated to the Futurity. Eight years after he bought the farm, Colonel Young (he, too, acquired the title) was America's leading breeder of the 1890 season when 110 horses he bred won 378 races and $335,150. Among the many thoroughbreds with which he was associated, Young is best remembered as the owner of Hanover and breeder of Broomstick.

He purchased Hanover from F. C. O'Riley, who had bought him after the break-up between the Dwyer brothers, and it was while standing at McGrathiana that the horse became the leading North American sire. Broomstick,

who came along later, was sold as a youngster; after a distinguished racing career, he sired more stakes winners (sixty-six) than any stallion in American history. (Much later, after McGrathiana had been sold to E. D. Shaffer and renamed Coldstream Stud, among the horses bred there was Bull Lea, sire of more $100,000 winners than any stallion in world history.)

Milton Young was active in every phase of turf affairs: at one time or another part owner of a race track, president of the Western Turf Congress, and Chairman of the Kentucky Racing Commission. His infectious enthusiasm for thoroughbreds was passed along to his sons, Tom and Jack. A young partner of his, Thomas Piatt, also became a famous breeder.

All that glitters is not gold, but on the other hand, gold isn't the only metal that glitters, and Marcus Daly (1841–1900) made his huge fortune from copper by way of silver. A native of Ireland who came to the United States as a boy of fifteen, he went west to become a pick and shovel miner in California, and later was employed by "silver kings" J. G. Fair and J. W. Mackay. While investigating silver deposits at Butte, Montana, Daly discovered rich copper deposits underneath, and the great Anaconda strike was on. The Daly empire soon encompassed railroads, timber, power plants, banks and a newspaper.

By conservative estimate the "Copper King" was estimated to have spent $1,000,000 on outside purchases of horses alone, which does not include horses he bred himself nor the funds he furnished to finance race tracks at Anaconda and Butte, which were operated by noted racing officials Ed Tipton, manager, and J. B. Ferguson, starter. For Monmouth Park's historic stakes program, which drew 2,786 entries in 1891, Daly was the leading nominator with 219 eligible horses, which topped by 13 nominations the powerful Eastern stable of J. A. and A. H. Morris.

The best horse owned by Daly was Hamburg, whose herculean weight-carrying feats as a two-

146

year-old under the ownership of John E. Madden already have been recounted. After this brilliant season, Hamburg was sold to Daly for $40,000 and turned over to trainer Billy Lakeland. The colt was a glutton, both for feed and for work, according to turf historian Vosburgh, and Madden had learned the hard way how to handle him, giving him twice the ordinary amount of exercise. It cost Daly the Belmont Stakes before he caught on, but Hamburg won the Swift, Realization Stakes and Brighton Cup after that loss and was acknowledged champion again at three.

Daly's other good ones included Tammany, who hit his best stride as a four-year-old; the Suburban winner, Montana, and Senator Grady, who had the misfortune to be foaled the same year as Domino, Dobbins and Henry of Navarre, but who managed to earn his oats nevertheless.

In addition to his huge Bitter Root Stock Farm in Hamilton, Montana, which was established in 1890, the Copper King maintained Apperfield Stud in France and another farm in England. The handling of such an empire entailed obvious problems in logistics, and although Ogden, possibly the best horse Daly ever bred, was officially registered as an English foal, it was rumored that he actually had been imported *in utero* and was born in a railroad car on a siding outside the Utah city for which he was named. (More likely, he may have been weaned in a freight car.) Ogden won the 1896 Futurity in record time of 1:10 for the old short course of 1,263⅓ yards.

Bitter Root was among the first stud farms to have its own resident veterinarian: Dr. Edward W. Hagyard, who acted as general advisor to Daly, and who later joined his father, Dr. E. T. Hagyard, as partner in the veterinary firm which in modern times is the equivalent of the Mayo Clinic in its field.

After his death, the dispersal of Marcus Daly's thoroughbred and trotting stock realized $865,550, the top price of $60,000 being paid by W. C. Whitney for Hamburg.

CHAPTER TWENTY-NINE

IN THE LAST HALF OF THE 1870s New Yorkers suddenly discovered the Atlantic Ocean, and Coney Island became a popular summer resort. William Engeman, owner of a large strip of waterfront property, took advantage of it by building a race track at Brighton Beach which opened in June 1879. Although it was modestly conceived, its success from the very first day was so spectacular that more and more meetings were added until Brighton became the scene of racing virtually all year round.

Simultaneously with the opening of Brighton, a second track for this playground was being planned. Having been check-reined in the management of the track which bore his name, Leonard Jerome gathered a group of outstanding members of the younger set and proposed building a new track in what had become the favorite recreation area of New York. In 1879 the Coney Island Jockey Club was formed with Jerome as president, and plans for a fancy race course at Sheepshead Bay were formulated. In the meantime Prospect Park Fair Grounds, which had been used primarily for trotting, was leased and two brief but successful race meetings conducted there.

The opening of the new track the following year fulfilled the fondest expectations, and Sheepshead Bay soon became the most popular track in America. In 1884 the Suburban Handicap was inaugurated and the course was enlarged to a circumference of 1⅛ miles, biggest in the nation at the time. (Vosburgh tells of the Maryland owner Frank Hall, watching his candidate for the first Suburban work

over the new track and timing him in 1:55 for the circuit. He was dolefully scratching his head until trainer A. J. Joyner reminded him that the horse had run 9 furlongs.) The Suburban caught the public fancy at once and became a popular medium for future book betting such as later was to be conducted on the Santa Anita Handicap and Kentucky Derby.

Salvator appeared in 1888 at Sheepshead Bay for the inaugural of the Futurity, a race which resulted in enormous purses; more often than not the Futurity winner was the leading money winner of the season, regardless of his other accomplishments, and his stable also led the owners' list. The race reached its peak nineteenth-century value in 1890 when August Belmont's Potomac collected $67,675, an especially appropriate victory since Belmont died before the year was out, after having seen his turf fortune reach its crest.

Another important Sheepshead Bay fixture which continued to exist was the Realization Stakes (Salvator won the inaugural of this one in 1889) later named the "Lawrence Realization" in honor of J. G. K. Lawrence, who succeeded Jerome as, president. It replaced the American Derby as the richest event in the land for three-year-olds.

Historic races were only a part of Sheepshead Bay's heritage to the sport, however. The track re-introduced turf course racing—and a former resident of the land on which Sheepshead Bay was built, James E. "Sunny Jim" Fitzsimmons, has been a traditional fixture, too.

Having enjoyed success with their racing stable and in the betting ring, in 1885 the

Grandstand of the Coney Island Jockey Club at Sheepshead Bay.

Dwyer brothers formed the Brooklyn Jockey Club, with Phil Dwyer as president.

The old Prospect Park track was re-built and the new club dovetailed its racing days with Sheepshead Bay—which at the time ran on Tuesday, Thursday and Saturday—so that New Yorkers had racing available every weekday.

Gravesend was functionally conceived and well located. It became immensely popular and profitable. The Brooklyn Handicap, patterned after the Suburban, was instituted in 1887, the inaugural won by Dry Monopole, and this race received an equally enthusiastic reception.

Other of today's stakes races born in Brooklyn include the Gazelle, Tremont, Great American Stakes and the Dwyer (which originally was named the "Brooklyn Derby").

From the day the track opened, until it closed in 1910, Phil Dwyer served in the stewards' stand. Of him it was said: ". . . his presence there inspired universal confidence. He was a man of rugged fairness and his shrewd good sense was absolute proof against hysteria. Securing his vote to a disqualification was as difficult a process as extracting an eye tooth. He always contended that getting a horse down in front was such a hard proposition, the

149

evidence of fouling should be positively over-whelming to justify the setting aside of a winner's claim to the big end of the purse."

When in 1887 the City of New York decided to purchase Jerome Park and construct a reservoir on the property, the indefatigable Leonard Jerome enlisted the support of John A. Morris in the construction of a substitute race course where the American Jockey Club could continue to operate. A magnificent park in Westchester County, comprising 330 acres, was promptly acquired and the lorgnette set soon had a new home.

Morris Park, which opened in 1889, was everything its predecessor had been and then some, with a 1⅜-mile race course (longest in America) and palatial facilities. The lawn between the grandstand and the track sloped so that all spectators might have an unobstructed view, and a straightaway course was built diagonally across the infield. It was formally named "The Eclipse Course," but after the California mare Geraldine set a new world's record of 46 seconds for 4 furlongs in the first race over it, and it was noted that the course had a slight downhill slant, some references to a "toboggan slide" appeared in the newspapers. Morris, not a petty man by any account, took the name for one of the track's feature races and the Toboggan Handicap has remained a popular spring event of the New York season.

As a corresponding feature to the Suburban and Brooklyn, Morris Park inaugurated the Metropolitan Handicap in 1891 and, as Jerome Park had been abandoned the preceding year, it also inherited the Belmont Stakes, Withers,

Club house at Morris Park, most fashionable of the New York tracks.

Ladies, Nursery, Juvenile and Champagne Stakes. Such long-standing events as the Matron, National Stallion Stakes and Grand National Steeplechase were instituted at Morris Park.

The Brooklyn Jockey Club had established the track at Gravesend as a business proposition and, operating on small property with low overhead, in a heavy concentration of population, the club's profits were tremendous.

Apparently taking their cue from their neighbors, in 1894 the Queens County Jockey Club, headed by T. D. "Cab" Reilly, David Holland and Robert Tucker, opened Aqueduct, where economy was carried to an extreme—Vosburgh described the clubhouse as "a shanty held up by stilts." The next year Captain William Carter, a tugboat skipper, endowed the club with a large sum of money to sponsor its big handicap race and the Carter Handicap joined the parade. Encouraged by this gesture, and by the large crowds which patronized Aqueduct, the management remodelled it into a fine racing plant, 1⅛ miles around with a chute which permitted 1¼-mile races involving only one turn, a backstretch 90 feet wide and an 80-foot homestretch.

Its convenient location made Aqueduct very popular with racing fans, and its commodious size and the exceptional quality of its soil caused it to be a great favorite with trainers.

CHAPTER THIRTY

THE LAST DECADE OF THE nineteenth century is fabled in song and story, and on stage and screen, as a carefree period in our history. Life was prosperous, effervescent; opportunity was limitless, and, having overcome the struggle for existence that palled its formative years, America was ready to relax and have fun. Recreation no longer was despised as a weakness. The national scene was crowded with glamorous figures and exciting adventurers. The most glamorous figure of all, Lillian Russell, later organized a racing stable under the name of "Mr. Clinton," the name being taken from that of her birthplace, Clinton, Iowa. The accent was on energy, laughter, speed and optimism, and racing went along with the Gay Nineties up to the hilt.

As Pierre Lorillard expressed the temper of the times: "I don't want to race anything but two- and three-year-olds . . . racing old horses is unsatisfactory. The stakes are of no value as a rule . . . After a colt has passed three years old I don't want him and shall sell mine as fast as they reach that age . . . I had rather race two-year-olds than any other class. It is more interesting. You get tired of the same old horses."

In 1891 the two-year-old, His Highness became the first horse in history to win more than $100,000 in a single season. That same year there was foaled a colt who was to take the most generous helping on record. This was J. R. and F. P. Keene's Domino.

Old Kingston had become the nation's leading money winner the hard way; he ran until he was eight years old and had started more than 100 times before he passed Hanover. The richest purse he ever earned was $6,635 in the Select Stakes—as a two-year-old—and thereafter his bank account piled up surely, but slowly.

A lot of water went under the bridge during Kingston's long career, and before he retired times had changed. In fact, he was still in action at the age of nine when Domino abruptly knocked him off his throne. It took Domino exactly three months and one day to do it. As a two-year-old, he averaged more per race than Kingston had averaged per season.

Domino is the only horse ever to have become America's leading money winner in his first season of racing, and he stayed at the top of the list longer than any thoroughbred in history.

DOMINO, 1891

(Himyar–Mannie Gray, by Enquirer)

The word was out concerning Domino's phenomenal speed before he entered competition, and for his debut in a purse race at Gravesend May 22, he was an odds-on favorite. He won this one easily by six lengths, then swept through five rich stakes in quick succession before going to the post for the richest of them all, the Futurity, at Sheepshead Bay, August 29.

From an original list of 812 subscribers, 20 went to the post. Because of their previous victories, Domino and Richard Croker's Dobbins were each penalized 12 pounds and shared top weight of 130.

The large field presented a problem. There was a thirty-four minute delay at the post, until

Domino, a whirlwind on the track and a phenomenon at stud.

starter James Rowe lined the jockeys up against the fence and threatened to fine the next offender $1,000, after which "the flag fell to a grand start." Domino raced wide much of the way and lost considerable ground, but he got up at the end, under a desperate ride by Fred Taral, to win by a head from Galilee, with Dobbins only another head away in third place. First money of $48,855 made Domino the richest horse in the country.

This race had an interesting aftermath. It will be recalled that the Dwyer brothers had purchased Kingston "just to get him out of Hanover's way." Well, J. R. Keene had purchased a promising looking colt named Hyderabad just to get him out of Domino's way, and in the Futurity Hyderabad had gotten very much *in* the way: he had fallen. Most witnesses agreed that Dobbins, who was given a very erratic ride by Patsy McDermott, had knocked him down, but Dobbins' owner saw it otherwise. He challenged Keene to a match a couple of weeks later which was accepted. Then,

thinking that Domino needed a rest more than Dobbins did, Croker taunted Keene at a party the evening of the Futurity about his colt's inability to run good races close together. (The Futurity had been Domino's seventh start of the season, but for Dobbins it was the eighteenth.)

Keene rose to the bait and agreed to a return bout two days later, on August 31, same track and same distance, although this time both colts carried only 118 pounds and Dobbins was ridden by Simms.

This race stands as the most futile endeavor on record. It ended in a dead heat—and, because it was a private match, arranged by the owners themselves, as distinguished from a duly scheduled event sponsored by the racing association, under the special rule which governed this type of race all bets were off and the purse was cancelled entirely.

In his next start, the Matron Stakes at Morris Park in September, Domino carried 128 pounds 6 furlongs over the straightaway in

153

1:09 to break a track record which had been set by a three-year-old carrying only 105½ lbs. Thus, the "Black Whirlwind" closed out his first campaign undefeated. (Officially, Domino was brown, but that color is difficult to distinguish from black, particularly if the horse sweats, which Domino did profusely.)

Domino began his three-year-old season with a narrow victory in the Withers Stakes at a mile, after which he finished ninth in his first attempt at a longer distance, the 1½-mile American Derby won by Rey El Santa Anita. Since Taral had kept Domino far back in the early running to conserve his speed—and the colt had emerged from the race with a bleeding foot—it was easy to make excuses for this loss. When Domino followed with four straight wins he again came to be regarded as invincible by his admirers, although a lingering doubt remained concerning his stamina. Accordingly, a race was arranged against Henry of Navarre, winner of the Belmont Stakes and the best distance colt of this generation, for Gravesend, September 15, 1894. It was at the "compromise" distance of 1⅛ miles, both colts carrying 122 pounds, and according to a contemporary account it resulted in "one of the most brilliant equine contests ever witnessed on the American turf."

There was a spirited contest in progress on the sidelines, too. Horace Wade describes this one in his book, *Tales of the Turf,* in part as follows:

> Riley Grannon was contemporaneous with Pittsburgh Phil, but there was a marked difference between the two men. Phil was of the cold and phlegmatic type; Riley was warm and sociable. Phil worked hard at his handicapping; Riley was open to any "hot tip." Phil could watch a race with the stolidity of a cigar-store Indian; Riley would jump about like corn popping on a hot stove.
>
> When Domino met Henry of Navarre . . . the two temperaments, as far apart as the poles, grappled . . . Riley Grannon did not think anything on the turf could whip Henry of

Navarre, while Pittsburgh Phil as emphatically liked Domino. As Phil moved from book to book, betting on Domino, Riley was right behind him, matching him dollar for dollar on Henry of Navarre. Phil finally turned to the youngster:

> "Riley, he said, "let's quit piking. How much do you want to bet on this race?"
>
> Grannon never flinched. "I've got $100,000 that says Henry of Navarre will win," he proposed.
>
> That was a race to see as Pittsburgh Phil and Riley Grannon stood side by side on the lawn watching the two thoroughbreds flash along the backstretch. Phil stood calmly, eating a nickel package of figs, while Riley waved his arms like a semaphore . . .

It *was* a race to see; following is the description from the *Live-Stock Record:*

> . . . Henry of Navarre drew the pole. They wheeled once and were sent away with Domino on the outside and a few feet back. There was no advantage, however, for Doggett took a strong pull on Henry of Navarre and as they passed the grand stand Domino crossed in front, took the pole and accepted the challenge to make the pace. Domino led around the turn by a length and a half. Both were under a pull.
>
> When they struck the backstretch Henry of Navarre moved up to Domino gradually and a wild yell went up from the chestnut colt's supporters. "He's got him already," was the cry. The black was not beaten, however. They swung around the turn as one horse and neither jockey had as yet made a move. As they neared the head of the stretch Henry of Navarre's head slowly crept to the front. Taral was beginning to ride Domino and the hearts of his followers began to fail them. As they straightened for the home run Henry of Navarre was half a length in front.
>
> Suddenly Taral was seen to straighten up in the saddle. Then the cruel whip descended upon the black's side with a swish that could be heard almost above the yells of the crowd. "Domino is beaten!" yelled the backers of Henry of Navarre. "Not yet!" answered Domino's supporters. Under the whip and spur

Domino's black muzzle began to creep up again. Slowly and surely he gained on the chestnut, on whom Doggett was still riding with hands and feet.

At the furlong pole Domino was on even terms with Henry of Navarre. Then Doggett raised his whip and the horse under him shot forward in response. Only for a moment, however, for the black was at his head again, struggling gamely for the victory. Whip and spur were applied mercilessly. The horses strained every nerve and muscle and the jockeys were using every art at their command to urge the game animals along.

Twenty lengths from home the black faltered for a fraction of a second, and Henry of Navarre again led by a neck; but Taral rode like the Dutch demon that he is, and the lost ground was recovered—and no more. The excitement was intense. Neither horse could gain an inch on the other. Stride for stride they ran to the finish, and, amid tremendous enthusiasm, they flashed by the judges on exactly even terms. The judges were unable to separate them, and a dead heat was declared . . .

The time was 1:55½, over a track classified as good, but still sticky from heavy rainfall the night before.

Under the rules which prevailed for regularly scheduled events, in the case of a dead heat in a dash race, either owner could demand a run-off "at an interval of not less than twenty minutes," but after a conference between the Keenes and Byron McClelland, owner of Henry of Navarre, it was decided to divide the purse.

Pittsburgh Phil (George Smith) and Riley Grannon undoubtedly had their own method of settling such impasses, but the public bettors had no such option. Total bets were split down the middle; and as Domino had been a heavy favorite, his backers lost money: They received $3.50 return on each $5 bet, while those who wagered on Henry of Navarre received $6.50.

Domino had proved his gameness beyond a shadow of a doubt, but there had been few, if any, misgivings on that score in the first place. As to stamina, the doubt lingered. Another special race—this one at 1⅛ miles—was arranged for October 6 at Morris Park in which the four-year-old Clifford was added to the field. In a superlative exhibition of grit, Henry of Navarre overtook Domino, then repelled a challenge from Clifford to win by three-quarters of a length as Domino fell back to finish ten lengths astern of Clifford.

Keene still was not convinced, and he entered Domino in the 1¼-mile Suburban Handicap the next year. The colt finished fourth. Henry of Navarre beat him again by a neck at 1⅛ miles in September, and in the final start of his career, Domino finished dead last at 1¼ miles to Henry of Navarre, Clifford, Sir Walter, and Rey El Santa Anita.

Because of his brilliant speed and stirring courage, some excuses were found for all of Domino's losses, but the cold statistics indicate simply that 9 furlongs was his absolute limit. It is customary to set forth a horse's racing record according to seasons; departing from this practice and breaking down Domino's career according to distance reveals definite strata of performance, as follows:

Range	Starts	1st	2nd	3rd	Un-placed
1 mile or less	19	18	1	—	—
1⅛ miles	3	1	1	1	—
More than 1⅛ miles	3	0	0	0	3
($193,550)	25	19	2	1	3

In sprints he was practically invincible—the one race he lost was the Fall Handicap as a four-year-old, when he carried the heaviest load of his career, 133 pounds, conceding 24 to the three-year-old filly, The Butterflies, who had won the Futurity the year before and who was, according to Vosburgh, "one of the fleetest bits of horseflesh that has ever been stripped." At the in-between distance, Domino was an in-between horse, and beyond that he was out of his depth. Nevertheless, no one can chip at the inscription on his gravestone:

"Here lies the fleetest runner the American turf has ever known, and one of the gamest and most generous of horses."

The inscription makes no mention of Domino's accomplishments at stud—which is easy to understand. The horse died in 1897, at the age of six, just a few months after his first foals were born.

When his foals did reach racing age, though, they made history. Domino left only twenty offspring, of which eight were stakes winners. From this tiny foundation a towering structure arose, and the blood of the "Black Whirlwind" earned honors throughout the racing world. That Domino founded a strong male line is astounding from the standpoint of raw mathematical probability. Of his nine sons, four were gelded and one died, leaving only four capable of carrying on the line; however, one of these sons, Commando, was as unusual in this respect as his sire.

The unprecedented rapidity of Domino's rise to wealth was in a way poetic—his co-owner, James R. Keene, was the breeder of Kingston, but had been unable to keep that horse because he temporarily had lost his fortune.

CHAPTER THIRTY-ONE

R. KEENE." VERY FEW PERsons, not even his own son, addressed James R. Keene otherwise, in direct discourse, that is—undoubtedly he was sometimes mentioned in less dignified terms in conversations of which he was not a part. Call him what you will, his was the name that rang out most frequently on the American turf between the Civil War and World War I.

The breeder of Kingston and co-owner of Domino was no newcomer to the spotlight. He had been around the course before, all the way, and with Domino he was beginning his second tour.

Considering the vagaries of the stock market in the last half of the nineteenth century, one would assume that however strong a penchant a man might have for risky investment and fast action, he could give it full expression on Wall Street. Nevertheless a large number of financial tycoons also were among the leading figures in racing; after dabbling with millions in their offices, they would relax by tackling the equally challenging business of racing or breeding horses. Prominent among these men in every respect was James Robert Keene. He had his ups and downs on Wall Street, but in racing it was practically nothing but up.

A native of London, Keene came to this country as a boy with his parents who settled in Shasta, California. He worked at a variety of jobs, including teaching school and editing a weekly newspaper, until the great Bonanza mining strike in Nevada in the 1870s. Keene was in his mid-thirties at the time, settled in San Francisco with his wife and two children.

But within about five years he was a multimillionaire.

As it happened, the nucleus of his fortune was horses (and mules). He began a supply business servicing the mines, and after amassing a modest amount of capital, he returned to San Francisco where he obtained a seat on the stock exchange. His knowledge of mining stocks enabled him to run $10,000 up to an estimated $6,000,000 by 1875, at which point, on advice of his physician, Keene took a long ocean voyage. The next year Keene left for New York by private railroad car, and although there were no ocean breezes, this trip, too, had a tonic effect; before leaving California he had sold short 10,000 shares of New York Central stock, and by the time he arrived at his destination he had made $200,000 profit.

A lean, bearded, intense man—he looked almost like a cartoon of the shrewd Yankee businessman—Keene's activity on the stock market led him to be regarded with a mixture of grudging respect and bitter hatred, and in his first two years on Wall Street, he is said to have made a profit of $9,000,000. He was forty years old when he obtained his first race horse, the three-year-old Spendthrift, which he bought from Daniel Swigert for $15,000 in a package deal that included the colt's younger brother.

As has been recorded, Keene came into racing with the avowed purpose of breaking up the monopoly of George Lorillard, and in this venture there was no delay at the post. In his first start for his new owner, Spendthrift was "pulled double" to allow his stablemate, Dan Sparling, who carried Keene's betting money, to win the Withers Stakes, and the stable ran one-two as Lorillard's 2-to-5 favorite, Harold, finished out of the money. (As a result of this incident, the rule requiring a "declaration to win" was put into effect.) A few days later, Spendthrift won the Belmont Stakes from Lorillard's Monitor, and the Keene colt went on to become champion of the season. He also won the Jersey Derby, Champion Stakes, and adding insult to injury, the Lorillard Stakes, despite being turned around at the start of the latter.

That same year, Keene sent his friend, William Bathgate, to Kentucky to purchase yearlings, and one of two yearlings Bathgate bought from R. A. Alexander turned out to be Foxhall, named for Keene's son.

Having made his fortune, Keene was thinking of returning to England, and he sent there a division of his stable which included Foxhall. The colt, managed by Richard Ten Broeck, was an immense success in Europe. In addition to becoming the only American-bred horse in history to win the Grand Prix de Paris, Foxhall won five stakes races in England, including the Cesarewitch, Cambridgeshire and Ascot Gold Cup. According to Foxhall Keene, his father won $350,000 wagering on his namesake, and thereupon swore off betting.

This rectitude with respect to gambling did not extend to Keene's stock market activity, however, and in 1884 he was flat broke. When he had made his grand entrance into New York eight years earlier the notorious Jay Gould had boasted, "Keene came East in a private car, I'll send him back in a boxcar," and by 1884 he had succeeded, at least figuratively speaking, in making good his threat. When Keene tried to corner the Chicago wheat market, Gould put pressure on his .other holdings, forcing Keene to cover until he ran out of cash. Keene was forced to abandon his plans for retirement to a lordly life in England and to sell out the horses he had been carefully collecting, among which was Kingston.

Although devoid of money, Keene still possessed his shrewd mind and intense determina-

Foxhall Keene, golfer, automobile driver and horseman.

tion. Four years later he became associated with William Havemeyer in the sugar market and by 1891 he was again a lion of Wall Street and re-entered racing. He operated on a much more expansive scale during this second phase, becoming a significant breeder as well as owner.

With his brother-in-law, Major Foxhall Daingerfield, in charge, he purchased the noted Castleton Farm near Lexington, Kentucky, which had been established by John Breckinridge, Attorney General in the cabinet of Thomas Jefferson. Under Keene's ownership Castleton regained its former prominence and then some, although Domino, the most influential horse associated with the stud, was not bred there.

Foxhall Keene had purchased the colt as a yearling from Major Barak Thomas for $3,000, and after Domino had turned in a couple of sensational trials, as Foxhall explained in his memoirs, Mr. Keene came to him and said, "Foxie, it is ridiculous for you to have a great horse like Domino, while I have only middling ones. Let's merge our stables and form a partnership." (Those fast trials were believed to have caused the trouble Domino later had with his legs—he raced in four red bandages—and trainer Albert Cooper was replaced by Billy Lakeland.)

Young Keene was of great assistance to his father in their racing venture, and quite an expert in his own right, as well as an all-around athlete. Despite his disavowal of betting on horses, the senior Keene offered to stake $100,000 on his son against any man in the world in a contest involving ten different sports. This confidence is the more noteworthy when it is considered that Foxhall was not a large man. He once volunteered to ride Domino because regular jockey Fred Taral had whipped the colt so unmercifully that Domino hated the sight of him, and a blanket had to be thrown over Domino's head before Taral could mount. It wasn't just talk on Foxhall's part, either.

A competent football player and boxer at Harvard, Foxhall Keene was a golfer and racing car driver of international stature, and an equestrian (polo, steeplechasing and fox-hunting) of universal renown. Before he was seventeen he was America's leading rider over the sticks—professional or amateur—and in 1887 he won 79 of the 101 races he contested. His later accomplishments included victories in the Pelham Gold Cup and Bibury Cup, and captaincy of America's international polo team.

The Keenes, as will be seen, made a number of curtain calls on the stage of racing history.

CHAPTER THIRTY-TWO

LTHOUGH DOMINO'S VICTORY in the 1893 Futurity made him the nation's leading money winner, this was the exceptional occasion when the Futurity was not the richest race of the season. The big money that year was in Chicago, where the World's Columbian Exposition was in progress and Washington Park, in keeping with the festive atmosphere that prevailed, held a twenty-five-day race meeting during which purse distribution averaged $11,172 daily. (By comparison, daily average purse distribution at the Coney Island Jockey Club meeting, which ranked second that year, was $9,330.)

Domino had gone west with the crowd, and paid his fare by winning the Hyde Park Stakes for two-year-olds, but the main objective of the stable's invasion of Chicago was the American Derby for three-year-olds; the Keene entry of St. Leonards and Chorister was favored to win.

This was the richest race that year: the Washington Park management had guaranteed a gross purse of $60,000, with $50,000 to the winner, $7,000 to second and $3,000 to third. As it turned out, the race would have gone down in history if the purse had been only $100.

The huge purse lured runners from throughout the country, headed by the Keene pair, and one from England. As a commentary on the quality of the field, quite a bit of sentimental money was riding on the locally owned J. E. Cushing couple of Lookout and Boundless, winners of the Kentucky and Arkansas Derbies, respectively, earlier that year, but this entry nevertheless was fourth choice in the wagering, at odds varying between 6- and 8-to-1. Fifteen colts went to the post—and for a time it looked as though that was as far as they were going to get.

The American Derby, according to *Inter-Ocean:*

. . . would have been called on schedule had not Ed Corrigan been determined that Gideon and Daly should have none the best of him as regards their jockey, Monk Overton, whom he claimed on an old contract. The result was that at 3:40 a change of jockeys was ordered on Ramapo [Gideon and Daly's horse], and, after a long delay, the services of Thorpe were secured to ride the horse. At 4:17 P.M. the most carefully selected lot of three-year-olds ever sent to a race were called out.

. . . the shout of admiration as they passed could have been heard by the crowds who were viewing the spectacle with glasses on the roof of the main building at the World's Fair . . .

When they arrived at the post the trouble began . . . why a starter like Pettingill should take almost two hours to get them off is a mystery . . . There is no doubt that the best horse, St. Leonards, was beaten by this tiring process . . .

In the hour and thirty odd minutes at the post there were twenty-five breaks, in which one or more horses ran from an eighth to a sixteenth of a mile. Twenty-five eighths of a mile both ways would be six miles. In fifteen of these breaks, St. Leonards was among the first three, and usually the first. It is safe to say, therefore, that St. Leonards ran three miles before the race . . . During this time Garrison on Boundless, Penny on Oporto, and Miller on Aldebaran, dismounted for one reason or the other . . .

. . . Chorister was so little pleased with the tiring work that he got rather free with the heels . . .

One thing about St. Leonards: he was persistent. When the official break finally came, at 5:50—more than two hours beyond the scheduled time, and after the horses had been at the post more than one and a half hours—he shot to the front again. However, the Cushing stable employed the classic one-two punch; Lookout soon took over the lead, as Garrison kept Boundless well in hand back in the pack, biding his time.

The favorite kept hammering away at Lookout, and eventually regained the lead after a mile had been run in 1:44¼, but the latter had served his purpose well. Exhausted from his duel, St. Leonards had nothing left when Garrison made his move on Boundless as the field rounded into the stretch for the final drive. After putting eight lengths between his mount and St. Leonards, the "Snapper" cooly nodded to the crowd while Boundless sauntered past, then turned around in his saddle to smile at Taral.

Time for the mile and one-half was 2:36 and, although the conditions of the race provided for penalties and allowances, all fifteen runners carried scale weight of 122 pounds except Tyro and the imported colt, Strathrose, who got in with maiden allowances at 115 pounds. Obviously confused by the rhubarb, if not the strange environment, Strathrose grabbed last place during the first furlong and held on to it throughout; the English invader was pulled up when the race was half over.

Victory by the home team, of course, made the occasion that much more glamorous. As the description continued:

Judging from the applause, the result seemed to be a popular one. Mr. Cushing was faint from excitement and had to be supported into the stand, where he received the congratulations of the officials. Mr. Brewster called for three cheers, which was given heartily, and Mr. Cushing was presented with a check for $50,000, which he waved before the crowd.

Jockey Garrison was also nearly mobbed by excited friends, and carried into the clubhouse on the shoulders of a number of admirers.

The sole sour note in the proceedings had been the start, and although it was quickly forgotten in the enthusiasm immediately after the race, it subsequently returned to haunt Charles Pettingill. One of the finest officials in the sport, he is unfortunately most frequently recalled in connection with two celebrated fiascos. Years later, after he had moved into the stewards' stand and become somewhat rusty at starting, he was called upon to fill in at his old job when the regular starter became ill; he it was who sent the field away in the race that resulted in the only defeat suffered by Man o' War.

The 1893 American Derby was covered from every angle. One Chicago newspaper assigned a lady reporter to narrate those aspects of the gala affair which might be of particular interest to feminine readers, but the social flavor somehow was obscured. "Elegantly dressed . . . refined women," she wrote indignantly, "were knocking against women who were betting and swearing." (A true reporter, in order to acquire first-hand identification with the subject, she primly offered to bet 50 cents, and was chagrined when bookmakers would not accept anything less than a dollar.)

An enterprising New York journalist covered the scene at the Coney Island clubhouse, where James R. Keene and Mike Dwyer listened to a description of the race over a specially installed wire. He wrote:

When the news came that a start had been finally effected, Mr. Keene got up near the instrument, after poking M. F. Dwyer in the ribs and telling him not to get over-anxious about the race. The faces of the two men to whom the race meant so much were a study. During the recital of the positions of the horses at different points in the race, Mr. Dwyer never said a word. Mr. Keene was, on the other hand, the anxious man, and even while the announcer would tell that St. Leonards was among the leaders and that he was ahead of Don Alonzo after the first half mile had been past, Mr. Keene would bend forward anxiously and inquire:

"Did anyone say anything about Chorister?"

At last there came the final announcement as to the running of the horses: "St. Leonards in the stretch by a head, Lookout second, Clifford third." That was the last before the winner was announced. Mr. Keene stood like a statue. There was $50,000 close at hand.

"The winner," said operator McKenna. Then he waited an instant. It seemed many minutes to the listeners, who stood silent as at a grave, with not a noise of any kind to disturb the fateful announcement. The color faded from the cheeks of Mr. Keene in spite of himself, and his face took on a marble color such as is rarely ever seen on the cheeks of that great operator, who plays with millions as children do with pennies. He bit his cigar as a steadier, held his breath, as did everyone else, and then came from the operator:

"Boundless wins!"

"Where the devil did he come from?" went up in chorus, for he had not been mentioned in the description of the race.

St. Leonards had his opportunity for revenge the next Saturday in the Realization Stakes at Sheepshead Bay, but this resulted in a double upset. S. S. Brown and J. W. Roger's unnamed colt by Troubadour—Sunbeam won by a head from St. Leonards with Boundless out of the money. Garrison, who shifted from Boundless to St. Leonards for this race, also exchanged his hero's laurel wreath for goat's horns.

"The victory of the Sunbeam colt . . . and the second defeat of St. Leonards was . . . certainly due to injudicious riding on the part of Garrison," stated the New York *World*. The article continued:

The fault was not altogether Garrison's, however. Garrison was asked to reduce so that he could ride at 115 pounds. He spent the night in a Turkish bath and came to the track looking like a ghost. He had taken off six or eight pounds in the bath and was as little able to do justice to his mount as a convalescent fever patient would have been. He was not himself physically or mentally, and he rode accordingly . . .

Both James R. Keene and his son Foxhall saw the race from the club-house and were disgusted with Garrison's ride. Foxhall Keene refused to speak to Garrison after the race, and his father was extremely bitter in his criticism.

No one who looked at the race intelligently could doubt for a moment that St. Leonards was ridden execrably, and that he ought to have won easily by a length or more; but at the same time the unfortunate "Snapper" did the best he knew how, and his errors were entirely due to his weakened condition . . .

Why in the *World* everyone was so upset is not very clear. The winner, later named "Daily America," had set a new track record of 2:50⅗ for the 1⅝ miles.

When Boundless returned to Chicago he received a rude welcome—Clifford beat him in a modest purse race at Hawthorne Park while conceding him 12 pounds.

Although he won the richest victory, Boundless was by no means the biggest star of the rich Washington Park meeting which drew such outstanding performers as Aetna Stable's Rudolph, and the Kendall Stable's fillies, Maid Marian and Yo Tambien.

Over-all honors went to Frank Van Ness's three-year-old colt Morello, who beat most of the members of his generation in the Drexel Stakes and Dearborn Handicap and then wound up with a resounding victory against older horses in the Wheeler Handicap on closing day, setting a new track record of 2:05 for 1¼ miles. Morello had not been nominated for the American Derby, but he had defeated Boundless earlier that year in the Hawthorne Derby. All in all, he was a remarkable bargain, for he had cost only $110 as a yearling and went on to win 24 races and more than $80,000 during his first two seasons.

The World's Fair meeting was in the nature of a final glorious fling for Washington Park because it already had been decided to suspend racing at that track. In the opinion of the operators, there was too much racing in Chicago (Hawthorne ran 260 days that year) and

162

if it could not be done properly, they preferred that it not be done at all. After the 1894 meet Washington Park suspended operation. The gesture was more chauvinistic than effectual because "Blind John" Condon's new Harlem track stepped in with mixed programs of running and trotting races, and Hawthorne and Harlem operated under a synchronized arrangement which provided Chicago with six days of racing per week.

CHAPTER THIRTY-THREE

LONG WITH THE CHANGE FROM heat racing to dash racing and the transition from an essentially private diversion to public entertainment, dependent for its existence upon popular support, there was another great transformation apparent in racing before the sport rounded the turn of the century. Jockeys began to come into their own.

Earlier there had been some famous riders, such as Gilpatrick, Simon, Laird, Cato and Abe, but by and large the jockey was regarded as a mere accoutrement of the horse. Sometimes the name of the winning rider was mentioned parenthetically in the summary of a big race, but it was not considered to be a highly pertinent portion of the report; often the identification consisted merely of some such vague reference as "Mr. Porter's boy," and the riders of horses which did not win were ignored completely in race summaries. As the nineteenth century drew to a close, the identity of the jockey assumed greater and greater importance, and in many cases the little men became Goliaths.

The growing recognition of jockeys can be attributed to several factors, one obviously being the American democratic spirit which demanded that ability be recognized regardless of a person's station in life. The change in the style of racing also served to increase the importance of jockeys, although there is room for argument on this score. The rider in a 4-mile heat race did not exert as much influence on the result as did the jockey in a dash race. True, the 4-mile rider had to be strong enough to rate his horse, and he had to

have a good sense of pace, but these qualities could be developed by practice and used more or less automatically; and if a jockey happened to be outsmarted at the start, or encounter some misfortune during the running, there was plenty of time available to make up the lost ground. In dash racing, on the other hand, a few yards lost could mean the difference between victory and defeat, and with a larger number of horses contesting such races, riding tactics played a vital part in the results. The jockey who was smart and quick-witted could employ these talents to more advantage.

Finally, as the amounts of money involved increased, both in the form of purses and wagering, quite naturally the strategic importance of the jockey increased accordingly. Many of these jockeys became public heroes, and five of them in particular became institutions.

Least spectacular in personality, but a screaming sensation according to cold statistics, was Isaac Murphy (1859-1896), the gentle young Negro who had a natural rapport with horses that bordered on the occult. Born Isaac Burns in the center of the horse country, Fayette County, Kentucky, on the universal birthday of thoroughbreds, January 1, 1859, he subsequently assumed the surname of his stepfather. Disdaining indiscriminate use of whip and spur, Murphy got the most out of his mounts by coaxing and nursing, never asking them to do more than win—which they did with fantastic frequency, as his lifetime record of 628 victories in 1,412 races will attest. Murphy's over-all 44 percent winning average has never been approached.

164

Isaac Murphy, top rider of the 19th century, whose lifetime percentage has never been equalled.

The sensitive, long-armed jockey set records by winning the Latonia Derby five times, American Derby four times and Kentucky Derby thrice. His Latonia record is untouched. His Kentucky Derby feat stood nearly half a century before it was duplicated by Earl Sande and subsequently surpassed by Eddie Arcaro. Murphy's four American Derby victories in five years (which included the first three runnings of that event) still stands as a record, although Arcaro won an equal number over a longer period. Three of Murphy's American Derby winners were owned by Lucky Baldwin, who paid him $10,000 a year to guarantee first call on his services.

As has been noted, the sad-eyed, soft-spoken rider also was regular jockey for Salvator, although he didn't ride that horse in his race against time. Other of Murphy's feats included a clean sweep of the 4-race card at Detroit on July 4, 1879.

In the off season Ike would hit 130 pounds or more, and rigid dieting undoubtedly weakened him. He died of pneumonia less than a year after he retired from the saddle, only slightly more than thirty-seven years old— officially. Actually, he was two years younger, according to home-town accounts; apparently he was only fourteen when he first came on the tracks, and to cover up that immaturity padded his age a couple of years.

Another colored jockey prominent in Murphy's era was "Monk" Overton, who set a record by winning six of seven races at Washington Park in 1891—which record was later exceeded by a Negro, James Lee, who won six of six at Churchill Downs in 1907.

A contemporary of Murphy was Jimmy McLaughlin (1861-1927), leading rider for four straight seasons, 1884-1887, who enjoyed correspondingly concentrated success in the Belmont Stakes: McLaughlin won this race six times in seven renewals, 1882-1888, a unique monopoly. The husky man behind the handlebar moustache also won the Kentucky Derby in 1881 with Hindoo, and he was a frequent rider of Miss Woodford and the other stars of the Dwyer brothers' stable. (McLaughlin trained as well as rode Hindoo during their invasion of Kentucky.) He had the mount on Salvator when that colt won the inaugural Realization Stakes, and just about every other great race came McLaughlin's way at one time or another; he took the 1885 Preakness with Tecumseh and the 1891 Futurity aboard His Highness. McLaughlin, too, had a perfect day in the saddle, at Nashville on October 10, 1878, when he won all three races on the program, including one event that was decided in two heats.

A powerful man of dignified demeanor, except for his muscles McLaughlin looked more like a banker than an athlete. According to Vosburgh, he used to exercise the gelding, Checkmate, a notoriously hard puller, with nothing but a halter.

"You'll get that boy killed some day," said Johnny Hyland to Checkmate's trainer, James Rowe.

"Jimmy is a strong boy," was Rowe's nonchalant reply.

Jimmy was a big boy, too, and he had to lose 17 pounds to ride Bob Miles in the 1885 Kentucky Derby, which was contested under "Southern weights" of 110 pounds. He finished out of the money as Murphy won with Buchanan.

As riders often do, McLaughlin lost his battle with weight. Although he attempted several comebacks, finally he had to abandon his career at thirty-one. He then became a racing official.

Whether McLaughlin personally selected his own son-in-law is not known, but his daughter later married Tommy Burns, who had broken in as a true "boy" at 75 pounds, and never went much beyond 100 at maturity. Burns was leading jockey for the 1898 and 1899 seasons, and later went to Germany. He was killed in an elevated train accident shortly after his return from Europe.

Overlapping the latter parts of Murphy's and McLaughlin's careers were those of the two great whipping masters, Fred Taral (1867-1925) and "Snapper" Garrison.

The hatred held for Taral by his most famous mount, Domino, because of the furious whippings the colt received already has been mentioned. Besides Domino's conquests, the slashing Taral won the Kentucky Derby with Manuel in 1899, the Preakness twice in succession with Assignee and Belmar in 1894-1895, and the Belmont Stakes, also with Belmar.

The three-year-old classics which now constitute the Triple Crown were of very modest value in Taral's day and his most noteworthy feat was winning the far richer Handicap Triple in 1894 with Dr. Rice in the Brooklyn Handicap, and Ramapo in the Metropolitan and Suburban. He rode Hamburg in that colt's spectacular victory as a two-year-old under 135 pounds in the Great Eastern Handicap. A real workhorse, Taral accepted approximately 5,000 mounts during his American career, an amazing number at the time, and he won more than 1,000 races.

Described as "a strongly built little man, with a cheerful face and honest blue eyes corroborative of the character his performances in the saddle have earned for him—that he always rides as straight as a string," the demon Dutchman pulled down $12,000 a year from Walcott and Campbell for first call, and an additional $8,000 from the Keenes for second call. He needed it. Taral was a great pal of former heavyweight champion, John L. Sullivan, and the pair were known as "Big and Little Casino."

When the fashion among American jockeys for riding in Europe was in full swing, Taral went to Germany and was a successful jockey in that country, and later a trainer, until World War I.

It was not so much the races he won as how he won them that brought Edward "Snapper" Garrison (1868-1930) his great fame. His ability to come from behind and snatch victory in the last jump made his name a household word and the term "Garrison finish" a part of racing's vocabulary. Since he did not win as frequently as Taral in the great events which have survived to this day, Garrison's name doesn't show up often in modern tabulations, but he did win one Belmont with Foxford, a Realization with Tammany, and two Suburbans, with Raceland and Montana. He rode the great mare Firenzi to several notable triumphs, and there was his victory on Boundless in the richest American Derby.

Tall and trim in his well-cut clothes with field glasses casually slung over a shoulder, Garrison appeared to be a college student or young man about town when he arrived at the

Fred Taral.

Edward H. "Snapper" Garrison.

track, but he underwent metamorphosis when he donned silk. Despite his long legs, he rode with a very short stirrup, and curled over until he resembled a hunchback. "Gripping the horse tightly with his knees, and working hands and body in unison with the motion of the animal, he . . . seems literally to lift his mount and shove it along by sheer nervous strength," was the way one reporter described his style.

Garrison also waged a constant war with weight, but he didn't have to struggle too hard. When he announced he no longer would accept mounts at less than 115 pounds, Marcus Daly still kept him on retainer at $15,000 a year. Garrison also followed McLaughlin's example by becoming a racing official after retirement; he was an owner and trainer, too.

That Garrison should lend his name to racing's vocabulary is especially appropriate, since both he and McLaughlin were protegés of "Father Bill" Daly, a trainer who became more famous for developing jockeys than horses.

William C. Daly (1837-1931) was a native of County Cork who came to America as a boy of seven; he lost a leg while working in a stone quarry near Hartford, Connecticut, and became a bartender until he saved enough to buy a horse. He began as a driver of trotters, but shifted to thoroughbreds and his first star jockey dropped into his lap, literally, as Mrs. Daly had picked up McLaughlin as a waif. (Garrison was an equally easy discovery, for he came from nearby New Haven.)

Daly also turned out such other renowned riders as Winnie O'Connor, Danny Maher, Harry Griffin, Patsy McDermott, the Lamley brothers, Johnny Daly and "Daredevil" Fitzpatrick.

Daly was very strict, and had a reputation in some quarters as a bit of an eccentric; he also was in hot water with the stewards on occasion, but in bringing along riding talent he had no equal.

The gayest figure on the American racing scene during the Gay Nineties was James Todhunter Sloan (1874-1933). What he lacked in

"Father Bill" Daly, the trainer who specialized in developing jockeys.

verted into "Tod" and the boy himself later added the sonorous decoration when he entered public life.

Although he had two older brothers who were jockeys, Tod Sloan's entry into public life was as assistant to a balloonist at county fairs; however, when he didn't rise in this profession as quickly as he had anticipated, Tod followed the advice of his brother Cassius ("Cash") and went to the racetracks. From the very beginning, the youngest Sloan seemed to appreciate that he was someone special, insisting on going it alone as soon as he could and refusing to accept the security of a contract employer. In later years he would accept "commitments," provided the fee was sufficient, but he never allowed himself to be tied down in the customary manner. He was the first jockey known to have demanded—and received—a percentage of the purse in addition to his regular riding fee.

Because of his abnormally short legs, Sloan rode in a high crouch; the "monkey-on-a-stick" style was his trademark. This in itself would have been sufficient to gain him a certain amount of passing notoriety, but it was genuine ability which earned him lasting fame. Sloan had an amazing sense of pace and was daring to the extreme. His arrogant airs so annoyed rival jockeys they sometimes deliberately plotted against him, but Sloan never was intimidated.

He was as much a prima donna as any of the great figures of the theatre with whom he loved to associate. During his periods of affluence, Todhunter was accompanied by a personal valet and several trunkloads of clothes wherever he traveled, and a contemporary rider of Sloan's, A. W. Booker, says that he affected a clean change of linen between races. Booker also remembers Sloan striding into the Grand Union Hotel at Saratoga demanding the finest accommodations in the house. When told that the premier suite had been reserved by J. R. Keene (who, off and on, was Sloan's employer) the breezy little jockey put his size-two foot

size he more than compensated for in grandiose behavior; he was as famous off the track as he was on, nor was his fame confined merely to one country. The dandy little jockey hobnobbed with such glittering personalities as Diamond Jim Brady and Lillian Russell on this side of the Atlantic, and on the other side was at one time personal jockey to the Prince of Wales. (He also mingled with gamblers, and, although he didn't exactly get himself ruled off the English turf, he was unofficially notified that his jockey's license would never be renewed.)

Sloan's middle name is a commentary of a sort on his irrepressible personality. As a child in Bunker Hill, Indiana, he was nicknamed "Toad" because of his small size; this was con-

Tod Sloan in his dandy days.

Tod Sloan (center) in his later years, with actors Buster Keaton (left) and Harold Lloyd at Tijuana.

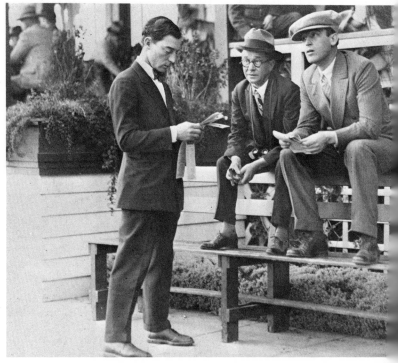

down. He calmly ensconced himself in the suite and notified the hotel clerk that Keene could seek other lodging when he arrived.

Regardless of his unusual seat, and his off-track monkey business, Sloan's eccentricities did not impair the talent he had for peak performance, although he was, if possible, even more flamboyant in the saddle. Because of his travels back and forth across the Atlantic, his American record on the bare face of it is not all it could have been, but he did win the Futurity, the Brooklyn Handicap and the

Lawrence Realization over here, and the 1,000 Guineas, Ascot Gold Cup and other important races in England. In 1898 he rode 166 winners from 362 mounts for a phenomenal 46 percent average. He had a perfect five-for-five day at Gravesend on May 28 that year, and the following season, in a triumphant appearance at the Ingleside Track in California, he announced to local newspaper reporters that he would duplicate this feat. The local jockeys resolved to take him down a peg or two, but on March 21, 1899, Sloan accepted five mounts and won five races. When California turf writers ridiculed his fastidiousness and accused him of being afraid to ride in the mud, he challenged a group of them to name the day. They did, and Sloan rode the entire program on a muddy track; he won three races and was second in the other three—after which he resumed his policy of riding mostly on dry tracks. After retiring as a rider, Sloan tried his hand at training, but when World War I broke out he was asked to leave England as an "undesirable alien."

Perpetually enamored of the theatrical world, he was married twice, both times to actresses. He became a bookmaker, and when that was outlawed he went into vaudeville and took a few bit parts in movies. His progress after the war was, in general, downhill.

Although he maintained contact with racing, it was largely through the generosity of friends, and his last official recognition came a year before he died when Sloan was arrested for violating anti-gambling laws. As a stunt, he had acted as starter for a turtle race.

Trainers, too, emerged as personalities in their own right during the last half of the nineteenth century, although, because their work was performed more in the background, they did not receive the wild adulation that was accorded jockeys.

Many of them, such as David McDaniel, John Harper, the McClelland brothers (Byron, J. W. and Wallace), T. G. Moore, E. V. Snedeker, Green B. Morris and John E. Madden would have been well known in any case as owners. Others, such as Ed Corrigan, were primarily owners who trained a little on the side. Still others represented various mixtures between the outright owner and the professional trainer: John Rogers, Jacob Pincus, James Rowe, Ed Brown, R. Wyndham Walden, Thomas J. Healey, Billy Lakeland, A. J. Joyner, J. J. Hyland, Sam Hildreth, William Preston Burch and Henry McDaniel. A number of them, notably Hildreth, Rowe and Lakeland, also had been jockeys.

Most successful of these men, by his own reckoning, was R. W. Walden, who, in the years 1872-1898, trained 200 individual winners of $1,367,796.50. The huge stable of J. A. and A. H. Morris provided the biggest entry on his tally sheet, 75 winners of $710,333.50, including Russell, Reckon, St. Florian, Correction, The Friar and Mars. That, plus the previously described stable of George Lorillard (50 winners of $452,267) was enough to put Walden over the million-dollar mark, and he also had an impressive record in his own name and with horses of a few miscellaneous clients.

While several of the foregoing trainers had completed their careers by the Gay Nineties, many of them were just starting out or only then getting into full stride; they will turn up later in history.

Representative of the noted owner–trainers whose careers straddled the turn of the century was Green B. Morris (1837-1920), a calm, gentle soul, whose turf activity extended over a long period of time and a vast quantity of geography.

Not related—by a long shot—to the wealthy Eastern family of the same name, Green Morris was a poor Mississippi country boy who moved to Missouri at an early age, and received his professional groundwork as a bullwhacker and driver of prairie schooners in the wagon trains to California. Because he had to earn his capital bit by bit, he was a relatively senior citizen when he first appeared in thoroughbred records, as owner and trainer of a mare named Zuzu at Mobile in 1869, but he quickly compensated for his late start. Racing at times in partnerships—James D. Patton of Missouri and James B. Haggin were his two best known partners—and at times on his own, Morris was a familiar, and extremely popular figure from coast to coast.

In 1882 he saddled Apollo for an historic upset in the Kentucky Derby over the heavy favorite, Runnymede, owned by Morris's good friends, the Dwyer brothers. (There were three kinds of betting available: Apollo, lumped with seven other runners in the "field" was 6-to-1 in the auction pools, but was on his own at 10-to-1 in the books and 33-to-1 in the mutuels. The short price they offered testifies to the respect bookmakers had for Morris, who was a formidable gambler despite his mild disposition.)

The next season Morris sent out runner-up Drake Carter (that was the year the winner, Chinn and Morgan's Leonatus, tried to eat the Derby roses) and in 1885 the Morris-Patton stable finished second again with Bersan, "the Horned Horse," so called because of unusual bony protrusions over his eyes. Favor, their only other Derby starter, was fourth in this same race.

Sir Dixon, the star two-year-old of 1887 which Morris sold to the Dwyer brothers the following year—or, rather, which Mike Dwyer took from him in exchange for $20,000, as has been related—was the most brilliant horse Morris ever owned. However, his greatest breadwinner was Strathmeath, winner of numerous stakes, who retired after 133 starts with 59 wins, 33 seconds, 19 thirds and $114,958.

Strathmeath's most notable victory, in the 1891 American Derby, was generally attributed to his trainer's painstaking methods. Washington Park had been hit by heavy rains the night before, and Morris took jockey George Covington on a complete inspection tour of the 1⅛-mile track just before the race. Covington's next trip around, on Strathmeath's back, was much quicker, as he steered the gelding in and out to avoid soft spots, and won by two lengths.

Strathmeath was later ridden in a greatly publicized race by Covington's brother, "Little Major" Covington, who weighed only 50 pounds, give or take a couple of ounces for meals. His petite physique and cherubic countenance notwithstanding, the Major was not altogether a doll. In the 1892 Labor Day Handicap at Sheepshead Bay, the crowd became enraged as Snapper Garrison, the big bully, riding Marcus Daly's Montana, apparently crowded Major Covington and Strathmeath onto the rail. However, although he won by a nose, it was Garrison who stormed into the stewards' stand after the race and complained that the Little Major had been tugging on Montana's bridle all during the last furlong. His accusations were labelled "wild" and "ridiculous," as it was believed no jockey, let alone Covington, could handle two horses in the heat of a stretch drive, and, moreover, if such tactics were attempted they would be glaringly obvious to officials and spectators alike. Subsequent history and the film patrol proved otherwise, and in his small way the Major apparently was a pioneer of a sort.

Strathmeath figured in yet another incident, which also illustrated the affection in which his owner was held. In 1894 he ran a dead heat with Mike Dwyer's Don Alonzo in a handicap on which Dwyer had bet $10,000 at 1-to-2. Under the rules, either owner could demand a run-off, or they could let the result stand, in which case all wagers would be divided 50-50 between bettor and book, as has been explained. Dwyer, who under this arrangement would get back only $7,500 of the $10,000 he put up, demanded a run-off; Morris, insisting that his faithful old six-year-old should not be subjected to further effort, refused, and quietly instructed the groom to return Strathmeath to his barn. Dwyer then calmly swallowed his $2,500 loss and sent word to the stewards that a mutual "agreement" had been made to allow the dead heat to stand.

In partnership with Haggin, Morris owned Star Ruby, an elegantly-bred English son of Hampton–Ornament, which Haggin intended to put to stud. The horse was chiefly a sprinter, but to enhance his appeal as a stallion Haggin entered him in the 4-mile Thornton Stakes at the Bay District course in 1896. With no time for an orthodox preparation, Morris instructed his jockey carefully: as the only two other starters fought for the lead (which takes a lot out of a horse, regardless of how fast he's running) Star Ruby ambled languidly along

172

in the rear, at one point falling half a mile behind by some estimates. Then, in the last mile, still fresh as mint, Star Ruby ran his usual race—a sprint of 6 furlongs. Covering the last three-quarters of the marathon in 1:15, he went by the exhausted leaders with disdainful ease, as spectators rubbed their eyes in wonderment.

Other good horses owned and/or trained by Green B. Morris included the Brooklyn Handicap winner, Judge Morrow; Fellowplay, Knight Templar, Mintzer and Freeman.

In 1902, Morris broke the "millionaire's monopoly" by heading the owners' list. He had the leading money-winning stable at the Gravesend meeting and was runner-up to F. C. McLewee at Brighton Beach, while the same season, clear across the country, he also ranked second to the Burns and Waterhouse stable at the New California Jockey Club meeting. In addition, the 1902 Preakness was won by Old England, a colt bred by Haggin, but flying Morris's purple and white colors.

A very dignified, gracious looking man, Morris's appearance belied his lack of formal education and polish, but according to one anecdote, he barely could read. As the story goes, Morris and Bill Daly were talking with a group of friends one day when a Western Union boy rushed up with a telegram. Daly couldn't read it, but studied it a long time while everyone anxiously awaited announcement of the important news. Finally, he passed it along to Morris, saying, "Ain't it hell, Green? Here, you read it."

Morris studied the paper an even longer time before passing it back with the simple remark, "It sure is Bill, pure hell." The contents of the message are still unknown.

Another new-fangled contraption eventually ended Morris's long career, fifty-one years after he had saddled his first winner.

Having lost his last horse, a selling plater, and down on his luck, the eighty-three-year-old trainer still made the racing circuit, and one August evening, outside the gates of Saratoga, he was struck down by an automobile and died the next day of a punctured lung.

If one personality must be chosen as the embodiment of the spirit of the Gay Nineties, it's only fitting that it should be a lady. Her name was Imp.

The daughter of Wagner–Fondling, by Fonso, foaled in 1894, was bred and owned by D. R. Harness of Chillicothe, Ohio, and trained by C. E. Brossman. As a two-year-old she went through a fairly normal campaign, winning four of eleven starts, but the next season she became the talk of the nation by reason of starting in no less than 50 races. She won "only" 14, but was in the money 33 times.

Imp's early racing had been in the Midwest and in her four-year-old season she was shipped to New York for a crack at the big-name horses in the Suburban. Although she failed that time she returned the following year at five and won this great race, plus several others. (There was a long delay at the post for the 1899 Suburban and jockey Nash Turner relieved Imp of his weight part of the time by standing her near the rail and resting his foot on it.)

A solid black mare except for a white diamond between her eyes, Imp caught the public fancy by her courageous tilts against mere males, and every time she won, which was often, the band on the lawn struck up "My Coal-Black Lady," a popular tune of the period. Although the custom of having "days" for celebrities had not yet been established, the city of Chillicothe declared a public holiday when the "Coal Black Lady" returned home that autumn; there was a band, and a parade, headed by Imp and Pete Clay in the orange-and-black silks which had been famous since shortly after the Civil War, when the partnership of Harness and McConnell had raced such stars as Vauxhall, General Duke and Bayonet.

By the end of her illustrious career, Imp had started in 171 races. She won 62, was second in 35 and third in 29, for earnings of $70,119.

Her trainer, Charles Brossman, later became editorial writer for the *Thoroughbred Record*.

THE JOCKEY CLUB

Theodore Roosevelt recommended as the best formula for maintaining peace and order, "Speak softly and carry a big stick." The Jockey Club, which came into being seven years before the Rough Rider moved into the White House, subscribed to the same theory, with emphasis on the last clause. Under the circumstances, it had to.

Before the Gay Nineties, every race track in America operated under its own individual rules. Although there was a certain amount of reciprocity among tracks concerning serious rule violators who were completely banished from the sport, not many bothered to keep tabs on minor offenders, and a person suspended by one association could merely transfer to another track, sometimes within the same city, and duck the punishment. Moreover, each track could decide its own racing dates, and simultaneous meetings in the same area, destructive to all parties concerned, were fairly common.

The forfeit list was another headache. Following the English system, horses nominated to sweepstakes remained eligible unless declared out, and when the race finally was run,

Imp, the "Coal Black Lady," winner of 62 races and darling of racing fans during the Gay Nineties.

the owner was liable for various fees that had become due during the interval. Many owners reneged on payments, and in one instance the Futurity was actually worth only 60 percent of its ostensible value. Owners in arrears were barred from racing at the particular track involved, but often as not could continue racing elsewhere. (This problem does not exist today, as the American "installment plan" has replaced the old forfeit system. Horses are automatically struck out of engagements for sweepstakes unless the eligibility fees are paid in advance of various deadlines set forth in the conditions.)

Finally, there was the appalling confusion in the matter of names. Every horse of any pretension to quality had a regiment of namesakes tagging along after him—there were "Januses," "Eclipses," "Partners," "Messengers" and "Travellers" in profusion, of both sexes. The same lack of ingenuity was evident in the selection of more pedestrian titles, and historian Hervey counted 102 different females named "Fanny" this or that, and 139 "Johns," in the first two volumes of the *American Stud Book*.

Recognizing the need for some central authority, in 1890 Pierre Lorillard invited representatives of track management and stable owners to a dinner to discuss the problem, and the result was the formation the following year of the Board of Control, consisting of seven members: D. D. Withers (Monmouth), J. G. K. Lawrence (Sheepshead Bay), P. J. Dwyer (Gravesend), John A. Morris (Morris Park), and stable owners A. J. Cassatt, John Hunter and James Galway.

This organization was making some headway, but after a reduction in purses a few years later, a group of owners and trainers held a protest meeting at which it was agreed that the tracks were too heavily represented on the Board of Control. James R. Keene proposed a new organization, patterned after the English Jockey Club, which would be composed of men more interested in the sport in general

than in individual race meetings. In 1894, the Jockey Club, which absorbed the Board of Control, was incorporated. It consisted of fifty members and was managed by seven stewards: Hunter, Keene, August Belmont II, J. O. Donner, Dr. G. L. Knapp, Col. W. P. Thompson and F. K. Sturgis.

Hunter was the first chairman; he was succeeded the next year by Belmont, and there have been but four since: Sturgis (1924-1930), William Woodward (1930-1950), George D. Widener from 1950-1964, when he retired and was succeeded by Ogden Phipps.

The original Jockey Club ran the whole show, frequently with an iron hand. Combining legislative, executive and judicial functions, it wrote the rules of racing, enforced them and interpreted them as a court of last appeal. It also licensed jockeys and trainers, appointed officials, allotted racing dates, kept the forfeit list, and in 1896 took over publication of the *American Stud Book*.

Any track which refused to accept the Jockey Club's authority was classified as an "outlaw," and horses which ran there could not run at other tracks until reinstated by the Club. The list of outlaw horses on occasion would include more than 1,200 names.

It was an awesome concentration of power, and the Jockey Club wielded it with gusto. Many of its actions have been criticized, some with justification and some without. If at times the decisions of the old Club were arbitrary or harsh, such behavior was to some extent a reflection of the times. Conduct that would be considered outrageously high-handed by modern standards was the norm in many walks of life during those years—for example, a trainer who was dissatisfied with a jockey's performance was more apt to haul the boy into the tack room and apply a whip to the seat of his dissatisfaction than to register a formal complaint with officials. The men who founded the Jockey Club were giants of their day—in industry, finance, politics and sport— and they moved in keeping with their roles.

Over the years the power of the Jockey Club has been reduced gradually. As the state racing commissions, beginning with that in New York in 1895, came onto the scene, functions formerly performed by the Jockey Club have been taken over until the commissions write rules of racing, issue licenses, assign dates to tracks and act as courts of appeal from the decisions of track officials.

Yet the voice of the Jockey Club has gained correspondingly, and what it used to accomplish with its big stick it is able to accomplish by precept and example. Its advice is sought in practically all matters pertaining to the sport, and usually followed.

In this connection, it is significant that New York, where the Jockey Club headquarters are located, was the last state to take control of licensing. This came about in 1951 when Jules Fink, having been denied a license by the Jockey Club, successfully sued in civil court to have the decision set aside. The court held that authority to issue licenses should not be vested in an essentially private organization, and that the state racing commission, appointed by the governor, more properly should assume this province. Having won his case, Fink applied to the New York State Racing Commission for a license. It was refused.

Among the primary functions of the modern Jockey Club is maintenance of the *Stud Book,* the official registry of thoroughbreds and their names. No horse, regardless of alleged bloodlines, is considered a thoroughbred unless it is registered, and a complex system of checks and cross-checks is in effect to safeguard purity of the breed.

The Jockey Club also fostered the "Universal" system of horse identification, which is analogous to the fingerprint method of identifying human beings, and just as foolproof. Every horse has a "chestnut" (or "night-eye") on the inside of each leg, no two of which have been found to be exactly alike. Occasionally, the night-eye might be lacking, but that in itself is an identifying feature. Also,

in extremely rare cases two night-eyes might be so similar that the difference cannot be detected by the naked eye. However, the odds against the similar night-eyes being located on corresponding legs of different horses are pretty long; the odds against all four night-eyes being similar *and* located on corresponding legs are astronomical—there are no such animals.

The Jockey Club's School for racing officials, originated by Marshall Cassidy in the 1930s, provides a pool of qualified personnel from which race tracks can make selections when vacancies occur.

Among numerous other services rendered by the organization, it administers racing colors for most states, acts as a clearing house for agency contracts, contingency agreements and similar matters, and maintains a breeding bureau at Avon, New York.

The original Jockey Club was limited to fifty members, nearly all of whom were New Yorkers and/or closely identified with New York racing. In addition, there was an unwritten law that no member be primarily dependent upon racing for his wealth; it was all right to own a large stable or breeding farm and include a race track or so among one's other holdings, but anyone connected with the sport in an essentially professional way apparently did not qualify for membership.

In modern times, this, too, was changed, and the composition of the Jockey Club became more realistic. Although it still is oriented predominately around New York, there is somewhat wider geographical representation among the members, and as racing grew bigger and more complicated, several professionals were added to the group.

THE SECOND BELMONT EMPIRE

August Belmont, Jr. (1853-1924) was thirty-seven years old when his father died, and up to that time his interest in racing had been relatively casual. The senior Belmont was survived by three sons and a daughter; Perry, the eldest son, was regarded as the horseman of the family, but August, Jr. was the one who kept the Belmont name alive.

Then, as now, race horses were regarded as fiduciary hot potatoes, and executors of the Belmont estate immediately ordered a dispersal of the stable and stud, which was accomplished in two stages: the yearlings and racing stock went on the block at the Nursery Stud in Babylon, Long Island, in December, 1890, about a month after Belmont's death; and the breeding stock was sold the next autumn at Tattersalls' arena in New York City. It was the largest dispersal on record to that time as the 131 horses in the two sales were auctioned for $639,500.

The season's leading money winner, Potomac, topped the first sale on a bid of $25,000 from Mike Dwyer, who said he didn't really want the colt but thought he was going too cheap. Potomac won $36,040 the next year before Dwyer sold him to S. Sanford & Sons, but he was by no means the best bargain of the sale. David Gideon paid $3,400 for a yearling, who turned out to be His Highness, winner of $106,900 as a two-year-old in 1891, to break the former record held by Potomac.

The highest bid at either sale was made by Charles Reed, who jumped auctioneer William Easton from $50,000 to $100,000 in one step to purchase the imported English stallion St. Blaise. Another buyer at the second sale was Colonel Jacob Ruppert, who paid $30,000 for a son of St. Blaise; however, the future owner of the Yankees struck out, for the colt started in only one race and ran unplaced.

St. Blaise—sire of Potomac and St. Leonards —was America's leading stallion at the time of his sale, and Reed stood and tipped his hat several times to the applause which followed his historic bid. The horse was a failure thereafter. Even his record price didn't survive very long, and it was only by a stroke of fate that Reed avoided involvement in that case.

Another breeder of transcontinental proportions during that period was William

O'Brien Macdonough, whose farm in Menlo Park, California, was near Leland Stanford's Palo Alto Stud. Although he bred his fair share of good ones, Macdonough unfortunately owes his niche in history to a monumental disappointment, which to some extent he brought upon himself. A young man of inherited wealth, in contrast to the majority of his colleagues in the West who had dug up their own fortunes, he was something of a dilettante, more inclined to the theoretical than the practical. (One of his close friends was the Australian bloodlines theorist, Bruce Lowe.) When it was announced that the undefeated English Triple Crown winner, Ormonde, was for sale, Macdonough evidently was most interested in obtaining the highest-priced animal in the world. The horse had been sent to Argentina, and in 1892 Charles Reed departed by steamer to look him over. Macdonough quickly negotiated a sale by cablegram for $150,000—topping Reed's record price for St. Blaise, and leaving that gentleman at sea. Before coming to North America, Ormonde was returned to England to be bred to some mares Macdonough owned there, so expenses of the transaction were increased another $20,000 or so.

Macdonough's farm was named Ormondale in honor of the great race horse who was to reside there, but after he finally was installed, Ormonde proved to be almost sterile. However, he did sire the Futurity winner Ormondale, as well as the good horses Ormonde's Right and Beau Ormonde, and his owner never complained about his misfortune. (One of the stallion's English sons, Orme, founded a great male line, and the bones of Ormonde himself were returned to England after his death.

Although both Perry and O. H. P. Belmont had made some purchases at the sale of their father's horses, August II (who discarded the "Jr." after the senior Belmont's death) was the biggest buyer among the brothers. He already had resolved to establish a second Nursery Stud.

Young Belmont received an immediate return on one of his investments, a filly he purchased for $11,000, Lady Violet, won six stakes as a two-year-old the next season.

The first true headliner he owned, though, was Hastings, whom he bought in 1895 from the partnership of Gideon and John Daly for $37,000, after the colt had shown considerable class at two. The next year, Hastings won the Belmont Stakes and Toboggan, and he developed into an outstanding handicap horse at four, although his temper was ferocious.

Belmont also bought Henry of Navarre as a four-year-old for $35,000 and owned him when he won the Suburban. Other successful horses he raced during his early turf years included Don de Oro, Margrave, Octagon and Firearm. However, Belmont went into temporary retirement following the death of his wife in 1898, and his horses ran in the name of trainer J. J. Hyland. For the moment, Belmont was preoccupied with other business. This preoccupation was to cost Belmont the best year of one of his best horses. Beldame, a daughter of Octagon foaled in 1901, was bred by Belmont, but in her two-year-old season she was leased to Newton Bennington. At three, she won twelve of fourteen starts, and the only horses which finished ahead of her were older males. On the other hand, besides dominating her own sex, she defeated males frequently, and all in all compiled an amazing record; Belmont had her back at four, but—required to make large weight concessions in some of her races—she only won twice. She retired with seventeen wins and $102,570.

Unlike his father, who might have been dashing in personality but was conservative in his approach to business, August II was a plunger who liked to get in on the ground floor, or, to be literal, under the ground. He is remembered in connection with subterranean projects, and he almost went under himself with the Cape Cod Canal in later years. However, at the turn of the century he was involved in the first subway system for New York City, and it was this interest which led him to take the track against W. C. Whitney.

CHAPTER THIRTY-FOUR

WHO AMONG THE MANY PILLARS of the American turf was the most influential, is a question that could be argued interminably, but few will dispute that no man exercised so profound an influence in so short a time as William Collins Whitney (1841–1904), who was directly associated with the turf for only six years.

Unlike his foe on the track and in Wall Street, James R. Keene, who had immigrated to America; and his business antagonist who later became his close friend, August Belmont, II, who was a first-generation American, W. C. Whitney was born into a family which had been established in this country for more than 200 years. His father, James Whitney of Conway, Massachusetts, was a member of the State House of Representatives from a solid, prosperous old New England family and William Collins, born in 1841, was raised in the Puritan tradition. He attended Williston Seminary, Yale, and later the Harvard Law School. At that time, there was no formal curriculum leading to a degree, and after leaving Harvard, Whitney read for the law in the office of Abraham Lawrence in New York City for a year, following which he was admitted to the bar. Three years later, he married Flora Payne, whose brother, Oliver Hazard Payne, had been one of his friends at Yale.

Whitney dove right into politics and compiled a distinguished record for exposing fraud and for bringing increased efficiency to various patronage-ridden agencies. He was instrumental in establishing full-time fire departments to replace the old volunteer companies,

which were organized more as distribution centers for political favor than for accomplishment of their mission; rival companies sometimes would argue over which had the right to put out a fire (and to loot the premises in the process) while the object of the dispute burned. Later, as corporation counsel of New York City, Whitney drew praise for his spirited defense of fraudulent claims against the city, which his predecessor had handled so sluggishly that the odds against New York City in any court suit were about 9-to-1. Whitney whipped things into a more reasonable line.

In the field of national politics, Whitney was the foremost supporter of Grover Cleveland, who was elected President in 1884. When Cleveland appointed Whitney Secretary of the Navy, it aroused criticism from Democrats and Republicans alike, since his father-in-law, Senator Henry B. Payne of Ohio, owned considerable stock in Standard Oil Company, but Whitney brought to his new post the same zeal for reform and efficiency that had characterized his earlier public service. He left the Navy Department in far better shape than he received it; even a Republican, T. B. Plumb of Kansas, praised Whitney's work in an address to the Senate.

As Cleveland was a bachelor when he took office, the Whitneys carried much of the official social load during the early years of his Administration. (When President Cleveland did marry, the bride, Frances Folsom, was a close friend of Mrs. Whitney and Whitney was best man at the wedding.) The Whitneys had five children: Harry Payne, William Payne (who later dropped the William), Pauline, Olive

William Collins Whitney (left) and trainer J. W. Rogers giving instructions to jockey Redfern.

(who died at an early age) and Dorothy. Diplomat John Hay, later to become Secretary of State in the Administration of McKinley and Theodore Roosevelt, and his wife were frequent guests of the family, and their daughter Helen subsequently married Payne Whitney.

Although Cleveland received a popular majority in the 1888 election, the electoral college vote went to Benjamin Harrison, and Whitney left public service for good. When Cleveland was returned to office four years later for the second half of his unique split tenure, Whitney was offered a position as Secretary of State or Ambassador to England, but he refused. He was embarked on an entirely new life.

In 1884, the year of Cleveland's first election, Whitney had become a director of the New York Cable Railway Company, in which he soon acquired a controlling interest. While he was in Washington, the business was left to

180

the capable ministrations of Thomas Fortune Ryan, one of the most awesome operators in the history of Wall Street. Having seen his family's small farm laid waste by the Civil War when he was a boy, Ryan, like Scarlett O'Hara, resolved never to go hungry again. In any case, when one of his friends said that Ryan would never be happy until he had cornered all the money in the world, Whitney replied that, if Ryan lived long enough, he would. Through a complicated series of mergers and capitalization schemes, in the course of which James R. Keene, for one, got his fingers burned to the extent of an estimated $5,000,000 (and which, years later, was the subject of an investigation by the New York Public Service Commission) the Whitney–Ryan combination acquired virtual control of surface transportation in New York City. In 1900, when August Belmont II espoused the subway system, there was reportedly a fierce battle between him and the Whitney–Ryan team. However, the rival companies eventually merged and the three men became friends.

Although he did not become actively identified with racing until he was fifty-seven years old, W. C. Whitney had shown an interest in horses throughout most of his life. He owned a number of trotters which he used for his private driving (and often as presents to friends); he served as Director of the National Horse Show; he had been one of the incorporators of the Jockey Club and an original member of the Turf & Field Club. When he came into racing, he did so at an all-out gallop. In the book, *The Spell of the Turf,* trainer Samuel C. Hildreth relates that Whitney abruptly approached him one afternoon in 1898 and asked him if he would train a stable of horses for him. When Hildreth inquired as to when Whitney would like an answer, the latter replied, "Now."

Whitney was connected with, and made money in, numerous other businesses, and the weight of these responsibilities, plus some personal cares, presumably is what caused him,

once he decided to enter racing, to do so with such intensity.

In 1893 Flora Payne Whitney had died and in 1896 Whitney was remarried, to Mrs. Edith S. Randolph, a widow. Although there had been an interval of more than three-and-a-half years since his sister's death, Oliver Hazard Payne looked upon the second marriage as disrespect for her memory. He severed relations with Whitney and urged the children to do the same. Payne was a bachelor and the Whitney children were his closest relatives; Payne also was one of the largest individual stockholders in Standard Oil and he threatened to cut off the children in his will if they stuck by their father. (There was no question of anybody starving to death under either arrangement, since both men were multimillionaires, but Payne's fortune was by far the larger.)

Harry Payne and Dorothy Whitney took their father's side in this clash, while Payne and Pauline aligned themselves with the uncle, although when Whitney first entered racing his horses ran in the colors of Sydney Paget, Pauline's husband. Whitney's own racing silks were acquired with characteristic conciseness. He took a liking to the colors of Englishman George Lambton, arranged to buy them on the spot, and the Eton blue jacket with brown cap have been prominent on the American turf ever since. In modern racing, these colors are borne by the stable of C. V. Whitney, grandson of the original American owner.

It is often said that money can't buy success, but in Whitney's case it certainly produced a reasonable facsimile. With Sam Hildreth as trainer and the astute John E. Madden as turf consultant, Whitney almost instantaneously reached the top in racing, although his financial returns didn't balance the expenditures. His first horses ran in Paget's name, as noted, but by 1900, when he began campaigning in his own name, Whitney's stable included fifty-five horses, divided into three divisions. In 1901 he led the winning owners in America with earnings of $108,440 (besides winning

181

the Epsom Derby with Volodyovski), and he was leader again in 1903 with $102,569. The first top year was achieved with horses he purchased, mostly from Madden or under his advice, but the 1903 stable included horses bred by Whitney at La Belle Stud in Kentucky, which he leased.

Among the performers owned by Whitney were Jean Beraud (Withers and Belmont), the steeplechaser Shillelah, Plaudit, Admiration, Kilmarnock, Ballyhoo Bey, Yankee, Endurance by Right, Blue Girl (leading money winner of 1901, $64,105), Nasturtium, Goldsmith, Morningside and King Hanover.

ENDURANCE BY RIGHT, 1899

(Inspector B.–Early Morn, by Silvester)

Endurance by Right was classified by Vosburgh as the "greatest two-year-old filly that has appeared within the past fifty years." She won 16 of 18 starts, never being defeated by a member of her own sex—and one of her losses was in the Flatbush Stakes which Whitney had elected to win with her stablemate, the colt Nasturtium. Endurance by Right began her career in the Midwest, and when she came East the Saratoga handicapper greeted her with 122 pounds for a race against both colts and fillies. She won. She also won the Great Eastern Handicap under 126 pounds and the Holly Handicap under 130, conceding 32 pounds to the minimum. For the White Plains Handicap, Endurance by Right was assigned 132 pounds, the highest ever for a two-year-old filly, but she did not run.

The metropolitan New York racing circuit reached its full development near the turn of the century. William H. Clark, a trotting enthusiast, had a track at Yonkers which primarily was intended for that form of sport, but after he won the 1899 Brooklyn Handicap with Banastar, he changed horses and requested dates for a thoroughbred meeting. Clark died before the track opened, but the meeting went off in 1900 under the direction of Phil Dwyer.

Except for sporadic trotting meets, the track was then idle for several years. In 1907, after the abandonment of Morris Park left Westchester County without a running horse track, James Butler purchased the property and Empire City, managed by Matt J. Winn, joined the big-time circuit. (Many years later, the track was to revert to its original purpose of harness racing, and today it is the site of Yonkers Raceway.)

As it became increasingly apparent that the best substitute for a key to the U. S. Mint was a race track on Long Island, in 1901 the Metropolitan Jockey Club was formed, W. H. Reynolds president, and two years later "the people's track" opened at Jamaica.

Although the original tracks on the island had been efficiency models, leaving embellishments to the Westchester tracks which catered to the carriage trade, Jamaica incorporated a number of luxury features. It boasted a grandstand with a seating capacity of 9,000 and a clubhouse with accommodations for 1,500, plus a huge dining room and a covered paddock. The track itself was 1 mile in circumference, shaped like a goose egg, with a sandy loam composition similar to Aqueduct's, which drained easily—it was quite common for races to be won in better time over a sloppy track than over a fast track.

Although Jamaica's esthetic pre-eminence lasted less than two years, throughout its existence it remained the people's track. Sportswriters of a later generation, after the track had piled up a lot of mileage, took to kicking it around like an old football, seldom referring to it without including such words as ramshackle or dilapidated, but even this abuse was administered in an affectionate manner. Racing fans treated it pretty much the same way. The Jamaica patron was a breed unto himself: a raucous, aggressive creature notorious for the audibility of his observations concerning horses, jockeys and racing officials. (Because of the peculiar shape of the track, the finish line was on a slant, and unless a horse won by five lengths or more, the official result invariably was greeted by howls of protest.)

However, the Jamaica fan also was intensely loyal, and year-in, year-out the track enjoyed higher attendance than its fancy new neighbor. That new neighbor was, of course, Belmont Park which made its grand entrance onto the racing scene in 1905.

It has already been related how the American Jockey Club, which included the most fashionable and wealthiest elements in racing, had moved its headquarters from Jerome Park to Morris Park in 1889.

That luxurious track had been "built to stand for a century," but it buckled under the strain of unfavorable legislation only seven years later, and in 1895 the New York Jockey Club, which had been holding the Morris Park meetings, was dissolved.

Headed by August Belmont II and James R. Keene, a new organization known as the Westchester Racing Association was formed, which leased Morris Park and conducted successful race meetings there. However, the insecurity of the lease arrangement, plus growing agitation to transfer operations to Long Island, led to a decision to build a new track. In 1904 the association purchased 650 acres at Queens, Long Island, and construction was begun on Belmont Park.

The huge track, named for the senior August Belmont, opened the following year with his son as president. It was by far the most magnificent establishment of its kind in America, with a 650-foot grandstand; an opulent clubhouse containing dining rooms, bedrooms and balconies; a truly functional administration building, and a separate turf and field club. In keeping with the magnitude of the place, the track itself was 1½ miles in circumference with a 7-furlong straightaway, and adjacent to it was a 1-mile training track.

The famous sweepstakes of Jerome Park and Morris Park, which over the years had acquired classic status, were transferred to Belmont, and on the gala opening day, May 4, 1905, Sysonby and Race King made the occasion especially historic by running a dead heat for the Metropolitan Handicap. (The first race that day was won by Blandy, owned by the track president.)

Belmont Park stands as a monument to a number of men. Vosburgh, who was the track's first handicapper, credits August Belmont II and James R. Keene with having spurred organization of the Westchester Racing Association; in his book *Giants of the Turf*, Dan Bowmar III lists Belmont, W. C. Whitney, Thomas Hitchcock, E. D. Morgan and J. P. Morgan as the principal moving spirits behind construction of Belmont Park.

That this elegant racing plant came into being at all is a testimony to the love for racing held by these gentlemen, since the combination of Belmont, Keene, and Whitney was otherwise more naturally suited to production of a Tower of Babel.

It's doubtful that any of the numerous horses he owned furnished Whitney more satisfaction than Ballyhoo Bey, who in 1900 performed a notable "Horatio at the Bridge" feat, then did an encore.

In Commando, James R. Keene obviously owned the best two-year-old of the season, but he had neglected to keep him eligible to the rich Futurity because Commando had been so unimpressive looking as a weanling. However, Keene did have a potent entry of Olympian, Cap and Bells, and Tommy Atkins deputizing for him, and they went off as 7-to-10 favorite.

Against them Whitney had Elkhorn and Ballyhoo Bey, the latter a pet of his although still a maiden. (After the colt failed to win his first start, Hildreth had been replaced by Madden as trainer.) Ballyhoo Bey, with his maiden allowance, was in the Futurity at only 112 pounds against 129 on prestige-laden Tommy Atkins. However, Whitney had persuaded Tod Sloan to come back from England to ride the colt, and that did the trick.

Winnie O'Connor, Milton Henry and Harry Spencer, riders of the Keene horses, plotted to trap Sloan, but the little jockey made amateurs of them as he won by one and a half lengths.

The shoe was on the other foot a week later when Ballyhoo Bey had to concede 5 pounds to Tommy Atkins in the Flatbush Stakes—but Sloan was on the same colt. Again there was a concentrated effort to box Sloan in, and this time a considerable amount of rough contact ensued, but Ballyhoo Bey won by a head from Atkins and Spencer. After the race every jockey was hauled before the stewards.

Spencer—known as "the Iceman"—was hot enough on this occasion, and he accused Sloan of a deliberate foul, but the stewards allowed the result to stand. Foxhall Keene, stating that ·the whole affair was "robbery arranged," threatened to boycott the Coney Island Jockey Club forever, but before he could scratch any entries, Spencer had ridden Voter to victory in the Ocean Stakes, the very next race on the program, as Sloan finished out of the money on Whitney's Rush, which caused Keene to cool out considerably.

Whitney later offered a return race under Flatbush conditions but it never materialized. For one thing, Ballyhoo Bey was so injured that it was not feasible. To add an ironic twist to the affair, the two times he bristled Keene's beard were the only races Ballyhoo Bey ever won. Moreover, he was a son of Kingston, the great horse which Keene had bred but sold, and which had haunted him before.

Whitney didn't get to see the Futurity, as he was en route from England at the time. Nevertheless, in a gesture of sublime confidence (Ballyhoo Bey was a maiden, remember) he consulted with the navigator as to what time by the ship's clock the Futurity would be contested in New York. It turned out to be shortly before 7:00 P.M. Whitney arranged for a banquet at that hour, at which guests were asked to join a toast to Ballyhoo Bey, "the winner of the Futurity," following which Whitney made a speech of acknowledgement.

As August Belmont had died on the crest of the wave—in a year when his stable set a new

earnings record, and a colt of his breeding scored a notable victory in the Futurity, richest race in history—so it was with William Collins Whitney, who died early in February 1904. His stable had led the list in the recently completed 1903 season, and in the year of his death it set a new earnings record, although the horses were leased to Herman B. Duryea and raced in his name. Also, a filly bred by Whitney won the 1904 Futurity, not so rich as it had been in Potomac's year, but her victory, if anything, turned out to be even more notable: Artful was her name, and she administered the only defeat of his career to James R. Keene's mighty Sysonby—a final post-mortem shot in the rivalry between the two turf titans.

From his brief formal connection with the sport, Whitney left a remarkable legacy: a first-rank racing stable and stud, revitalization of Saratoga, participation in the Jockey Club and construction of Belmont Park, and—most important of all—establishment of a family tradition that has been maintained on both sides of the Atlantic by his children and grandchildren.

The elder of Whitney's sons did not step into his father's shoes in the ordinary meaning of that expression. Harry Payne Whitney (1872–1930) had been wearing a fairly sturdy pair of his own for several years before he took title to the family heritage. In partnership with Duryea, and under the wing of Madden, he had owned the good colt, Irish Lad, in 1902. An all-around sportsman, prominent in yachting and polo, he had married the well-known sculptress Gertrude Vanderbilt in 1896, which represented a merger between two great American racing families.

Harry Payne Whitney, thirty-three years old when his father died, had been a Phi Beta Kappa at Yale, and already had shown considerable business acumen. He had amassed a tidy fortune of his own, and any doubt that he intended to carry on in racing was dissipated at the auction of his father's thoroughbred stock in October of 1904. Hamburg, who had been purchased by W. C. Whitney for $60,000 at

Artful, the filly who inflicted the only defeat of his career on Sysonby.

the Marcus Daly dispersal, elicited an offer of that same sum from Milton Young, the bidding having gone up at $10,000 a crack. Whitney quickly jumped it another $10,000, and the stallion was his for $70,000. He also purchased sixteen mares and another stallion, for total expenditures of $183,900.

At the dispersal of the racing stable, Whitney bought several more horses, including Artful and Tanya. After her Futurity victory, Artful had achieved further recognition by setting a new American record of 1:08 for 6 furlongs on the Morris Park straightaway while carrying 130 pounds—and Artful was the only reason Tanya wasn't hailed as the best filly in America.

As a three-year-old Artful made three starts for her new owner without being defeated, after which the daughter of Hamburg was retired to stud with six wins and two seconds (both times to a stablemate) in eight starts, for earnings of $81,125. Tanya that year won the Belmont Stakes and ran second to Sysonby in the Lawrence Realization.

In 1905, the first year Whitney raced a full stable in his own name, he topped his father's best season by winning $170,447. Besides the two fillies, the stable included a huge 1,300-pound son of Hamburg named Burgomaster, who won a number of stakes and followed in the hoofprints of his sire by winning the Great Eastern Handicap under a healthy package, 130 pounds. Burgomaster the next season gave Whitney his second Belmont Stakes in two tries.

The stable was eminently successful during these early years—with such other stars as Perverse, Stamina, Dinna Ken and Baby Wolf —but Whitney had to wait a long time before his name appeared in first place on the money-winning list. Along with every other owner of a stakes horse during this period, he suffered from spots before his eyes. The spots were blue ones on a white jacket, carried by the horses of James R. Keene.

Mr. Keene cleaned house in the early twentieth century, as the racing scene became what his son described as a parade of galloping Dominoes. Although he had not himself been successful at more than 9 furlongs, there was nothing in Domino's appearance which suggested the "pure sprinting" type. He was powerfully developed, but leggy, not of the blocky construction which usually denotes a strictly short-running horse; he had a fine profile and the nicely tapered barrel often found in stayers. His limitation as to distance evidently was more mental than physical in origin: he simply could not be persuaded to nurse his blazing speed.

This theory was borne out by his previously mentioned son, Commando, who followed up his championship two-year-old season by winning the Belmont Stakes in 1901. Although the race was then only 1⅜ miles, a furlong shorter than it later became, it was nevertheless a test of stamina. Also, that same year, Foxhall Keene took Domino's daughter, Cap and Bells, to England, where she won the Oaks over the full 1½ miles by ten lengths.

All the Keenes' horses did not have Domino blood, however, and one of the exceptions was Sysonby—rated by a veteran turf writer, Neil Newman, as among the three greatest thoroughbreds he had seen in a career that encompassed forty-seven years.

SYSONBY, 1902
(Melton–Optime, by Orme)

Having bought Sysonby's dam, in foal, at the dispersal of Marcus Daly's stock, Keene was therefore the colt's official breeder of record. However, Foxhall Keene (who named the horse after his favorite hunting lodge) states in his memoirs that his father wanted to sell Sysonby as a yearling, but he talked him out of it. The future champion ran into another possible stumbling block when Keene wanted to send him to England, but trainer James Rowe wrapped the colt in a blanket and pretended he was too sick to travel.

Sysonby stayed home—but he traveled in style. He romped through four straight races

186

Sysonby, whose entire career was marked by odd twists of fate.

before Artful beat him in the Futurity, which was not a true bill according to Foxhall Keene, who testified that Sysonby had been doped and a groom had confessed to the deed.

On only one other occasion did a rival extend Sysonby: his debut as a three-year-old when Race King ran him to a dead heat in the 1-mile Metropolitan Handicap on opening day at Belmont Park. To say it was a moral victory for Sysonby would be an understatement. The massive bay had not raced for seven and a half months, while for Race King it was the seventh start of the season. Three-year-old Sysonby carried 107 pounds, against 97 on his four-year-old opponent, which in May amounted to a 30-pound concession on the scale.

In his first experience at a distance greater than 6 furlongs, Sysonby grabbed the lead and, despite his long layoff, held on well enough to avoid defeat as Race King nailed him right on the post. The excellent filly, Colonial Girl, was five lengths back. The fractions tell the story —:24⅗, 49⅗, 1:14⅗ and 1:41⅗. Sysonby was dead tired, but dead game in that final quarter.

Thereafter the only excitement he provided, other than the visual pleasure of watching his enormous stride gobble up ground, was in the Great Republic Stakes at Saratoga, when he was left at the post. The field—and a good one it was—ran about 100 yards ahead before Sysonby finally took off, but, as Vosburgh described it, ". . . overhauling them at every stride, he was with them at the end of the first quarter of a mile. The next instant he was in the lead. People shook their heads. 'The effort was too great; he'll stop,' they said. But no; he drew away; Oiseau and Broomstick were racing for their very lives, but the great powerful strides of Sysonby kept him in the lead, and he won, amid a scene such as has seldom been witnessed at the historic ground . . ."

Sysonby closed out his campaign by beating the same two rivals in the 2¼-mile Annual Champion Stakes, winning by four lengths "with a stride as regular and seemingly as powerful as the piston-rod of a locomotive . . ." That was his average victory margin, for except in his races against Artful and Race King, he invariably had daylight showing behind him at the finish.

Broomstick came near being a stablemate of Sysonby. Keene had owned his dam, but sold her to Milton Young under the impression she was barren. The next year, she foaled Broomstick, who, like his sire, Ben Brush, was a hard little horse to beat. Racing for Captain S. S. Brown, he set an American record of 2:02⅘ for 1¼ miles, and upon his retirement to stud became a tremendously successful sire for H. P. Whitney—another trick of Fate on Keene, especially in view of what happened to Sysonby.

Sysonby went into winter quarters as the toast of the turf, but he never came out again. He contracted a mysterious skin ailment, and

in June, 1906, he died in his stall at Sheepshead Bay of septic poisoning. He was buried at the track the next day—with more than 4,000 spectators in attendance—but his bones later were exhumed and articulated; they now are on exhibit at the Museum of Natural History.

Besides those already mentioned, there were numerous other good horses when the twentieth century was coming away from the starting barrier—Advance Guard (the "Iron Horse" who won 48 of 162 races), Africander (Belmont Stakes; first three-year-old to win the Suburban), Laureate, McChesney, Keene's own Delhi (Belmont Stakes), Waterboy (who was in slings for three months because of a dislocated hip, but made a successful comeback), The Picket, Hamburg Belle (Futurity), Dandelion, Mohawk; the full brothers Dick Welles, Ort Wells and Dick Finnell; Hermis, Running Water, Jack Atkin (who won with 140 pounds up, conceding 47 to the runner-up), and many others. One in particular, who shone brightly during Belmont Park's first year of operation and for several seasons thereafter, was D. C. Johnson's awesome sprinter, Roseben.

It is often said, quite accurately, that weight can stop a freight train, but it took a lot of weight to stop "The Big Train" himself, Roseben. This gelded son of Ben Strome derived his name from his size—he lacked only an inch of standing 18 hands—and his blazing speed, similar to that displayed by the other famous "Big Train," baseball pitcher Walter Johnson, who came along a couple of years later.

Roseben, foaled in 1901, was a four-year-old when he won the transplanted Toboggan Handicap at Belmont's inaugural spring meeting, and he returned that autumn to win the Manhattan Handicap, 6 furlongs in 1:11⅗, while carrying 147 pounds. He conceded 42 pounds to the runner-up, the three-year-old Aeronaut.

In addition to these stakes, Roseben won a number of overnight races under 140 pounds. The art of handicapping was then in full flower, and there was a version of all-age con-

Roseben, the "Big Train," who won several times while carrying 147 pounds and whose record of 1:22 for seven furlongs stood for decades.

tests in vogue, wherein weights were assigned the day before the race and the owner was allowed one hour to decide whether to take it or leave it.

In 1906, for example, his owner took 144 pounds for a race on September 14 and Roseben won it. He took 150 pounds for another race four days later and the horse finished second. On October 12 Roseben repeated his Manhattan Handicap victory, under an identical 147 pounds, winning easily by six lengths. Four days after that, in an allowance race at Belmont Park, he got in with a mere 126 pounds and set an American record of 1:22 for 7 furlongs, clicking off fractions of :23$\frac{4}{5}$, :44$\frac{4}{5}$ and 1:10$\frac{2}{5}$ en route.

On November 5 at Aqueduct, the huge gelding for the third time packed 147 pounds to victory at 6 furlongs (conceding 57 pounds to the runner-up) and a week later he won the 7-furlong Bayview Handicap in the mud, under a 146-pound impost.

Again, as a six-year-old on July 17, 1907, at Brighton Beach, Roseben was assigned 147 pounds. Trying for his fourth victory under such a burden, he covered the 6 furlongs in 1:12$\frac{1}{5}$—and once more the Big Train rolled in on time.

Roseben roared across the pages of racing history for several seasons. Seven furlongs was about as far as he could go, but on those short hauls he could deliver enormous loads. When he finally retired, he had started in 111 races, of which he won 52, was second in 25 and third in 12 for earnings of $74,910.

It was nearly thirty years before Roseben's 1:22 American record for 7 furlongs was equaled by Clang at Arlington Park in 1935, and another dozen years passed before Honeymoon broke the record, at Hollywood Park. Roseben's mark still survived as the Belmont Park track record until Bold Ruler erased it in 1957, more than half a century later.

Besides those heavy weights, the Big Train carried a lot of responsibility. Dave Johnson was once asked how much he customarily bet on his horse. The owner of Roseben, who appeared startled by such a superfluous question, replied simply: "Whatever I have."

The numerous other good horses notwithstanding in the first decade of the twentieth century, there still was no getting away from the spots on the Dominoes.

The Keene stable led the winning owners for four successive seasons, 1905-1908, setting two earnings records in the process, $228,724 in 1905 and $397,342 in 1907.

A. H. Morris (left), Robert Walden (center) and T. J. Healey.

Commando's second crop of foals, which came racing in 1906, included Peter Pan and Superman, and the stable had another top two-year-old that season in Ballot, a son of Voter. Between races, Rowe would exhibit them to an admiring audience. On the distaff side, there was Court Dress, a daughter of Domino's other son, Disguise, who had five wins and a second in six races at two. Commando, as had Domino, died prematurely, after having sired only twenty-seven foals, but the line went on.

Peter Pan verified his sire's performance at three by also winning the Belmont, and stepping on his heels was the next year's crop of Commandos—which included Peter Quince, Celt and the mightiest of them all, Colin.

COLIN, 1905

(Commando–Pastorella, by Springfield)

It has been recorded that turf writer Neil Newman ranked Sysonby among the three best colts he ever had seen. The other two were Man o' War and Colin.

Colin, like Sysonby, started only 15 times before his racing career came to an untimely end, but unlike Sysonby, Colin never lost a race. He swept through twelve races as a two-year-old, winning them all in the clear except the Eclipse Stakes, in which Beaucoup was second by a head. Colin had bucked shins, but won nevertheless. At three, he started only three times. He beat Fair Play and King James with ease in the Withers, then came another close call in the Belmont Stakes, when Fair Play ran him to a neck. This time, too, there were reasons: Colin had come back gimpy from a preparatory work, and there had been a question whether he would run at all; when he did run, it was not under optimum conditions.

"Weather bad; track sloppy," was the succinct description in the official chart, but according to a more detailed narrative, there was a blinding rainstorm in progress when the horses came onto the track, and portions of the race could not be seen (no time was taken).

"A furlong from the home turn the field came into view again," said a contemporary account, which continued:

. . . Colin was seen to be in the lead by several lengths. He was apparently outrunning the others and very easily . . .

Robert Cooper was hopelessly beaten and King James was lengths back of Fair Play, but coming to the home turn Fair Play began to close on Colin . . .

Would Colin stick that last trying furlong? . . . Fair Play kept creeping up on the

Colin, undefeated winner of 15 races, at exercise under Marshall Lilly (who always wore a derby at work).

outside, but Colin came again and hung on with wonderful gameness and endurance.

The finish for the Belmont Stakes is below the judges' stand . . . The great crowd did not know this, and when Colin reached the usual finishing point he was well in front of Fair Play. It thought the race was over . . .

The race was not over. There still remained a desperate struggle of fifty yards between Colin and Fair Play. Notter himself did not remember the proper finish and it was a far closer thing at the real point than at the judges' stand. But Fair Play was thoroughly beaten and Colin was almost out himself . . .

Apart from the unusual, 1⅜-mile distance of this event, until 1920 racing at Belmont Park was in a clockwise direction, opposite to the pattern at other American tracks.

Goodwin's official chart also states, "Notter nearly lost the race by mistaking the finishing line and pulling up," but Colin's jockey denied this accusation and said that the colt was slowing down because his leg hurt. Colin stated once more, in the Tidal Stakes three weeks later, which he won easily. He was then sent to England, but the leg went wrong, and he raced no more.

How good was Colin? On the record, it is hard to say, especially since the colt most capable of testing him happened to be his stablemate, Celt (who was sparingly but successfully campaigned while Colin was active). On the other hand, those who saw Colin run could never forget him. Colonel Phil T. Chinn, whose experience covered some seventy years and many good horses, from Salvator through Kelso, steadfastly maintained that Colin never had an equal. Chinn chaperoned the horse on his trip to England, and, to him, the clincher was the evaluation of Colin by the noted English trainer, Sam Darling: the highest tried horse he had ever seen.

191

The boy who rode Colin in the majority of his races was no less sensational than his mount, and his, too, was a meteoric career: brief, but brilliant.

Walter Miller first appeared in the official jockey standings as a fifteen-year-old in 1905, when he was credited with 176 winners. The following season he breezed past the hitherto mythical goal of 300 winners with scarcely a glance—by the end of the year he had won the fantastic total of 388 races.

The youthful jockey accepted 1,348 mounts during his record-breaking season, and the next

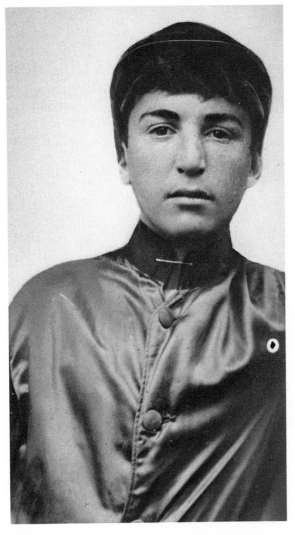

Walter Miller, first jockey to ride 300 winners in one season.

year, when he rode Colin in all but one race of the colt's undefeated juvenile campaign, he took on fewer assignments, 1,194, but again broke through the barrier with 334 winners. He was as consistent as he was spectacular, for in each of these seasons his winning average was 28 percent.

Miller's fame rests almost completely on this intense two-year splurge. He carried on another season in this country before joining the general exodus to Europe, but in 1908 he dropped off to 194 winners and Joe Notter had replaced him as Colin's jockey.

During his streak, Miller swept five-race programs at Brighton Beach July 28, 1906, at Benning November 24 of that same year, and at Oakland February 27, 1907. He also rode five winners on a six-race card at Benning.

An all-around athlete, Miller was the star second baseman of the Sheepshead Bay jockeys' baseball team, and he once was given a tryout with the Oakland club of the Pacific Coast League. Another well known second baseman, John McGraw, was a close friend of his, and the jockey sometimes worked out with the Giants. (Quite a few jockeys of this era were proficient in other sports; Winnie O'Connor, leading rider of the 1901 season, was an accomplished boxer and held a bicycle speed record.)

Miller's immediate successor as saddle champion, Vince Powers, challenged his records with 324 winners in 1908, but thereafter they were not approached for more than forty years. (Powers later became leading steeplechase jockey.) Some old-timers like to say Miller's records still would be standing were it not for the more numerous riding opportunities available to modern jockeys, yet, among the latter day saddle champions, Bill Hartack has duplicated Miller's winning percentage, and Bill Shoemaker has exceeded it twice. (Several other jockeys also have ridden better than 28 percent winners, but didn't win a riding title in the process.)

Nevertheless, in its time the performance of Miller stood out like the Washington Monu-

Beldame, brilliant filly of the 1904 season.

ment, and the intervening years have not dimmed its brilliance appreciably.

The rumblings of the earthquake which was to cause the near collapse of racing mingled with the sound of Colin's hoofbeats. Qualified as well as any man to sense a soft market, James R. Keene, in common with a number of other owners, began to shorten his holdings. Nevertheless, the good ones kept coming his way.

A year behind Colin came the champion two-year-old, Maskette, by Disguise, a filly who won the Futurity and lost only one race in six starts, while conceding actual weight to the leading colt, Sir Martin.

The next season, 1909, the Keene stable had another two-year-old champion in Sweep. This small brown colt was by Ben Brush, whom Keene had purchased from Mike Dwyer as replacement for Domino, and out of a daughter of Domino himself. Sweep continued to dominate his generation the next season at three, while his "nephew," Novelty, bred by Keene but racing for Sam Hildreth, was the best two-year-old, winner of eleven races, including the Futurity and a handicap under 135 pounds. (Keene's own best 1910 juvenile, Iron Mask, was runner-up to Novelty in the rich Hopeful Stakes and Saratoga Special.)

Novelty, by Kingston, in a way was symbolic of the over-all change that was taking place in racing. As he went from Keene to Hildreth so did the national leadership, and the era of Keene's domination came to an end.

In fact, the entire sport was coming apart at the seams.

CHAPTER THIRTY-FIVE

JAMES R. KEENE WAS PERsuaded to acquire his first horses because of the fear that George Lorillard was going to "break up racing," and in due time there was greater concern lest Keene himself might break it up. Before the Civil War, there had been occasions when it was thought that Wade Hampton or W. R. Johnson, by developing almost invincible stables, might destroy the sport; and quite likely before the origin of recorded history, as some unremembered Arab chieftain sped across the desert on a particularly fast steed, one onlooker turned to another, and said, "Abdul is going to break up racing."

The man who finally came nearest to accomplishing the demolition job did not own a race horse. He was a politician: Charles Evans Hughes.

Although best remembered for his close 1916 Presidential race against Woodrow Wilson, to the racing fraternity Charles Evans Hughes is notorious as the man who brought on a blackout. Anti-racing legislation was nothing now nor was it entirely undeserved. In the latter part of the nineteenth century the sport had grown so rapidly and in such helter-skelter fashion that it got out of hand. Race tracks were popping up like dandelions all over the country, and many of them tried to milk a good thing beyond all reason.

Today, eyebrows are raised every time the Northern racing season is extended further into the winter months, but at least programs are called off during inclement weather. In 1880 the races at the Guttenburg Track in New Jersey were run during a "blinding snow storm" on January 3. The best time for 6 furlongs recorded that day was 1:28. The next year, at Mike Dwyer's New Jersey Jockey Club, on December 20, according to the official report, the "races were run in a dense fog. Neither the horses, jockeys, nor numbers on the telegraph board could be seen." The year after that, at Gloucester City, New Jersey, another program was run off in snow and ice on December 26. This was the 91st day of a 176-day continuous meeting which had begun September 1, 1890, and did not end until April 4, 1891, with racing on both Christmas and New Year's Day.

In the St. Louis area, there was racing all year around—night and day. Alex Ullman's track in East St. Louis, Illinois, ran a 364-day meeting in 1893 which came to an end only because there was no more calendar; the 108-day 1894 meeting began immediately thereafter, with free train service from downtown provided.

Across the river in Missouri, racing under electric lights was introduced in 1892-1893, and this new-fangled form of sport also was tried in the nineteenth and early twentieth centuries at several other places: Savannah; Maspeth, Long Island; Algiers, across the river from New Orleans; Covington, Kentucky; and Mystic and Combination Parks in Boston. Maspeth offered five afternoon races and five more commencing at 8 p.m.

Not only were some of the tracks running all year round, but so were some of the horses. On the theory that a horse which could run 12 miles a day in heat racing ought to be a dozen times as active in dash racing, some owners stretched their racing strings to the

"Big Ed" Corrigan, stormy petrel of the Midwestern turf.

limit. The most active horse during the 1888 season was Jim Nave, who started 65 times and won three races; the next year Vivian won two of 64 starts; and in 1890 John Jay S. collected four victories in 76 races.

Frequently, race tracks ran in direct competition with a neighbor, and even such organizations as the American Turf Association and Western Jockey Club, whose purpose was to promote harmony among the various tracks, went to war with each other.

There were also political aspects. The closing of Washington Park was not solely the result of Chicago being flooded with racing days—the refusal of the owners to play ball with politicians also was a factor. Ed Corrigan, owner of Hawthorne, managed to precipitate an actual shooting war with competing Garfield Park. He persuaded the mayor of Chicago to crack down on Garfield, which was within the city limits, and leave Hawthorne alone. On September 6, 1892, several hundred police

raided Garfield Park and arrested customers, track officials and horsemen alike; some of the jockeys were loaded into the patrol wagon while still wearing racing silks. James M. Brown, who formerly had been a sheriff in Texas, refused to accept the arrest and in the fight which followed he killed two policemen before they shot him. Garfield Park was closed down and never reopened.

Finally, some tracks, finding it impossible to make ends meet by legitimate means, took over control of the books on their grounds, and what had been at best a disorganized situation became at worst an impossible mess.

Unfortunately public indignation did not discriminate between the good tracks and the bad, and in the sweeping reforms which followed, the innocent were washed away along with the guilty.

After only one season of operation, the fabulous new Monmouth Park, where Salvator had set his record against time, was forced to close and its meeting was transferred to New York. Monmouth reopened in 1892 but after it ran a 46-day meeting in 1893, repressive legislation forced it to close again, forever. St. Louis, Kansas City and Nashville were caught in the net, as was the Benning track in the nation's capital, despite an effort by the latter to escape the onus of the ugly image by renaming itself the "Washington Horse Show and Racing Association." (In a further effort along these lines, the track later tried a comeback under the name of the "Washington Riding and Hunt Club.")

An anti-racing measure came before the Louisiana legislature in 1908, the same year Governor Hughes swung his axe in New York, and it, too, was passed, but not without opposition. The Locke Bill, as the Louisiana measure was called, looked to be a dead heat in the morning line, and it was reported that someone doped the food of two senators who favored its passage. Sick though they were, they showed up in the legislature the next day and survived a long harangue, calculated to

195

wear them out, until 3:00 P.M., at which time a vote was forced; prodded by their cohorts, they were barely able to raise their heads and utter a feeble "aye" as the measure went through, 21 to 19.

The original Santa Anita track lasted only two years before it, too, received a political knockout. The instrument in this case was the Walker-Otis Bill.

The world record for brevity, though, was set by Rockingham Park. Anticipating the death of racing in New York, a group headed by John "Bet-A-Million" Gates, Andrew Miller and John Drake built a track in Salem, New Hampshire. While the track still was under construction, a group of citizens, including the men who had sold the land on which it was built, began stirring up opposition. After Rockingham finally opened on June 28, 1906, amidst great fanfare, it lasted exactly two days. On the third day a task force of sheriffs from Manchester arrested all the bookmakers and carted them away. According to turf writer Tom Shehan, the episode stands out in New Hampshire history as the first occasion the local residents had tasted breast of guinea hen and champagne. The owners of the track had planned an elaborate banquet in the clubhouse that evening, and a special train of Pullman cars brought out distinguished visitors, including the great dance team of Irene and Vernon Castle. After the raid, everyone took the train back to Boston, leaving the feast for the townspeople.

The 1897 edition of *Goodwin's Official Turf Guide* had listed 314 race tracks running that year in the United States (some of which conducted more than one meeting) and 43 in Canada. By 1908 (the last edition before the *Daily Racing Form* replaced the *Guide* as official custodian of racing's records) these figures had dropped to 25 race tracks in the United States (California, Kentucky, Louisiana, Maryland, Massachusetts, New Jersey, New York, Virginia and the District of Columbia) and six in Canada.

(In 1897, these 314 tracks were located in 29 of the United States, the Oklahoma Territory and the District of Columbia. In 1963, as a comparison, there were 98 tracks in 26 states.)

Finally, on June 11, 1908, Governor Charles Evans Hughes, after leading a long fight to get it through the legislature, signed the Hart-Agnew Bill into law, and betting became illegal in New York. Because this bill, as it was written, left a number of loopholes, racing was able to stagger on for a time with wagering conducted on an oral man-to-man basis. However, in 1910 a new law prohibiting oral betting was passed, and under the Director's Liability Act, race tracks were made responsible for its enforcement. Racing was completely blacked out in New York for the next two years; some county fairs even cancelled such innocuous events as hog-calling contests, fearful that patrons might wager on the outcome and the fair management be held liable.

A misconception exists to this day concerning the extent of racing's blackout. It was not nationwide by any means. In fact, as the following table will show, during the 1910 and 1911 seasons there was actually more racing in America than during the years immediately preceding and following.

Year	Racing Days	Number of Races	Purse Distribution	Average Purse
1909	724	4,510	$3,146,695	$698
1910	1,063	6,501	2,942,333	453
1911	1,037	6,289	2,337,957	372
1912	926	5,806	2,391,625	412
1913	969	6,136	2,920,963	476

As can be seen, although the number of races increased during the blackout in New York, at the same time national purse distribution decreased, and it was the blow to quality racing which hurt. Other tracks, in states where racing still was legal, were only too eager to fill the void, but the void was too big.

The old Members Clubhouse at Pimlico.

Notable exceptions to the general rule were Canada, Maryland and Kentucky, where racing improved during the New York hiatus.

Woodbine, which had been fairly close to the pace before the blackout, seized the lead from Belmont Park in the matter of daily average purse distribution and retained it for eight successive years. In 1911 Canadian tracks ranked one-two-three in this respect, and for the first time since such statistics had begun to be maintained, the leading money winner of the season, Star Charter, was a Canadian-campaigned horse. The leading stable, although owned by J. W. Schorr of Tennessee, owed its position to operations in Canada.

Pimlico, which had fallen on hard times during the 1890s owing to competition from New Jersey, and had staggered along for a while with short meetings, mostly steeplechasing, came back to life. As the bigest, if not the

only, game along the Atlantic seaboard, it became enormously popular and prosperous, and the passage of a Maryland pari-mutuel law in 1912 served to strengthen its position. Baltimore developed quite an impressive racing circuit all its own as Laurel was opened in 1911, Havre de Grace in 1912 and Prince George Park (later named Bowie) in 1914. Through the 1920s Pimlico was the perennial leader among American tracks in daily purse distribution, and it continued to vie for the leadership until Chicago and California made their way into the picture and, finally, once again competition developed in New Jersey.

What gain there was to Kentucky racing as a result of the New York ban was offset many times over by the damage to Kentucky's far more important breeding industry. Then, as now, the state owed its position as national breeding center largely to investment of outside capital in its stock, and with the Northern and Far Western market for thoroughbreds virtually eliminated, Kentucky suffered a more severe economic blow than many states where the sport had been eliminated entirely.

Yearling prices tumbled alarmingly, down to a low of $230 in 1911. Foreseeing the debacle, Colonel Milton Young had sold his fabled McGrathiana Stud and its stock in 1908, receiving only $80,360 for 489 lots. At those prices, he couldn't bear to see some of them go, however, and bid on several himself; a few years later he was back in business.

The ubiquitous Ed Corrigan sold his Kentucky stock about a month later, receiving only $22,995 for 92 horses which included McGee, later to become sire of Exterminator, for $1,300. He was on the point of stopping the sale, but he didn't, nor did he bid any in himself and get back in business. The next year he was bankrupt.

The swashbuckling tycoon, whose turf empire had included a stable of 70 to 80 horses, a 503-acre Kentucky breeding farm and interests in race tracks in Chicago, Hot Springs, New Orleans, Kansas City, St. Louis and California, listed assets of $13,653 against liabilities of $174,100, with "Bet-A-Million" Gates as his principal creditor. The Hawthorne track went to Thomas Carey for $2,000 cash, the remainder being set off against notes Carey had endorsed for Corrigan.

Also in 1909, J. B. Haggin sold large consignments in Argentina ($85,000 for 119 lots) and Germany ($17,747 for 34 lots) but he brought back 26 horses from England because prices for others sold there had been too low.

If Governor Hughes had known anything about racing, which is doubtful, he still could not have timed his blow at a more telling moment. He crippled the value of the American thoroughbred when its prestige was at its height, and, although racing was resumed within two years, the hangover from the experience lasted much longer.

Under normal conditions, the British could be expected to take a patronizing view of American thoroughbreds, and, rightly or wrongly, disdain any thought that they might become competition for their own products. However, isolated noises begun by the horses of Richard Ten Broeck, Pierre Lorillard and James R. Keene in the previous century reached a steady roar exactly at the time the Hart-Agnew Bill was going through the New York legislature. In 1908, American-bred Rubio won the Grand National Steeplechase; August Belmont II's American-bred Norman won the 2,000 Guineas; and Richard Croker's Rhodora, out of the American-bred mare Rhoda B. (on the heels of a victory of her half-brother Orby in the Derby the previous year) won the 1,000 Guineas and was an unlucky loser of the Oaks when another filly fell in front of her. These victories could not be lightly dismissed.

Not only American horses, but American jockeys and owners were figuring prominently throughout Europe. Following the lead of Johnny Watts (four Epsom Derbys), Tod and Cash Sloan, Johnny and Lester Reiff, Lucien Lyne, Danny Maher, "Skeets" Martin and others, American riders were making their presence felt. In France the stable of William K. Vanderbilt was mopping up during 1908; Sea Sick ran a dead heat for the French Derby and Northeast won the Grand Prix de Paris, richest race in the world, before a crowd of 180,000 at Longchamp. Besides Vanderbilt and Croker, such noted owners as H. P. Whitney, the Keenes, H. B. Duryea and Thomas Hitchcock, Jr. were active abroad.

As the American victories piled up, certain alarming prospects began to occur to our British cousins. As an English correspondent expressed it, ". . . though we are as yet a free trade country the Jockey Club can impose whatever restrictions it pleases, and if the present trouble in America should continue, so that a rush of American stables to England might be threatened, some rule to bar any such invasion would seem to be necessary . . . The best known American owners . . . are welcome . . . but there is another class of American owner whose presence here is undesirable."

Pleading crowded conditions, the English refused to issue licenses to train at fashionable Newmarket turf headquarters, and among those invited to stay away was Richard Croker, whose trainer, Enoch Wishard, already had collided with British stewards.

The former Tammany leader, who had returned to his native Ireland to live after losing power in the 1901 New York elections, might have been displeased, but dispirited he was not. Croker set up shop at Glencairn Stud in Ireland, and in 1914, shortly after the death of his first wife, at the age of seventy-three he married a twenty-three-year-old singer, described as a descendant of British royalty on her father's side, and on her mother's side the granddaughter of a Cherokee Indian chief.

More than an invasion of American owners, the English feared an invasion of American bloodstock. J. B. Haggin had been shipping some horses there for sale—the Grand National winner, Rubio, had been one of them, sold for the sum of $75—and Haggin alone was capable of flooding the British market. If owners of other large American studs took up the practice, the English thoroughbred stood a good chance of being swallowed.

Accordingly, in 1913 the English Jockey Club passed the Jersey Act, which made a horse ineligible for registration as a thoroughbred in its stud book unless it traced in all lines to animals previously registered therein. This served to classify the vast majority of American horses as technically half-bred, and their names in pedigrees were indicated by a Maltese cross. The reaction of most Americans to this demeaning classification was mild to begin with—they had more serious difficulties confronting them—but indignation increased over the years as the act remained in force when there no longer was any need for it.

The logic of the act was indefensible in the first place. For example, because her sire happened to have been taken across the Atlantic, and she was registered in the *General Stud Book* before the Jersey Act, Americus Girl was considered a thoroughbred—an exceptionally good one, in fact, ancestress of a classic family that included Mahmoud. Yet, horses which had remained in America and did not get under the wire before the act was passed, were barred from the English stud book because of that same blood.

The situation became increasingly ridiculous, especially when French horses of "tainted" American ancestry began monopolizing England's traditional classic events, and in 1949 the Act was modified so as to permit registration of horses which could prove "eight or nine" crosses of "pure" blood and were otherwise acceptable. Never Say Die, whose great-grandfather, Man o' War, would have been denied registration, has proved eminently acceptable. Presented to the British National Stud by his American owner, Robert Sterling Clark, after he had won the Derby and St. Leger, he was the leading stallion in England for the 1962 racing season.

BRIGHT FACES IN A DARK PICTURE

Matt Winn's monument is a horse race, and his trademarks were a cigar and a twinkle (usually a smile, but sparks when the occasion demanded). However, the deepest imprint made on the American turf by Winn was that of a Moses who led the sport through trying times. On second thought, bulldozer would be a better characterization.

A native of Louisville, Martin Joseph Winn (1861-1949) watched the inaugural Kentucky Derby on May 17, 1875, standing on the seat of his father's grocery wagon. At about that same time he discarded his first name in favor of Matt, and ended his formal education; as a fourteen-year-old he took a job as a bookkeeper, later became a traveling grocery salesman, and then went into the tailoring business. It was his business ability and personality rather than any status in the racing world which led to an invitation in 1902 to join a group being organized by Charles Price to buy financially tottering Churchill Downs for

$40,000. On the other hand, Winn, whose only previous connection with the sport had been as a bettor, was reputed to have wagered on two winning 100-to-1 shots the same day several years earlier, so Price probably figured that here was a man who couldn't miss.

He was correct. Winn's two most important contributions to the sport, from a cosmic viewpoint, were both longshots in the sense that neither was a result anticipated from calculations beforehand.

The first of these episodes is well known. Along with the popular trend among public officials, the mayor of Louisville in 1908 decided suddenly to enforce a law against bookmaking, just as Churchill Downs was ready to open. The track obtained a restraining order, and the upshot of the litigation which followed was a ruling by the Court of Appeals that, although bookmaking was illegal, pool selling was not. Winn remembered the old pari-mutuel machines that had been used at the Downs during the 1880s, and dusted off those which could be found on the premises. After scouring the country by telephone and telegraph, he located another one in a pawnshop, a couple in New York and others here and there until by Derby day, May 5, eleven machines had been installed. It was an eye-opener for Winn and everyone else when the mutuels attracted $67,570 in wagering, while conventional auction pools amounted to only $12,669. The payoff on Stonestreet's Derby victory was $123.60 for a $5 ticket, which looked very attractive, too, and the machines found a permanent home. Other tracks saw the light, and pari-mutuel betting became the wedge through which racing was restored in most states, and eventually the only permissible method in all states. (Oddly, New York, the first state to try the system, was the last to adopt it.)

Matt Winn's other notable effect resulted from his fighting spirit. Dissatisfied with the racing dates assigned to Churchill Downs by the Western Turf Association, he bolted that

James Butler and Matt J. Winn, partners in race track management.

organization and joined with nine other tracks to form the American Turf Association. The bitter war between the two rival combines, during which tracks deliberately were assigned competing dates to hurt each other's business, was a strong factor leading to establishment of the Kentucky State Racing Commission in 1906. The commission took the initiative away from the tracks and ended the suicidal competition, another precedent which was followed by other states and which has been of inestimable value to racing over the years.

Winn joined Churchill Downs as a vice-president in 1902, and by 1904 was appointed general manager. He immediately undertook enlargement of the facilities, which included addition of the huge clubhouse with its twin spires, and from the outset the Kentucky Derby was his pride.

When Winn came into racing, the big events for three-year-olds were the American Derby, Realization and Belmont Stakes, with the Derby and Preakness also-rans in the purse department. The American Derby went the way of all racing in Chicago in 1904, and during the troubled period in the East, Winn seized the opportunity to make the Kentucky Derby the most valuable event of its kind in the land. In later years, the Kentucky Derby lost its monetary leadership, but it always remained reasonably close to the top, and its prestige was so firmly established that it continued to be the most sought-after race in America.

Winn's fighting instinct came into play again in New York, when he succeeded in getting approval for Empire City over the objection of August Belmont, II, and this was the beginning of a lifelong friendship between Winn and Empire City's owner, James Butler (another who had started out in the grocery business). Nineteen hundred seven was a busy year for Colonel Winn, for he also managed both tracks in New Orleans: City Park—where young John Blanks Campbell was beginning his career as a racing official—and Crescent City.

Described by a friend as the "only Irish diplomat" he had ever seen, Winn employed this talent in 1909 when he managed a track in Juarez, Mexico, at which Pancho Villa was an occasional visitor. According to Colonel Phil Chinn, without militating against the legitimate winners, there were times when the track dipped into its own funds to give Villa a "winner" after a race had been run. Winn himself had quit betting when he made racing his business. (Butler was behind this track, too, and when he mentioned the project to Harry M. Stevens, founder of the catering company of that name, realizing that if racing was to be saved everyone had to pitch in, Stevens said, "Put me down for $100,000." The Juarez track was not a success, and closed in 1916, but it kept a lot of racetrackers going while it lasted.)

A great promoter with an inimitable flair for publicity, Winn also was associated (at one time or another) with the Mexico City track, Laurel, Douglas Park, Lexington, Latonia, Fairmount Park, Washington Park and Lincoln Fields.

He had an indestructible faith in growth, and operated at only one speed—full steam ahead. During World War II, when the government requested cancellations of big sporting events, to ease the transportation problem, Winn replied that if two spectators showed up the Kentucky Derby would be run; but he withheld sale of box seats to patrons who resided outside of Louisville. The 1943 "Streetcar Derby," won by Count Fleet, was the result, and the Derby preserved its record as the oldest continuously run race in the United States.

Having licked every problem he faced, there were few challenges left for Matt Winn. However, the man who had seen every running of the Kentucky Derby since its inception, wanted particularly to see the 75th, Diamond Jubilee, renewal in 1949. On the first Saturday in May, he saw Ponder make his memorable charge to victory through the long, long stretch at Churchill Downs, and in October that year, at the age of eighty-eight, Matt J. Winn went under the wire.

PAN ZARETA, 1910

(Abe Frank–Caddie Griffith, by Rancocas)

Racing at Juarez automatically evokes the name of Pan Zareta, the fabled filly who began her career at the Mexican track and turned in some of her most brilliant performances there. Foaled in Sweetwater, Texas, owned by J. H. and H. S. Newman, and trained by the latter, the busy filly campaigned from border to border and beyond. From Juarez she ranged up into Canada—Fort Erie, Windsor, Connaught Park, Woodbine, Blue Bonnets—with forays into such widely scattered other racing centers as Coeur d'Alene, Idaho; Salt Lake

City, Butte, Montana; Dallas, Douglas Park and Churchill Downs in Louisville, New Orleans, Hot Springs, Devonshire, Lexington, Latonia; and, after the blackout ended, at Jamaica, Aqueduct and Empire City in New York.

At Juarez she equaled the American record of 1:04⅗ for 5½ furlongs while carrying 126 pounds as a three-year-old, then lowered it to 1:04⅖, and then equaled her own new record; it was there, two years later, that she set a world record of :57⅕ for 5 furlongs which stayed on the books for thirty-one years, and it also was at Juarez that she won a race at 6 furlongs in 1:11⅘ while packing the very unladylike burden of 146 pounds. It wasn't "Mexican weight," for she subsequently won with 142 pounds at Oaklawn Park and under 140 pounds both in New Orleans and at Empire City.

Although she had a favorite track, "Panzy" was impartial to jockeys and trainers. She won for a number of different riders, including Johnny Loftus, G. Burns, Mack Garner and the 1912 champion, Pete Hill, and also was saddled at times by E. Foucon and E. T. Colton.

She was fast, she was beautiful and she was smart. Serene as a queen in the saddling paddock, she had her mind on business when she got to the post—as other horses milled around, Pan Zareta watched the starter, and when he said, "Come on," she was long gone.

Definitely partial to quick starts and short distances, Pan Zareta nevertheless could be rated when the occasion demanded, and she came from behind to win many of her races; sprint specialist that she was, she set a track record of 1:39 for a mile at Oaklawn.

By the end of her career, this distaff equivalent to Kingston had won more races than any filly in American turf history. Her record in 151 starts was 76 wins, 31 seconds and 21 thirds, for earnings of only $39,082.

Hers was the story of the dark days of racing: hard work, low pay and plenty of travel to find what work there was. The richest purse she ever earned was $1,050, but, as has become increasingly evident over the years, in the appraisal of class, money isn't everything.

The bustling life of the racetrack was all the mare ever had known, and she was destined never to know another. While in training as an eight-year-old, Pan Zareta contracted pneumonia and died. She was buried in the infield at the New Orleans Fair Grounds; thus, she receives a sort of memorial tribute around Thanksgiving Day each year, as the ground in which she lies begins to vibrate to the tempo of pounding hooves, and another race meeting begins.

Time records fell like raindrops at Juarez, and there can be no doubt that the track was exceptionally fast, but neither can there be much doubt that some of the records were broken by exceptional horses. In 1914 Pan Zareta was defeated by Jefferson Livingston's Iron Mask in 1:09⅗ for 6 furlongs, and three months later this six-year-old gelded son of Disguise picked up 150 pounds and clipped a full second off the filly's 5½-furlong mark by running the distance in 1:03⅖; in the latter race he conceded 58 pounds to last-place Bing. A relic of the last Keene stable who had been acquired by Harry Payne Whitney before being sold to Livingston, Iron Mask boasted numerous track records elsewhere, and his Juarez performances stood as world records for many years. (Iron Mask also took a shot at Salvator's mile record while in Mexico, but his pacesetters got in the way and he missed by nearly 4 seconds.)

He, too, died of pneumonia while still in training as an eight-year-old.

CHAPTER THIRTY-SIX

THE MAN WHO DISPLACED James R. Keene in 1909 as owner of America's leading stable was a professional horseman, and nothing else, throughout his life. He was literally born into the sport.

A native of Independence, Missouri, Samuel Clay Hildreth (1866-1929) was the youngest of ten children in the family of Vincent Hildreth, an itinerant horse trader and racing man, who farmed a little on the side as necessary to meet stable expenses.

Young Sam negotiated his own first horse trade, with a rich neighbor, at the age of five and a half, and made $750 on the transaction.

However, at about the same time, he received instruction in one of the ruder facts of life. Having heard that Jim Brown, the previously mentioned ex-sheriff of Lee County, Texas, was a man who could not resist an opportunity to bet on a horse race, Vincent Hildreth moved his entire family to Texas to challenge Brown to a match against Red Morocco, a mare of Hildreth's whom he considered unbeatable.

After a long trip, which involved several days delay in order to join other travelers before passing through Indian country, the Hildreth caravan reached Texas. A match was arranged for $5,000 a side, which represented the entire Hildreth family fortune. Red Morocco's regular jockey conveniently disappeared, and she was ridden in the race by a boy who came highly recommended by the local citizens, but whose performance fell considerably short of his references. Not only did

Brown's mare win, but Vincent Hildreth had to sell Red Morocco to him to finance the family's retreat from Texas. The bitter lesson stuck in the mind of Sam Hildreth all his life, and it became his policy in later years never to name a jockey for a match race beforehand if it could be avoided.

Sam Hildreth's "grammar school" curriculum consisted of riding for his father in quarter horse races in which he sometimes was opposed by a slightly older jockey named Charles Curtis, who became Vice-President under Herbert Hoover; Hildreth and Curtis remained lifelong friends.

By the time he was seventeen, Sam Hildreth had become too heavy for riding and he turned to training. Already he had acquired a yearning for the glamorous thoroughbred, who raced over longer distances for bigger purses than the quarter horse, and, as there was no demand for persons of his background at the big tracks, Hildreth financed his own way by becoming a blacksmith, then, as now, a surprisingly lucrative profession. It was not long until he was operating one of the most active stables in the country, which he trained himself.

Like his father, Hildreth was a two-fisted betting man, but Sam was so successful that bookmakers often refused his money. As a result, Hildreth employed betting commissioners (nicknamed "beards" because of the disguises some of them affected) to place wagers for him, a common, and perfectly legitimate, practice of the period. Many of his local bets were placed by Frank James, the ex-train robber who had gone straight under an assumed name and was negotiating with the governor of Missouri for terms of surrender. (James also at one time raced a string of horses in Tennessee and rode in an event for gentlemen jockeys.) For out-of-town bets Hildreth called upon his close friend, William Allen Pinkerton, partner with his brother in the detective agency of that name which had been founded by their father.

Although he campaigned for the most part in his own name, Hildreth at various periods trained the horses of Ed Corrigan, Lucky Baldwin, W. C. Whitney and E. E. Smathers. The last named was a prominent trotting horse owner who entered the thoroughbred sport by buying out the entire Hildreth stable and signing the trainer himself to a contract. Their best horse was McChesney, an awkward-looking, but smooth-running colt who, shortly after the sale, won a $100,000 bet for Smathers by winning the Harlem National Handicap under 127 pounds.

The best horse Hildreth ran in his own name was King James, champion handicap horse of the 1909 season. As a contemporary of Colin, Fair Play and Celt, King James had relatively slim pickings as a young horse, but as a four-year-old he blossomed forth with ten victories and two seconds in twelve starts. His most notable feat that year was a sequence of victories in Los Angeles. He won the California Handicap at 1¼ miles on a heavy track February 13, while carrying 129 pounds; nine days later, dropping down to 6 furlongs in distance but going up to 142 pounds in weight, King James won the Speed Handicap in 1:11⅘.

It was an amazing demonstration of versatility, for in the beaten field for the Speed Handicap were two of the greatest sprinters in the history of the American turf: the previously described Roseben, then an eight-year-old, was runner-up under 139 pounds, and five-year-old Jack Atkin finished sixth under 148 pounds.

Jack Atkin was even more active than Roseben. He started 136 times, won 56 races and was 31 times second and 19 times third to earn $85,130. Although his forte also was sprinting, he did stretch out enough to win the Metropolitan Mile in 1908. The horse's owner, Barney Schreiber, was one of the most popular turfmen in America, maintaining his Woodlands Stud in Missouri even after restrictive legislation made it an unprofitable venture. Schreiber's general fortunes were on the wane in the last years of his life, but he held on to Jack Atkin to the very end, and the two died within a few months of one another.

Besides King James, Hildreth's 1909 stable included the three-year-old Joe Madden, who won only five races but was never out of the money in fifteen starts. One of his victories was the Belmont Stakes, and Joe Madden's earnings of $44,905 were the highest of any horse that year. Slightly less successful financially, but considerably more consistent, was Fitz Herbert, another three-year-old in the Hildreth stable who also started fifteen times, winning fourteen and placing second in the other. By themselves, King James, Joe Madden and Fitz Herbert earned more money than any other stable that year.

The sensational Novelty came to the races in 1910 and made Hildreth the leading owner for the second time, assisted by Dalmatian, a horse the trainer had purchased from Perry Belmont for only $400.

When the blackout descended in New York the following season, Hildreth took his stable to Canada, and although there was an alarming 69 percent drop in his earnings, he still remained America's leading owner for the third successive year.

Disgusted by the actions of the New York legislature, Hildreth sold his entire stable to New York piano manufacturer Charles D. Kohler toward the end of the 1911 season, and staying on as trainer, took it to France. Except on special occasions, foreign-bred horses were not allowed to run in French flat races at the time, so Novelty, Restigouche and others were converted to jumpers. Both Restigouche and Novelty's dam, Curiosity, ended up as calvary mounts for French officers during World War I.

Mr. and Mrs. Samuel C. Hildreth and Mr. and Mrs. J. W. Schorr at Memphis in 1902.

The sellout to Kohler marked the end of Hildreth's independent operation and thereafter he was chiefly a private trainer. When Kohler died two years later, Hildreth returned to America as trainer of August Belmont II's stable, where his greatest successes were yet to come.

Nothing succeeds like success, and when Hildreth reached the top of the owners' standings he had the two best jockeys in the country under contract at the same time: Eddie Dugan, the leading money rider of the 1909 season,

and Carroll Shilling (1886-1950), who succeeded him the next year.

Novelty's rider, and Hildreth's number 1 boy, was Shilling, regarded by that noted trainer, and a number of others, as the best jockey ever seen on the American turf. By reputation, Shilling had a bad temper, but according to Hildreth, "he never showed it while riding in my colors. What he did show was every riding quality that a finished horseman could possess—an almost uncanny ability to break two-year-olds away from the post,

Carroll Shilling.

judgment of pace that made you think he must have a stop-watch ticking before his very eyes, a seat so light that he was like a feather on a horse's back, and a knack for getting every ounce out of his mount, whether at the barrier, the half post or the finish. He was a master-mechanic astride a horse, with natural riding instincts that his boyhood on the cattle ranches of Texas had brought to the utmost."

To other observers, Shilling showed other colors, and in 1912, as the finale of a series of incidents, he was ruled off for life because of rough riding. With 969 wins from 3,838 mounts, his lifetime average was a shade better than 25 percent, but in the 1911 season he achieved a peak of 36 percent.

His knowledge of horses led to jobs as exercise boy and stable foreman, but Shilling was unsuccessful in a long series of attempts to be reinstated as a jockey. He became more and more morose and soured on the world, took to drinking and in 1948 was picked up on a vagrancy charge in Maryland.

Two years later his body was found lying beneath a van parked outside Belmont Park in mid-January. Apparently it had been there for several days, and the official report attributed death to "natural causes."

The career of Sam Hildreth was curiously intertwined with that of John E. Madden (1856-1929), the man who replaced him as trainer of Ballyhoo Bey when both were associated with the powerful W. C. Whitney turf organization.

A native of Bethlehem, Pennsylvania, Madden was far too burly to have been a jockey, which was the usual introduction to the sport for great trainers of that era, nor for that matter was he a trainer in the usual sense of the word. In his ability to condition a horse for a race, he had few equals, but from the beginning his horizon encompassed considerably more territory. His aim was toward the management side, and he achieved it.

A powerful man, who in his youth was an accomplished boxer and a professional foot racer, Madden could have made a successful career of either of these pursuits but he preferred to utilize his brains more than his brawn. He began his turf activities with trotters and achieved considerable success in that branch of sport before turning to thoroughbreds, and he maintained a bilateral interest in both breeds for the rest of his life.

Coupling a discerning natural eye for a horse, with a profound knowledge of bloodlines which he gained through intensive study, Madden became the greatest trader the American turf has ever known. As his good friend, John Hervey, expressed it, "Many of his big sales were famous and will long remain so. And in many cases they were the result of a carefully thought-out and expertly stage-managed *modus operandi*. In all of these affairs, Madden was emphatically his own *deus ex machina*. He invented the plot, arranged the scenery, provided the lines and the cues, and pulled the wires . . ."

If a likely horse came along, but the price was too high for Madden by himself, he usually could induce someone else to come in with him as a partner. It frequently turned out so well for both parties concerned that Madden, had he so desired, could have done a brisk business merely as a turf consultant. However, he remained active in other fields.

His success in 1897 as owner and trainer of Hamburg, the huge colt which he had purchased for $1,200 and subsequently sold to Marcus Daly for $40,000 after Hamburg had won virtually an equal sum ($39,950) as a two-year-old, was a shining example of the Madden touch. Daly won a further $22,428 with the horse before he was retired; then, as has been recorded, Hamburg was sold for

$60,000 to W. C. Whitney, and still later Harry Payne Whitney paid $70,000 for him at the sale of his father's horses. Hamburg represented a healthy profit every time he changed hands, and Madden's reputation was enhanced accordingly.

In the same crop as Hamburg was Plaudit, a light-bodied, unimpressive colt bred by Dr. J. D. Neet and racing in the name of the noted colored trainer, Ed "Brown Dick" Brown. Despite his frail appearance, Plaudit won the Emerald Stakes at Cincinnati in his third start, and Madden bought him. For his new owner and trainer, Plaudit won the Nursery and Champagne Stakes and scored his notable victory over the four-year-old Ben Brush (another alumnus of the Ed Brown stable) in an all-age race at Brooklyn. The next season Plaudit won four stakes races for Madden, including the Kentucky Derby.

Although Hildreth left W. C. Whitney shortly after Madden replaced him as trainer of Ballyhoo Bey in 1900, there were no hard

Noted trainer A. J. Joyner (left) with John E. Madden, owner, trainer and leading breeder of his day.

feelings among the three men. Many of Hildreth's best subsequent horses were purchased from Madden, and on occasion Madden bought horses from Hildreth.

In 1905 Madden announced his intention to give up racing and concentrate on breeding. Hamburg Place, his stud farm in Kentucky, named for the horse which had brought him such good fortune, was developed into the nation's leading equine production center. During the New York blackout, while other breeders were retrenching or selling out entirely, Madden expanded, taking advantage of the bargain prices that prevailed. In 1912 he bought out all the mares, foals and yearlings of Colonel E. F. Clay's noted Runnymede Farm, plus a half-interest in the leading sire, Star Shoot. (Madden later acquired complete ownership of the stallion.)

Some of his own mares were farmed out to other breeders on shares to make room for the additions, and many a future supplier of racehorses got his start in this way. (Economic note: Madden estimated it cost $250 to raise a thoroughbred until the age of two at his place, but that an average farmer, who maintained a less pretentious establishment, ought to be able to do it for $156.)

During his lifetime, it was said that John E. Madden bred more winners than any man in turf history. Statistics on breeders were not tabulated until after World War I, but for the first ten years after such statistics became available, Madden headed the list according to number of races won; he also ranked at the top several times according to the amount of money won by horses he had bred.

Madden's fame is most popularly associated with the Kentucky Derby as in his own name he bred four winners of that event—Old Rosebud, Paul Jones, Zev, and Flying Ebony—and in partnership with Vivian Gooch of England he bred the first Triple Crown winner, Sir Barton. All five of these horses were foaled in the same barn at Hamburg Place.

Madden had a distinguished record in connection with the Belmont Stakes as, besides Sir Barton and Zev, he bred Joe Madden, The Finn and Grey Lag. Both Grey Lag and Zev were trained by Hildreth.

Madden was fond of quoting epigrams: "The family is greater than the individual" (although he later strayed away from this precept) . . . "Breed the best to the best and hope for the best" . . . "Opinions die; only the records live on." Madden's own record has survived very well. Although he was noted primarily for the quantity of winners he bred, there was an adequate number of quality horses among them. Besides those already mentioned, they included Princess Doreen, leading money winner of her sex at the time she retired; Sir Martin (an older half-brother to Sir Barton), who was champion two-year-old colt of 1908 and later started favorite for the Epsom Derby in England but fell during the running; Spinach, Boniface, Joy Smoke, Fayette and the great trotting mares Nancy Hanks and Hamburg Belle (there also was a prominent thoroughbred of the latter name). At the time of his death Madden had bred eight winners of $100,000 or more, and ranked in a tie with August Belmont II for leadership in this respect.

Neither of his two sons showed an inclination to carry on the vast breeding business Madden had built up, and in 1926 he dispersed most of his stud and returned to the race track at the age of seventy, retaining just enough breeding stock to supply the needs of his stable. The 139 horses at the sale brought $446,200.

Madden also announced an intention to sell Hamburg Place, but did not follow through. He died three years after his return to the track, and the great breeding farm he founded has been passed along to his grandsons, one of whom, Preston Madden, is managing it. The barn where five Kentucky Derby winners were foaled still is in operation.

When the curtain descended on New York racing in 1911 the American stable of James R. Keene disappeared forever. He ran a few horses in England with some success that season, but so far as he was concerned, in the United States the show was over.

Castleton Stud was sold to David M. Look that same year, and the entire crop of foals was put up for sale as yearlings the following season. Charles Kohler bought the thirteen fillies for $15,000. The sixteen colts also were sold as a package, for $25,000, to a buyer identified by the *New York Telegraph* as banker William A. Prime, but a couple of weeks later they were advertised for sale at auction by trainer Frank E. Brown, who had acted as agent in the transaction.

By sale time there was a rumor that E. R. Bradley actually was the owner of the horses, and, as he was a prominent bidder at the auction, some talk arose that Bradley was trying to run up the prices on his own stock. The gentleman gambler, whose chief stock in trade was his reputation for absolute integrity, had a ready explanation. A personal friend really had purchased the yearlings, said Bradley, acting on his advice, and when the friend had second thoughts about the investment, Bradley bailed him out. "I had made it a practice never to advise anyone to do a thing that I would not do myself," commented the colonel, who never did mention his friend by name.

As the auction turned out, there was no ground for complaint. The entire group was sold for $57,650 and it included several individuals who were each worth several times that sum. Among the four Bradley purchases were the two highest priced colts of the sale, at $14,000 and $11,000, neither of which amounted to much, but he got Boots and Saddle for $5,800, and his lowest priced purchase, at $1,600, was Black Toney, a successful race horse and famed foundation sire of Bradley's Idle Hour Stock Farm.

There were other bargains. For $1,700 James Rowe, as agent for H. P. Whitney, obtained Pennant, winner of the next year's Futurity and also a great stallion after his retirement, sire of the immortal Equipoise. At the same $1,700 figure John Gray acquired Luke McLuke, who did not race at two, but won the Belmont Stakes at three for owner John W. Schorr of Memphis, who had the leading stable of 1912 and had tried to get Bradley to go in as partner with him on the entire group in the first place. (As it was, Bradley, who could have owned the complete lot for $25,000, paid $32,400 for only four of them. He got his money back on the other twelve, so his acquisitions were on the house.)

Shortly after the sale of his yearlings, Keene sold six of his best brood mares to Phil T. Chinn, agent for W. K. Vanderbilt, and Chinn was negotiating for the sale of Colin and Ballot when Keene died.

The executors of his estate thereupon took over and began liquidating what was left of the Keene turf empire. Ballot was sold privately to John E. Madden, Ben Brush was sold to Senator Johnson N. Camden and the 1912 crop of foals was bought by James Butler. The remainder were consigned to auction at Madison Square Garden in September, 1913, but before that date 28 of the horses were destroyed in a fire at Kingston Farm, where they were being boarded. When the last of the stock went under the hammer there were 45 horses left. They elicited total bids of $229,000, excellent prices for the time (the sale average of $5,088 broke the record which had been set at the Marcus Daly dispersal in 1901) but nevertheless bargain prices considering the quality of the stock.

Peter Pan topped the auction at $38,000 bid by James Rowe as agent for Payne Whitney, who later presented the stallion to his brother, Harry Payne Whitney. Colin, at $30,000, was next, going to Price McKinney, the biggest buyer at the sale, who also took four other stallions. H. P. Whitney got the best of the weanlings, as for $2,200 Rowe obtained Dominant, leading two-year-old money winner of the 1915 season.

There were numerous other notable purchases of which two in particular deserve mention. A. B. Hancock, who had been standing Celt at his Ellerslie Stud in Virginia under a lease arrangement, bought the stallion for $20,000, and a syndicate composed of Charles W. Moore, John Ed Barbee, Kinzea Stone and Dr. J. C. Carrick bought Sweep for $17,500. Both these stallions subsequently headed the American sire list. (At the dispersal of Charles Kohler's Ramapo Stud breeding stock at Sheepshead Bay a couple of days later, the leading two-year-old sire, Uncle, was purchased by Hal Price Headley for $38,500, but the Kohler mares averaged only $938.)

Thus the books were closed on probably the most influential, and certainly the most controversial figure in the history of the American turf. Despite such "disasters" as the premature deaths of Domino, Commando and Sysonby, and the untimely injury to Colin, Keene could boast of having bred five successive Futurity winners and six winners of the Belmont Stakes in a fourteen-year period from 1901-1914. He also launched the stud careers of the founders of the three strongest American male lines— Spendthrift, Domino and Ben Brush—and through yet another quirk of fate the strength of these lines was carried on largely through the agency of his great business and turf rivals, the Belmonts and the Whitneys.

The late Colonel Phil T. Chinn, who had dealings with Keene both on and off the track, while reminiscing over the Ballyhoo Bey– Tommy Atkins rhubarb, once told the author, "James R. Keene was the toughest, meanest . . . no, son, don't say that. He was sometimes hard on people, but the man *loved* horses."

Keene and his brother-in-law, Foxhall Daingerfield, ran as an entry to the end. Two days after Keene died, Major Daingerfield went, too, and the greatest partnership of the American turf was dissolved. It was said that during their long association Keene had only once visited his Castleton Stud (although his son, Foxhall, spent much time there) and the management of this noted establishment had been entirely the province of Daingerfield. The oft-

Harry Payne Whitney (left) and James R. Keene, each of whom led the owners' standings many times.

210

James Rowe, a leading trainer as well as a leading jockey.

wounded Confederate cavalry hero was a member of the Kentucky Racing Commission at the time of his death. He also had become an eminent student of bloodlines and the author of numerous papers on breeding. One of his theories was that horses must have peace and quiet, and he allowed none of his employees at Castleton to exhibit signs of hurry or excitement.

Although Keene was survived by only a bachelor son and a daughter, Daingerfield had five daughters and two sons. A daughter, Elizabeth, became a recognized expert on thoroughbred farm management. A son, Algernon Daingerfield, became secretary of the Jockey Club and a grandson, Keene Daingerfield, is a noted modern racing official.

Along with many of the Keene horses, the best of the Keene men wound up in the stable of H. P. Whitney. Although Keene had been associated with several trainers, the one who tightened the cinch on Commando, Sysonby, Colin, Maskette, Sweep and other great horses,

and who trained the stable during its unprecedented four-year tenure at the head of the owners' list, was James Rowe (1857-1929).

Not only was Rowe a towering figure in American turf history, he could almost be characterized as the cement which held racing history together during the shaky transition period.

A native of Fredericksburg, Virginia, Rowe was a ten-year-old boy working behind the newsstand of the Exchange Hotel in Richmond, and exercising horses for the hotel's livery stable, when Colonel David McDaniel picked him up as a prospective jockey.

The boy's reward for his first victory was a striped stick of peppermint candy and permission to stay up until 9 o'clock that evening. As a fourteen- and fifteen-year-old in 1871, Rowe was America's leading jockey and he retained his championship for two more seasons. He guided Harry Bassett to his previously described triumph in the Saratoga Cup of 1872, won successive renewals of the Belmont Stakes with Joe Daniels and Springbok in 1872 and 1873, and rode such other McDaniel stars as Hubbard and Katy Pease.

Rowe was still a growing boy of naturally powerful physique—the muscles of his calves could be seen bulging under the tight-bottomed trousers fashionable in that era—and he was not cut out to remain a jockey for life. In 1874, both his parents having died meanwhile, Rowe declared his independence from McDaniel and went on his own. Since the rules did not permit him to ride races for another employer during that year, he joined P. T. Barnum and rode at the Hippodrome. As soon as he was able, he returned to the track, but by this time the boy jockey had become a boy trainer. He was an immediate and equally sensational success in that profession.

After brief associations with David McCoun, and the Davis Brothers of West Virginia, Rowe became connected with the Dwyer Brothers at the beginning of their march toward the top. In the stable at the time were such good ones

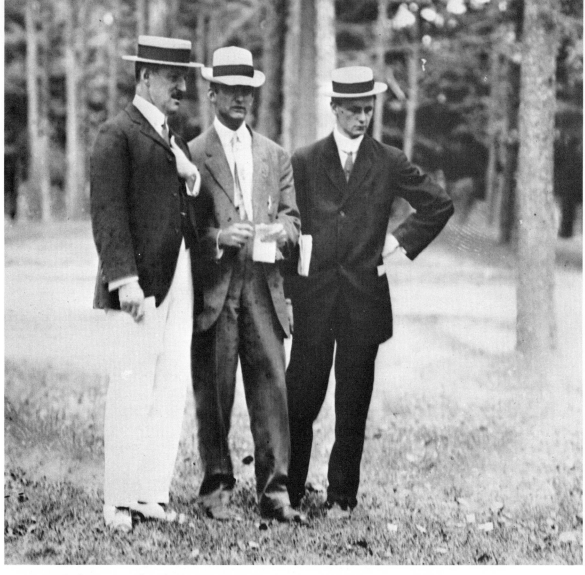

Turf patron and sculptor Harry LaMontagne (left) with Preston and Shelby Burch, members of a notable family of trainers.

as Bramble and Runnymede. Rowe trained them and such later stars as Luke Blackburn, Hindoo and Miss Woodford. A dispute with the Dwyers concerning the last-named great filly caused Rowe to resign, and he became a racing official. He was a successful starter of the old flag school, and a steward before he re-entered the training profession, first with the stable of the original August Belmont and, after the latter's death, as conditioner for the sensational Keene racing string.

Rowe joined Keene too late to train Domino, but he handled such other great runners as Sysonby, Colin, Commando, Peter Pan, Maskette and Sweep. He once stated that for his epitaph he would like just three words: "He trained Colin."

By 1913, when he was salvaging what pieces he could of the crumbling Keene empire, Rowe already had earned his niche in history as a success in three distinct careers. However, he was just getting his second wind.

CHAPTER THIRTY-SEVEN

HAD JAMES R. KEENE LIVED SIX months longer, he would have seen the return of his beloved sport to New York. While the horses from his estate were being sold piecemeal, and several months before the final big auction, thoroughbred racing was revived at Belmont Park. It was not racing in the lavish style that Keene had known, but it was, nevertheless, sport—in fact, an extreme form of it.

Certainly there was never a more enthusiastic throng than the 35,000 people who turned out at Belmont Park on May 30, 1913, to welcome back racing. Old friends greeted one another effusively, and even perfect strangers nodded and smiled. As the bugle broke a three-year silence to summon the horses for the first race, the forty-piece band broke into "Auld Lang Syne," and a great cheer reverberated over Long Island. After the five-year-old mare Ella Bryson led all the way to win the first event on the program for a $430 purse, she was greeted by an ovation that would have done credit to a Futurity winner of former years.

Some of the traditional features were missing, notably the bookmakers shouting their odds, but nobody seemed unduly upset, certainly not enough so as to dampen the festive atmosphere. What betting there was consisted of oral wagers "among friends," which the courts had ruled to be permissible, and, as has been pointed out, everyone was very friendly. Since the track had expected only about 15,000 attendance, programs and grandstand badges were quickly exhausted, and an estimated 5,000 patrons had to be turned away; this too was taken in relatively good humor.

There being no revenue from betting, purses were supplemented by an Owners Fund, subscribed to by prominent sportsmen. Among the original donors named were August Belmont II, James Butler, Frederick Johnson, H. K. Knapp, Charles Kohler (deceased by the time the track opened), H. T. Oxnard, Thomas F. Ryan, John Sanford, H. P. Whitney, George D. and Joseph E. Widener, and Richard T. Wilson, although others responded to the call. Total net distribution for the six races that first day was $4,600 which included the Metropolitan Handicap at $2,500-added.

There also were some new features on revival day at Belmont Park. Herman R. Sinkerstein and Samuel Kornblum of Brooklyn were arrested for making a bet and arraigned a few minutes later before Justice Louis Raisig. With Nassau County District Attorney Charles Wysong, who also conveniently happened to be available, acting as prosecutor, the "court" was called to order in one of the rooms under the grandstand. Sinkerstein and Kornblum thus joined the army of unsung heroes in racing's fight for survival. It was a vast army, of heartwarmingly cosmopolitan composition, which included, besides the contributors to the Owners Fund and others already mentioned, such men as bookmaker Melville Collins, who in 1908 allowed himself to be arrested in a test case staged by the Jockey Club, and won a decision which delayed implementation of the blackout for three years; Paul Shane, who put anti-gambling legislation to a pressure test after the blackout, and many others.

WHISK BROOM II, 1907

(Broomstick–Audience, by Sir Dixon)

Even the racing had a special flavor at Belmont Park's reopening, as, regardless of its modest value, the Metropolitan Handicap went to one of the most worthy winners in the history of that traditional fixture.

The Metropolitan was the first start in his native country of H. P. Whitney's American-bred Whisk Broom II, a colt which Whitney had purchased as a yearling and sent to England under trainer A. J. Joyner during the blackout. Whisk Broom II had raced in that country with considerable success for four seasons, and even before he showed his wares to the home folks he had captured the fancy of the American public.

A rich, golden chestunt, standing 16½ hands and splendidly proportioned, he excited tremendous admiration in the paddock. There was a buzz of approval as the name of Joe Notter went up as Whisk Broom's rider (Whitney also had taken over Keene's old jockey). As Notter, too, only recently had returned from Europe, it was a particularly appropriate combination for homecoming day. Whisk Broom started an 8-to-5 favorite in the friendly discussions touching on the likely outcome of the forthcoming test of skill.

When the six-year-old stallion, carrying 126 pounds, closed about ten lengths to win the race going away, the admiration turned to adulation and 10,000 hats and an equal number of handkerchiefs went into the air. Whisk Broom's time of 1:39 for the Metropolitan Mile was not especially impressive, but on June 21, he toted 130 pounds to victory in the Brooklyn Handicap in new track record time of 2:03⅖ for 1¼ miles, finishing well in hand.

Since the big horse had shown such clear-cut superiority over his opposition, handicapper Vosburgh threw his weight into the proceedings and assigned Whisk Broom 139 pounds for the Suburban Handicap a week later.

This race, on June 28, 1913, was the most startling performance of all. With his stablemate Nightstick setting the pace, Whisk Broom II lay second under double wraps until the far turn, where Meridian and G. M. Miller moved up to join him. Notter then sent the odds-on favorite along the rail, and at the same time Meridian and Lahore launched a challenge. This time Whisk Broom II felt the sting of the whip through the stretch, and he pulled away again to win by half a length from Lahore, with Meridian third.

The tumult engendered by the contest came again, too, when 2:00 was hung out as the official time. According to this clocking, despite his enormous load, Whisk Broom II had completely shattered his own track record, and the American record of 2:02⅘, held jointly by Broomstick (his own sire) and Olambala, as well.

The crowd greeted this information with loud applause, and the professionals with snorts of disbelief. Other than the official timer, not a single person who held a watch on the race had caught it that fast. Among the horsemen who clocked it, James Brown made it closest to the official time at 2:01⅗. Others had it even slower than that. Matt Allen and James Fitzsimmons recorded 2:02⅖; William Garth,

2:02⅗; Hugh Penny, 2:02⅘; Thomas J. Healey, 2:03; Kimball Patterson, 2:03⅕; and E. J. Albright, 2:03⅖.

However, the timer stuck by his guns and August Belmont stuck by him, so the 2:00 flat went into the record book.

This mark, which stood as a world record for many years and as an American record for nearly half a century, was a subject of dispute during all that time. The start had been straggling, and some observers reported that the flagman had been slow giving his signal. Others theorized that the timer snapped his watch about 200 yards short of the finish (this race also was run clockwise).

The truth of the matter probably can best be determined from the fractions—:24, :47⅕, 1:12, 1:36⅘ and 2:00. According to these fractions, Whisk Broom II ran the final quarter in 23⅕ seconds, which, especially considering his weight, historian John Hervey observed was "unbelievable."

Whether he ran the distance in 2:00 or 2:03, Whisk Broom II was conceding 44 pounds to his stablemate and an average of 27 pounds to his other four rivals. (Frederick Johnson's Cock o' the Walk, who finished last under 111 pounds, went on to become champion three-year-old of the season.)

Whisk Broom II was, moreover, the first horse in history to win all three of the big New York handicaps, a series which today is known as the handicap triple crown, and it was forty years before the mighty Tom Fool duplicated this feat.

Owing to the unusual circumstances which prevailed, all these races were run at Belmont Park in 1913, and they were Whisk Broom II's only starts in America. Having won $9,625 in this country, he retired to stud the next season and became a very successful stallion.

Although it extended from May 30 to July 5, the first meeting of the Westchester Racing Association comprised only eighteen days of racing. After it closed, the Metropolitan Jockey Club conducted a brief meeting, three days a week, but again at Belmont Park since Jamaica had not yet reopened.

In August, when Saratoga time rolled around, racing was resumed on an everyday basis. (Another advantage to the Saratoga meeting was that the arm of the law was neither so eager nor so long; although Belmont Park had sold off a bit of land during its idle period, it still spilled over from Nassau County into Queens, and there had been *two* sheriffs prowling the premises during the meetings there.)

Racing was conducted on a more normal basis when the sport moved up to Saratoga, but it could not be said that everything was the same again, nor, for that matter, was it ever to be. Apart from the obvious changes in purse structure and wagering procedures, which in time were repaired to their former state, and the subtle change in the carefree atmosphere of the place, which made a comeback but never really challenged the spirit of the Gay Nineties, there were the missing faces, many of them gone forever.

At Saratoga this was felt with particular keenness; General Stephen Sanford (1826–1913) had died in February, just a few months before the sport was revived. The carpet manufacturer from Amsterdam, New York, had been a staunch supporter of Saratoga racing since the track first opened. He raced horses only of his own breeding, and began his campaign each year at the Saratoga meeting, preceded by a special holiday of races at his Hurricana Stud, for which his 3,000 millworkers were given the day off. No matter which important real races the Sanford horses were being trained for, they ran in these trials, and the contests were as serious as though a Derby were at stake.

A native of Mayfield, New York, and a graduate of Georgetown and West Point, General Sanford owned a number of good runners, many of whose names reflected his love for upstate New York. Molly Brant and Mohawk II are easy to identify, but Sanford named others more obscurely, such as Danoscara, Chactanund and Caughnawaga.

A pillar of the turf of the old-fashioned variety, Sanford's appreciation of tradition is reflected by the fact that trainer Hollie Hughes stayed with the family for three generations, through son John, and on to grandson Stephen.

ROAMER, 1911

(Knight Errant–Rose Tree II, by Bona Vista)

There was no Whisk Broom to race at Saratoga Springs the summer of 1913, but there was another historic horse to welcome back the sport after the blackout.

Roamer was the product of a chance mating; his dam was blind and while she ordinarily would have been booked to the Runnymede Farm home stallion, Star Shoot, that would have resulted in two blind parents, so the mare was sent to Star Shoot's "teaser" instead. The resulting offspring was a useful but definitely unsensational two-year-old at Pimlico and in Kentucky, until he was brought East by Woodford Clay and sold to Andrew Miller.

The gelding found his legs at Saratoga and popped up to win the Saratoga Special. Although it was his only stakes victory that particular season, Roamer turned out to be one of the original "horses for courses," and in following years he kept the old spa bubbling. He won the Saratoga Handicap three times (carrying 129 pounds in his third victory), the Travers Stakes, the Merchants' and Citizens' Handicap and Saratoga Cup at his favorite stamping grounds, and his stakes victories elsewhere included the Carter, Yonkers, Municipal and National Handicaps, carrying 132 pounds in the last-named event. Racing for seven seasons, he started 98 times and won 39 to earn $98,828.

It was at Saratoga as a seven-year-old, on August 21, 1918, that Roamer crowned his career in an exhibition race against Salvator's time record of 1:35½ for the mile. Carrying 110 pounds, Roamer quickly lost his pacesetter and clicked off fractions of :23⅗, :46, 1:10⅕, and 1:34⅘ to set a new record. This was the last mark for a popularly run distance established in a race against time, as all subsequent recognized records were made during actual competition.

Although James Rowe, as trainer of H. P. Whitney's American stable, saddled Whisk

Roamer, one of the first outstanding horses to emerge after the New York blackout.

Broom II for his undefeated career on this side of the Atlantic, it was Andrew Jackson Joyner (1861–1943), who had trained the horse during his English career. Along with Hildreth and Rowe, Joyner enjoyed status as a dean of his profession at a comparatively early age.

A native of Enfield, North Carolina, Joyner was too big to aspire to a career as a jockey, yet, as did all children of that period, he rode a great deal in his youth. His father was a physician who died when Joyner was a boy, and he went to work, first as a postal clerk, then as a stable boy for William Wyche. He then moved on to the stable of W. P. Burch and rose to the job of foreman before he went on his own as a trainer.

He saddled his first winner at Saratoga in 1884, and in the late 1880s, for the partnership of Davis and Hall, won numerous good races with Oriflame, a supposed cripple which they had acquired from August Belmont. Later, Belmont engaged Joyner as his own trainer.

Joyner's subsequent patrons included David Gideon, W. A. Chandler, James B. Haggin, and Perry Belmont. The latter's Ethelbert, winner of the Realization and Metropolitan, was one of the best horses Joyner developed. His next big stars were James B. Haggin's Waterboy and Sidney Paget's Hamburg Belle, and then Joyner became trainer for August Belmont II.

He led the trainers' list in 1908 when his charges included Fair Play, and later that year went to England with the Whitney stable. It was there that he developed Whisk Broom II, a colt he had purchased from Captain Harry Brown and resold to Whitney.

Shortly after his return from England in 1915, Joyner took over the stable of George D. Widener and this association lasted until the end of his life. At the period under discussion, when American racing was emerging from the gloom, as was true of his two good friends, Rowe and Hildreth, many of Joyner's greatest successes were yet to come.

Like a patient returned from a hospital, by 1914 American racing, although by no means recovered, began to show signs of getting back its strength. It had been a hard fight, with severe casualties. Numerous tracks never did reopen, including Brighton Beach, Sheepshead Bay and Gravesend; Belmont Park retained the Suburban, Futurity and other Sheepshead Bay fixtures, while the Brooklyn Handicap, Derby (soon to be renamed Dwyer Stakes) and similar traditional Gravesend races were taken over by Aqueduct.

The fight was not over, but an air of confidence and faith in the future began to stir. Yearling averages which had hit their low average of $230 in 1912, had built back up to $654. Average purse distribution, which in 1911 had dropped to $372, and during the New York blackout had hovered at a figure less than half what it had been before the Hughes law, had gone into a slow but steady climb; in 1914 the average purse was $512 and on the way up.

Headed by John E. Madden, who named 106 mares, H. T. Oxnard with 54 and August Belmont II with 49, nominations to the next season's Futurity had exceeded 500, and lady owners—Mrs. Lily A. Livingston and Mrs. Payne Whitney—were among the nominators.

Apart from statistics, there were other vigorous signs for racing. Sam Hildreth was back in action with August Belmont II's Stromboli, winner of eleven races, including a victory in the Baltimore Handicap over Roamer, the season's leading money winner. The first of numerous Kentucky Derby winners from J. E. Madden's famous foaling barn turned up in H. C. Applegate's Old Rosebud, who collected considerably more than just roses, for the purse that year had been boosted to $10,000 added, making it the richest event for three-year-olds in America.

There were some clouds visible, but far away on the horizon. In the summer of 1914, those Americans still left in Europe as stragglers from the great evacuation were given added encouragement to return to the fold; it was time for another Saratoga meeting and, besides, Europe was getting uncomfortable. However, America was to have a few more years before she became involved directly in World War I.

The former Keene horses were very much in evidence in 1914 as J. W. Schorr won three stakes, including the Belmont, with Luke McLuke, whom he had acquired at the Bradley sale of Keene yearlings. This colt was a strong factor in making Schorr leading money-winning owner for the second time, and his son, J. F. Schorr, leading money-winning trainer for the first time. The Schorrs were an unusual combination in that, before he began training for his father, the son also had been stable jockey. The senior Schorr was a native of Germany who made his fortune in the brewery business in Memphis, Tennessee, and among his other good runners was one named Ed Crump.

Luke McLuke was of additional interest, too, as a son of Ultimus, an intensely inbred stallion who never had raced. Foxhall Keene had arranged the mating: between Domino's son, Commando, and Domino's daughter, Running Stream.

James Butler also had a good year with the youngsters he had purchased from the Keene estate, which included the filly Comely and the colt Pebbles, the latter a winner of five stakes as a two-year-old.

Pebbles wasn't the champion of his division, however. Harry Payne Whitney, who signaled his intention of getting even deeper into the horse business by buying a portion of Elmendorf Farm, boasted an undefeated two-year-old filly called Regret. Bred at Brookdale Farm in New Jersey, which Whitney leased, Regret started only three times, as a two-year-old, but they were all stakes and she won them all—the Saratoga Special, Hopeful and Sanford. She met Pebbles twice, and it is significant that all of her races were against colts . . . giving males their comeuppance was her specialty.

CHAPTER THIRTY-EIGHT

WHEN MATT WINN SET ABOUT to make the Kentucky Derby the most talked-about race in America, he wasted no time. In 1911 the $2 mutuel ticket was introduced, and two years later Roscoe Goose rode T. P. Hayes's Donerail to victory in new track record time for the biggest payoff in history, $184.90. The next year the Kentucky Derby pulled away from the Latonia Derby in value. In 1915, Winn saw his dream more than realized.

The winner's purse for the Belmont Stakes that year sank to $1,825, the lowest value in history, and the Preakness—which Pimlico had not yet begun to emphasize—was at its lowest twentieth-century value, $1,275. Not only was the Kentucky Derby the richest three-year-old event in America, but the winner's purse reached a record sum of $11,450.

Whereas until that time the Derby had been essentially a Kentucky race, or at best a Midwest race, it now had become a national classic which attracted the top three-year-olds from all areas.

Kentucky was duly impressed.

". . . Notables of the turf world from all sections of the country were present in the greatest gathering (40,000) ever assembled at Churchill Downs," wrote a local reporter. "Representation of the East was greater by far than for any previous running of the Derby," and listed were such prominent visitors present as H. P. Whitney, James Butler, Schuyler Parsons, Jr., Andrew Miller, H. K. Knapp, Price McKinney, James F. Johnson, Foxhall Keene, James Corrigan, F. R. Hitchcock, Thomas Monahan, R. J. Mackenzie, G. A.

Cochran, Preston Burch, Phil Dwyer and Thomas Street.

Also taking cognizance of the great occasion, the Kentucky Racing Commission, headed by chairman Johnson N. Camden, was represented by its entire membership at Churchill Downs. Matt Winn's publicity cup was brimming over before the race started.

REGRET, 1912

(Broomstick–Jersey Lightning, by Hamburg)

Already there was a tradition well established that no three-year-old filly could beat colts at a mile and a quarter in May, but Regret proceeded immediately to shatter tradition by going to the post a warm favorite, despite the fact that she had not raced since the previous August. After all, she had defeated colts at two carrying 127 pounds and with her sex allowance, her Derby weight was only 112.

It was the most chivalrous Derby ever run, for the lady led every step of the way. As they passed the grandstand the first time around Regret was in front by half a length followed by Pebbles and Sharpshooter; a grueling mile later they came around again in the same order, only by this time Regret had increased her margin to two lengths and Pebbles was an equal distance in front of Sharpshooter. For an instant, just a brief one, Pebbles had challenged at the five-eighths pole, but Notter had only to loosen his reins a bit and the filly moved away.

"Behind Regret trailed the greatest field that had ever worn silk in this premier turf event," stated one enthusiastic reporter.

219

Regret, filly winner of the Kentucky Derby, who never lost a race to a member of her own sex. Joe Notter up.

The undefeated filly kept her record intact by winning the Saranac Handicap in August, after which she was retired for the season.

In her final start at three, Regret raced in the colors of L. S. Thompson, owner of Brookdale Farm, where she had been foaled. On the day before the Derby, the *Lusitania* had been sunk by a German submarine off the Irish Coast, and among those who went down (with heroic fortitude, according to accounts of the disaster) was Whitney's brother-in-law, Alfred Gwynne Vanderbilt. For a time there had been speculation that Regret would be withdrawn from the Derby, but Whitney let her go and thereafter turned his stable over to Thompson who ranked as the leading owner that year. (This was the second time the Whitney family eschewed an official title, as it will be recalled that in 1904 the stable was leased to H. B. Duryea following the death of W. C. Whitney.) Borrow, a tough old gelding who had been a stablemate of Whisk Broom II over in England, was the leading money winner of the 1915 season with $20,195, and Regret's full brother, Thunderer, won the Futurity.

The next year Regret attempted to duplicate her feat of winning a 1¼-mile race first time out, but after an absence from competition of nearly a year, she was dead last in the Saratoga Handicap won by Stromboli. She won next out, however, and concluded her campaign after only two starts.

As a five-year old, for the first time in her life, Regret competed in events exclusively for fillies and mares, and she won all three such races she contested. Her only loss that season was a second by a nose to her stablemate Borrow, while conceding him 5 pounds actual weight, in the fabulous Brooklyn Handicap of 1917. The nine-year-old gelding beat three Kentucky Derby winners that day—Regret, Old Rosebud and Omar Khayyam—plus such other stars as Stromboli, Roamer, Boots and Chicle.

Regret retired for good with nine victories and one second in eleven starts for earnings of $35,093. No member of her sex ever finished in front of her . . . and, of course, she always will be remembered as the only filly to win the Kentucky Derby: a feat without parallel in eighty-nine years.

In 1914 there had been a sample three-day meeting in Chicago (during which Gin Rickey and Modesto Boy each won a race every day of the meeting, and Santa Maria won twice) and, encouraged by its reception, in 1916 the Illinois Jockey Club staged a thirteen-day meeting at Hawthorne Park beginning July 15. Like the comeback in New York, this one operated under no-betting rules, but the reaction was equally enthusiastic.

". . . the largest crowd ever within the gates of Hawthorne Race Track, not excepting even when racing was at its best in the Windy City," turned out for the festivities, according to a local report, which continued, "the people began to gather as early as ten o'clock this morning. By post time for the first race, there was not an inch of vacant space anywhere within the inclosure. The vast crowd seemed to go wild when the horses came on the track for the first race, and they realized that racing was on in Chicago again. The orchestra struck up 'America,' and hats and canes were thrown in the air as the horses paraded to the post past the grandstand for the inaugural dash. Pandemonium broke loose again when the small but select Derby field paraded to the post, and the cheering was deafening while the horses were running the big race."

The big race was the American Derby, which had been borrowed from abandoned Washington Park for the occasion, and Foxhall Keene had brought his colt, Churchill, all the way from New York to add the prestige of his presence to the proceedings. However, Churchill went to the post gimpy and "cut little figure in the running," as Weber and Ward's Dodge spurted away to win by six lengths from Faux-Col in new track record time of 2:04⅗.

As had been the case at Belmont Park's reopening, there was certain offstage byplay at Hawthorne. Captain W. T. Duhain had a force of 100 Pinkertons policing the track, assisted by Cook County Sheriff John Traeger with 50 deputies. The sheriff's force made 28 arrests during the day, of which 18 were dismissed immediately. The meeting was not repeated the following year—and the track was used by the government during World War I—but,

heartened by its popularity, a new Illinois Jockey Club arose, which reopened Hawthorne in 1922 and it has been running ever since.

Dodge went on to become the leading three-year-old money winner of the 1916 season. The son of Jim Gaffney—Flora Willoughby, by Florist, also won the Latonia Derby and Autumn Handicap, and beat James Butler's Spur in the Saranac Handicap.

Toward the end of the season Dodge was purchased for $17,500 by A. K. Macomber, who was operating on all fronts that year; the Lawrence Realization, which was revived in 1916, was won by Macomber's Star Hawk, who earlier in the season had been beaten only a neck by George Smith in the Kentucky Derby.

August Belmont II's Friar Rock cut the widest swath among Eastern three-year-olds by winning the Belmont Stakes against his own age, and defeating older horses in the Brooklyn and Suburban Handicaps and Saratoga Cup. This colt was a son of the English triple crown winner, Rock Sand, whom Belmont had imported to the United States at a cost of $125,-000 (and which he resold a few years later for the same price). Imported horses were very prominent on the American racing scene in 1916, as the war in Europe had made for bargain prices. Star Hawk was imported as were the good two-year-olds Hourless and Omar Khayyam, who were to become great rivals the following season.

Among the older horses Emil Herz's eight-year-old import, Short Grass, started twenty-seven times and won eight races, including four stakes, a remarkable performance for an entire horse of that age. (Short Grass was far from being the most active senior runner that season, as G. E. Phillips's Budweiser, foaled at the turn of the century, was still going strong: the sixteen-year-old gelding still had enough foam to start forty-one times, and win seven. He continued to race, and win, two more seasons.)

In summary, racing was emerging from its convalescent period and beginning to sprout anew. Purse distribution was considerably healthier and the leading money winner of the season, regardless of age, was R. T. Wilson's Campfire, the champion two-year-old who earned $49,375 with six wins and two seconds in nine starts. His victories included the Great American, Sanford, Saratoga Special, Hopeful and Futurity Stakes.

The most unusual "race" which took place during 1916 was the contest between Wilson and H. G. Bedwell for leading money-winning owner. It was just as exciting as any equine contest on the track that year, for it was decided late in the season and the finish was unbelievably close. Richard Thornton Wilson (1867–1929), of the prominent New York banking family, was a steward of the Jockey Club, president of Saratoga, a director of Belmont Park; a member of the Knickerbocker, Union, Racquet and Tennis, Brook and other fashionable clubs; and an in-law of the Astors and Vanderbilts. Long an enthusiastic supporter of turf affairs, he had helped nurse Saratoga through the trying days of the blackout, and in 1916, when Campfire, a colt of his own breeding, became the season's leading money winner, Wilson's turf fortunes were at their zenith. When his horses went into winter quarters that autumn, it was thought that Wilson could not fail to head the owners' list.

Harry G. "Hard Guy" Bedwell (1874–1951) was a native of Roseburg, Oregon, whose father had died soon after he was born. Cast on his own, Bedwell was first a cowboy, then he drifted into Colorado, where he opened a livery stable; at the same time, he rode in running races and drove in harness races. He returned to California as a trainer and had some success with a horse named Los Angeleno, but most of his winners were of the sort whose names never made the record books. Operating with a large stable of claimers, Bedwell compiled a remarkable record. In 1909, the first year after he moved East, he saddled 122 winners to become the country's leading trainer. In 1912 he earned the title again and was to retain it for an unprecedented six years in succession, but 1916 was the first year he figured in any monetary compilation.

After the Wilson stable had been put up for the winter, Bedwell kept plugging away bit by bit. Of the fifty-two horses he campaigned that season, the leading money winner, Manokin, gleaned only $8,330. On December 29 at Havana, Mr. Sniggs picked up $25 for finishing third and King Tuscan earned $400 by winning the last race of the day, and when the final tabulation was in, Bedwell had nosed out Wilson by just $65.

CHAPTER THIRTY-NINE

IT WAS SOME TIME BEFORE the effects of World War I were felt at home, and although the struggle was a bitter one it was relatively brief. There was a slight drop in the number of races contested in 1917, and a sharp drop the next year, but so far as it affected the general growth of American sports, the war was but a bump in the road. Racing in particular suffered less than it had during previous conflicts, as this one was fought exclusively on foreign soil and American horses were not so greatly involved.

In 1917 there was another close battle for leading owner, as Willis Sharpe Kilmer, with a small stable and good luck, was nosed out by A. K. Macomber (1875–1955), with a large stable and bad luck.

"King" Macomber was just getting started in his turf career, but he purchased everything that caught his eye. In 1917 his racing string earned $68,578, despite a succession of misfortunes that would have done in an ordinary stable. North Star III, Boots, Dodge and Ed Crump had been expected to lead him to an extraordinary year, but none of them delivered; moreover, Liberty Loan also went awry after a brilliant victory in the Latonia Derby.

A native of Pasadena, Macomber became one of the guiding lights of the Western turf, although he lived a large part of his life in France. He was instrumental in the campaign to bring racing back to his home state, and through the lean years when there was no racing to speak of, with his brother, Dr. H. J. Macomber, he operated Mira Monte Stock Farm in San Jose. After buying W. K. Vander-

bilt's noted French stud, Haras du Quesnay, Macomber funneled many fine European horses to California, including Masked Marvel II and Sun God II. Although 1917 was the only season he topped the list of winning owners in America, he continued to enlarge his turf operations, and at one time had 150 race horses in various parts of the world.

In 1917, Macomber's American stable had thirty-six horses. Kilmer, who finished less than $4,000 behind him, did so thanks almost exclusively to one colt, Sun Briar, the leading money winner of the season with $59,505. The imported two-year-old won five races, all stakes, including that season's richest prize, the Hopeful, which had a net value to the winner of $30,600.

H. G. Bedwell won his seventh training championship (sixth in succession) and the leading rider of the season was a future racing official, Willie Crump, who won 151 races despite being suspended for a time by his contract employer, E. W. Moore, who also was Crump's stepfather.

Old Rosebud refuted the dogma, "they never come back," by winning fifteen races as a six-year-old after a sojourn of nearly three years on the Texas prairies. He had broken down in the Withers Stakes on May 30, 1914, and did not re-enter competition until February 18, 1917. He headed the handicap division (horses older than three) in earnings with $31,720.

The sensation of the early part of 1917 was the three-year-old Omar Khayyam, who, racing for Billings and Johnson, in May had become the first imported colt ever to win the Kentucky

Derby. Subsequently sold to Wilfred Viau, he also won the Brooklyn Derby, Kenner, Travers, Lawrence Realization Stakes, the Saratoga Cup and the Havre de Grace Handicap.

In the Brooklyn Derby and again in the Realization, Omar Khayyam had defeated August Belmont's Hourless, a colt originally intended for Belmont's European racing stable but brought to this country because of the war. Hourless, in his turn, had won four races, including the Withers and Belmont Stakes, and two handicaps under 130 pounds. His defeat in the Brooklyn Derby was attributed to the muddy going, but his loss in the Realization caused trainer Sam Hildreth to erupt. There were only three horses in the race, but jockey Jimmy Butwell had managed to get Hourless in a pocket and lose his whip in the bargain. Despite these misfortunes Hourless was only a nose behind Omar Khayyam at the finish.

The fuming Hildreth persuaded Matt Winn to put on a special event at Laurel (which that impresario modestly christened the "American Champion Stakes") and on October 18, 1917, a crowd estimated at from 15,000 to 20,000, said to be the largest ever gathered at a Maryland track, jammed Laurel to witness the great contest. They saw what Hildreth described as "the most remarkable horse race I have ever seen."

The first surprise came before the horses entered the paddock. It had been assumed all along that Hourless would be ridden by regular jockey Butwell, but ten minutes before saddling time Hildreth sent assistant trainer Mike Hackett to the jockeys' house to offer the mount to Frankie Robinson. This young rider, who had risen from obscurity to top the saddle standings the year before, was as surprised as anyone else by this last-minute change, but he eagerly accepted the opportunity.

The next surprise came at the snap of the webbing, when Everett Haynes went to the front immediately with Omar Khayyam, the horse who ordinarily liked to come from behind. This was a match, however, and, as Haynes well knew, in contests of this sort ordinary tactics do not necessarily apply. As the so-called plodder went the first half in 47 seconds flat, the crowd sensed this was to be an unusual race. Hourless at this point was trailing two lengths behind, under double wraps. Robinson continued to stalk the leader until they reached the turn for home, where he turned Hourless loose. The brown son of Negofol cut down Omar's margin with every stride, but the flying leader refused to collapse. At the eighth pole, Hourless poked his nose in front for the first time and slowly drew away to win by slightly more than a length.

Bert Morgan

Hourless, winner of the celebrated match against Omar Khayyam.

The final time of 2:02 was a new track record, but the fractions were what made the race remarkable. They were :$23\frac{2}{5}$; :47, 1:$12\frac{2}{5}$, 1:$38\frac{2}{5}$ and out in 2:02. The last quarter had been covered in $23\frac{3}{5}$ seconds, and since Hourless had been behind at the end of a mile, he ran this final quarter even faster than that.

Whisk Broom II's world record had been disputed because his final quarter in 23⅕ seconds was "unbelievable." However, he had covered the first mile in 1:36⅘, whereas Hourless was coming off a much slower mile and carrying 126 pounds, 13 less than Whisk Broom had been laboring under; and Hourless's fantastic time for that last quarter never was called into question.

When the track announcer shouts, "Here he comes!" and a great stretch runner begins to pass his rivals through the home lane, it does appear that he is accelerating, but an analysis of the fractions shows that in the vast majority of races over an appreciable distance, winners which come from behind are really slowing down—only not so much as the others. It is a rare horse indeed that truly can accelerate after running a mile, and the performance of Hourless remains a landmark in racing history. (As was true of other races during this period, Hourless's $10,200 winner-take-all purse was donated to the Red Cross.)

That was Hourless's last race. He injured himself in training the next spring and was retired to stud. Omar Khayyam started twice more in the 1917 season. He won the Pimlico Autumn Handicap, but then his stablemate Westy Hogan, a supposed sprinter, threw a new track record of 2:31⅘ at him in the 1½-mile Bowie Handicap; Omar, under top weight of 130 pounds, finished second. He raced on for two more seasons during which he won only three of his fourteen starts, although one of these victories was in a Liberty Bond Handicap while carrying 132 pounds.

Robinson continued on to win his second riding title the next year, then his career came to an abrupt end. On April 4, 1919, while aboard Roederer in the seventh race at Bowie, the brilliant jockey was killed when a horse named Garbage crossed in front of him and caused a four-horse spill.

The year 1917 marked the end of the most successful monopoly on record of a major stakes event by an individual owner, as Joseph E.

Seagram's filly, Belle Mahone, won the King's Plate. The noted distiller, nearing the end of his days, was lying in a Waterloo, Ontario hospital at the time, but, the war notwithstanding, King George V took time out to send him a congratulatory cablegram.

The procedure was by then a well-established routine, for Belle Mahone was the fifteenth winner of Canada's great race owned by Seagram. The man whose turf activity amounted to a history of racing in Canada had won eight renewals in a row, beginning with the appropriately named Victorious in 1891, and he had seen the Plate grow from a winner's purse of $407 to Belle Mahone's $6,125.

Seagram succeeded William Hendrie—the owner who broke his original winning streak in the Plate—as president of the Ontario Jockey Club, and served for thirteen years. He also was a member of the Canadian Parliament, and was one of the few North American members of the English Jockey Club. Horses carrying his black-and-yellow jacket paid visits to winner's circles across the border, too, as he often campaigned his stable in the United States.

The year after Seagram's last victory, there was no racing in Canada—that is, except for the Plate. To preserve its continuity, it was run as a special feature of the Red Cross Horse Show, and won by Springside, a colt owned by George M. Hendrie.

August Belmont II was sixty-five years old in 1917, but his version of retirement was to volunteer for Army service. Commissioned a major, his job entailed procurement of supplies (including mules) for the AEF. In order to devote his time completely to his Army duties, Belmont decided to sell that year's entire crop of Nursery Stud foals. His wife, the former actress Eleanor Robson, liked to name the Belmont horses, and it was she who had named one of the brood mares Mahubah, an Arabic saying meaning "May good things be with you."

On March 29, 1917, Mahubah foaled a chestnut colt by Fair Play which Mrs. Belmont reportedly intended to name "My Man o' War" in honor of her husband. However, when it was decided to sell all the yearlings the following season, this touch of personal sentiment was eliminated, and he went into the auction ring simply as Man o' War.

On January 1, 1918, Willis Sharpe Kilmer gave a birthday party. The site was the wealthy sportsman's Sun Briar Court, a lavish estate in Binghamton, New York, named for Kilmer's two-year-old champion of the season just past, and the guest of honor was Sun Briar himself. Although he was not yet fully mature, this son of Sundridge–Sweet Briar II, by St. Frusquin, already had been firmly enshrined by his enthusiastic owner. Visitors were invited to inspect the new covered exercise track and the fancy clubhouse, which included a display of memorabilia pertaining to the colt whose third birthday was being observed. In addition to a large oil painting of Sun Briar, there was the $5,000 cup which had been his trophy for the Saratoga Special, the shoes he wore in the Hopeful Stakes, and the whip which jockey Willie Knapp had carried during his 1917 campaign, during which he won five of his nine starts. According to an article in the *Binghamton Press,* this whip had touched Sun Briar's aristocratic flank but once, in the Grand Union Hotel Stakes, when the colt had stumbled but had come on again to win, including among his victims the ultimate Futurity winner Papp.

However, the most notable souvenir associated with Sun Briar was acquired several months after his gala birthday party, and it was far too big and much too active to fit into a display case.

The Kilmer champion was being pointed for the Kentucky Derby, but when he ran a dull third in a prep race at the Association track in Lexington on April 25, it was decided that he needed more work under simulated race conditions. Accordingly, Kilmer purchased from J. Cal Milam, for a reported price of $10,000, a three-year-old gelding named Exterminator, who had won only $1,350 the previous season.

That the new acquisition was intended strictly as a trial horse was emphasized when Exterminator began to show up so well in the workouts Kilmer became annoyed by suggestions that he might make a better Derby candidate than Sun Briar. He issued a public statement that the gelding had been purchased strictly as a trial horse and added, "I do not consider Exterminator in the same class with Sun Briar."

Fate took a different view, though, and Sun Briar—who had ringbone—went lame before the big race. Kilmer also had sent Nelsweep south as a standby Derby candidate, but at post time on May 11, it was Exterminator who carried Knapp onto the track sporting the Kilmer colors, green, brown sash and orange sleeves.

Starting as the longest price on the board at nearly 30-to-1, the ugly duckling splashed through the mud to win by a length from Escoba and Viva America, as the heavy favorite, War Cloud, finished fourth, thirteen lengths away.

EXTERMINATOR, 1915

(McGee–Fair Empress, by Jim Gore)

Thus was born the greatest equine Cinderella story in American history. The Derby was the ungainly gelding's three-year-old debut, and in fifteen starts that year he was out of the money only once. Racing on through the age of nine, he became a great popular favorite despite his appearance (Vosburgh called him "an unattractive gelding . . . as lean and hungry looking as Caesar described Cassius. High in bone and low in flesh . . .")

The huge (16-3) angular running machine, affectionately dubbed "Old Bones" by the public, started exactly 100 times. He won 50 races, was second in 17, third in 17, and unplaced in only 16 for earnings of $252,996. Nothing bothered him except possibly the absence of his mascot, a pony named Peanuts. He won at sixteen different race tracks in three different countries at distances ranging from 5½ fur-

Exterminator at the time of his Brooklyn Handicap victory as a seven-year-old.
Albert Johnson up.

longs to 2¼ miles under weights up to 138 pounds.

He was especially formidable over long routes. He won the 1¾-mile Saratoga Cup four times in succession, setting a record of 2:58 which he lowered himself to 2:56⅗, after which he was conceded a walkover the following season. He won the 2¼-mile Pimlico Cup three times in a row and set a record of 3:53 in that one. He won the 2-mile Autumn Gold Cup at Belmont Park twice and his time of 3:21⅘ for that distance was an American record.

Exterminator was leading money winner of the handicap division—in which a horse is penalized for winning by being assigned higher weights in subsequent races—four straight seasons, an attainment that defies the imagination, even with the records staring one in the face. During his long career, Bones was trained by nine different men, and won for all of them.

In the book, *Boots and Saddles,* J. K. M. Ross, whose father's stable raced against Exterminator frequently, made the observation: "I cannot believe that Exterminator's prowess and consistency in distance racing (i.e., over 1½ miles) will ever be surpassed." The late

Grantland Rice did not qualify his admiration for the great gelding: he considered him a better all-around performer than Man o' War.

Perhaps the most significant tribute, however, is that indicated by the *American Racing Manual,* official bible of the sport, which includes among its many features a twentieth century "Hall of Fame." As racing has grown and statistics relating thereto have become more voluminous, space requirements have been so demanding that when a new horse enters the Hall of Fame, an old one must leave to make room. Since his time, hundreds of horses have won more money than Exterminator, and the hammering on the door has been fierce. Moreover, as a gelding, whose name is not kept fresh through the exploits of his descendants, and because his exceptionally long racing record takes up more than the usual amount of space, from a purely callous standpoint Exterminator would be the most convenient elimination. At the time of writing, Old Bones is still in there.

Although his brilliance was certainly dimmed by his stablemate's heroic performance, Sun Briar was not eclipsed entirely. After losing his first four starts as a three-year-old, he finally rounded into form and won the Delaware Handicap and Travers Stakes, the latter race being the only time that year Exterminator was out of the money. Sun Briar's time of 1:36⅕ was the fastest mile ever run in actual competition, as distinguished from Roamer's record of 1:34⅘, which had been set in a race against time. After the close of the Saratoga meeting Sun Briar broke this record, too, by running a mile in 1:34 flat, using two pacemakers, but as no formal arrangements had been made beforehand, it was not generally recognized. (Track superintendent William A. Myer verified the time, but stated that the Saratoga track was at least 2 seconds faster than when Roamer had set his record.)

In his lone victory as a four-year-old the next year Sun Briar, carrying 128 pounds, beat Exterminator, 120, by a length, in the Champlain Handicap, although the chart noted that Exterminator was "not hard ridden and probably best at the weights."

W. S. Kilmer boasted that he put Henry McDaniel (1867-1948) on the map, but the records suggest that the effervescent patent medicine tycoon, who made his millions purveying Swamp Root (good for anything, apparently, except ringbone), was off pitch in this diagnosis. In fact, just the opposite seems to have been true.

Henry McDaniel was literally born on a race track at Secaucus, New Jersey, owned by his father, Colonel David McDaniel, who was America's leading owner from 1870-1874, during which period he won three successive Belmont Stakes and four successive Saratoga Cups with Harry Bassett, Joe Daniels and Springbok. (The last-named horse, after winning the Saratoga Cup in 1874, ran a dead heat with Preakness for the same race the next year.)

Henry McDaniel was only seventeen when he took his first job as trainer, for the two-horse stable of M. E. Clark of Louisville, at a salary of $12 a month. (McDaniel later explained he had "no expensive habits" which, since he was his father's son, is easily under-

"Uncle Henry" McDaniel, member of a famous family of horsemen and trainer of Sun Briar and Exterminator.

stood.) Henry's salary was doubled when he patched up a broken-down gelding named Forest to win four races in a row, but when Forest subsequently ran into a fence at Washington Park, the stable went out of business. Operating a public stable at times and as a private trainer off and on, McDaniel conditioned horses owned by B. J. Treacy of Lexington, Lucky Baldwin, John E. Madden, Charles Head Smith, Gus Straus, G. C. Bennett, Tichenor and Newgass, Louis Cella, R. L. Thomas, the Davies brothers' Thorncliffe Stable and other patrons, who ran the gamut from bookmaker to owners of race tracks— some of them were both. The better-known horses McDaniel had developed before he joined the Kilmer stable included the American Derby winner Rey el Santa Anita, Rey del Carreras (later named "Americus"), Myrtle Harkness, the Tennessee Derby winner Abe Frank (sire of Pan Zareta), and Mentor and Rustle, respectively, the sire and dam of Wise Counsellor.

Although Kilmer was the actual purchaser

of the French-bred colt named Sunday, who later became Sun Briar, at the 1916 Saratoga yearling sales, he was said to be bidding on McDaniel's recommendations. In a gesture of sublime optimism, before Sun Briar ever had started in a race, Kilmer sent McDaniel to Europe to buy mares for his court against the day the horse would retire to stud. (Kilmer later increased the scope of his operations to include Remlick Hall and Court Manor Stud in Virginia.) Among the mares McDaniel brought back was Contessina, future dam of Reigh Count. It was also McDaniel who selected Exterminator to become Sun Briar's stable companion, but the trainer left the Kilmer stable in 1921 while Exterminator was still in the middle of his fabulous career, and was replaced by former jockey Bill Knapp.

McDaniel trained successfully for R. L. Gerry and then J. K. L. Ross before he was persuaded to return to the Kilmer stable in 1927, reportedly at an unprecedented salary plus attractive fringe benefits. This second association didn't last long, either, as the two men broke up because of a disagreement concerning the sale of Reigh Count.

McDaniel went on to train for Gifford A. Cochran, Joseph E. Widener, Mrs. F. Ambrose Clark, A. G. C. Sage, a third term with Kilmer (at $40,000 a year this time), Walter P. Chrysler, Jr. and Mrs. C. Oliver Iselin, before his long career ended.

"Uncle Henry" was one of the turf's most durable characters—there was a span of sixty-two years between his first and his last winner —as well as one of the most colorful.

When a kibitzer asked him how he possibly could start Sun Briar with those ringbones, McDaniel casually replied that he removed them before each race. On another occasion, when he was training for Widener, he had in his stable a horse by Stefan the Great. McDaniel, giving the old college-of-hard-knocks try at the foreign pronunciation, referred to the horse as a son of Stoppin' the Great.

Ultimately, the stallion thus identified was sent back to Europe.

PART FOUR

WORLD WAR I
TO WORLD WAR II

CHAPTER FORTY

H. G. BEDWELL WAS ACCUSTOMED to success, but not to the limelight. After his great 1916 season, when he had been leading owner as well as leading trainer, Bedwell sold out his stable and took over as private trainer for the wealthy Canadian businessman, yachtsman and war hero, Commander J. K. L. Ross.

The heir to the Canadian Pacific Railway fortune was in the process of putting together a powerful stable, and, reminiscent of A. K. Macomber, Ross purchased any likely looking runner he happened to see. Although Macomber's stable had improved greatly in the 1918 season, his luck had not, for Ross nosed him out in the owners' rankings with $99,179.

Cudgel, a horse for whom Ross paid $30,000 shortly after Bedwell entered his employ, was the first true stakes star to fall into the veteran trainer's hands, and there was some speculation concerning how Bedwell would react to the responsibility associated with such a valuable property.

Bedwell took it in stride, and so did Cudgel. As a four-year-old, the son of Broomstick won nine races, including the Brooklyn Handicap under 129 pounds and two other handicaps under 130. As a five-year-old Cudgel won five more races under weights up to 132 pounds, and during his tenure in the Ross stable he defeated such formidable rivals as Exterminator, Sun Briar, Johren, Roamer and George Smith.

H. G. "Hard Guy" Bedwell, leading owner of 1916, seven times leading trainer numerically and twice leading trainer financially.

BILLY KELLY, 1916

(Dick Welles–Glena, by Free Knight)

The horse that was to give Bedwell his biggest headache came along a year after the purchase of Cudgel, when Ross picked up the two-year-old Billy Kelly early in the 1918 Saratoga meeting. The young gelding, already winner of six races in eight starts for W. F. Polson, was even more sensational under the black-and-orange Ross colors. Ridden by Earl Sande, Billy Kelly won eight of his next nine races. He evoked memories of Hamburg by winning the Eastern Shore and Grab Bag Handicaps

Sir Barton, first winner of the American Triple Crown.

under 135 pounds and the Sanford Stakes under 130; he also defeated a field of older horses in the Columbus Handicap. Billy Kelly's only loss after his sale was by a head to the season's leading money winner, J. W. McClelland's Eternal, in the McLean Memorial at Laurel, October 28, a special event at $10,000 a side, the proceeds from which were donated to the Red Cross.

Over the winter pressure built up in anticipation of another encounter between these rivals in the following year's Kentucky Derby, which in 1919 for the first time was raised to an added value of $20,000. The pressure was not eased when, a few months before the race, what Ross's son described in his memoirs as "an insignificant, yeasty-faced little man" approached his father in a Broadway restaurant and offered to bet that Eternal would beat Billy Kelly in the Derby. Thinking in terms of $50 or so, Commander Ross accepted the challenge and requested the stranger to identify himself and name the amount. The little man, who seemed miffed at not being recognized, was the notorious gambler Arnold Rothstein, who only months later was to be connected with the Black Sox baseball scandal. The amount he named was $50,000.

It was a horse-and-horse bet concerning only Billy Kelly and Eternal, but there was a stipulation that in order for either man to win, his horse must finish among the first three. By the time the Ross stable arrived in Louisville, where it was greeted by a crowd of reporters and photographers, the strain was beginning to tell on the normally complacent and well-padded Bedwell. "He became almost impossibly irascible, kept his mouth plugged with cigars or chewing gum, his face screwed in frowns," wrote the younger Ross. "He lost weight almost visibly and by Derby Day was a walking wraith . . ."

SIR BARTON, 1916

(Star Shoot–Lady Sterling, by Hanover)

That 1919 Kentucky Derby was won by a colt who went to the post a maiden, Sir Barton, whose weight assignment was so low (110 pounds) that jockey John Loftus was 2½ pounds overweight in the race. Taking the lead immediately, Sir Barton never looked back, and scored the first victory of his career by five lengths.

It was a happy result for trainer Bedwell, since Sir Barton was a stablemate of Billy

234

Kelly, and it was a happy result for owner Ross as Billy Kelly finished second (the first such one-two result in Derby history) to win the bet with Rothstein. Eternal, a slight favorite in the betting, finished tenth. Sir Barton went on to become the biggest money winner of the season, never out of the money in thirteen starts, eight of which he won—the Derby, the Preakness, Withers, Belmont Stakes, Potomac, Maryland and two Pimlico fall serial races.

The expression "triple crown" was not in use in America in Sir Barton's day. The term originated in England, where it was applied to the 1-mile Two Thousand Guineas, 1½-mile Derby and 1¾-mile St. Leger Stakes, a series of races over a wide range of distance and well spaced in the calendar. The races which today comprise the American triple crown grew up as independent events, close together in distance and in the calendar. Nevertheless, at the time of Sir Barton's achievement, it was duly noted that he was the first horse in American history to have won the most important races for three-year-olds in Kentucky, Maryland and New York and, of course, in later years when the Derby, Preakness and Belmont Stakes began to be associated as a series, Sir Barton was firmly entrenched in history as the original winner of the American triple crown.

Billy Kelly also had a good year in 1919—as did Cudgel—and Ross was leading owner for the second successive season with earnings of $209,303, the greatest total since the withdrawal from the turf of James R. Keene. H. G. Bedwell also was the leading money-winning trainer for the second successive time.

The successful team was broken up after one more season. Bedwell left the Ross stable because of a tangle resulting from efforts to get jockey Carroll Shilling reinstated. Ross, along with several other prominent horsemen, at first supported the idea, but when it came to a question of outright war with the Jockey Club (or, more specifically, with August Bel-

Commander J. K. L. Ross, first owner to finish one-two in the Kentucky Derby and first to win the Triple Crown.

235

mont II) he withdrew his sponsorship. Bedwell continued the fight, and was himself suspended in Maryland and New York; although the racing commission, overruling the track stewards, quickly reinstated him in Maryland, Bedwell was not licensed in New York for many years.

Despite the impressive total amassed in 1919 by the Ross stable (twenty-six horses, of which twenty-four earned money and twenty-one were winners) it was not lacking for competition. There was a pair of flashy two-year-olds on the scene—Glen Riddle Farm's Man o' War and C. E. Rowe's filly, Miss Jemima, winner of eight races, seven of them in succession. Moreover Sam Hildreth, who had gone into business for himself again when Belmont went into the Army, gave Ross and Bedwell a good run for their money.

Before they parted company, Hildreth purchased from Belmont the colt, Lucullite, who had been a promising two-year-old until his leg bone was splintered by a kick from another horse. The son of Trap Rock didn't show much at three, but he came back at four to win nine races for Hildreth, including a victory over Sir Barton and Sun Briar in the Mount Vernon Handicap. He also ran Billy Kelly to a head, while spotting him 11 pounds, in one of the most thrilling renewals of the Toboggan Handicap on record.

Also a winner of nine races that season was Purchase, a three-year-old son of Ormondale, whom Hildreth had bought from George D. Smith. Classified by Hildreth as "the best horse I ever trained, and I say that without any strings to it," and described by Vosburgh as "one of the most exquisitely beautiful of racehorses . . . to describe Purchase properly would be to exhaust the superlative," the magnificent 16-hands 1-inch chestnut was a case of handsome does as handsome is. He beat Sir Barton in the Dwyer, Eternal in the Southhampton Handicap and won the Saranac Handicap under 133 pounds, the Huron under 134. He started in eleven races that season, and ran second in the two he didn't win, to earn $33,710.

Laverne Fator, leading money-winning jockey of the 1925 and 1926 seasons.

Purchase was not the top winner of the Hildreth stable, however, as another former Belmont colt, Mad Hatter, winner of four races and never out of the money in seven starts, included among his victories the inaugural Latonia Championship, richest event of the season. That one alone was worth $45,090 to Mad Hatter, and this son of Fair Play whipped Sir Barton in the Pimlico Autumn Stakes, although Mad Hatter had a 21-pound pull in the weights.

Fair Play himself had gotten cunning as he grew older, and as a four-year-old was virtually worthless as a race horse because of his vicious temper, but a number of his sons raced well, if somewhat erratically, at handicap age. Mad Hatter was one of them. At four, it was his turn to win nine races (he lost about an equal number because of his antics) and he defeated both Sir Barton and Billy Kelly at weight-for-age in the forerunner of what was to be the Pimlico Special.

Hildreth had made some astute deals in horseflesh, but his shrewdest financial coup

236

of the 1919 season was the purchase of a jockey's contract. The price was $15,000, and the transaction was made after Hildreth had seen the boy ride just once, but it was a bargain. The jockey was Laverne Fator (1900-1936).

A strong, broad-shouldered lad, who stood less than 5 feet and weighed under 100 pounds, Fator was discovered riding on the half-milers of his native Idaho by Stuart Polk, who took him to Cuba for seasoning before unleashing him in the United States. Fator was a sensation in his first season on the big time, and it was he who won most of the big races for Hildreth in 1919. Although he later was leading money-winning rider two seasons in succession, Fator never led the jockey list from the standpoint of number of winners, and there were good reasons. His career overlapped those of Buddy Ensor and Earl Sande—for a time he and Sande were under contract to the same employer—besides which Fator had a wealth of other competition in his own backyard.

He had two brothers who were jockeys, one of whom, Mark, topped the standings in 1922. Mark Fator was succeeded as riding champion by Ivan Parke, foremost member of an even larger brother act—also from Idaho. Ivan Parke, who followed up his 1923 leadership by taking both the numerical and financial title in 1924, had four jockey brothers— Chuck, Burley, Monte and Vasco. (All of the Parkes became prominent in modern racing, as trainers or racing officials.)

CHAPTER FORTY-ONE

N THE HISTORY OF BASEBALL, Allison Danzig and Joe Reichler tell of the amusing results when the Washington Senators during the 1950s invited everyone who had seen the great Walter Johnson pitch his first major league game to sit in a special section of the grandstand. It had been about fifty years since Johnson had made his major league debut, but more than 8,000 fans applied for seats, a number that is especially remarkable when it is considered that official attendance at the original game was only 2,841.

An even more pronounced parturitional phenomenon exists in regard to Man o' War. Although attendance at Saratoga on August 13, 1919, a Wednesday, was 20,000, there are at least three times that number of persons who can "remember" the Sanford Memorial Stakes in which Man o' War met his only defeat at the hands of the aptly named Upset. And, although a $5,000 auction price can accommodate only a limited number of under-bidders, if to the number of fans who saw the Sanford Stakes is added the number of owners and trainers who "almost bought Man o' War" as a yearling, the resulting total would tax the facilities of new Aqueduct.

MAN O' WAR, March 29, 1917

(Fair Play–Mahubah, by Rock Sand)

Pursuant to the plan announced by August Belmont at the time he went into the Army, the entire crop of Nursery Stud yearlings was offered for sale at Saratoga on August 17, 1918. The twenty-one youngsters realized an average price of $2,474, and although Man o' War brought more than double this average, he was not the most sought-after yearling. Joseph E. Widener bid $14,000 for Fair Gain, F. M. Taylor bid $13,600 for Rouleau and Man o' War went to the Glen Riddle stable on a bid of $5,000. It was a high price for the time, but it was the greatest bargain in racing history. Man o' War won 20 races in 21 starts and retired as America's leading money winner. His complete racing career is tabulated in the appendix.

Except for his single defeat, the huge chest-nut won all of his races by open daylight. He set all of his eight time records—three world records, two American records and three track records effortlessly. Normally it requires two horses to break a record, one to force the other to run faster than usual. "Big Red" was under no pressure to set his records; he ran fast for the sheer joy of it, and he didn't shave or clip existing records—he shattered them.

In the Lawrence Realization, which he won by 100 lengths, he lowered the previous world record by 6⅘ seconds; in the Kenilworth Cup he lowered the track record by 6⅖ seconds and in the Belmont Stakes his time was 3⅕ seconds faster than the former world record. He was never in a drive at the finish of any of his twenty victorious races; he was running easily at the end, according to the official charts, except for his furious but futile charge in the Sanford.

This loss to Upset, to whom he was conceding 15 pounds, is the most discussed race of Man o' War's career, although it wasn't such

Man o' War as a three-year-old with jockey Clarence Kummer, who rode him in all but one of his record-smashing victories.

a shock at the time. Golden Broom, for example, coming off an impressive win in the Saratoga Special, was conceded a reasonable chance (5-to-2) before the race, and preoccupation with Mrs. Jeffords' colt undoubtedly was a factor in the result. Regular starter Mars Cassidy was not in the stand that day, and substitute C. H. Pettingill sent two of his fields away in what were officially described as "poor" starts; the Sanford was one of them. Finally, Man o' War got caught in a pocket.

The chart description of the race reads, "Start, poor and slow . . . Upset followed the leader closely from the start, moved up with a rush in the last eighth and, taking the lead, held on gamely when challenged and just lasted long enough to withstand Man o' War's challenge. The latter began slowly, moved up steadily to the stretch turn, where he got into close quarters, and came to the outside in the final eighth, and, responding gamely to punishment, was gaining in the closing strides.

Upset defeating Man o' War in the 1919 Sanford Stakes,
the only race the champion ever lost.

Golden Broom showed great speed in pace-making, but tired when challenged . . ." (The four other horses in the race never figured in the running.)

Man o' War had beaten Upset before in the U. S. Hotel Stakes, and he beat him again five times afterwards. That no one took the champion's defeat seriously is illustrated by the fact that ten days later Man o' War met Upset again in the Grand Union Hotel Stakes. Although he had to concede 5 pounds to the colt which had just defeated him, Man o' War was an odds-on favorite, while Upset went off at 6-to-1.

On the other hand, in August of 1913 the Sanford Stakes was merely another race in which a high-flying two-year-old had been trapped and had his wings clipped, a common-place occurrence. Man o' War had not yet become a legend, his great record-breaking feats still lay in the future, and it is significant that at the end of the season he was being compared to exceptional two-year-olds of the past, no more. Too many juvenile sensations, some with records comparable or superior to his, had wilted in their subsequent careers to cause anyone to go overboard on Man o' War.

It was in later years, after the horse had gone on to greater glory, that the Sanford assumed its overriding importance, which, to at least some extent, contributed to a tragic aftermath.

In 1919, John Loftus had the best season experienced by any jockey since Joe Notter had reaped his harvest of gold with the 1908 J. R.

Keene juggernaut, headed by Colin. Loftus didn't ride many races, but he didn't have to. With 177 mounts, he won 65 races, including Sir Barton's sweep of the Triple Crown and Man o' War's victories. Loftus's mounts that year won $252,707, and his 37 percent winning average still stands as an unmolested record among leading money-winning jockeys. But Loftus never rode another race after 1919.

It was common practice for the Jockey Club —or state racing commissions, as the case might be—to deny, or table, applications for licenses, without informing the applicant of the reasons therefor, except in rare instances in which civil suits were filed. Sometimes, after a license had been refused for one or more seasons, it was granted in subsequent seasons— and quite often the same individual might be given a license in one state but not in another. It was the custom among most jockeys and trainers who had been denied a license to simply wait it out and reapply some other time, or some other place.

The applications for licenses to ride in 1920 of both Loftus and Upset's jockey, Bill Knapp, were denied. As time went on there were rumors that this action was in some way connected with Man o' War's loss of the Sanford Stakes, although no evidence ever was produced to support the theory. On the contrary, Loftus had ridden Man o' War in three more races after the big upset, and Knapp obviously had fulfilled perfectly his primary obligation of trying to win. (As Knapp stated recently, he could have gone away from Golden Broom earlier, but waited until the sixteenth pole so as not to give Man o' War enough time to catch up after he got clear. He also remarked about the system that prevailed of reviewing applications for licenses: "Trainers, owners, anybody could knock you, and you never knew about it or had a chance to answer.")

Both boys weighed around 112 pounds, and had to hit the road often to make that, so their riding days were numbered anyway. Each turned to training (Knapp took over Exterminator) and were granted licenses.

Nevertheless, Loftus became identified more as the "guy who lost that race on Man o' War" than as the jockey who won nine races with him, not to mention the victories with Sir Barton and other horses.

Knapp was for years a respected official (at Saratoga, among other tracks) and recently returned to training. Loftus was elected to the National Jockeys' Hall of Fame at Pimlico in 1960, but could not be located for the installation ceremony.

It was as a three-year-old that Man o' War took on his Olympian aura, and as a three-year-old he won his most thrilling victories. His closest call, if it can be called that, came in the Dwyer Stakes (ex-Brooklyn Derby). The Harry Payne Whitney stable included a collection of three-year-olds which would have been awesome in any other year—Upset, John P. Grier, Damask, Wildair and Dr. Clark—and at one time or another each of them was pitted against their tormentor. For the Dwyer, John P. Grier, like Upset a son of the mighty Whisk Broom II, was sent out to do battle alone.

There was talk before the race that trainer James Rowe thought he had a good chance this

time at the weights (108 on Grier against 126 on Man o' War) and talk that Man o' War's trainer, young Louis Feustel, was not too happy with his colt's condition. "Lay along with Grier all the way, and if you find you can win, don't try to ride him out, but win by a length or two lengths," were Riddle's instructions to jockey Clarence Kummer, according to Vosburgh. "Mr. Feustel tells me Man o' War isn't screwed up right tight, and I don't want more use made of him than is necessary to win."

The huge crowd which thronged Aqueduct included many who never before had seen a horse race, but were drawn to the track by a desire to see a champion in action. They saw one and perhaps two.

Full of spirit and accompanied by a pony, Man o' War stepped onto the track. John P. Grier was equally lively, but jockey Eddie Ambrose, seeking to get as much advantage as he could from the 18-pound difference in weight, was in no hurry to get to the post. When they finally did arrive, there was a two-minute delay while starter Mars Cassidy aligned the rivals . . . and they were off.

Although Man o' War, on the inside, bounded into an immediate lead, John P. Grier just as quickly moved up to join him, and they raced as a team, through the first quarter in :23⅗, through the half in :46, through 6 furlongs in 1:09⅗—faster than Thunderer's track record for sprinting that distance, and there still remained 3 furlongs more to go.

One of them had to crack—and Grier was the logical candidate—but after they entered the stretch still lapped on, the unbelievable happened. It was John P. Grier who began to

Man o' War beating John P. Grier in the Dwyer Stakes

inch away, getting his head in front at the three-sixteenths pole.

Down came Kummer's whip as the struggle continued through the mile in 1:36, and Man o' War regained the lead. Realizing his colt had given his all, Ambrose didn't punish Grier further, and the champion drew away in the final stages to win this one, as he did all the others, "easily," by nearly two lengths.

This race also had its aftermath. The next time he met Man o' War, in the Travers Stakes, John P. Grier ran the poorest race on his record, and it was said in later years that "Big Red" had broken his heart, that Grier never was the same after his jousts with Man o' War.

The observation is partially true, in that John P. Grier was not the same colt afterward—he was much better. The Travers was his last tilt against Man o' War, and a month later Grier launched the longest winning streak of his career, four straight, including the Edgemere Handicap, the Aqueduct Handicap in new track record time for $1\frac{5}{16}$ miles and the $1\frac{1}{2}$-mile Annapolis Handicap. As a four-year-old the next season he won the Queens County Handicap under 127 pounds in new track record time.

Before he met Man o' War, John P. Grier never had won a stakes race and his earnings amounted to $7,840. Subsequent to his encounters with the champion, Grier won four stakes events and $28,463; there was nothing wrong with his heart that could not be cured by getting away from the long shadow cast by Man o' War.

According to Man o' War's owner, the colt's greatest race was in the Potomac Handicap as a three-year-old when he carried 138 pounds, highest weight of his career. When the barrier rose, Man o' War was being held by an assistant starter and he broke to the right, losing about three lengths, but despite his heavy burden he overcame the deficit to win easily by one and a half lengths going away, breaking the track record on a surface officially fast, but cuppy.

If Man o' War's weight was impressive, the concessions he was making were more so. To runner-up Wildair, winner of that year's Metropolitan, he conceded 30 pounds; to Blazes, who finished fifteen lengths behind Wildair in third place, and who later was to beat John P. Grier in the Maryland Handicap and to win the Laurel Stakes from The Porter and Sir Barton, he conceded $33\frac{1}{2}$ pounds; and to last-place Paul Jones, winner of that season's Kentucky Derby and Suburban Handicap, he conceded 24 pounds.

Man o' War's final start, in a special match race against Sir Barton for an $80,000 purse at Kenilworth Park, Canada, was such a cakewalk it is generally conceded that Sir Barton was off form. Nevertheless, the Ross colt was coming off a string of four straight victories—in the Rennert Handicap under 132 pounds; the Saratoga Handicap under 129 (in track record time beating Exterminator, Wildair. The Porter and Mad Hatter); the Dominion Handicap under 134 pounds; and the Merchants' and Citizens' Handicap under 133 pounds, in new American record time of $1:55\frac{3}{5}$ for $1\frac{3}{16}$ miles. Sir Barton never won another race after his match with Man o' War, but he raced creditably enough in the Maryland fall handicaps.

As had been done in the case of American Eclipse, various details concerning Man o' War were faithfully recorded for posterity. The high-spirited, muscular colt had been a terror to break to saddle, but once he learned that the human beings who intruded upon his majestic presence wanted only that he should run—which is what he intended doing on his own account—he became tractable enough.

In training, his day began at 3:30 A.M., when he was given his first meal, $2\frac{1}{2}$ quarts of clipped oats mixed with a little cut hay. Because of his voracious appetite, he was fed with a bit in his mouth. At 7:30 he was brushed and massaged; the bandages he wore at all times except in action were removed, and his feet washed; his face, eyes and nostrils were sponged and he was rubbed with a soft cloth.

During this activity, he was docile, yet playful. He was very fond of his caretaker, Frank Loftus, and sometimes showed off for visitors by fetching his hat and carrying it around. Like all horses, Man o' War loved sugar and begged for it; he also was fond of oranges.

At 8:30, morning exercise began. On Mondays, Wednesdays and Fridays, ridden by Clyde Gordon, Man o' War would be jogged half a mile and cantered a mile and a half. Tuesdays, Thursdays and Saturdays were work days—at distances and speeds specified by trainer Feustel, depending upon coming races.

After work, on warm days, he was washed with a mixture of alcohol, arnica and witch hazel; then he was rubbed thoroughly, his feet were picked clean, his hooves washed and he was left to rest in his stall.

On work days, the colt was given walking exercise from 4:00 to 4:30 P.M. and at 5:15 received his final ration of feed, 5 quarts, making a daily total of 12 quarts. On alternate days, the evening meal was varied, and a mash consisting of crushed oats and bran substituted. Thrice a week, at intervals of ten days, he was given a tonic of equal parts oil meal, cream of tartar and sulphur. At 8:30 P.M., he was left alone for the night.

Racetrackers have four classic standards to evaluate a horse: how fast could he run, how far could he go, how much did he carry, and who did he beat?

That Man o' War could run fast and far, under heavy weight, is obvious. In all his starts he either carried or shared highest weight on the scale, except his second race, when the assignments were even but Ralco's jockey was 1½ pounds over weight.

As to whom he beat, the answer is simple: every horse that ever took the track against him. The quality of his opposition might look somewhat pale in Man o' War's presence, and the quantity admittedly was sparse. In his 21 races, "Big Red" faced only 48 individual opponents; although some of them tackled him more than once, most of them did not, and a lot of others avoided him entirely.

Apart from the Sir Barton match, which was scheduled as such, there were five other occasions when only one horse could be found to oppose Man o' War. In the Stuyvesant Handicap, all his opposition was scratched, and R. T. Wilson threw in Yellow Hand as an added starter just to provide a race. (This colt was an ex-claimer who later developed into a good handicap runner, and Wilson sold him for a nice price to Charles Stoneham, owner of the New York Giants.)

Man o' War answered all the questions of greatness that can be put to a race horse, with the possible exception of one: the ability to beat his elders in open competition. Sir Barton was the only older horse "Big Red" met.

In the fall of 1920 the Kentucky Jockey Club offered to put up $50,000 for a match between Exterminator and Man o' War, but Riddle refused it. This caused some sniping, but the owner of Old Bones had everything to gain and nothing to lose, while Riddle was tinkering with destiny: he already had decided to retire Man o' War.

The story goes that Riddle had asked Jockey Club handicapper Walter Vosburgh how much weight his colt would be expected to carry in handicap racing if he remained in training as a four-year-old. Vosburgh could not provide a specific answer, since that depended upon the caliber of the opposition, but he assured Riddle that he would assign Man o' War more than he ever had put on any horse before. As the horse already had carried 138 pounds as a three-year-old, to proceed further would have been to tempt fate.

Physically Man o' War was a glowing chestnut, almost red, standing 16 hands 1⅝ inches. He girthed 71¾ inches and weighed 1,100 pounds in training (at the end of his three-year-old season he was up to 1,150 and as a stallion his weight reached 1,370 pounds). He had a straight profile, large nostrils, stout neck and a broad chest. His barrel was unusually long, his hind legs straight and his gaskins exceptionally powerful looking. He stood over a lot of ground and strode over considerably more; estimates of his stride varied between 25 and 28 feet although, oddly, it never was officially measured.

Measurements, however, cannot convey the picture of this colt who inspired such expressions as "look of eagles" and "living flame." Neither tape nor scale could capture the tremendous vitality that he exuded. As the late Joe Palmer expressed it, "Even when he was standing motionless in his stall, with his ears pricked forward and his eyes focused on something slightly above the horizon which mere people never see, energy still poured from him. He could get in no position which suggested actual repose, and his very stillness was that of the coiled spring, of the crouched tiger."

Man o' War never raced in his native state, but he was shipped to Kentucky and made his last appearance under silks in a gallop at the old Association track in Lexington. Before being sold as a yearling, America's most famous horse had been raised by Mrs. Elizabeth Kane, who had carried on as manager of Nursery Stud after the death of her husband, Edward. When Man o' War retired, he entered stud at Hinata Stock Farm under supervision of another noted lady farm manager, Miss Elizabeth Daingerfield.

Later Riddle built Faraway Farm and established Man o' War there under the management of Harrie B. Scott. While more pedestrian horses shared the universal birthday of January 1, "Big Red's" actual foaling date, March 29, was duly observed as a special occasion. He received telegrams, carrots and other tokens of recognition from all over the country.

Talented writers and eloquent speakers did their best to find phrases to express adequately the glory of this great horse. It fell to a groom, Will Harburt, who did not become associated with Man o' War until some years after his retirement, but who digested thoroughly every iota of his greatness, and was his constant companion thereafter, to devise the description which fit best. Man o' War, as Will never tired of telling the thousands who came to see him, was "de mostest hoss dat ever was."

The owner of Man o' War was a sportsman of the old school. Samuel D. Riddle (1861-1951) was born in Glen Riddle, Pennsylvania, a textile mill town named for his family's ancestral home in Scotland. After graduation from Swarthmore College, Riddle entered the family textile business and was very active in hunting and steeplechase racing as a young man. Sometimes, he would use the mount he rode in competition as transportation to and from the meet. He raced a few horses in partnership with steeplechase trainer John Howard Lewis, who had been a classmate of his at school, and the first important horse the partnership developed was Swarthmore, named for their alma mater. Swarthmore, whose dam was said to have been bred by Ulysses S. Grant, ran in the colors of artist Harry Stull. Yankee Witch, winner of the Rosedale and Spinaway Stakes in 1916, was the first stakes star to wear the black and yellow of Glen Riddle Farm, and next came Man o' War, who through his own exploits and those of his offspring kept the silks prominent.

Riddle's idea of racing, as gleaned from thorough experience as a rider and trainer as well as an owner, was that the best horse should win. Years after Man o' War's retirement, when Riddle was guest of honor at the annual testimonial dinner of the Thoroughbred Club of America, he remarked, "Now and then a horse who can't keep up with his own shadow . . . will win over a really speedy animal, because of the unfair and unintelligent distinction in the matter of weights carried."

With the exception of Friar's Carse, Big Blaze and Whetstone, virtually all Riddle's stakes winners were descendants of Man o' War, and they were numerous: the Belmont Stakes winner American Flag, the Alabama Stakes winner Maid at Arms, the Belmont and Jockey Club Gold Cup winner Crusader, the Matron Stakes winner Taps, the Travers Stakes and Saratoga Cup winner War Hero, the Realization winner War Glory and the pair who joined Man o' War in the stallion barn, War Relic and the Triple Crown winner War Admiral.

Mrs. Riddle's niece was the wife of Walter M. Jeffords, and the Jeffordses also enjoyed great success with the descendants of Man o' War. Originally the two families shared Faraway Farm, but later it was separated into two divisions.

Riddle often was criticized for his management of Man o' War's stud career. The great horse, who was the first to command a $5,000 service fee, was maintained largely as a private stallion, and it has been theorized that his record as a sire would have been far more impressive if he had been permitted larger and more varied books of mares.

A number of fabuolus offers, reportedly in the million-dollar range, were made for Man o' War, but the most staggering one came from Texas. Fort Worth cattle baron and oilman W. T. Waggoner handed Riddle a blank check to be filled in with whatever amount he desired, but that, too, was turned down.

Will Harburt, who had quite a way with words as well as with horses, said, "Lots of folks can have a million dollars, but only one man can own Man o' War. Stand still, Red."

Whatever the caliber of Riddle's stewardship, in 1942 Man o' War replaced his own sire, Fair Play, as the leading progenitor of all time in money won by his offspring (although this distinction disappeared with the general increase in purse values after World War II). When the records were all in, Man o' War had sired sixty-two stakes winners, a total exceeded only by Broomstick's sixty-six, and Big Red's get had earned more than $3½ million.

The long list of stars includes, besides those already mentioned, Mars, Scapa Flow, Edith Cavell, Bateau, the Kentucky Derby winner Clyde Van Dusen, Salaminia, War Beauty, Identify and Fairy Manhurst.

The mathematical odds against any great horse reproducing exactly his own quality at stud are astronomical. Man o' War came reasonably close at that, with War Admiral, and it might be noted that this greatest of "Big Red's" sons was out of "one of those Riddle mares."

The Riddles had no children, and when Riddle died, predeceased by his wife, the bulk of his estate was left to a fund for the establishment of a hospital in Media, Pennsylvania. Faraway Farm continued in operation for a number of years after his death, and the profits from the sale of yearlings and the stud fees of War Admiral and War Relic were contributed to this fund.

While he was in the Army, August Belmont continued to sell off stock from his Nursery Stud, and the turf fortunes of other men besides Riddle and Jeffords were boosted or founded thereby. Most of the yearling crop which followed Man o' War's, in 1919, was sold to A. B. Hancock, and later resold. Included in this batch was Sporting Blood, who began his career in the colors of Redstone Stable (*nom de course* of gambler Arnold Rothstein) but reached his peak under the ownership of cartoonist H. C. "Bud" Fisher, creator of "Mutt and Jeff."

The 1920 crop was purchased by E. F. Simms, James W. McClelland and Henry Oliver, and among the good developments from that piece of business were Chatterton, Lucky Hour, Missionary, Horologe and My Play. The latter was a full brother to Man o' War (Mahubah was never bred to any stallion except Fair Play) whom Belmont considered the pick of the lot, and whom he had intended to keep for himself. As he explained, "His brothers and sisters are in other hands, but this one will be 'my play' in the great game of which we are all so fond," yet the colt was sold along with the rest. He wasn't a patch on his older brother, and for that reason is sometimes referred to as a disappointment, but My Play won nine races including the Jockey Club Gold Cup, which, at 2 miles under weight-for-age conditions, is as definitive a test of intrinsic class as there is in the United States.

CHAPTER FORTY-TWO

IT IS A CURIOUS COINCIDENCE that so many great athletes—Babe Ruth, Bill Tilden, Jack Dempsey, among others—burst upon the scene almost simultaneously shortly after World War I. In racing it was Man o' War who got the twenties off to a roaring start, as he ripped through his undefeated three-year-old season to a new American record for earnings, but even his brilliance did not obscure the members of his supporting cast.

Exterminator, Boniface, Sir Barton, The Porter, Mad Hatter, Billy Kelly, Naturalist and others of the older stars were still going strong.

Besides the three-year-olds who have been mentioned in connection with their races against Man o' War, W. R. Coe's imported filly Cleopatra turned in a brilliant campaign during which she was out of the money only once in fifteen starts. The daughter of Corcyra earned $46,731 including a victory over John P. Grier and other star males in the Latonia Championship.

Among the 1920 two-year-olds, there were three undefeated colts. Whitney had the champion in Tryster, a son of Peter Pan who won all six of his starts, including the Juvenile, Youthful, Keene Memorial, Saratoga Special and Kentucky Jockey Club Stakes, to lead his age division in earnings with $49,925.

Not far behind him was Leonardo II, owned by J. W. McClelland. Although the son of Sweep won only four races, one of them was the rich Hopeful Stakes, a sterling achievement quite apart from the value of the purse, for Leonardo II had undergone scarcely any preparation for it. After winning his first three starts with ease, the colt had developed a lameness, and his training for the Hopeful consisted of standing with his foot in a tub for ten days.

Whitney had an exceptional two-year-old filly in Prudery, also by Peter Pan, who won five of her eight races, and had two seconds: to Tryster in the Saratoga Special and to Leonardo II in the Hopeful. She was not the leading money winner of her sex, however, as the distaff division that year was monopolized by Walter J. Salmon, who had a pair of tomboys, Step Lightly and Careful, who thought nothing of beating colts. Step Lightly, by Ultimus, topped her division in earnings with $40,471 thanks to a victory in the Futurity. Careful, a daughter of Wrack, won twelve of seventeen starts and $34,383, including such races as the National Stakes and Eastern Shore Handicap. Both fillies were ridden by Frankie Keogh.

The other undefeated juvenile colt was Inchcape, who started but twice. Sam Hildreth and Harry F. Sinclair had formed a racing partnership, and they bought Inchcape after his maiden victory for $115,000, a record price at the time for an animal that age. The colt started only once for the partnership, winning the Tremont Stakes by seven lengths, after which he broke down. The next year, he raced once more, won by ten lengths, and broke down again.

Inchcape was bred by John E. Madden, who had supplied Hildreth with many good horses in the past, but the colt was owned by J. H. Rosseter at the time of his sale. Madden and Rosseter were partners in the ownership of

Inchcape's sire, Friar Rock, under an agreement whereby the stallion would stand alternating seasons at Madden's Hamburg Place in Kentucky and Rosseter's Wikiup Ranch in California. The latter establishment was one of the most grandiose in the world, with a $50,000 barn built of the finest quality redwood and mahogany. Rosseter insisted on nothing but the best, and the contractor who built the barn reportedly made a tidy nest egg just on material which had been rejected as unfit for the structure which housed Rosseter's horses. The colorful Californian became so enamored of Friar Rock that Madden had to resort to a court order to get the stallion back when his turn came.

The loss of Inchcape was a severe blow, but it was softened considerably almost immediately. While Inchcape might have been any kind of horse, it is doubtful that he could have been much better than his replacement, Grey Lag, another Madden-bred who was brought to the races by Max Hirsch and purchased by Hildreth after a victory in the Champagne Stakes.

With all the enthusiasm of a child with a new toy, Sinclair was snapping up every horse that caught his fancy. When he also purchased Rancocas Farm, the old Lorillard showplace, and began an elaborate program of restoration, the pace began to tell on Hildreth, who was by this time merely a wealthy man, not a multimillionaire. The two men came to an amicable dissolution of the partnership. Sinclair took over as owner and Hildreth stayed on as trainer, and the following season Grey Lag brought immediate fame to a new set of racing silks: the green and white of Rancocas Farm.

As the earnings of the stars of the 1920 season suggest, so far as racing was concerned the golden age of sports was not merely an expression. Purse distribution had begun a steady climb, which was to last until the end of the decade. Off the track there were other signs that augured well for racing's economic outlook. Ed F. Simms, the breeder of Leonardo II and the owner of luxurious Xalapa Farm, paid $150,000 for the stallion Prince Palatine. Joseph E. Widener purchased 213 acres of the Elmendorf tract as Kentucky breeding headquarters, and a few years later, with his nephew George D. Widener as partner, he acquired an additional 530 acres. Emil Herz paid $910 an acre for Kingston Farm and changed the name to Short Grass Farm.

Highlights of the year 1921 were numerous, but it will be remembered as the year Colonel Edward Riley Bradley took title to the Kentucky Derby; the season Rancocas Stable began a three-year reign at the head of the owners' list, which culminated in a new earnings record; and a year in which yet another undefeated two-year-old appeared upon the scene.

Since he had won the Kentucky Derby in his first try, with Regret in 1915, Harry Payne Whitney had become the biggest subscriber to the race. He was represented whenever possible, and by more than one candidate on several occasions, but a repeat victory in the Louisville classic proved to be elusive. The Whitney coupling of Thunderer and Dominant had been a heavy favorite in 1916, but George Smith knocked them off; again in 1920, the three-horse entry of Upset, Damask and Wildair had been a strong favorite, but it was Paul Jones who pulled the upset. For the 1921

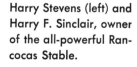

Harry Stevens (left) and Harry F. Sinclair, owner of the all-powerful Rancocas Stable.

renewal, the first at an added value of $50,000, Whitney sent his top colt and filly from the preceding season, Tryster and Prudery, who started at odds of 11-to-10. The race became known as the "battle of the entries," because the second choice was the Xalapa Farm Stable pair of Leonardo II and Bon Homme, while the field included yet another entry, owned by E. R. Bradley, at fourth choice in the wagering.

The contest for the major prize was between the Bradley horses, as Behave Yourself won by a head from Black Servant, with the Whitney horses getting the minor awards, Prudery third and Tryster fourth.

Bradley thus became the second owner in history to run one-two in the Derby, a feat he was to repeat in the near future; all told he racked up four victories in this race and his trainer, H. J. Thompson, earned the nickname "Derby Dick."

The Bradley entry finished six lengths clear of their nearest opposition, so there was no need for jockey Charles Thompson to put Behave Yourself into an all-out drive to nip his stablemate at the end. Black Servant, ridden by Lawrence Lyke, had led all the way up to this point, and the story arose that Lyke and Thompson had a fight in the jockeys' quarters after the race. It also was said that Bradley had made a huge bet on Black Servant in the winter book, which he lost through Thompson's impulsiveness, but according to Olin Gentry, who worked for Colonel Bradley at Idle Hour and became manager of the place under its later identity of Darby Dan Farm, neither story was true.

Green and white were definitely in fashion during 1921. These colors, which had flashed one-two in the Kentucky Derby on the Bradley horses, also were flown in a different combination by the runners of Rancocas Stable, which earned a money championship for Harry F. Sinclair in its first year of action.

Heading the stampede was the three-year-old Grey Lag. This son of Star Shoot—Miss Minnie, by Meddler, won nine of his thirteen starts and was unplaced only once to head his division with $62,596. In addition to beating his contemporaries in such races as the Belmont Stakes, Dwyer, Empire City Derby and Knickerbocker Handicap (under 135 pounds), he beat his elders in the Brooklyn Handicap. Victory in the latter race always has been a mark of distinction for a three-year-old, and in the case of Grey Lag it was particularly so. His 112 pounds was the highest weight successfully carried in the Brooklyn thus far by a horse of his age, and his victims included the cream of the handicap division—John P. Grier, Exterminator, Captain Alcock, Audacious, Mad Hatter, Blazes, Eternal, Paul Jones

Grey Lag (Earl Sande up) equaling the American record of 1:49 for 1⅛ miles in the 1921 Dwyer Stakes at the old Aqueduct.

and Donnacona. The chestnut colt's toughest victory that year was against his own age, however, in the Devonshire International Stakes in Canada versus Black Servant.

Grey Lag took the lead at the start, but Sande took him back and allowed Black Servant to set the pace. After the Bradley colt had reeled off the first 6 furlongs faster than track record time, Sande began gradually to close the gap. All through the stretch it was inch by inch, with Grey Lag getting up just at the wire to win by a nose in new Canadian record time of 1:50 for 1⅛ miles.

That was Grey Lag's eighth victory in succession, but the enormous effort exacted its toll. Neither he nor Black Servant won another race that season, and both of them were beaten in the Latonia Championship by Sporting Blood.

Grey Lag's contributions to the Sinclair coffers were generously supplemented by such good runners as Mad Hatter, Kai-Sang, Thundercloud, Valor, Krewer, Dominique, Cirrus, Lord Brighton, Rose Brigade and old Purchase, but the top money winner of the season was a two-year-old belonging to another stable.

MORVICH, 1919

(Runnymede–Hymir, by Dr. Leggo)

Morvich was bred by sugar baron Adolph B. Spreckels at his well-appointed Napa Stock Farm near San Francisco. However, Morvich, who was not a potential beauty contest winner, happened to be foaled the same year as Runstar, another son of Runnymede, who was the apple of his owner's eye. Thus it was that the awkward-looking, knobby-kneed Morvich was sent east with trainer C. W. Carroll and made his debut in the Suffolk Selling Stakes. He started at 30-to-1, which was possibly the greatest overlay in history.

The California colt won by ten lengths and thereupon was sold to trainer Fred Burlew, who entered him in another selling stake. This time Morvich was odds-on, and won by six lengths.

Sam Hildreth warned Burlew that if he ever started the colt in a claiming event again, it would be the last he'd see of him. The warning was unnecessary, for Burlew realized he had struck gold. After Morvich won an allowance race by five lengths, the trainer sold a half-interest in him to Wall Street financier Benjamin Block, and the colt raced under the ownership of the B & B Stable for his next three starts, all of which he won easily.

Up to this point Morvich had won six races by an average of nearly five lengths, leading all the way, without once being put to a drive. Block bought out Burlew's interest—retaining him as trainer, however—and the colt was shipped to Saratoga to make his debut in stakes competition.

His introduction to that brand of racing, in the United States Hotel Stakes on August 6, resulted in a close call, as jockey Frank Keogh on Morvich was all out to win by a neck from Kai-Sang, ridden by Earl Sande, after Morvich had been crowded close to the rail in the stretch. When the same rivals met in the Saratoga Special a week later, however, Morvich won easily by two lengths. Although the jockeys were changed for the Hopeful Stakes on August 31—Albert Johnson on Morvich and Laverne **Fator on Kai-Sang—the result was identical,** as again the California colt won easily by two lengths, carrying 130 pounds.

Morvich, unbeatable for 12 races, was never able to win the thirteenth. Albert Johnson up.

Morvich had not been nominated to the New York Futurity, won that year by Bunting, so he was shipped down to Maryland where he made even more money than would have been possible in New York. Pimlico inaugurated its Futurity in 1921 as the richest race in the nation. After winning the Eastern Shore Handicap under 130 pounds in September, Morvich closed out his juvenile campagin on November 5 by adding the Pimlico Futurity to his collection. Beyond the winner's purse of $42,750, the race was of added significance in that, while Morvich had won his previous races as a front runner over sprint distances, this one was at a mile and he had come from behind to win.

His harvest for an unbeaten campaign of eleven starts was $115,234, the first time since Colin that a two-year-old had won more than $100,000. Indeed, Morvich's over-all juvenile record had been surpassed only by that great horse. He went into winter quarters being compared to Colin, Man o' War, Salvator, Hindoo, Luke Blackburn and other immortals of the past.

The only problem that confronted Block at the outset of Morvich's three-year-old season was to decide which big race he wanted to win. The Preakness and Kentucky Derby, both with $50,000 added, were run on the same afternoon in 1922. Block chose the Derby for his colt, and, although Morvich had not started in more than six months, he was made a heavy favorite. He won the race in his usual style, taking the lead soon after the start and staying in front all the way. Johnson had him under a pull when he crossed the finish one and a half lengths clear of his nearest rival, Bet Mosie, the first occasion, except for the time Kai-Sang had cornered him at Saratoga, that any horse had finished closer than two lengths to Morvich.

Following this victory, which made it an even dozen, the black son of Runnymede was hailed as a super horse. He never won another race.

Start number 13 was the Carlton Stakes, in which Morvich finished second to Harry Payne Whitney's Whiskaway. Although his undefeated string had been snapped, Morvich did not lose much prestige, since he was conceding the winner 15 pounds in this race, and had beaten Whiskaway as a two-year-old; moreover, finishing behind Morvich in the Carlton was J. S. Cosden's French-bred Snob II, who a few weeks earlier had won the Withers Stakes from R. T. Wilson's Pillory.

As Pillory had won both the Preakness and Belmont, this threw the three-year-old championship picture into a turmoil, and Matt Winn into ecstasy.

The renowned promoter scheduled the Kentucky Special at $50,000-added to be run at Latonia on June 24 under Derby conditions, designed to establish supremacy among the three-year-olds. Although Morvich again was the favorite, Whiskaway won this one without a weight concession, Thibodaux was second, Morvich third and Pillory fourth.

In his final two starts, each time under 130 pounds, Morvich's mantle of invincibility was reduced to tatters. Surf Rider beat him easily in a two-horse race at Saratoga, and in the Fall Highweight Handicap, won by the filly Careful, Morvich ran dead last—the only race since his debut in which he was not favorite, the first time he had finished out of the money and the last race of his career.

His suspicious-looking legs finally had given out, but his sad ending notwithstanding, the colt from California had written a brilliant chapter in turf history, and his performance was a tribute to those Westerners who carried on during the lean years, which lasted much longer in their area than in the East. Besides Spreckels, Rosseter and Macomber, they included such men as Baron Long (who stood Runnymede at stud), John Marchbank, Norman Church, Hamilton Cotton, John McKee, H. D. "Curly" Brown, Charles Perkins and others. (As a final footnote to the story of Morvich, Runstar, the colt Spreckels had retained in preference to Morvich, did come through. On March 30, 1924, as a five-year-old, he beat seventeen rivals in the Coffroth Handicap at Tijuana to earn $43,650, the richest purse ever offered to horses of handicap age up to that time.)

Pillory finally won out in the helter-skelter scramble among the three-year-olds of 1922, but the real stars of that racing season were in the handicap division, the old-timers who had helped launch the golden age of sports.

For Exterminator it was the best season of his distinguished career. As a seven-year-old he won ten races and $71,075, a sum never before approached by a horse of that age.

Racing returned to Chicago for good in 1922 and on September 30, at Hawthorne Park, a delirious crowd of 25,000 and a 100-piece band turned out to celebrate. The main act on the program was an exhibition by Exterminator; in theory, he was running against Dodge's track record for 1¼ miles, but in practice no one expected him to come close on a track that only recently had been covered with weeds. Old Bones took 2:10 to run the distance, but as the "victory wreath" was draped across his well-worn withers, the cheering lasted fully ten minutes.

Grey Lag had a remarkable season for a handicap horse, winning five of his six starts, including the Mt. Kisco Stakes, Empire City, Queens County and Saratoga Handicaps. His only loss was a second to Exterminator in a memorable renewal of the Brooklyn Handicap. Ridden by Laverne Fator and carrying 126 pounds, the four-year-old Grey Lag dogged the pace of Polly Ann until the stretch turn, where he took the lead and began to draw away. Exterminator, ridden by Albert Johnson and carrying 135 pounds, had been in close pursuit all the way, and he roared up in the stretch to challenge his younger rival. Grey Lag was a head in front at the stretch call, but it was Exterminator by a head at the end.

Six-year-old Mad Hatter started 21 times, and despite frequent displays of the temperament associated with the sons of Fair Play (or, to put it another way, the grandsons of Hastings), he was in the money 16 times and won five races, including the Champlain and Metropolitan Handicaps and a second renewal of the two-mile Jockey Club Gold Cup.

Down at Tijuana, where excellent sport was being provided for Southern California racing fans, a star of the meeting was C. B. "Cowboy" Irwin's seven-year-old Motor Cop.

Several noteworthy two-year-olds made their bows in 1922. W. S. Kilmer was back on the scene with a filly named Sally's Alley, who set a new seasonal earnings record for her sex by winning $94,847, with victories in the Clover Stakes, New York Futurity and a division of the Pimlico Futurity, which race attracted so many entries that it had to be split. Another branch of the Whitney family was in evidence as the good two-year-old Cherry Pie ran in the colors of Greentree Stable, which was the racing name of Mrs. Payne Whitney. Cherry Pie was destined to lower the competitive record for a mile to 1:35⅖ the following year.

Among numerous other promising juveniles were Bud Lerner, Blossom Time and one which was destined to make the world sit up and take notice, Zev.

CHAPTER FORTY-THREE

IT MIGHT BE SAID THAT MAN o' War was made a gift of the American money-winning championship, i.e., a special purse of $80,000 was dangled before him and he had to beat only one horse to get it.

Turn about is fair play, and the colt which displaced Man o' War in the financial standings did so by virtue of another special event of even more generous proportions. In 1923 Zev won more money in a single season than any other American horse had won during his entire career. He led Rancocas Stable to the top of the owners' rankings for the third successive year, and the stable earnings also were a new record. Zev provided more than 60 percent of the Rancocas total, and the biggest item in his bank account came from his match with Papyrus.

Although only the two horses participated, it was the richest race in world history. The match between Man o' War and Sir Barton had been a winner-take-all proposition; that between Zev and Papyrus guaranteed a slightly larger purse to the winner, and even the second horse received more than $20,000.

ZEV, 1920

(The Finn–Miss Kearney, by Planudes)

A brown colt, named for Sinclair's attorney, Colonel William Zeveley, Zev had been an adequate two-year-old but nothing special. He started five times before winning his maiden race, following which he won an allowance event, the Grand Union Hotel Stakes and the Albany Handicap. He then finished third to Dunlin and Goshawk in the Hopeful Stakes,

and second to Sally's Alley in the Futurity, to wind up his campaign with four victories in twelve starts and $24,665.

He served notice that things were going to be different at three when, in his first start, after seven and a half months' absence from competition, he beat older horses in the Paumonok Handicap, but this flash of brilliance was offset when he ran twelfth for the Preakness in his next start. The race was too bad to be true, and it wasn't. Zev had been kicked by another horse while waiting for the start, and he came back three days later to win the Rainbow Handicap.

Four days after that he led all the way to win the Kentucky Derby at odds of 19-to-1. He was then shipped East for the Withers, Belmont Stakes, Queens County Handicap, an allowance race at Belmont and the Lawrence Realization Stakes—all of which he won, defeating Preakness winner, Vigil, twice in the process.

American pride in native achievements in all forms of sport was boiling over during the 1920s, and in 1923 officials of Belmont Park issued an invitation to Ben Irish to send over his Epsom Derby winner, Papyrus, to race against the champion American three-year-old. The inducement was £20,000 ($80,600) to the winner and £5,000 consolation prize to the other contestant. (The total purse of the International Race was £25,000 of which £20,000 went to the winner and £5,000 to the second. The pound was worth $4.03 that year.) After considerable hesitation, and not a little trepidation in view of the hazards involved, on the 22nd of September Papyrus sailed from England on the *Aquitania*.

After eight days at sea, during which his box had to be kept under surveillance to prevent admiring fellow passengers from feeding him oranges, bananas and nuts, Papyrus was led down the gangplank in New York amidst a scene such as seldom has been duplicated. Few movie queens could boast a more enthusiastic reception, and Papyrus was himself a budding cinema star, for there had been a great clamor for film rights to the match, and as a novelty it was to be broadcast over radio. The dock was packed with excited onlookers, while passengers and crew lined the rail of the great steamer, and all cheered loudly as the English colt was led down the gangplank and walked into a motor van for the drive to Belmont Park, preceded by a police escort.

Trainer Basil Jarvis, on his own as Irish had not accompanied him, had exactly three weeks in which to prepare his charge for the contest, against an American opponent not yet definitely decided upon.

Although it had been assumed all along that America would be represented by Zev, the colt broke out with hives a couple of weeks before the race and an effort was made to substitute My Own. This son of King James, owned by Admiral Cary T. Grayson's Salubria Stable, had been a moderate two-year-old, but was undefeated in his first five starts at three. How-ever, Zev quickly recovered from his indisposition, and the contest was made firm: Derby winner against Derby winner.

Papyrus, meanwhile, had missed a couple of days training because of a hot ankle, but had recovered sufficiently to electrify the public with a 9-furlong workout in 1:50⅖—just 1⅕ seconds slower than Man o' War's world record—two days before the race. In a classic exhibition of British *sang-froid* Jarvis cabled Irish that the horse held "a good sporting chance of winning."

On October 20, the day of the race, the English trainer was confronted with another emergency. On Friday evening rain had begun to fall and by Saturday morning the Belmont track was a quagmire. Jack Joyner and other American trainers advised Jarvis to put mud calks on Papyrus, but the English trainer, thinking that his colt was being subjected to enough strange circumstances as it was, decided not to risk a last-minute change.

Ridden by the champion British jockey Steve Donoghue, and wearing the smooth English plates he had worn all his life, Payprus went to the post a slight favorite. Ignoring the special enclosure that had been set up for the occasion, the superstitious Hildreth saddled Zev in a spot

Zev beating Papyrus in the first of the great international races at Belmont Park in 1923.

under the trees he had been using for years, and the American colt, with Sande roosting in the saddle, followed the Englishman onto the sloppy track as the huge throng roared its enthusiasm.

At the start, Papyrus jumped into a lead, but Donoghue quickly took him under wraps and waited for Zev to move up where he could keep an eye on him. Sande was only too happy to accommodate, and from there on out Donoghue was able to watch Zev without having to twist his neck. Bounding along smoothly, the American colt kept drawing out straight ahead while Papyrus, unable to take hold in the slippery going, struggled vainly in his wake. "I first realised that Papyrus would not win after they had gone four furlongs," said Jarvis later. The Englishman was standing next to his American counterpart during the running, and as the horses rounded the stretch turn, with more than a quarter of a mile to go, Hildreth felt a tug on his sleeve. Jarvis already had turned away from the contest in progress and was extending his hand. "I congratulate you, Mr. Hildreth" he said, "it's your race, my horse is beaten."

Zev crossed the finish five lengths clear in 2:35⅖ for the 1½ miles. It had required 1:54 to negotiate the first 1⅛ miles—3⅗ seconds slower than the time Papyrus had registered in his workout on a fast track.

Jarvis then returned home to a barrage of criticism, while on this side of the Atlantic Zev was hailed as a national hero. There was some private opinion to the contrary, however, with Admiral Grayson prominent among the demurrers.

My Own had extended his undefeated skein to six races by winning the Maryland Handicap the week before Zev's victory, and Grayson thought his colt should have represented America, but his argument was drowned out as Zev won the Empire City Autumn Championship on October 31 by four lengths.

Grayson shipped My Own to Kentucky in an effort to trip Zev in the 1¾-mile Latonia

Championship. There was a surprise in store for everyone, as Carl Weidemann's In Memoriam won by six lengths, with Zev second, ten lengths in front of My Own. This led to a challenge for another match and, after scoring his eleventh victory of the season at Pimlico, Zev returned to Kentucky to meet In Memoriam at Churchill Downs. With a beautiful exhibition of timing, Sande waited until the last instant before challenging, and got Zev's nose in front just at the end of the 1¼-mile race. A lot of spectators felt that the Weidemann colt had won (and some still do) but in the records it is Zev by a nose.

There was anticipation of a renewed rivalry between Zev and In Memoriam at four, but the son of McGee started only once the next year. Zev made seventeen starts as a four-year-old, winning only six, but he padded his already unprecedented earnings further to retire with the following record: 43 starts, 23 wins, 8 seconds, 5 thirds and $313,639.

In addition to Zev's financial championship as a three-year-old, the earnings of Rancocas Stable that year amounted to $438,849, also a new record, surpassing the winnings by James R. Keene in his best season. However, 1923 was a disastrous year for Rancocas otherwise, as forty-one horses, including the stallions Inchcape and Cirrus, were destroyed in a fire at the farm.

There was further trouble brewing. While Zev was still in action, a Congressional investigation began in connection with the Teapot Dome oil leases. The affair dragged on for years; Sinclair was tried on charges of conspiracy with Secretary of the Interior Albert B. Fall to defraud the government; he was acquitted of these charges, but nevertheless served a few months in prison after being adjudged guilty of contempt of Congress for refusing to testify.

In spite of this experience, Sinclair later served on the Petroleum Industry War Council during World War II, and, although 1923 was its last season of leadership, Rancocas

Stable hovered near the top for many years afterward.

Old Grey Lag also had his tribulations. Retired to stud with great fanfare after his distinguished racing career, he had proved to be virtually sterile, getting only a few foals in several years. He was put back in training as a nine-year-old, but, although he won some overnight races, the spark was gone, so he was retired again, this time, given to a friend of Sinclair who promised him a comfortable home. However, the friend died, and Grey Lag —unknown to Sinclair, who was busy with his own problems at the time—was sold at auction. His name appeared among the entries for a claiming race up in Canada in 1931, when Grey Lag was thirteen years old. As soon as Sinclair learned of this, he sent an agent to purchase the horse.

Grey Lag didn't win during his third racing career, but before the agent found him he had picked up a third place; he closed out his record, finally, with $136,715, from 25 victories in 47 starts.

For a long time it was a widely held belief that horses were color blind. However, F. M. Taylor, who welcomed the van which carried Grey Lag home for the last time said that the old horse nearly threw a fit with delight when he saw the familiar green and white buckets of Rancocas. He was around them for the rest of his life, for he never left home again.

On a horse, according to both Ring Lardner and Damon Runyon, there never was a handy guy like Sande. As Zev's jockey, he would have been the leading money-winning rider of the 1923 season more or less automatically, but Earl Sande chose this as the most active season of his career, other than the year he broke in as an apprentice, and he set new records both in number of stakes races won (39) and amount of purse money ($569,394).

These records are the more noteworthy because what was an active season for Sande consisted of only 430 mounts, about half the number many other jockeys accepted. He,

like such roughly contemporaneous riders as Fator, Ensor, Albert Johnson, Linus "Pony" McAtee, Mack Garner and Raymond "Sonny" Workman, was a money rider who concentrated on the stakes events. They monopolized the financial standings, while, after Ivan Parke, a series of boys who came and went took turns at the top of the numerical standings; few of the latter group managed to achieve a 20 percent winning average, in contrast to money jocks who seldom dropped below that average.

Earl Harold Sande was a money rider personified. He twice exceeded 30 percent and maintained a lifetime winning average of 26 percent. He wasn't a native of Idaho, but he was born in the nearby state of South Dakota, and broke in at the fairs in Idaho, Utah and Arizona before taking his first official ride, at the Fair Grounds in New Orleans on January 5, 1918. Like Tod Sloan, Sande knew he was good, and became something of a prima donna, though not nearly so flamboyant as his predecessor, and he, too, became well acquainted with the stewards. At the time of his conquests with Zev, his career still had several distinguished, and several bumpy, years to go— but this was the apex. Not for three decades was another jockey to win 39 stakes in one

L. S. Sutcliffe

Sarazen, the gelding who outran his pedigree by setting a record for 1¼ miles.

season, and that when there were four times as many races on the calendar.

While Zev was sweeping nearly everything before him in the three-year-old division, a trio of two-year-olds was doing a pretty good job of their own within their respective sectors.

In New York, George D. Widener's St. James, a son of Ambassador IV–Bobolink II, by Willonyx, won the U. S. Hotel Stakes, Saratoga Special and Futurity (the first horse since Domino to succeed with 130 pounds up) to top his division in earnings with $89,385.

In Kentucky, Wise Counsellor, a son of Mentor–Rustle, by Russell, owned first by T. C. Bradley and later by J. S. Ward, after finishing second in his first start roared through four straight stakes victories at Latonia and Churchill Downs to collect $60,610.

More impressive than either of these two, although he earned less money, was Phil T. Chinn's Sarazen, a son of High Time–Rush Box, by Box. He was undefeated in ten starts, including the Champagne Stakes, Oakdale Handicap, National Stakes and—most unusual of all—a victory over older horses in a weight-for-age race at Pimlico. Like Zev, Sarazen had won a special match race, and also like Zev, both he and Wise Counsellor were to participate in a series of international races the next year.

Although it had been a disappointment, the Zev–Papyrus match sparked a general interest in international racing and in 1924 French perfume manufacturer Pierre Wertheimer brought his French champion Epinard to the United States for a whole series of races. It was a rare gesture of sportsmanship, pitting the invader against the best America had to offer over a variety of distances, at a different track each time. And, although Epinard failed to win a race, he covered himself with glory.

The French four-year-old, trained by Eugene Leigh and ridden by Everett Haynes, made his first American start at Belmont Park on September 1 where Wise Counsellor (then owned by Fred Burton) beat him by less than a length, 6 furlongs in 1:11⅘, with August Belmont's Ladkin three lengths farther back. On September 27 at Aqueduct the distance was a mile, the time was a fast 1:36⅖ and the winner was Ladkin by only a nose, as Epinard took second by one and a half lengths from Wise Counsellor with Zev fourth and My Own fifth. At Latonia on October 11, Epinard was the favorite, but Sarazen threw a track record at him.

Sarazen, who had been sold to Mrs. William K. Vanderbilt III's Fair Stable, chose this moment to repudiate his pedigree. The son of the intensely inbred High Time, a line which was noted for pure speed and nothing else, ran the 10 furlongs in 2:00⅘ as Epinard was a length and a half behind, nosing out that year's Belmont Stakes winner, Mad Play, for second. The winning time not only broke the Latonia track record by 1⅗ seconds, but in view of the dispute concerning Whisk Broom II's American record it was hailed by many horsemen as the fastest performance of its sort ever seen in this country. Having completed his series of special engagements, Epinard was entered in the Laurel Stakes a week later, but finished out

Epinard, the "bridesmaid" of the 1924 international match races, never won but nevertheless acquitted himself nobly.

of the money as Wise Counsellor was the winner.

To return to Sarazen: as a gelding he was not eligible to a number of the richer races in his youth, but Matt Winn had been standing by with his customary $50,000 which he added to the purse of the third International Special in order to attract the best possible field, so Sarazen led his division in earnings despite the discrimination against him. He raced on for four more seasons and led the handicap division in 1926; when he retired after 27 victories, with $225,000, he was among the top five American money winners.

CHAPTER FORTY-FOUR

T HE CLASSIC PLOT FOR A WORK of fiction that deals with horse racing features an animal of humble circumstances who plunges through to win the Kentucky Derby and thereby enables his widowed owner to pay off the mortgage on the old homestead.

BLACK GOLD, 1921

(Black Toney–Useeit, by Bonnie Joe)

It is doubtful that Black Gold's owner was burdened by a mortgage at the time he scored his richest victory—the colt himself would have remedied that the previous season when he won $19,163—but she was a widow, and of adversity she certainly had her share.

The hero of racing's most romantic true story could not have had a more suitable background. Black Gold's dam, Useeit, was an unfashionably bred daughter of Bonnie Joe–Effie M., by Bowling Green, who as a two-year-old had come into the possession of R. M. Hoots, who campaigned her at the small Western meetings. Her earnings were modest, but her performance

was prodigious. She won 34 races and, within her limit—which was around 6 furlongs—she could hold her own with the best, although the fabulous Pan Zareta managed to defeat her several times.

Hoots became exceedingly fond of his little breadwinner, and paid the penalty for his sentiment. When the mare was claimed by Tobe Ramsey at Juarez in 1916, Hoots refused to give her up. He was ruled off the turf and sent Useeit back to the farm. Hoots died the following year, but his widow kept the mare. After Useeit had foaled a couple of winners, Mrs. Hoots, who lived in Oklahoma and proudly traced her ancestry to an Indian tribe, shipped the mare to Kentucky to be bred to Colonel E. R. Bradley's fashionable stallion, Black Toney. The name of the resulting foal was a natural one to be chosen by a resident of Oklahoma in those days, when everyone in the state could dream of sudden wealth from the oil that gushed from the land like streams of black gold.

Black Gold's saga began and ended at the New Orleans Fair Grounds. Trained by Harry Webb, who also had trained his dam, the colt

Black Gold, winner of four Derbies.

won his first start there on January 19, 1923, and went on to win a total of nine races in eighteen starts as a two-year-old. Foreshadowing his big moment, his only stakes victory that season came at Churchill Downs on the same day Zev won the Kentucky Derby.

When he came out at three the next season, Black Gold won six races in succession. After taking a couple of allowance races at Jefferson Park, he moved up into stakes company for the Louisiana Derby. Going to the lead at once, he splashed through the mud to win by six lengths from a field of ten rivals, including representatives of several large Eastern stables. After a hollow, eight-length victory in the Derby Trial Purse, Black Gold started as a heavy favorite for the Kentucky Derby at Churchill Downs, May 17, but this one was not so easy.

The Gallaher Brothers' Chilhowee, ridden by Albert Johnson, polished off Rancocas Stable's Bracadale after entering the stretch, and headed for the wire, but Jimmy Mooney went to work on Black Gold and the colt got up in time. It was one of the more exciting finishes to the Derby, as Black Gold was just half a length clear of Chilhowee, who took second by a nose from Beau Butler, a head in front of Altawood, and fifth-place Bracadale was only a head behind him.

Black Gold ranged farther north to win the Ohio State Derby at Maple Heights Park in Cleveland next out, and then his winning streak was broken. Chilhowee, the colt who had fought him so hard at Churchill Downs, beat him in a preliminary race and again in the Latonia Derby. Chilhowee was a bearcat, and Latonia was his favorite course. He set a new American record of 1:48⅖ for 1⅛ miles at the northern Kentucky track on October 14, and four days later set another American record of 2:54⅗ for 1¾ miles.

Black Gold added three more victories later that year, including the Chicago Derby at Hawthorne, in which the favorite, Ladkin, finished fourth, to wind up the season with the unique achievement of having won a Derby in each of four different states.

Black Gold proved to be sterile after two seasons at stud and was returned to the track. He raced briefly as a six-year-old, but couldn't win, and in his first race as a seven-year-old at the Fair Grounds, where he had begun his career five years earlier, he broke his leg. He was humanely destroyed and buried in the infield beside the old friend of the family, Pan Zareta.

Among the two-year-olds of 1924, Master Charlie, an English-bred colt owned by William Daniel of Chicago, slashed clear across the continent to win the championship. After taking the Tijuana Futurity he came East to New York and won the Colorado, Hopeful and Remsen Stakes, then won the Kentucky Jockey Club Stakes in the Midwest.

Fillies were especially prominent that year. Harry Payne Whitney uncorked a formidable quartet of juvenile fillies—Maud Muller, Mother Goose, Elf and Swinging, who swept through the Eastern stakes for their division, in some cases taking all three places. Mother Goose won an historic renewal of the Futurity, in a field of twenty-nine runners which included the top colts Stimulus and Single Foot.

Among the three-year-old fillies, H. C. Fisher's Nellie Morse was the leading money winner ($60,250) thanks to a victory in the Preakness, but she was hard pressed by Princess Doreen who started eighteen times and won eight, including the Kentucky Oaks, Coaching Club American Oaks, Labor Day, Falls City and Covington Handicaps to earn $51,370.

Ladkin, winner of the second International Special, was the last top horse raced by August Belmont II. Quite a few turf notables, including A. B. Spreckels, Ed Corrigan, James Shevlin, Frank Kelly, and William Hendrie, had passed away during 1924, and on December 9, Belmont joined them.

259

Princess Doreen, the mare who supplanted Miss Woodford after 40 years as leading money winner of her sex.

Having completed his tour of duty with the Army, Belmont had resumed an active role in racing in 1922, with his horses trained by Louis Feustel, who at the same time continued to train for S. D. Riddle. This, the third distinct phase of Belmont's turf activity, was on a more limited scale. He kept some of his stock and sold some, and again he went through the experience of seeing horses he had bred perform well for other owners. Among the good ones who got away were Dunlin, Osprey, Peter King, Catalan and Mad Play, the latter a full brother to Mad Hatter, who also went to the Rancocas Stable, for whom he won the Belmont Stakes.

Some of those Belmont retained for himself turned out well, too, such as Messenger, the filly How Fair, Lucky Play, Ordinance and, of course, Ladkin.

The influence of Belmont as a breeder was further spread by a decision of the executors of his estate to sell out his entire stock after his death. Ordinance was sold privately to Mrs. Payne Whitney for an undisclosed sum (estimated in excess of $50,000) and the rest of the racing stable to railroad tycoon W. Averell Harriman. The future Ambassador to Russia and to Great Britain, Secretary of Commerce and Governor of New York paid a reported price of $225,000. Harriman had begun his racing activity as a partner with G. H. Walker in the ownership of Log Cabin Stable; when the partnership later was dissolved, Walker took that name and Harriman assumed Arden Farm as his *nom de course*.

The Belmont yearlings and breeding stock were bought by another transportation magnate, Joseph E. Widener, whose fortune was based on the Philadelphia Street Railway system. He paid an estimated $100,000 for the yearlings (which included ultimate stakes winners Chance Shot, Arc Light, Canaan and Broadside) and $350,000 for the breeding stock. As he was already well supplied at his own Elmendorf Farm, Widener scheduled an auction of the Belmont breeding stock at Nursery Stud on the day before the 1925 Kentucky Derby. Special trains were run to Lexington to accommodate the crowd which attended the sale, and the results were historic. Widener more than doubled his money as the three stallions and sixty-five broodmares realized a total of $782,000, although he himself paid the top prices: $100,000 for the stallion Fair Play, who was then twenty years old, and $40,000 for the mare Qu' Elle est Belle II.

August Belmont II was the last autocrat of the American turf as a whole. Men equally prominent, equally powerful (and autocratic) within their own orbits, and men more successful in racing financially were to come along later, but the day of nationwide domination by individuals ended with Belmont.

Long before his death Maryland and Kentucky, for example, had declared their independence from the Jockey Club. The racing commissions in these states wrote their own rules of racing, taking into account local aspects of the sport, and otherwise went their own ways in administrative procedures. Maryland in particular—or, more specifically, Pimlico—had chafed under the long reins extend-

ing from New York, especially during the years of the blackout and the period immediately following, when Pimlico was the No. 1 track in the country.

Belmont came along at a time when racing needed a few firm foundations on which to build, and he had served his purpose well. At the time of his death racing was big enough and strong enough to stand by itself.

August Belmont II lived long enough to see the first crop by Man o' War come to the races, and there were seven two-year-old winners among them, the first of whom was American Flag. Had Belmont lasted just a bit longer, he would have seen this colt top the three-year-old division and make Samuel D. Riddle the season's leading owner. In 1925, the year the Nursery Stud was broken up, American Flag was undefeated in four starts including the Belmont Stakes.

Riddle led the owners' list with an amazingly small stable, seventeen horses, but eleven of them were by Man o' War. Besides American Flag, they included the stakes winners Maid at Arms, Taps, Crusader and Corvette. In addition, such of Big Red's offspring as the sisters Florence Nightingale and Edith Cavell (both out of a mare named The Nurse), Mars

Louis Feustel (left), trainer of Man o' War for Samuel D. Riddle, later also took over the racing string of the great colt's breeder, August Belmont II (right), most influential turf figure of his era.

and By Hisself did well for other owners, giving Man o' War a total of nine stakes winners out that season.

PRINCESS DOREEN, 1921

(Spanish Prince II–Lady Doreen, by Ogden)

Princess Doreen had been bred by John E. Madden and she raced for the Audley Farm of Montfort and B. B. Jones. Following her good sophomore season, as a four-year-old in 1925 she won eleven of twenty-five starts and collected $69,220, to become the first filly since the blackout years to top the handicap division in earnings.

Princess Doreen thereby ousted Miss Woodford as the leading money winner of her sex in American racing history. Although she padded her lead with two more years of successful racing, 1925 was her biggest season. She hit her peak late in the summer in the Cincinnati area, when she won a remarkable series of races carrying high weights against males. At the new Coney Island Jockey Club she won the Western Hills Handicap on August 25 under 126 pounds. At the same track on September 7 she won the Cincinnati Enquirer Handicap under 129 pounds. Five days later she was across the river at Latonia for the Covington Handicap, which she won under 130 pounds. A week after that one, with her weight up to 133 pounds, she won the Autumn Handicap, conceding 12 pounds to the four-year-old gelding Gibbons, and defeating the good three-year-old colt Captain Hal among others. In all of these races Princess Doreen made large weight concessions to male horses, among them Brown Sugar, San Utar, Sir Peter, and Kentucky Cardinal. She also won the Bowie Handicap that year, under 118 pounds, from Aga Khan and My Own.

As a five-year-old she was just as active, though somewhat less successful; she started twenty-six times and won six, including the Latonia Inaugural and Saratoga Handicaps,

beating Sarazen in the latter. At six, the mare with the iron constitution started a dozen times more and added the Independence and Greater Chicago Handicaps to her string of stakes successes. She retired after 94 starts with 34 victories, 15 seconds and 17 thirds for earnings of $174,745.

Princess Doreen represented the crowning achievement for trainer Kay Spence, a former jockey from Fairbury, Illinois, who in 1918 had broken H. G. Bedwell's long reign as leading trainer in number of winners. Spence stayed on top in that category in 1919, and in 1920 tied with S. A. Clopton for the lead. Although he began, as Bedwell had done, with mostly claiming horses, a number of stakes stars came his way before his career ended in 1936. The best of his earlier horses was Hodge, and he later trained Gallant Knight and The Clown. Princess Doreen was one of five winners of the Kentucky Oaks saddled by Spence.

POMPEY, 1923

(Sun Briar–Cleopatra, by Corcyra)

Good as she was, Princess Doreen was not the leading money winner of 1925, for the richer plums were being offered to two-year-olds, and there was a pair of good ones ready to pick them up.

Pompey, a home-bred colt owned by W. R. Coe's Shoshone Stable and trained by W. H. Karrick was the year's top winner with earnings of $121,630 coming from seven wins and two seconds in ten starts. His victories included the East View, U. S. Hotel, Hopeful Stakes and the Futurity, the latter the richest event of the season.

Canter, a son of Wildair, bred and owned by J. E. Griffith, and trained by Harry Rites, came close in earnings with $113,948, from eight wins in eighteen starts, but he lost to Pompey on all four occasions they met. Canter won six stakes, the principal one being the Pimlico Futurity.

American Flag, Man o' War's first champion son, with jockey Albert Johnson.

The 1925 Belmont Stakes winner, American Flag, started but four times that year, as noted. The first two classics were won by colts of similarly brief tenure, both owned by Gifford A. Cochran and trained by W. B. Duke.

The Preakness, contested first that year, was won by Coventry, a son of Negofol, bred by E. F. Simms. Ridden by Clarence Kummer, Coventry won by four lengths, although he was fifth choice in the wagering, coupled with two other horses as part of the mutuel field.

The Kentucky Derby was won by Flying Ebony, a son of The Finn, bred by J. E. Madden. Flying Ebony was second choice in the wagering—but that was because he, too, was part of the mutuel field, which in the Derby included no less than nine runners. It was the first Derby broadcast on radio. There

were 8½ miles of Pullman cars in "Derby Village," where the special excursion trains were parked, which visitors used as their "hotel" during their stay in Louisville. Many had come to Kentucky for the Belmont dispersal the day before, and it was at the sale that Cochran had decided to start Flying Ebony, only after he learned the services of Earl Sande were available. Even so, Cochran refused to go home that night for fear that his friends would persuade him to withdraw the colt.

Cochran had paid good prices for both Coventry and Flying Ebony at the yearling sales, and both colts, after returning their big installment, called it even. The Derby was the last victory in Flying Ebony's career; the Preakness was the only victory in Coventry's racing career.

CHAPTER FORTY-FIVE

N ABOUT THE MIDDLE OF THE decade characterized as the golden age of sports, racing underwent a boom. This was particularly evident in Canada, where the sport had come to the fore during the blackout in the New York area, and had begun to expand greatly after World War I. Stamford opened in 1923; followed by Lansdowne, Long Branch, and Whittier Park in 1924; and in 1925 Chinook Park, Edmonton, Polo Park, Saskatchewan and Victoria Park were added to the list.

In Ohio, Ascot Park opened in 1922, Beulah Park in 1923 and in 1925 ThistleDown and Coney Island (now River Downs) joined the parade.

In Illinois, Hawthorne had started the ball rolling with an "oral betting" meeting in 1922. It was joined by Aurora Downs the next year; in 1925 Fairmount Park opened its gates, down in the southern part of the state, across the river from St. Louis, Missouri; and Peoria began racing in 1926. The big twins—Washington and Arlington Park—were coming, as was Lincoln Fields.

Out in California, racing was still across the border in the southern part of the state, as the Tijuana meeting continued to supply good sport. In the northern part of the state A. B. Spreckels formed the Pacific Coast Jockey Club, which remodeled Tanforan; the track opened in 1923 for two years of betless meetings after which it closed again, but it generated new hope and it was not long before racing was to return to California on a permanent basis.

Racing gained a new foothold in 1925 as the Miami Jockey Club, managed by Luke Cassidy, opened a fifty-one-day meeting at Hialeah. The Florida boom was at its height and in its first season of operation average purse distribution at the new track was only slightly less than at the Fair Grounds. Seminola Park, Pompano and Tampa opened in the state the next year.

Nineteen twenty-six was a noteworthy year from several standpoints. It was Man o' War's year, as with three crops of racing age, his get won $408,137, to exceed the previous stallion record by more than $100,000. Leading the battle was Glen Riddle Farm's three-year-old home-bred, Crusader, biggest money earner of the year, with $166,033 from nine wins and four seconds in fifteen starts. He launched his victory march in unusual fashion, by running away and hiding from his older stablemate and kinsman, American Flag, in the Suburban Handicap. Against his own age group he won the Belmont Stakes, set a new track record of 2:29⅗ in the Dwyer, which had been lengthened to 1½ miles, and another track record of 2:02 for 1¼ miles in the Cincinnati Derby, for which the field included the four top money winners of the season. Finishing behind Crusader were Walter J. Salmon's Display, E. R. Bradley's Boot to Boot and Chula Vista Stable's Carlaris.

The last-named colt, owned by W. T. "Fatty" Anderson, had created a sensation earlier that season at Tijuana by winning the Coffroth Handicap against older horses on February 22 for a net purse of $70,700, a truly amazing achievement for a three-year-old at that stage of the year. He won seven other races at the meeting, among them the Tijuana Derby, also in record time.

Crusader's winning streak was snapped when he was left at the post in the Travers, but he later added the Huron Handicap, Jockey Club Gold Cup, Havre de Grace, Maryland and Riggs Handicaps to his record.

Man o' War's other big winners were Scapa Flow (three wins including the Futurity), Mars (six wins, including the Travers), Edith Cavell (five wins, including the Coaching Club American Oaks, Latonia Oaks and Pimlico Cup) and Gun Boat.

Although he had only one offspring of Man o' War in his stable, and that a filly, 1926 also was Harry Payne Whitney's year, as he became the second owner in history to amass more than $400,000 in one season. His enormous 58-horse racing string gathered $407,139, although the stable included no stars of the first magnitude where racing of that particular season was concerned.

It also was a good year for E. R. Bradley, whose Idle Hour Stock Farm ranked second on the list of winning owners. In addition to successes in other stakes, his busy B's made a specialty of winning Derbies: Bagenbaggage and Boot to Boot finished one-two in the Louisiana Derby; Bagenbaggage won the Latonia Derby; Bubbling Over and Bagenbaggage took first and second in the Kentucky Derby; and Boot to Boot won both the Ohio State Derby and American Derby. The $25,000-added Fairmount Derby also would have been added to the collection, but Earl Sande turned in one of his most brilliant rides on J. E. Widener's Haste to nose out Bagenbaggage, as Boot to Boot finished third.

Bubbling Over was the best of the lot, undefeated in a brief campaign of three starts. Following his easy romp in the Kentucky Derby, which lured Mayor Jimmy Walker down from the sidewalks of New York to make the trophy presentation, the colt went wrong and never raced again.

Boot to Boot was the most active of the group as well as the most productive, for in the American Derby he won the largest purse in history up to that time.

Chicago shouldered its way into the racing picture with a vengeance in 1926 as two big new tracks opened, Washington Park in Homewood and Lincoln Fields in Crete.

The old Washington Park had been dismantled in 1906, and when oral betting was declared legal in Illinois in 1924, efforts were begun immediately to provide Chicago with another luxury track. A group headed by Tom Bourke and R. M. Sweitzer began construction at Homewood, an ideal location easily accessible to a heavy concentration of population. Opened on July 3, 1926, the new Washington Park track was 1⅛ miles around with a homestretch 90 feet wide and 1,320 feet long. A special chute extended from the backstretch that enabled horses to run a mile while making only one U-turn, and since that time the vast majority of the world's fastest miles have been run at Washington Park.

On opening day county and state officials threatened to arrest anyone who patronized co-operative betting booths. Although Judge Ira Ryner issued a restraining order, track authorities were still somewhat dubious and the booths were kept closed for the first three races. Six of them were opened to test the ground for the fourth race, and when nothing happened, the meeting was on. For Derby Day, July 31, it was in high gear.

Display, a son of Fair Play who even as a youngster had begun to display the temperament for which his sire was notorious, was favorite for the American Derby, with Boot to Boot and W. R. Coe's versatile filly, Black Maria, also well supported. Albert Johnson kept Boot to Boot under a hard hold as he allowed C. E. Durnell's Bolton to set the pace for the first 1¼ miles, and when the pacesetter folded Boot to Boot went on to win by two lengths. Display closed in the final stages to take second and Black Maria finished third. The time of 2:30⅖ was automatically a new track record for 1½ miles, since the distance had not been run before, and Boot to Boot received $89,000 for his work. The minor purse awards swelled the gross value to $106,000.

When its meeting closed Washington Park ranked eighth in daily average purse distribution with $13,390, which, as it turned out, was over-generous. Washington Park lost money on the meeting, and although it was eventually made good, the fabulous winner's check for the American Derby bounced on first presentation. Lincoln Fields, which held its inaugural meeting immediately afterward, was slightly lower in distribution but much more successful, as it drew greater attendance. Washington Park had the location, but Lincoln Fields had Matt Winn. Not long afterwards, Winn organized a syndicate which purchased Washington Park and put it on a sounder financial basis.

In 1927 Chicago racing came to full flower with the opening of Arlington Park in a fashionable suburb north of the city. Built by H. D. "Curly" Brown, it was the most ambitiously planned project yet conceived, consisting of a 9-furlong main track, a 1-mile track inside of that and a figure-eight steeplechase course and polo field further inside. Among the other accoutrements were a golf course and tennis club. In its first year of racing, under the auspices of the American National Jockey Club, Arlington ran a brief sixteen-day meeting in the last half of October, yet it took rank immediately as a center of major sport. Pari-mutuel wagering had been made legal in Illinois on July 1, 1927 and the last half of that year the state received $436,559.60 in taxes. Racing had found a permanent home in Chicago.

Arlington, however, also had a shaky financial experience getting started, and a group of Chicago businessmen headed by Otto Lehman, John Hertz and Charles McCulloch took over the operation about a year after it opened.

Although he did not maintain ownership very long, Arlington Park was the culminating achievement of "Curly" Brown (1863-1930), one of the most colorful figures of the period. In addition to maintaining Brown Shasta Ranch near the snow-capped mountain in California from which the name was derived, Brown was even more prominent as a builder of race tracks. He helped found Laurel, the City Park Track in New Orleans, Moncrief Park in Jacksonville, Clear Lodge in Montana and Oriental Park in Havana. (Cuba was a favorite winter haven for baseball players who wanted to let off steam away from the baleful eye of Commissioner Kenesaw Mountain Landis, and Charles Stoneham and John Mc-Graw both owned stock in Oriental Park.)

In the book *Sport's Golden Age,* Bryan Field relates an anecdote concerning Brown's activity in Cuba. The officials who ran Oriental Park soon learned that the local citizens had no appreciation for the subtle nuances of the rules of racing. If they bet on a horse and he came home first, they wanted their money with no questions asked, and every time there was a disqualification a near riot resulted. Hence, a tacit understanding arose, whereby, in deference to the customers, no winner was disqualified, although the offending jockey was ruled off permanently, but Brown was at the track in the early days before this happy compromise had been figured out. On one of the rare occasions when the stewards changed the order of finish, there was some gunplay during which a Cuban was badly wounded. Brown was arrested and locked up in Havana's Morro Castle.

As time wore on, and all efforts to bring Brown to trial met with the *mañana* treatment, his friends began to get worried. When the long race meeting was nearing its end, and there still was no action, the matter was taken up with a high Cuban official who, sympathetic though he was, informed his supplicants that so far as he knew no one ever had left Morro Castle except in a coffin.

That advice was good enough for the race-trackers. After salting the necessary palms and disguising themselves, a group of horsemen entered the prison one evening and came out carrying a coffin.

The next day Brown was safe in Florida.

The decision of John Daniel Hertz (1879-1961) to buy into Arlington Park the next year

266

undoubtedly was influenced by the excellent showing of his wife's racing stable in 1927.

The protagonist of a typical Horatio Alger story, Hertz had come to this country from Austria (that part which later became Czechoslovakia) as a five-year-old boy, and went to work immediately selling newspapers for a penny each on the streets of Chicago. He received his first lesson in business when a kindly customer explained to him that, although his prices were attractive, it was difficult to sell morning papers after the afternoon editions were out.

The lesson stuck. Hertz left school in the sixth grade to become a copy boy for the *Chicago Daily News*. While in his teens he supplemented his income in "amateur" boxing bouts for which he received $10 an appearance, and the young impresario also managed the good featherweight Benny Yanger. Shortly after Hertz was married in 1903, a newspaper merger caused him to lose his job.

That was opportunity in disguise for Hertz. He became an automobile salesman and within a few years was able to buy into an agency. Stuck with a number of second-hand seven-passenger Comet Flyers that had been taken in trade, Hertz conceived the idea of renting these cars, and soon he organized a taxicab business in Chicago, which, along with various other forms of car and truck rental services, was the basis of a tremendous fortune for Hertz.

Having been interested in racing since his days as a sportswriter, Hertz began campaigning a stable in the early twenties in the name of his wife, with the yellow cab motif incorporated in the racing silks.

ANITA PEABODY, 1925

(Luke McLuke–
La Dauphine, by The Tetrarch)

At their Leona Farm in Cary, Illinois, the Hertzes bred Anita Peabody, leading money winner of the 1927 season (which gave their home state a boost in breeding as well as in racing). Winner of six races in seven starts, the filly included in her string a victory in the Futurity for a new record purse of $91,790. (Boot to Boot's record reward for the American Derby had lasted only a year; Anita's was to last no longer. During the next few seasons, the phrase "richest purse in history" was to become overworked.)

The four-horse entry of Harry Payne Whitney, headed by Victorian, was favored for the 1927 Futurity, but Anita Peabody, ridden by Chic Lang, took the lead and held it all the way to win by a nose from her stablemate Reigh Count, who was receiving a 5-pound concession from the filly, and probably could have won if jockey Mack Garner had so desired.

Not only was the Futurity the richest race yet contested, but September 17, 1927, at Belmont Park was the richest day of racing ever staged, as $172,030 was dispensed in purses. There were two other stakes on the program: the Grand National Steeplechase, won by Greentree Stable's Jolly Roger, and the Jockey Club Gold Cup, won by Arden Farm's Chance Play.

With all that money at stake, no one was conceding an inch, and in two of the stakes races there were claims of foul. The rider of fourth-place Petee-Wrack lodged a complaint against Anita Peabody in the Futurity, which was not allowed, and Frederick Johnson's Brown Bud finished first in the Gold Cup, but was disqualified for interference.

REIGH COUNT, 1925

(Sunreigh–Contessina, by Count Schomberg)

Although the Futurity was his first placing in a stake, Reigh Count went on to win the Kentucky Jockey Club Stakes and Walden Handicap before the year was out. He was favorite in the Pimlico Futurity and might have won it also except for yet another instance of rough riding—this one among the most discussed episodes of its kind in turf history.

Walter M. Jeffords's filly, Bateau, ridden by Earl Sande, smashed Reigh Count into the rail on the far turn, as Glade went on to win the race from Petee-Wrack.

To most observers it appeared that Sande deliberately had cut off the favorite. However, the Handy Guy, jacket in hand, reported to the stewards alleging that Lang had tried to bring Reigh Count through where there was no room, and had torn the buttons off his jacket in the process.

The officials refused to accept this version. Bateau, who had finished third, was disqualified, and Sande's license was revoked. Since he had been the rider of Chance Play in the Jockey Club Gold Cup, Sande came out even on the over-all exchange that fall.

Joseph E. Widener, Sande's contract employer at the time, paid the jockey's expenses for a trip to Europe, and his license was restored after his return—a more or less academic gesture as it developed, for Sande retired from the saddle almost immediately and took up training. Nevertheless, the affair remained a *cause célèbre* for years to come, Hertz stoutly maintaining that Reigh Count had been deliberately fouled, and Jeffords just as stoutly maintaining the opposite.

Hertz was attracted to Reigh Count by his fighting spirit. In one of the colt's earlier races, Hertz had noticed Reigh Count attempt to bite a rival trying to get past, and the ex-boxer decided that was the kind of horse for him.

Reigh Count had not won a race until his seventh start, and Hertz bought him from Willis Sharpe Kilmer after that maiden victory "for a pittance." The sale of this colt was a factor which led trainer Henry McDaniel to quit the Kilmer stable a second time.

Despite the great success of the Hertz duo, they did not completely overshadow the two-year-old class of 1927, for that crop also included the sensational colt, Dice, who was in action only two months, but undefeated in five starts during that period, four of them stakes. The son of Dominant had been bred by Harry

Payne Whitney, but sold to the Wheatley Stable of Mrs. Henry Carnegie Phipps and her brother, Ogden Mills, which was just getting started in racing about that time. Turned over to James Fitzsimmons for training, after winning his maiden race on April 25, Dice, in succession, won the Keene Memorial, Juvenile, Hudson and Great American Stakes. In the Hudson he carried 127 pounds and in the Great American 130, conceding 20 pounds to Sun Edwin, who finished second but was disqualified.

Dice apparently was headed for further accolades when he died suddenly of a hemorrhage. His veteran trainer, who already had been saddling winners for more than a quarter-century, was to continue his notable training career that much longer before he got another two-year-old he considered the equal of Dice: Nashua.

The sale of Dice did not weaken the Whitney Stable seriously as once again it led the owners' list. Punsters had a field day as the Whitney sweep was accomplished mostly by offspring of Whisk Broom II and Broomstick. His top five money winners were by those two stallions, including the Preakness winner, Bostonian, and Kentucky Derby winner, Whiskery. After having won the Kentucky Derby with the first candidate he sent to the post, Regret, and having sent sixteen more horses in quest of the roses without success during the intervening eleven years, Whitney finally won another renewal—Whiskery, it turned out, was his last candidate in that event.

Fred Hopkins, "the Boy Wonder" of the training profession saddled Whiskery and Bostonian for their big scores, but the 47-horse Whitney stable was operated in divisions that year, under head trainer James Rowe, so the financial leadership in this category went to W. H. Bringloe, trainer of the E. F. Seagram stable, which included Sir Harry, winner of the rich Coffroth Handicap.

Runner-up in the owners' standings was the Greentree Stable of Whitney's brother, Payne, but its owner missed the stable's most successful season as he died in May before most of the principal races had been contested.

The turf career of Payne Whitney (1875-1927) was relatively brief. When William Collins Whitney had died, he left only a token portion of his estate to his younger son, but Payne was heir to a much larger fortune from his uncle, Oliver Hazard Payne. As one of the wealthiest men in the United States, he occupied himself more with business affairs, and it was his wife who was responsible for Greentree Stable. For a number of years Helen Hay Whitney, who adopted the pink-and-black racing silks from a favorite gown, raced only steeplechasers, but as she accumulated horses, she began to try some of them on the flat. Her husband, who was a steward of the Jockey Club and a stockholder in Belmont Park, always was interested in the stable and toward the end of his life became an active partner. Greentree had finished second to Rancocas Stable in the record-breaking 1923 season, but the earnings in 1927 were considerably more thanks to Jolly Roger's victory in the Grand National Steeplechase, and the exploits of the two-year-old filly, Glade, who won the Matron Stakes and the controversial Pimlico Futurity. Although the stable dropped in rank for a couple of seasons after Payne Whitney's death, it was not broken up. Continued in operation by his widow, and subsequently the Whitney children, it went on to even higher rank.

Among the numerous other noteworthy aspects of the 1927 season were the performances of the full brothers Chance Shot and Chance Play, who just about matched each other in earnings with $89,527 and $86,800, respectively. Their kinsman Display had the most active season of his long career, with seven wins in twenty-five starts. Before he retired at the age of seven Display was known as the "Iron Horse," by virtue of 103 starts, of which he won 23, finished second in 25 and third in 27, for earnings of $256,526.

In addition to Anita Peabody in the juvenile division, there were several formidable distaff runners among the three-year-olds. Hal Price Headley's Handy Mandy (sold later that year to Three D's Stock Farm) won the Latonia Derby in 2:28⅗, thus breaking Man o' War's American record for 1½ miles, and followed up with a victory over her own sex in the Latonia Oaks under 130 pounds. Marshall Field's Nimba, known for her beauty as well as her class, became the second filly to win the Realization—and the first to score a clear victory, as her predecessor, Vexatious, had won by disqualification. Nimba also won over her sex in the Coaching Club American Oaks and Alabama Stakes. Allan Gallaher and Sewell Combs' Mary Jane won the Kentucky Oaks from Handy Mandy, and beat colts in the Raceland Derby.

Also in 1927, descriptions of races were broadcast over loudspeakers at the Bowie meeting and the voice of Clem McCarthy was heard in the land. The Fair Grounds also adopted a public address system for its meeting.

Although he was not the season's leading money winner, Reigh Count definitely was the star of 1928. The leggy chestnut won three in a row at the beginning of the season, including the Kentucky Derby and Miller Stakes, but it came up mud for the Travers and Reigh Count finished last as Petee-Wrack took the laurels. The Hertz colt then won the Huron Handicap, set a new track record of 2:55 for 1¾ miles in the Saratoga Cup, although Display was his only opponent; won the Realization, and wound up his campaign by winning the Jockey Club Gold Cup. That race also was his farewell to the American turf, for the following season he raced in England, where he won the Coronation Cup and was second in the Ascot Gold Cup, after which he was returned home to enter stud.

The leading money winner of 1928 was Marshall Field's two-year-old colt High Strung, who won five of his six starts to net $153,590. The bulk of this came from his victory in the

Futurity which that year reached yet another record value to the winner of $97,990. The son of the intensely inbred High Time was regarded as strictly a colt of early speed, but his time of 1:19 was a record for the unusual Futurity distance (somewhat short of 7 furlongs) and he followed up by setting another record for the Pimlico Futurity, running the mile in 1:39 for a winner's purse of $50,750. However, his subsequent racing career was undistinguished.

Harry Payne Whitney's three-year-old Victorian, a full brother to Whiskery, went through a very active campaign of twenty starts. He won ten and was second in four to net $126,750, his most notable score being a victory in the Preakness by a nose over Edward B. McLean's Toro. The latter colt, plus LeMar Stock Farm's Misstep, and W. S. Kilmer's Sun Beau were prominent in the classic division.

Washington, D. C., newspaper publisher McLean had a well-balanced stable that year which included, besides Toro in the three-year-old division, the good juvenile Neddie and handicap horse Jock, the latter two probably the best sons of Colin to come to the races. McLean, who was the leading owner of the 1928 season, reached that eminence by a rather unusual route. Other owners who had bobbed up to the top suddenly had done so by virtue of lavish purchases of proven horses, but McLean had built up his stable from the ground floor; his top money winners were horses he had bred himself.

A noticeable feature of the 1928 season was the increase in stakes money available to older horses. The accent on youth continued, of course, but stakes open to older horses were getting richer and richer. The biggest ones were scheduled by the winter tracks, whose meetings were run early in the year, at a time when two- and three-year-olds ordinarily would not be expected to have established any significant form. Nevertheless, the richest all-age race in America, the Coffroth Handicap at Tijuana, for two successive seasons had gone to

a three-year-old—Carlaris in 1926 and Sir Harry in 1927. In 1928, however, Crystal Pennant, a four-year-old son of Pennant, owned by Walter Hoffman's R. C. Stable, grabbed the first prize of $92,700. In so doing, he earned more money in a couple of minutes than any previous member of the handicap division had won during an entire season.

The New Orleans Handicap at the Fair Grounds, which had been raised to $50,000-added, was won by William Daniel's imported four-year-old Justice F., who earlier in the meeting had won two other stakes.

As the season wore on, these horses had faded and most of the remaining laurels were gathered in by Hal Price Headley's Mike Hall and Jospeh E. Widener's Osmand.

A gelded bay son of Hourless, Mike Hall had been the hero of a rags to riches climb as a three-year-old the previous season, when, after racing for a $2,500 claiming price, he developed to the point where he set a new American record of 1:40⅗ for a mile and 70 yards at Latonia in October. In his last start of the year he won the Latonia Cup in American record time of 3:38⅗ for 2¼ miles. As a four-year-old in 1928 he earned $77,685 with five wins in sixteen starts. His victories included the Dixie Handicap, Lincoln Fields Special, Great Lakes Handicap, Washington Handicap and a repeat in the Latonia Cup.

Another gelding, Osmand, had been a stakes winner both at two and three, and although he was regarded as chiefly a sprinter, he had run Whiskery to a head in the Kentucky Derby. He proved that he was a sprinter as a four-year-old—one of the very best. The chestnut son of Sweeper–Ormonda, by Superman, brought back memories of Roseben, both by his appearance (Osmand stood 16-2) and his performance. He won six of eight starts including the Toboggan, Carter, American Legion and Laurel Handicaps, and he also stretched out to win the 1⅛-mile Havre de Grace Cup from Sun Beau and Crusader.

Both Mike Hall and Osmand were destined

270

H. P. Whitney on his favorite polo pony, Cottontail.

for greater triumphs in the future. As a five-year-old Osmand won only four races, but they included the nation's three most definitive sprint tests: he scored a second victory in the Toboggan, carrying 129 pounds; a repeat victory in the Carter, carrying 132 pounds, and then won the Fall Highweight Handicap with 140 pounds. By the end of his career he had won 23 of 37 races and $157,975, an enormous sum for a horse classified as a sprinter.

Mike Hall was taken to England by his breeder, R. M. Eastman, the next year, without any appreciable measure of success. But, after returning from abroad, as a six-year-old in 1931, he won the first race in America with a guaranteed winner's purse of $100,000: the Agua Caliente Handicap, which had replaced the Coffroth on the winter racing scene. He finally retired after 73 races, of which he won 19, with earnings of $213,430.

Mike Hall was not the first handicap horse to win $100,000 in one season, however, for the build-up in purses had continued while he was abroad.

The wave of prosperity was still going strong as America entered the last year of the golden decade. In 1929 the final meeting was held at Tijuana, which was replaced at the end of the year by the Agua Caliente track in the same area. The Coffroth Handicap was raised in added value again, to $100,000. Sunshot Stable's five-year-old Golden Prince equaled the track record to grab the lion's share of this 1929 purse, $98,250, and as he was successful in several other races that season, he wound up with $121,600—by far the most money ever earned by a horse older than three. He was the first handicap runner to earn more than $100,000 in one season.

The 1929 Futurity Stakes reached an unprecedented value, with a record total of 2,139 nominations at the day of closing, and 17 survivors going to the post at $1,000 each, the net value to the winner, Harry Payne Whitney's Whichone, was $105,730—the first six-digit award in history. As the Grand National Steeplechase (won by Arc Light) and Jockey Club Gold Cup (Diavolo) again were run on

The first race in history with $100,000 *added* to the purse was the 1929 Coffroth Handicap at Tijuana, for which starter Marshall Cassidy sent 22 horses away from the barrier. The winner, Golden Prince (post position 11), equaled the track record of 2.02⅗ for 1¼ miles and collected $98,250.

The crowd of 30,000 at Tijuana for the 1926 Coffroth Handicap, won by Carlaris.

Futurity day, although there were only six races on the program, purse distribution at Belmont Park reached $181,010—a record which was destined to stand a long time.

Whichone, a son of Chicle–Flying Witch, by Broomstick—and hence a full brother to Mother Goose—won four other races that year to easily top his division with $135,455. In his own stable, however, there was a colt by John P. Grier named Boojum who was just as impressive, or perhaps more so. So fast that he was difficult to keep sound, Boojum won just one stake, the Hopeful, in which he set a new American record of 1:17 for 6½ furlongs.

It was a Whitney year all around. He occupied his customary position at the top of the owners' standings; young James Rowe, who was taking over the stable from his elderly father, headed the trainers in money won; and although Phil T. Chinn's Himyar Stud bred the most winners in 1929, for the fourth successive season Whitney was leading breeder in amount of money won, and he set an all-time record of $825,374 which was to stand until after World War II.

In the three-year-old division, the Preakness, run before the Derby in 1929, was won by Walter Salmon's Dr. Freeland, and the Derby by H. P. Gardner's Clyde Van Dusen, a colt named in honor of his trainer. As it developed, neither Dr. Freeland nor Clyde Van Dusen won another stake that year and the champion three-year-old emerged in E. R. Bradley's Blue Larkspur, winner of the Withers and Belmont Stakes after a fourth place in the Derby. In Chicago, Arlington Park inaugurated the Classic Stakes as a companion feature to Washington Park's American Derby, and Blue Larkspur moved West to win this, too, for a net purse of $59,900, with Live Oak second, Clyde Van Dusen third and Dr. Freeland fourth. The Bradley colt headed all horses, regardless of age, in earnings that season with $153,450.

Mack Garner on Blue Larkspur.

Another good three-year-old was The Nut, a son of Mad Hatter, who lived up to his name so far as personality was concerned, but was sensible enough to win the Realization and Latonia Championship among other races.

The feminine star (if she could be called that—she stood 17 hands and was more muscular than many colts) of 1929 was Rose of Sharon, bred by Senator Johnson N. Camden, but raced in the colors of trainer D. E. Stewart. The daughter of Light Brigade was out of the money but once in fourteen starts, of which she won ten, including several victories over colts. Rose of Sharon died of "shipping fever" (probably pneumonia) before the year was out, and the $50,000 insurance paid was one of the highest sums on record at the time.

Wheatley Stable's Diavolo, who won several stakes besides the Jockey Club Gold Cup, was the top performer in the handicap division. Sun Beau, ridden by Frank Coltiletti, turned in a notable performance in the Hawthorne Gold Cup, which he won in new track record time of 2:01⅗ for 1¼ miles. He defeated Misstep and Diavolo at level weights, and among those unplaced was the sentimental favorite, Karl Eitel, only three-year-old in the field, owned by Chicago alderman, John "Bath House" Coughlin.

By odd coincidence, in 1929 Sun Beau duplicated almost exactly his earnings of the previous season by banking $79,755. At the time, nobody realized where he was headed, but he was getting there steadily.

If there had been a prize for assiduousness in 1929, however, Sun Beau wouldn't have been in the running. Closing out his career that season was the venerable Tippity Witchet, a fourteen-year-old gelding by Broomstick–

Lady Frivoles, by St. Simon. His life record: 266 starts, 78 wins, $88,241.

In 1929 there occurred the most enthusiastic effort ever staged to promote racing. Other owners from time to time had promoted one-day race meetings on their estates for various worthy purposes, but William T. Waggoner built a $2-million track and subsidized an entire race meeting. The owner of 600,000 acres of cattle land "spoiled" by oil wells (Waggoner didn't like anything that inhibited the growth of grass) for years had been fighting for the legalization of racing in Texas. To demonstrate that the people wanted the sport, he opened Arlington Downs, midway between Fort Worth and Dallas, and on November 6, 1929, an eleven-day race meeting was launched, during which the $70,700 purse distribution was underwritten by him.

The big-spending Texan, in partnership with his two sons, raced as the Three D's Stock Farm—and his experience in 1929 was an example of partial poetic justice, for in the beginning of the year, months before Arlington Downs opened, Three D's stable had enjoyed particularly good fortune at the Fair Grounds meeting, winning the Louisiana Derby with Calf Roper and the New Orleans Handicap with Vermajo.

Waggoner also proved his point, since racing was made legal in Texas in 1933. It did not survive long, but America's greatest racing fan was spared that experience. He died before the curtain descended again.

During World War II many a neophyte naval aviator received his instruction in emergency landing procedures over the Arlington Downs track, and utilized the adjacent auxiliary field for his first solo flight.

CHAPTER FORTY-SIX

DDLY, THOUGH IT WAS TO wreak havoc among individuals, the Depression in its peculiar way was to contribute markedly to the growth of racing. Pari-mutuel taxation, modest as it was by modern standards, already had proved to be a convenient source of revenue to state governments. It was, moreover, a painless source, at least in theory, since it applied only to those who presumably could afford to pay it. As the Depression grew worse, more and more states turned to racing to pump up their deflated coffers: while other businesses were cut back, racing expanded greatly.

It was not the usual sort of business expansion, resulting from healthy operating figures. On the contrary, purse distribution—the accepted index of prosperity—dipped drastically, but the number of tracks increased. Of course, a few went out of business, and others hit dangerously low ebbs, but the overall trend was one of growth.

Of the tracks still in operation, 34 were in existence on Black Tuesday, 1929; between that day and the beginning of World War II, 24 new tracks came into being, an increase of 70 percent in numbers during America's blackest economic period.

Many persons prominent in the sport died in 1929, David Gideon being among the first to go, in February, at the age of eighty.

On August 2, James Rowe completed the course, and for the first time in its history, the flags at Saratoga were flown at half-mast in respect to a horse trainer.

In September, Sam Hildreth joined his old friend and foe, and the following month the ranks of racing officials underwent a similar loss with the death of Mars Cassidy, dean of his profession. The famed starter, who sent fields on their way at all the New York tracks, and had done so at other tracks in such scattered racing centers as Kentucky, Florida and Mexico, had established a notable dynasty before he passed on; his sons Marshall, George and Wendell all went on to become prominent officials in their own rights.

John E. Madden, who had shared so much success with Hildreth, answered the last call on November 3, and just before the year ended Richard T. Wilson, president of Saratoga who had ordered the flags lowered for Rowe, breathed his last.

A few trainers from racing's Old Guard were left—notably Jack Joyner and Tom Healey—and even fewer owners. Foremost among the latter was Harry Payne Whitney, and he was to experience just one more racing season.

Powerful as it was, the impact of the stock market crash could not effect immediately the stability of racing's prosperity left over from the golden age, and in 1930 purses remained near the peak values they had reached in the 1920s. One colt gathered a sufficient share of these purses to become America's leading money winner.

When Epinard had been racing so impressively all over America in 1924, it occurred to several breeders that the French horse might make a good stallion. It occurred to A. B. Hancock that a horse who beat Epinard might make an even better one, so in 1925 he organized a syndicate to purchase Captain Jefferson Davis Cohn's Sir Gallahad III, who had defeated Epinard in a match in France. One of the syndicate members was William Woodward, owner of Maryland's historic Belair Stud, and he reaped immediate benefits.

Gallant Fox was in the French stallion's first crop of American foals. A bay colt out of the Celt mare, Marguerite, who already had produced Petee-Wrack, as a two-year-old Gallant Fox was among the top ten members of his generation, but not outstanding. He won the Flash and Junior Champion Stakes, placed in the U. S. Hotel Stakes and ran third in Whichone's Futurity. Lively as a puppy and just as inquisitive, Gallant Fox was out of the money only once in seven starts that year, when he was left at the post for the Tremont Stakes while he gazed at an airplane.

At three it was a different story. "The Fox of Belair," as he came to be known, opened the season with a victory in the Wood Memorial Stakes at Jamaica. Next he journeyed to Pimlico and won the Preakness, for which the cities of Baltimore, Washington and Philadelphia emptied themselves to see the "local boy" perform. Governor Albert C. Ritchie of Maryland presented the trophy, and Vice-President Charles Curtis watched the race from Woodward's box.

The 1930 Preakness was the first classic race started out of the "machine," as the newly installed device at Pimlico was called, although such starts previously had been effected elsewhere, and experiments along this line had been in progress for years.

As early as 1894 races were started from a "gate" at Maspeth, New York, and, judging from the description, its failure to catch on was due not so much to any inherent defects of the contrivance itself as to ill-conceived application of the idea. A gong was sounded three times—once as a signal to line up, the second time to alert the jockeys and the third time as the "gate" was swung out of the way—and one can but visualize the tension that must have prevailed in a field of high-strung animals by the third time that gong sounded.

A gate with separate stalls for each horse, designed by William Murray, was tried out at Bowie in the early 1920s; Marshall Cassidy experimented with a movable gate later during that decade; the Jarvis-Waggoner gate was sampled at the Lexington meeting in 1927; and the Bradley–Stewart stalls were used at the Fair Grounds for the 1928 meeting, when Colonel E. R. Bradley was in control of the track.

Of the early gates, those developed by John Bahr and W. C. Waite were the ones which survived. The use of the Bahr gate at the 1929 Hawthorne fall meeting generally is accepted as the origination of the practice on a permanent basis, and 1930 was the first season during which starting gates of one kind or another were in general use throughout the country—although the New York tracks, waiting until they had been thoroughly tested elsewhere, didn't adopt them until a year later.

As is true of most breaks with tradition, the starting gates were not greeted with universal acclaim. In some of the early models, the doors were opened electrically, and a circuit failure resulted in a ragged start, or no start at all for one or more horses. In most later versions of the gate, however, the stall doors are held closed by electromagnets working against a spring, hence an absence of current would be apparent at the time a horse is loaded into his stall. When the modern starter presses his "sticks" together, he is shutting off the electricity rather than turning it on, and a power failure subsequent to loading therefore would cause a start, not prevent one. The doors would all fly open, perhaps not at the optimum instant, but at least at the same instant.

No remedy has been found for the objection that the gates obscure from view one of the most vital portions of a race, and, moreover, a number of veteran trainers maintain that the sudden acceleration from a standing start puts too great a strain on a horse's underpinning.

Gallant Fox, the first American thoroughbred to be recognized as the world's leading money winner, and the only Triple Crown winner to sire a Triple Crown winner.

On the other hand, the gate has practically eliminated long delays at the post, injuries through kicking and other shortcomings of the old-fashioned start, and, in any case, it quickly became a standard part of the American racing scene.

From Pimlico, Gallant Fox went to Churchill Downs, where the machine also had been installed, plus several other innovations. Governor Flem D. Sampson proclaimed May 17 a holiday throughout the Commonwealth of Kentucky, and the extra added attraction this particular year was the presence in person of Lord Derby himself, whose ancestor was the eponym for races of this sort all over the world. A special pagoda had been built in the infield to house the distinguished visitor, which was fortunate, since many members of the crowd were pelted by rain. Gallant Fox won easily by two lengths from Audley Farm's Gallant Knight over a track classified as "good."

Back to New York went the Fox for the Belmont Stakes and a meeting with the previous year's champion, Whichone, who had skipped the tour of the provinces and sharpened himself for the forthcoming clash with a four-length victory in the Withers. In the Belmont Stakes, Gallant Fox beat him by three lengths, and became the second winner of the American triple crown.

Gallant Fox had become a celebrity, nor was his crowd appeal diminished by the fact that in his three-year-old campaign he was being ridden by Earl Sande, America's most famous jockey, who was making a comeback after two years away from competition.

Another victory in the Dwyer, and the triumphant procession headed out to Chicago where another extravaganza was brewing. The largest crowd in the history of Illinois racing, 43,000 by actual turnstile count and an estimated 50,000 all told, including Governor Emmerson, jammed Arlington Park for the Classic Stakes on July 12. The track offered a $10,000 bonus to the winner of the Classic, provided he should also previously have won

277

Governor Franklin D. Roosevelt and Mrs. Roosevelt (rear seat) are welcomed to Saratoga by track president George Bull. The future president saw Jim Dandy upset Gallant Fox in the Travers Stakes.

the Preakness, Kentucky Derby, Belmont Stakes or American Derby.

Gallant Fox qualified for the bonus, but he almost caught a tartar. Gallant Knight, who had been his closest pursuer in Kentucky, gave him an even harder fight in the Classic; the son of Bright Knight stuck to Gallant Fox almost every step of the way, and the champion had only his neck in front at the end, although Sande stated afterward that Gallant Fox merely had been loafing.

Having won the major races of four different states, traveling the old-fashioned way despite his vicarious interest in aircraft, the Fox was shipped back East.

Governor Franklin D. Roosevelt of New York had missed the Belmont, but he showed up at Saratoga for the Travers Stakes August 16, in which the Belair champion was to encounter Whichone for the second time that year. The throng for this race was too big to be counted accurately—it more than packed the premises, and some automobiles were abandoned 2 miles away from the track gate, as their occupants got out and walked.

The sun was shining for the big race, but an earlier rain had left the track very heavy, and only two other horses came out to face the principals. Neither of these—Sun Falcon at 30-to-1, and Jim Dandy at 100-to-1—was conceded any sort of chance. A son of Jim Gaffney, owned by the young California sportsman Chaffee Earl, trained by J. B. McKee and ridden by F. J. Baker, Jim Dandy had come to Saratoga as a two-year-old, and almost exactly a year previously had won the Grand Union Hotel Stakes, over the same type of footing, at odds of 50-to-1, for his only stakes victory of the season. Apparently nobody in the vast throng awaiting the Travers with such anticipation remembered that race. This race they never forgot.

Whichone and Gallant Fox went right off into a torrid duel, with Sonny Workman on the Whitney colt taking care to keep Gallant Fox and Sande on the outside. The "Handy Guy" also was pretty adept with his feet, and it was widely believed that to allow him to get inside in a close struggle, where he could lock legs with a rival, was to concede the race.

278

Man O' War, by Fair Play – Mahubah
painting by F. B. Voss

Gallant Fox, by Sir Gallahad III – Marguerite

painting by T. Ivester Lloyd

There was no opportunity for shenanigans in the Travers, however, and as the top pair drifted wide in the stretch, their jockeys preoccupied with each other, along came Jim Dandy on the rail. Exhausted from his battle with Whichone, Gallant Fox could offer only token resistance, and Jim Dandy beat him by eight lengths. Although he did come in ahead of Sun Falcon, Whichone collapsed entirely. He broke down and never raced again.

It not only was Jim Dandy's only stakes victory, it was his only victory of any kind in 20 starts that season.

Two weeks later, Gallant Fox earned his diploma by defeating older horses in the Saratoga Cup, and then came another stirring race. Seeking revenge for the Travers, Workman paid off the colt's regular rider to get the mount for the Lawrence Realization on James Butler's Questionnaire, an excellent son of Sting who won eleven races that season.

Again Workman grabbed the inside path, and Questionnaire led until the stretch, where Gallant Fox ranged alongside; for an instant, the champion appeared ready to sail on by, but Questionnaire refused to quit. Then Gallant Fox seemed to tire, but he came again and through the stretch it was stride for stride to the bitter end of the 1⅝-mile contest. Gallant Fox, in front by a neck at the sixteenth pole, had his head in front at the wire, as Questionnaire also had come again—a rare race, indeed, in which two horses each make two moves.

The first 1½ miles had been run in 2:28⅖, faster than Handy Mandy's American record for that distance, and the final time of 2:41⅕ had been bettered only by Man o' War.

It was reported that Workman and Sande had a fight in the jockey's quarters after this race, but they later were good friends.

No horse in world history ever had won $300,000 in a single season, but when Gallant Fox closed out his career with a victory in the Jockey Club Gold Cup, it pushed his earnings for the year to $308,275. His grand total, including his two-year-old season, was $328,165, a new American record. In 17 starts, he won 11 races, was second three times, third twice and unplaced but once.

Owner William Woodward (1876-1953), banker, lawyer, diplomat, was a native of New York and graduate of Harvard, who had served as secretary to Ambassador Joseph Choate in London, and acquired a taste for racing in that country. After returning to America around 1903, he bought a few mares and began breeding thoroughbreds; and during World War I, while French bloodstock was being sold away on all sides, for a modest outlay he obtained a group of mares which were to establish great families in America.

In 1910 he inherited from his uncle, James T. Woodward, the great 3,000-acre Belair Stud, which had been founded by Governor Samuel Ogle in Maryland years before the Revolution, and Woodward's turf activity increased from then on. He had owned several good horses (and had sold several better ones than those he kept) before Gallant Fox came along, including the hardy filly Priscilla Ruley, who started twenty-seven times as a three-year-old in 1924 and won ten races, among them the Alabama Stakes.

The year 1930 was a particularly important one in Woodward's turf career, as that November he succeeded Frank K. Sturgis as chairman of the Jockey Club. Gallant Fox was Woodward's first super star, but he was not the last.

His nickname notwithstanding, the "Fox of Belair" actually was born at the Claiborne Farm in Paris, Kentucky, of Arthur Boyd Hancock (1875-1957), Woodward's longtime friend, partner and turf advisor.

Hancock, who became the master horse breeder of his time, was born into the business at Ellerslie Stud in Charlottesville, Virginia, owned by his father, Captain R. J. Hancock. After college—he attended Johns Hopkins and was graduated from the University of Chicago—he went straight into livestock farming, assisting his father at Ellerslie. When young

Arthur Boyd Hancock, Sr., founder of America's most successful breeding farm.

Hancock's wife inherited a large tract of land in Kentucky, he established Claiborne Farm there, and, following the death of his father, for many years he ran both places, probably the largest operation of its kind under the direction of one man. Ellerslie was at first his main headquarters, but Hancock gradually shifted to Kentucky, until eventually the Virginia farm was sold.

Most of the horses he bred raced for other owners, and Hancock also provided boarding facilities for many of the country's leading breeders and owners. Although not the originator of the stallion syndicates (actually, by a strange quirk, one of the earliest formal syndicates of record was formed in 1923 by a group of Englishmen who bought the American-bred Tracery) Hancock was a pioneer in their development, and certainly he originated the most successful early syndicates in America.

Sir Gallahad III set a new sire record in Gallant Fox's year; he later was to become leading sire three more seasons and leading broodmare sire twelve times.

It's difficult to think of James Edward Fitzsimmons as anything other than "the Sage of Sheepshead Bay," but the world's most successful horse trainer, born on the land that later became a noted race course, began his turf career unobtrusively enough. He was a dishwasher in the track kitchen at the age of ten.

He tried riding for a time, but as he himself phrased it, "I was vaccinated for jockey, but it didn't take." He rode his first winner in 1890, but it was ". . . a bad ride. The horse was a sixteenth of a mile in front in the stretch, and I started whipping him."

After his saddle career ended, Mr. Fitz was urged to give up the barnstorming race track life and take a job jockeying a streetcar around Philadelphia, but he stayed on the track as a trainer. Beginning with Agnes D. at Brighton Beach on August 7, 1900, Fitzsimmons had developed numerous winners, including Dice and Diavolo for Wheatley Stable.

Gallant Fox was the first of numerous champions Fitzsimmons was to train for Bel-

Sir Gallahad III, leading sire four seasons and leading broodmare sire 12 seasons.

Sunny Jim Fitzsimmons and Mrs. H. C. Phipps, owner of Wheatley Stable.

air, and perhaps the most expressive single clue to his personality lies in the circumstance that his association with Belair, and with Wheatley, never was interrupted. "Sunny Jim's" rule was to take good care of his owners.

By the time he retired on June 15, 1963, shortly before his eighty-ninth birthday, after an association with the sport of more than three-quarters of a century, Mr. Fitz had saddled winners of more than 2,300 races. Because formal training records were not maintained during the early years of his career, the total of his purse winnings must be estimated, but the figure is in excess of $13-million. There are authentic records of stakes races, however, and James Fitzsimmons saddled 149 stakes winners during his time, some of whom won repeatedly in added money competition.

In the matter of gubernatorial accolades, public recognition—and money—Gallant Fox ran far ahead of the pack in 1930, but that is not to say the pack didn't include prize articles. Outstanding among these was Equipoise, never out of the money in sixteen starts —except for one race in which he was disqualified and another in which he dumped his rider. He won eight races and $156,835 in his first season.

Although his earnings did not approach Gallant Fox's, Equipoise was the second leading money winner of the year, and his contribution enabled Workman to achieve a measure of revenge by topping Sande on the jockey's financial list. The son of Pennant also made Harry Payne Whitney leading owner (only slightly ahead of Belair) in his last season on the turf.

In that same crop there were so many good horses—Twenty Grand, Jamestown, Mate, Epithet, Vander Pool, etc.—that historian Hervey dubbed it an *annus mirabilis*, similar to the 1886 season when Kingston, Hanover, Tremont and Firenzi had appeared simultaneously.

George D. Widener's Jamestown became only the fourth colt in history—and the second this century, the other having been his sire, St. James—to win the Futurity while carrying 130 pounds, as Equipoise ran second under equal weight and Mate third under 122 pounds in a tight finish. Jamestown won six of seven starts in 1930, and his only loss was a second to Epithet in the Hopeful, while conceding the winner 13 pounds.

Vander Pool, a son of Campfire, owned by Mrs. M. P. Allen's Tennessee Stable, was undefeated in eleven starts. He began his campaign in January, an unusual procedure in those days for a two-year-old of stakes class, and collected six stakes events, although in the Youthful, Equipoise beat him by a city block, only to be disqualified.

The Whitney colt was the sounding board of his generation, and the chief claim to two-year-old fame of A. C. Bostwick's Mate was a victory by a head over Equipoise in the Champagne Stakes, carrying 119 pounds against 132 on Equipoise. Mate beat Twenty Grand at level weights in the Walden, and also won six other races including the Breeders' Futurity at Lexington.

Greentree Stable's Twenty Grand, with an 11-pound pull in the weights, beat Equipoise in the Junior Champion Stakes, and then at level weights engaged him in two of the most thrilling contests in turf annals. Since two-year-olds ultimately are apt to turn out this way or that way, the foregoing is pretty lofty language to apply to a juvenile event, but these races took place late in the season, and the juveniles involved were rather special.

In the Kentucky Jockey Club Stakes October 16, Twenty Grand and Equipoise drove through the entire stretch head and head, neither giving an inch. They went under the wire together in 1:36, having run the fastest mile ever accomplished by two-year-olds, and the fastest by horses of any age at Churchill Downs. Twenty Grand was the winner.

In the Pimlico Futurity in November, Equipoise was turned sideways at the break and virtually left at the post, but he charged through the mud to make up ground, and won by half a length from Twenty Grand, with Mate a neck away third. It subsequently was learned that Equipoise had thrown both front plates during the race.

His owner didn't see Equipoise's great victory, for Harry Payne Whitney had died on October 26. As had been the case the previous year, death removed quite a number of familiar faces from the scene in 1930, including Gifford Cochran, Snapper Garrison, Clarence Kummer, Curly Brown, C. J. Enright, Ed Tipton, Samuel Ross and George Long.

At the time of his death Whitney's stable had accumulated close to $4 million in earnings, and he had bred the winners of more money than any individual in history. His passing marked the end of an era. The Golden Age was over.

There were to be other popular champions, but not for a long time was any to receive the crown-prince treatment that had been accorded Gallant Fox, to say nothing of the rich purses. There were to be large throngs at race tracks, but the atmosphere was not to be so relaxed and gay. The desperation bettor was to become more a part of the picture, and the general attitude of the crowds began to reflect the fact that life was grim.

CHAPTER FORTY-SEVEN

COLLEAGUES WHO SPECIALIZE in other sports sometimes accuse turf writers of sycophancy, because of their seeming preoccupation with names of the wealthy. Yet, although racing has developed into a sport of the people—the King of Sports, as the slogan goes—it began as the Sport of Kings, and over the years it has been held together by those who could, and would, stand the gaff of hard times.

The tradition begun by William Collins Whitney, for example, survived the blackout when many other stables collapsed; it survived World War I, as less powerful (or less dedicated) owners pulled in their horns; and in 1931, as purses began to shrink, the two top stables in the country were operated by W. C. Whitney's grandson and daughter-in-law, respectively. C. V. Whitney was the leader, followed closely by the Greentree Stable of Mrs. Payne Whitney.

Their dominance was shaken in the early part of the racing season, however.

MATE, 1928

(Prince Pal–Killashandra, by Ambassador IV)

Over the winter there had been great anticipation of a renewed rivalry among "the miracle crop" as three-year-olds, and this came about in the Preakness Stakes on May 9. Twenty Grand had a new trainer, as Tom Murphy, the former harness horseman who had saddled him as a two-year-old, had been succeeded by James Rowe, Jr.

The Greentree colt, who had opened the year with a win over Clock Tower in the Wood Memorial, was slightly favored for the Preakness over Equipoise, who had won his first out, but then had finished dead last, obviously hurting, in the Chesapeake Stakes won by Anchors Aweigh. Mate, beaten two noses by Ladder and Panetian in his seasonal debut, was third choice.

Only seven paraded to the post for the Preakness, a small field which gave promise of a truly run race, but just the opposite materialized. Still undecided whether he was going to be a halfback or fullback, Equipoise swerved at the start, then plowed straight ahead. He ran into a jam caused by Soll Gills at the first turn, in which Twenty Grand also suffered interference.

Clock Tower, Ladder and Mate enjoyed clear sailing, and were in the order named at the end of a mile, where the leader tired and jockey George Ellis drove Mate to the front. Twenty Grand, after overcoming further interference from his own stablemate, Surf Board, launched a bid from sixth place that carried him past Ladder, but Mate held him safe by one and a half lengths. Equipoise also made a game move after getting back in stride, but tired at the end to finish fourth.

That was his last effort of the season, as Equipoise developed a quarter crack before the next Saturday's Kentucky Derby and was withdrawn.

TWENTY GRAND, 1928

(St. Germans–Bonus, by All Gold)

For the 1931 Kentucky Derby, which was broadcast overseas as well as in America, the

284

Mrs. Payne Whitney leading in Twenty Grand (Charles Kurtsinger up) after the 1931 Belmont Stakes. J. H. Whitney (straw hat) is following at left.

three-horse Greentree entry of Twenty Grand, Surf Board and Anchors Aweigh was an odds-on favorite, with Mate a well-supported second choice.

The surprise of the race came when jockey Frank Coltiletti drove Dixiana Farm's long-shot, Sweep All, into the lead on the stretch turn, but Charles Kurtsinger merely had been biding his time on Twenty Grand. After a mile in 1:37⅗—relatively casual time at other tracks, but sensational at Churchill Downs—Twenty Grand blazed through the stretch to win easily by four lengths in 2:01⅘, a new track record by 1⅖ seconds. Sweep All held on for second, and Mate was three lengths behind in third place after an uneventful trip.

The two principal adversaries went their separate ways from Louisville. Twenty Grand added more feathers to his cap by winning the Belmont Stakes by ten lengths from Sun Meadow and Jamestown, and then the Dwyer, conceding 14 pounds to runner-up Blenheim (an American colt, not to be confused with an imported English stallion of the same name).

Mate enhanced his reputation by winning a thrilling American Derby by a nose from Pittsburgher, carrying 126 pounds to 118 on his rival, and equaling a track record (2:04⅕) that had been set by a four-year-old under only 98 pounds.

Then came the rubber meeting in the Arlington Classic, for the biggest purse offered three-year-olds that season, $73,650. Mate, this time ridden by Al Robertson, turned in his most brilliant performance; he broke the track record to win easily by four lengths in 2:02⅖ as Twenty Grand, the odds-on favorite, failed by a neck to wrest second place from Spanish Play.

That was their final encounter, although each remained in training. Twenty Grand emerged with the season's honors, as he was undefeated during the rest of his campaign, winning four more stakes. Mate also won four more stakes, but he lost more than he won, albeit in tough company under heavy weights.

Twenty Grand made a brief campaign at four, then was retired to stud. He proved to

285

be sterile, was put back in training at seven, and after winning one race he left the track for good with a bank balance of $261,790.

Mate also raced through the age of seven, and at the end of a much more active career, seventy-five starts, he entered stud with $301,-810. He sired the steeplechase champion Elkridge, among others.

TOP FLIGHT, 1929

(Dis Donc–Flyatit, by Chicle)

Females are supposed to be the unpredictable sex, but among the two-year-olds of 1931 there was no such confusion as existed among the three-year-olds, thanks to a filly. Twenty Grand and Mate were waging a tight battle for earnings as well as for honors when a young lady breezed right by them both.

In seven starts—all stakes—Top Flight never met defeat. In less than five months she won more than any two-year-old in history, and her $219,000 made her the richest member of her sex not only in America, but in the world.

Bred by Harry Payne Whitney, raced by his son, trained by T. J. Healey, and ridden by Robertson and Workman, the delicate-looking but robust-running filly began her career in the conventional manner, against members of her own division. After winning the Clover in the mud, and Arlington Lassie Stakes by five lengths, coming within ⅕-second of the track record, she took on colts in the Saratoga Special and beat them as well. Two more victories over the fillies in the Spinaway and Matron, and she was back amongst the colts for the Futurity. Packing 127 pounds, conceding actual weight to all but one of her rivals, and getting only her 3-pound sex allowance from Tick On, she romped home by two and a half lengths.

Her speed having been demonstrated, her stamina was put to test in the Pimlico Futurity November 7. Top Flight held on grimly to win

Top Flight, undefeated two-year-old champion of 1931, whose $219,000 stood as a juvenile earnings record until years after World War II. Raymond "Sonny" Workman up.

by a neck from Tick On, with the next year's Kentucky Derby winner, Burgoo King, third in the field of twelve. It was the only occasion that year a rival finished within a length of the flying filly.

The next season Top Flight became demure. She still was a terror, but strictly within her own group. She started in five filly-and-mare events and won them all: the Acorn Stakes, Coaching Club American Oaks, Arlington Oaks, Alabama Stakes and Ladies Handicap. In four starts against male rivals she failed to finish in the money, but she picked up pieces of the purse in two of them by finishing fourth.

She ended her brief career with 12 wins in 16 starts and $275,900—plus a distinction she shared with her predecessor, Regret, of never having lost a race to a member of her own sex.

SUN BEAU, 1925

(Sun Briar–Beautiful Lady, by Fair Play)

When Zev retired in 1924 as leading American money winner with earnings of $313,639, there was some argument whether he might not also be the world's leading money winner. The French horse, Ksar, had ended his career shortly before with $335,340, but, in accordance with the European system of reckoning, this sum included the value of various trophies he had won. Zev had received a $5,000 gold cup for his match with Papyrus, plus a miscellaneous assortment of hardware at other stops along the line, but none of this was reflected in his official total. There was also to be considered the fluctuating value of the franc during the early 1920s.

When Gallant Fox retired in 1930 with $328,165, the Jockey Club had instituted a new rate of exchange whereby Ksar almost disappeared among the also-rans with an adjusted total of $134,702. The Belair colt was the world's leading money winner according to American bookkeeping procedure, but the argument nevertheless continued.

Sun Beau ended it the next year. The W. S. Kilmer home-bred seemed to do everything backwards, but he got there just the same. Whereas the typical thoroughbred gathers the bulk of his bankroll in his first two seasons of racing, when purses are larger and weight is not so much a factor, for Sun Beau these were his least profitable seasons. In practically a straight-line progression, he got richer as opportunities grew worse, as follows:

Age	Starts	1st	2nd	3rd	Un-placed	Earnings
2	4	1	0	1	2	$ 1,150
3	23	8	5	1	9	79,909
4	14	6	2	4	2	79,755
5	19	9	3	3	4	105,005
6	14	9	2	1	2	110,925
	74	33	12	10	19	$376,744

Moreover, within each season Sun Beau's progress followed the same over-all pattern, i.e., a slow beginning and a strong finish. He earned 60 percent of his total in the months of October and November. (With the exception of his last season, his earnings prior to September could be thrown out with scarcely a noticeable effect on his record.)

At the beginning of his final, and most successful campaign, Sun Beau was sent to Caliente for the rich $100,000 handicap. He won two preliminary races, but was unplaced in the big one as Mike Hall popped up from nowhere to grab it. In April, very early for him, Sun Beau won the Philadelphia Handicap and another race at Havre de Grace, then moved up to Arlington Park for the clincher.

On July 18, the day Mate set his 1¼-mile track record in the Classic, Sun Beau won a 1⅛-mile overnight race in 1:49⅖, equaling Blue Larkspur's track record. The next week Sun Beau broke Mate's brand new record by winning the 1¼-mile Arlington Cup in 2:01⅘. On August 1 he followed up with the Arlington Handicap and emerged ahead of Gallant Fox by a slight margin.

Willis Sharpe Kilmer with his world's leading money winner, Sun Beau.

Subsequently he added to his total with a second to Plucky Play in the Hawthorne Handicap, then reversing that decision in the Lincoln Handicap, while conceding Plucky Play 15 pounds, and a second to Twenty Grand in the Saratoga Cup.

For his final flourish, he returned to the scene of his biggest triumphs, and won his third successive renewal of the Hawthorne Gold Cup, defeating Mate and Plucky Play.

The year 1931 also saw a landmark decision in the development of racing jurisprudence and the disappearance from the turf of what had been America's most powerful stable.

Before the Burnt Hills Handicap at Saratoga August 13, an obscure race worth $900 to the winner, the stewards ordered that Rancocas Stable's Ladana be scratched. The stakes-winning filly had been poisoned in a crude and cruel manner; she was frothing at the mouth and there were blisters where the substance (reportedly chloral) had been applied too heavily. There was, moreover, unexpectedly

heavy wagering on Admiral Cary T. Grayson's Happy Scot, who subsequently won the race by a head—his first win in six starts that year.

Without imputing guilt to owners or trainers of any of the horses involved, the stewards of the Jockey Club notified trainer Frank Taylor that the entries to overnight races would not be accepted from Rancocas Stable during the remainder of the meeting.

Racing split wide open in its reaction to the case, especially after a stable boy reportedly confessed to the act, was fired by Taylor in a rage and then disappeared. On the one hand, it was deemed intolerable that a man could be punished for a misdeed with which he was not shown (or even implied) to be connected in any way—on the other, it was hailed as an example of proper discipline. The official stand was that participants in the sport were obligated not only to refrain from wrongdoing themselves, but to protect the public who paid admission to the races and wagered on their outcomes, from being victimized, regardless of who perpetrated the actual deed. Immediately, speculation arose as to whether favorites who lost in various other races about that time also had been poisoned.

This was not the first incident of its kind (in less formal environments many a trainer had been quietly invited to hit the road or else) but it was a celebrated case that brought forth explicitly the issue of public interest, and the responsibility of protecting it. This doctrine was to play a prominent role in the future, when circumstances were less clear-cut and disciplinary action more severe.

Shortly thereafter the entire Rancocas racing stable of twenty-five horses was sold at auction —(Ladana bringing second highest price of $9,500).

Owner Harry F. Sinclair stated that he had been contemplating retirement for some time, owing to the press of other business and the difficulty of managing his large breeding operation since the death of Hildreth two years earlier, but it was widely rumored that in private he was fuming. The sale was directed by Christopher J. FitzGerald, a prominent racing official and impresario, who included in the announcements pertaining thereto that a comeback by Rancocas (eighth-ranked stable of the 1930 season) in the near future was "taken for granted" by Sinclair's friends. Later that same year, the Rancocas yearlings were sold, and in 1932 the breeding stock of the vast farm also went on the block—with the exception of Zev and Grey Lag.

CHAPTER FORTY-EIGHT

W R. COE'S LADYSMAN, A HOME-bred son of the 1925 champion, Pompey, led the 1932 two-year-olds with $111,435. Trained by Bennie Creech, and ridden by Bobby Jones (a high-cheeked boy of patrician copper features, said to be a descendant of Montezuma) Ladysman won five of nine starts, including the inaugural Arlington Futurity, U. S. Hotel, Grand Union Hotel and Hopeful Stakes. He was blocked in the Belmont Futurity (although writer Neil Newman accused Jones of getting lost on the Widener Chute) and ran second to Lee Rosenberg's Kerry Patch. The latter colt did not win another stakes event in a long campaign, but it was a nice score for Kerry Patch's trainer, Joe Notter, who in his jockey days had won two Futurities.

Swivel, a huge filly who raced first for her breeder, Mereworth Farm, and later for Adolphe Pons, with J. R. Pryce as trainer, headed her class with $71,755. She won only four of fourteen starts, but among them were the Rosedale Stakes and the rich Pimlico Futurity.

In the three-year-old ranks, E. R. Bradley's Burgoo King, trained by Derby Dick Thompson and ridden by Eugene James, quickly got two legs on the triple crown but proceeded no further. The Kentucky Derby that year planted itself on the first Saturday in May, ahead of the Preakness, an order which has prevailed ever since. Burgoo King, ridden by Fator, had been a listless second to his stablemate Brother Joe, ridden by James, in his sophomore debut at Lexington, and Bradley switched

jockeys for the Derby. The son of Bubbling Over duplicated his sire's performance with an easy five-length victory, but a week later he was all out to win the Preakness by a head from Tick On, as Boatswain was just another nose away third. Burgoo King had not been nominated to the Belmont, but wouldn't have won it in any case, as he went wrong after skidding to sixth place in the Withers, won by Boatswain over a sloppy track.

The leader of the season, with $145,940, turned up in Morton L. Schwartz's Gusto, a home-bred son of American Flag, trained by Max Hirsch and ridden by Silvio Coucci. He won just four of his sixteen starts, but his wins included the American Derby and Classic in Chicago, and the Jockey Club Gold Cup.

Belair Stud's Faireno won six stakes, the Belmont among them, and, as has been related, Top Flight had no trouble among the fillies—but all the youngsters were overshadowed in 1932 by exceptional performers in the handicap division.

EQUIPOISE, 1928

(Pennant–Swinging, by Broomstick)

Noblesse oblige. As Top Flight had filled the gap admirably when Equipoise was sent home for repairs in 1931, so did he take up the slack when the filly's earnings tapered off the next year. Equipoise led young C. V. Whitney's 59 horse stable to another season at the top, with $403,681.

As a four-year-old, the "Chocolate Soldier" roared back like a tidal wave. Trained by Fred Hopkins and ridden by Sonny Workman,

Equipoise, the "Chocolate Soldier," the most memorable of a bumper crop of foals. Sonny Workman up.

he opened the season by winning seven races in a row, ranging in distance from 5 furlongs to 1¼ miles, six of them handicaps.

He won the 5-furlong Au Revoir Handicap under 126 pounds; the 6-furlong Harford by three lengths under 128, conceding 21½ pounds to runner-up Happy Scot; the 6-furlong Toboggan under 129 pounds, conceding 21 to Ironclad; the Metropolitian Mile by two and a half lengths under 127, and then was shipped to Arlington Park.

On June 30, 1932, in his Chicago debut Equipoise won the Delavan Handicap under 128 pounds in 1:34⅖, establishing a new world record for the mile, and ending forever the dual standard, as he not only bettered Jack High's 1:35 set in competition, but he erased Roamer's 1:34⅘, which had been set in a special race against time. Both previous record-holders, incidentally, had carried 18 pounds less than Equipoise. (On the other side of the coin, Arlington had installed a special chute for mile races, and the track was especially fast;

Volette set a new track record for 5½ furlongs and Tred Avon a new 7-furlong record the same day Equipoise made his mark, and within a month three other new track records were on the books.)

Raised to 129 pounds for the Stars and Stripes Handicap on July 4, Equipoise won that one from Tred Avon and Dr. Freeland, conceding them 22 and 19 pounds, respectively. The Arlington Gold Cup five days later, at weight for age, was a respite after all those handicaps, and he won it by four lengths from Gusto and Mate.

It was back to the handicaps for his next start, and his string was snapped. Saddled with 134 pounds, he failed by a neck to catch Plucky Play, who was in receipt of 23 pounds and showed his gratitude by running the fastest 1¼ miles of the meeting, 2:02⅕.

Two races under allowance conditions—Saratoga's Wilson and Whitney Stakes—proved to be romps for Equipoise. Then, dropping down drastically in distance, from 1¼ miles to 6 furlongs, and carrying 129 pounds, Equipoise threw in his only poor performance of the season, when he was unplaced in the Severn Handicap.

The "Chocolate Soldier" then gave Gallant Sir 21 pounds and a licking in the Havre de Grace Cup, ran third to Jack High and Gallant Sir in the Laurel Stakes, and was second by a head to Tred Avon in the Washington Handicap, making weight concessions all around.

As a five-year-old, T. J. Healey having succeeded Hopkins as trainer, Equipoise duplicated his sensational performance of the previous season by again winning the first seven starts of his campaign, including a second Metropolitan Handicap under 128 pounds, the Suburban Handicap under 132 and the Arlington Handicap under 135. He had a second and third in the events he failed to win.

At six, carrying 130 pounds or more in all but one race, again he never finished out of the money. He came home first four times in six tries, although he was disqualified after winning the Metropolitan Handicap by two lengths. This race later became the denouement of a popular play and movie, *Three Men On A Horse.*

Equipoise started three times at seven, then was retired after 51 starts, 29 wins, 10 seconds and four thirds, with earnings of $338,610. He ranked second on the list of the world's leading money winners.

By substituting equivalent modern purse values of actual races won by horses of the past, a surprising number of old-timers emerge as millionaires, and it is often said that a particular horse would have been on top, but he was born a few years too soon.

The case of Equipoise is doubly ironic. Not only was he born too soon—he also was born too late. He would have been the world's leading money winner if he had come along at a different time a few years either way.

Purse values were on the way down while he was in his prime, and a lot of races he won had been more valuable before, and became more valuable later. Add to that his absence from competition during most of his three-year-old season, customarily the most profitable one in a thoroughbred's life, his three disqualifications, the time he lost his rider, and his bad foot, and his climb is remarkable.

He was rough and tough and could win at any distance from 4 furlongs to 1¾ miles. Among his lesser distinctions he was considered "one of the best assistant starters in the business." Horses who ordinarily might be expected to cut up at the post, went docilely to their stations and stayed out of the way when the "Chocolate Soldier" was around.

PHAR LAP, 1926

(Night Raid–Entreaty, by Winkie)

Equipoise was not the only horse who was caught in the bight of shrinking purses. Before he began his comeback as a four-year-old there appeared in the West an enormous gelding considered by many experts—including jockey Eddie Arcaro, New York State Steward Francis Dunne and Marshall Cassidy, who succeeded his father as dean of American racing officials —as the greatest thoroughbred ever to race on the American continent. What is more striking, the horse concerned gained his lofty stature in exactly 2 minutes 2⅘ seconds.

Phar Lap was foaled in New Zealand. Bred by A. F. Roberts, he was sold as a yearling for the equivalent of about $800 to the partnership of Davis and Telford. His name meant lightning in the language of the aborigines, and that's exactly what he was in America—one quick stroke of devastating brilliance. Before he crossed the ocean, however, he had compiled a long and distinguished record in Australia, and was that country's leading money winner.

After a modest two-year-old season, Phar Lap won thirteen races at three, including both the Australian Jockey Club and Victoria Derbies and St. Legers, the Rosehill Guineas and other important stakes. At one point during the season he won nine consecutive races; he set records of 2:03 for 1¼ miles, 2:16¼ for

292

The carcass of Phar Lap on display at Belmont Park in 1932.

1⅜ miles, 2:29½ for 1½ miles and 3:49½ for 2¼ miles.

As a four-year-old Phar Lap won fourteen consecutive stakes, including the Melbourne Cup under 138 pounds. In the century-plus history of Australia's greatest race, only three times has it been won under higher weight. At five the big gelding was eight for nine, his sole loss having been in the Cup, in which he carried 150 pounds and the winner carried 98.

When he sailed for America, Phar Lap boasted 36 victories in 50 starts, for earnings of $282,200 at the prevailing rate of exchange. Success in "the hundred thousand," as the big handicap at Caliente was commonly called, would make him the world's leading money winner.

Phar Lap arrived in California a few months in advance of the race and then underwent the most peculiar training regimen ever seen in

293

America. No fast trials, no blowing out, none of the accepted works. In fact, much of the horse's exercise wasn't on the track. Trainer Tom Woodcock rode Phar Lap over the countryside, much as a rancher would ride his cow pony, up and down sandy hills, over rocky ground and through mesquite. Marshall Cassidy, who was starter at Caliente, tried to persuade Woodcock to school Phar Lap out of the stalls with a Maxwell barrier, but although the horse had no experience at this type of start, his trainer disdained practice sessions. Phar Lap would come away properly, he said.

The biggest shock of all came on the day of the race, when jockey Billy Elliott mounted Phar Lap an hour before post time and paraded him around the infield, in the hot Mexican sun, under his full assignment of 129 pounds, "to get him accustomed to the weight." On Phar Lap's frame—16-3 and 1,450 pounds—it was a feather.

Eleven horses paraded to the post on March 20, 1932, for one of the most sensational contests ever seen. Among its numerous other features, the Caliente track boasted the world's largest collection of starting chutes, one for every conceivable distance. The start of the Caliente Handicap was effected from the 1¼-mile chute, and true to his trainer's prediction, Phar Lap emerged with his field. However, he went immediately to the outside for an inspection tour of the 1⅛-mile chute which slanted into the track a furlong farther on, and passing the grandstand the first time around he was fully 50 yards behind the pack. Having satisfied his (or his jockey's) curiosity, Phar Lap then bounded into the lead. From sixth place after half a mile had been run, he had moved to first place before the end of 6 furlongs. Going around the home turn Elliott allowed Reveille Boy to draw up almost alongside, then away went Phar Lap again. He crossed the finish eased up, two lengths clear of Reveille Boy, who was carrying 118 pounds. In his effortless romp, the gelding from New Zealand had set a new track record of 2:02⅖, breaking

the mark that Mike Hall had established the year before under only 116 pounds.

The Caliente track was not exceptionally fast that day. Of the fifteen races on the program (the big one was the thirteenth), none of the others was won in time anywhere near a track record. In the race immediately following Phar Lap's victory, Eddie Arcaro won on Wizardry in 2:07⅕ for the same distance. The winner of the last race required 2:08 for 1¼ miles.

Phar Lap's purse was $50,500. Caliente had run into financial troubles, and had been forced to chop planned purse values in half, "the hundred thousand" included. Had the race been run according to its original conditions, Phar Lap would have been world's leading money winner—as it was, he had boosted his total to $332,250 and was within what appeared to be easy striking distance of Sun Beau's record. Tracks all over the country were vying with one another to schedule rich races that would attract the super-horse, and Bowie offered $10,000 just to have him gallop around the track under silks.

On the morning of April 4 a group of reporters who had driven the 30 miles out to Menlo Park from San Francisco to see the great horse were somewhat peeved when they were instructed to come back later. When they did return that afternoon, Woodcock met them with tears streaming down his face, and informed them that Phar Lap was dead.

Apparently he had been poisoned. There was a great uproar, but an autopsy revealed that Phar Lap had not been "got at," as had been suspected. He had eaten either some bad feed, which had developed fungus, or some forage that had been sprayed with insecticide; cause of death was acute enteritis. His huge carcass was mounted by a taxidermist and exhibited at Belmont Park on Futurity day, after which it was sent home to Australia.

That there were no hard feelings toward America on the part of Phar Lap's immediate entourage is evident from the fact that both

Woodcock (who trained some horses for W. S. Kilmer) and Elliott stayed over until their visas expired. Feeling among the general public ran a different course, however. As recently as World War II fists flew on several occasions when American servicemen in the Pacific theater mixed socially with their ANZAC allies. After a few beers, quite often the question which had been eating away for a decade would come out: "Tell me, Yank. Why did your people poison Phar Lap?"

The autopsy also provided a possible clue as to what made Phar Lap tick. The great gelding's heart weighed 14 pounds, compared to the 9-pound heart of another thoroughbred which was dissected at the same time.

CHAPTER FORTY-NINE

OR RACING, 1933 WAS ROCK bottom. Average purse distribution per race hit its modern low of $672 (that includes first, second, third and, where applicable, fourth money) and whereas in past seasons half a dozen horses had been winning $100,000 each, Mrs. John Hay Whitney's two-year-old Singing Wood was 1933's leading money winner with $88,050, lowest total since World War I.

The son of Royal Minstrel won only three of nine starts, and only one stakes race, but that was the Futurity (in which he was ridden by Bobby Jones, who apparently by this time had learned the intricacies of the Widener Chute). Although he placed in four other added money events, that New York victory alone was enough to put Singing Wood at the head of the list, for there was no other race of comparable value. The Pimlico Futurity was suspended in 1933–1934.

The two-year-old colts did not sort themselves out with any precision. Handicapper Walter Vosburgh, who began his Experimental Free Handicap—a sort of class standing—with this crop, had another son of Royal Minstrel on top, Greentree Stable's First Minstrel, winner of only three races in eleven starts, including the Sanford and Junior Champion Stakes. In addition to performance at two, the Experimental reflected possibilities as a three-year-old, and Vosburgh also ranked the Brookmeade Stable pair of Cavalcade and High Quest near the top, which proved to be a sound prediction.

Among the fillies Mata Hari, owned by Charles T. Fisher's Dixiana stable, was rated best (better than the colts, if her 5-pound sex allowance were counted, as she was at 122 pounds, against 126 on First Minstrel). The daughter of Peter Hastings won five of eight races, including the Arlington Lassie in her own division, and Breeders' Futurity and Kentucky Jockey Club Stakes against colts. Mata Hari had competition within her own stable, for Far Star beat her in the Arlington Futurity, and Constant Wife also was impressive. Other good two-year-old fillies that year were E. R. Bradley's Bazaar and C. V. Whitney's pair of Jabot and High Glee.

Equipoise clearly dominated the handicap division, despite what was, for him, a brief campaign. His only two losses were a third to Dark Secret and Gusto in the Jockey Club Gold Cup, and a second to Osculator, spotting him 28 pounds, in the Havre de Grace Handicap.

The three-year-olds were as jumbled as the juveniles, with Brookmeade's Inlander on top in the money standings after an active but in and out campaign of twenty-four starts, four wins, two stakes, the Classic and Travers. The big races went in various directions—the Belmont to Hurryoff, the American Derby to Mr. Khayyam, the Preakness to Head Play and the Kentucky Derby to Brokers Tip.

Discounting completely the ability of the Kentucky Derby to generate publicity, the 1933 renewal would have been the most talked-about horse race of its era had it been any race at any track.

According to all accepted criteria, the winner didn't belong in the race. Like Sir Barton, he was a maiden in quest of America's most difficult prize, but unlike Sir Barton, he was not backed up by a supposedly superior stablemate, nor did he go on to confirm his status with other victories after the run for the roses. The Kentucky Derby was the only race Brokers Tip ever won, and there were plenty of questions concerning that victory.

How an astute Derby team like Bradley and Thompson came to be represented in the Churchill Downs classic by such a colt is a mystery, except that his connections were astute. As a foal Brokers Tip was close to a cripple; he suffered from calcium deficiency and walked on his hind pasterns, a condition that was corrected by wrapping his legs in wet leather which stiffened into a splint as it dried, and by corrective shoeing. That he got to the races at all is a miracle, and in four starts as a two-year-old he failed to win, although he did finish third in the Cincinnati Trophy, won by Head Play.

Trained by former champion jockey, Willie Crump, and owned by Mrs. Crump, Head Play had been among the leaders of his division at two, and won his three-year-old debut impressively. Various offers were made for the son of My Play by owners seeking a Derby prospect, but not until the day before the race was he sold, to T. P. Hayes, acting as agent for Mrs. Silas B. Mason, for $30,000 plus 15 percent of the Derby purse, should he win. The Masons were not able to see their new acquisition perform, since they had gone to Baltimore to watch The Nut in the Dixie Handicap, run on the same day.

The 1933 Kentucky Derby, destined to be clipped in value for the next few years, was the last renewal for the time being at $50,000-added, but a relatively sparse crowd attended. Wagering on the race was the lowest it had been since World War I, only $229,312, compared with three times that sum before the crash; the W. R. Coe entry of Ladysman and Pomponius was favorite; Mrs. M. H. West's Catawba Stable entry of Mr. Khayyam and Good Advice was second choice, with Head Play the best backed "individual" at slightly more than 5½-to-1. Bradley, who usually sent an entry to the post, often as favorite, and who twice had seen his colors flash first and second across the finish, was represented only by Brokers Tip, still a maiden after having finished second in his prep race. The odds of about 9-to-1 on the son of Black Toney reflected not so much the crowd's opinion of him as the reputation of his owner and trainer, and the presence in the saddle of the country's latest riding sensation, Don Meade.

Head Play, ridden by Herb Fisher, went quickly to the lead and maintained it the first mile, bearing out on the stretch turn and entering the home lane some distance out from the rail. Brokers Tip, after trailing the field the first half-mile, had moved up by this point and Meade sent him through the opening. Head Play then swung back toward the rail, and the two colts locked together near the furlong pole; from that point on they raced as a team, while their jockeys engaged in a violent fight.

As their mounts strained ahead unattended, Meade and Fisher could be seen tugging and pushing at one another, although who was doing what to whom wasn't clear, and immediately after they crossed the finish, Fisher slashed Meade across the face with his bat. Brokers Tip was declared winner by a nose, but even while Meade was posing him in the winner's circle Fisher was clicking up the steps to claim foul.

The stewards gave him short shrift. They had seen the fiasco out on the track and already had reached a decision: both riders were guilty, but since they had finished four lengths clear of third place Charley O, and no other horse had been affected, the result was allowed to stand. Meade and Fisher each were suspended thirty days, and five more days were tacked onto Fisher's sentence when he attacked Meade as the latter entered the jockeys' quarters.

Reactions to this unprecedented battle varied. Mrs. Mason, on the basis of accounts she received of the affair, was all for disqualifying both horses, but Colonel Bradley insisted Fisher had started it. After careful study of the newsreel movie (film patrol had not yet been installed) he stated that all Meade had done was try to fend off Fisher, who had grabbed Brokers Tip's saddle cloth.

A celebrated photograph of the finish taken by Louisville photographer Wallace Lowery, who was lying under the rail, shows Fisher reaching out to grab Meade's boot, and the latter trying to push his arm away. Head Play's neck was turned to the right, indicating that in leaning over, Fisher was pulling on that rein and leaving the left rein loose while the jockey's left arm was otherwise occupied. Brokers Tip was looking straight ahead at that instant.

In their subsequent careers, however, the verdict went the other way so far as both riders and both horses were concerned. Ridden by Charley Kurtsinger, Head Play the next week won the Preakness by four lengths, as Brokers Tip finished last, nor did the Bradley colt ever earn another cent. Head Play raced successfully in later years, winning the Suburban and San Juan Capistrano Handicap among other races.

So it was with the jockeys. Fisher continued to ride for several seasons and became a trainer after retirement. Meade also rode with great success, for some years in the future, but he eventually became a notorious transgressor who was ruled off the turf for life, and repeated attempts at reinstatement proved futile.

As a final oddity in connection with the 1933 Kentucky Derby, it was the last renewal won by the man whose name was almost synonymous with the race.

"I am a speculator, race horse breeder and gambler," replied Colonel Edward Riley Bradley (1859–1946) to a question from Senator Huey Pierce Long at a Senate com-

Head Play (left) and Brokers Tip strain toward the finish of the 1933 Kentucky Derby as their respective jockeys, Herb Fisher and Don Meade, engage in a furious struggle.

Courier-Journal and Louisville Times

mittee hearing less than a year after Brokers Tip won the Kentucky Derby. The four-time winner of America's most famous race, who made no bones about any aspect of his profession, might also have added, "and a philanthropist and a gentleman."

Born to a family of Irish immigrants in Johnstown, Pennsylvania, Bradley worked in the steel mills as a youth, and while still in his teens went west to seek his fortune. He didn't strike gold, but in the gambling houses which abounded in that country he acquired a knowledge of odds which proved to be an adequate substitute.

For a time in the 1880s he made book at tracks in the Mississippi Valley—St. Louis, Memphis and Hot Springs—and he gradually obtained interests in gambling casinos in various parts of the nation. The most famous was the Beach Club in Palm Beach, Florida, which he established in partnership with a brother, John, and where a stringent code of ethics was scrupulously observed.

On the advice of his physician to spend more time in the open, Bradley bought a selling plater in Chicago just before the turn of the century, but his first horse of stakes caliber was Bad News, purchased from the partnership of Woodford and Buckner in 1903. This gelding (so named in the hope that he would travel fast) was responsible for the Bradley policy of giving his later runners names that began with the letter B, a policy that resulted from a gambler's superstitious reluctance to change a successful pattern rather than an infatuation with the sound of Bradley's own name.

Anybody with enough money can buy a ready-made thoroughbred. The real gamble in racing is rolling your own, and as a man who naturally played odds, it was just a matter of time before Bradley began breeding horses. He purchased Ash Grove farm near Lexington, Kentucky, and, with Barry Shannon as manager, it was developed into the expansive, but model Idle Hour Stock Farm. Nothing was too good for the Idle Hour horses, and every new idea that come along was at least tested. (Bradley once tried spectacles on a horse with poor vision.)

Along more practical lines, Bradley financed an improved stall gate and was credited with introduction of the fiber skull cap for jockeys, predecessor of the modern safety helmet, which saved many a rider from injury. (On the track, that is. Quite a few boys, following the human inclination to resist anything that is good for them, tried to get around the edict to wear skull caps. They received their lumps from some clerks of the scales, who used to "inspect" for caps merely by standing at the door and rapping each jockey over the head with a policeman's billy as he left for the paddock.) In the mid-twenties, Bradley purchased a controlling interest in the Fair Grounds, and made the New Orleans track the winter racing capital of America until Hialeah, in which he also owned an interest, became prominent.

The nucleus of Bradley's breeding success was the stock he bought from the J. R. Keene estate, but he later added notable imported animals, including La Troienne, who became the most successful modern foundation mare in America. When the Idle Hour horses were sold after the death of their owner, this carefully collected stock spread a considerable amount of success among other owners.

Bradley tried for the Kentucky Derby six more times after Brokers Tip's year; five of his candidates failed to get so much as a part of the purse, and one of them, Bimelech, ran second in possibly the biggest upset in the history of the race. But being a gambler, Bradley could appreciate such things: Bimelech and Blue Larkspur he regarded as the two best colts he bred, and neither could win the race he dominated.

Offsetting to some extent the gloomy outlook for the future, ten states authorized racing with pari-mutuel wagering in 1933. The various legislatures were motivated primarily by a need for revenue, but they had been shown that the public wanted racing.

299

In Florida, the Miami Jockey Club track, which was opened by Joseph Smoot in 1925, was functional enough (it was one of the first at which the grandstand, instead of being built parallel to the track, was faced on a slant to afford maximum visibility of the homestretch) but it was as far removed from the Taj Mahal as some of the other Florida real estate developments of the 1920s. After Joseph E. Widener and a group of associates bought the property, several changes were made before it opened the 1931 meeting under the name of Hialeah Park. In addition to a general sprucing up of the premises, the main track had been increased from a mile to 9 furlongs in circumference, and an infield hurdle course had been added. When pari-mutuels were made legal in Florida that year, the Widener group completely renovated the entire plant at an estimated cost of more than $2-million, converting it into a veritable garden.

An ally of Widener in his efforts to have a pari-mutuel law passed in Florida was William V. "Big Bill" Dwyer, a promoter who, besides interests in several tracks, ran a string of night clubs and a shuttle service to rum-runners to keep them supplied. (Earl Sande once sang at his Stork Club, and for a time Dwyer had an ex-dancer in charge of his racing stable.)

Dwyer, William Gallagher and Frank Bruen, who had been manager of Hialeah, were the controlling forces behind Tropical Park, which opened at the end of 1931, and they quickly began a dispute for preferred mid-winter racing dates. Widener threatened to bar all horses which raced at Tropical from participation in the richer Hialeah meeting, but the conflict was resolved when Tropical split its meeting.

The inaugural pari-mutuel meeting at Hialeah in 1932, which introduced the Australian totalisator, was not an unqualified success, but in 1933 the handle increased to a daily average of $178,637 and the State of Florida received $308,532 from the forty-five-day meeting. Owing to its ambitious purse distribution, the track itself did not make a profit (stockholder

E. R. Bradley estimated it would have except for the banking moratorium which was in effect) but the future looked excellent. The State of Florida had nothing to worry about in any case, and other areas sat up and took notice.

Joseph Early Widener (1871–1943), the man who brought Hialeah to flower, was the son of wealthy Philadelphia meat packer, street railway magnate and art patron, P. A. B. Widener. Although his father tried to direct his equine interest toward show horses, young Joseph early decided that the more definitive competition of racing was to his liking, and before he was out of college he owned some steeplechasers. He campaigned a stable of jumpers trained by J. Howard Lewis until the New York blackout, when he moved to France, and Widener's red and white racing silks were familiar sights in that country and England as well as in America.

Upon his return to America, he began racing on the flat and took an active interest in all turf affairs. He established headquarters at Elmendorf Farm in Kentucky, became a steward of the Jockey Club in 1920 and in 1925 succeeded August Belmont II as president of the Westchester Racing Association after the latter's death. Widener immediately set about refurbishing mammoth Belmont Park, and in this, as well as at Elmendorf and at Hialeah, his taste for French culture was evident. (Other instances of French influence were the pari-mutuel system, and the saliva test of horses which Widener fostered in this country.)

Widener enjoyed considerable success in flat racing, with Osmand, the Futurity winner Chance Sun and the Belmont Stakes winners Chance Shot, Hurryoff and Peace Chance, and an equal success in steeplechasing. Among the noted jumpers he owned were Lizard, Duettiste, Arc Light, Fairmount, Best Play and Bushranger. Widener also bred a number of top stars who raced in other colors.

As head of the major tracks at both ends of the East Coast, and vice-chairman of the

Jockey Club, Widener was the most influential molder of turf affairs in his day. When the Thoroughbred Club of America began the practice of recognizing men who had made beneficial contributions to the sport at an annual testimonial dinner, the first two guests of honor were Bradley and Widener.

The states which adopted racing legislation in 1933 were California, Michigan, New Hampshire, New Mexico, North Carolina, Ohio, Oregon, Texas, Washington and West Virginia. Many of these states had existing tracks, where racing began immediately, but others had to wait on track construction before the new laws could be implemented.

Among the tracks which resumed operation in 1933 were Rockingham Park, where Lou Smith two years earlier had been unable to complete a meeting using certificate betting; Coney Island in Cincinnati; Charles Town, West Virginia; Longacres, Washington; Houston, Texas, and Detroit Fair Grounds. Arlington Downs and Tanforan, which had been running meetings around the law, continued operations.

As Hialeah had shown the way in the East, Tanforan, under the leadership of Adolph Spreckels, John Marchbank, William P. Kyne and Joseph Murphy, pioneered in California.

In 1928 the track had conducted a twenty-day betless meeting, but was dark the following year when this proved too costly. It came back strong in 1930 with "options," a complicated system whereby one purchased what amounted to a share of stock in the actual horse, which could be sold for a profit if the horse won. These meetings drew enormous crowds (estimates ran up to 25,000) and proved conclusively that California wanted racing.

For the 1928 Tanforan meeting, the horse, Wirt G. Bowman, owned by Baron Long, was flown up from San Diego; he started on the second day of the meeting, came back a week later to win, and raced five times in all during the session.

When conventional racing came to California in 1933, Tanforan led the nation in gross purse distribution with $475,975. The daily average was not especially impressive, for there were 122 days of sport under the auspices of three distinct racing associations, but it was the first step in the revival of another major racing state.

CHAPTER FIFTY

IN 1934 THE DUNNIGAN—CRAWford bill eased the burdens on the existing New York tracks, and in other states other race courses either opened or reopened under the encouragement of parimutuel laws, among them Bay Meadows, Narragansett, Oaklawn Park, Tampa, Dallas, Alamo Downs in San Antonio and, at the end of the year, Santa Anita.

E. R. Bradley and J. E. Widener were very much on the racing scene as owners of Balladier and Chance Sun, respectively, two of the best two-year-old colts of the season, and the top juvenile fillies were Calumet Farm's Nellie Flag and Bradley's Black Helen. Dominating the racing picture, however, was the Brookmeade Stable of Mrs. Isabel Dodge Sloane, who became the first woman ever to head the winning owners' list. The Brookmeade racing string trained by Robert A. Smith, numbered forty-one horses including the veteran Okapi; the speedy Psychic Bid, who was among the leaders of the two-year-old division and boasted a victory over older horses; and a raft of top three-year-olds: Time Clock, Good Goods, High Quest and the champion of the season, Cavalcade.

CAVALCADE, 1931

(Lancegaye–Hastily, by Hurry On)

Imported *in utero* from England by F. Wallis Armstrong, Cavalcade was foaled at his breeder's Meadowview Farms in Moorestown, New Jersey, and sent through the Saratoga yearling sales, where Bob Smith bought him for $1,200. As a two-year-old he won only two of eleven starts, but Vosburgh saw enough promise in him to rank him second on his Experimental Free Handicap at the end of the year. (Young Alfred Gwynne Vanderbilt should have shared in any trophies that might have been awarded for perspicacity, however, for he bought Discovery from Adolphe Pons, agent for Mereworth Farm, after an even less impressive two-year-old season.)

A dark brown, almost black, colt standing nearly 16 hands, Cavalcade equaled Osculator's record in winning his first 1934 start at Havre de Grace, a mile and 70 yards in 1:41⅘. Just three days later he broke Mr. Khayyam's track record by winning the 1₁/₁₆-mile Chesapeake Stakes in 1:43⅗, with Agrarian second and Discovery third.

Coupled with his stablemate, Time Clock, who earlier had won the Florida Derby, Cavalcade started a heavy favorite for the Kentucky Derby May 5, and won it handily by 2½ lengths from Discovery, with Agrarian third. It was an especially gratifying victory for jockey Mack Garner, who in his twenty-year career had tried for the Louisville classic many times, but never before had made it.

Calvacade was coupled with another stablemate, the Wood Memorial winner High Quest, for the Preakness the next Saturday, and that colt was the only one to beat him all season. Although Cavalcade came with a rush entering the stretch, making up more than three lengths rounding the turn, his partner refused to quit. High Quest continued to fly toward the finish and won by a nose over Cavalcade, with Discovery in third place, a length behind the Brookmeade pair.

Cavalcade, champion of the 1934 season, with trainer Robert A. Smith.

High Quest didn't win another race that year, and Cavalcade didn't lose another. With High Quest going for the Eastern money (he dumped his rider in the Withers, won by Singing Wood, and ran second to Peace Chance in the Belmont), Cavalcade concentrated on the Midwest. Conceding eight pounds to Discovery, he beat him by two lengths in the American Derby, and then made a triumphant appearance in Detroit.

The city had pulled out all the stops: June 16, the day of the Detroit Derby, was practically a holiday; the purse had been set at $25,000-added, the best horse in the country was entered and Clem McCarthy was brought in to broadcast it. For 1 minute 12⅘ seconds the Michigan fans thought they had been sold a bill of goods as the distinguished invader, who went off a 1-to-2 favorite, was in eleventh place after 6 furlongs, with just one rival behind him.

"Cavalcade is beaten; he can't win," growled McCarthy as the horses turned for home with the Brookmeade colt in tenth place, about eight lengths off the pace, but with a brilliant burst of speed the favorite shot to the front to win handily by one and a half lengths, setting a new track record of 1:58⅕ for the 1³⁄₁₆ miles. Discovery was eleventh.

At Arlington July 14, where 30,000 fans jammed the track for the Classic, Cavalcade again was to meet Discovery, the Vanderbilt colt having scored a sensational victory over older horses in the Brooklyn Handicap since

303

their last encounter. Second to last with only half a mile remaining, Cavalcade roared to the front before the stretch call, and won easily by four lengths.

As other horses had been before him, Cavalcade was hailed as an invincible wonder following this victory, and as had been the case with some other horses, Cavalcade never won another race.

Plagued by a succession of injuries, he was taken out of training as the leading money winner of the year with $111,235; attempts to bring him back at four, and again at five, proved abortive; he did not win. Meanwhile, Discovery came into his own during those years.

Two other notable racing careers were interrupted abruptly in 1934, under circumstances more tragic, since the interruptions were permanent.

CHASE ME, 1929

(Purchase–Mayanel, by Lucullite)

Chase Me, owned by Mrs. John Bosley of Maryland, was a gelded son of Purchase who had become the human interest story of the decade. So unsound looking as a foal that there was no attempt to make a race horse out of him, he was turned over to the Bosley children as a family pet. They taught him tricks—how to play dead and how to beg for food—as though he were some overgrown puppy, which in disposition he was. As Chase Me developed into an attractive animal, teen-aged Sara Bosley won a number of ribbons with him in horse shows, but there was no thought of racing until he was pressed into service as a work companion for a supposedly better horse. The unbelievable happened. Chase Me was so good that he was put into training and in his first season of racing—as a four-year-old—he was undefeated in six starts, including the Bryan and O'Hara Memorial Handicap.

He came out again at five, and won his first start, then was entered in the Metropolitan Handicap against the top members of the di-

vision. Chase Me was moving with a rush on the turn for home when suddenly he fell. As the remainder of the field went on across the finish, he roused himself and stood on three legs, with the fourth one, hopelessly shattered, dangling weirdly under him. Led by a groom, Chase Me hobbled painfully off the track, and the sound of the pistol shot that ended his undefeated career was scarcely noticed over the uproar of the crowd.

That was *the* Metropolitan Handicap, the one which Equipoise had gone on to win by two lengths, only to be disqualified for swerving into Mr. Khayyam.

DARK SECRET, 1929

(Flying Ebony–Silencia, by King James)

Although he was not quick enough to be a champion, Wheatley Stable's Dark Secret, after a modest two-year-old season, developed into a top stayer—according to trainer Jim Fitzsimmons, the best he ever handled.

Following a juvenile campaign during which he won just two races, Dark Secret captured eight races at three, including the Kenner Stakes and Potomac Handicap. At five he was even better; among his nine wins were the Brooklyn, Empire City, Merchants' and Citizens', Manhattan and Washington Handicaps, Laurel Stakes and Jockey Club Gold Cup.

Distance racing was his specialty, and in addition to the 1¾-mile Saratoga Cup, he added repeat victories in the 1½-mile Manhattan Handicap and 2-mile Jockey Club Gold Cup to his tally sheet as a five-year-old, but with the last-named race his record was closed.

On a muddy track at Belmont Park September 15, only Faireno (also trained by Fitzsimmons) and Inlander came out to face Dark Secret. He entered the stretch in the lead, and appeared capable of winning without difficulty when there was a hitch in his stride. With Faireno straining beside him, Dark Secret continued on to cross the finish; he won by a head, but came to a painful halt immediately there-

Dark Secret, with a fractured leg, winning the 1934 Jockey Club Cup.

after; his leg, too, had been broken, and he also was humanely destroyed. To compound the tragedy, plans already had been made to retire Dark Secret to stud after the Gold Cup. It would have been his last race anyway.

As the 1934 season drew to a close, Santa Anita Park began its meeting on December 25. Built on the site of the old Lucky Baldwin estate, with a Spanish-American architectural motif that harmonized with its surroundings, the fancy new plant boasted a grandstand with a seating capacity of 8,000 plus a clubhouse that could accommodate 450. The track was 1 mile around, with chutes for 7-furlong and 3-furlong "baby" races, and the equipment was the most modern available. On Christmas Eve a pinto pony could be seen running back and

forth across the finish line, to test the new camera above the press box, which was capable of taking photographs that could be printed within three minutes.

A crowd of 25,000 welcomed the sport back to Los Angeles the next day. Winner of the featured Christmas Handicap was C. V. Whitney's three-year-old filly, High Glee, representative of but one of several big eastern stables which were on the grounds.

Beyond its modern facilities, novelty and position as a new center for winter racing, the main attraction at Santa Anita was the ambitious purse schedule. Breaking ground—since there had been no racing in the area for a quarter of a century—the track nevertheless announced a program that ranked it among the country's top ten in daily average distribution. Heading the cluster of stakes was the Santa Anita Handicap at $100,000-added, in a year when the main fixtures at long-established tracks were cut back from their customary, and smaller, values.

The original "hundred thousand" at Caliente had lasted only one year before it was halved for Phar Lap's renewal, then halved again for the next two runnings, both won by Norman W. Church's Gallant Sir, who broke Phar Lap's track record in his first win. Thereafter, the race quietly expired.

Horsemen didn't think the Santa Anita race would set any longevity records either—but they were not going to be absent while it lasted. The big handicap drew the greatest collection of horses ever to assemble at one track.

Trailing clouds of glory, over the mountains they came, and the roster of candidates sounded like a muster of the hall of fame: Equipoise, Twenty Grand, Mate, Head Play, Cavalcade, Statesman, all the way from England, Time Supply, Faireno, Top Row, Ladysman, Gusto, Tick On, Riskulus and others, accompanied by the ex-steeplechaser, Azucar.

Cavalcade never made it to the post at Santa Anita. Equipoise finished second to Sweeping Light in his first Western start, then beat Twenty Grand in another prep race, but the "Chocolate Soldier," who loved to run on the rail and would grab it whether it was otherwise occupied or not, was disqualified for lugging in.

When the great day arrived, February 23, 1935, despite his top weight of 130 pounds, Equipoise was a heavy favorite to capture the biggest purse in world history.

Inaugural running of Santa Anita Handicap. For three-year-olds and upward. By subscription of $100 each, which shall accompany the nomination, starters to pay $1,000 additional to the winner, with $100,000 added, of which $10,000 to second, $5,000 to third and $2,500 to fourth. Weights December 15, 1934. No penalties. Starters must be named through the entry box the day preceding the race . . . One mile and a quarter. Entries closed December 1, 1934, with 70 nominations.

Twenty of the seventy original nominees started. Head Play caused a delay at the post, refusing to enter the stall gate, so he was allowed to start from the outside. Don Meade sent Ted Clark winging to the front in a scorching pace—:22⅖, :45, 1:10 and 1:36 for the mile—but "Iceman" George Woolf, after biding his time for 6 furlongs, moved Azucar up and went on to win easily by two lengths over Ladysman, with Time Supply third and Top Row fourth.

Neither Equipoise (seventh) nor Twenty Grand (tenth) was prominent at any stage. The former, his chances of overtaking Sun Beau as world's leading money winner now shattered, was retired to stud. The latter never won another race.

The winner's final time of 2:02⅕ was a new track record—the previous record having been set four races earlier on the same program—and his $108,400 share of the purse was a new world record. Azucar didn't win another race that year, but the Irish-bred son of Milesius, as a gelding, stayed in training and was a stakes winner again at eight and at nine.

Contrary to pessimistic prediction, Santa Anita's "hundred thousand" did set a longevity record. It became the major event of the winter season, and gave the leading stakes stars an incentive to remain in training after their three-year-old season, instead of retiring at the height of their popularity.

The practice of assigning weights long before the running added a special flavor to the event. As horses who had been assigned light burdens developed into runners of unsuspected class, and vice versa, the complexion of the race was constantly changing, giving it an aura of expectancy and drama that was invaluable from a publicity standpoint. This practice was not conducive to uniformly valid results, and several lightly rigged strangers made off with

Dr. Charles H. Strub, dynamo of southern California racing.

As the Kentucky Derby is inevitably associated with Matt Winn, so is the name Santa Anita linked with that of Dr. Charles Henry Strub (1884–1958). A native of Hollister and graduate of Santa Clara, Strub finished dentistry school at the University of California and was practicing that profession when he learned the franchise of the San Francisco Seals baseball team was for sale. A former Sacramento player himself, he helped organize a group to buy the team, which he developed into the most profitable minor league outfit in the country. Paul Waner, Earl Averill and "Lefty" Gomez were among the players Strub sold to the majors for healthy sums.

When it became known that California finally was going to pass a pari-mutuel law, after unsuccessful attempts to build a track in the San Francisco area, Strub was invited to join a group of Southern California businessmen, headed by Leigh M. Battson, in organizing the Los Angeles Turf Club. Anita Baldwin had made plans to construct a track on the estate she had inherited from her father, and when she abandoned the project, the Battson–Strub group stepped in. Movie producer Hal Roach was the track's first president, with Strub general manager.

From the outset, Strub went his own way. In the depths of the Depression, he inaugurated a lavish purse program, which, at Santa Anita, was possible. In an era when ostentatious display of wealth was frowned upon, he loaded his track with every symbol of luxury he could find. While other tracks disseminated complimentary passes to the extent that payment of admission was the hallmark of a rube, Strub insisted—on the ground that no one appreciated anything he got free—on a tight gate policy.

A somewhat controversial figure, Strub had an unerring instinct for pleasing the public, although he was unpopular with a number of horsemen. Having himself survived the San Francisco earthquake when his career as a dentist was budding, and having suffered in

the purses—for a time, the Big 'Cap resembled more a South American fiesta than a North American horse race—but this, too, added to the romance of the great race.

In later years, as other rich races became available and owners could afford to take the Santa Anita Handicap or leave it alone, weight assignments were moved nearer to the running, but the old wide-open event, in its heyday, was the best possible medicine for what ailed racing at the time.

the stock market crash and recovered, Strub wasn't especially patient with anyone who felt sorry for himself.

Strub never missed a trick, and, popular or not, he was respected. Like Belmont or Widener in the East, in California he was the man to see when anything needed doing.

"Strubville," as Santa Anita later was nicknamed, not only got off the ground, it flourished. Easterners used to joke about it as a place where people came to gawk at the movie stars—Bing Crosby, later founder of Del Mar, was one of the original stockholders—rather than watch the horses. For whatever reason, people at least came, and the horses ran, for some of the biggest purses in America. Santa Anita became a frequent leader in daily average purse distribution until displaced by its crosstown colleague, Hollywood Park.

DISCOVERY, 1931

(Display–Ariadne, by Light Brigade)

One of the few top horses of handicap age who did not contest the 1935 Santa Anita Handicap was A. G. Vanderbilt's Discovery, but then he was an exceptional animal in many respects. As it turned out, he was the best of the season. Although he had assistance from stablemates in his young owner's huge, 68 horse racing string, Discovery was the prime factor in making Vanderbilt the season's leading owner with $303,605, and J. H. "Bud" Stotler the top trainer in money won.

After Cavalcade departed the scene the previous summer, Discovery won five more stakes, including the Rhode Island Handicap in world record time of 1:55 for 1¾₆ miles. The next season, the son of the "Iron Horse" proved

Discovery, great weight-carrier of the thirties, who despite his brute strength was known as a gentleman.

Sagamore Farm

308

to be of pretty solid construction himself, and without the spells of incorrigibility to which his sire had been subject.

Discovery did not begin his four-year-old campaign until May, when he was fifth in the Toboggan Handicap, won by his stablemate, Identify. After four more losses, beginning on June 22 at Aqueduct he launched a sensational winning streak of eight races, six of them handicaps. He scored a second victory in the Brooklyn Handicap by eight lengths in the new world record time of 1:48⅕ for 1⅛ miles; he equaled the 1³⁄₁₆-mile track record in beating Azucar by thirty lengths for the Detroit Challenge Cup; he won the Stars and Stripes Handicap by six; the Butler by one and a half, carrying 132 pounds; the Bunker Hill by fifteen, under 131; the Arlington Handicap by five lengths, carrying 135 pounds, in 2:01⅕, another new track record; the Wilson Stakes by six, and the Merchants' and Citizens' Handicap by two lengths, packing 139 pounds.

For the Narragansett Handicap, Discovery was again assigned 139, and Top Row beat him by one and a half lengths with a 19-pound concession, but Discovery came back to win the Whitney Stakes and Hawthorne Gold Cup.

In the Massachusetts Handicap, conceding 22 and 30 pounds, respectively, to the first two, Discovery was beaten a neck and a nose by Top Row and Whopper in new track record time. Top Row did not have Discovery's number, as it might appear, for he had finished behind the handicap champion as often as he did in front—with Discovery giving away the weight.

Discovery closed out his campaign with a twelve-length win in the Cincinnati Handicap under 132 pounds, and a fourth in the Washington Handicap under 138. In little over five and a half months he had started nineteen times and won eleven, for earnings of $102,545.

As a five-year-old in 1936, Discovery embarked on the most remarkable weight-carrying venture of his era. In fourteen starts that year,

he went to the post ten times with 130 pounds or more on his back, and his burdens for the season averaged more than 132. He won the San Carlos Handicap under 130, the Inchcape under 135, the Brooklyn with 136 and the Saratoga with 132 pounds. The weight-for-age Wilson and Whitney Stakes were his other victories. He did not win, but he carried 143 pounds in the Merchants' and Citizens' Handicap.

The big horse, 16-1 and 1,180 pounds in racing condition, who was ridden regularly by Johnny Bejshak, retired with 27 victories, 10 seconds and 10 thirds from sixty-three starts, for earnings of $195,287. Like Equipoise, he came along at an unfortunate time, but more so. Equipoise, for example, received $22,300 for winning the 1932 Stars and Stripes Handicap; for his 1935 victory in the same race, Discovery received $9,000.

Few horses ever monopolized a major stakes event as Discovery did the Brooklyn Handicap. At three he won under 113 pounds, the most ever carried to victory by a horse of that age; at four he won it in world record time, and at five he won with 136 pounds, as much as any horse ever carried to victory in that event.

Discovery became even more powerful looking after he retired to stud; the crest most stallions develop to some extent, he developed until his neck seemed as big around as the average horse's body. Despite his appearance of brute strength—and the reputation other members of his line had for temper—both Vanderbilt and his farm manager, former football star Ralph Kercheval, characterized Discovery as a "gentleman."

As had the handicapper's lead, the weight of years lay lightly on the big horse, and he enjoyed a long and distinguished stud career. Vanderbilt, when asked what was the secret breeding formula behind his success in racing, used to say, "Breed a mare to Discovery." Later, when the horse was getting along in years, the formula was revised: "Breed a stallion to a daughter of Discovery."

OMAHA, 1932

(Gallant Fox–Flambino, by Wrack)

Discovery was not the leading money winner in 1935, for the season boasted America's third Triple Crown winner in Omaha, a chestnut colt from the first crop by Gallant Fox, the pair of them being the only father–son combination in history to sweep the three-year-old classics that comprise the series. Omaha, like his sire, was bred and owned by Belair Stud, and trained by Fitzsimmons. He won only once as a two-year-old, but when he came out at Jamaica the next April, he won his debut at a mile and 70 yards. In the longer Wood Memorial later that month he was third to Today and Plat Eye.

The Kentucky Derby on May 5 was viewed as anybody's race, particularly since showers had dampened the track; the crowd eventually settled on the filly Nellie Flag, who was reputedly a good mud runner, as a lukewarm fa-vorite, with Omaha second choice at a shade longer odds, 4-to-1. Plat Eye set the pace for 6 furlongs, but by the end of a mile Omaha and jockey Willy Saunders were coasting along in front, and in the stretch it was just a ques-tion of how great the winning margin would be. It was only a length and a half, but it was maintained easily as Roman Soldier came in second and Whiskolo third.

The Preakness a week later was nothing but a workout as the Belair bullet cruised home by six lengths, Firethorn second, Psychic Bid third. Nevertheless, it was the second fastest Preakness run up to that time.

It is an exceptional horse who can success-fully drop down quickly from routes to sprints, and Omaha attempted something of the sort by starting for the Withers Mile on May 25. Fox-catcher Farm's Rosemont beat him, and as often happens when a 1-to-2 favorite fails to deliver, a mild uproar ensued; the Belair runner

Omaha, Belair Stud's second Triple Crown winner, with jockey Earl Sande

Citation, by Bull Lea — Hydroplane II

painting by Richard Stone Reeves

Round Table, by Princequillo – Knight's Daughter

painting by Richard Stone Reeves

was condemned in some quarters as a lucky colt who owed his previous success to inept competition.

Actually, after his juvenile season the long-striding Omaha never won except at distances beyond a mile. He met Rosemont again in the 1½-mile Belmont Stakes June 28, which Omaha won easily by one and a half lengths from Firethorn, with Rosemont another eight lengths astern. That completed the triple crown, and wrapped up the three-year-old championship.

The son of Gallant Fox next attempted to go out of his division in the Brooklyn Handicap, but he ran into Discovery and his world record. King Saxon was second, and Omaha third.

Returning to his own age group, with Wayne Wright in the saddle, Omaha won the Dwyer with ease, spotting 12 pounds to runner-up Good Gamble, and finished the season with a notable victory in the Arlington Classic, which brought his earnings for the year up to $142,255. Before 40,000 hoarse fans, he came from sixth place at the half-mile pole to win going away handily in 2:01⅖, a new track record, which was erased a week later by Discovery, but which stood as the best performance by a three-year-old under scale weight for a number of years.

The only others carrying scale weight in the 1935 Classic, incidentally, were E. R. Bradley's fillies, Bloodroot (third) and Black Helen (fourth). The last named, a pint-sized daughter of Black Toney–La Troienne, was yet another sensation of the season. She beat colts in March in the Florida Derby, won the Coaching Club American Oaks from fillies, then beat colts again in the American Derby. Toward the end of the year, Black Helen and Bloodroot ran one-two in the Maryland Handicap, as Firethorn finished third.

In the Midwest there was a hot sprinting rivalry between Brownell Combs' filly Myrtlewood, and John F. Clark, Jr.'s gelding Clang, both three-year-olds. The filly erased Iron Mask's world record for 6 furlongs, running the distance in 1:09⅗; Clang equaled Roseben's world record of 1:22 for 7 furlongs; and when Myrtlewood beat him twice, two match races were arranged at 6 furlongs. She won the first, at Hawthorne, by a nose in 1:10⅘, just a tick off her own track record, and at Cincinnati October 12 Clang beat her by a nose in 1:09⅕, to break her world record.

To mention briefly the juveniles of the star-studded 1935 season, and the most important victory of each, the leading money-winning colts were Marshall Field's Tintagel (Futurity), Bomar Stable's Grand Slam (Arlington Futurity), and H. P. Headley's Hollyrood (Pimlico Futurity), although C. V. Whitney's Red Rain (Hopeful) was ranked at the top of John B. Campbell's Experimental Free Handicap. Milky Way Farm's Forever Yours (Lassie and Spinaway) was a standout among the fillies.

Standing out purely because of activity (although he won a modest stake) was a colt named Seabiscuit, who started 35 times in his juvenile season.

311

CHAPTER FIFTY-ONE

RACING WAS BACK ON ITS FEET in 1936. The number of races declined—actually, levelled off would be a better term, since the drop was slight—but distribution and the average purse went up. Yearling prices took an encouraging leap and the over-all business curve adjusted into a gentle upward slope it was to maintain until the boom following World War II.

The Santa Anita Handicap drew five fewer starters than the inaugural, but so far as Reno, Nevada, horseman A. A. Baroni was concerned, the purse difference was technical. The trainer as well as owner of the winner, Top Row, he received a special bonus of $7,500 for his saddling chore, which swelled his booty to $112,100, the highest ever. (Winning jockey Wayne Wright received a $1,500 bonus, too.) Baroni, who originally had claimed the son of Peanuts for $3,500, had turned down an offer of $75,000 for Top Row three weeks before the race; before he retired, the horse won a total of $213,890.

The Santa Anita meeting got the season off to a fast start, as Airflame set a world record of :33 for 3 furlongs. Later in the year, Indian Broom at Tanforan lowered the 1⅛-mile world record to 1:47⅗, Primrose Day at Longacres set a new world record of 3:34 for 2¹⁄₁₆ miles and at Belmont Park Pompoon won the Futurity in 1:16⅖, a record for 6½ furlongs on a straightaway.

It was a star-studded season, and the most successful collection of them were in a galaxy, the Milky Way stable of Mrs. Ethel V. Mars.

Mrs. Mars first attracted attention when she spent more than $100,000 at the 1935 Sara-toga yearling sales. She came back the next year to spend an even larger sum, for her 43-horse stable, more than half of them two-year-olds, was making her the second woman in history to head the owner's list, with $206,450.

The widow of a candy manufacturer, whose 3,000-acre Milky Way Farm in Pulaski, Tennessee, was named for the company's most famous product, had enjoyed sweet success with Forever Yours, champion filly of 1935, who also was named for a candy bar, and one of the better colts in her 1936 racing string, Nation's Taste, was named in a radio contest.

There was no single individual dominating the stable, which was trained by Bob McGarvey. The top three money earners were all juveniles: Reaping Reward, winner of the U. S. Hotel, Kentucky Jockey Club Stakes and New England Futurity; Case Ace, winner of the Arlington Futurity and two other races in a brief campaign of only four starts; and the filly, Talma Dee, winner of the Selima Stakes.

Heading the stable's sparse three-year-old contingent was The Fighter, winner of three stakes at Arlington Downs, the biggest of which was the Texas Derby on April 18. Milky Way had a three-horse entry going in the race, including Doran and Sangreal besides the winner. Sangreal set the stage by dueling for the lead with A. G. Tarn's Rushaway for the first mile, at which point The Fighter came on in the last furlong to win easily as his stablemate dropped back to last. Rushaway, winner that year of three other Derbies (Louisiana, Illinois and Latonia) held on for second, and the Arkansas Derby winner, Holl Image, was third. It was the fifth straight victory for The Fighter, a son of Bull Dog.

312

Mrs. Ethel V. Mars, whose "Stars of the Milky Way" dominated the 1936 season.

BOLD VENTURE, 1933

(St. Germans–Possible, by Ultimus)

One May afternoon in the 1920s, while an enthusiastic crowd roared its approval as the winner of the Kentucky Derby was led into the charmed circle to be draped with roses, a reporter in the infield was struck by a jarring note in the festive scene. A little girl, sitting astride her pony, with tears streaming down her cheeks, had averted her eyes from the pageant that occupied everyone else's attention. In reply to the reporter's questions, the girl explained that her father, Max Hirsch, was the trainer of one of the horses which had just been defeated.

By 1936 Mary Hirsch was a licensed trainer in her own right. She did not have an entry in the Kentucky Derby, but she owned the contract of a promising young apprentice named Ira Hanford, and she loaned the boy's services to her father, who was saddling M. L. Schwartz's Bold Venture for the event. At the time it seemed rather a dubious favor, since Bold Venture never had won a stake, and no apprentice ever had won the Derby, to say nothing of the competition the neophyte pair had to face.

Virtually all the Derby winners from the winter tracks gathered together at Churchill Downs May 2, with Joseph E. Widener's Brevity, who had equaled the world record for 1⅛ miles in the Florida Derby, an odds-on favorite. A. C. Taylor's Indian Broom, who promptly had lowered Brevity's record in the Marchbank Handicap, was second choice at more than 5-to-1, and it was any price on the others.

There was a jam immediately after the start, during which Brevity was knocked to his knees, Granville lost his rider, and Indian Broom was blocked in the first quarter. Bold Venture also got into close quarters, but Hanford quickly extricated him and they were in the lead going down the backstretch. By the time he entered "heartbreak lane," the Schwartz colt had more than a length to spare over Indian Broom, as Brevity came charging up, racing wide. The favorite passed Indian Broom and ate into the leader's margin all through the stretch, but the end came too soon. Bold Venture won by a head.

In view of the unusual incidents at the start, and since Charley Kurtsinger, who finished seventh on the Santa Anita Derby winner He Did, claimed that a spectator had leaned over the rail and snatched his whip as a souvenir, the result of this race was regarded as something less than ironclad.

However, two weeks later in the Preakness, Bold Venture, this time ridden by George Woolf, again got in a jam at the start, but

Granville, elected Horse of the Year in the first championship poll.

stormed up from seventh place at the half pole to win. It took the newly installed camera to decide the issue, as he finished just a nose in front of Granville, who had been up front at the end of 6 furlongs and came again in the stretch after Bold Venture passed him.

In 1936, the photo-finish camera came into general use, and surprisingly (or maybe not), there was a drastic increase in the number of dead heats. As recently as 1933 there had been only one; in 1934 there were 6; and in 1935, as the camera was in the experimental stage, an all-time record of 20 dead heats were recorded. In 1936 the number jumped to 115, and by World War II it had passed 300. (In September of 1936, the New York State Racing Commission ordered eye tests for all placing and patrol judges.)

Undefeated in his three outings that year, and with two legs on the Triple Crown, Bold Venture bowed a tendon right after the Preakness and was retired.

GRANVILLE, 1933

(Gallant Fox–Gravita, by Sarmatian)

In 1936, *Turf and Sport Digest* and *Daily Racing Form* began conducting polls to determine the season's champions, and Granville was elected the first Horse of the Year according to both.

The second successive champion sired by Gallant Fox, he, too, sported the white jacket and red dots of Belair Stud. Granville, like Omaha, won just once as a two-year-old, and he was even slower coming around at three. He won an overnight race in his 1936 debut, but before losing jockey Jimmy Stout in the Derby, he had been defeated by Teufel in the Wood Memorial. After his close second in the Preakness, Granville took on older horses in the Suburban Handicap and again was second, to Firethorn. With the Belmont Stakes June 6 he began a winning streak of six races which completed his seasonal campaign and

314

career. Cutting the finish fine was his great specialty.

In the Belmont, Granville beat John Hay Whitney's Mr. Bones by a nose, Hollyrood third, as Brevity ran unplaced in his final start of the year. In the Arlington Classic, the order of finish among the first three was exactly the same, although Granville this time spotted Mr. Bones 5 pounds and beat him by more than two lengths.

He won the Kenner by a neck from Memory Book, and the Travers by a head from Sun Teddy on a muddy track; the stewards investigated that one, but decided it was a case of mutual guilt between the Calumet Farm colt and Granville, and allowed the result to stand.

If Granville owed his title to any one performance, that was his next win, a victory over Discovery at weight for age in the Saratoga Cup. The handicap champion obviously was not himself (perhaps off balance under his light burden of 126 pounds) but Granville won by eight lengths under a pull. The Belair colt bruised an ankle winning the Lawrence Realization, also under a hold, and completed the season with seven wins in eleven starts, never out of the money, for earnings of $110,245.

Granville concluded what appears to have been a mysterious genetic metamorphosis. After siring two straight champions, as well as the excellent Flares, in his first two crops, Gallant Fox was hailed as a sensational sire, but he went downhill from there. Nor, did either of his champion sons distinguish themselves at stud; Omaha was sent to the Jockey Club Stallion Station in Avon, New York, and Granville became an Army remount stallion.

In other categories of the *Daily Racing Form* poll, Discovery was named best handicap horse and Bushranger the top steeplechaser.

Jerry Loucheim's Pompoon, by Pompey, was champion two-year-old with six wins and two seconds in eight starts. Trained by C. F. Clarke, and ridden by Harry Richards in his principal engagements, he won the National Stallion, Junior Champion and Futurity Stakes. (At Saratoga, Maedic was king, however, as he won all five stakes for his division at the meeting.)

Hal Price Headley's Apogee, a daughter of Pharamond II, trained by his nephew Duval A. Headley, topped the juvenile fillies by virtue of victories in the Arlington Lassie, Fashion and Old Colony Stakes.

The exceptionally consistent High Fleet was the best three-year-old filly, never worse than second in thirteen starts, of which she won eight. The daughter of Jack High, owned by George D. Widener, trained by W. F. Mulholland, and ridden to her biggest score by Johnny Gilbert, won four stakes including the New England Oaks and Coaching Club American Oaks.

Myrtlewood, the sensational speedster of the previous year, came back fast as ever in 1936, and the daughter of Blue Larkspur, trained by R. A. Kindred, was voted champion sprinter. In ten starts, she won eight, of which seven were stakes events. Ridden by George South, she won the Lakeside Handicap at Washington Pork in 1:35⅗, which equaled the track record for a mile and was a world record for a female. In the Motor City Handicap she set a new track record for 1¹⁄₁₆ miles, and in the Cadillac Handicap a new track record for 6 furlongs, both at Detroit.

Two other sprinters of extraordinary proportions were on the scene in 1936. Myrtlewood's old rival, Clang, campaigned in the East, where the son of Stimulus, trained by W. R. Sallee and ridden by Ed Litzenberger, won the Carter Handicap and showed that he, too, could stretch out a bit by also winning the 1¹⁄₁₆-mile Yonkers Handicap.

Fast as they were, Myrtlewood and Clang operated best under skeleton rig compared to George D. Widener's Sation; as a six-year-old, the son of Galetian still was formidable enough to win the Jamaica Handicap under 128 pounds, and finish second in the Toboggan with 135, the Carter and American Legion with 132.

On October 15, 1936, racing began at

Keeneland Race Course.

Keeneland Race Course in Lexington, Kentucky. When the Association track had closed after more than a century of operation in 1933, the breeding capital of America was left without a place to race, and in 1935 Major Louie A. Beard, manager of the Whitney thoroughbred interests, called a meeting at the Lafayette Hotel of those interested in the welfare of the sport. The upshot was the organization of the Keeneland Association, with Hal Price Headley as president, dedicated to establishment of a center of sport for sport's sake. As a non-profit enterprise, subscribed to by persons interested only in having a race track in operation in the Bluegrass, Keeneland was something of a community project, but by no means entirely so, since many of the contributors were residents of other areas who were sympathetic to the general idea.

The first move was the purchase of 147 acres from John Oliver "Jack" Keene (1870–1935) one of racing's legends. Not related to James R. Keene, he had been everywhere horses race and done everything that can be done on a race track. He saddled his first winner at Nashville in 1897, Max Hirsch up, and his numerous ventures included a foray into Japan and a trip to Russia, where he won many races since his were the only horses wearing aluminum shoes. When he settled down at his family homestead, Keene dreamed of developing the place into a haven for horses and horsemen, with an elaborate combination stable and living quarters, which would serve as a sort of perpetual open house. According to the accepted anecdote, he was very particular about the size and shape of stones that went into his gate, so that by the time he had finished scouring the countryside for precisely the right ones, there were enough left over to build his huge structure; an estimated twenty years and $400,000 went into it.

This unique structure, which was converted into the clubhouse, was the nucleus of Keeneland Race Course; the other features were a $1\frac{1}{16}$-mile main track, an infield track of sand for training and a grandstand, the whole of which was laid out in a natural, country style.

Its founders hoped to make Keeneland into a "Saratoga of the South" or an American equivalent of the Royal Ascot meeting. Everything was done to promote this aim, and the track did acquire a special flavor all its own. No extremely rich stakes were offered (although in modern times some valuable ones were instituted), but large stables from all over the country co-operated by sending high-class runners to contest what was available.

For years Keeneland operated under a special pari-mutuel rule in which the state did not participate, because of the track's non-profit status. However, this exemption was withdrawn and it became a conventional track, but all profits from the business were turned over to a fund for educational and charitable purposes.

316

WAR ADMIRAL, 1934

(Man o' War–Brushup, by Sweep)

A good big horse can beat a good little horse, so the saying goes, but occasionally an individual comes along who causes such sayings to go out the window. War Admiral, Triple Crown winner and Horse of the Year in 1937, was that sort of individual. Neither big nor red, he was by no means another Man o' War, but the little brown colt was probably the best runner ever begotten by his famous sire.

Bred and owned by Samuel D. Riddle, trained by George Conway, and ridden by Charley Kurtsinger, War Admiral stood 15 hands 2 inches, and resembled his dam, the tiny Brushup, in appearance. As a two-year-old he had been near the top of his generation. After winning a maiden and an allowance race, in his first stakes effort he finished third to Pompoon and Fencing in the National Stallion Stakes. Fairy Hill beat him in the Great American, then War Admiral won the Eastern Shore

Handicap by five lengths for his only added-money victory as a juvenile. His last start of a brief campaign was in the Richard Johnson Stakes, in which he ran second to Bottle Cap.

As a three-year-old, although his campaign was interrupted by injury, War Admiral was never beaten, nor was he fully extended more than once. He won his seasonal debut at Havre de Grace by two and a half lengths, then followed up with a runaway conquest over the Flamingo Stakes winner, Court Scandal (by Royal Minstrel out of The Colonel's Lady), in the Chesapeake Stakes. The Flamingo Stakes was the new name for what had been the Florida Derby, and as the Santa Anita Derby winner, Fairy Hill, also was in the beaten field for the Chesapeake, Riddle for the first (and only) time in his life decided to try for the Kentucky Derby.

The mission was accomplished with no strain. After an eight-minute delay at the post, much of it caused by himself, War Admiral shot into the lead immediately after the start

War Admiral, champion of the 1937 season. (Photo taken as a stallion.)

and was already under restraint when he passed the finish line first time around. Kurtsinger merely had to adjust the advantage as he saw fit, and his mount was still in hand when they came under the wire again. Pompoon made a rally to finish second, but without threatening the leader, and Reaping Reward was third. Trainer Conway accepted the trophy from Governor "Happy" Chandler, shook hands with Vice-President John Garner, then put his charge on a car for Maryland that same evening.

The Preakness, a week after the Derby, was the same story, but with the climax radically revised. Again War Admiral took the lead promptly, but he lost ground on the turns, and Wayne Wright, who had replaced Harry Richards as Pompoon's jockey, launched his challenge earlier. Slipping through on the inside, Pompoon was on even terms with the favorite in the last sixteenth, but War Admiral put his head in front and held it there the rest of the way. It was a more decisive victory than the margin suggests, however, as Pompoon was giving every ounce while Kurtsinger appeared to be keeping something in reserve, merely brandishing his whip at War Admiral during the drive. The field straggled in eight lengths behind the first pair.

The last, and theoretically most difficult of the Triple Crown series, the Belmont Stakes, was the easiest for War Admiral. The only trouble encountered by the Riddle colt was of his own making, as he repeatedly broke through the stall gate, causing another eight-minute delay at the post. When the official start finally was effected, he scurried to the lead from his outside post position as though he were embarking on a 6-furlong jaunt instead of a 1½-mile run. Kurtsinger soon restrained him, however, and the Riddle colt clicked off the quarters evenly to win by three lengths from Sceneshifter, with Vamoose a further ten lengths away third. The winner's time of 2:28⅗ equaled the American record.

As War Admiral marched back to scale,

seemingly none the worse for his exertions, he left a trail of blood behind him; a portion of his off forefoot had been sheared away, apparently during his antics at the start. He had run the race without noticing the injury.

It was four and a half months before he started again, but he came out good as ever for a purse race at Laurel late in October, which he won by two and a half lengths from the Suburban winner, Aneroid. Four days later Man o' War's little son defeated another field of older horses in the Washington Handicap; then, again with only a four-day rest, he closed out his season on November 3 with a win over his contemporaries in the inaugural of the Pimlico Special. There were anxious moments in the latter race as Masked General, under a feathery 100 pounds, outran the heavily laden Admiral (128) until the turn for home, but when the leader flew wide on the turn War Admiral came through to win by one and a half lengths.

He went into winter quarters undisputed champion of the season with $166,500, the bulk of it having come from the Kentucky Derby and Preakness, which in 1937 were restored to their former values of $50,000-added.

SEABISCUIT, 1933

(Hard Tack—Swing On, Whisk Broom II)

War Admiral commanded a handsome sum for his eight appearances, but he was not the year's leading money winner, for 1937 was the most profitable of Seabiscuit's numerous seasons of racing. Although he raced nearly twice as often as the champion, for Seabiscuit it was a relatively light campaign.

The hard-working two-year-old, who had escaped the claiming halter only to be sold at three, had developed into a good winner for Mrs. C. S. Howard that year, but gave no real indication of what he was going to be eventually. He broke a couple of track records, but these were at Bay Meadows, a track which had been in operation just two seasons.

As a four-year-old the son of of Hard Tack, trained by Tom Smith and ridden by Red Pollard, finally came into his own. Never before in his active life had Seabiscuit managed to win more than two races back to back, but in 1937 he won eleven of fifteen starts, including seven handicaps in a row.

He began the season (or, rather, resumed it, since he did not close out his three-year-old campaign until mid-December) in February at Santa Anita with a victory in an overnight handicap, in which Rosemont finished fifth. The Foxcatcher Farm horse had upset Omaha in the Withers at three, and Discovery in the Narragansett Special at four—and as a five-year-old Rosemont chose Seabiscuit as his victim. When the stakes money appeared on the line, the son of The Porter reversed the earlier decision; he won the San Antonio Handicap as Seabiscuit ran fifth. An epic sequence of frustrations for Seabiscuit in the Santa Anita Handicap began when Rosemont, under a beautiful ride by Harry Richards, threw in a final quarter that shaded 25 seconds, to make up a deficit of nearly six lengths and win by a nose.

There was some consolation in that part of the cream had been skimmed off the top of the world's biggest purse, in order to double the minor awards, so Rosemont received $90,700, while Seabiscuit's second money of $20,000 was the largest sum he had ever earned in one race. With Rosemont out of the way, Seabiscuit won the San Juan Capistrano Handicap by seven lengths, setting another new track record of 1:48⅘ for 9 furlongs. He followed up with scores in the Marchbank and Bay Meadows Handicaps before departing for the East.

Although he had won with 127 pounds in his last race in California, the Howard colt got into the Brooklyn Handicap with only 122, against 127 on the favored Rosemont. The latter (destined never to win another race) was no factor as Seabiscuit won by a nose from equal-weighted Aneroid. Another victory, under 126 pounds, in the Butler Handicap, and Seabiscuit was up to 129 for the Yonkers at Empire City. He won by four lengths in 1:44⅕, on this occasion breaking a track record that had been standing twenty years. The revitalized colt's richest and most significant win of the season came next, when he carried 130 pounds in the Massachusetts Handicap at Suffolk Downs, winning by a length from the giant Chilean horse, Caballero II, who carried only 108.

At this point, Seabiscuit was within one victory of matching Discovery's eight-race winning streak, but the Narragansett Special, as it was for Discovery, was his undoing. The Hawthorne Gold Cup, for which Seabiscuit had been assigned 128 pounds, was run the same day, but his board of strategy elected to send him after the Rhode Island race, under 132; Calumet Dick and Snark, both with large weight concessions, beat him back to third.

Down to 130 pounds for the Continental Handicap at Jamaica October 12, Seabiscuit ambled home by five lengths and became the season's leading money winner. A dead heat with the speedy Heelfly in the Laurel Stakes four days later increased his total, but late that month War Admiral passed him in earnings. A meeting between the two outstanding horses of the season had been anticipated for the Washington Handicap, but Seabiscuit was thrown off his work schedule by a muddy track, and he skipped the race.

He regained his financial leadership, after War Admiral retired for the season, by winning the Riggs Handicap by a neck from Burning Star, carrying 130 pounds and setting a new track record of 1:57⅖ for 1 3/16 miles. In his final start of the year, Seabiscuit, 130, lost the Bowie Handicap by a nose to William Ziegler, Jr.'s outstanding mare, Esposa, 115, who in 1937 enjoyed the most successful season of her career. The five-year-old daughter of Espino, trained by Matt Brady, had won seven earlier stakes events, and her time of 2:45⅕ in the Bowie was a new track record for 1⅝ miles.

Seabiscuit headed west with $168,580, the

Joseph E. Widener presents the trophy to owner Hal Price Headley following Menow's victory in the 1937 Futurity. Trainer Duval Headley is at right.

first horse of handicap age to lead the seasonal financial rankings since the blackout days. His encounter with War Admiral had been deferred, but not cancelled. It was to come a year later.

The ladies, who had been increasingly prominent in recent seasons, dominated the owners' standings in 1937, as Seabiscuit's owner, Mrs. Charles Howard, ranked first with $214,519, Mrs. Mars's Milky Way Stable second and three others were among the top ten: Mrs. Emil Denemark, whose stable created a sensation in Florida by several times winning more than one race on the program; Mrs. Ethel D. Jacobs, whose husband continued his amazing stint as leading trainer; and the Greentree Stable of Mrs. Payne Whitney.

Despite atrocious luck, Milky Way gave the Howard stable a tussle, finishing less than $5,000 away. Reaping Reward broke down in the Latonia Derby, but carried on to win it. Sky Larking, winner of three stakes including

320

the Hopeful, was regarded as the champion two-year-old when he broke his leg during the running of the Champagne Stakes and had to be destroyed. However, the well-balanced stable also included Tiger, who won the inaugural Washington Park Futurity and ran a dead heat (giving away 5 pounds) with Teddy's Comet in the Arlington Futurity; Mars Shield, filly winner of the last Texas Derby, plus the Kentucky Oaks; Case Ace, Mountain Ridge, Well Rewarded and Military.

Champion two-year-old of the season in the final voting was Hal Price Headley's Menow, who atoned for losses in the Chicago futurities by winning the Champagne and New York Futurity, the latter in world record time of 1:15⅕ for 6½ furlongs on a straightaway. The Headley stable also included Whopper, a huge colt who made a successful return to competition after an operation to remove kidney stones.

Mrs. Edward Friendly's Jacola, Wheatley Stable's Merry Lassie, J. H. Whitney's Inhale and Calumet Farm's Theen were prominent among the two-year-old fillies, and King Ranch's Dawn Play, winner of the American Derby from colts as well as the Acorn and Coaching Club American Oaks, stood out among distaff three-year-olds. W. J. Hirsch's four-year-old Columbiana, trained by her owner, won a notable victory in the Widener Challenge Cup, forerunner of the race that was to become the Eastern equivalent of the Santa Anita Handicap. Although War Admiral completely overshadowed the three-year-old colts, Whitney's Flying Scot, Mrs. C. Oliver Iselin's Strabo and J. W. Parrish's Dellor had impressive records.

CHAPTER FIFTY-TWO

THE ANTICIPATION OF A BATTLE between Seabiscuit and War Admiral was a fever that permeated the country during 1938. There were other horses running, and good ones, too, but this pair had captured the public imagination: two kinsmen from opposite sides of the tracks: War Admiral, bred in the purple, by Man o' War out of a granddaughter of Ben Brush; his rival. Seabiscuit, by a son of Man o' War out of a great granddaughter of Ben Brush. By spring there were firm offers from both Belmont Park and Arlington for a $100,000 match between them. Neither came off—primarily because Riddle and Howard (who had taken title to Seabiscuit from his wife) were too cautious. Seabiscuit, in particular, was several times scratched from races when conditions were not right—but the clamor for a showdown between them continued, until another match was arranged, with the Horse of the Year title at stake.

Ordinarily, such a race would not have been necessary, for a younger colt had established a strong claim to such honors by March.

STAGEHAND, 1935

(Sickle–Stagecraft, by Fair Play)

A maiden in eight starts as a two-year-old, Stagehand was purchased for $8,000 from Joseph E. Widener by Dayton, Ohio, paper manufacturer Maxwell Howard (no relation to Seabiscuit's owner) because he liked the colt's older brother, Sceneshifter. Within about two months, Stagehand had guaranteed Howard a

position as leading owner of the season, Earl Sande a ranking as leading money-winning trainer and helped Nick Wall gain a corresponding title among the jockeys. Quite a feat for an eight-horse stable, only four of which were winners, but Stagehand was quite a horse, as by himself he contributed $189,710.

He got started immediately, on January 1 at Santa Anita, running second in a 7-furlong maiden race; then he won three overnight events in succession, significantly, all of them at a mile. (He never did win at a shorter distance.)

In his next start, on February 22, Stagehand, ridden by Jack Westrope, beat a good group of previous stakes winners in the $50,000-added Santa Anita Derby, which he won by half a length from Dauber, Sun Egret third.

Since he had been a maiden at the time weights were assigned, Stagehand was in the "hundred thousand" at the allowable minimum of 100 pounds, but on the scale of weights for March that was equivalent to 122 pounds on a four-year-old or 123 on an aged horse. Seabiscuit, who had disappeared from the work tabs for a while, emerged from hiding and finished second by a nose to Aneroid in the San Antonio Handicap, carrying 130 pounds, the same weight he had been assigned for the big one; for his first out, it was a sparkling performance, so he started favorite in the Santa Anita Handicap March 5.

The race was almost a duplicate of the previous year's renewal. Seabiscuit, ridden by Woolf, reached the lead in the stretch, but the long-striding Stagehand, ridden by Wall, running the final quarter in less than :24⅖ seconds, made up about three lengths to win by a nose. The time of 2:01⅗ was a new track record, and Pompoon, who had received such heavy play in the future books that one of them took him off the board, finished six lengths behind Seabiscuit.

No three-year-old, before or since, accomplished such a notable double as Stagehand. No horse had paid through the nose so heavily as Seabiscuit, for his nose at Santa Anita alone had cost the future world's leading money winner $148,075.

Stagehand's string of wins was snapped in his next start, but he did not fade away thereafter as some other stars of the winter season had done. He finished third in the Kentucky Derby Trial, won by his stablemate The Chief, but developed fever and was declared out of the main event. When he returned to action in the Dwyer, he was again third, but The Chief was again the winner, and next the pair ran one-two against older horses in the Brooklyn Handicap.

Running on his own, Stagehand equaled the track record for 1⅛ miles in winning the Empire City Handicap July 9, after which he was unplaced in the Classic and Travers, although he picked up fourth money in each. Bull Lea and Purple King, both getting concessions, beat him a head and a neck in the Thornton Memorial Handicap, but Stagehand reversed this decision by beating Bull Lea in the Narragansett Special a week later, again conceding weight. On September 10, Westrope tried new tactics with the stretch-running colt, allowing Stagehand to go to the front earlier than usual, and the result was a victory in the Narragansett Governor's Handicap and another track record, 1:49⅖, for 9 furlongs. That closed out a campaign of fifteen starts, eight wins, two

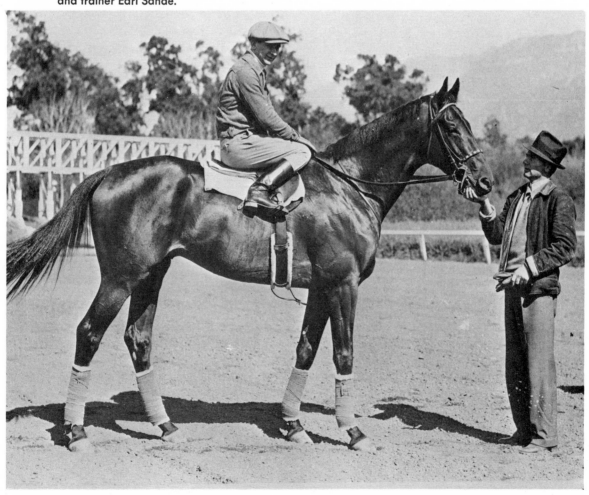

Stagehand, only three-year-old to win the Santa Anita Handicap, with Jack Westrope up and trainer Earl Sande.

seconds and three thirds, and Stagehand had never failed to bring home at least part of the purse.

Following the end of the Santa Anita meeting, Seabiscuit went to Mexico for an improvised but pale revival of the Caliente Handicap, which he won. In April, carrying the highest weight of his career, 133 pounds, he won the Bay Meadows Handicap in new track record time of 1:49 for 9 furlongs. He went to New York for the proposed $100,000 match with War Admiral at Belmont Park, but lost his edge and the race was called off. He went to Boston for a shot at War Admiral in the Massachusetts Handicap, but the track came up mud. Heading west again, he stopped off in Chicago, where the track was slow but he started anyway, with 130 pounds, and War Minstrel beat him by three and a half lengths with a 23-pound pull in the weights. At the inaugural meeting of the new Hollywood Park, again with 133 pounds, Seabiscuit won the first running of the Gold Cup.

He got his first taste of match racing at Del Mar in August, in a special event against the Argentine-bred Ligaroti, owned by Binglin Stock Farm, stable name of Bing Crosby and Lin Howard, the son of Seabiscuit's owner. It turned out to be one of his toughest races. Under 130 pounds, he won by a nose in 1:49, breaking the previous track record by 4 full seconds, as Noel Richardson and George Woolf flailed each other in a manner reminiscent of the 1933 Kentucky Derby. Both jockeys were suspended for the remainder of the meeting.

Seabiscuit then went back to Chicago, but weather interrupted his training and he was withdrawn from the Hawthorne Gold Cup. Continuing east to Belmont Park, the five-year-old bay, who had not won at a distance beyond 1¼ miles (and never did), two days off the train finished third in the 1½-mile Manhattan Handicap, conceding 20 pounds each to Isolater and Regal Lily. Plans to go against War Admiral in the 2-mile Jockey Club Gold Cup were thereupon dismissed, and Seabiscuit went

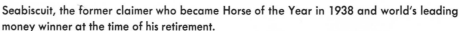

Seabiscuit, the former claimer who became Horse of the Year in 1938 and world's leading money winner at the time of his retirement.

to Maryland. He won the Havre de Grace Handicap and was defeated by the three-year-old filly Jacola in the Laurel Stakes, she ridden by Wall and carrying 102 pounds to his 126. That was on October 15, by which time a match against War Admiral already had been scheduled.

Patrons at Pimlico in 1938 may have noticed a slim young man here and there about the premises, standing in line at the mutuel windows, awaiting his turn at the concession stands, and otherwise being ubiquitous. This was Alfred Gwynne Vanderbilt, who had purchased a block of stock in the track the year before, and added to it that year until he had a controlling interest. The Pimlico vice-president, soon to be president, was operating on the unorthodox principle, for an executive, that the best way to feel the public pulse was to get among them oneself. With other tracks offering larger sums to bring together the two most glittering stars of the period, it was he who swung the deal, and the $15,000-added Pimlico Special, winner-take-all, was set for November 1. The owners of Seabiscuit and War Admiral had posted $5,000 forfeit to guarantee the appearance of each horse.

War Admiral also had trouble finding a comfortable spot for his 1938 debut, for Riddle steadfastly refused to accept 130 pounds without a tightener. Finally, an allowance race materialized in which the colt was required to carry only 122, and he was off to a remarkable season.

On the day Seabiscuit was beaten by Stagehand in the Santa Anita Handicap, War Admiral picked up his 130 pounds and won the Widener Handicap, big race of the winter in the East. As Riddle was as fastidious about weight as Howard was about track condition, War Admiral stayed on the shelf three months after this victory because no suitable races were available.

When the Belmont race with Seabiscuit was called off, War Admiral was entered in the Suburban, at 132 pounds, but was scratched after rains the night before the race left the track muddy. (As it happened, the track dried out to an extent that Snark won the Suburban in 2:01⅖, fastest time of the year for 1¼ miles.) As though to silence critics—and there were plenty of them—Riddle accepted 132 pounds for the Queens County Handicap a week later in which War Admiral beat Snark, giving him 6 pounds.

Once more a public hero, the son of Man o' War was shipped to Boston, where it was expected he would meet Seabiscuit in the Massachusetts Handicap, for which both horses had been assigned 130 pounds, but because of the heavy track the Western horse was scratched forty-five minutes before post time. War Admiral went, and for the only time in his life finished out of the money, as Menow (107 pounds) danced to an eight-length victory with Wall in the saddle. Busy K. (107) was second by a neck over War Minstrel (106), who beat the Admiral by a nose.

An eight-length win over Fighting Fox and Esposa in the Wilson Stakes, at weight for age, failed to get War Admiral out of the doghouse, but when he picked up 130 pounds and won the Saratoga Handicap after only three days' rest, making concessions all around, he was restored to grace. With Wayne Wright and Maurice Peters substituting for Kurtsinger, who had been injured, the 1¼-mile Whitney Stakes, 1¾-mile Saratoga Cup and 2-mile Jockey Club Gold Cup, all at weight for age, were merely romps for War Admiral. He was hailed as king of the turf when he headed south for Pimlico.

The agreement stipulated that the track must be fast, and on the morning of November 1, Jervis Spencer, chairman of the Maryland Racing Commission, accompanied by steward A. G. Weston, personally walked around the Pimlico track, nodded affirmatively to Vanderbilt, then stepped over to a microphone and announced that the race between War Admiral and Seabiscuit would be run. By 10 o'clock, when the gates were opened, there was a crowd

325

standing in line, and by afternoon 40,000 fans had packed themselves into the relatively small plant, well more than half of them standing-room customers.

The battle was on: $1\frac{3}{16}$ miles, both horses at 120 pounds. War Admiral, the giant killer, the good little horse; against Seabiscuit, another of the same stripe—they were about equal in height, but the Californian was heavier in frame. Large crowds surrounded the contestants in the paddock as Kurtsinger, undoubtedly well supplied with instructions, mounted for his first ride on the champion *pro tem* since July. Woolf, the Iceman, after conference with Silent Tom Smith, was relaxed; he gave Seabiscuit a casual, friendly swat on the rump before he mounted, and his chief concern seemed to be finding a place to spit without hitting a spectator.

Clem McCarthy, whose broadcast of this race has been made into a record, already was vibrating with excitement. War Admiral was a pronounced favorite at 1-to-4; Seabiscuit was 11-to-5. (It wasn't until after the race that everyone suddenly seemed to recall that War Admiral was attempting a difficult shift from routes to a shorter distance—dropping down $6\frac{1}{2}$ furlongs from his last previous race—while Seabiscuit was going the other way, coming off a race at one mile.)

Out of deference to War Admiral's aversion to the gate, a walk-up start had been agreed upon, and George Cassidy had been imported from New York to do the honors. They began moving toward the start, but Woolf, not liking the looks of things, reined to one side. Another try, and Kurtsinger wasn't ready. The third time, and they were off.

The shocking upset of advance calculations was evident immediately. War Admiral, who habitually shot straight into the lead, was outrun from the start, as Seabiscuit, from the outside post position, darted to the front while Woolf beat a tattoo on him. Still whipping rapidly, Woolf steered his mount over and grabbed the rail, hugging it around the first turn. Kurtsinger, after a futile attempt to forestall this maneuver, settled down to a chase. On the backstretch, Woolf moved Seabiscuit out slightly, presenting an inviting hole, but Kurtsinger knew better. He took War Admiral to the outside, and as he drew abreast his rival a great cheer went up. At the end of 6 furlongs they were even, at the end of a mile Seabiscuit was a head in front, in midstretch it was half a length and then, suddenly, War Admiral surrendered. Seabiscuit crossed the finish four lengths in the clear, the new champion. The time—:$23\frac{3}{5}$, :$47\frac{3}{5}$, 1:$11\frac{4}{5}$, 1:$37\frac{4}{5}$, 1:$56\frac{3}{5}$—was a new track record.

Both War Admiral and Seabiscuit were eligible to the Rhode Island Handicap at Narragansett Park, and the management offered to increase the purse by $25,000 should they both contest it. War Admiral went up and won it, under 127 pounds. Seabiscuit, assigned 3 pounds more, stayed put.

The next year, War Admiral was pointed for a repeat victory in the Widener, and Seabiscuit again was sent after the Santa Anita Handicap.

After winning a 7-furlong prep in near-record time in February, 1939, War Admiral developed laryngitis and was taken out of training. He later injured an ankle and was retired permanently with earnings of $273,240, having won 21 of his 26 starts, finished second three times and third once. The winner-take-all Pimlico Special was the only race in which he did not get part of the purse.

Seabiscuit finished second in his prep race, pulling up lame. He was withdrawn from the Santa Anita Handicap which was won in his absence by his stablemate, Kayak II. An ankle injury kept Seabiscuit out of action the rest of that year, but in 1940 he came back briefly to win the San Antonio, and, at long last, carrying 130 pounds, the Santa Anita Handicap. He won the latter race from Kayak, who didn't really argue the issue when it became apparent Seabiscuit was home free. Seven years old, Seabiscuit retired as world's leading money winner with the following record: 39 starts, 33 wins, 15 seconds and 13 thirds, for earnings of $437,730.

Toward the end, as Seabiscuit drew near the earnings record, Willis Sharpe Kilmer threatened to put Sun Beau back in training in an attempt to regain his financial title, but as Seabiscuit was no colt, and Sun Beau was eight years older than he, no one (probably not even Kilmer) took it seriously.

The scene was crowded with stars in 1938, among them the two-year-old champion, William Ziegler, Jr.'s El Chico, a son of John P. Grier, trained by Matt Brady, and ridden by Nick Wall, who went undefeated in seven starts, all of them stakes: the Youthful, Dover, Great American, U. S. Hotel, Saratoga Special (equaling the track record of 1:10⅗ for 6 furlongs), Hopeful and Junior Champion Stakes. His average winning margin was more than three lengths, and in none of his races did any rival finish within a length of him, but El Chico was the exception in that he never was hailed as another Man o' War. He looked like a yearling filly—not an especially large one at that—and every time he won from rivals who towered over him, spectators shook their heads in disbelief. (His fabulous juvenile season was the little colt's one taste of glory, for after a disappointing three-year-old campaign, he broke two sesamoid bones and was destroyed.)

Because he was so small, El Chico had not been kept eligible to the futurities. In his absence, the Belmont Futurity was won by airplane manufacturer W. E. Boeing's Porter's Mite, a colt who prepped for the event by setting a new world record of 1:14⅖ for 6½ furlongs (straightaway) in the Champagne. W. L. Brann's Challedon won the Pimlico and New England Futurities; Thingumabob, owned by the Manhasset Stable of Mmes. Charles S. Payson and Thomas Laughlin,

won the Arlington Futurity, and seemed destined for a top season when he injured himself in the Sanford Stakes and had to be destroyed, and other good two-year-old colts were George D. Widener's Eight Thirty and Belair Stud's Johnstown. The top juvenile fillies were Woolford Farm's Inscoelda, Widener's Dinner Date, King Ranch's Ciencia, Longchamps Farms' Donita M. and E. R. Bradley's Big Hurry.

St. Louis merchant Herbert M. Woolf, owner of Woolford Farm, had an excellent year as his Lawrin—bred in Kansas—won the Kentucky Derby, to the dismay of the crowd which had backed Fighting Fox, Bull Lea and Menow in that order, and to the consternation of the Churchill Downs band, which by that time had forgotten how to play any tune but "Bred in Old Kentucky," and stood mute for an embarrassing interval. The occasion was the beginning of an awesome combination—trainer Ben Jones and jockey Eddie Arcaro. Lawrin, a son of Insco, also won the Hialeah, Flamingo, Hollywood Trial Stakes, and a special invitational race at Hollywood Park for which the winner's share was $40,000. Townsend B. Martin's Cravat, W. S. Kilmer's Nedayr and W. P. Stewart's Pasteurized were good three-year-old colts besides those already mentioned; and the better fillies included Brookmeade's Handcuff, the previously described Jacola, and Mrs. Walter M. Jeffords's Creole Maid.

The handicap division, of course, was dominated by Seabiscuit and War Admiral, although honors were due Esposa, who added three more stakes to her collection (all at the expense of males, naturally); to Snark, a son of the speed sensation Boojum, who accomplished a neat coupling by winning the 6-furlong Toboggan and 1¼-mile Suburban the same season; and to T. D. Taggart's Marica, who beat Esposa twice while conceding weight.

CHAPTER FIFTY-THREE

BY 1939 RESIDENTS OF THE Free State had become so proud of a native-bred horse that when he appeared on a track they began singing "Challedon, My Challedon" to the tune of "Maryland, My Maryland." The repetitiousness of the refrain was appropriate, for the colt was elected Horse of the Year twice in succession.

However, before Challedon attained his exalted stature, there was a lot of groundwork to be done.

KAYAK II, 1935

(Congreve–Mosquita, by Your Majesty)

South America nearly took it away in 1939 before Maryland made a move, as the sensation of the winter season was a colt who proved to be a more than adequate substitute for none other than the great Seabiscuit himself. Imported from Argentina by C. S. Howard, Kayak II had been foaled in August, in accordance with the system that prevails south of the Equator, where seasons and the universal birthday are opposite to those in the northern hemisphere. Hence he was six months "behind his age" in the United States, but despite his disadvantage the smooth-running brown colt won five races as a "two and a half year old" racing against threes; they were not such as to cause any fanfare, however, and at the end of 1938 Kayak II was assigned only 110 pounds for the next year's Santa Anita Handicap.

When he glided to a new track record winning the San Carlos Handicap at 1 1/16 miles in February, under identical weight, it appeared

that Howard had the proverbial lock on the big one two weeks later. Such proved to be the case. Although Seabiscuit (who would have had to carry 134 pounds) was withdrawn, Kayak II, John Adams up, romped to another new track record, 2:01⅖.

Efforts were made to lure the South American to Mexico, and to the East, but he remained in California until the Hollywood Park

Charles S. Howard with his South American record breaker, Kayak II. (American Stock)

meeting. The latter track, which had opened the previous year amidst dire predictions that it would never go (summer racing in Southern California was incongruous—too much competition from the beaches and other resort activity), had prospered, taking its place immediately among the national leaders in purse distribution. Kayak II duplicated his crosstown performance by winning two stakes at Hollywood, the American Handicap and the Gold Cup, both in new track record time, carrying a respectable 125 pounds in the latter.

He was easily the richest horse in the country when he finally was shipped to the opposite coast, where he was to meet Challedon.

JOHNSTOWN, 1936

(Jamestown–La France, by Sir Gallahad III)

The eventual Horse of the Year also had as much, or more, competition than he could handle right in his own age division during the first half of 1939. Johnstown, winner of seven races, including four stakes, as a two-year-old, made an impressive entrance as a three-year-old by defeating older horses in the Paumonok Handicap April 15. Next he set a new track record of 1:40⅘ for a mile and 70 yards in an overnight race at Jamaica, then followed up with another victory over his contemporaries in the Wood Memorial. In May, the Belair Stud colt started as an odds-on favorite for the Kentucky Derby, and won, leading all the way, with never a rival within hailing distance. Jimmy Stout, who had been dumped by Omaha, had a rocking chair ride this time; Challedon finished second—but eight lengths away.

In the Preakness, over a muddy track, the tables were turned as Challedon won from Gilded Knight and Volitant, with Johnstown unplaced for the only time that season.

For the Withers the track was fast and so was Johnstown, as the big bay won under a strong pull, six lengths ahead of Hash. The Belmont Stakes at 1½ miles on June 3 capped a remarkable exhibition of versatility as the colt, who had been fast enough to beat his elders at

William Woodward, Sr., owner of Belair Stud and chairman of the Jockey Club, leading in Johnstown (Jimmy Stout up) after the 1939 Belmont Stakes.

6 furlongs less than two months earlier, now won the "Test of Champions" in an easy gallop, covering the route in 2:29⅗, and finishing five lengths ahead of his nearest rival, Belay.

In the Dwyer two weeks later, Johnstown again was confronted by Challedon. There was a sizzling duel for about 3 furlongs, after which Johnstown drew farther and farther away; Stout had to go to work on him toward the end, as the lightly weighted Sun Lover launched a challenge, but Johnstown won by a length in 1:48⅖ for the 9 furlongs, just a tick off Discovery's track record, while Challedon wound up six lengths behind Sun Lover.

It was reported that Johnstown while running had begun to "make a noise"—the race-tracker's catch-all term for respiratory ailments of any description—but the colt continued to train brilliantly and was shipped to Chicago for the Classic in July. After leading for a mile in 1:36, he tired badly, and Challedon went on to win, although he was under pressure to stave off Sun Lover by a neck.

Johnstown finished third, six lengths behind the runner-up, and although he remained in training for some time thereafter, eventually the reluctant announcement came that he was being retired. Challedon and Johnstown had defeated each other twice, and it was take-your-pick between them. Judging by the odds when they raced against one another, most people were picking Johnstown—but Challedon went farther.

CHALLEDON, 1936

(Challenger II–Laura Gal, by Sir Gallahad III)

Challedon was bred by Branncastle Farm, a partnership between his owner and Robert Castle—both advertising men—who had imported his sire, Challenger II, from England on the advice of Christopher J. FitzGerald. Foaled at Brann's Glade Valley Farm in Frederick, Maryland, Challedon grew into a big, robust colt, not really exceptional in size (16 hands 1 inch) but he appeared larger than he

actually was because of a commanding presence. This in some measure probably accounted for his great popularity.

As a two-year-old, he made a name for himself in the last half of the season. Trained by ex-jockey L. J. Schaefer, he won four races in six starts; he finished twelfth in a field of fifteen in his first stakes attempt, the Eastern Shore Handicap in September, but he then won three futurities in a row; the Maryland, New England and Pimlico.

His debut as a three-year-old was a third to Gilded Knight and Impound in the Chesapeake Stakes, following which were his three encounters with Johnstown in the Derby, Preakness and Dwyer. (In fifteen starts that season Challedon competed exclusively in stakes events.)

On the heels of his defeat in the Dwyer, he was again third, in the Kent Handicap to Sun Lover and Eight Thirty, both of whom were carrying less weight. After this race, George Seabo, who had been his regular jockey, was replaced by Harry Richards. In their first outing, the new team won the Yankee Handicap in new track record time from Hash and Silent Witness, and on July 12 Challedon was sent against older horses in the Massachusetts Handicap. That was his only time out of the money, as Fighting Fox was the winner, followed by Pompoon and Burning Star, although Challedon, beaten six lengths in all, did save fourth money.

After his Classic victory over Sun Lover in Chicago, Challedon was assigned 128 pounds for the Thornton Memorial Handicap, and Porter's Mite, rigged at 116, upset him by one and a half lengths. It was the pride of Maryland's last defeat; on September 2, he took his biggest step toward the championship.

Kayak II had come east, accompanied by his stablemate Sorteado, a good enough horse in his own right, and the pair of them went off a 1-2 favorite for the Narragansett Special, despite Kayak's package of 128 pounds, 10 more than Challedon's, and a 3-pound concession ac-

Challedon, first horse to be elected overall champion for successive seasons. George Woolf up.

cording to the scale for September. The race had a heavy Latin flavor for the first 6 furlongs as Sorteado, Ligaroti and Kayak led the file; the last-named took over the lead in the next quarter, but Challedon, after trailing for half a mile, rolled up in the stretch and won by three. It had been so easy that sarcastic comments arose about "California form," but Silent Tom Smith opened his mouth enough to explain that Kayak had bruised a heel.

Returning to Chicago, Challedon beat older horses again—the few that faced him—as he became the first three-year-old ever to win the Hawthorne Gold Cup. He received surprising opposition from Gridiron and Chief Onoway, who finished lapped on him, as a trio of sophomores led the way across the wire.

If there had been an award for travel, Challedon would have won that, too, since his next appearance was home in Maryland, before an enthusiastic crowd that cheered him to another victory over an all-age field, by four lengths in the muddy Havre de Grace Handicap. The colt

by this time was much sought after as an attraction, and Brann sent him to Kentucky for a special race at Keeneland honoring the late E. J. Tranter, a famous bloodstock salesman and auctioneer, who owned the Fasig-Tipton Company and originated the Saratoga yearling sales. The race was open to all ages, but only three-year-olds contested it, as Challedon set a new world record of $1:54\frac{3}{5}$ for $1\frac{3}{16}$ miles, winning by four lengths from Greentree's Hash, who was fresh from victories in the Edgemere Handicap and Lawrence Realization. Back in Maryland, Challedon won the Maryland Handicap in a canter, and commenced preparation for his final start of the year, a showdown with Kayak in the Pimlico Special. Since their Narragansett race, the Howard colt had proved he could run in the East with an authoritative win over Hash in the Continental Handicap.

Cravat also was in the Pimlico Special field, but played no part in the result, since the race quickly developed into a match between the big two. Arcaro, riding Challedon for the first time, pulled a surprise by sending the big colt to the front at once, taking a path somewhat out from the rail to avoid sticky footing; while Woolf, who had ridden Challedon to his world record at Keeneland, but now was back on Kayak, did not contend for the lead. He brought the South American up to even terms on the turn for home, however, and entering the stretch Kayak was slightly in front. It was one of those classic battles, stride for stride through the lane, two top colts and two ace jockeys giving their all, but the longer-striding Challedon slowly pulled away to go under the wire half a length clear. It was his sixth successive stakes conquest, and his earnings for the year reached $184,535.

Howard wanted another try at the champion in the Bowie Handicap, but Challedon was sent immediately into winter quarters, while Kayak, in a sterling performance, broke his fifth track record of the season, winning from Heelfly in a gallop, time for the 1⅝ miles, 2:44⅖.

EIGHT THIRTY, 1936

(Pilate–Dinner Time, by High Time)

Another who finished the 1939 season with an impressive winning streak was George D. Widener's home-bred Eight Thirty, who ended his campaign with five successive stakes victories.

At two, the chestnut son of Pilate had won three races, including the Christiana and Flash Stakes. He had also finished first in the Albany Handicap, but was disqualified.

At three he was slow rounding into form. After his second to Sun Lover in the Kent (Challedon third), Eighty Thirty won a hard-fought battle with Day Off in the Diamond State Stakes, and was given a rest until the Saratoga meeting in August.

He proved invincible at the Spa. In the Wilson Mile, at weight for age, he defeated the distinguished older horses Pompoon, Main

Eight Thirty, as a stallion, with his owner, Jockey Club chairman George D. Widener.

Man and Fighting Fox. Just three days later, on August 5, he beat another field of his seniors in the Saratoga Handicap. Back in his own division, he won the Travers in the mud with ease, finishing five lengths ahead of Sun Lover, and wound up with a victory over the older mares Shangay Lily and Handcuff in the Whitney Stakes. A sore hind leg removed him from the scene at that point, but he was to be back the next season, tilting with Challedon.

BIMELECH, 1937

(Black Toney–La Troienne, by Teddy)

By and large two-year-olds are not considered as candidates for Horse of the Year, since they rarely compete outside of their own age division. It was not Colonel E. R. Bradley's fault that Bimelech wasn't considered for the title in 1939, for after the colt had beaten everything in sight within his own group, Bradley challenged all comers, but there were no takers.

The last son of the Idle Hour stallion Black Toney, Bimelech was a full brother to Black Helen and Big Hurry, and as such was regarded with special attention. By the time the colt entered training both Bradley and trainer William Hurley, who had replaced the deceased Thompson, agreed he was one of the best they ever had seen, regardless of breeding.

From the outset, Bradley had his eye on the next year's Kentucky Derby, and the eighty-year-old owner campaigned his hope for a fifth victory cautiously. Bimelech didn't show silk until late June, when he sped to a three-length victory at Suffolk Downs; in mid-July, ridden by F. A. Smith, he won another overnight race at Jamaica by six lengths. Along with Boy Angler, he was shipped to Chicago for the Arlington Futurity, but Bradley withdrew both colts when the Illinois Racing Commission refused to grant a license to Don Meade, Boy Angler's intended jockey.

Back in New York, Bimelech was entered in the winner-take-all Saratoga Special; his vaunted speed was tested fully as the Vanderbilt filly Now What—champion of her sex that year and already winner of three stakes—carried him a fast half in :46⅕, after which the Bradley colt drew away to win by three lengths, Briar Sharp second, Andy K. third and the filly fourth.

A son of Jack High, owned by the Millsdale Stable of M. L. Emerich and Tony Pelleteri, Andy K. was the winner of the Arlington Futurity, but he had a habit of bearing out; he lost considerable ground in the Special by so doing, although not enough to affect the result.

That habit cost him the rich Hopeful Stakes, however, for Bimelech was bothered at the start and had to thread his way between horses to reach a contending position, which he did not attain until well in the stretch, at which point Andy K. was winging along more than two lengths ahead. In spite of Longden's best efforts to keep him straight, Andy K. drifted wider and wider, practically to the outer rail, and Bimelech was able to get up in time, winning by a neck in the only close finish he was to experience all season.

Because of a wet track, Bradley refused to let Bimelech start in the Champagne Stakes, which in his absence was won by Andy K., who, relishing the straightaway Widener Chute, finished six lengths clear of his closest rival.

The Futurity a week later over the same course would settle the issue, and the old Colonel left his sickbed to see it. From a vantage point high in the grandstand, attended by doctor and nurse, Bradley watched his pride and joy lead all the way to go under the wire one and a half lengths clear as Smith still had a lapful of horse left. Andy K., after a poor start, moved up for a time, but tired and finished next to last; it wasn't a true bill on him.

Bimelech took another futile trip, this one to Rhode Island for the New England Futurity —but he was scratched when the track became muddy. He then journeyed to Pimlico for a test of stamina in that track's 1¹⁄₁₆-mile Futurity November 4. Smith had to whack him a few times when he tried to loaf, but Bimelech won easily by four lengths from Rough Pass, with the New England Futurity winner, Straight Lead, third, another five lengths away.

It was then that Bradley issued his challenge to any horse in training, Challedon and/or Kayak II preferred, "for money, marbles or chalk," for a race at a mile and 70 yards or 1¹⁄₁₆ miles at weight for age. Since any older rival would have had to concede Bimelech at least 20 pounds by the scale of weights—and his contemporaries already had seen more than enough of him—no one wanted any part of such a race, so Bimelech went home as the heaviest future book favorite for the Kentucky Derby in history. He was assigned an unprecedented 130 pounds on the Experimental Free Handicap.

A number of other horses made their marks in 1939. King Ranch's Ciencia, ridden by Carroll Bierman, became the first filly to win the rich Santa Anita Derby; Belair Stud's six-year-old Isolater was an excellent stayer and assisted materially in putting his stable at the head of the owners' rankings; Mrs. F. Ambrose Clark's Lovely Night was another of the exceptionally good three-year-olds, as was James Cox Brady's filly, War Plumage, and Woolford Farm's Unerring.

The juvenile division included Joseph E. Widener's Roman, Arnold Hanger's pair of Roman Flag and Dit, who finished one-two in the Breeders' Futurity; Ral Parr's Victory Morn and Jack Keene's War Beauty; also, C. V. Whitney was back in action with Flight Command.

In 1940, the first full year of the war in Europe, almost all of racing's vital statistics continued their slight climb, except the average price for yearlings, always the most sensitive barometer of anticipated conditions. In the countries already involved in the war, of course, racing was in a turmoil, and importations from abroad increased. Among the prominent animals acquired by Americans were the undefeated English Triple Crown winner, Bahram,

purchased from the Aga Khan by a syndicate composed of A. G. Vanderbilt, Walter Chrysler, Jr., Sylvester Labrot, Jr. and James Cox Brady; Mahmoud, winner of the Epsom Derby in record time, acquired also from the Moslem ruler by C. V. Whitney; the Cesarewitch winner, Hunter's Moon IV, and the leading Australasian stallion, Beau Pere, both purchased by Louis B. Mayer; Heliopolis, imported by E. D. Shaffer of Coldstream Stud; Rhodes Scholar, Easton and Hairan.

The biggest single development was the institution of pari-mutuel wagering in New York, where expectations were exceeded as more than $100-million went through the machines, and purse distribution went up accordingly.

Along the racing front Challedon gained his second championship, never finishing out of the money in seven starts, of which he won five, carrying 130 pounds or more except in two weight-for-age events. Skipping the rich winter handicaps, and thereby causing considerable conjecture as to his condition, he did not come out until July, when he won an overnight race at Suffolk Downs, in preparation for the Massachusetts Handicap. That rich event, however, for the second year in a row proved to be his low point. He ran into a seasoned Eight Thirty, who equaled Seabiscuit's track record in winning by a length from Hash, while Challedon, carrying 130 pounds and conceding 4 to the winner and 15 to the runner-up, was another one and a half lengths away.

It was Challedon's turn to revise the records next out, as only ten days later, clear across the continent, he broke Kayak II's track record in the Hollywood Gold Cup, covering the 1¼ miles in 2:02 under the heaviest burden of his career, 133 pounds. Eight Thirty wasn't there, but the field represented the best in the West; Specify was second, Can't Wait third and the favored Kayak unplaced. A month later at Saratoga, only two rivals went to the post against Challedon in the Whitney Stakes at weight for age, but after Isolater pulled a surprise by setting the pace, Challedon went all out and was very fortunate to beat him a nose. Not long afterward, Lou Schaefer announced his resignation as trainer of the Brann stable, and Don Cameron replaced him.

After the Hollywood Gold Cup, Brann had decided that never again would he allow his horse to carry more than 130 pounds, but he did accept that maximum load for the Narragansett Special September 21. The Maryland colt reached the lead in the stretch, but tired under his burden, and was unable to withstand the closing rush of Hash (122), who beat him by half a length.

Challedon, who never had attempted a distance greater than 1¼ miles, was withdrawn from the 2-mile Jockey Club Gold Cup coming up September 28, in which he would have had to carry only scale weight of 125 pounds, the explanation being offered that the purse was not worth it. However, a new stake, the New York Handicap, at 2¼ miles, was scheduled for the following week at $50,000-added, and Challedon was withdrawn from that on the assumption that he would be assigned too much weight. On Gold Cup day, the Maryland colt accepted 130 pounds and won the $15,000-added Havre de Grace Handicap by three lengths, spotting 20 pounds to second-place Honey Cloud, 18 to third-place Masked General and 22 to Volitant, the only other starter. Assigned 4 pounds less for the following week's $50,000 race—which drew seventeen starters in spite of the dearth of distance horses—Challedon nevertheless was kept out of it.

The prospective field for the Pimlico Special having evaporated through retirement or injury, a last-minute invitation was issued to Myron Selznick's Can't Wait, a good five-year-old who had been coming along all season to the extent that he won four stakes events. On a dreary, drizzly day, Challedon led all the way to beat him by two lengths.

That was the end of his 1940 campaign, and his tenure as champion. Out of action as a five-year-old, Challedon returned at six, but won

only two of thirteen starts, and then went to stud. His final record was 44 starts, 20 wins, seven seconds, six thirds, $334,660.

Eight Thirty won more money ($81,450) than Challedon during their mutual four-year-old season, thanks directly to his victory over the champion in the rich Massachusetts Handicap, the only occasion they met. Before that race the Widener colt had won the Toboggan with 127 pounds, conceding 14 to runner-up War Dog; finished fourth to Third Degree, Can't Wait and War Dog in the Metropolitan, while carrying top weight of 128 pounds; won the Suburban Handicap under top weight of 127, defeating Can't Wait and Third Degree; and run third in the Brooklyn, again under top weight, 130 pounds, conceding 11 to the winner, Isolater, and 19 to Can't Wait.

Following his conquest of Challedon at Suffolk Downs, Eight Thirty won the Wilson Mile at weight for age, then was third to Sickle T. and Hash in the Saratoga Handicap, conceding them 19 and 12 pounds, respectively. His leg was again troublesome, so his campaign was ended without his having been tried beyond 1¼ miles. (He came back the next year to win the Toboggan under 129 pounds and the Metropolitan under 132, his only two starts.)

The "people's choice" in the 1940 handicap division was Mrs. Marie Evans's four-year-old gelding, Shot Put, a son of Chance Shot, who had run with a $2,000 claiming tag in his youth. Starting 33 times, the ex-plater won nine races, of which five were stakes: the Kentucky, Lincoln, and Bryan and O'Hara Handicaps at conventional distances, and the New York and Exterminator Handicaps at distances beyond 2 miles. An extraordinary stayer, Shot Put shattered the Belmont track record for 2¼ miles in the New York Handicap, winning in 3:48⅘ (the previous record for this seldom-contested route having been 3:51, set in 1908). Among several marks he set at Washington Park was a world record of 4:48⅘ for 2¾ miles. Shot Put performed best under light weights, however. The best routers of the season with their weight up were Belair Stud's three-year-old Fenelon and the aged Isolater, who staged an unusual two-horse walk-over in the Saratoga Cup. Another big money winner of the handicap division was Le Mar Stock Farm's Many Stings, winner of both the McLennan and Widener Handicaps during the Florida season.

Bimelech was the leader among the three-year-olds of 1940, but he failed in his primary mission. Not making his debut until April 25 in the Blue Grass Stakes, which he won easily from his sole real opponent, Roman, he was entered five days later in the Derby Trial. He won this by two lengths from Milky Way Farms' Gallahadion.

Although the Kentucky Derby purse had been raised to $75,000-added, Bimelech had frightened off all but seven opponents, and he started at 2-to-5. After Bimelech had taken an expected lead in the stretch, Gallahadion came roaring up from fourth place under the urging of Carroll Bierman to win by one and a half lengths. It was all Bimelech could do to save second by a nose from Dit.

In the Preakness the next Saturday, Bimelech led all the way to win easily by three lengths from Mioland, as Gallahadion finished third. There followed another unaccountable upset in the Withers, as Bimelech had all he could handle prompting the pace of Roman, while Corydon, coming from last place at the halfway point, passed them both in the stretch to win by a length and a half, Bimelech again saving the place just by a nose. After this debacle, the work was poured to Bimelech in the next few weeks in preparation for the Belmont Stakes. He won that race, but only after a hard fight; Your Chance finished lapped on him, and Andy K. was a surprisingly close third. Century Note was eight more lengths behind Andy K., while Gallahadion and Corydon brought up the rear.

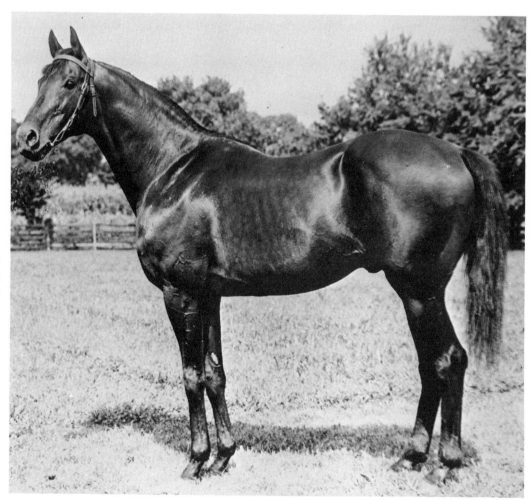

Bimelech, victim of the biggest upset in modern Derby history. (Photo taken as a stallion.)

336

In the Arlington Classic Dixiana's Sirocco, winning his only stake of the season, headed a straggling procession across the finish line, seven lengths ahead of Gallahadion, who, in turn was three ahead of Bimelech, who led Dit by eight. It later was learned that Bimelech was suffering from an injured foot, and he was taken out of training—he, too, returned the next season, but, after finishing fourth in the Widener, the only occasion he was out of the money, he was retired for good.

Among Bimelech's contemporaries, C. S. Howard's Mioland was his nearest rival for over-all honors, having won the San Juan Capistrano Handicap before he met the Bradley colt in the Preakness; and the American Derby, Potomac and Westchester Handicaps afterward. Roman turned out to be an excellent sprinter, and H. C. Hill's gelding, Sweepida, was tops in the West with victories in the Santa Anita Derby, Will Rogers, Golden State Breeders and Bay Meadows Handicaps.

There was no real champion among the three-year-old fillies of 1940. Starmount Stable's Damaged Goods (so named because she had been injured as a yearling while narrowly escaping from a stable fire) won both the Acorn and Coaching Club American Oaks, beating the best of her age and sex in these events, but she lost many more races than she won, her record having been four wins in nineteen starts. Salaminia and Fairy Chant each won more money and more stakes, the former taking the Alabama, Ladies (beating older mares) and Gallant Fox (beating older colts), while Fairy Chant won the Santa Margarita Handicap from older mares in February, and subsequently won the Pimlico Oaks, Gazelle Stakes and Beldame Handicap. At one time or another, each of the above fillies defeated each of the others during the season.

The juvenile championship of 1940 was split, Woodvale Farm's Our Boots winning one poll, Calumet Farm's Whirlaway the other.

Our Boots was never out of the money in a light campaign of six starts. He won only one stake, the New York Futurity, in which he carried 119 pounds, against 122 on runner-up King Cole and 126, the maximum, on third-place Whirlaway. Finishing unplaced were the New England Futurity winner, Bushwhacker; the Washington Park Futurity winner, Porter's Cap; the Arlington Futurity winner, Swain, and the National Stallion and U. S. Hotel Stakes winner, Attention.

Whirlaway was three times out of the money in a heavy campaign of sixteen starts, of which he won seven, including the Saratoga Special, Hopeful (Attention second), Breeder's Futurity (Our Boots third) and Walden Stakes, the last-named race being at $1\frac{1}{16}$ miles, the longest distance two-year-olds were required to run. In the Pimlico Futurity, at the same distance, both Our Boots and Whirlaway had been upset by Bold Irishman.

Whirlaway in action was more impressive than Whirlaway on his record, however, as the colt lost several times through bearing out, dawdling at the start or other foolishness; when he finally made up his mind to run, he could turn it on, and it was agreed that he would be harder to beat at longer distances the next season, especially if his manners should improve.

Crispin Oglebay's Level Best, a daughter of Equipoise, who was equally agreeable to whipping males or females, was the best juvenile filly of the season, winner of six stakes events. Her nearest rivals were Joseph E. Widener's Misty Isle and Valdina Farm's Valdina Myth, both of whom also won from masculine competition.

The year 1940 was one of particular significance in the Midwest as, at opposite ends of the circuit, events transpired which were to establish racing on a sounder basis than ever before.

In New Orleans, the Fair Grounds had undergone severe losses, and the track was put up for sale. However, a group headed by Sylvester Labrot, Jr., Anthony Pelleteri and William Helis obtained an option on the property and the auction (actually scheduled for January 2, 1941) was called off. A number of local citizens were persuaded to join the operation of the famous old winter track as a civic venture, and under the direction of Labrot, Herbert Schwartz and John S. Letellier the Fair Grounds got back on stride.

In Chicago, circumstances were not so dire, but racing nevertheless received a boost as Washington and Arlington Parks, hitherto rivals, were formed into a team. A syndicate headed by John D. Allen purchased control of Arlington Park, and Benjamin F. Lindheimer (1891-1960) was given the reins to both tracks.

A native of Chicago, Lindheimer had begun as an assistant to a building contractor and later became a successful real estate developer on his own. Interested in all forms of sports (he was a good southpaw pitcher himself) he made notable improvements at Washington Park, which he took over in 1935. Under the new arrangement he was able to coordinate the meetings of the two big Chicago tracks into what amounted to one continuous program, making the Windy City a self-sufficient racing capital within itself. Lindheimer's influence in his area was analogous to that of Dr. Strub in Southern California. He, too, was a great innovator and deft at pleasing the public.

CHAPTER FIFTY-FOUR

ONTRARY TO WHAT MIGHT have been expected, the effect of World War II on racing was to increase its prosperity. There were some opposite effects, of course—the difficulty of procuring strategic materials delayed construction of race tracks in New Jersey, where the sport had been made legal, and, at the request of Army officials, Santa Anita postponed its meeting—but the over-all trend was expansion. The entertainment business in general underwent a boom in which racing participated—nothing to compare with the boom that was to follow the war, but nevertheless quite remarkable at the time. Racing's vital statistics, which had been in a gentle climb, turned sharply upward; purse distribution in 1941 reached a record total of nearly $18-million, more than $2-million greater than the previous year's sum, which also had been a record.

Another new era in thoroughbred racing was on the way, and the stable which was to dominate the sport to an extent not believed possible under its modern, far-flung structure, charged to the top for the first time in 1941. Thirty-five horses carried the devil's red and blue silks of Calumet Farm into combat during the season, surging to a new record of $475,091 in stable earnings, breaking the old Rancocas mark. Leading the charge was Whirlaway, top money winner of the year, who by himself earned more than any other entire stable. His winnings alone also would have been enough to make Ben Jones the leading money-winning trainer, and Blenheim II the leading sire. Eddie Arcaro missed being the leading money-win-

ning jockey by a narrow margin, because he was under suspension a good part of the year, but he topped the stakes riders easily. All of this, thanks to the one colt who, like Challedon, was elected Horse of the Year twice in succession.

WHIRLAWAY, 1938

(Blenheim II–Dustwhirl, by Sweep)

For a time at the beginning of his three-year-old campaign, it appeared that Whirlaway was not going to make delivery on the promises he had given at two.

After winning his sophomore debut at Hialeah in February by only a head, Whirlaway finished third twice in a row, a disappointing performance for the winter book Kentucky Derby favorite, made more so by the fact that the colt, noted for his stretch drive, was losing ground at the end in each of these defeats. Whirlaway made some amends by winning his next two races, but only by a neck; he still hadn't shown any of the verve that had characterized his two-year-old form, and with five races under his belt at three he was yet to be tested in stakes competition.

The first such race was a fiasco. In the Blue Grass Stakes at Keeneland, after wresting the lead from Our Boots, Whirlaway still was on top entering the stretch, and for an instant appeared ready to bound away to victory; instead, he reverted to his old habit of bearing out, and fell back so fast he was defeated by six lengths, as Our Boots continued on to win.

In the Derby Trial, he again refused to maintain a straight course, and he was defeated, although he did recover after bearing out and was gaining on the winner, Blue Pair, at the end. On both the occasions he had run out, Whirlaway was ridden by Calumet's contract jockey Wendell Eads, a boy still fresh from the apprentice ranks. For the Kentucky Derby, Ben Jones obtained the services of Eddie Arcaro, under contract to Greentree Stable, but granted permission to ride for Calumet when Greentree did not have a competing horse.

Arcaro was introduced to his mount during morning work hours in an unusual manner. To find out whether his new rider could prevent the colt from veering to the outside, Jones, astride a fat stable pony, planted himself a few feet out from the rail and told Arcaro to ride Whirlaway through the hole. As the jockey later described his feelings, "I couldn't see enough room, but I thought if the old man was game enough to sit there, I'd be game enough to try it." He tried it, and made it.

The jockey was startled again in the paddock just before the Derby when Jones, mumbling something about "I'll fix that so-and-so," yanked out a knife—but he used it only to cut away the inside cup from Whirlaway's blinkers, thus providing the colt with unrestricted vision out of his left eye. Jones's decision was not so impulsive as it appeared to be, because early that morning he had confided his plan to two newspaper reporters.

Warren Wright with Whirlaway, the horse that led Calumet Farm to the first of its many championship seasons.

The 1941 Kentucky Derby was a memorable race in more ways than one. Both his recent conquerors, Our Boots and Blue Pair, were in the field, but Whirlaway nevertheless was a lukewarm favorite, with the Santa Anita Derby winner, Porter's Cap, second choice. It was testimony to the Calumet colt's popular appeal, the flair he had—once he decided to run—that made him appear invincible, and no race was more illustrative of "Mr. Longtail's" special personality than the one he ran the afternoon of May 3, 1941.

Dispose, winner of the Flamingo, led for the first mile, but when Whirlaway launched his drive from fourth place it was all over but the ticket cashing. His tail (which lacked not more than an inch of touching the ground when he stood still) streaming behind him, he ran the final quarter in a fantastic :23⅗ seconds to win by eight lengths as Staretor, longest shot on the board at 36-to-1, was second by a neck over Market Wise, the early contenders having given up. The winner's final time of 2:01⅖ broke the former track record set by Twenty Grand ten years before, and Whirlaway was not once touched with the whip—Arcaro was looking over his shoulder in the final yards for competition that never materialized.

With Arcaro again in the saddle, Whirlaway was an easy winner by five and a half lengths in the Preakness, after which Eads rode him to a victory against the older horses Mioland, Hash and Your Chance in an allowance race on May 20—an unusual preparation for the Belmont Stakes. The latter was merely a workout for the Calumet comet, as only three rivals challenged him in the 1½-mile contest; after piling up a seven-length lead before the race was half over, Arcaro took Whirlaway in hand and they sauntered home to win the Triple Crown.

With no apparent opposition in sight from active horses, Whirlaway began running against history; the earnings record for one season, established eleven years before by Gallant Fox, seemed his for the taking, as he galloped to

another victory in the Dwyer Stakes, although Market Wise made him hustle for it.

Shipped to Chicago for the Classic, Whirlaway, ridden by Eads, won an easy prep race, but gave his backers a scare by once again going wide on the turn for home. Arcaro having been suspended for a rough ride at Empire City, Alfred Shelhamer was awarded the mount for the Classic itself; he kept the colt straight enough, but Mrs. Parker Corning's Attention, ridden by Carroll Bierman, ran one of his best races to win by one and a half lengths. All eyes thereupon were turned to Attention as the only

The finish photograph of the 1941 Saranac Handicap in which War Relic (top) seemed to be closest to the wire but actually Whirlaway (nearest camera) was the winner.

341

Market Wise beating Whirlaway for the 1941 Jockey Club Gold Cup in the new American record time of 3:20⅘ for two miles.

colt who could stop the juggernaut, but the son of Equipoise went wrong and did not race again that year; as it happened, there was enough competition for Whirlaway from other sources, and the six-race winning streak that ended with the Classic was the longest he ever was to enjoy.

In the Saranac Handicap, carrying 130 pounds, he was opposed by War Relic, 117, fresh from a new track record conquest of older horses in the rich Massachusetts Handicap; the Riddle colt entered the stretch with a narrow lead, and as Whirlaway turned for home spectators waited for his electric burst of speed. Instead, they saw the favorite head for the outside rail, while Alfred Robertson frantically tried to get him aimed at the proper target. Whirlaway finally came on course and reached War Relic just at the end. It took the camera to decide the issue, and even that decision was not reassuring. A near riot resulted when the print was posted, since it looked as though War Relic, next to the rail, really had won; however, under a magnifying glass (which few horse players include as standard equipment) what appeared to the naked eye as a hoofprint in the track could be identified as Whirlaway's flaring nostril, and by that margin he had won.

The Travers, in the mud against only two opponents, was an easy victory for Whirlaway, and his second trip to Chicago had a happier result as he won the American Derby from Bushwhacker by nearly three lengths. In the Narragansett Special, however, he again met War Relic, and this time there was no question concerning the outcome. Ted Atkinson on War Relic stole the race by setting an artificially slow pace—1:14⅗ for the first six furlongs,

1:39 for the mile—and when Whirlaway launched his famed stretch run that had been so devastating against exhausted pace setters, he found a fresh horse up front who had enough left for a devastating run of his own. War Relic won by four and a half lengths, and although he was receiving an 11-pound concession, Whirlaway carried only 118, so weight was not the deciding factor.

After an easy eight-length victory from just two opponents in the Realization, Whirlaway lost the 2-mile Jockey Club Gold Cup by a nose at level weights to the formidable stayer, Market Wise, who lowered the Belmont track record by a full second to 3:20⅘.

That was the final start of an active season for the champion; he had missed Gallant Fox's record for annual earnings, but was destined to exceed all other horses in career winnings before another year had passed.

ALSAB, 1939

(Good Goods–Winds Chant, by Wildair)

The twenty starts made by Whirlaway in 1941 was an exceptionally large number for a stakes horse, but that year's juvenile leader, Alsab, was in action even more often; he raced 22 times, but then wasn't regarded as a stakes horse at first. By the time he finished, though, he had won 15 races, more than any two-year-old on record.

A colt of vastly different origin from the home-bred Whirlaway, who was by an Epsom Derby winner out of a mare who had produced the excellent Reaping Reward, Alsab was sold by breeder Tom Piatt for only $700 at the Saratoga yearling sales, and his name was a

342

contraction of that of his purchaser, Chicago attorney Albert Sabath.

In his first start, the bay colt finished just about where an animal with that price tag would be expected to finish: fourteenth in a field of fifteen. Thereafter, throughout his exhaustive campaign, he never failed to bring back part of the purse. Running in the colors of Mrs. Sabath, trained by August "Sarge" Swenke, and ridden by a succession of jockeys but most regularly by Bobby Vedder, Alsab progressed steadily through the year.

He did not win an added money event until his eleventh start, the Joliet Stakes at Lincoln Fields, which he took by five lengths. He followed up with a seven-length triumph in the Primer Stakes at Arlington; then, after a long trip to Suffolk Downs, he lost the Myles Standish Stakes by half a length when Eternal Bull set a new track record.

That was the Sabath colt's last defeat of the years. Two weeks later Alsab equaled the track record in the Mayflower Stakes (Eternal Bull third) and a remarkable, ten-race winning streak was launched. He won the Hyde Park Stakes by five lengths, equaled the track record in the Washington Park Juvenile, won the rich Washington Park Futurity and Prairie State Stakes. Moving east to Maryland, he was assigned 126 pounds for the Eastern Shore Handicap, and Colchis (117) almost sneaked off with the victory, but Alsab drove up in the last strides to make it a dead heat.

The Futurity, designed as the race to settle the question of two-year-old supremacy, was by this time beginning to shape up as a hollow affair (apart from the money involved) since Alsab was not eligible, nor was the season's other sensational juvenile development, Mrs. Ben F. Whitaker's Requested, winner of the Youthful, Tremont, Great American, East View Stakes, Wakefield, Babylon Handicaps and Cowdin Stakes.

Accordingly, a match between this pair was arranged at Belmont Park early during Futurity week, at the Futurity distance of 6½ furlongs, scale weight of 122 pounds, but over the main course instead of the straightaway Widener Chute. Tracking a blazing pace set by Requested, Alsab drew abreast at the eighth pole to pass the 6 furlongs in 1:09⅘, then drew out to win by three and a half lengths in 1:16, more than a full second faster than the track record, set by a four-year-old under lighter weight, that had been standing twenty-one years.

Four days later, Some Chance, who had been defeated by Alsab during the Keeneland spring meeting, won a hard-fought Futurity from Devil Diver in 1:16⅘, over the straight course.

The Champagne Stakes a week later gave the Futurity colts a chance to tackle the upstarts who had stolen their thunder, but only Amphitheatre—fifth in the big race—availed himself of the opportunity. Alsab won by

Alsab with jockey George Woolf up, owner Albert Sabath and trainer Sarge Swenke (with cigar).

seven lengths from Requested, with Flaught third and Amphitheatre fourth; while not a track record, the winner's time of 1:35⅖ was the fastest mile ever run by a two-year-old anywhere. (Taking no chances for Alsab's three-year-old season, his owner nominated him to the next year's Kentucky Derby on October 14.)

Although Alsab was invited to the Pimlico Special—an unprecedented honor for a two-year-old—his owners decided to keep the colt within his own division. He won the 1¹⁄₁₆-mile Spalding Lowe Jenkins Stakes by four lengths from Colchis, and, after surprising resistance from Bless Me, to whom he was conceding 9 pounds, Alsab closed out his campaign with a win by a neck in the Walden Stakes.

Other headliners of the 1941 season and their principal victories included the two-year-olds Sun Again, who led a three-horse sweep by Calumet Farm in the Arlington Futurity; Devil Diver, winner of three stakes including the Hopeful, and the Pimlico Futurity winner Contradiction. Champion filly was A. G. Vanderbilt's Petrify, winner of the Matron and Arlington Lassie, although she was defeated by Miss Dogwood in a special race at Keeneland. Foxcatcher Farm's Ficklebush won the Selima Stakes, richest race for juvenile fillies.

In any other year it would have been difficult to deny a championship to Louis Tufano's Market Wise, a three-year-old son of Brokers Tip, trained by G. W. Carroll, who started 26 times and won 11, including seven stakes: the Wood Memorial, Rockingham Park, Edgemere (new track record for 1⅛ miles), Gallant Fox, Governor Bowie (new track record for 1⅝ miles) Handicaps, and Pimlico Special—besides his track record thriller over Whirlaway in the 2-mile Gold Cup. The three-year-old fillies established reigns according to territories: W. H. LaBoyteaux's Imperatrice in the East, Joseph E. Widener's Misty Isle in the Midwest, and Louis B. Mayer's Painted Veil in the West; the Coaching Club American Oaks went to Level Best, but it was her only stakes victory that season.

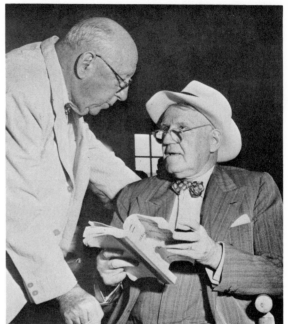

Walter Salmon (left) whose Mereworth Farm topped the breeders' standings eight times confers with Tom Piatt, breeder of Alsab.

Circle M. Ranch's Big Pebble was voted handicap champion in one poll, and C. S. Howard's Mioland in the other. Big Pebble, trained by W. B. Finnegan, ranged from coast to coast, winning the McLennan and Widener Handicaps in Florida, the Hollywood Gold Cup in California and the Washington Park Handicap in Chicago. Mioland also made a trip across country, but his victories all came in his home territory; he won the New Year, San Antonio, San Pasqual, San Juan Capistrano and American Handicaps, and his several placings included a second to Bay View in the Santa Anita Handicap. Fenelon, Pictor, Haltal and Foxbrough also ranked near the top of the handicap division, and the leader among the older fillies was Fairy Chant.

Although he was defeated by Alsab in two of their three encounters, and yet another colt, Shut Out, won more money than either of them during 1942, Whirlaway was once more Horse of the Year. Unlike some previous handicap champions, who put together impressive winning streaks and/or successfully carried crushing loads, the temperamental Calumet colt never won more than twice in succession that year, nor did he triumph under exceptional burdens. He did win five races with 130 pounds up, but he lost four at that same weight, and also lost both races in which he attempted a heavier assignment.

On the other hand, Whirlaway never lost more than two races in succession during 1942, and he was never out of the money, while the same could not be said for Alsab. Moreover, Whirlaway retained that certain aura of untapped resources, which gave the impression he could have won several races that he actually didn't, and, finally, he emerged from his in-and-out exhibition as the world's leading money winner.

With that goal in mind, Whirlaway had been shipped west for the Santa Anita Handicap, but racing in Southern California, which had been postponed, later was cancelled outright, and Santa Anita was turned over to the Army. (The track became the biggest ordnance center in the West during World War II; Hollywood Park, Tanforan and Golden Gate Fields also went into war service.) Thus Whirlaway missed several lucrative opportunities in Florida, and the colt, who according to Ben Jones needed a lot of racing to stay in shape, did not get back in action until April at Keeneland.

Devil Diver, only a three-year-old, beat him a head in the Phoenix Handicap, then Sun Again, also three, beat him half a length in his next start, but both these events were at 6 furlongs, and Whirlaway had not enough time to unravel his patented late run. Mr. Longtail then swept from behind to win both the Clark and Dixie Handicaps; he appeared on his way to an all-conquering parade when Market Wise, in receipt of 5 pounds, defeated him soundly in the Suburban. Carrying 130 pounds in the 7-furlong Carter Handicap, not his best distance, Whirlaway made up six lengths in the stretch, but still was third to Doublrab (120)

and Swing and Sway (113). Taking advantage of the lightest weight he carried all season, 122 pounds, Whirlaway next set a new track record of 1:49⅖ for 1⅛ miles at Aqueduct, following which he won the Brooklyn Handicap under 128 pounds. In the Butler, under 132, he was second to the five-year-old stallion, Tola Rose, at 103.

On July 15, when he carried 130 pounds to victory over the Irish-bred Rounders in the rich Massachusetts Handicap, the $43,850 winner's purse pushed him past Seabiscuit's earnings to a new record total of $454,336. As frosting on the cake, Whirlaway covered the 9 furlongs in new track record time of 1:48⅕. Again he was hailed as a super-horse, and again he was tumbled from his pedestal as the three-year-old Rounders, under 103 pounds, defeated him in the Arlington Handicap, Whirlaway unable to handle his 130-pound assignment on the sloppy track. Two successive wins under 130 pounds, in the Trenton Handicap at the new Garden State Park, and the Narragansett Special, restored his reputation and set the stage for the long awaited race against Alsab. The latter colt originally had been scheduled to compete in the Special, but was scratched, a radical departure from the way he had been handled early in the year.

Despite his rigorous juvenile campaign, Alsab came out on February 7 as a three-year-old, picking up 128 pounds for the Bahamas Handicap and finishing sixth. He then was fourth in an overnight race and third in the Flamingo— beaten eight lengths by Requested and Redthorn—but this poor showing against his contemporaries did not prevent Alsab's owner from taking on an even bigger project: the colt was entered against older horses in the Widener Handicap March 7. The explanation offered for this unusual gambit was that Alsab belonged to the people and they deserved to see him run. Notwithstanding the criticism which greeted his owner's actions, Alsab acquitted himself well enough; he finished fifth, but less than two lengths behind the winner, in the slowest Widener ever run (except one renewal over an off track). The Rhymer, who won by a head from Best Seller, required 2:05⅕ to make the 1¼-mile journey.

Alsab, who began the season looking quite jaded, began to pick up in appearance—he was racing himself into condition—and in his remaining nineteen starts that year he never failed to earn part of the purse, although it was not until his ninth outing that he garnered a winner's share. Colchis beat him both in the Chesapeake Trial and Chesapeake Stakes, following which Alsab was a sluggish third to Valdina Orphan and Sun Again in the Kentucky Derby Trial.

In the Derby itself, after dawdling near the rear for half a mile, Alsab closed well in the final strides to take second from Valdina Orphan, but he still was two and a quarter lengths behind the winner, Shut Out, who covered the distance in a slow 2:04⅖.

The Preakness on May 9 was different. Coming from second to last, and superlatively ridden by Basil James, Alsab drove past the field to win going away by a length, as Requested and Sun Again dead-heated for second, Colchis finished fourth and Shut Out fifth. The time, too, was more impressive: 1:57, ⅖-second off the track record and the fastest up to that time for the race. When he followed up with an easy victory in the Withers, Alsab was considered to have put all his troubles behind him, but in the Belmont Stakes June 6 Shut Out was walking away from him at the end, winning by two lengths in 2:29⅕, time which had been bettered only by War Admiral.

A week later, Alsab was fired for a blind splint, but where an ordinary horse would have been out of action for a longer time after such an operation, he was back in action at Washington Park August 8. A fourth and two wins in lesser events came his way, then he won the rich American Derby by three and a half lengths. In the final start of his Chicago swing, he was second in the Washington Park Handicap to the tough old gelding, Marriage, conceding him three years in age and 7 pounds.

Blenheim II, the imported Epsom Derby winner, sired Whirlaway in his first American crop.

Such are the vagaries of horses, jockeys and tracks that match races often don't pan out as planned, but the $25,000 winner-take-all race between Alsab and Whirlaway at Narragansett Park September 19, 1942, was cut from a perfect pattern. A mile and three-sixteenths, weight for age: Whirlaway, 3-to-10, with 126 pounds including George Woolf; Alsab, 8-to-5, 119 pounds, Carroll Bierman up. Both colts the same size (15-3, about 1,000 pounds) but otherwise as dissimilar as horses can be: Whirlaway, chestnut; Alsab, bay; Whirlaway, sleek and arrogant looking, with a pronounced development of the withers accentuating a well-tapered barrel, the epitome of the classic horse; Alsab, good enough looking, although he wouldn't stand out in a group, shorter coupled, and an obvious hard worker when running, in contrast to Whirlaway's apparently effortless style.

The younger colt took the lead as Woolf contented himself with tracking tactics for a mile, using Alsab as a windshield. In the stretch, Woolf brought Whirlaway to the outside for the grim task of overhauling the leader. Inch by inch the gap was reduced, as the crowd screamed encouragement to the favorite, but Alsab refused to quit. The two horses went under the wire together, Whirlaway with all four feet off the ground, gathering for the next stride, and Alsab with his hind legs just hitting, preparing to thrust forward. An instant either way and the decision could have gone either way—as it was, the official photo showed Alsab the winner by a nose.

The next Saturday, Whirlaway, in his second attempt to carry 132 pounds, was defeated by the five-year-old Bolingbroke (115) in the celebrated renewal of the Manhattan Handicap, in which the son of Equipoise set a new world record of 2:27⅗ for 1½ miles. Two days later, Alsab won the 1⅝-mile Realization easily, for his first victory beyond 1¼ miles.

Sequels to successful projects don't often turn out as well as the originals, but when Whirlaway and Alsab met again in the Jockey Club Gold Cup October 3, same jockeys and weight for age, another unforgettable performance took place. Again Alsab entered the stretch in front, spurting to a one-and-a-half-length lead, and again Whirlaway began to eat into his margin stride by stride; on this occasion his inexorable drive paid off, as he passed his younger rival to win going away by almost a length. Bolingbroke was eight lengths out of it, and The Rhymer another fifteen behind him.

That seemed the answer then—2 miles was too far for Alsab—but another Saturday brought another race, and another result. In the 2¼-mile New York Handicap October 10, Whirlaway had the lead in the stretch, but the Calumet colt, carrying 130 pounds and ridden this time by Jack Westrope, was unable to withstand either Alsab (121), who won by a head, or the longshot Obash (106), who finished second by one and a quarter lengths. On the scale, Alsab had 2 pounds the best of it from Whirlaway.

They went their separate ways thereafter. Whirlaway won the Washington Handicap, walked over for the Pimlico Special, was second to Riverland in the Riggs Handicap, then won the Governor Bowie and Louisiana Handicaps. He started twice without winning the next year and retired with the following record: 60 starts, 32 wins, 15 seconds, nine thirds, earnings of $561,161.

Alsab went for the Gallant Fox Handicap in an attempt to even the score with Shut Out, but Dark Discovery, with a 24-pound concession, beat him by a length, as Shut Out finished fourth and pulled up lame. A third to Riverland and Tola Rose in the Westchester, and a win in the Victory Handicap ended Alsab's campaign. He also came back the next year, and the year after that, but never won another stake. He retired after 51 starts, 25 wins, 11 seconds, 5 thirds and ten unplaced efforts with $350,015.

SHUT OUT, 1939
(Equipoise–Goose Egg, by Chicle)

The wartime curtailment of the rich Southern California meetings notwithstanding, purse distribution reached another new high in 1942, and for the first time in history three horses won more than $200,000 each in the same season. Leader of them all was Shut Out with $238,972 from eight wins and two seconds in twelve starts. In addition to his victories in the Kentucky Derby and Belmont, he won the Blue Grass Stakes, Yankee Handicap, Arlington Classic (richest race of the season, $69,700 to the winner) and Travers Stakes. His Derby time was slow, but Shut Out set a new track record of 1:55⅖ for 1¾₆ miles in the Yankee Handicap, and his winning time of 2:01⅖ in the Classic was just ⅕-second off Discovery's track record; he also chased Valdina Orphan to a new track record in the Dwyer, giving him ten pounds. Although he had somewhat the edge in his encounters with Alsab, the latter was voted best three-year-old because of his performance in all-age competition. (Shut Out beat older horses in overnight racing, but his stakes victories were scored only within his age group.)

The Greentree colt nevertheless led his stable to a championship season, helped trainer John Gaver to the money-winning leadership in his profession, and put Equipoise at the top of the sire list. (There were other beneficiaries, too. Mrs. Whitney, Gaver and Arcaro donated all or part of their shares in the Belmont Stakes purse to a war relief fund.) Other stakes winners in the Greentree racing string were The Rhymer, Corydon, Swing and Sway, Devil Diver and Trade Last.

Equipoise set a new record (posthumously) as his get won $437,141. Besides Shut Out, he was represented by stakes winners Bolingbroke, Attention, Swing and Sway, Equifox, Level Best, Lotopoise and Equipet.

Like everyone else connected with Greentree Stable, jockey Eddie Arcaro topped the financial

Shut out (Eddie Arcaro up) being led in by trainer John Gaver after winning the 1942 Belmont Stakes.

rankings of his category in 1942, but other than that it scarcely could have been termed a good year for America's ace jockey.

Arcaro had an excellent chance to tie Isaac Murphy's long-standing record by winning his third Kentucky Derby, but, given his choice of mounts between Shut Out and Devil Diver,

348

he chose the latter and finished sixth. Later that year his license was revoked.

Born in Newport, Kentucky, not far from Latonia Race Course, of Italian ancestry, Arcaro had come a long way since he broke in during the Depression. There was an interval of eight months between the time he accepted his first mount at Bainbridge Park in Cleveland on May 18, 1931, and the time he rode his first winner, Eagle Bird, at Caliente on January 14, 1932.

When Arcaro did reach the top of his profession, he was in personality not unlike Whirlaway, the colt he rode with such success: brilliant, but temperamental—headstrong and unpredictable.

His Latin fire flared up in the Cowdin (formerly Junior Champion) Stakes on September 19, 1942. Arcaro, riding the favored Occupation, was bumped by Venancio Nordase on Breezing Home after the break, and he set out to get revenge. As soon as he could draw abreast of Breezing Home, Arcaro smashed Occupation into him; Slide Rule avoided the pile-up to win, and Occupation finished second but was disqualified (his only time out of the money that year).

Of rough riding he was guilty, but none could accuse Arcaro of evasive testimony. When questioned concerning his actions, he was quoted as having stated forthrightly that he was trying to kill him. His license was thereupon revoked, and the star jockey, making $1,000 a week, became an exercise boy at a reported salary—tops for that profession—of $165 a month.

Arcaro accepted his comedown in the world. He stayed on the ground exactly a year—with no assurance that he ever would regain his license—and when he did return to the saddle it was as a chastened soul. "Banana Nose" gave way to such nicknames as "Heady Eddie" and "The Master"—and, as shall be seen, Murphy's record for riding Kentucky Derby winners, as well as numerous other records, eventually fell to the new Eddie Arcaro. At the time he re-

tired—of his own volition—after a thirty-one-year career, Arcaro had won more money than any jockey in world history; unlike some earlier riders, who had squandered their fees as fast as they came in, George Edward Arcaro retired as a highly respected dean of his profession, and a millionaire in his own right.

Belair Stud's Vagrancy, winner of eleven races, was such a standout among the fillies of 1942 that she not only was elected champion three-year-old of her sex, but was awarded the handicap title as well. Her victories included the Pimlico, C. C. A. and Delaware Oaks, Gazelle, Test and Alabama Stakes (by disqualification of Bonnet Ann), Beldame (dead heat with Barrancosa), Ladies and Queen Isabella Handicaps. The three-year-old colts, besides those already mentioned, included Apache, Thumbs Up and With Regards.

Another of the season's interesting developments was T. H. Heard, Jr.'s six-year-old gelding, Boysy, who discovered New Jersey, and won three stakes at the newly opened Garden State Park, plus a couple of others elsewhere.

Among the two-year-olds, John Marsch's Occupation barely missed joining the $200,000 club, as he earned $192,355, with nine victories and three seconds in thirteen starts. A specialist at the rich ones, he won the Arlington, Washington Park, Belmont and Breeders' Futurities, plus the Washington Park Juvenile Stakes; his seconds were in the Pimlico Futurity, Joliet and Primer Stakes. However, Occupation did not win at the ballot box, for Mrs. John D. Hertz's Count Fleet ended the season on a high note that could not be denied. Never out of the money in fifteen starts, he won the Wakefield Stakes in July, then was second in Occupation's Washington Park Futurity and third in the New York race. A week later he startled the world by winning the Champagne Stakes in 1:34⅘, a new track record for Belmont Park and a new world record for a two-year-old. Subsequently, he won the Pimlico Futurity by five lengths from Occupation, equaling the track record of 1:43⅗ for 1¹⁄₁₆ miles, and the Count put a finishing flourish to his juvenile season by winning the Walden Stakes by thirty lengths.

Hal Price Headley's Askmenow won the two-year-old filly championship, with a victory in the Selima and several placings in stakes, including a second place, between Occupation and Count Fleet, in the Futurity. Other good youngsters included the colts Devil's Thumb (bargain of the year, a $3,000 yearling who won $62,875 at two) and Blue Swords, and the fillies Fad, Good Morning and Our Page.

Thoroughbred racing went all out in the war effort. The Turf Committee of America, formed in the spring of 1942 with Herbert Bayard Swope as chairman, announced a goal of $2,000,000 as the sport's contribution to war relief; by the end of the year this goal had been easily surpassed, and within the next three seasons more than $16½-million had been collected through special days of racing, setting aside of certain percentages of regular purses and race-track profits, and outright donations.

A war baby which became a permanent part of the racing structure was the Thoroughbred Racing Associations, Inc., an organization of tracks originally designed primarily to foster co-operation in the war effort. The TRA continued after the war as a trade association to promote harmony and enforce ethics in all phases of race track operations. On the recommendation of J. Edgar Hoover, one of his former associates in the Federal Bureau of Investigation, Spencer J. Drayton, was hired after the war to organize the Thoroughbred Racing Protective Bureau, which performs a service to racing analogous to that performed for the federal government by the FBI.

Through its elaborate horse-identification system, the TRPB virtually eliminated ringers in American racing; and its fingerprint system prevents undesirables from breaking into the sport under false names.

Another important racing organization that developed during this period was the Horsemen's Benevolent and Protective Association. Actually founded before the war, in the summer of 1940, it was known originally as the Horsemen's Retirement Fund, and its chief activity consisted of buying up old horses considered no longer fit for racing.

This proved to be impractical, and the organization was revised so as to include other functions. As the new name suggests, it provides disaster relief funds to horsemen, and performs other similar services. It also acts as a trade union, conducting negotiations with tracks for purse distribution formulae, and on occasion has called strikes. Representatives of the HBPA also present their viewpoints at various conferences pertaining to proposed changes in the rules of racing, and so forth.

It was apparent in 1943 that World War II would be longer than its predecessor, and the United States adapted itself to wartime conditions. Racing at Tropical Park was called off in mid-meeting, and the Hialeah session cancelled entirely when the Air Force took over the track. The inactivity in Florida caused an overflow of horses at the Fair Grounds in New Orleans, the only major winter racing center left in operation, although it, too, was utilized by the armed services during the off-season. Among other tracks shut down was Delaware Park.

Rubber and gas were the big items that year. Racing dates were granted contingent upon parking lots being kept closed, and horse-drawn vehicles were put back in commission at some tracks. A general shifting about of race meetings took place to accommodate transportation requirements. The Arlington Park meeting was transferred to Washington Park; the Maryland associations conducted a combined meeting at Pimlico; Keeneland held its meeting in another city, Louisville; Saratoga moved to Belmont Park, and Empire City—in what was to become a semi-permanent arrangement—shifted to Jamaica. The infields of some idle tracks were converted into victory gardens; other track properties became defense plants.

350

War bond sales and relief days continued to be commonplace features at American tracks, and racing's special war fund passed $8½-million.

Because of the difficulty in transporting horses, the Fasig-Tipton Company held its annual yearling sales in Kentucky, with results so successful that it led to formation of the Breeders' Sales Company, which continued to hold auctions in Lexington after the war.

Restrictions on movement could not stem the tide of racing's popularity, however, as a new afternoon leisure class—the swing shift workers—kept pouring into the tracks that were open. Although the number of horses in action during 1943 was the smallest in seven years, they competed for another record high purse distribution.

With one notable exception, there was a division of opinion as to championships in every category in which there was duplicate voting in 1943.

The Triangle Publications poll awarded the title of best two-year-old colt to George D. Widener's Platter, a lightly campaigned son of Pilate, who won just two races in seven starts, but whose victories came in the Pimlico Futurity and Walden Stakes, both at 1 1/16 miles. *Turf and Sport Digest* elected John Marsch's Occupy, a full brother to the previous season's Occupation, who completed a unique succession of successes by siblings when he duplicated his brother's victories in the Washington Park and Belmont Futurities. The son of Bull Dog also was runner-up in the Arlington (to his stablemate, Jezrahel) and Breeders' Futurities, Primer and Prairie State Stakes, to lead the division comfortably in earnings with $112,949.

Brownell Combs's Durazna was voted champion juvenile filly in one poll, Calumet Farm's Twilight Tear in the other. The tomboy Durazna, also by Bull Dog, and out of the famed sprinter Myrtlewood, won all three of her stakes events from male competition— the Prairie State, Hawthorne Juvenile and Breeders' Futurity—beating Occupy in two of them. Twilight Tear won only one stake, the Lassie, but in it she beat a good field, including her stablemate, Miss Keeneland, subsequent winner of the Selima Stakes, in which Twilight Tear was second while carrying eight pounds more weight.

Clustered right with the above trio was Beatrice Maguire's Bee Mac, a daughter of War Admiral, who topped all juvenile fillies in earnings with $44,900; she won the Spinaway from her own sex and the Hopeful from colts. Longchamps Farm's Mrs. Ames, A. B. Hancock's Whirlabout, Lazy F. Ranch's Cocopet and C. V. Whitney's Boojiana rounded out a tight group in which honors were spread around rather evenly.

It was take your pick in the handicap class also, as Market Wise and Devil Diver shared the palm. Whirlaway's old nemesis, Market Wise, "the magnificent cripple" who had been trampled on in a paddock as a foal and never could be relied upon to be sound from one day to the next, won the Massachusetts Handicap and Narragansett Special, besides placing in other stakes. Devil Diver won the Toboggan, Metropolitan, Carter and Brooklyn Handicaps.

Neither of the top pair earned as much as Marriage, Coward and Dupuy's hard-working gelding, who took home $86,875, winning the New Orleans, American, Des Plaines and Arlington Handicaps. Louisiana Farm's Riverland, another active gelding who won the Dixie Handicap in record time among other races, would have been a factor, too, had not his career been cut short in mid-season, when he broke a bone and had to be destroyed. Apache, Don Bingo, Rounders, Thumbs Up, Bolingbroke, Shut Out and several others completed a well-diversified battery of handicap runners.

Distaff honors went to Calumet's Mar-Kell, winner of the Washington's Birthday, Top Flight, Cinderella and Beldame Handicaps.

George Widener's Stefanita, by Questionnaire, was elected champion three-year-old filly, by virtue of an impressive string of victories in the Test, Alabama Stakes, New England Oaks, Ladies, Lady Baltimore and Bryan and O'Hara Memorial Handicaps. Hal Price Headley's Askmenow also boasted quite a record, winning the Pimlico Oaks, Arlington Matron, Beverly Handicaps, and the American Derby. She led the fillies in earnings with $98,625.

The three-year-old colts presented the only clear-cut picture. There were several worthy ones, but none of them approached the unanimous choice as 1943 Horse of the Year, Count Fleet.

COUNT FLEET, 1940

(Reigh Count–Quickly, by Haste)

At the end of the 1942 racing season, John B. Campbell in his weights for the Experimental Free Handicap assigned Count Fleet 132 pounds—more than any horse before or since. He was right, to the ounce, or, if anything, a little light.

Contrary to a popular notion, handicap weights are not absolute quantities designed to position a horse in some sort of cosmic hierarchy; rather, they are relative in nature, and express an evaluation of the individual animal in his specific circumstances. In other words, the 132 pounds assigned to Count Fleet was in no way an intended comparison between his ability and that of, say, Bimelech, who was assigned 130 pounds a few years earlier, or of Native Dancer, who was to be assigned 130 pounds some years later. The weight represented an expression of Count Fleet's presumed ability measured against his own prospective

opposition—in this case, the 1940 crop of foals.

Count Fleet murdered his opposition. As a three-year-old, nothing came within three lengths of him, and those which got that close did so purely on sufferance. As testimony to his brilliance, his unanimous selection as Horse of the Year was based on less than two months' activity.

He made his debut in an allowance race on April 13, winning easily by three and a half lengths. He won the Wood Memorial by the same margin in the same manner; the Kentucky Derby handily by three; the Preakness easily by eight; the Withers easily by five, in 1:36 for the mile on a muddy track; and the Belmont Stakes on June 5, completing the Triple Crown, by twenty-five lengths. He was 1-to-20, the legal minimum odds, in both his last starts, and caused a minus pool of $15,-912.02 in the Belmont.

The distinguishing feature of pari-mutuel wagering is that under ordinary circumstances the patrons bet against one another, not against the track. All money is lumped into a pool— from which the state government and track deduct a percentage as their take—and what is left is divided among the holders of winning tickets. In the usual case the track is not in any way concerned with the outcome of a race, since the losers are the patrons who have made unsuccessful wagers—it is their money that is paid out to the winners.

However, state laws require a guaranteed minimum profit on every successful wager—in the case of Count Fleet, it was 5 percent. Under natural conditions he would have been held at

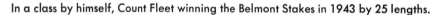

In a class by himself, Count Fleet winning the Belmont Stakes in 1943 by 25 lengths.   Sirico

much shorter odds; as it was, he was such a heavy favorite that not enough money was bet on his rivals to provide the guaranteed profit, and the track was required to make up the difference.

Only two rivals had dared to face Count Fleet in the Withers and Belmont; the latter race was so obviously at his mercy that rider Johnny Longden gave it some element of competition by letting Count Fleet run at the track record. The colt began to shorten stride near the end, and was allowed to finish on his own steam—in 2:28⅕, not as fast as the track record (2:27⅗, set by Bolingbroke as a five-year-old, while carrying 11 pounds less weight), but ⅖-second faster than the previous record for that particular race. It subsequently was learned that Count Fleet had struck himself during the running, and the resulting injury ultimately led to his retirement.

How good Count Fleet was never will be known for certain. Longden, who went on to become the rider of more winners than any jockey in world history—and rider in the most races—rated Count Fleet the best horse he had ever seen. The only jockey to ride the Hertz colt in a race, Longden also exercised him at times, and he later stated that once, just once, he turned the brown flash loose for an instant, to satisfy his curiosity concerning how fast Count Fleet really was—but felt such a surge of power that he took him in hand again almost immediately, fearful of the consequences.

Count Fleet was no beauty (for one thing, his pasterns were too long for most tastes) but in action he was superb. Fast enough to cover 6 furlongs in 1:08⅕ (an unofficial record) in a workout on the Belmont Park straightaway at two, he could run far enough to win by twenty-five lengths at 1½ miles. Because of his premature retirement, he never carried handicap weights, and as to the horses he beat, the same could be said of him as was said of Man o' War—everything that crossed his path.

His most persistent pursuer was Allen T. Simmons's Blue Swords, winner of the Eastern Shore, Remsen and Ardsley Handicaps at two, and runner-up to the Count in the Champagne,

John D. Hertz and Count Fleet.

Wood, Kentucky Derby and Preakness at two and at three, but Blue Swords' career also came to an untimely end because of injury. The other horses Count Fleet left in his wake as a three-year-old included W. E. Boeing's Slide Rule, winner that year of the Swift Stakes, Arlington Classic, Experimental, Peter Pan, Jerome, Interborough and Westchester Handicaps; W. L. Brann's Dwyer winner, Vincentive; Foxcatcher Farm's Realization winner, Fairy Manhurst; Dixiana's Amber Light, winner of the Louisiana Derby and Test Stakes; and Havahome Stable's Eurasian, winner of the Travers Stakes, Jersey and Gallant Fox Handicaps. That season's other good three-year-old—Boone Hall Stable's ex-claimer Princequillo (Saratoga Cup, Saratoga Handicap, Jockey Club Gold Cup)— never faced Count Fleet, and had not won a stake race at the time the son of Reigh Count retired.

The career of Count Fleet was a quick flash of intense brilliance; the career of his jockey was a steady glow sustained over an amazingly long period. John Eric Longden was born in Wakefield, England, on St. Valentine's Day, 1910 (or thereabouts), but moved to northwestern Canada while still quite young. His early schooling involved equines—as a boy Longden was a "grease pig" who led the donkeys which hauled coal out of a mine. While labor in a coal mine is not generally considered a healthy environment for children, in Longden's case it developed a powerful pair of shoulders and arms that were to be well-utilized in later life.

In his teens he left the coal mines and took to "Roman riding"—guiding two horses from a standing position, with one foot on each—at one point winning fifteen such races in a row. The next step was thoroughbred racing, but it was a hard one to negotiate. Hopping a southbound freight in company with R. H. McDaniel, later to become the country's leading trainer, Longden got off at Salt Lake City in 1927, and his first victory was scored at that track on October 4 aboard a $300 claimer named Hugo K. Asher. It was the nine-year-old gelding's only win in thirty-three starts that year, and Longden's visits to the winner's circle were not much more frequent in those early days. In 1928, his first full season, his winning average was a meager 7 percent. Not until 1932 did his first real break come: a victory in the Agua Caliente Derby with Bahamas. (At that same meeting, incidentally, Longden finished fourth in the race won by Eagle Bird, which introduced young Eddie Arcaro to the winner's column; he also got a good southern exposure of Phar Lap, for he and Bahamas finished next to last in that great gelding's celebrated Caliente Handicap.)

The world's winningest jockey credited Percy Pike, George Schilling, Al Tarn (later to become Longden's father-in-law), Charley Leavitt and E. A. "Sleepy" Armstrong for giving him encouragement during those hard years when others recommended that he try some other profession. By 1936 Longden was up to more than 200 winners, and he played a prominent role in one of the season's most publicized episodes: riding Rushaway, owned and trained by Tarn, Longden won the Illinois Derby at Aurora Downs May 22, and the very next day, several hundred miles away, the same combination won the Latonia Derby in northern Kentucky.

In 1938 Longden won his first of several national championships with 236 winners, and in 1943—assisted materially by Count Fleet's haul of $174,055, largest of the year—he set a new record of $573,276 in earnings by his mounts, breaking Sande's mark that had been established twenty years earlier. (Longden credits John D. Hertz with much of his later success, and in at least one season the taxi tycoon's contribution was monumental; he had the jockey under contract at $1,000 per month but had occasion to assign him only two mounts during the year—which figured out at $6,000 per ride.)

The hard-working little man, who believed it was just as important to become acquainted

354

with his mounts in morning workout periods as it was to ride them in races, was thirty-three years old in Count Fleet's big year. There was talk then of his retirement, but Longden, despite an adequate share of spills and injuries, stayed in the saddle. His career wasn't even halfway complete. Following his great season with Count Fleet, Longden became a U. S. citizen.

He kept going until he was a grandfather—in fact, he won numerous races after receiving "instructions" in the paddock from his own son, Vance, who became a successful trainer. What Johnny Longden had to offer—brains—didn't wear out with the years. Not much of a stylist esthetically, he was a great one tactically. On the logical assumption that the shortest way around is the quickest, he grabbed the rail when he could, and ran in front, thus avoiding possible pockets or interference; it required a special sense of timing, but "The Pumper" was noted for the built-in clock in his head. On the other hand, on a mount which did not have the speed to set the pace, Longden could come from behind to win, and a good deal of his continued popularity with trainers lay in his ability to size up a horse's capabilities for them.

An athlete's legs determine the length of his career; Dempsey, Ruth, Budge—they all had to retire when their legs began to give out. However, as Longden explained, he always got four new ones every time he went to the post.

CHAPTER FIFTY-FIVE

THE WARTIME CONDITIONS under which racing had been conducted continued in 1944; the effect, if anything was more pronounced. Race meetings were subject to approval by local War Manpower Commissions, which established ceilings on the number of personnel that could be employed, and investigated to insure that none of them were vital to the war effort in other jobs. Gasoline and tires still were rationed, and race meetings continued to be adjusted in locale so as to accommodate the transportation problem.

Nevertheless, a number of tracks reopened in 1944. Hialeah and Tropical Park resumed their meetings, much to the delight of Eddie Arcaro, who swept the board in rich Florida stakes, winning the Flamingo with Greentree Stable's Stir Up, and the Widener and Tropical Park Handicap with the same stable's Four Freedoms. However, Arcaro scarcely could have been more pleased than young Bobby Permane, who on each of three successive days rode five winners at Tropical. Hialeah registered the first million-dollar daily mutuel handle in Florida history, then surpassed it; before the season ended, the record was $1,038,361.

Gulfstream Park, purchased in bankruptcy for $100,000 by James Donn, who also agreed to assume the track's outstanding liabilities, held a meeting later in the year.

Racing was resumed in Delaware and Southern California, after some difficulties on the West Coast. Dates were granted to both Del Mar and Hollywood Park, but rescinded by the manpower commission, which later reconsidered and permitted a meeting at Hollywood beginning in November. More than 40,000 sport-starved patrons jammed the premises opening day, and new daily wagering records were set with headlong frequency. After a Western record of $1,813,272 was established, it was broken several times, passing $2-million and $2½-million until finally, on closing day, yet another plateau was passed as the handle hit $3,290,356. The feature that happy day was the Hollywood Gold Cup, won by Happy Stable's Happy Issue, the first filly to triumph in this race, who broke Challedon's track record by covering the 10 furlongs in 2:01⅗.

The experience of Hollywood Park was an example of what was going on all over the country. Every national record toppled as attendance reached almost 18-million and total mutuel handle exceeded $1-billion. Why such surges should occur at a time when transportation facilities were at their lowest ebb was not fully understood—beyond the obvious circumstances that more people had more spending money than ever before, and a mood of frantic gaiety pervaded the country—but it led Matt Winn to observe that customers couldn't have been kept away with baseball bats.

Purse distribution made a fantastic leap from $18½-million to $29-million, the largest increase in history. Because of several tracks coming back into action, there was some increase in the number of races, but not nearly enough to account for the huge rise in gross vital statistics. Average purse distribution reached a new high value of $1,516.49.

Individual monetary records also tumbled.

The $601,660 won by Calumet Farm was a new record; Ben Jones headed the money-winning trainers with an identical total, also a record; Warren Wright (Calumet's owner) bred the winners of a record $990,612; and jockey Ted Atkinson, leader in both numerical (287) and financial standings, set a new record of $899,101 in the latter category. (He accepted 1,539 mounts, a record for a leading jockey.)

As a corollary to the rich purses, there was a drastic increase—and obviously an unanticipated one, since owners and trainers complained bitterly—in the number of horses claimed. From 2,293 the year before, in 1944 the claiming halter was slipped onto 4,010 horses, a jump of 75 percent.

The war was evident in other ways. Racing added another $8-million to its special relief fund. In addition to such outright gifts, war bond sales again were part of the racing scene; at a number of tracks, including all those in New York and also Hollywood Park, purchase of a war bond was good for free admission.

The term, "ranks of owners," had assumed a literal connotation, as various winners during the year were identified as belonging to Ensign Townsend B. Martin; Lieutenants Ogden Phipps, Edward Lasker, G. H. Bostwick and J. M. Roebling; Lt.-Commander Theodore D. Buhl; Colonel C. V. Whitney and Captain Harry F. Guggenheim.

It is traditional when men go off to war for women to take over on the home front. Female cab drivers and streetcar conductors no longer were considered unusual in 1944, and Rosie the Riveter had inspired a song. Detroit used women as mutuel clerks, and Hollywood Park, in keeping with its policy of hiring recently discharged veterans as much as practicable, announced proudly that it was the first track with a WAC on the payroll.

So it was with horses. In each of the last two years of the war, a filly was elected Horse of the year.

TWILIGHT TEAR, 1941

(Bull Lea–Lady Lark, by Blue Larkspur)

The first of numerous champions to be sired by Bull Lea, Twilight Tear never had been out of the money in six starts at two, winning four, including the Lassie. She shared honors with Durazna in the voting for champion two-year-old filly, but on his Experimental Free Handicap, John B. Campbell ranked her below her own stablemate, Miss Keeneland, as well as Durazna. At three, however, Twilight Tear's eminence was unchallenged by any rival of any age or either sex.

Three-year-olds ordinarily are not sent against their elders early in the season, nor are fillies often sent against colts, but in 1944 trainers were taking their racing where they found it, and Ben Jones never was one to be a slave to dogma under any circumstances.

J. C. Meadors

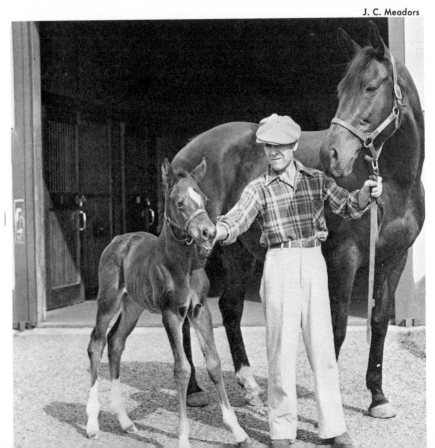

Twilight Tear, first filly to be elected Horse of the Year with her foal, who later gained fame as the stakes winner A Gleam, dam herself of A Glitter.

The Leap Year Handicap at Hialeah on February 29 was Twilight Tear's first start of the season—against older males. She finished third to the six-year-old gelding, Mettlesome, and four-year-old colt, Adulator, beaten two lengths. Thereafter, "Suzie," as she was known to her stable hands, embarked upon an amazing winning streak. For eleven straight races no rival —male or female—finished within a length of her.

After three victories in overnight races in Florida and Maryland, she won the Rennert Handicap and Pimlico Oaks in Baltimore, the Acorn Stakes and Coaching Club American Oaks at Belmont Park, and the Princess Doreen Stakes at Washington Park, in the latter race dropping down successfully to 6 furlongs from 1⅜ miles in her previous start.

The Skokie Handicap July 7 was her first outing against colts since her seasonal debut; ridden by Lee Haas, who had replaced Conn McCreary as her jockey, Twilight Tear thumbed her nose at the boys to win by one and a half lengths from Sirde, while conceding him seven pounds actual weight, with Challenge Me, in receipt of 15 pounds, third. The time of 1:22⅗ was ⅗-second faster than the previous track record, and among the also-rans were Occupy and the winner's stablemate, Pensive. In an overnight race at 1 mile, as a prep for the Arlington Classic, the flying bay filly had no trouble winning from Pensive, Appleknocker and Challenge Me.

The Classic that year had attracted 144 nominees, more than the Kentucky Derby, and the Chicago race also might have boasted a larger winner's purse had the field been of reasonable size. However, there was no stampede among owners to contribute starting fees to the already swollen coffers of Calumet Farm, which was represented by the formidable entry of Twilight Tear and Pensive, so only three other contestants went to the post. Carrying 114 pounds—even on the scale with the rest of her rivals, but getting a 7-pound concession from Pensive—the filly led all the way to win

handily by two lengths for a net purse of $62,050. Walmac Farm's Old Kentuck was second, Pensive third, Challenge Me fourth and American Eagle last. (Among those who participated in the winner's circle ceremony after the Classic was the Mayor of Parnell, Missouri, Lieutenant Horace Allyn Jones, on leave from duty in the Coast Guard for the occasion; in peacetime, he was better known as Jimmy Jones, assistant to his father as Calumet Farm trainer.)

By her rich Classic victory Twilight Tear earned the maximum penalty, 6 pounds, for her next start, the Alabama Stakes on August 8, and it cost her dearly, as her winning streak was snapped. Belair Stud's Vienna, whose previous performance entitled her to the maximum allowance, got in at 114 pounds against 126 on the champion. Ridden by Jimmy Stout, the daughter of Menow uncorked a relentless stretch drive, coming from last place and making up eleven lengths in the final half-mile, to win by almost a length. Twilight Tear, who had set the pace throughout most of the 1¼ miles, had no difficulty saving second.

Having started at least once, and frequently more often, during every calendar month since February, "Suzie" was given a rest. She came out again October 2 and won a 5½-furlong handicap down the Widener Chute under top weight of 126 pounds in 1:03⅖, ⅗-second off the track record but the best time recorded that season. Ten days later, again carrying 126 pounds, with Doug Dodson as jockey, she won the Queen Isabella Handicap at Laurel by five lengths, conceding 8 pounds actual weight to the runner-up, the four-year-old filly, Good Morning.

For the Maryland Handicap against three-year-olds on October 21, Twilight Tear was assigned 130 pounds; when it came up mud it was generally expected that she would be withdrawn, but start she did, and for the first time in her life ran out of the money. The winner, under 109 pounds, was Brookmeade's filly, Dare Me; Miss Keeneland, 110, was second;

and William Helis's colt, Aera, finished third under 106 pounds. Twilight Tear did get part of the purse by finishing fourth. (In May she had defeated Dare Me by four lengths in the CCA Oaks at level weights.)

The final start of Twilight Tear's campaign was the Pimlico Special at weight for age, which she won easily by six lengths from the season's handicap champion, Devil Diver, as the only other starter, Megogo, finished another ten lengths away.

The next year it was intended to send Twilight Tear after Top Flight's distaff earnings record, but she bled in her first start and was retired with 18 wins, two seconds, two thirds and $202,165 from 24 starts.

A big, but not masculine-looking filly, Twilight Tear stood 16 hands, about an inch taller than her stablemate, Pensive. She was correspondingly bigger than the colt in other dimensions, longer bodied, larger in girth, and she outweighed him. She also outran him.

PENSIVE, 1941

(Hyperion–Penicuik II, by Buchan)

Pensive is remembered as the colt who came closer to the Triple Crown, without winning it, than any other horse in history. Other horses have won two of the three classics that comprise the series—but they either were eliminated as Triple Crown possibilities earlier in the game through a loss in the Derby or Preakness (e.g. Shut Out, Bimelech, Johnstown, Twenty Grand) or did not make it to the post for the Belmont (Bold Venture) or were defeated more emphatically. Pensive still was in the running until the last quarter-mile of the Belmont Stakes—in fact, he was in the lead—and he missed the Triple Crown by only half a length.

A chestnut son of England's "mighty atom," Hyperion (who had won two-thirds of that country's Triple Crown in his own racing days) Pensive was imported *in utero* by A. B. Han-

cock, who sold his dam to Wright before the colt was foaled.

At two, Pensive raced only five times, winning two overnight races, finishing third in the Champagne and Oden Bowie Stakes and fourth in the Futurity.

He came out on March 1 at three. After a third, then a second, then a first in overnight competition, the Calumet colt took on older horses in the Rowe Memorial Handicap at Pimlico April 12; he won by a head from six-year-old Porter's Cap, as Calumet also took third with Sun Again. In the Bowie Handicap three days later, however, Pensive encountered old Tola Rose, who once had defeated Whirlaway, and the seven-year-old stallion gave Pensive the same treatment, defeating him by three lengths.

Pensive thereupon returned to competition within his own age division. After winning an allowance race, he ran second by a nose to Mrs. A. J. Abel's Gramps Image in the Chesapeake Stakes. Pensive was ridden by Conn McCreary, a jockey noted for his come-from-behind style, but tactics did not account for this loss; the Calumet colt had reached the leader in the stretch, and simply was not able to get past.

It was a different story in the Kentucky Derby, however, as McCreary brought Pensive from fifth place at the quarter pole to win going away by four and a half lengths; Broadcloth was second; the heavy favorite, Stir Up, was third, and Gramps Image unplaced. A week later, on May 13, Pensive won the Preakness by three-fourths of a length from Platter, Stir Up again third. That was the last victory of Pensive's career.

For some years the Belmont Stakes had been lagging behind its companion classics in value. Although the net to the winner was not that much lower—because of the stakes fees and method of dividing the purse—the added value had been half that of the Preakness and one-third that of the Derby. For the 1944 renewal Belmont Park threw in some more negotiable cash to go along with the prestige that accrued to the winner of the "Test of Champions." The added money of the Belmont Stakes (and several other races) was raised to $50,000 for the first time. The lion's share appeared to be Pensive's for the taking, and he went off at 1-to-2.

Everything proceeded according to script for 1¼ miles, by which point Pensive had taken the lead and was heading for the coronation ceremony. However, William Ziegler, Jr.'s Bounding Home, ridden by G. L. Smith, rolled up on the outside to win by half a length.

Pensive started eight more times that year without winning, and was retired to stud. If his change in form seems abrupt, it might be noted that Bounding Home started ten times in 1944 after the Belmont Stakes without winning, came back the next season and failed to win in twelve starts, and did not win another race until June 8, 1946—twenty-eight starts and more than two years later. The Belmont remained the only stakes victory he scored in his life. Perhaps *c'était la guerre.*

Pensive was nosed out in earnings (and defeated more decisively than that in the voting for best three-year-old colt) by Alfred Parker's By Jimminy, a son of Pharamond II, trained by J. W. Smith. The first colt since Stagehand to be acknowledged best of his group without a victory in at least one of the Triple Crown races—nor could he match Stagehand's distinction of having defeated older horses—By Jimminy nevertheless was the most consistent performer of his lot, winner of seven races in eleven starts to earn $162,635. He won the Shevlin (beating Who Goes There and Stir Up), Dwyer (beating Stir Up, Lucky Draw and Bounding Home), Travers (beating Bounding Home), American Derby (beating Pensive) and Lawrence Realization (beating Bounding Home). On the other hand, Who Goes There beat him in the Withers and Stir Up beat him in the Empire City Stakes—at level weights, whereas By Jimminy had been receiving weight in his victories over them—

so there was no clearly defined order of precedence.

Stir Up, besides the Flamingo and Empire City Stakes (in which he set a new track record of 1:56⅕ for 1³⁄₁₆ miles) won a division of the Experimental Free Handicap and a division of the Wood Memorial Stakes. George D. Widener's Lucky Draw won the other division of the Wood, as well as the Peter Pan and Jersey Handicaps.

Other three-year-old colts who rose to the top at one time or another during the season were Christiana Stable's Megogo (who set a new American record of 4:20⅕ for the seldom-contested distance of 2½ miles), Abe Hirschberg's Black Badge (who acted as though he owned Detroit and had a good share in Miami), Mrs. J. B. Burnstein's Okana (best in the West) and Occupy, not as impressive as he had been at two, but good enough to win the Jerome and Autumn Handicaps.

What honors Twilight Tear left among the three-year-old fillies were taken by Louis B. Mayer's Whirlabout, winner of the Gazelle and Test Stakes, Yankee, Diana, Mary Dyer and Correction Handicaps, and New England Oaks. Others in this division included the two who beat Twilight Tear, Dare Me and Vienna, plus Longchamps Farm's pair of Donitas First (Beldame and Ladies Handicaps) and Mrs. Ames.

Getting better as he got older, five-year-old Devil Diver was voted champion handicap horse of the season, this time in both polls, after seven wins in twelve starts and $64,265—all of it earned in stakes competition. The son of St. Germans successfully covered a wide range of distances under hefty burdens, winning the Paumonok with 130 pounds, the Toboggan with 134, both at 6 furlongs; the Metropolitan Mile with 134, the American Legion Handicap with 136, the Whitney and Wilson Stakes, on up to the 1½-mile Manhattan Handicap.

Leading money winner among horses older than three was Mrs. Edward Mulrenan's First Fiddle, winner of exactly half his sixteen starts, for earnings of $124,105. His weight ceiling was 126 pounds, but he set a new track record of 1:49⅗ for 1⅛ miles in the Grey Lag Handicap under 119, won the Queens County Handicap under 126, the Massachusetts under 124 and the Butler under 126.

Four Freedoms, a stablemate of Devil Diver, was hard to handle in the winter, winning the Palm Beach Handicap besides the Widener and Tropical Park Handicaps; later in the year he took the Brooklyn to give Greentree excellent coverage in the all-age races. Actually, Four Freedoms was bred by John Hay Whitney's Mare's Nest Stud; when Colonel Whitney entered the service, he had turned over his racing string to his mother's Greentree Stable.

Old Bolingbroke, seven, ended his career with victories in the 1¾-mile Saratoga Cup (his second) and 2-mile Jockey Club Gold Cup. He never set any records for weight lifting, but over a distance of ground at weight for age he had been awesome.

W-L Ranch's Paperboy, C. C. Turner's Bon Jour, Brown Hotel Stable's Seven Hearts, A. S. Hewitt's Some Chance, Marriage, Allen Drumheller's Georgie Drum, Sun Again, Howard Wells Equifox and Denton and Burt's Gay Dalton (winner of five stakes in Mexico City) also were prominent, but the race of the year was provided by three good sprinters, who ran a triple dead heat for first place in the Carter Handicap, June 10.

After running with the pack for three quarters, Joe W. Brown's five-year-old Brownie, ridden by Eric Guerin (115) took a slight lead in the last furlong; Belair Stud's four-year-old Bossuet (Stout, 127) sliced between horses and Ziegler's five-year-old Wait A Bit (G. L. Smith, 118) came storming up the outside. The placing judges called for a photo, looked at it for a long time, then called for the stewards. These supreme officials verified that the three horses indeed had crossed the finish at the same instant; an announcement was made to that effect and the next problem was posting the winning prices on the mutuel board. This was solved by a hastily painted hand sign. The winners' time was 1:23⅖ for 7 furlongs over a sloppy track.

It was the first such dead heat recorded in American stakes racing, and, considering the spread of weights, a remarkable feat of handicapping. Actually, a wager on any one of four horses would have been successful, since Bossuet was coupled in the betting with his stablemate, Apache, top weighted at 132.

Besides his part-interest in the Carter, Bossuet that year won the Fleetwing and Valley Forge Handicaps, while Brownie won the Princeton and Bay Shore Handicaps. All three

Triple dead heat finish of the 1944 Carter Handicap, won by Bossuet (top), Brownie (center) and Wait A Bit (nearest camera).

Carter winners had been or were to be prominent in stakes racing for several seasons.

In addition to championship of her own age, Twilight Tear was voted best handicap filly of 1944. The senior members of this division included the four-year-old Hollywood Gold Cup heroine, Happy Issue, also winner of the Hawthorne and Vanity Handicaps, and Mrs. M. E. Miller's hard-working six-year-old Traffic Court, winner of eight races in twenty-five outings, including the Beverly, Churchill Downs, Kentucky and Falls City Handicaps.

The 1944 racing season featured not one, but two undefeated stakes-winning two-year-old colts, one of whom campaigned exclusively in the East and the other in the Midwest. At the end of the season, it was an open-end debate as to which was the champion; Walter M. Jeffords's Pavot, having won more races and more money, and having defeated more rivals, won the election.

PAVOT, 1942

(Case Ace–Coquelicot, by Man o' War)

Trained by Oscar White, and ridden in most of his important races by George Woolf, Pavot did not enter competition until June, but he came onstage with a flourish, setting a new track record of 1:05⅕ for 5½ furlongs at Delaware Park in his debut, which he won by eight lengths. In his next start, the Christiana Stakes, he lowered his own mark to 1:04⅖. He cruised through the Mayflower, U. S. Hotel, Saratoga Special and Grand Union Hotel Stakes, winning them all by open daylight. In the Hopeful, his first attempt beyond 6 furlongs, Esteem finished within half a length of him, and speculation arose that Pavot was essentially a speedball who had reached his limit. However, Woolf blamed the performance on his poor ride, and in the Futurity September 30, at the same 6½-furlong distance, Pavot carried top weight of 126 pounds to victory by two lengths. He retired for the year with eight wins and $179,040, leading money winner of the season regardless of age.

FREE FOR ALL, 1942

(Questionnaire–Panay, by Chicle)

John Marsch's Free For All, trained by Burley Parke and ridden by Otto Grohs, went five-for-five in 1944 for earnings of $109,575.

He, too, won his debut by eight lengths, and four days later won the Hyde Park Stakes in new track record time of 1:04⅗ for 5½ furlongs. His only close call of the season came on July 11 in a prep race for the Arlington Futurity in which his stablemate, Errard (carrying 10 pounds less weight), finished lapped on him, and Edward J. Lasker's invader from the East, Flood Town, was just a nose behind Errard. In the Futurity itself, however, Free For All strode away from actor Don Ameche's Sir Bim to win by two and a half lengths, as Errard and Flood Town were unplaced.

The little brown colt's final start was in the Washington Park Futurity, for which only three rivals besides his entry-mate came out to face him. He won this one by one and a quarter lengths from Icangetit to complete the most remarkable monopoly in modern racing history. For three years in succession, Marsch had won both the rich Chicago futurities: with Occupation in 1942, Jezrahel (Arlington) and Occupy (Washington Park) in 1943 and Free For All in 1944.

One of the great disappointments of the season was the fact that Pavot and Free For All never met. The latter was shipped East, but developed sore legs and was sent to Kentucky for application of the firing iron, after which he was turned out for the remainder of the year.

Free For All, who stood right at 15 hands, re-entered competition at three, but broke down in the 1945 Derby Trial after having won his first out. Pavot lost his first two starts the next season, but disproved the notion he was a sprinter by winning the Belmont Stakes at 1½ miles. However, he did not win another race that season. Again, he was relegated to the ranks of the sprinters (a lucky sprinter, of course, in view of his Belmont victory) and again he confounded the experts by coming back as a four-year-old and winning the Sussex, Massachusetts Handicaps, Wilson Stakes and 2-mile Jockey Club Gold Cup. He retired finally with 14 wins in 32 starts and $373,365.

Other top two-year-old colts of 1944 included Calumet's Pot o' Luck (Champagne Stakes and Pimlico Futurity), C. C. Tanner's Best Effort (three stakes including the Cowdin), Maine Chance Farm's War Jeep; Errard and Flood Town (who won stakes besides losing to Free For All); and George D. Widener's Plebiscite.

Idle Hour Stock Farm's Busher was the champion two-year-old filly of 1944, as well as the leading money winner in that category, with $60,300. She had an unusual campaign.

Colonel Bradley was approaching his eighty-fifth birthday, and was unable to withstand the buffeting about of a race track crowd. He had a special place on the roof of Belmont Park which could be reached by elevator and which afforded him a good view of the races. As a result, except for her final start, Busher raced only at Belmont.

After winning her maiden race on May 30, she was idle until racing returned to New York City in August. She won an allowance event, then was fourth in the Spinaway—behind Price Level, Ace Card and Safeguard—closing fast at the end after a tardy start. Following a change in jockeys—Ferril Zufelt to Eddie Arcaro—Busher next won the Adirondack Handicap from War Date and Leslie Grey (Ace Card unplaced) then she met her second defeat. Nomadic, with a concession of 11 pounds, beat the Bradley filly a head in a tune-up for the Matron Stakes.

Busher avenged both her defeats as she won the Matron by a neck from Twosy, with the top-weighted Price Level third and Nomadic fourth. The trip to Pimlico for the rich Selima Stakes, won easily by three lengths from Ace Card, closed out Busher's juvenile activity.

Crispin Oglebay's Price Level won three other stakes besides the Spinaway; Mrs. Walter Jeffords's Ace Card won two stakes and placed in two; and Greentree's Expression won the Lassie.

Death dealt a particularly severe blow in 1944. Again, casualty reports from overseas

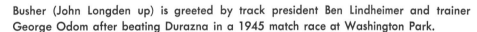

Busher (John Longden up) is greeted by track president Ben Lindheimer and trainer George Odom after beating Durazna in a 1945 match race at Washington Park.

included names familiar to racegoers. Among those listed as killed in action were trainer Edward Haughton, Jr., owner C. J. Amendola, jockeys Herbert Chinn and Warren Hawley and former racing commissioner Pearson Jones. War losses other than in combat included jockey George King, and Thomas Hitchcock, the world-famous polo player and member of one of racing's most prominent families, who died in an airplane crash.

The home front was diminished, too, as among those who passed on were the last two surviving trainers from the rebuilding period after the Civil War: Charles E. Brossman, eighty-three, who had trained the great mare, Imp, and Thomas Jefferson Healey, seventy-eight, whose associations had been varied and successes many. The noted runners saddled by Healey since his first winner in 1888 included Olambala at the turn of the century, through Campfire, Pillory, Display, Top Flight and Equipoise (he took over the latter horse as a five-year-old). Charley Boots, Fred Burton, Maxwell Howard (Stagehand's owner), Henry Buck and William and Robert Shelley, father and son, were others to die during the year.

Finally, Mrs. Payne Whitney, owner of Greentree Stud and Stable, succumbed in September after having been in poor health for several years. A quiet, gracious sportswoman, who published poetry in addition to her interest in sports, she was known and admired as the First Lady of the American Turf. Her son, Colonel John Hay Whitney, had been captured by the Germans, and less than two weeks before her death, Mrs. Whitney heard the welcome news that he had escaped when a train taking prisoners from France to Germany had been attacked by American forces. The son, who had been maintaining Mare's Nest Stud, and his sister, Joan (Mrs. Charles Shipman Payson), a partner in Manhasset Stable, announced before the year was out that they would continue the Greentree establishment.

Two days before Christmas, 1944, James F. Byrnes, Director of War Mobilization and Re-

conversion, issued a request that racing in the United States be suspended entirely. According to his statement:

> The operation of race tracks not only requires the employment of manpower needed for more essential operations, but also manpower, railroad transportation, as well as tires and gasoline in the movement of patrons to and from the track, and in the movement of the horses . . . The existing war situation demands the utmost effort that the people of the United States can give . . . The operation of race tracks is not conducive to this all-out effort. Therefore, with the approval of the President, I urge that the management of these tracks take immediate measures to bring the present race meetings to a close by January 3, 1945 . . . I am confident that the management . . . can be depended upon to take action without the necessity of recourse to other measures.

In other Allied countries closer to the scene of combat, racing had resumed, but Byrnes's request followed a surprise offensive launched by the Germans in the Ardennes Forest area, and his announcement coincided with the American counterattack that touched off the Battle of the Bulge. In the United States leaders of the sport pledged their co-operation. Tropical Park, the Fair Grounds and Sportsman's Park (Arizona) were the only U. S. tracks in operation at the time; they closed shop on January 2, and racing in the United States came to a complete halt.

Byrnes recommended that the ban be lifted on V-E Day. After having surrendered to Russia several days earlier, on May 7 the German high command accepted Allied terms of surrender. The documents were signed on May 8, the ban was lifted the next day and three days later a field of horses was off and running at Narragansett. Santa Anita, Jamaica and Delaware followed in short order and the most amazing splurge in history was underway.

Despite the short year—less than eight months—every over-all record relating to the sport was broken. National attendance ap-

Barry Whitehead

The colorful history of Tanforan, California's oldest existing track, included a period during World War II when the infield was occupied by Navy barracks.

proached 19½-million and mutuel handle $1.4-billion. There were more days of racing (2,480) than ever before, and, of course, more races contested (19,587). The largest number of horses ever to appear in one season (14,307) were in action, and they competed for a new record purse distribution of more than $32-million, nor was the swell in purses solely the result of numerical increases elsewhere, for the average purse distribution per race (and per horse) also reached unprecedented values. On the breeding side of the industry, the number of yearlings sold at auction did not attain pre-war levels, but the financial picture was just as good; the 986 animals sold elicited total bids exceeding $5-million, a new record gross, and the resulting average of $5,146 far surpassed all previous records.

Jamaica still was preening itself on having registered a $3-million mutuel handle on opening day in New York, when Belmont Park came along with a $4-million day; before the year was out Belmont had posted a world record of $5,016,745 for a single day's wagering.

All these records were the more remarkable when it is considered that a ban on the transportation of race horses by common carrier stayed in effect until the Japanese surrender in August.

Racing was disrupted, but by no means dismayed. The Kentucky Derby, having been held in abeyance during the shutdown, was run in June; unable to work in the Preakness during its regular spring meeting, Pimlico held a special one-day meeting June 16 with five stakes on the program—the Preakness, Pimlico Oaks, Nursery Stakes, Dixie and Jennings Handicaps.

BUSHER, 1942

(War Admiral–Baby League,
by Bubbling Over)

In March of her three-year-old season, Busher was sold by E. R. Bradley to Louis B. Mayer for a reported price of $50,000; as racing had not yet been resumed, the filly campaigned only in her new owner's French blue and pink colors that year. George Odom became her trainer and Longden her regular jockey.

Ready to go shortly after Santa Anita opened, she won an allowance race on May 26 by five lengths, followed up with an easy, seven-length victory over her sex in the Santa Susana Stakes, then won the San Vicente Stakes, her first outing against male competition, by one and a quarter lengths. The latter race was marred by Quick Reward, who lost his rider at the start and ran loose through the field, but Busher was bothered as much as any of her rivals. As was indicated by the time of 1:36⅗, fastest of the year at Santa Anita, the race wasn't slowed down seriously.

There was a touch of irony in her next race, the Santa Anita Derby, for she lost by half a length to Bymeabond, an ex-stablemate of hers who had been sold by Bradley to J. Kel Houssels of Nevada. At that she was not disgraced as she was spotting the colt 2 pounds actual weight (7 on the scale) and Bymeabond received one of George Woolf's better rides, than which there were no better.

Sharing top weight of 126 pounds with Happy Issue (two years her senior) Busher won the Santa Margarita on July 4 from her own stablemate, Whirlabout, with Canina third and Happy Issue unplaced. Three weeks later she was in Chicago, where she won the Cleopatra Handicap against her own division,

then scored a resounding victory by four and a half lengths in the Arlington Handicap August 4 over the best field that could be mustered, including older males.

In her next start, carrying 128 pounds in the Beverly Handicap (the equivalent of 134 on an older horse) Busher finished third to Durazna (116) ridden by Woolf, and Letmenow (102). The salient attribute of War Admiral's little daughter, however, was she always took revenge: throughout her career, no horse ever defeated her without subsequently being defeated by Busher. In a special race at equal weights against Durazna August 29, during which the lead changed several times in a thrilling spectacle of gameness, it was Busher who began to draw away at the end, to win by three-fourths of a length.

Having failed to stop Busher earlier in the summer with Twosy and Pot o' Luck, Calumet Farm sent its mighty gelding, Armed, against her in the Washington Park Handicap September 3. Carrying 115 pounds against 120 on her rival (which amounted to a 6-pound concession if the age and sex difference is taken into account) Busher defeated Armed by one and a half lengths in new track record time of 2:01⅘ for the 1¼ miles.

This was the perfect last act in her Chicago run. Busher returned to Hollywood Park (whose meeting was held in the autumn that year, since Santa Anita had led off in the summer). Quick Reward gave her a rude welcome, when with jockey Tony Skoronski on his back, he defeated her by a head in the Will Rogers Handicap, carrying 112 pounds to the filly's 123. For what consolation it provided, second money brought Busher's lifetime earnings up to $276,120 and she thereby displaced Top Flight as the world's leading money winner of her sex.

The Hollywood Derby two weeks later brought her multiple compensation: she evened the score with both colts who had defeated her, earned the biggest purse of her career and broke Top Flight's remaining record for earnings by a filly in a single season. Carrying actual top weight of 123 pounds, Busher won by one and a half lengths from Man o' Glory, with Quick Reward second and Bymeabond unplaced, for a net purse of $40,470. A week after that, under top weight of 126 pounds, she easily won the Vanity Handicap from older fillies and mares to bring her 1945 total up $273,735, tops for the year.

One of her legs had developed a filling, and she was taken out of training for a year. She attempted a comeback at five, without success, and was retired after having compiled the following record: 21 starts, 15 wins, three seconds, one third and only twice unplaced, $334,035.

In the voting for the best three-year-old filly, Busher was a unanimous choice. However, racing in the East that year was a filly destined eventually to replace her as world's leading money-winning female, Gallorette. Another exceptional filly was Maine Chance Farm's War Date, winner of the Princess Doreen Stakes, Modesty, Arlington Matron, Beldame and Ladies' Handicaps: she was associated with an exceptional stable.

Among the colts of classic age, Hoop, Jr. was the most interesting, not only because of his provocatively brief racing career, but because of his unusual background. He was the first yearling ever bought by Alabama (and Florida) contractor Fred W. Hooper, who paid $10,200 for the son of Sir Gallahad III. After two wins and placing three times in modest stakes events in five starts at two, Hoop, Jr. had developed osselets, so Hooper in June decided to put him aside and save him for the next year's Kentucky Derby. (There is nothing like the optimism of an owner with his first race horse.) The colt's ankles were fired, and after being turned out at Hooper's Alabama farm during convalescence, he was put back in training at Hialeah during the shutdown, under the supervision of Ivan Parke. Late in May, Gallorette won their mutual three-year-old debut, as Hoop, Jr. came in

fourth, the only occasion in his life that more than one rival finished ahead of him. For the Wood Memorial he was drawn into the second division, which he won in 1:45. (Jeep defeated Gallorette in the first division, covering the distance in ⅘-second slower time.)

Ridden by Arcaro in the Kentucky Derby over a muddy track, Hoop, Jr. took the lead going past the grandstand first time around and increased it thereafter, winning easily by six lengths from Pot o' Luck and Darby Dieppe. Hooper's classic comment was, "I never thought I'd make it this quick." (Through 1963 he had not made it again, but the tall Alabaman still had an amazing record in the Kentucky Derby; his next two starters in the race, Olympia and Crozier, both finished second.)

A week later in the Preakness, Hoop, Jr. stayed in third place during the early running, began to move up in the stretch, then gave way suddenly near the end to finish second to Polynesian. The Hooper colt pulled up lame, with a bowed tendon, and that ended his career with four wins and four seconds in nine starts for earnings of $99,290.

Mrs. P. A. B. Widener's Polynesian, trained by ex-steeplechase rider Morris H. Dixon, also had an adventurous life. After losing his first three races as a two-year-old, and bucking shins, he had developed azoturia (a condition horsemen describe as "tie-up," a tenseness of the loin muscles which makes urination difficult). Turned out on a farm, he apparently had recovered from the basic ailment but was left with a psychosomatic trauma: he stood perfectly still in his paddock for fear that movement would cause him pain, and had to be more or less dragged back and forth to his stall. Dixon was toying with the idea of cracking him across the rump just to see what would happen when the problem was taken out of his hands; a group of hornets stung the colt and Polynesian became a runner. Put back in training he won five of his remaining seven starts, including a division of the Sagamore Stakes, and was never out of the money.

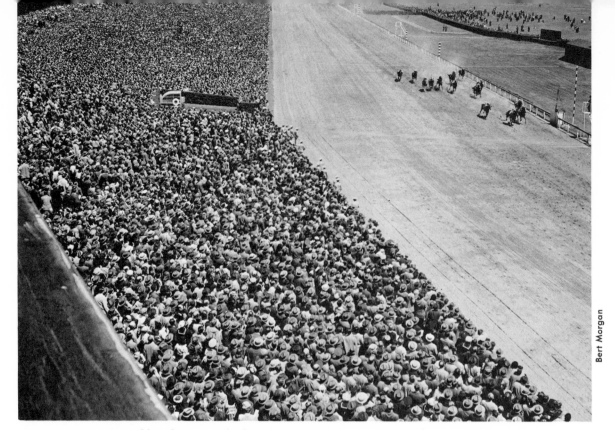

Record-breaking crowd of 64,670 at Jamaica on Memorial Day in 1945 after the war-time blackout had been lifted.

At three, the son of Unbreakable finished third to Jeep and Greek Warrior in the Experimental Free Handicap and fourth in Hoop, Jr.'s division of the Wood. Skipping the Derby, he defeated Pavot in the Withers, and his front-running victory in the Preakness followed, Wayne Wright guiding him in both instances. Later that season he won the Saranac Handicap and in subsequent years became the top sprinter on the American scene, and quite proficient at medium distances.

At four Polynesian won eight races including the Toboggan, Roseben, Rumson (130 pounds), Pageant (126 pounds, equaling the world record of 1:09⅕ for 6 furlongs), Turf and Field, Scarsdale and Riggs Handicaps. At five he won nine more races, among them the Fighting Fox, Atlantic City Inaugural, Wilmington, Oceanport, Long Branch, Omnibus, Camden and Janney Handicaps, carrying up to 129 pounds over distances out to 1⅛ miles, and setting several records at the newly built New Jersey tracks. He retired with 27 wins (including one burst of five straight stakes vic-

tories in his final season of competition), 10 seconds and 10 thirds in 58 starts, for earnings of $310,410—and achieved great fame as a sire.

Returning to the 1945 season, Fighting Step, a son of Fighting Fox owned by Murlogg Farm, was voted best of the colts after a campaign of fifteen starts during which he was out of the money only once (in the Kentucky Derby). Trained by C. C. Norman and ridden by George South, the colt won seven races, including the rich American Derby, from his contemporaries and the Autumn Handicaps at both Churchill Downs and Hawthorne from his seniors, to earn $106,915. In the American Derby, K. Doe-Doe dumped his rider at the start and ran loose in the field, but Fighting Step was in front all the way and unconcerned with this development.

Calumet Farm's Pot o' Luck won more money ($149,220) but was not as consistent. He won only five of his 21 starts, although his wins were the Arlington Classic and Lawrence Realization within his division, and the Ben

Ali, Governor Bowie Handicaps and Jockey Club Gold Cup from mixed-age fields. He finished third in Fighting Step's American Derby and the champion finished third in his Classic.

Other three-year-olds of prominence included Maine Chance Farm's War Jeep; William Helis's Greek Warrior, Pavot; J. M. Roebling's Wildlife; Mrs. Louis Rabinowitz's good stayer, Reply Paid; Sunshine Stable's Buzfuz; and Walter M. Jeffords' Trymenow.

Among older horses, the sensation of the season was created by Mrs. Ethel D. Jacobs's four-year-old Stymie, a colt which had been claimed by her husband for $1,500 as a two-year-old. After only seven wins in 57 starts in his first two seasons, as a four-year-old he blossomed into the champion and leading money winner of the handicap division, with earnings of $225,375, a new record for a horse older than three.

Calumet Farm's gelding, Armed, another who had waited until maturity to show his class, also was impressive, but since both Armed and Stymie were to achieve greater renown in the postwar era, their careers will be sketched more fully in a following chapter.

Devil Diver came very near taking the "handicap triple crown" in 1945, a season during which he carried steadying weights. After winning the Paumonok Handicap under 132 pounds, and finishing second in the Toboggan under 135, he won the Metropolitan (129) and Suburban (132)—but in the Brooklyn Handicap, again carrying 132, he was defeated by Stymie with the aid of a 16-pound concession.

First Fiddle (Fleetwing, Massachusetts and Trenton Handicaps) and Thumbs Up (San Pasqual and Santa Anita Handicaps) also scored points in the voting for the championship, and other notable performers included Apache, Equifox, Olympic Zenith, Rounders and True North. The last-named, holder of the straightaway Widener Chute record of 1:08⅕ for 6 furlongs at Belmont Park, ran the distance in 1:08⅘ in 1945 to win the Fall Highweight Handicap under 140 pounds.

Distaff members of the handicap brigade who received honorable mention were Durazna (winner of the Clang and a division of the Sheridan Handicap besides her conquest of Busher in the Beverly) and Milcave (Vineland and Bryan and O'Hara Handicaps).

Fred Wyse's two-year-old Air Rate, a gelded son of Deliberator, trained by R. Lentini, won the first event for his generation at the Fair Grounds January 1 (run in the morning to avoid conflict with the Sugar Bowl football game) then continued through the season undefeated in seven starts, five of them stakes: the Myles Standish, Mayflower, Garden State, Newport and Connors Memorial. (The Garden State Stakes in 1945 was not the same as the heavily endowed race of that name which later came into being; the earlier one, formerly the Walt Whitman Stakes, was a 6-furlong event, but it carried a reasonably large value at that—$30,250 to the winner.)

However, the story of 1945's juvenile division is Maine Chance Farm, owned by Mrs. Elizabeth Nightingale Graham, better known in the business world as Elizabeth Arden. Mrs. Graham had raced horses before—as Mrs. T. J. Lewis and for a time under the assumed name of "Mr. Nightingale" —but in 1943 she had changed the name of her stable and launched an expensive building program: in a three-year period from 1943-1945 she spent $669,500 at the yearling auctions. Expensive purchases are one thing— hers also were astute—and in the 1945 season alone she retrieved the bulk of this sum as Maine Chance hit the top of the owners' standings with $589,170.

Flying the red, white and blue Maine Chance colors that year (the red later was changed to cerise) were the champion two-year-olds of both sexes, Beaugay and Star Pilot. The filly Beaugay, a unanimous selection as best of her age regardless of sex, won

"Silent Tom" Smith, trainer of Seabiscuit and other exceptional racers.

her first six starts in succession, including the Fashion, Polly Drummond, Arlington Lassie, Princess Pat and Matron Stakes, to earn $105,910. Her only defeat came in the Futurity, when the daughter of Stimulus ran into the rail and fell.

That race was won by her stablemate, Star Pilot, a son of Sickle, who topped the juvenile division in earnings with $165,385. Winner of exactly half his dozen races, his other stakes

victories were in the Hopeful Stakes, Ardsley Handicap and Pimlico Futurity.

Also in the Maine Chance string was Lord Boswell, a colt by Boswell, who won the Remsen and Endurance Handicaps and was rated at the top of the Experimental Free Handicap at the end of the year with 128 pounds. Other two-year-old stakes winners in the stable were Knockdown (Cowdin Stakes), Colony Boy (Walden) and They Say (Juvenile).

Of the 24 horses which sported the Maine Chance silks during 1945, 18 were two-year-olds, five were three and only one was a four-year-old.

Tom Smith trained the stable until November, when his license was revoked for alleged administration of ephedrine to Magnific Duel, winner of a race at Jamaica on November 1. Roy Waldron took over as Maine Chance trainer until the end of the year, when he was succeeded by Tom's son, James Smith.

The Maine Chance monopoly notwithstanding, there were a couple of good two-year-olds in other stables. Dixiana owned the Arlington Futurity winner, Spy Song, and Dr. Eslie Asbury had the Washington Park Futurity winner, Revoked. The latter colt received his name in an unusual manner. After being sold for $41,000 as a yearling, he was turned back because of suspicious breathing; the colt won $67,650 in his first season.

PART FIVE

THE POSTWAR YEARS

CHAPTER FIFTY-SIX

WHEN THE REMARKABLE FIG-ures for the 1945 season had been compiled, those observers of racing with an analytical bent shook their heads and wondered—if all those records could have been established in eight months, what would have happened in a full year? In 1946 they found out.

In the first full season after the war, every single gross record pertaining to American racing was again shattered, and the modern era of the sport began again from scratch. Since, after a shaky settling down period, new over-all financial records were to be set in each succeeding year during the postwar period, as racing continued its growth; the reader is referred to the appendix for the specific figures.

The foregoing should not be construed as an indication that another golden age was in the starting gate. The bubble was to burst in the near future, and much of the "growth" resulted from desperation measures to pump it back up through "lateral expansion" (more racing days) and "vertical development" (more races per day). A number of new tracks came into the picture, contributing significantly to the rise in statistical summaries. In 1946, however, with one notable exception, there was no hint of gloomy days.

Ted Atkinson, once more the leading jockey according to both races won (233) and money won, in 1946 became the first rider in history to hit the million-dollar range as his mounts earned $1,036,825. The studious, gentlemanly native of Toronto, nicknamed "The Professor"

off the track, was known as "The Slasher" on it, his trademark being an arm pointing straight at the sky, ready to descend with the whip. Still hustling although he was at the top, Atkinson rode in 1,377 races.

However, the jockey best known as a money rider had no opportunity to participate in the unprecedented largesse. When Please Me stumbled in the fourth race at Santa Anita January 3, 1946, jockey George Woolf was jerked over his neck and hit the ground head first. The riderless horse did not fall—in fact, he ran on to finish first—but "The Iceman" never regained consciousness.

George Woolf never set any records of the conventional sort, although he led the country in number of stakes victories in 1942 (twenty-three) and 1944 (fourteen). Also a native of Canada (Cardston, Alberta) he was the diametric opposite of Ted Atkinson so far as activity was concerned. In an eighteen-year career Woolf averaged slightly more than 200 mounts per season, and in his later years he accepted considerably fewer than that number. Woolf was the jockey's jockey.

His numerous scores in rich races included three successive victories in the Futurity, American Derby, Hollywood Gold Cup (the first three renewals) and Harve de Grace Handicap. In less concentrated form, he also won the Preakness, Realization, Hopeful, Jockey Club Gold Cup, Santa Anita and Arlington Handicaps—plus a number of overnight races, for he did not disdain mounts from small stables. (The Kentucky Derby was one race Woolf never won, despite nine tries at it.)

Brusque, aloof and tersely outspoken, "The Iceman" was held in awe by many, yet he was a persuasive salesman when called upon. He had an agent, but arranged a good many of his rides himself, and, as a person who moved in a direct line all the way, he was somewhat contemptuous of contracts and such; to him, a verbal agreement was ironclad, nor did he brook deviations from the straight and narrow in any form.

"The Iceman" just as aptly could have been nicknamed "The Sandman," for Woolf possessed that most valuable asset to any athlete, the ability to relax. He could turn sleep on and off like a faucet. As other jockeys might pace the floor nervously while waiting for their race to come up, Woolf might snooze. When the time came, he could rouse himself, yawn, stretch, amble down to the paddock and climb aboard. After a ride that gave palpitations to spectators, he was quite capable of going promptly back to sleep.

The new-found prosperity in 1946 was evident in many ways. The Kentucky Derby, Preakness, Belmont Stakes, Santa Anita Derby and Hollywood Gold Cup were raised to an added value of $100,000—and it was announced that the original "hundred thousand," the Santa Anita Handicap, would be boosted as necessary in added value to guarantee at least that sum to the winner, exclusive of second, third and fourth money. At the bigger tracks, grooms and exercise boys were awarded a $20 bonus for each winner, and a $10 fee for each starter, regardless of where it finished. Yearling sales were phenomenal as an all-time record average of $5,909 was realized.

One notable exception to the general trend was manifested in New York, where the surplus money quickly was evaporated when, at the request of Mayor William O'Dwyer, an additional tax of 5 percent was imposed on pari-mutuel wagering to provide revenue to city and county governments. The municipal government of Saratoga followed suit and— although the O'Dwyer Bite, as it was known,

later was gradually rechanneled into the state coffers—it has not been removed nor is there any indication that such action is contemplated. As early as July of the first year it was in effect, the state tax commission reported a drop in revenue; it became more drastic as the season progressed, and toward the end of October the racing commission announced that wagering was down nearly $129-million and attendance off 705,792 from comparable figures of the previous year—a sharp contrast to reports from other areas. Because there were thirty-eight more racing days in 1946, New York made up some of this gross loss, but despite the longer season, there still was a $41½-million drop at the end of the year. In the more revealing area of daily averages, attendance was down 14½ percent and wagering diminished by 27 percent.

How much of the business decline in New York was due to the Bite could not be determined precisely, since competition arose in the form of two glamorous new tracks which opened that year in New Jersey, Atlantic City and Monmouth Park, the latter track reviving some of the stakes events that had been run at the original Monmouth. (Saratoga, New York's vacation track, was hardest hit by the decline; daily average wagering at the upstate oval was less than half what it had been in 1945.)

For the country as a whole, though, everything was emphatically bigger than ever before —and faster. Even time records fell with extraordinary frequency in 1946, as the sport appeared to be grooming itself for the new era. At the end of the Santa Anita meeting, the names of ten new horses appeared among the holders of a track record (some of them sharing a record for the same distance), eight new names made the corresponding list at Tropical Park, six at Washington Park and six at staid old Saratoga (not counting steeplechase events).

Numerous changes took place in racing during the years that followed World War II, but there was no significant alteration in the basic structure of the sport, such changes as there were having been essentially modifications within the existing framework.

The commercial aspect, which had been accentuated over the years, became yet more pronounced as racing expanded. It was no longer just a sport; it was a major national industry, representing enormous investments not only in race tracks and horseflesh, but in such allied businesses as feed companies, van lines, veterinary service and farming. As financial partners in the venture, state governments took more than a casual supervisory interest in its affairs—revenue from racing, $94-million in 1946 and growing ever since, was a vital source of income.

The business approach was apparent on the track, too, as horses were regarded as investments rather than as implements of a hobby. One noticeable effect was in the attitude toward weight. Objections to high weight assignments were nothing new, but as purses grew larger and larger the few pounds that could mean the difference between victory and defeat assumed greater importance. Moreover, as the value of breeding stock, especially stallions, rose sharply, in addition to the purse itself there was to consider the effect of a possible defeat on a horse's reputation when he should be retired to stud. In 1946 stud fees already were on the rise, but even so Bull Lea, a proven sire of a champion in his first crop, was advertised at a fee of $1,000, and $1,500 was about tops for any stallion; by 1960, as bloodstock breeding had developed into a huge industry of itself, and syndicate ownership of stallions had become more prevalent, $10,000 stud fees were not a rarity, some applied to horses as yet untried at stud, and beyond that price range there were stallions standing at private contract.

The owner whose interest was strictly sporting—who would seek out the putative champion at all costs and challenge him, or, if he happened to own the champion himself, would accept whatever poundage was assigned just to find out how good the horse really was—still was around, but he was losing ground. Rich purses were available in such profusion that it was easy for the owner of a logical challenger to give the champion a wide berth, and for the owner of the champion to shop about for suitable weights. At some tracks weight ceilings (explicit or tacit) were put into effect, whereby it was understood that no horse would be required to carry more than 130 pounds, for example. This practice came in for considerable criticism—and it also inspired spirited defense. It boiled back down to the basic element of horse racing—difference of opinion—*is* it sporting, really, to arrange a contest so that an inferior runner under a feathery load is enabled to defeat a champion handicapped by a heavy burden?

The proliferation of racing in general, and the increase in number of rich purses, made it more difficult to establish definitively the various champions at the end of each racing season, since, racing each within his own orbit, several runners could compile impressive records without ever facing one another. No longer were there certain races of such overwhelming value that they were assured of attracting the best eligible horses from all over the country. On the other hand, paradoxically, as transportation by air became common, it was easier to arrange meetings between horses from different areas, and quick invasions for one big purse became common. There were several air shipments of horses in 1946, including one trans-Atlantic flight and one from South America.

Supplementary nominations, through which an owner who had failed to nominate at the original time of closing was permitted to enter a horse in rich stakes races at the last minute, became more the vogue in the postwar era of thoroughbred racing, and the pros and cons of this policy were argued with vehemence. One school of thought contended that the practice was equivalent to allowing a poker player to see his last card before he had to decide whether or not to get in the game; true enough, the owner who came in late had to pay a stiff penalty for the privilege, but he did not do so unless he stood a reasonably good chance of winning it back, plus the pot the others had been building up all along. The opposite viewpoint maintained that a race was designed to determine the best horse, not the luckiest owner—and animals like Alsab, El Chico and others should not be denied participation in the most important races just because their owners had failed to nominate them far in advance.

Claiming races, already subject to a wide variety of conditions, underwent further embroidery. As large sums became available for purse distribution, for a time the tracks were able to scale purses over an appreciable range of racing class, but as the minimum purse became more popular the scale was pinched. When the minimum went up, and there was constant agitation for it to be raised, the lower and higher classes of horses were crammed closer together—in many cases the difference in value to the winner of a $5,000 claiming event and a $2,500 race was negligible, if there *was* a difference.

More than ever before, claiming price came to represent an arbitrary classification as to relative racing ability rather than an appraisal by the owner of a horse's real market value. In 1946 Roman Carnival was claimed for $17,500, highest price on record at the time and one that would have bought a good stake horse not many years before; by 1960 there were races for "selling platers" running with a $50,000 tag. At the other end of the ladder, because of more frequent opportunities to race, a good solid $3,500 horse had as much, or more, earning potential than, say, a $20,000 claimer, and complaints were heard when these good breadwinners were haltered. Numerous elaborate methods of discouraging indiscriminate claiming became popular—including, among others, the "optional" race,

in which horses that previously had been exposed to the halter could run without being subject to claim, at the option of the owner.

Finally, fourth money by this time having become standard, the purse was divided further in some areas; fifth money was awarded at a few tracks, on down to eighth money, in certain rich races.

The rapid increase in the scope of racing was not without its more serious problems. A rash of ringer cases were detected in 1946, as the Thoroughbred Racing Protective Bureau swung into high gear in its first full season of operation, but within a few years tight controls and improved procedures for identifying horses eliminated this problem.

Stimulation continued to be a sore spot, not only in cases of willful skulduggery, but more often through innocent mistakes, accidents and misunderstanding. The "suspension" of Tom Smith, leading money-winning trainer of 1945, became a *cause célèbre* when the affair was taken to court. (Technically, Smith was not suspended; his license was revoked, which paved the way for an appeal.) It was testified that the alleged stimulation of Magnific Duel had consisted of eight squirts of a nasal spray containing ephedrine, which Smith had purchased at a drugstore without prescription, and which he used on himself as well as his horses. An expert witness for the defense stated that the amount of ephedrine thus ingested would not have affected the physical performance of a flea, and, moreover, it was brought out that on the day in question Smith hadn't ordered the horse's nose to be sprayed in the first place. This last aspect was somewhat irrelevant to the specific case, but germane to the root of the stimulation problem as a whole. Under the rules (following precedent of the Ladana affair) a trainer could be held responsible for a horse's condition regardless of the acts of third parties; without imputing a connection with the actual stimulation one way or another, punishment was meted out for negligence in failing to protect the horse from tampering.

376

The case dragged on, and Smith lost his appeal, but by the time the legal machinery had finished grinding he had practically served his one-year term, and he soon was reinstated. (In the course of the hassle, Silent Tom did loosen up enough to comment wryly that if ever he had been inclined to use a stimulant, he wouldn't have wasted it on Magnific Duel—he'd have used it on War Date when she was running against Busher.)

Big targets are the easiest kind to shoot at, and the press in general enjoyed a picnic sniping at what was called the stuffy attitude of the Jockey Club and the New York State Racing Commission. However, there was also the issue of public interest. The official viewpoint was that to give an inch in security was to risk loss of a mile; that if substances innocuous enough in themselves were permitted, they could be used to mask the presence of more serious drugs; and that a rule was a rule, to be obeyed as a matter of course.

Onstage more or less concurrently with the Smith case was another which would have been hilarious had it not been for the distress it brought on the persons directly involved. Maryland had been using the New York laboratory for chemical analyses, but a zealous racing commissioner, in an effort to double check, caused samples to be sent to another analyst, who gave this report: five horses (four of whom had raced on the same day), including representatives of prominent stables under the control of reputable trainers, had shown positive for morphine. Appeals and lawsuits flew back and forth. It subsequently was brought out that a biological test had been used which was based on the reaction of mice. Samples from horses were injected into the rodents, and if a mouse's tail curled up into the shape of the letter S, it was classified as a morphine reaction. As the fate of gladiators in ancient Rome had been determined by thumb signals of the Caesars, the careers of these trainers had hung by a mouse's tail. It was demonstrated during the hearings that the jars containing the damning

samples could be opened without disturbing the protective seal, and it was suggested that the rubber gaskets on the jars were of such composition as to have possibly caused the samples to produce the reaction they did. Ultimately, all the suspensions were overruled in court.

Various remedies for the perplexing problem were advanced. The receiving barn, where horses scheduled to race were held in isolation, was one of them, but, beyond the disinclination to subject a high-strung animal to unfamiliar experience just before he raced, trainers objected to being held responsible for a horse that was taken out of their custody. A mobile testing laboratory was instituted, through which horses could be given a saliva test *before* the race, and the trainer thereby relieved of responsibility if further chemical analysis indicated presence of unauthorized substances. This took the trainer off the hook, but it didn't do much for the horse, or the betting public.

As analytical techniques improved, and horsemen became more cautious about trying every new miracle medicine that came along without first ascertaining its chemical properties—lest it prove to be too miraculous—such fiascos ceased. However, two thorny issues persisted: whether a distinction should be made between drugs which hop a horse and those which are essentially pain killers or curative medications, which merely restore a horse to his natural capability; and who should be held responsible for administration of unauthorized substances by unknown parties.

Concerning the first issue, the point has been made that participants in all other sports are allowed reasonable medication—a golfer who has a headache can take an aspirin—so why should not horses receive the same consideration? The opposite stand is that a line has to be drawn somewhere, and the simpler the better. (At one hearing, an "interested party" sat throughout the proceedings ostentatiously sniffing a benzedrine inhaler, which at the time could be purchased by a child in any drugstore.)

Concerning the second issue, as of 1963 the absolute insurer rule, under which a trainer automatically is suspended if a horse in his care flunks a chemistry test, still was in effect in most states, although in some states he was entitled to a formal hearing before any official action was taken. Regardless of the assurance that punishments meted out under this rule are for sins of omission—failure to protect the horse—and do not imply wrongdoing on the part of the trainer, many trainers object strenuously to the damage inflicted on their personal reputations by inferred involvement in stimulation incidents. On the other hand, officials feel that the responsibility has to be fixed somewhere, and the trainer is the only logical candidate. While the general public might arrive at a conclusion of guilt through association, persons familiar with the problem are more understanding. (In this connection, it should be recorded that Tom Smith got back his job with Maine Chance Farm—several times.)

As speed records continued to be broken, various attempts were made to connect this circumstance with stimulation, but the hypothesis could not stand up under scrutiny. For one thing, horses kept on breaking time records after the incidence of stimulation dwindled to a trickle, and as winners they were tested for drugs all along at the time of their victories. A less sensational, but more logical explanation might lie in the fact that more horses were running against time records more often. Also, in the old days there had been a distinct break between summer and winter racing; horses did not reach peak condition until a race meeting was well along. In the modern era of year-around racing, at any given moment a high precentage of the runners are hard and fit, ready to go all out from the first day. Finally, addition of organic material and other techniques of race track maintenance have produced faster running surfaces.

As the controls against illegal use of drugs were tightened, some unscrupulous characters resorted to use of electric batteries and chaining; these practices were drastically reduced (and eventually practically eliminated) by the passage of rules which made mere possession of such equipment an infraction, and by the work of the TRPB and similar agencies in ridding the sport of undesirables.

All in all, racing accomplished a remarkable job of housecleaning during the postwar era, to the extent that it became by far the most thoroughly supervised of all sports.

Movies of races had been made at Santa Anita before the war, and as peace returned the Oswald Photo Patrol and Telefilm Service had been adopted by a number of other tracks throughout the country. Thus, races not only were under scrutiny by officials during the actual running, but they could be studied at leisure thereafter to detect any possible infractions that might have escaped notice in the heat of action. Rockingham Park tried a helicopter patrol, which followed the horses around and also made films of the race from close range. Hollywood in 1945 installed towers around the track from which movies were taken at close range, from various angles. Supplementing the regular officials, who watched over racing as a whole, that track introduced the Performance Observer system, a battery of twelve trained observers each of whom was assigned a specific horse to watch throughout the race—while the attention of the crowd and regular officials naturally tended to concentrate on horses that were in contention, every other runner, down to the last horse (and its jockey) was under surveillance at all times, to insure genuine performance throughout.

Designed originally as a "spy," the film patrol actually became a great friend to jockeys—indeed, a lifesaver—by promoting safe riding tactics. It also was a valuable educational tool; riders were able to study themselves in action, pick out mistakes and devise means of correcting them. The film also did a little spying on officials, indicating mistakes they might be

378

making, and it promoted higher-caliber performance in this field, too.

Purse distribution again made a record-breaking jump in 1946, from $32-million up to $49-million (an increase that very likely will remain a record) and there was a wealth of horses ready to run for it. Fourteen different horses earned more than $100,000 each during that season alone.

In 1946 Assault broke Gallant Fox's record for earnings in a single year; Armed set a new record for seasonal earnings in the handicap ranks and replaced Phar Lap as the world's leading money-winning gelding; Gallorette set a new record for earnings by a female of handicap age; and Stymie just kept rolling along. However, since the rivalry among these four

spilled over into the 1947 season, the other stars of 1946 will be introduced first.

Carrying on the family tradition of remarkable fillies, C. V. Whitney's First Flight was unanimous choice as best two-year-old filly, and a landslide winner in the balloting for champion two-year-old of either sex. The daughter of Mahmoud–Fly Swatter, by Dis Donc, trained by Sylvester Veitch, won five of her six races and was second in the other for earnings of $134,965. She equaled the Widener Chute record of :51 for 4½ furlongs in her debut, the Fashion Stakes; lost to Allen T. Simmons's Eternal War in the Juvenile; then won four in a row, including the Astoria, Matron and Futurity Stakes, covering the 6½ furlongs of the latter race in 1:15⅕, fastest

Hollywood Park, perennial leader among American tracks in daily average attendance.

time of the season. Her winning time of 1:08⅗ in the 6-furlong Matron Stakes was exceptional, too, although it was bettered later in the season by Bimlette, with the aid of a tailwind.

She didn't get a vote, but William Helis's Miss Kimo, by Hash, also had an impressive record, with victories in the Rosedale, Rancocas, King Neptune and divisions of the Polly Drummond and Pollyanna Stakes. Bimlette (racing in the name of John Bradley, brother of Colonel E. R. Bradley, who died that year), also won the Frizette; her stablemate, Bee Ann Mac, won the Selima; and W. H. LaBoyteaux's Pipette won the Spinaway, Colleen and Jeanne d'Arc Stakes.

Ridgewood Stable's Double Jay, a son of Balladier–Broomshot, by Whisk Broom II, trained by W. L. McCue, was voted best two-year-old colt of 1946. Never out of the money in ten starts, he won six, including the Newport, J. H. Connors Memorial, Garden State and Kentucky Jockey Club Stakes, to gather $77,550.

Mrs. Fred Hooper's Education, a speedy son of Ariel, far oustripped the other two-year-olds in earnings, winning $164,473, with ten victories in sixteen starts, among them the Hialeah Juvenile, Elementary, Prairie State Stakes, Washington Park and Breeders' Futurities, and Hawthorne Juvenile Handicap, equaling the track record of 1:10⅗ for 6 furlongs while carrying 126 pounds in the latter race. However, Double Jay beat Education by three lengths at a mile in the Kentucky Jockey Club Stakes.

Runner-up in the voting for best colt was Helis's Cosmic Bomb, who won the Arlington Futurity (beating Jet Pilot and Colonel O'F., with Education unplaced) and Cowdin Stakes (beating Colonel O'F., Brabancon, I Will, Donor and Phalanx among others). He was hotly pursued in the voting—and outrun on the track—by Bradley's Blue Border, who won the Grand Union Hotel Stakes in new track record time of 1:09⅗ for 6 furlongs (Cosmic Bomb unplaced) and beat the Helis colt by a nose in the Hopeful. Cosmic Bomb's jockey, Shelby Clark, was suspended for grabbing Blue

Border's saddlecloth in this race (Saratoga had not installed a film patrol as yet) and the colt was disqualified from second and placed last.

Other colts mentioned in the voting were Deering Howe's Donor (Sapling, World's Playground, Sanford, Champagne Stakes and Albany Handicap), Jay Paley's I Will (Great American, Wakefield, U. S. Hotel Stakes), C. V. Whitney's Phalanx (Remsen, Ardsley Handicaps, both longer than a mile) and Maine Chance Farm's Jet Pilot (Pimlico Nursery, National Stallion, Tremont Stakes and Pimlico Futurity).

On the Experimental Free Handicap, First Flight shared top weight of 126 pounds (highest ever assigned to a filly) with Cosmic Bomb and Double Jay, which ranked her 5 pounds the best with her sex allowance taken into account.

Assault was a unanimous choice as champion three-year-old, but colts in his division included such good ones as Foxcatcher Farm's Hampden (Chesapeake and Withers Stakes, and always close in the classic races); Mrs. W. M. Jeffords's pair of Mahout (Peter Pan, Jersey, Jerome Handicaps) and Natchez (Kent, Travers Stakes); John Marsch's Mighty Story (Peabody Memorial, Meadowland, Discovery Handicaps); and Maine Chance Farm's Lord Boswell (Blue Grass, Dick Welles Stakes).

In the filly division it was difficult to choose between E. R. Bradley's Bridal Flower and Louis B. Mayer's Honeymoon. Bridal Flower had the edge at the ballot box (18 to 11) and Honeymoon had the larger bank account ($193,705 to $118,530).

A daughter of Challenger II out of Bimelech's full sister, Big Hurry, trained by J. W. Smith, Bridal Flower won six times in fourteen starts; after winning the Gazelle Stakes in her own division, she beat her elders in the New Castle Handicap and a division of the Beldame, then won the Roamer Handicap from Assault.

Bridal Flower was the last Bradley champion. The noted turfman died 1946, and his racing and breeding establishment was purchased for $2,681,545 by a syndicate composed of King Ranch, Greentree Stud and Ogden Phipps. After dividing some of the horses among themselves, the syndicate resold the remainder of the estate. King Ranch retained part of the Idle Hour land for a Kentucky headquarters, and the other part was bought by Edward S. Moore, who relocated his Circle M Farm there. A weanling full brother to Busher was sold for $50,000, a record price for so young an animal, to Mrs. Elizabeth N. Graham, whose stable had nearly been wiped out earlier that year when a flash fire at Arlington Park destroyed 22 Maine Chance horses.

A daughter of Beau Pere—Panoramic, by Chance Shot, trained by Graceton Philpot, Honeymoon as a two-year-old had led an unusual parade across the finish in the California Breeders Champion Stakes, an event restricted to horses foaled in the state—the first three finishers were all owned by Mayer and sired by Beau Pere. At three, Honeymoon won the Santa Maria Stakes and Hollywood Oaks within her own classification, beat older females in the Sequoia Handicap, won the Golden State Breeders Handicap from elders of both sexes (although confined to California foals), and scored her most notable triumphs over male rivals in the Cinema Handicap (carrying 128 pounds), the Hollywood Derby and Drexel Handicap. She gained her greatest stature, however, in a race she lost; carrying equal weight of 113 pounds with Fred Astaire's five-year-old stallion Triplicate, in the 1¼-mile Hollywood Gold Cup, the filly was de-

The family act of the Parke brothers—Monte, Ivan, Charles, Burley and Vasco—continued after their riding days as four became trainers and one a racing official.

feated by only a neck in 2:00⅖, time which equaled the track record. Triplicate was a tough customer that year, as earlier in the season he had set a new track record of 2:28⅖ for 1½ miles in the San Juan Capistrano Handicap. Also, finishing a neck behind Honeymoon in the Gold Cup was Woolford Farm's five-year-old gelding, Historian, who had set a new track record of 2:01 for 1¼ miles in the Arlington Handicap, and who later equaled the world record of 2:40⅘ for 1⅝ miles in the Sunset Handicap.

Belair Stud had a formidable pair of three-year-old fillies in Bonnie Beryl (Empire City Stakes, Delaware Oaks, Comely Handicap and a division of the Jamaica) and Hypnotic (C. C. A. Oaks and Alabama Stakes). Other prominent members of the division included Helis's Earshot (Acorn Stakes, Lady Baltimore Handicap) and, to the confusion of racing fans, Hal Price Headley's Athenia and Edward Lasker's Athene, who finished one-two in the Cleopatra Handicap. Athenia also won the Misty Isle Stakes, Artful and Ladies Handicaps; Athene won the Modesty.

Perhaps the most eloquent commentary on the 1946 season lies in the fact that a horse which set six track records, all in stakes, did not earn a divisional championship. Two of the records were at the newly constructed New Jersey tracks, but the other four were accomplished at older courses and one was a world record.

George D. Widener's Lucky Draw, a five-year-old gelding by Jack High, trained by W. F. Mulholland, set new track records in the Butler Handicap at Jamaica (1³⁄₁₆ miles in 1:55⅕), Monmouth Handicap (1¼ miles in 2:01⅘), Merchants' and Citizens' Handicap at Saratoga (1³⁄₁₆ miles in 1:55⅖), Saratoga Handicap (1¼ miles in 2:01⅗), Narragansett Special (1³⁄₁₆ miles in 1:54⅗, breaking Discovery's track record and equaling Challedon's world record), and the Olympic Handicap at Atlantic City (1¼ miles in 2:02⅕, carrying 129 pounds). Lucky Draw also won the Sy-

sonby Mile in 1:35⅗ on a sloppy track, not a record, but the best time of the season at Belmont Park. Most amazing of all, the horse had not raced as a four-year-old because of a bowed tendon. His comeback netted $179,680.

In 1946, however, the champion of them all was a three-year-old colt from Texas.

ASSAULT, 1943

(Bold Venture–Igual, by Equipoise)

The first beneficiary of the hundred-grand purse policy that became popular after the war was Assault, who won three of them. The Triple Crown—worth $139,255 to Count Fleet during the war, $168,690 to Gallant Fox during the peak prewar period and $57,275 to Sir Barton long, long ago— brought $268,420 to the little Texan, and that did not constitute his entire income.

Foaled at the King Ranch, as a youngster Assault had stepped on a sharp object and run it through the wall of his hoof. He developed a peculiar gait that stayed with him even after the pain had long since disappeared, and his right front foot never grew to normal size. The wall was so thin it was difficult to find enough room to anchor a nail, and throughout his career shoeing him was a ticklish business.

As a two-year-old he had been what horsemen describe as "better than an empty stall," but he squeezed into the top twenty on the Experimental Free Handicap, after two wins in nine starts, one of them by a nose in the Flash Stakes.

The Experimental Free Handicap No. 1 (by this time two races had been inaugurated to test the previously theoretical weights) was Assault's first outing at three. He won by four and a half lengths, followed up with a victory in the Wood Memorial by two and a quarter lengths in a leisurely 1:46⅗ for 1¹⁄₁₆ miles and next ran fourth in the Derby Trial. Trainer Max Hirsch blamed this loss on himself, as the colt had been equipped with Oregon boots, which had filled with mud. (Although

Assault, the 1946 champion with jockey Warren Mehrtens.

Assault's running action did not include the limp he displayed at slower gaits, he did have a tendency to strike his legs.)

No excuses were needed for his next effort, when, under jockey Warren Mehrtens, he won the Kentucky Derby from Spy Song and Hampden by eight lengths on a slow track. He had a close call in the Preakness, when he took the lead sooner than was his habit, and was all out to stave off Lord Boswell by a neck in 2:01⅖, 5 full seconds away from the track record over an officially "fast" surface. The Belmont also was a rather slow race; after stumbling at the start, Assault recovered quickly and went on to win by three lengths from

Natchez in 2:30⅘ for the 1½ miles. He made it four straight in the Dwyer, again not running fast (1¼ miles in 2:06⅘) but again not being required to, as he won by four and a half lengths.

Shipped to Chicago for the Classic, the King Ranch colt ran an unaccountably poor sixth and last as Mrs. Al Gaal's The Dude registered his only stakes victory of the year, although the winner's time of 2:02⅗ was markedly better than anything Assault had come up against in the East. Hirsch reported that the colt apparently had been in pain after the race, and tests indicated a kidney ailment, so Assault was put aside for six weeks.

383

Upon his return to competition September 7, he finished third to Mighty Story and Mahout in the Discovery Handicap, conceding them 11 and 14 pounds, respectively. Mahout, with a 12-pound pull in the weights, then beat Assault by half a length in the Jersey Handicap, after which the three-year-old money king took on older horses for the first time in the Manhattan Handicap; Stymie and Pavot were the first two across the line, as Assault shared third place with Flareback. Bridal Flower beat him in the Roamer; and Stymie and Rico Monte led him home in the Gallant Fox Handicap, to run Assault's losing streak up to six races. Arcaro was thereupon called in for consultation.

Having concluded that Assault had been making his run too early, leaving nothing in reserve with which to repel challenges in the stretch, before the Pimlico Special Hirsch instructed his new boy to "Watch Stymie . . . never mind those other horses." Arcaro carried out orders up to a point, delaying his move until Stymie loomed alongside, but thereafter he was unable to watch any rival without twisting his neck, as Assault scampered to the front. He won by six lengths from Stymie, with Bridal Flower another three lengths away third. Eight days later he closed out his campaign with a two and a half length victory over Lucky Draw in the Westchester Handicap at Jamaica, carrying equal weight on the scale, in 1:56⅖ for the 1³⁄₁₆ miles.

In the voting for Horse of the Year, Assault won out over the formidable handicap champion, Armed, in both polls.

Assault represented the high point (but by no means the last peak) in the career of his trainer, Max Hirsch, a native of Fredericksburg, Texas, who had started out as a jockey when he was ten years old, racing down Main Street of his hometown. As a rider on the fair circuit he caught the eye of John A. Morris, who hired him to work on the ranch of A. H. and D. H. Morris, owners of the enormous racing stable, trained by Wyndham Walden.

When he was a boy of twelve, Hirsch stowed away with a shipment of horses to Baltimore; the Morrises gave him a job on the track and he became a full-fledged jockey. Weight caught up with him before he reached manhood, however, and at twenty he became one of the youngest licensed trainers on record.

He saddled his first winner, Guatama, at New Orleans in 1902, and his first stakes winner was Beau Claire (named in honor of his wife, Kathryn Claire) at the Benning track in Washington, D. C. in 1909. The blackout then hit, just as Hirsch was getting started, but he survived the ordeal, and in 1917 he won the Futurity with Papp. A few years later he sold Grey Lag to Harry Sinclair for $60,000 after the colt had won the Champagne Stakes, and Hirsch was on his way to success. Before Assault came along, he had made a name for himself with such horses as Sarazen, the Belmont Stakes winner Vito; and Assault's own sire, Bold Venture, winner of the Kentucky Derby and Preakness.

Besides King Ranch, Hirsch trained for Mrs. William K. Vanderbilt, Sam Mason, George Loft, Bernard Baruch, the Swartz brothers, the Sage brothers, Admiral C. T. Grayson, George Walker, Elizabeth Tailer, Frank Hampton, Arnold Hanger, Mr. and Mrs. John W. Hanes, John A. Bell (Sr. and Jr.), Edward Lasker, John W. Marr and other patrons. He was destined to develop many more star runners in the years that followed Assault.

Hirsch developed a couple of good trainers, too. His daughter Mary (Mrs. Charles McLennan) was a pioneer of her sex in the profession, and son William J. "Buddy" Hirsch also became a noted trainer.

ARMED, 1941

(Bull Lea–Armful, by Chance Shot)

A big brown gelding from Calumet Farm, Armed, was unplaced only once in eighteen starts, and he got fourth money on that occasion. He won eleven, and in ten straight races carried 130 pounds or more. One horse in one race (Buzfuz in the Sunshine Handicap) shared equal weight with him, and was defeated. In every other start Armed was making concessions to every rival.

He earned $288,725, equaled or broke four track records, lost one race in track record and another in world record time. A good year for any horse, it was sensational for a former lead pony.

Not very promising as a two-year-old, and of studdish disposition, making it virtually impossible to train him, Armed had been sent back to the farm to be gelded. He could have been raced earlier, but Calumet was more than adequately supplied with running stock, so the ex-colt was utilized as a lead pony for a time. He came out as a three-year-old for a brief campaign of seven starts, of which he won three, for earnings of $4,850.

After finishing unplaced in his debut as a four-year-old, Armed launched a fantastic streak, extending over three seasons, of 36 successive races during which he never failed to get part of the purse. In the remainder of 1945, he won six in a row, finished second four times in succession and completed the season with four more victories. Only three of his ten wins came in stakes—a division of the Sheridan, the Washington Park Handicap and Pimlico Special (beating First Fiddle and Stymie)—and his earnings of $91,600 were not exceptional for that season. He didn't carry epic weight, his only really big burden having been 135 pounds in the Fall Highweight Handicap, in which event such packages were not unusual; Armed finished second in the renewal won by True North under 140 pounds. At the end of the year Armed was runner-up to Stymie in the voting for best handicap horse.

In 1946, Armed won his first two starts, then was second by a neck to B. A. Murphy's Concordian in the McLennan Handicap, carrying 128 pounds to 116 on the winner. In those days weights for the Widener Handicap, like those for its Western counterpart, the Santa Anita Handicap, were assigned far in advance of the running, and Armed already had been allotted 128 pounds for Hialeah's big race. Concordian, however, had gotten into the Widener with an assignment of only 109, so Armed was required to accept a 7-pound shift in favor of the horse who had just defeated him. He beat Concordian by four and a half lengths, and professional as well as amateur handicappers have been chewing their pencils over that one ever since.

At Tropical Park, with 126 pounds up, Armed took both sections of the Double Event Stakes, setting a new track record of 1:48⅗ for 1⅛ miles in the first one, and duplicating exactly this performance a week later, conceding 15 pounds to Occupy and 18 to Historian, his nearest pursuers in the two races. Shipped up to Maryland, Armed found the combination of 129 pounds and a drop back to 6 furlongs too much for him, as Bobanet (116) defeated him by more than a length in the Harford Handicap at Havre de Grace. Five days later, however, Armed picked up the same weight and set a new track record of 1:43⅕ in the 1¹⁄₁₆-mile Philadelphia Handicap, as Elpis ran second and Bobanet third. Again going up in weight and down in distance, Armed was defeated in Pimlico's 6-furlong Jennings Handicap; with 132 pounds, he finished fourth in a blanket finish to New Moon (115), Brookfield (122) and The Doge (117), beaten three necks for it all.

Under 130 pounds each time, he won the Dixie Handicap by three and a half lengths from Stymie (124) then moved up to New York and took the 1¼-mile Suburban by two and a half from Reply Paid and Stymie, before heading west for Chicago.

Armed had bounced back immediately from his previous defeats, but he lost three in a row in Chicago. The first was the same story—more weight and less distance—as, under 132 pounds, he was third in the Equipoise Mile, won by Louis Schlosser's Witch Sir (110), with Old Kentuck (106) second, Armed finishing less than a length behind the winner. Historian, with an 18-pound concession, beat him by a neck in the Arlington Handicap, won in new track record time of 2:01; then Mrs. L. S. Donovan's Fighting Frank, with 21½ pounds advantage, beat him by daylight in the 6-furlong Quick Step Stakes.

Armed won his next two starts in Chicago (both with 130 pounds up) but his experience was a factor leading to establishment of weight ceilings and maximum spreads at Arlington and Washington Parks in the future. On August 3 he won the Sheridan Handicap in 1:35, a Washington Park record for a mile. On August 21, 1946, in the Whirlaway Stakes, appropriately enough, Armed brought his life-time earnings up to $342,875, thereby replacing Phar Lap as the world's richest gelding. On Labor Day he set a new track record of 2:01 in the Washington Park Handicap, which he won easily by nearly four lengths.

His trip to Rhode Island, where, still at 130 pounds, he finished third to Lucky Draw and Pavot (both at 123) in the world record Narragansett Special, closed out Armed's campaign. As was true of the horses who were to join him in the race for the top of the financial rankings, however, his career still had several seasons left to run.

STYMIE, 1941

(Equestrian–Stop Watch, by On Watch)

Stymie was the "people's horse" to end them all. There were several reasons for this: his bright chestnut coat; his thrilling come-from-behind tactics, his proud carriage (he ran with his head high, and appeared to sail majestically past his rivals), the fact that his owner came from Brooklyn, and the knowledge that he represented the rejected stone who made good.

Armed beating Honeymoon and With Pleasure in the Washington Park Handicap.

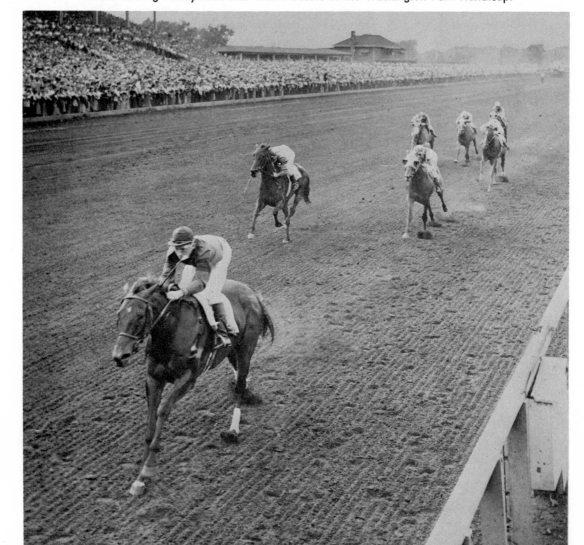

His ancestry was a factor, too, as he combined the blood of two popular favorites, Equipoise and Man o' War. Officially, Stymie was bred by Max Hirsch, the dam's owner of record at the time he was foaled, but actually Stop Watch had been turned over to King Ranch, without the formality of transferring papers, before he was born. The mating which produced Stymie was an example of the "line breeding" with which King Ranch owner Robert J. Kleberg, Jr. had been successful in developing the Santa Gertrudis breed of cattle—doubling up strong strains. Stymie's sire was by Equipoise out of a Man o' War mare; his dam also was by a stallion from the Domino line out of a mare by Man o' War— and, moreover, Stymie had two fairly close crosses to Broomstick. His was an American pedigree, with no foreign animals within the first three generations, a very unusual feature considering the fashion of imported bloodstock. (One of Stymie's great granddams had been foaled abroad, but she was of American parentage.)

These characteristics went unrecognized for a long time, however. Jacobs claimed Stymie in his wife's name for $1,500 in the colt's third start. He raced ten more times—beginning with a frustrating string of five successive seconds— for his new owner before winning, and even after that he continued to run in claiming events. Ten times Jacobs gave other owners (including King Ranch) an opportunity to second-guess him, and there were no takers.

Stymie more than paid for his oats in his first two seasons ($52,260), but principally through hard work; he started fifty-seven times, won only seven, and although he placed in stakes, he did not win any. At the end of 1944 he was turned out for a rest, which was extended by the shutdown in 1945. He emerged a different horse.

In nineteen starts at four he was out of the money but twice, winning nine of them to top the handicap division in the championship poll and in earnings, as has been noted. His first

stakes victory was in the Grey Lag Handicap, in which he beat Alex Barth by half a length, getting a 5-pound concession. With a 13-pound pull in the weights he was unable to handle Devil Diver in the Suburban, and Olympic Zenith beat him in the Queens County, with Stymie making the concession of 12 pounds. He met Devil Diver again in the Brooklyn, getting 16 pounds this time, and the earlier decision was reversed. This was the last time Stymie received a large concession.

During the remainder of 1945, he won the Butler Handicap, Saratoga Cup (beating Olympic Zenith at level weights), Continental and Westchester Handicaps; finished second in the Yonkers Handicap; and third in the Whitney Stakes, Merchants' and Citizens' Handicap and Jockey Club Gold Cup before meeting Armed for the first time in the Pimlico Special. The Calumet gelding won by four lengths from First Fiddle, with Stymie third and Gallorette fourth; however, Armed retired after that race and Stymie went on to score two of his most notable victories, the first time in his life he won two in a row. In the Riggs Handicap, Stymie beat First Fiddle and Pot o' Luck, and then he wound up his season with a stunning eight-length victory in the 2½-mile Pimlico Cup Handicap, beating Pot o' Luck and Trymenow, under 128 pounds, his first attempt to carry more than scale weight.

Stymie was given another rest prior to the 1946 season, and the formula worked again. As a five-year-old he was even more consistent than he had been the previous season, as he won eight races and was unplaced but once in twenty starts to earn $238,650. He definitely was no match for Armed, losing to the champion handicap runner on both occasions they met, receiving a concession each time—in the Dixie and Suburban Handicaps.

In his five meetings with Lucky Draw whoever had the weight advantage prevailed. Stymie had the misfortune to run into the Widener gelding when he was in his record-

Stymie, "the people's horse," with jockey Bobby Permane.

breaking streak, and concede him weight in the bargain. He lost to Lucky Draw, making concessions as follows: Butler Handicap (21 pounds), Monmouth Handicap (15 pounds) and Saratoga Handicap (5 pounds). However, in the Gallant Fox Handicap, when Lucky Draw had to concede him 3 pounds, Stymie was the winner in new track record time, as Lucky Draw was unplaced. Stymie also outfinished Lucky Draw in the Wilson Stakes while carrying less weight, although neither won.

With other rivals, Gallorette, Pavot, Snow Boots, King Dorsett and Assault, Stymie swapped decisions back and forth.

Stymie's stakes victories in 1946 included the Grey Lag Handicap (127 pounds, tying the Jamaica track record of 1:49⅗ for 1⅛ miles); Whitney Stakes; a walkover in the Saratoga Cup followed by wins in the Edgemere and

Manhattan Handicaps (the only time he won three races in succession during the same season); the New York Handicap under 128 pounds and the Gallant Fox (126 pounds, new Jamaica track record of 2:42⅘ for 1⅝ miles). He was second in the Dixie, Brooklyn, Monmouth Handicaps, Jockey Club Gold Cup and Pimlico Special; third in the Suburban, Sussex, Butler and Saratoga Handicaps. His sole unplaced effort came in the Wilson Stakes, in which he finished fifth, but was beaten by less than a length.

Like his fellow Texan, Assault, Stymie represented a landmark in the career of his trainer. Jacobs was firmly entrenched in history with his record of having led the nation in number of winners eleven seasons—including seven in succession—and his record (at the time) of 177 winners during the 1936 season. However, those feats had been attained with mostly

388

claiming horses, and the development of Stymie from a selling plater into a stakes star wrought a similar change in his trainer's career. In 1945, when Stymie blossomed, Jacobs disappeared from the top of the list of leading trainers according to number of races won; in 1946, as Stymie continued on his way, the Brooklyn redhead appeared at the top of the money list for the first time. The salmon pink and emerald green of Mrs. Jacobs, as well as the scarlet and white of Jacobs's frequent partner, Colonel Isidor Bieber, were to be seen in stakes races (and in winner's circles) more and more often in the future, later being joined by the colors of daughter Patrice Jacobs. The Jacobs success story was not confined to the track, for he developed a highly successful breeding setup also.

GALLORETTE, 1942

(Challenger II–Gallette, by Sir Gallahad III)

In 1955, in connection with the launching of its "Distaff Big Three" series of rich races for fillies and mares, Delaware Park sponsored a poll among members of the American Trainers Association to determine the ten greatest female runners in American history. When the votes had been counted, the name of Gallorette led all the rest.

It is rather ironic that Gallorette should be associated with a scheme to promote bigger purses for her sex—but eminently fitting. Since her time, fillies and mares have received greater consideration in the allocation of purse money (although not in proportion to their population, for, after all, they do constitute half the breed), but in her day such pickings were slim. There were a number of stakes events set aside exclusively for two- and three-year-old fillies, but beyond that age it was by and large a man's world. The big purses for horses older than three were wide open, and an ambitious filly or mare had to make her way against male rivals. (The first $100,000 race restricted to females—the New Castle Handicap, forerunner of the Delaware Handicap—did not come into being until long after Gallorette retired.)

Gallorette's dam, a non-winner in two dimensions (on the flat and over jumps) had once been sold for $250 and used as a hack. When the rage for daughters of Sir Gallahad III as prospective broodmares was in full swing, trainer Preston Burch bought Gallette and tried to race her. Faced with the familiar dilemma—if he ran her for too low a price someone would claim her because of her bloodlines, and if he ran her any other way she could not win—he retired her. W. L. Brann at the time was seeking to duplicate the pedigree nick that had produced Challedon (by Challenger II out of a Sir Gallahad mare) and Burch entered into an agreement with him whereby Gallette would be sent to the Brann stallion and they would alternate ownership of the resulting foals. Brann hit the jackpot, for the first foal was Gallorette.

She was turned over to Edward A. Christmas, member of a noted family of Maryland horsemen, for training. A big, growthy filly (16 hands 1 inch at maturity) she wasn't started as a two-year-old until September, and her juvenile campaign consisted of eight starts, of which she won three, and was never out of the money. At two, Gallorette won no stakes, but was second in the Maryland Futurity (limited to native foals) and third in the Selima.

As a three-year-old the big chestnut Amazon opened the season with a victory over ultimate Kentucky Derby winner, Hoop, Jr., then took on colts in the Wood Memorial, finishing second to Jeep. In her own category, she won the Acorn Stakes, Pimlico Oaks and Delaware Oaks in quick succession, in the process beating virtually all the Eastern fillies of consequence. Resuming her jousts with colts, she was nosed out by Wildlife in the Dwyer, while carrying the same weight, then won the Empire City Stakes from Belmont winner Pavot and others. Efforts were made to arrange a match between Gallorette and Busher at this point, but it never

Bert Morgan

Gallorette winning the 1948 Whitney Stakes.

materialized, which probably was just as well since Gallorette tailed off thereafter, failing to win in six subsequent starts, which included fourths in Stymie's Westchester Handicap and Armed's Pimlico Special.

In 1946 Gallorette started out by getting fourth money in Fighting Step's Excelsior and Stymie's Grey Lag Handicap, after which she won the Metropolitan from Sirde and First Fiddle, with Fighting Step, Polynesian and Buzfuz among the also-rans. Against her own sex she won the overnight Nimba Handicap easily, but in the Top Flight Handicap, carrying 128 pounds, she finished fifth, conceding 15 pounds to the winner, Sicily. A win in an overnight race and a second to Pavot in the Sussex Handicap led up to her most celebrated struggle with Stymie.

For the 1¼-mile Brooklyn Handicap June 22 Gallorette carried 118 pounds against 128 on Stymie, a 5-pound difference according to the scale. After following the pace for a mile, Gallorette (J. D. Jessop) and Stymie (Hedley Woodhouse) launched their bids virtually simultaneously, the stallion coming from farther back. According to Jessop, Stymie at one point

during the stretch drive got his head in front —which usually was the end for his rivals— but the filly would not quit and lasted to win by a neck.

Gallorette's other stakes victories that year were in the Bay Shore Handicap (giving 4 pounds actual weight to runner-up King Dorsett) and against her sex in a division of the Beldame (giving 13 pounds to runner-up War Date). Against male rivals, she was second in the Butler (by a head to Lucky Draw, who set another of his track records, while in receipt of 11 pounds actual weight; Stymie third), Wilson Stakes (by a neck to Pavot, carrying equal weight on the scale), Edgemere Handicap (to Stymie, conceding him 2 pounds actual weight) and Sysonby Purse, the latter technically not a stakes event, but worth $16,500 to winner Lucky Draw. The Brann filly also ran third in the Massachusetts Handicap for seasonal earnings of $159,160, by far the largest sum ever won by a female racing under handicap conditions. She was a near-unanimous choice as champion handicap filly, the only dissenting vote going to Louis B. Mayer's Be Faithful (Vanity and Beverly Handicaps).

CHAPTER FIFTY-SEVEN

URING 1947, FOR THE ONLY time in history, four different horses were listed as the world's leading money winner at one time or another—and, if distaff leaders are considered in a separate category, no less than six ultimate financial champions were under colors during the season. The colors were mostly devil's red and blue.

Calumet Farm's Whirlaway, the horse who had made those colors famous before he retired with record earnings of $561,161, still was the leader at the beginning of the year, but it was generally anticipated that he would be dethroned some time during the season—most probably by Stymie, who had finished out 1946 less than $50,000 away. Assault needed $120,000 to make it, and considering the normal tailing off in the income of rich three-year-olds when they become four and fall into the hands of the handicapper, it would require a bit of doing, since Assault had not been that sensational at three. As for Armed, he was a gelding and had lots of time.

Stymie also was in the handicap division, but he got better as he got older, contrary to all custom. As it turned out, he actually did win more money as a six-year-old than during any other season.

Whatever reservations had been held concerning Assault's intrinsic quality were dissipated as he opened his four-year-old season with five straight handicap victories, carrying more than scale weight in each, and extending his string of stakes, carried over from the previous season, to seven.

After a layoff of nearly six months, he came out for the 1⅛-mile Grey Lag Handicap under top weight of 128 pounds, to win by a neck from the seasoned Lets Dance (110) in 1:49⅗, just a tick off the track record. Stymie, making his second start of the year and carrying 126 pounds, finished fourth in his favorite event. (Stymie had won the Grey Lag twice, and each victory was a landmark in his career; his first stakes win, in 1945, and his first track record, 1946.)

Assault then moved down to Pimlico, where he won the Dixie Handicap under 129 pounds, beating the formidable South American stayer, Rico Monte, while conceding him 9 pounds. The next day, up in New York, Stymie won the Metropolitan Handicap and moved closer to the earnings record; one good purse would do it.

In the Suburban, however, Assault, carrying 130 pounds, won by two lengths from Natchez (120), with another tough South American, Talon, third under 113. Stymie was fourth, beaten ten lengths under 126 pounds.

It was the King Ranch colt who emerged as challenger now, and on June 21 Assault completed his blitz, winning the Brooklyn Handicap under 133 pounds by three lengths from Stymie (124) to become the world's leading money winner with total earnings of $576,680.

Meanwhile, Stymie had picked up a second to Gallorette in the Queens County Handicap, and subsequent wins in the Questionnaire and Sussex Handicaps, the latter in new track record time at Delaware, put him on top July 5. A week later, however, he met Assault for the fourth time that year and an historic battle ensued.

Assault had been assigned 135 pounds for the 1 3/16-mile Butler Handicap, against 126 on

Hialeah Clubhouse, 1925 season.

Stymie, 121 on Rico Monte, 117 on Gallorette and 111 on Risolater. Kleberg and Hirsch accepted the assignment, and Assault went to the post. The field being essentially a collection of stretch runners, there was no early pace to speak of; the first 6 furlongs were run in 1:13⅘, the mile in 1:38⅗. As they turned for home, Gallorette, Assault and Stymie made their runs, and the King Ranch colt became sandwiched between the other pair. Having literally to bull his way into contention, overcoming interference from Gallorette, he refused to flinch from the tight quarters, and under a masterful ride by Arcaro, Assault went on to win by a head from Stymie, thereby regaining his crown. The time of 1:56⅗ was the fastest of the year at Jamaica.

If the polls had closed at this point, Assault might have been elected Horse of the Decade; as it was, he did not make Horse of the Year.

Armed began the 1947 season before either of his chief rivals. He won four straight in Florida, including the McLennan and Widener Handicaps under top weight. In the former race he carried 130 pounds, conceding 12 to runner-up Reaping Reward, winner of the previous year's American Derby; and in the Widener he carried 129 pounds to a new track record of 2:01⅗, spotting 7 pounds to Talon and 14 to Lets Dance. It was his second straight victory in the Widener, and it continued what

was to be a remarkable monopoly by Calumet Farm of this particular race, begun by Bull Lea and continued by his descendants.

A flight to California for the Santa Anita Handicap proved futile, as the gray Chilean ghost Olhaverry (116) charged from far back to victory while Armed (130) finished fifth, behind Stitch Again (112), Pere Time (108) and See-tee-see (114). Armed lost it all by less than two and a half lengths in the blanket finish—the first time in 37 races he had failed to share in the purse.

Returning to Florida, on March 22 Armed won the Gulfstream Park Handicap with 129 pounds in new track record time of 2:01⅗. Before either of the others had left the barn, he amassed nearly $100,000, passed Assault and was breathing down Stymie's neck. In May, Atlantic City offered a $50,000 purse, winner take all, for a special race among the Big Three, provided all participated. What with the difficulty attached to guaranteeing the appearance of a specific horse, ready to run, on a specified date in the future, conventional two-horse matches are hard enough to arrange. Three-horse contests are that much more so, and this one never came off. On June 5—and timing is important, since some acrimony resulted from the affair as it finally was consummated—a revised offer was made that applied only to Armed and Assault. This one did not occur either, but it set the pattern for subsequent offers, by Washington Park and Belmont Park, in which Stymie was eased out of the picture. At this particular juncture the Jacobs horse had lost four of his five starts, including two defeats by Assault while receiving a weight concession. Morover, he never had defeated Armed in their encounters of previous seasons.

However, before the big match finally did materialize, the cages of both principals had been rattled. In Chicago, Armed once more found the distance too short and the weight too high—not to mention the company being too fast—as, carrying 132 pounds, he was defeated in the Domino Handicap at Arlington Park by Brolite Farm's With Pleasure, who, with an 18-pound concession, ran the 6 furlongs in 1:09⅘. Armed, of course, had been out of action three months, but a week later, with Armed down to 130 and With Pleasure up to 116, the Brolite Farm (Oscar Breault) colt won by a neck in the Equipoise Mile, covering the distance in 1:35.

Armed took his revenge July 4 in the Stars and Stripes Handicap, packing 130 pounds over the 9 furlongs in new track record time of 1:49⅕, as With Pleasure, carrying 13 pounds less, finished second. Again loaded with 130 pounds, Armed won the 1¼-mile Arlington Handicap July 19; but early in August, as he went up in weight to 132, he went down in defeat again to With Pleasure, who beat him in the 1-mile Sheridan Handicap, this time with only an 8-pound advantage.

The ceiling at the co-ordinated Chicago tracks was 132 pounds for distances at a mile or less, but 130 over longer hauls, so Armed's burden was lightened 2 pounds for the Whirlaway Stakes August 20, and With Pleasure was assigned scale weight of 126. Armed defeated him by half a length in a thrilling duel, setting a new track record of 1:48⅗ for the 1⅛ miles.

Ben Lindheimer meanwhile had offered $100,000 for an Armed–Assault match, still ignoring Stymie, although the Jacobs horse had come back after his defeats to hand Assault his first loss of the year, at level weights in the Gold Cup at Belmont Park July 19. This race, however, had been at 1⅝ miles, a distance particularly to Stymie's liking, whereas the proposed match was at 1¼ miles, and in their encounters at medium distances Assault always had been the winner. The match had been scheduled for August 30, but shortly after his arrival in Chicago, Assault came out of a work in unsatisfactory condition and it was cancelled.

Armed then liquidated his account with With Pleasure; picking up his customary 130 pounds, he won the Washington Park Handicap September 1 by more than three lengths, as Honeymoon (111) insinuated herself between the arch rivals to take second by one and a quarter lengths from With Pleasure (123). Then it was on to the East for the long-awaited first meeting with Assault, which finally had been fixed for Belmont Park on September 27.

A lot of trainers detest the thought of match races, and the one between Armed and Assault is a good illustration why. It is one thing to stage an impromptu match between a couple of horses racing fit and campaigning on the same circuit, whose paths probably would cross in the normal course of things—e.g. Clang and Myrtlewood—but quite another to put on an extravaganza at long range. An owner can withdraw from a conventional race without causing a furor if his horse does not appear to be just right, but in a match the pressure to stay in is fierce, since one scratch means everything is cancelled and the public is disappointed.

The monumental meeting between Armed and Assault began to tarnish weeks before the great moment. Following his victory over Assault in the Gold Cup, Stymie won the Massachusetts Handicap July 30 and regained the financial leadership. He continued to click along in his usual fashion—winning and losing, but making money all the time—a third to Rico Monte and Gallorette in the Whitney Stakes, a win in the Aqueduct Handicap (carrying 132 pounds).

This took the frosting off the match, which had been expected to settle monetary supremacy, among other questions, because Stymie was now more than $100,000 ahead of both Armed and Assault. Regardless of which horse won the exclusive race, he would not catch Stymie in the pocketbook standings. A great clamor arose at this point to declare Stymie in, but even while it was in progress Stymie (134) was defeated again, by the mare Elpis (114), in the Edgemere Handicap. Bay Meadows also offered to stage a $100,000 race involving any or all three eastern horses against the West Coast star, Cover Up.

Five days before the match Armed was defeated by Polynesian in a 6-furlong overnighter. The morning of that day Assault began to limp on his "good" front leg, and it was found that a splint, which had been there for some time, was bothering him. He responded to treatment, and, after issuing a statement concerning his colt's condition, Kleberg decided to let him run. It was agreed among those concerned that it should be a betless exhibition, however, and the purse donated to charity.

On September 27 the match went off, both horses at scale weight of 126 pounds. Armed led throughout the 1¼ miles, to win easily by eight lengths. Assault gave what he could, getting within two lengths of the leader at the end of a mile, but Arcaro did not pursue the issue when it became apparent the cause was hopeless.

Half an hour later that same afternoon, at the same track, Stymie went to the post for the Manhattan Handicap. Top weighted at 132 pounds, he finished second by one and a half lengths to Rico Monte, who carried 123.

Assault's splint led to his immediate retirement for the season. Armed became the world's leading money winner when he brought his earnings up to $761,500 by winning the Sysonby Mile October 9, then he was retired for the year after an unexpected third in the Pimlico Special, won by his stablemate, Fervent, from Cosmic Bomb.

Armed's tenure as world's leading money winner was the briefest on record. Less than three weeks after he took over, Stymie, who had run a couple of uncharacteristically poor races in between, found his legs again and won the Gallant Fox Handicap from Talon and Miss Grillo on October 25 to boost his bankroll to $816,060. He went into winter quarters after starting once more, unplaced.

For the 1947 season, however, the honors definitely went to Armed, who had set another record of $376,325 for winnings by a member

Trainer Max Hirsch and owner Robert J. Kleberg of King Ranch.

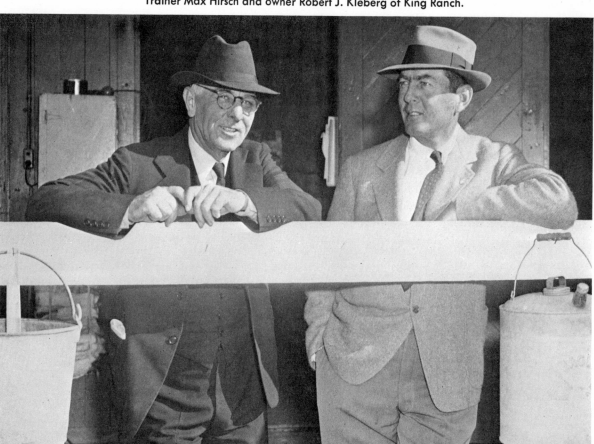

of the handicap division. He was elected Horse of the Year by a heavy majority, the only dissenting votes being two cast for Assault and one for Stymie.

All three of 1947's biggest stars raced on for two or three more seasons, but none approached his former stature, although Stymie, the horse who did best in the late stages, came closest.

Armed continued through age nine, but never won another stakes event. Assault (who proved to be sterile when tried at stud) raced through age seven, and the Brooklyn Handicap was his only stakes victory during his last three seasons of campaigning. Stymie had a fairly good season as a seven-year-old, winning the Metropolitan, Aqueduct and Sussex Handicaps (breaking his own track record)—and only once failing to earn part of the purse—but he cracked a sesamoid in mid-season. Brought back at eight, in an attempt to make him the first millionaire, he failed to win and was retired.

The summarized records of the three horses who for a time wore the world's financial crown are as follows:

Horse	Starts	Won	2nd	3rd	Unpl.	Earnings
Armed	81	41	20	10	10	$817,475
Assault	42	18	6	7	11	$675,470
Stymie	131	35	33	28	35	$918,485

Who was the best? That question will be argued forever on the basis of their over-all careers, although in their actual encounters Armed never lost to either Stymie or Assault.

Stymie, the top money winner, never was able to win more than three races in succession (and that included a walkover). Countless horses have done better than that, but then Stymie put three top *seasons* together, and very few horses have matched that feat. In his races against Assault, there was a definite break at 1¼ miles; up to that point the younger horse was the winner, beyond it Stymie.

Armed never won beyond 1¼ miles, one reason being that he never raced farther than that. Oddly, while Stymie was in general more responsive to weight changes, and Armed could run in record time with 130 pounds, Stymie won under 132 and Armed was stopped cold every time he attempted to carry that much. On the other hand, Armed's efforts under 132 pounds coincided with changes from longer distances to sprints, which is a difficult transition in itself. In the ability to carry weight, neither horse could match Assault's performances as a four-year-old in 1947.

In their later seasons, members of the Big Three bumped into one another a few times, but in races that were won by other horses. A summary of their unusual rivalry, including just races which resulted in victory for one of the horses concerned, is as follows:

Date	Event	Distance	Winner (Weight)	Loser (Weight)	Margin
November 17, 1945	Pimlico Special	1³⁄₁₆ miles	Armed (126)	Stymie (126), 3rd	6 lengths
May 10, 1946	Dixie Handicap	1³⁄₁₆ miles	Armed (130)	Stymie (124), 2nd	3½ lengths
May 30, 1946	Suburban Handicap	1¼ miles	Armed (130)	Stymie (123), 3rd	2½ lengths
September 25, 1946	Manhattan Handicap	1½ miles	Stymie (126)	Assault (116-124), 3rd	3¾ lengths
October 26, 1946	Gallant Fox Handicap	1⅝ miles	Stymie (126)	Assault (114-121), 3rd	4½ lengths
May 3, 1947	Grey Lag Handicap	1⅛ miles	Assault (128-129)	Stymie (126), 4th	2½ lengths
May 30, 1947	Suburban Handicap	1¼ miles	Assault (130-131)	Stymie (126), 4th	10 lengths
June 21, 1947	Brooklyn Handicap	1¼ miles	Assault (133-134)	Stymie (124), 2nd	3 lengths
July 12, 1947	Butler Handicap	1³⁄₁₆ miles	Assault (135)	Stymie (126), 2nd	head
July 19, 1947	Gold Cup	1⅝ miles	Stymie (126)	Assault (126), 3rd	1 length
September 27, 1947	Special Match Race	1¼ miles	Armed (126)	Assault (126), 2nd	8 lengths

Note: In the double weights opposite Assault's name, the first figure indicates the weight he actually carried, the second figure is the equivalent weight on an older horse according to the scale in effect at the time.

Not only did the handicap division monopolize the voting for Horse of the Year in 1947, but it cornered the market on broken financial records. Besides her victory over Stymie in the Queens County Handicap, five-year-old Gallorette also won the Wilson Stakes, mile in 1:35⅗, and finished second six times, third five times in added money competition, mostly against male rivals, to earn a further $90,275 and pass up Busher as the leading money-winning female thoroughbred in the world. Gallorette raced on at six the next year (during which she was sold to Mrs. Marie A. Moore) adding the Carter Handicap, Wilson and Whitney Stakes to her trophy cabinet to retire finally after 72 starts, 21 wins, 20 seconds and 13 thirds, with $445,535.

Zack T. Addington's Cover Up, trained by Ross Brinson, had an excellent year in 1947, winning eight races, five of them stakes, and $179,150. A four-year-old son of the unraced stallion, Alibhai, when he was right Cover Up was positively awesome in the ease with which he loped away from his opposition. He equaled the Tanforan track record of 1:52 for 1⅛ miles in the San Francisco Handicap, and in the Hollywood Gold Cup set a new track record of 2:00 for 1¼ miles, which also tied Whisk Broom II's disputed American mark for that distance and proved that the feat was possible—at Hollywood Park at any rate. The argument whether the distance could be run that fast at Belmont continued for many more years.

Pan de Azucar's Olhaverry, the senior señor (eight years old) from Chile who shut out Armed in the rich Santa Anita Handicap, also won the Argonaut Handicap in 1:42, a Hollywood Park record for 1¹⁄₁₆ miles. He was one of several notable performers that year from South America, three others of which were trained for North American owners by the tall, suave Argentinian, Horatio Luro. Arnold Hanger's Rico Monte beat Stymie at his own game several times as he won the Whitney Stakes and Saratoga Handicap at 1¼ miles, the Manhattan at 1½ miles and the New York Handicap at 2¼ miles. Mill River Stable's Miss

Cover Up, the western handicap star of the 1947 season. (Photo taken at age 11.)

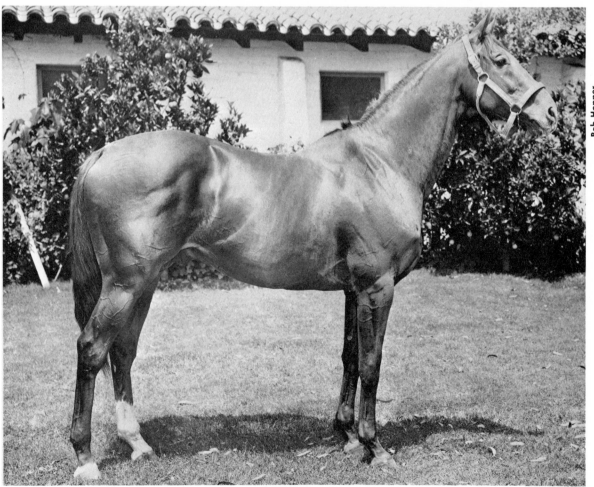

Grillo won the $1\frac{1}{8}$-mile Black Helen and Diana Handicaps, $1\frac{5}{8}$-mile Governor Bowie Handicap and $2\frac{1}{2}$-mile Pimlico Cup Handicap.

Carrying 124 pounds, she won the last named race so easily (the official margin was forty lengths) that jockey Conn McCreary stood straight up to grin and wave at the crowd in the last yards. It might have been that McCreary, known for his Garrison finishes, had suffered a touch of agoraphobia under such unfamiliar conditions, or perhaps he had battle fatigue from being so long in the saddle, for Miss Grillo strolled home in $4{:}29\frac{4}{5}$. She won this same event again the next year, however, in more than 15 seconds faster time, setting a world record of $4{:}14\frac{3}{5}$. Richard N. Ryan's Talon won the All American Handicap, dead-heated with Loyal Legion in the Merchants' and Citizens' and won the $1\frac{3}{4}$-mile Saratoga Cup. The general effect of this Latin domination of distance racing led U. S. breeders to reflect on the stamina of native stock.

Certainly there was no such concern regarding speed. Among older horses Honeymoon, winner of the Vanity Handicap in fast time, also set a world record of $1{:}21\frac{4}{5}$ for 7 furlongs at Hollywood Park which was equaled by Buzfuz three weeks later. Up at Golden Gate, Artillery and See-tee-see ran a dead heat for the Golden State Breeders Handicap in world record time of $1{:}41\frac{3}{5}$ for $1\frac{1}{16}$ miles. Later in the year Count Speed (a full brother to Count Fleet) lowered it to 1:41. On that same day, at the same track, the English-bred Fair Truckle set a new American record of $1{:}08\frac{2}{5}$ for six furlongs. With Pleasure (never out of the money in sixteen starts), besides his three victories over Armed, won the Quick Step Stakes at Washington Park in $1{:}09\frac{4}{5}$; the next month Rippey, another of that season's better handicap runners, lowered it by $\frac{2}{5}$-second. Among numerous other track records by various horses, Burning Dream set one of $1{:}48\frac{1}{5}$ for 9 furlongs in the American Handicap at Hollywood.

Elpis, the mare who beat Stymie in the Edgemere Handicap, also won the New Castle, Comely, Molly Pitcher, Hannah Dustin and Miss America Handicaps against her sex. Be Faithful was quite active for a mare, starting 23 times; while some of the California horses lost their form when shipped to the Midwest, she scored her major victories in Chicago, the Beverly Handicap and Hawthorne Gold Cup. Bridal Flower, one of the fillies obtained by King Ranch in the division of E. R. Bradley stock, won three stakes.

The Triple Crown went three ways in 1947. Maine Chance Farm's Jet Pilot, ridden by Eric Guerin, led from start to finish in the Kentucky Derby, holding on to stave off the closing rush of C. V. Whitney's Phalanx, who charged from fifth place in the stretch and just missed by a head. Calumet Farm's Faultless was only another head away in third place. Faultless, ridden by Doug Dodson, won the Preakness

Phalanx, champion three-year-old of 1947.

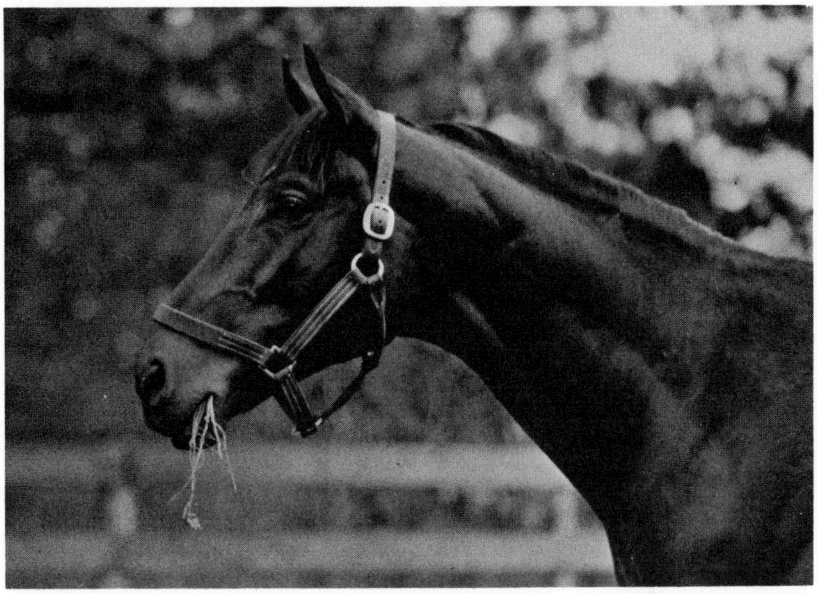

Marshall Hawkins

from E. O. Stice & Sons' Santa Anita Derby winner, On Trust, as Phalanx was third and Jet Pilot fourth. Phalanx, ridden by South American jockey, Ruperto Donoso, won the Belmont Stakes by five lengths from Tide Rips and Tailspin. A notable exception to the evident trend away from stamina among native-breds, the tall bay son of Pilate, out of Jacola, by Jacopo, trained by Syl Veitch, also won a division of the Wood Memorial, the Dwyer and Empire City Stakes, and beat older horses Talon and Stymie at weight for age in the 2-mile Jockey Club Gold Cup. Phalanx, un-placed only once during 1947, was voted champion three-year-old of the season in both polls.

Runner-up in the voting was Calumet's Fervent, a chestnut son of Blenheim II who was small but strong. He missed the classics because he had been fired for a splint in February, but he made up for lost time after he did begin running in June. In ten starts, he was never out of the money, and he won the Skokie Handicap, Dick Welles Stakes and American Derby, plus the Pimlico Special.

Cosmic Bomb, third in the voting, beat his fellow sophomores in the Drexel, Discovery, Roamer (128 pounds) Handicaps and Lawrence Realization, and won the Trenton Handicap from his elders in new track record time of 1:48⅗ for 9 furlongs. Faultless, winner of the Flamingo, Blue Grass Stakes, Derby Trial and Withers, besides the Preak-ness, also received a vote in the poll. Jet Pilot won the Jamaica Handicap before his Derby victory, but he bowed a tendon after the Withers later in May and was sent to stud. Double Jay, ranked in a tie for head of the class the previous season, won the Jersey, Ben Franklin, Riggs and Prince George Autumn Handicaps as a three-year-old.

But Why Not, another filly acquired by King Ranch from the Bradley estate, was the leading distaff money winner of 1947, with $225,300, and a landslide choice in the voting for best three-year-old filly. In fact, she was so good

that she also nosed out Gallorette in the handi-cap division poll. The daughter of Blue Lark-spur won the Pimlico Oaks, Acorn and Alabama Stakes within her own classification, beat her elders in the Arlington Matron and a division of the Beldame Handicap, and knocked off Fervent and Cosmic Bomb in the Arlington Classic. She lost only two races to members of her sex, and in return defeated both her conquerors more than once.

Second in the poll was Mrs. Walter M. Jeffords's Snow Goose, who won the other division of the Beldame and, with the aid of an 8-pound concession, beat But Why Not in the 1½-mile Ladies Handicap, as such stalwart older mares as Miss Grillo and Gallorette finished behind the top pair. Miss Kimo won the Cleopatra and Artful Handicaps, Misty Isle Stakes in new track record time of 1:22⅕ for 7 furlongs at Washington Park, and Vineland Handicap in 1:42⅗, equaling the Garden State Park record for 1¹⁄₁₆ miles. Circle M Farm's Cosmic Missile won the Jasmine, Ash-land, Gazelle Stakes and Tambour Handicap, and was second to J. J. Watts's Harmonica in the C. C. A. Oaks, in which Snow Goose fin-ished third and But Why Not fourth.

Ben Whitaker's Carolyn A., named for Eddie Arcaro's daughter, beat colts in the Louisiana Derby, but Phalanx—ridden by an unsentimental Arcaro—defeated her in the Wood Memorial. First Flight, champion of the generation as a two-year-old, won only two of six starts at three, one of them the Monmouth Oaks, however.

What with the performance of Assault, plus the prize horses the stable had drawn in the distribution of former E. R. Bradley stock, it became fashionable in 1947 to speculate upon what a fabulous record King Ranch would have compiled if only Stymie had not been allowed to slip away in his youth. King Ranch had a good enough record as it was, and if Stymie, too, had been sporting the brown silks with the famous white running W cattle brand, the stable would have exceeded a million dollars in earnings. Nevertheless, that would not have altered the standings, for Calumet Farm in 1947 became the first stable in history to pass that figure, as forty wearers of the devil's red and blue gathered in $1,402,436, more than double the previous high for a stable (which also had been set by Calumet). One of the few financial records to survive an appreciable length of time in the postwar era, this still was standing unmolested at the end of the 1963 season.

Calumet also bred the winners of $1,807,-432, almost double the previous record (which also had been held by Calumet); home stallion Bull Lea sired winners of $1,259,718, almost double the previous record; and trainer H. A. "Jimmy" Jones saddled winners of $1,334,805, well more than double the previous record. Jones's mark also still was high at the end of 1963.

Although Calumet was well represented in the three-year-old and older divisions—with Twosy, Pep Well and Pot o' Luck, in addition to the previously mentioned Armed, Fervent and Faultless—in the two-year-old division the stable was overwhelming. Citation was a unanimous choice as champion colt, and nearly so in the voting for over-all honors, as the only dissenting ballot was cast for his stablemate, the champion filly Bewitch.

Citation lost only one race, but there were extenuating circumstances. As is true of all breeds of animals, including mankind, the female often is more precocious than the male, and Bewitch, a brown daughter of Bull Lea who fully justified her name in appearance, achieved her stature sooner than Citation. Making her debut at Keeneland April 10 she won by six lengths in :46⅕, just a tick off the track record for the Headley Course at the odd distance of 40 feet less than half a mile. Taking on colts a week later, she equaled the track record in the Thoroughbred Club Dinner Purse, and continued undefeated through five more races. She won the Debutante Stakes at Churchill Downs by eight lengths; beat colts

Bull Lea, the Calumet Farm Stallion who rewrote the record books.

again in the Hyde Park Stakes at Arlington June 16, again winning by eight lengths; set a new track record of 1:04 for 5½ furlongs as she won the Pollyanna Stakes by five lengths; won the Arlington Lassie by nearly three lengths, and the Princess Pat by exactly that margin, the latter two races being the filly equivalents to Chicago's rich futurities.

Citation meanwhile had won five straight. Four of them were overnight races, in one of which he set an Arlington Park record of :58 for 5 furlongs, and just one was an added money event, the Elementary Stakes, in which he spotted 12 pounds to runner-up Salmagundi.

When the rich Washington Park Futurity came up August 16, Calumet fired a broadside. Joining Bewitch and Citation in the salvo was Free America, whose chief claim to distinction in that company was that he was *not* undefeated (he was caught in a tangle and lost his first start in a race won by Whirl Some), another stablemate. Free America had won his next three races, including the George Woolf Memorial Stakes.

Jones was noncommital before the race, apparently not caring who came home first so long as Calumet won and they trooped across the finish one, two, three—Bewitch winning by a length from Citation, with Free America only a head farther back. Whenever a horse loses to a stablemate, the validity of the result is questioned. In the Washington Park Futurity, Citation (ridden by Steve Brooks) moved from fourth place after ½-mile, seven lengths off the pace, to make up six lengths in the final quarter. Free America (ridden by Jack Westrope) came from dead last after the first quarter, and sixth place after a half, to gain about ten lengths in the final quarter. On the other hand, Bewitch (Doug Dodson) won "ridden out"—which is to say under less than all-out effort—while the colts were described as having finished "driving." The filly won in 1:10⅗, fastest clocking registered in the event up to that time, and she carried 119 pounds, conceding actual weight to all her male rivals

except sixth-place Piet. Citation and Free America both were at 118, which amounted to a 4-pound concession on the scale. (Because of their precocity, two-year-old fillies get a sex allowance of only 3 pounds, compared to the 5 pounds allowed older females until September 1 each year.)

On the record, making up more ground than he actually did would appear to have been an impossible task for Citation, but on the track it did seem to a number of observers that he could have done so. It made no difference, as the discussion about the relative merits of the top pair soon was dissolved. Having drawn out her undefeated string to eight races, Bewitch finished first again in her next start, the Matron Stakes, but was disqualified for interfering with Ghost Run. Brookmeade Stable's Inheritance was declared the winner, Vaudeville was moved up to second and Ghost Run to third, as Bewitch was placed last. Dodson was suspended for his ride.

Ridden by Al Snider, who had been his jockey earlier in the season, Citation next won the Futurity Trial, and then the Futurity itself, beating Whirling Fox by three lengths, with Bewitch another neck away third. Conceding 1 pound to the winner and 9 to the runner-up, at no time did the filly appear capable of catching Citation. She was retired for the season after that race, and a few weeks later was fired for a popped osselet.

With Dodson up, Citation finished out the year with another win in the Pimlico Futurity, run over a muddy track. The stable picked up more Maryland money as Whirl Some, deputizing for Bewitch, won the Selima and Marguerite Stakes.

Bewitch, who would have broken Top Flight's juvenile earnings record if she had not been disqualified in the Matron, topped all 1947 two-year-olds in winnings with $213,675, and Citation led the colts with $155,680. Both Calumeteers were destined to become leading money winners of their respective sexes in the world.

Calumet couldn't be everywhere at once, and King Ranch had another Bradley-bred star in Better Self, winner of the East View Stakes and Saratoga Special, and runner-up to Citation in the Pimlico Futurity. Texan Ben Whitaker's My Request won the Juvenile, National Stallion, U. S. Hotel, Grand Union Hotel and Cowdin Stakes. C. B. Bohn and P. A. Markey's Piet won the Arlington Futurity, Richard Johnson and Spalding Lowe Jenkins Stakes. Stanley Sagner's Saggy won the Aberdeen, Ral Paar, Eastern Shore and Wakefield Stakes; the son of Swing and Sway set a new world record of :51⅖ for 4½ furlongs at Havre de Grace, although there was some question as to its accuracy since the manual clockings were slower than that registered by the electric timer. Greentree Stable's Star Bout won the Christiana, Great American and Flash Stakes; Circle M Farm's plum from the former Idle Hour stock was the Hopeful Stakes winner, Relic; and C. V. Whitney's home-bred Vulcan's Forge took the Champagne.

Ranked second to Bewitch among the juvenile fillies was Mrs. Laudy Lawrence's Bellesoeur, winner of four races in six starts, including the Spinaway and Astarita Stakes, and second in the other two—to Whitney's Ghost Run in the Demoiselle, and to E. P. Taylor's Spats in the Schuylerville Stakes.

By 1947, the wartime boom had ended, and other areas besides New York learned the hard lesson that increasing taxes hurts business. Racing underwent a general recession as sixty-three tracks reported drops in that important index, daily average mutuel handle. Purse distribution, however, was up, partially because of an increase in number of racing days, and partially because it had been predicated to some extent on the halcyon conditions of the previous year. Caught by this pinch—and other items of expense which had grown to new proportions—many tracks eliminated the bonuses to grooms and exercise boys. This action resulted in strikes; some of the dissatisfied employees allied themselves with the Teamsters Union, and the state Labor Relations Board in New York was unable to effect an amicable settlement.

The TRA (tracks) and HBPA (horsemen) did not see eye to eye on a code of conduct agreed upon by the former organization, particularly a clause which provided that acceptance of stall assignments at a race track constituted tacit approval of the purse distribution schedule. The HBPA also exchanged sharp words and threats with individual tracks, some of which objected to basing purse money on a fixed percentage of mutuel handle (a practice which eventually was to become almost standard.) A boycott was invoked against at least one track, and further squabbling resulted when some HBPA members refused to honor it.

That summer there was an outbreak of swamp fever in New England which created a panic as other tracks established embargoes against horses from that area. Approximately twenty horses died from the disease, and about

The Coaching Club at their 1947 meeting. Front row (seated): F. Ambrose Clark, Robert J. Kleberg, Lewis E. Waring, Samuel D. Riddle, William Woodward, Reginald W. Rives, George D. Widener, Cornelius V. Whitney, J. Henry Alexandre, Robert E. Strawbridge, Jr., Austen Gray and John A. Morris. Back row: William du Pont, Jr., Walter M. Jeffords, William C. Langley, John C. Clark, W. Plunket Stewart, Crispin Oglebay, F. S. von Stade, James Butler, Dunbar Bostwick, William H. Bolton, Franklin B. Voss, Reginald B. Rives, Robert J. Turnbull and Robert Goelet. Bert Morgan

as many more were destroyed on suspicion. The TRA and HBPA, working together on this problem, offered $2,000 as compensation for destruction of each horse that had been exposed; some owners accepted it, others did not, insurance rules being one of the principal objections. (H. G. Bedwell, owner of the stakes winner, Prognosis, reportedly valued at $40,000, was one of the owners who did not accept the plan, and the horse later died.)

Racing in New England was disrupted beyond recognition, particularly at Rockingham Park, where the disease was discovered. Other tracks felt the blow, and lack of sufficient entries forced Narragansett to cancel many stakes races, including the $50,000 Special. Before the panic subsided an estimated 960 horses at Rockingham had to be cleared by health authorities for shipment to other states. One of the tests was injection of blood from a suspected victim into a test animal, which involved delays of up to two months to await possible reaction.

Besides such organizations as the TRA, HBPA and the Jockeys' Guild, donations to help fight the problem were made by numerous individuals, including several stewards of the Jockey Club and Walter Annenberg, publisher of the *Daily Racing Form*.

Standing behind the impressive array of Calumet chargers who demolished all records in 1947 was a quiet, smallish man wearing rimless spectacles and a gray Homburg; to look at him one would never dream that here was the most powerful figure in American racing. Other men had achieved comparable positions of domination, but most of them at sporadic intervals, and all of them when the sport was more localized. It was not believed possible for an individual to attain an equivalent prominence—and maintain it—under modern conditions, as the scope of major racing expanded from coast to coast and border to border.

A native of Springfield, Ohio, Warren Wright (1875-1950) received his education in public schools, after which he attended business college. At fifteen he became office boy for the Calumet Baking Powder Company, and in 1899 succeeded his father, William Monroe Wright, as president. Under management by the son, the company was developed to the extent that it was sold for an estimated $40-million before the Depression. The elder Wright had begun Calumet Farm as a trotting horse establishment, but when Warren Wright inherited the place in 1931 he sold off the trotters and began collecting runners. Some years before Calumet colors became standard equipment for winner's circle ceremonies, Wright was one of the group of Chicago businessmen who rekindled Arlington Park, and in 1937 he was elected a member of the Jockey Club.

A methodical person, who approached his turf venture with the same attitude of efficiency that would apply to business, Wright sought out the best in everything, associating himself with the finest advisors, and purchasing the highest quality stock. To some extent he benefited from Depression prices—for example, the Preakness winner, Nellie Morse, later dam of Nellie Flag and a notable foundation mare, cost $6,100—but Wright could not be classified as lucky because he also paid higher prices for worthless horses. Bull Lea, his greatest bargain, was purchased as a yearling for $14,000, a modest price in view of his later accomplishments, but in 1936 that was a large sum. Only three yearlings sold higher that season (all of them bought by Mrs. Ethel V. Mars, and very few persons ever outbid her). That same year Wright joined with A. B. Hancock in the importation of Blenheim II at a cost of $225,000. Whirlaway was in the stallion's first American crop, and Calumet was on its way.

Although he had been preceded by some good ones, notably Nellie Flag (trained by B. B. Williams), Whirlaway really began the long parade of champions—Mar-Kell, Twilight Tear, Pensive, Armed, Bewitch, Citation—extending far into the future and an unmatched sequence of stable leaderships. Calumet Farm led the list of winning owners twelve times during the period 1941–1963; the first stable to win a million dollars in a single season, it had done so six times before another stable reached that level. During the same period, Calumet was leading breeder according to amount of money won fourteen times—including eleven years in succession. (It led the numerical list only once, which makes the financial record more impressive.) The first farm to breed winners of more than a million dollars, it subsequently broke this record by going over the $2-million mark, another record still not surpassed.

As is true of all big outfits, the Calumet racing string had to be curtailed to keep it down to workable size. Because of the resounding success of its own stable, the idea took hold that "Calumet never lets a good one get away," and many horsemen were wary of any animals the farm was willing to sell. Simple subtraction of the sum credited to Calumet on the owners' list from the sum credited to the farm on the breeders' list indicates that a number of good ones did get away. For example, from 1947, the stable's first million-dollar season, through 1961, Calumet bred the winners of about $20-million and owned the winners of slightly more than $13-million. The precise difference for the fifteen seasons is $6,888,798, which is to say that the farm's "culls" averaged $453,920 each year.

This does not take into account sums earned by horses Calumet stable acquired from other breeders, but the amount is insignificant, and in any case would be applied on the culls' side of the ledger.

From the time the stable began racing under its present name in 1932, which includes the formative period of low income, through the end of 1963 Calumet runners had won 1,855 races, including 412 stakes events, and $17,023,166.58.

The impressive statistics were put together by a tightly knit team, organized by Wright, extending from Ben and Jimmy Jones at the track, to manager J. Paul Ebelhardt (and later Melvin Cinnamon) at the farm and Mrs. Margaret Glass in the office. An operation that successful does not become so without certain refinements, however, and the gross stable earnings listed above, for instance, vary somewhat from official records. When a horse wins a stakes race, his purse encompasses fees from rival owners, which often include odd cents. These sums are rounded off to the nearest even dollar in official records, thus eliminating 33¢ here or adding 25¢ there in the totals. The Calumet office accounted for this money, which over the years amounts to $8.58 net.

It is said the mark of a top executive is to so arrange his program that it can be carried on in his absence. After the death of Warren Wright in 1950, Calumet Farm continued on its successful way, under the direction of his widow (who later married movie producer Gene Markey), Calumet Farm led the owners list 5 more times in 13 years, and not until 1963 did it slip from the top twenty.

Haden Kirkpatrick, editor of the *Thoroughbred Record,* summarized Wright's influence in an obituary:

> . . . he played the game the way all games should be played, with a fierce devotion to the main objective, content with nothing but paramount achievement. In a sport that has its integrity sometimes questioned, his was above the reproach of even the most scurrilous critics. The world knew, and there was never a doubt, that when the Calumets went down as they sometimes did, they went down leveling with all turrets blazing.
>
> That element of uncompromising endeavor was doubtless Warren Wright's greatest gift to American racing. For the devil red, not merely a symbol of the ultimate aristocracy of the turf, became also the proud banner of the $2 bettors. They believed in it, and they worshipped the horses that bore it. Wherever the Calumets were running, the clerks, the salesmen, the laborers could turn out in full confidence, with their little bills in their hands, secure in the knowledge that whether they rode with Wright or against him, his entry was going to blast for all the money, and intended either to get it or crack wide open trying.

The best description of the man whose success was so closely interwoven with that of Calumet Farm that no distinction is possible, lies in his nickname: Plain Ben.

Born in Parnell, Missouri, the son of Horace Jones, a banker and cattle rancher, Benjamin Allyn Jones (1882–1961) attended State Agriculture College of Colorado (later to become Colorado A & M) and was well known in his own right both as a breeder and trainer long before he joined the Calumet forces. He saddled his first winner, Errant Lady, for a $200 purse at Oklahoma City in 1909, and was an active trainer on the Southwest circuit, including Juarez in the days of Pancho Villa, as well as owner of the Jones Stock Farm. By 1913 Jones was standing the stallions Blues and Harrigan, and had thirty-two mares on the farm. He soon became one of the nation's leading breeders from the standpoint of number of winners, ranking among the top ten from 1922-1931. He enjoyed great success with the offspring of the stallion Seth (Adam–Purity, by Deceiver). There was Dolly Seth, Seth's Hope (62 wins and 101 placings in 327 starts), Senator Seth, General Seth, Colonel Seth, right on down through the ranks to Private Seth, many owned or trained by Jones, and the stallion himself was a leading sire in number of races won by his get.

In 1932, the year Calumet Farm began operating under that name, Jones took over the Woolford Farm stable, with whose Lawrin he scored his first Kentucky Derby victory in 1938. The next year, he joined Calumet and went on to shatter all records by saddling five more winners of America's most sought-after race, not to mention the numerous other records he established. After his son Jimmy assumed active management of the stable, Calumet added two more Derby winners, for a grand total of eight by the Jones boys, seven for Calumet.

As was the case with the Calumet organization in general, the transfer of the reins from Ben to Jimmy was accomplished smoothly, with no interruption in the stable's overwhelming power, and by no means the least of the senior Jones's contributions to the sport was the development of such a son.

Ben Jones was not an unquestioning subscriber to the Foxhall Daingerfield theory of complete equanimity in the presence of horses, lest nervousness or excitement be communicated to the high-spirited animals. According to Eddie Arcaro, when Hill Gail became fractious in the paddock before the 1952 Kentucky Derby, Big Ben hauled off and clouted him on the snout to "settle him down." The colt, described by the jockey as a "real nut," went on to win number six for his trainer.

On the other hand, Jones was a man of infinite patience and diligence. While some trainers maintain headquarters in the tack room (and some in the track kitchen) Jones usually could be found sitting astride a pony, staring reflectively at a set, not merely while they were working out, but during the walking to and from the track as well. Like many trainers, he was a strong believer in the value of fresh grass, and took every opportunity to graze his horses, in the infield or on whatever patch of turf was available in the barn area. This routine chore customarily is assigned to an assistant, but it was not by Ben Jones. As turf writer Len Tracy observed, the most vivid picture of the famed trainer is evoked by his characteristic behavior on those cold spring mornings shortly before Derby time, when others had sought shelter.

With his galoshes buckled, that ratty-looking knitted muffler knotted about his throat, overcoat tails blowing in the wind, Jones would be standing outside the Calumet barn, holding his prospective best horse of the moment by a shank, watching the fellow munch grass, an hour at a time, while the trainer studied and studied the least little thing that would tell him something more about this horse.

Nothing too much trouble, nor too trivial—where a horse was concerned—to engage Plain Ben's fullest attention. And therein lay much of his success.

Although the only racing stable to crack the million-dollar range in 1947 was Calumet (and this was to remain true for many years) the farm was not the sole breeding establishment to achieve this figure. Louis B. Mayer was second-ranked breeder of the season with $1,277,377 and horses bred by Idle Hour Stock Farm earned $1,226,597.

As was the case with the Idle Hour horses, most of those bred by Mayer were running for other owners. On February 27, 1947, the movie tycoon had sold out his racing stable in the most fabulous horse auction ever conducted. In the best traditions of a Hollywood premiere, 7,000 spectators and bidders jammed Santa Anita race track (no ordinary sales arena could accommodate the throng—it was reported that there were 15,000 requests for tickets) and when the evening sale ended 60 horses-in-training had been sold for a record-shattering sum of $1,553,500—the average $25,891. Bidding on the big guns—Stepfather ($200,000), Busher and Honeymoon ($135,-000 each), and Be Faithful ($100,000)—was broadcast over three radio networks.

There was more to come. Still riding the crest of post-war enthusiasm, early in 1948 Mayer's 39 newly turned two-year-olds realized

The noted California mare, Honeymoon, with her five-day-old colt who later became the stakes winner Honeys Alibi.

Lloyd Maclean

$1,033,250 for an average of $26,493. Not until 1950 was liquidation of his vast holdings completed, by which time 248 thoroughbreds had been auctioned for $4,479,650. Interspersed among these auctions were the private sale of Beau Pere for $100,000 to a syndicate headed by Leslie Combs II, and, when the twenty-year-old stallion died shortly thereafter, the sale of Alibhai to the same undaunted syndicate for $500,000. Busher, who had been reacquired by Mayer, was sold again, this time for $150,000 to Mrs. E. N. Graham, which brought the grand total value of Mayer's stock to $5,229,650, not counting possible undisclosed private transactions, nor his farm at Perris, California.

As the head of MGM—whose name was perennially at the top of the list of individuals with highest incomes published by the Bureau of Internal Revenue—explained his action, his horse business was getting too big. Mayer later returned to it on a restrained scale.

CHAPTER FIFTY-EIGHT

THE SLIDING-BACK PROCESS continued in 1948 as a heavy majority of race meetings (fifty-seven of seventy-seven) reported decreases in daily mutuel handle from the previous year, these decreases being especially serious since 1947 had been a bad year, too. Whereas the tracks alone had borne the brunt of the earlier recession, in 1948 aggregate revenue to the states also was down, for the first time since the Depression.

In New York particularly, the Bite, plus the competition from New Jersey, was painful, and despite addition of eight more racing days, gross wagering was off nearly $20-million, and the state suffered a loss in income of more than $1¼-million. Nevertheless, authority of municipal governments to tax pari-mutuel handle was extended past the original deadline. Maryland also felt the effect of competition, and statistics dropped in proportion.

Outstanding individuals aren't hampered greatly by averages, however, and in 1948 Calumet Farm again was able to exceed a million dollars in earnings; Jimmy Jones also passed this barrier for the second time; Bull Lea set another record, $1,334,027; and Eddie Arcaro, utilizing Calumet mounts to a significant degree, set a new monetary riding record of $1,686,230.

The only new high mark not affiliated with the number-one stable was that broken by trainer William Molter, operator of one of the large public stables that had become increasingly in vogue since the war. As conditioner for more than a dozen different patrons, Molter for the third successive year saddled the most winners during the season, and his total of 184 surpassed the former record of 177 held by Hirsch Jacobs. The ex-jockey, a native of Texas, led every major meeting on the West Coast; he also gave Jones a run for the money by becoming the second trainer to pass the million-dollar mark, as his charges earned $1,015,547, compared with $1,118,670 credited to the Calumet trainer. Molter teamed frequently with leading jockey John Longden (319 wins).

These were modest accomplishments stacked against that of the year's leading horse, however, who was largely responsible for the successful season enjoyed by Calumet. In 1948 Citation earned $709,470, considerably more than the amount won in a single season by any entire stable before he came to the races.

CITATION, 1945

(Bull Lea–Hydroplane II, by Hyperion)

At the end of the 1947 season Jockey Club handicapper John B. Campbell assigned Citation 126 pounds on the Experimental Free Handicap, top weight, but equal on the scale with his stablemate, Bewitch (121).

As noted in connection with Count Fleet, these weights pertain only to the specific crop of two-year-olds involved—there is no intended comparison between horses of different years (nor are such comparisons feasible). However, 126 is the customary highest weight for a normal season, and Citation, ranked 3 pounds ahead of Better Self and Relic, was not evaluated as so outstanding in his crop as had been, for example, Count Fleet, who was assigned

132 pounds, 5 more than his nearest contemporary (Devil's Thumb) or First Flight, who also had been assigned 126, which, considering her sex allowance, rated her 5 pounds superior to the rest of her crop.

At the end of Citation's three-year-old campaign, the veteran racing secretary revised his estimate—Campbell stated that he considered the colt 15 pounds better than any other member of his generation—at least.

Other experts were not so conservative. In addition to being unanimously acclaimed Horse of the Year in the voting conducted by Triangle Publications, Citation was elected champion of the handicap division by a heavy majority. In the *Turf and Sport Digest* poll for best of the season, he received 161 of 163 votes cast. The rules governing the two polls differed. On *Turf and Sport Digest* ballots, horses were classified strictly according to age, the handicap division being limited to horses older than three. In the Triangle voting, age of itself was not a criterion, and three-year-olds who went out of their division and competed successfully against older horses were eligible for the handicap title besides championship of their own group. Several three-year-old fillies

(Vagrancy, Twilight Tear, Busher and But Why Not) thus had won overlapping honors, but Citation was the first colt to do so. In fact, he won every title for which he was eligible except that of best sprinter, finishing second in this classification to his stablemate, Coaltown. However, voting was based on performance at sprint distances, at which Coaltown competed more frequently than Citation; there was no real suggestion that any horse was superior to Citation at any distance, and the trainer of both colts scoffed at the suggestion Coaltown could beat his stablemate "doing anything."

Certainly, no three-year-old ever compiled a comparable record. In action from early February until mid-December, making twenty starts—an exceptionally heavy campaign for a stakes horse—Citation lost just one race, but put together a string of fifteen successive victories (ultimately, extended to sixteen), longest winning streak in the history of modern racing.

In 1948 he won at distances ranging from 6 furlongs to 2 miles; over fast, good, sloppy, heavy and muddy tracks; ridden by three different jockeys, at nine different tracks in seven different states—Florida, Maryland, Kentucky, New Jersey, New York, Illinois and California.

Citation, the turf's first millionaire.

Citation with jockey Al Snider.

In the matter of all-age competition, Citation wasted no time. Whereas three-year-olds ordinarily are not sent against their elders until late summer or autumn, he opened his campaign against a field of older horses on February 2. The scale of weights calls for large concessions to youngsters at this time of year, and while the 113 pounds carried by Citation might not seem heavy, it was the equivalent of 128 on a four-year-old, or 130 on an animal older than that.

Citation thus shared top weight on the scale with his stablemate, Armed (130), and made large concessions to the others. He won handily by a length in 1:10⅗ from Kitchen Police (five, 110) with Say Blue (four, 107) third. The also-rans included the formidable mare Rampart (six, 113) and Armed.

His sophomore debut was only an overnight race, but on February 11 Citation whipped another field of his elders in the Seminole Handicap, covering the 7 furlongs in 1:23, fastest time of the year at Hialeah, while carrying 112, top weight on the scale. He won by a length from Delegate (four, 123), with Armed third. The other victims were Tavistock, Faultless, Round View, Buzfuz, Wide Wing and Gestapo.

Although he was technically a three-year-old, Citation had been foaled on April 11. Chronologically, he was still two months short of his third birthday when he won his second race against mature horses.

Al Snider had been riding Citation while Doug Dodson rode Armed in their mutual races, but when the horses parted company—Citation going back to his age group in the Everglades Handicap, and Armed in the Widener a few days later—Snider got the mount on both, and Dodson quit the stable.

Citation won the Everglades easily from the only two rivals that faced him, and he followed up with a victory against a larger field in the rich Flamingo Stakes by six lengths, in 1:48⅘ for the 1⅛ miles. As Florida had not yet revised its scale to winter values, the Calumet colt carried 126 pounds in both these February events, in the Flamingo conceding 8 pounds to runner-up Big Dial.

The Flamingo was Snider's last ride on the champion. Early in March, while on a fishing trip off the Keys with trainer C. H. "Tobe" Trotter and Canadian businessman Don Fraser, he disappeared. Although the boat later was recovered—and some notes signed "Al S.,"

409

evidently the work of a prankster, eventually were washed ashore in a bottle—no authentic trace of any of the men ever was found.

It was Saggy who inflicted on Citation his only defeat of the year when next they met, in the Chesapeake Trial at Havre de Grace April 12. The track was muddy and the distance only 6 furlongs. Saggy took the lead at once with Hefty prompting the pace. As Citation went outside to challenge, Hefty carried him very wide, and after he got clear there remained two lengths to make up on Saggy. Citation failed, by a length, but Eddie Arcaro, riding the colt for the first time, admitted afterward he had feared to demand the utmost from his mount on the muddy track, in view of the important races coming up.

As to how seriously the public took this defeat, Citation had been 1-to-3 in the Trial, but went off at 1-to-5 in the Chesapeake Stakes at 1 1/16 miles five days later. He was an easy winner by four and a half lengths from Bovard, as Saggy finished last. On this occasion, Saggy had the excuse; he injured himself in the running, and did not start again until the last day of June, when he again came out of the race lame. That finished his career. Citation thereupon embarked on a casual spree amongst his contemporaries, polishing off a couple of jinxes in the process. No horse had won America's prize races both at two and at three—the Futurity and Kentucky Derby—nor had any winner of the Derby Trial gone on to win the big race itself. Having already taken the Futurity the previous season, Citation further taunted fate with a romp in the Derby Trial on April 27, at odds of 1-to-10. What followed is a collector's item in the field of horseplayers' psychology.

It was the annual custom of Matt Winn, a decent interval after Washington's Birthday, to carefully survey the three-year-old picture and then announce portentously that this year's Kentucky Derby, all things considered, looked to be wide open. In 1948 the words stuck in his throat, especially since he had a message of somewhat conflicting text to impart: only win betting would be permitted on the Derby.

Citation was being joined in the race by a stablemate, Coaltown, who had been kept out at two because of a throat condition, but was undefeated in four starts as a three-year-old. Another of Bull Lea's tribe, Coaltown had equaled the 6-furlong Hialeah track record of 1:09 3/5, beat older horses in the Phoenix Handicap in April and, as a tightner, had won the Blue Grass Stakes from a field of Derby candidates in new track record time of 1:49 1/5 for 1 1/8 miles at Keeneland. Although the owners of four other horses had the temerity to enter the Derby, Winn was taking no chances. A minus show pool every track could accept as one of the risks of the game—but a minus place pool on top of it was too much.

Betting on the Kentucky Derby opens in the morning at Churchill Downs, and continues at special windows until preceding races on the program have been run off. There are blackboards in remote recesses of the vast rambling old plant where the cognoscenti (and the hardy) can learn approximate odds resulting from advance Derby betting, but to the bulk of the crowd out front no information can be furnished until the tote board is freed of its use in connection with earlier races. When the board finally did blink the Derby odds, Ben Whitaker's My Request (carrying Texas money, no doubt), was favorite, and the Calumet entry second choice. Presumably, thinking the entry would be at such prohibitively short odds that it was senseless to wager on it, the early bettors had been pouring in money on the Whitaker colt, not without logic, since My Request was coming off four straight wins as a three-year-old, including a clean sweep at Jamaica of both Experimental Free Handicaps and the Wood Memorial. However, neither his manner of winning nor his times were comparable to either of the Calumets, and the throng at Churchill Downs set about doing what it could to bring matters back into line.

410

By post time the entry was 2-to-5, as My Request drifted out to almost 4-to-1.

It was the biggest odds-on overlay in history, as Citation romped home handily, three and a half lengths ahead of Coaltown, with My Request another three lengths away third. The fourth Derby victory for both Arcaro and Ben Jones, it enabled the jockey to break Isaac Murphy's record, and the trainer to tie that set by Derby Dick Thompson.

No horse ever had an easier time winning the Triple Crown than Citation (oddly, it has not been won since). He won the Preakness easily by five and a half lengths from Vulcan's Forge, with Bovard and Better Self the only other starters. While awaiting the third leg of the crown, Citation kept in shape with an eleven-length victory in the Jersey Stakes, conceding 12 pounds to each of his nearest pursuers, Macbeth and Bovard, and setting a new track record of 2:03 for 1¼ miles at Garden State Park.

Apparently in the hope that there might be a hole in his stamina—which had not yet been thoroughly tested—seven rivals took him on in the Belmont Stakes, and he beat them by eight lengths, Better Self finishing second and Escadru third. The Derby had been run on a sloppy track, and the Preakness on a heavy one, so the clockings were inconsequential. Citation won the Belmont in 2:28⅕ for the 1½ miles, not menacing the track record which had been set by Bolingbroke as a five-year-old under 11 pounds less weight, but equaling Count Fleet's record for the event.

Shipped to Chicago, Citation came against older horses again in the Stars and Stripes Handicap July 4, and it turned out to be one of his hardest races. Carrying 119 pounds in the 9-furlong event, the equivalent of 129 on a mature horse, he was giving away 3 pounds by the scale to his stablemate, Fervent, and actual weight to everything else. After trailing the early pace set by Knockdown and Loujac (the latter the only other three-year-old in the field) Citation went to the front entering the stretch, but he didn't draw away in his usual style. Whereas in his previous races Arcaro had been able to urge him on with merely a cluck, or at most a couple of frugal whacks, this time he had to let him have it with the bat. The end result was a two-length victory in 1:49⅕, tying Armed's track record, with Eternal Reward (five, 116) second and Pellicle (five, 106) third.

Citation pulled a hip muscle in this effort, and as a consequence missed the Classic Stakes, but he was back in time to win a prep race on August 21, followed a week later by a front-running win in the American Derby in 2:01⅗, fastest time of the year at Washington Park, while conceding 8 pounds to stablemate Free America.

Returning to New York, he again tilted with older horses in the Sysonby Mile at weight-for-age. Citation trailed a blazing pace set by Spy Song, :45⅖ for the first ½-mile. Six lengths behind at this point, Citation released a phenomenal surge of power to attain a two-length lead at the quarter pole, covering the 6 furlongs in 1:10⅕, and drew out to win by three lengths from First Flight in 1:36, which equaled the fastest time of the year at Belmont. Coaltown, who had won the Jerome two weeks earlier in identical time, finished third in the Sysonby, followed by Star Reward, Spy Song and Natchez. It was the first occasion Citation and Coaltown had run together since the Kentucky Derby, and Belmont Park, faced with the same problem that had confronted Churchill Downs, permitted place betting; the pool was minus.

Having accomplished everything asked of him thus far, Citation's stamina was put to the ultimate test in the 2-mile Jockey Club Gold Cup, and he won by seven lengths from Phalanx and Beauchef, with Miss Grillo and Conniver among those in the beaten field. His next start also was over a route at weight-for-age, the 1⅝-mile Empire City Gold Cup, a $100,000 race which James Butler had created in the hope it would become an international championship contest. Stymie, Natchez and Assault had shut out the foreign representatives in the inaugural the previous year, and Citation, Phalanx and Carolyn A. ran one, two, three in 1948; foreign owners lost interest, and the race subsequently was reduced in value. Citation's other victims in the Gold Cup included Miss Grillo again; Better Self; Ace Admiral; the Irish St. Leger winner, Nathoo; and the Belgian representative, Bayeux. In both these routes, the smooth-running bay colt registered the best clocking of the year (3:21$\frac{3}{5}$ for 2 miles, and 2:42$\frac{4}{5}$ for 1$\frac{5}{8}$ miles) although the distances are not run often enough to make those figures significant.

"Big Cy's" time for the Pimlico Special also was quite respectable, in fact remarkable—for a walkover. It was all Arcaro could do to hold him down to 1:59$\frac{4}{5}$ as he pranced the 1$\frac{3}{16}$ miles without opposition (this being a winner-take-all contest).

The Special originally had been designed as the climax to the season, but Citation, gaining fast on Stymie in earnings, was aimed at the money crown. Shipped to San Francisco, Citation won a prep race from Bold Gallant December 3, then took on what the West had to offer in the Tanforan Handicap eight days later. Carrying 123 pounds, he won by five lengths from Stepfather (four, 110) with Seetee-see (five, 117) third, in new track record time of 2:02$\frac{4}{5}$ for 10 furlongs. (The two horses considered to have been the most logical challengers, Neil McCarthy's Shannon II and E. O. Stice & Sons' On Trust, had been withdrawn after weight assignments were announced. Both older horses, Shannon II had been assigned 127 pounds and On Trust 124.)

The victory at Tanforan moved the champion to within $50,000 of Stymie. It had been planned to keep Citation in California for the Santa Anita meeting, but he developed osselet trouble and was sent home to be fired. The first phase of his split career had ended.

It was inevitable that Citation, at the corresponding stage of his career, be compared to Man o' War, and it is axiomatic that such comparisons are futile.

Running time—a deceptive yardstick under the best of circumstances—in the case of horses who raced twenty-eight years apart, offers no basis for valid comparison. Man o' War ran with steel horseshoes over tracks that were in general slower than the surfaces Citation negotiated with aluminum plates. Man o' War shattered a number of records, Citation shaved a few—but they were horses of different types. "Big Red" was a gay, ebullient giant who squandered the energy with which he had been so copiously endowed; Citation was a slick, relentless running machine, of calm, efficient disposition, evidently content just with getting the job done.

Although he lacked the size, eye-catching color or flourish of his predecessor, the dark bay Citation was certainly a handsome animal of adequate proportions: 16 hands, 1,075 pounds, girthing 74 inches, with a stride that averaged 25 feet. He was put together so neatly that no single feature stood out, the total impression being one of smooth, muscular power. His nostrils were noticeably large and his eyes, set wide apart, held an intelligent expression; trainer Jimmy Jones reasoned that his intelligence might have been a factor in making Citation the colt he was.

Weight—often a reliable gauge—as applied to Man o' War and Citation is almost equally difficult to relate, reflecting as it does the sport of different eras. Man o' War averaged about 6½ pounds more per start as a two-year-old than Citation, and 5 pounds more at three; in fact, "Big Red," packed more weight as a juvenile than his modern counterpart carried as a three-year-old. However, in Man o' War's day, races were written so as to include both penalties and allowances—weight added for previous accomplishment or subtracted for lack thereof—whereas in modern racing the penalty has virtually disappeared, and allowances only are used to make adjustments. The 130 pounds Man o' War carried at two was not exceptional in his time (some of the colts he beat carried identical weight) although the 138 he lifted as a three-year-old, and the concessions he made, were exceptional. On the other hand, some of Citation's, "light" weights at three were so allotted because he was facing older rivals.

Except for one start in Canada (against restricted opposition, as Willis Sharpe Kilmer was fond of pointing out) Man o' War raced only in two states, Maryland and New York, which took in the major racing of his day, but which was a provincial domain compared to the modern sport. Citation laid his title on the line in seven states, north, south, east and west.

In 1920, when Man o' War was king, only 4,032 race horses saw action during the season; by 1948, the year of Citation, this number had increased to 20,254 potential challengers for the crown. Both horses could run fast and far, carrying the weights assigned in their time. Competent judges can be found to advance the merits of either one over the other.

Each was a great champion.

In the end the horses who beat Citation reached an awkward number, but in 1948 Saggy and Bewitch were the only ones who could claim that distinction. On the other hand, the horses defeated by Citation comprised a great majority of the better horses seen in action that year. Among the three-year-old colts who succumbed, Walmac Farm's Billings won the Peabody Memorial, Hawthorne Speed and Autumn Handicaps, Gold Cup, and Illinois Owners' Handicap. My Request, in addition to his sweep of the Jamaica spring stakes, won the Shevlin and Dwyer at Aqueduct that summer. Better Self won the Paumonok, Yankee, Discovery and Westchester Handicaps. Coaltown embellished his performance in the Blue Grass Stakes with wins in the Swift Stakes, Drexel and Jerome Handicaps, and among his placings was a second to the older Tre Vit in the Great Western Handicap, won in new track record time of 1:09⅕ at Washington Park. Vulcan's Forge triumphed in the Withers and

Providence Stakes; Maine Chance Farm's Ace Admiral won the Travers and Lawrence Realization; Sylvester Labrot, Jr.'s Bovard took the Louisiana Derby and Survivor Stakes; William Helis's Salmagundi won the San Vicente Stakes and Santa Anita Derby; and J. A. Goodwin's Papa Redbird won the Dick Welles Stakes and Arlington Classic.

The older runners who were beaten by the champion included the stayers Phalanx (2¹⁄₁₆-mile Daingerfield Handicap) and Miss Grillo (New Castle Handicap, 2¼-mile New York Handicap and 2½-mile Pimlico Cup in world record time) as well as the sprinter Delegate (Hialeah Inaugural, Palm Beach, Coral Gables, Steger and Hawthorne Sprint Handicaps). Stars of intermediate distances included Fervent (Ben Ali, Dixie, Equipoise Mile and Washington Park Handicaps); Fred W. Hooper's South American-bred gelding, Colosal (both sections of the Tropical Park Double Event, Whirlaway Stakes in record time of 1:48⅕ for 9 furlongs at Washington Park, and Vosburgh Handicap) and Knockdown (Excelsior and Queens County Handicaps).

Another of his victims was Conniver, voted best female member of the handicap division by a wide margin over Gallorette. A long, lean, snaky-looking giantess, at 17 hands Conniver towered over the males. Owned by Harry LaMontagne and trained by William Post, the daughter of Discovery–The Schemer, won the Vagrancy, Beldame and Comely Handicaps from her sex, and the Brooklyn in mixed company. Rampart, another of "Big Cy's" vanquished foes, won the Gulfstream Park, Black Helen (dead heat with Shotsilk, conceding her 24 pounds), Valley Forge, Boardwalk, Olympic, All American and Lady Baltimore Handicaps. Carolyn A. won the Correction, Firenze and Diana Handicaps, and First Flight took the Fall Highweight.

Prominent elsewhere on the scene in 1948 was the seven-year-old handicap horse Shannon II, imported from Australia after considerable discussion concerning a questionable ancestor in the eleventh generation of his pedigree. A bit slow in adjusting to his new home, he finished fast indeed, winning six stakes (though not in succession) and slashing time records as follows: San Francisco County Handicap (new Bay Meadows record, 1:55⅗ for 1³⁄₁₆ miles), Argonaut, Hollywood Gold Cup Handicap, Forty-Niners Handicap (1⅛ miles in 1:47⅗, new Golden Gate record, equaled world record), Golden Gate Handicap (1¼ miles in 1:59⅘, new American record, equaled world record), and San Francisco Handicap (1⅛ miles in 1:50⅘, new Tanforan record). Just before owner Neil S. McCarthy withdrew him from the Tanforan Handicap the stallion had been sold for $300,000 to a syndicate headed by Leslie Combs II.

Among the other good runners in the handicap ranks were Stymie, Talon (San Antonio and Santa Anita Handicaps) and On Trust (four stakes including Santa Catalina and Golden State Breeders Handicaps). Daniel Lamont's El Mono won the McLennan and Widener Handicaps, setting a new Hialeah record of 2:01 in the latter race, but he did not race beyond March; his owner was denied a license because of alleged bookmaking activity.

Handicap females besides those already mentioned, included Honeymoon (Vineland, Top Flight, Beverly, Queen Isabella Handicaps), S. S. Schupper's Miss Disco (Interborough, American Legion and New Rochelle Handicaps) and Harmonica, sold to Arnold Hanger during the year, and winner of the Hallandale and Suburban Handicaps.

Ben Whitaker had some success against Calumet, as Miss Request swamped Bewitch in the voting for champion three-year-old filly. In

Bewitch beating 17 rivals for the Modesty Stakes in 1948.

a remarkable campaign of twenty starts (which led to an award for trainer J. P. Conway) she won eight races, including the Delaware Oaks in her own division, the Ladies Handicap against elders of her sex (beating Gallorette and Honeymoon) and the Empire City Handicap from colts (beating Quarter Pole, Better Self and Ace Admiral).

Bewitch won the Ashland, Modesty Stakes, Cleopatra and Artful Handicaps. Others to receive consideration in the voting were King Ranch's Scattered (Pimlico and CCA Oaks), Havahome Stable's Sweet Dream (Gazelle Stakes), Lester Manor Stable's Compliance (Monmouth Oaks, Alabama Stakes) and Brookfield Farm's Itsabet (Prioress Stakes, Colonial, Wilmington Handicaps). The division also included Miss Mommy, Blue Helen and Grey Flight.

Joseph M. Roebling's Blue Peter, trained by ex-jockey Andy Schuttinger, was a landslide choice as champion two-year-old of 1948, after a campaign of eight wins and two thirds in ten starts, which he wrapped up with a string of seven straight victories. Having already set a new track record of :52⅕ for 4½ furlongs at Garden State Park, he won the William Penn Stakes in track record time of :58⅗ for 5 furlongs, the Garden State, Sapling, Saratoga Special, Hopeful Stakes and Futurity, the latter in 1:14⅗, a tick off the track record, but the fastest time ever registered for the event. He carried 126 pounds in his last two races, and topped his generation in earnings with $189,185.

Unfortunately, this colt, who promised to be War Admiral's best son, never raced again. He became ill at three and was taken out of training; after an apparent recovery, he was being brought back into racing condition as a four-year-old when he died from what was described as the equine equivalent of tuberculosis.

Second-best colt of the generation, according to the voting, was another son of War Admiral, also the victim of bad luck, but in his case not so disastrous, since he was saved for stud.

Maine Chance Farm's Mr. Busher, who had been purchased as a weanling for $50,000, was undefeated in his first three starts, including the National Stallion Stakes and Arlington Futurity, but he was injured in his next start, the Washington Park Futurity, and had to be retired. His brief career notwithstanding, the full brother to Busher more than won himself out with $83,875.

Fred Hooper had an effective pair in Ocean Drive (Hialeah Juvenile, Mayflower and Prairie State Stakes, plus the Futurity Trial) and Olympia (Primer Stakes, Breeders' Futurity and a dead heat with Ky. Colonel in the Joliet). Other male juveniles of note were Greentree's Capot (Champagne, Wakefield Stakes, Pimlico Futurity), J. A. Kinard's Johns Joy (Kenner, Kentucky Jockey Club Stakes, Hawthorne Juvenile Handicap), Woodvale Farm's Sport Page (East View Stakes, and close in others) and Mrs. F. Ambrose Clark's Algasir (Flash, Cowdin Stakes, Babylon Handicap), whom she bought during the year from the estate of A. C. Ernst for $106,000, a record auction price for a gelding. The Washington Park Futurity was won by Mrs. Ada L. Rice's Model Cadet, a son of Requested, making the stallion something of a sensation that year, as My Request and Miss Request were in his first crop. However, his fate was somewhat similar to that of Gallant Fox, for Requested never reached such heights again.

The juvenile fillies were led by Maine Chance Farm's Myrtle Charm, a lightly campaigned but heavily rewarded lass, who won her first three starts, including the Spinaway (by twelve lengths) and Matron Stakes, then was second in the Futurity against colts. Trained by J. W. Smith, she was from the first crop by Requested's old foe, Alsab.

Foxcatcher Farm's Gaffery (Schuylerville and Selima Stakes) was ranked second in this division, followed by Brownell Combs's Princess Pat winner, Sequence. Others of note were Ed Lasker's Pail of Water (Arlington Lassie), Mrs. Al Sabath's Alsab's Day (Pollyanna and

Marguerite Stakes), Allen T. Simmons's Eternal Flag (Viscaya and Astoria Stakes) and W. M. Jeffords's Green Baize (filly division of the National Stallion Stakes).

Trainers, an independent lot by nature and required by the demands of their profession to be possibly more so, did not always see eye to eye with Mrs. Elizabeth N. Graham, owner of Maine Chance Farm. Some grumbled that she insisted on using her Elizabeth Arden beauty lotions on the horses. However, in 1948 Mr. Busher, the record-priced weanling, justified his cost.

The champion filly, Myrtle Charm, winner of $64,830, also was a profitable yearling purchase, as she had been bought for $27,000 from Leslie Combs II. Finally, Royal Blood, a three-year-old in the Maine Chance Stable, in 1948 completed his second successive stakes-winning season to earn back his purchase price. Combs, as agent for Maine Chance, had bought this colt from Coldstream Stud for $50,000. Royal Blood went on to garner more than double that sum—and for years he was the only $50,000 auction yearling to have won himself out on the track.

CHAPTER FIFTY-NINE

THE RECESSION IN RACING, BY this time often referred to as a depression, continued in 1949, as reports from fifty-five race meetings showed a decline in business, compared with eighteen that showed a gain. The sport made frantic efforts to climb off the bottom, but lost ground withal. Despite 26,832 races during the season, the greatest number in history, gross vital statistics dropped and averages suffered even more. Again, New York and Maryland were among the areas hardest hit; the Preakness and Belmont Stakes were cut from $100,000 to $75,000-added, the Jockey Club and Empire City Gold Cups to $50,000. Pimlico abandoned four stakes events and, although the pinch was felt even in the Golden West, Santa Anita dislodged Belmont Park from its customary position as leader in daily average purse distribution.

A few tracks noted, with grim satisfaction, that losses in 1949 were not as severe as they had been the previous year, but some of these tracks were into their third successive declining season.

If the business side of the sport got nowhere fast in 1949, the racing side was equally inconclusive. There was plenty of activity, thrilling contests and exciting horses, but when it was all over it was difficult to decide who was leading whom where.

The leading money winners of the year, and there records, were as follows:

	Starts	1st	2nd	3rd	Unpl.	Earnings
Ponder, 3	21	9	5	2	5	$321,825
Coaltown, 4	15	12	3	–	–	276,125
Capot, 3	16	6	2	6	2	238,335

The voting for Horse of the Year in the Triangle Publications poll ran in exactly the inverse order of the above listing, while *Turf and Sport Digest* named Coaltown over-all champion. In the three-year-old division Capot was ranked ahead of Ponder in both polls, but on the race track Ponder beat him decisively three times, while Capot beat Ponder twice, once decisively and once narrowly. In their only other encounter, which neither won, Ponder outfinished the sophomore king by five lengths.

A marvel of consistency, Coaltown finished his second season of racing without ever having been out of the money, technically. In 1949 he won eight races in a row, six of them stakes, and one of these a walkover.

Neither Capot nor Ponder won more than two races in succession during the 1949 season —or at any time thereafter. There were good explanations for some of each colt's defeats, but the main reason, as it always is, was that some other horse covered the distance faster. However, although he had his troubles with the vulnerable Ponder, Capot had no difficulty handling the consistent Coaltown, and he did it at the right time.

417

Coaltown beat every other horse he met during 1949, including Ponder. The handicap champion, regarded as a sprint specialist at the beginning of the season, won easily in record times in longer races, but suffered two of his three losses at 1 mile, supposedly his pet distance, which he ran faster than any horse in history.

It was that sort of year.

COALTOWN, 1945

(Bull Lea–Easy Lass, by Blenheim II)

Coaltown began his winning streak in his first start of the season, a 6-furlong allowance race at Hialeah February 5. Nine days later, in another overnight race, carrying only 114 pounds, he won by ten lengths—eased up—to equal the world record of 1:47⅗ for 1⅛ miles.

Carrying 10 pounds more in the McLennan Handicap at the same distance the following week, he won by four lengths in 1:48⅖ from Faultless and Shy Guy. Coaltown already was in the Widener with 123—the gentle assignment evidently in deference to his presumed sprinting proclivity—but the extra furlong posed no problem as he covered the 1¼ miles in 2:02, winning by two lengths from the same pursuers, although the placings were interchanged. (In his Hialeah races, Coaltown was well under the 130-pound ceiling, but later that year the track announced that the policy of limiting maximum weights in its two big handicaps would be discarded. Coaltown was assigned 132 pounds for the next year's renewal of the Widener.)

He had to carry 128 pounds in the Gulfstream Park Handicap on March 19, but after stumbling at the start, he won easily by seven lengths from Three Rings (118) and Armed (116), equaling the world record of 1:59⅘ for 1¼ miles. At this point Coaltown again was being compared to Citation, and certainly the 1948 champion, still on the sidelines convalescing from his ankle injury, scarcely could have done better. Coaltown's weight was boosted to 130 when he moved up to Maryland, but that did little for his prospective opponents' morale, and he walked over for the Edward Burke Handicap.

At Jamaica on April 30, again under 130 pounds, he won the Gallant Fox Handicap, which had been reduced to 1³⁄₁₆ miles the previous season, by seven lengths in 1:56⅕, conceding 11 pounds to Vulcan's Forge and 17 to Three Rings. At Narragansett in June he carried the same weight over the same distance to win by twelve lengths, conceding 26 pounds to runner-up Grand Entry. With a little competition, it seemed Coaltown might have boasted a premier collection of world records.

He got the competition in his next start, the Equipoise Mile at Arlington Park on June 25, but not the expected result. To some extent Coaltown was facing the same problem that had dogged Armed—a drop in distance and an increase in weight, to 132 pounds—but that was not the whole story. Mrs. Helen Reineman's very fast Carrara Marble threw a half-mile in :44⅖ at him, With Pleasure took over to pass the 6 furlongs in 1:08⅗, and both stuck in there when Coaltown drew alongside in the

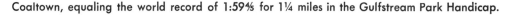

Coaltown, equaling the world record of 1:59⅘ for 1¼ miles in the Gulfstream Park Handicap.

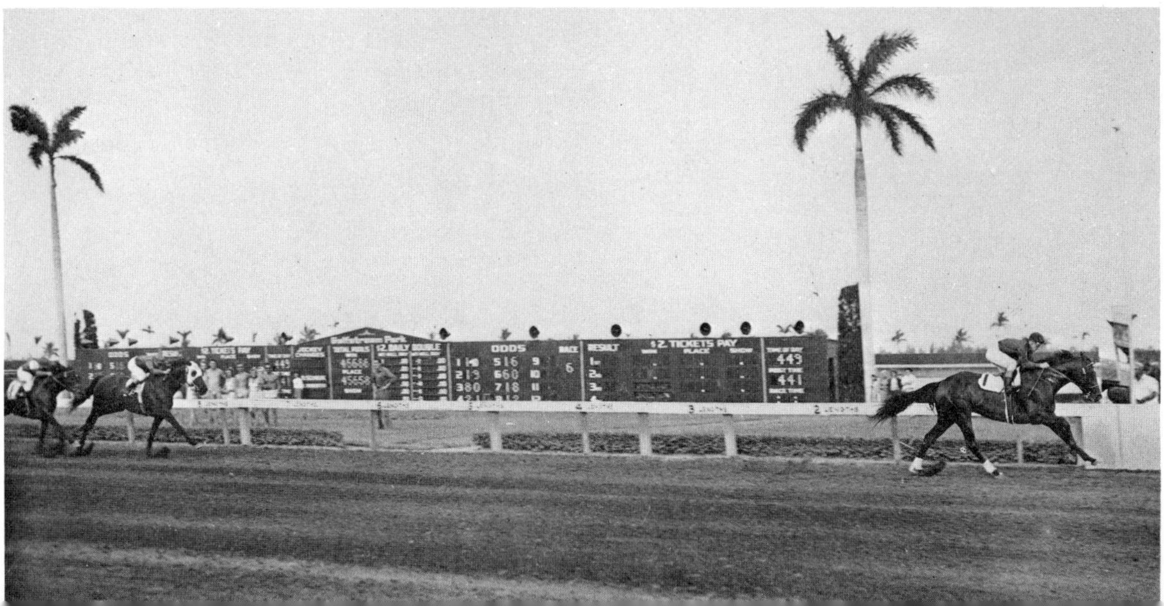

stretch. None had anything left when Star Reward (116) breezed by to win by three lengths in 1:35, Coaltown second and Carrara Marble third.

Throughout his winning streak, Coaltown had been grabbing the lead early, but it now appeared that if some rival could keep up with Coaltown, or, better yet, beat him to the lead, the champion could be had. However, such pat theories usually have a string attached; in the case of Coaltown, it was simply that very few horses could match his speed. In the 1⅛-mile Stars and Stripes Handicap. Delegate tried it, but Coaltown went to the lead in the first quarter, shook off the year's co-champion sprinter, and carried his 130 pounds on to victory by one and a quarter lengths in new track record time of 1:48⅖, as Armed (110) finished second and Star Reward (121) third. Still at ceiling weight in the 1¼-mile Arlington Handicap, Coaltown rushed to the front in the first furlong and won by three lengths from Star Reward, who was getting a 14-pound concession this time, as Armed ran third.

For the Whirlaway Stakes on August 20 Coaltown was left at 130 pounds, and he turned in the most glittering performance of his career, erasing Equipoise's world record as he covered the mile in 1:34, to win by two and a quarter lengths from Ponder, with Star Reward third, receiving 16 pounds from the winner. Washington Park was exceptionally fast that year. Ten days earlier J. A. Goodwin's Ky. Colonel had won the Sheridan Handicap in new world record time of 1:21⅖ for 7 furlongs, and two days later some of the shine was removed from Coaltown's feat when the three-year-olds Johns Joy (122) and Provocative (110) finished a nose apart in an allowance race, running a mile in 1:34⅕.

The handsome bay completed his Chicago tour with another victory under 130 pounds in the 1¼-mile Washington Park Handicap. The track was slow, the time 2:03⅘ and for the only time that season, not counting his losses, another horse finished lapped on Coaltown; this, however, happened to be Armed, and neither was under a drive. (Armed might very well have overtaken Stymie as leading money winner had it not been for his own stablemates.)

Coaltown was shipped back to the East, where he was to meet the horse who had his number, but before he emerged as challenger, Capot had first to deal with one of Coaltown's younger stablemates.

PONDER, 1946

(Pensive–Miss Rushin, by Blenheim II)

The diametric opposite of Coaltown, Ponder liked to do his running in the late stages of a race, and a number of his defeats could be attributed to his having waited until too late. As might be expected of such a colt, he was a maiden in four two-year-old starts, contributing only $400 in second money to the fabulous stable total. Ponder had begun so late in the year that his three-year-old season was really a continuation of his juvenile campaign, and on January 3, he left the maiden ranks with a victory at Tropical Park. He won twice more in Florida, but still was considered second to De Luxe as Calumet's candidate for the Kentucky Derby, assuming there would be one; neither

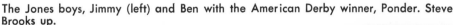

The Jones boys, Jimmy (left) and Ben with the American Derby winner, Ponder. Steve Brooks up.

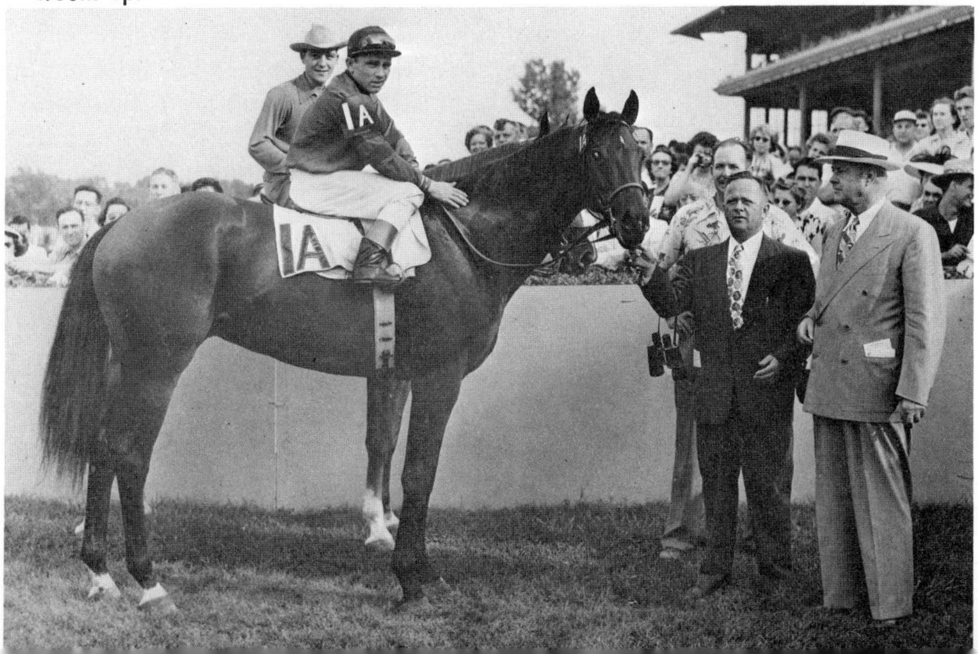

Jones made any bones about 1949 being a bad year. (At the end of the season there were only four champions in the Calumet barn.)

Ponder earned his chance to run in the main event with a surprising performance in the Derby Trial. Olympia, carrying 8 pounds more weight, beat him easily by more than a length, but that was Ponder's first start at so much as a mile, and he made up ground toward the end; also, he had rolled by Capot, to leave that colt five lengths farther back. It was enough encouragement to warrant a try at the Derby, especially in view of the stature of Olympia.

That son of Heliopolis was the hero of a celebrated aerial Odyssey. After finishing second to his stablemate, Ocean Drive, in the Hibiscus Stakes in Florida, Olympia was flown to California, where he won the San Felipe Stakes and was runner-up to Clifford Mooers' Old Rockport in the Santa Anita Derby. He then flew back across the country and commenced a sweeping operation up the East Coast, winning the Flamingo Stakes, both Experimental Free Handicaps and the Wood Memorial before his victory in the Trial.

He was, understandably, an odds-on favorite to capture the Kentucky Derby, too, but as it turned out, long routes were not his forte.

Olympia led for the first mile of the Derby, with Capot prompting the pace, as Ponder trailed the entire field for half a mile, moved up to twelfth at the end of 6 furlongs and then began running, reaching sixth place as the leaders turned for home. At this point Ponder cut loose with the sustained stretch drive that was to become his trademark; striding relentlessly past the leaders, he won by three lengths from Capot, as Isidor Bieber's Palestinian took third, Old Rockport fourth and Olympia faded to sixth. The final clocking of 2:04⅕ was nothing remarkable, but Ponder's performance was something to see. Following a slow first mile in 1:38⅗, the final quarter of the race was run in :25⅗ seconds. Since Ponder came from a charted nine and a half lengths off the

pace at the head of the stretch, he had run the last quarter in about :23⅘, one of the best finishing kicks on the books. It was victory number five for Ben Jones, and the first $100,000 race for veteran jockey Steve Brooks; and never again was a colt wearing Calumet colors allowed to go off in the Kentucky Derby at 16-to-1.

For the Preakness a week later, Ponder's odds had been slashed to 11-to-5, but by then it was time for another colt to take the limelight.

CAPOT, 1946
(Menow–Piquet, by St. Germans)

Capot had been rated near the top of his class at two, with his victory in the 1¹⁄₁₆-mile Pimlico Futurity promising better things when the distances stretched out at three. However, he was not a stayer in the typical sense, like Stymie or Ponder, who came from far back. Capot had plenty of early speed, he liked to run in front or close up and, according to jockey Ted Atkinson, resentment of restraint caused several of his losses.

The Greentree colt (whose name was a term from the card game, piquet) took on a large order for his three-year-old debut, finishing second to the veteran sprinter, Buzfuz, at 6 furlongs. He next won the Chesapeake Stakes from Slam Bang, then finished third to Olympia and Palestinian in the Wood Memorial before his trip to Kentucky. In the Preakness he avenged his Derby loss.

Until the Pimlico layout was changed prior to the 1959 meeting, the Preakness used to favor the speed horse, or, at least, it did not accommodate the stretch runner. The turns were tight, and the home stretch only 950 feet long, compared to the 1,234-foot stretch at Churchill Downs, for example. A horse fast enough to stay near the front sometimes could get home free before a late-running rival could fully catch up; and the Preakness on occasion has been won by colts of generally sprinting disposition who did not otherwise stay 1³⁄₁₆ miles, Polynesian being a notable example.

The 1949 champion Capot with Greentree Stable owners J. H. Whitney and Mrs. C. S. Payson, Ted Atkinson up.

Not that Capot was such a colt, but the Preakness was tailor-made to his style. After prompting the early pace of Noble Impulse for a fast mile in 1:36⅗, he took the lead in the stretch and staved off Palestinian's late rally to win by a head in new track record time of 1:56. Ponder, gaining momentum in the drive, finished fifth, three lengths and two noses farther back.

The next encounter between Ponder and Capot, the Peter Pan Handicap, was at a shorter distance, but around Belmont Park's sweeping turns. The favored Capot engaged in a duel for the lead with Curandero and Cochise, while Ponder made his customary slow start. He was able to uncork his late run, though, and went on to win from Colonel Mike and Old Rockport, as Capot faded to seventh. The winner was getting 5 pounds from the favorite, but Ponder beat Capot by ten lengths.

In the Belmont Stakes, Capot showed that he was more than just a speed horse, while Atkinson demonstrated he was a smart jockey. Ponder was the heavy favorite for this 1½-mile marathon, and he ran dead last for the first mile, as Capot set the pace. Atkinson kept the leader throttled down to a snail-like 1:15⅖ for the first 6 furlongs, 1:39⅗ for the mile and

he had enough horse left to withstand Ponder's challenge when it finally came. Ponder closed ten lengths in the final quarter, but Capot held him off by half a length to win in 2:30⅕, with Palestinian third. The last half of the long race had been run in ⅗-second less time than the first half.

The colts went separate ways after the Belmont, and each lost two races before they met again. Capot actually finished first in the Leonard Richards Stakes, but was disqualified because of a foul committed by his stablemate, Wine List; Sun Bahram was declared the winner, and Cochise moved up to second. Since he and Wine List were the only other starters, Capot was placed third officially, but as a disqualified horse he received no money. In the Empire City Handicap, Capot finished third, under 130 pounds, conceding 5 to the winner, Palestinian, and 17 to Reveille.

Ponder was fourth to the older Dandilly, With Pleasure and Royal Blood in the 6-furlong Myrtlewood Handicap, and third to his contemporaries, Admiral Lea and Johns Joy, in a mile overnighter, on neither occasion having the opportunity to utilize his chief weapon.

The Arlington Classic on July 30 was his final race with Capot, and it was no contest. Ponder won by three lengths from Admiral

421

Lea, with Palestinian another three lengths away in third place, while Capot beat only one horse, finishing fourteen and a half lengths behind the winner.

For Ponder, there followed his second to Coaltown in the world record mile; a victory over Ky. Colonel and Johns Joy in the American Derby, won in new track record time of 2:00⅖; a good third to the older Donor (118) and Vulcan's Forge (124) in the Narragansett Special, Ponder defeated by only a head and a neck under 119 pounds; a win in the Lawrence Realization, while conceding runner-up Blue Hills 16 pounds; and a victory over older runners Flying Missel and Miss Request at weight-for-age in the 2-mile Jockey Club Gold Cup. (Ponder made one more start in 1949, unplaced to Olympia in a 6-furlong race, but that was on December 26 in what amounted to a premature debut of his next year's campaign.)

For Capot, there followed a third to Halt and Daiquiri in an overnight handicap at Saratoga, in which he was defeated by seven lengths while giving away 16 and 20 pounds, respectively, to the top pair; then, a win by a nose in the Jerome Handicap from Arise and Double Brandy, giving them weight. Next, came his first encounter with Coaltown.

Few owners cared to sample Coaltown—or Capot—at a mile under any conditions, and for the weight-for-age Sysonby at Belmont Park October 5, Manyunk was the only other starter. Coaltown went to the front, as expected, but Capot stayed right with him, lapped on him all the time, never letting him get more than half a length clear. The battle continued through 6 furlongs in 1:10⅗, with Capot on the outside, drawing up to the leader's head. In the final furlong it was the three-year-old who drew away from his older rival, to win by one and a half lengths in 1:35⅗.

Ten days later, Capot finished third in the Grey Lag Handicap, conceding age and weight to Royal Governor and Three Rings, and next came the Pimlico Special. Although eighteen horses had received invitations, only three indicated an interest in running; trainer John Gaver let it be known that he would send Capot against either Coaltown or Ponder, but not both, so it evolved into a match. There was some question whether Ponder was ready to run, and anyway Coaltown was the logical candidate, since it presented him with an opportunity to avenge his earlier defeat.

Capot drew the inside for this race, and when he beat Coaltown to the first turn it was all over. The Greentree colt drew out two lengths, three, four, five—and crossed the wire twelve lengths ahead, Brooks having ceased to urge Coaltown when it became obvious there was no catching the 1949 Horse of the Year.

Although Ben and Jimmy Jones were among the most vocal critics of excessive weights (Coaltown had been eligible to the Suburban but was withdrawn when he was assigned 138 pounds) they would accept a handicap within reason. Coaltown that year won seven races under the ceiling weight of 130, setting records and conceding chunks to his opponents. Ironically, the only two stakes he contested at weight-for-age he lost.

As the Special was a winner-take-all affair, in his twenty-eighth start, for the first time Coaltown failed to get a piece of the purse.

To carry the three top names of 1949 to the conclusion of their careers, Capot won the Wilson Stakes in a brief campaign of only three starts as a four-year-old, and retired to stud with 12 wins from 28 starts and $345,260. He begat only six registered foals in his first crop, and the number dwindled further in succeeding seasons, until eventually he was gelded. (No scientifically proved connection was established, but Capot's problem was commonly called "St. Germans trouble." Twenty Grand and Assault, respectively a son and paternal grandson of that stallion, had been sterile, and Capot was his maternal grandson.)

Coaltown raced on two more seasons, with one victory at five, in Hollywood Park record time of 1:09⅕ for 6 furlongs, and two wins at six, including the Art Sparks Handicap. He retired with 23 wins from 39 starts and $415,675. St. Germans did not appear in his pedigree, but Coaltown was not very prolific either, siring thirty-eight registered foals in his first four crops, after which he was sold to France.

Ponder enjoyed another good year as a four-year-old, with five wins: the Santa Anita Maturity and Handicap, plus the San Antonio, Tanforan, Arlington and Marchbank Handicaps. He retired after one unplaced effort at five with 14 wins from 41 starts and $541,275. Ponder was from the first crop by Derby winner, Pensive, who died the year his son won, and Ponder's own stud career also was cut short by death—but he also sired Kentucky Derby winner Needles in his first crop, a three-generation sequence unmatched on the American turf (the only comparable dynasty being that of Reigh Count, which was not carried on through first crops).

Coaltown was a clear-cut winner in 1949 voting for best handicap horse. The runner-up was Mrs. Deering Howe's Donor, winner of the Saratoga, Manhattan and New York Handicaps, besides his victory over Capot in the Narrangansett Special. Walmac Farm's Volcanic, winner of the Hawthorne Gold Cup and Bidwill Memorial Handicap (equaling the track record for 1⅛ miles) on conventional dirt surfaces, also proved to be a pioneer specialist in grass racing, setting a slew of new records in that type of competition. He won the Meadowland Handicap in new American record time of 1:54⅘ for 1³⁄₁₆ miles, and Hawthorne Autumn Handicap in American record time of 1:35⅗ for 1 mile among his other notable grass course performances. Mrs. E. L. Hopkins's Three Rings won the Royal Palm, Queens County, Monmouth, Omnibus and Westchester Handicaps.

Ace Admiral won the rich Santa Anita Maturity, plus the Ventura, Argonaut, Inglewood, Children's Hospital and Sunset Handicaps,

lowering the world record for 1⅝ miles, previously held by Man o' War, to 2:39⅘ in the last-named event. Vulcan's Forge took the Santa Anita Handicap, as well as the Suburban in the East and Detroit Governor's Handicap in the Midwest. He had been bought by I. J. Collins from a paddock sale of C. V. Whitney horses; another bargain from the same sale was Abe Hirschberg's Dinner Gong, who won the San Antonio, Golden Gate Mile and La Jolla Handicaps, and once worked out 9 furlongs in world record time (he lost his next start).

My Request won the New Orleans, Excelsior and Edgemere Handicaps and ran a dead heat for the Le Compte; Loser Weeper took the Metropolitan, Vosburgh, Bay Shore and Valley Forge; Solidarity won the Hollywood Gold Cup in track record time and the Golden Gate Handicap; Better Self won the Carter and All American; and Double Jay set a track record in the 9-furlong American Handicap.

There was a tie for best sprinter between Woolford Farm's Delegate (Hialeah Inaugural, Seminole, Crete, Steger and New Rochelle Handicaps) and Mrs. Esther duPont Weir's Royal Governor (Wilmington, Brandywine, Fall Highweight, Interborough, Grey Lag and Questionnaire Handicaps). Other fast ones were Rippey (Paumonok, Toboggan, etc.), Royal Blood and the three-year-olds, The Pincher and Bolero.

In the distaff section of the handicap division, Bewitch made it a clean sweep for Calumet by winning her second seasonal championship. She won the Churchill Downs Inaugural, Misty Isle and Vineland Handicaps, and set a world record for a filly of 1:34⅖ in the Beverly Handicap at Washington Park shortly after Coaltown set his record. Bewitch also showed admirable consistency, placing numerous times while conceding weight. One of the three times (in thirteen starts) she was unplaced was a fourth in the 1½-mile Ladies Handicap under 126 pounds.

Miss Request (Beldame Handicap) was back on the scene, as were But Why Not (Firenze and Top Flight Handicaps) and Conniver (Butler). Others in the top echelon were Dr. Eslie Asbury's Brownian (Tulip, Detroit Governor's Lady and Falls City Handicaps) and Mrs. O. L. Nyberg's Irisen (Boardwalk and Capitol Handicaps). Miss Grillo was sent to stud after winning the San Juan Capistrano Handicap.

Four colts—Capot, Ponder, Palestinian and Olympia—completely dominated the voting for best three-year-old colt of 1949. Besides his Empire City Handicap victory and numerous placings, Palestinian won the Jersey Stakes. In addition to his other successes, Olympia took the Withers Mile.

Despite Ponder's loss to Capot in the voting for best colt, Calumet also had two sophomore champions, as Two Lea and Wistful shared the filly title. Although horsemen ignore paternal relationships, because the large number of offspring a stallion can beget makes it confusing, actually each of these fillies, in blood, was a half-sister to Coaltown. Two Lea was by the same sire, and Wistful (by Sun Again) was out of Coaltown's dam. Of the pair, Two Lea was by far more impressive, but Wistful more active and the winner of more money. Perhaps bored with the spectacle of the stable colors flashing across the finish line one-two, Calumet campaigned them independently with one exception.

In seven starts Two Lea had six wins and a second for earnings of $60,300. After winning two overnights and beating No Strings in the Princess Doreen Stakes, she lost by half a length to that filly in the Modesty, conceding her 9 pounds (with older fillies behind the top pair). Thereafter Two Lea was undefeated. She won the Cleopatra Handicap from Wistful, as No Strings was fourth, and finished her season with victories in the Artful Stakes.

Wistful won six of eleven and $92,360, her victories including the filly equivalents to the races which comprise the Triple Crown: the Kentucky, Pimlico and Coaching Club American Oaks.

The remaining fillies defeated just about all of each other at one time or another, but several boasted exceptional records. Mrs. Walter M. Jeffords's Adile won the Monmouth Oaks, Alabama Stakes and, in what was becoming more of a rare achievement as the number of races exclusively for females increased, won the Empire City Gold Cup from the older male stayer, Flying Missel. Gaffery won the Santa Susana Stakes in California and the Ladies' Handicap in New York; owned by boxing impresario James D. Norris, Spring Hill Stable's Nell K., won the Prioress, Acorn and Gazelle Stakes; and Hal Price Headley's Lithe took the Arlington Matron and Comely Handicaps.

The carousel aspect of 1949 racing influenced the juvenile division, as honors among the colts were divided—perhaps scattered would be the more accurate term. Hill Prince was a narrow winner over Middleground in the Triangle Publications poll, Oil Capitol fifth; in the *Turf and Sport Digest* voting Oil Capitol was a narrow winner over Hill Prince, Middleground fifth. Guillotine and Curtice were third and fourth in each ranking.

Middleground led (with a dead heat for second between Hill Prince and Oil Capitol) the Experimental Free Handicap, which combined predicted three-year-old performance along with assessment of accomplishments at two. In fact, there could be no reasonable caviling at any of the rankings; this was an excellent batch of youngsters, and, unlike some two-year-olds whose brilliance fades quickly thereafter (except for Curtice, who died in a fire the next year) this group continued to shine in subsequent seasons.

Thomas Gray's Oil Capitol, trained by Harry Trotsek, lost more races than he won, but he scored in a couple of the important ones and led the juvenile colts in earnings with $106,956. A gray son of Mahmoud–Never Again II, by Pharos, he had been purchased from Elmendorf Farm for $15,000 at the yearling sales, and he was destined to retire as the winner of more money than any previous auction yearling. He

424

Formidable stablemates, A. G. Vanderbilt's Bed o' Roses and Next Move, finishing one-two in the 1949 Demoiselle Stakes.

got a good start in his first season by winning six of thirteen starts, including the Keeneland Sales Colt and Gelding Stakes (a prophetic achievement), Breeders' and Pimlico Futurities. Oil Capitol's name derived from the fact that his owner came from Tulsa, Oklahoma. The origin of his dam's name, according to the late Joe Palmer in *American Race Horses*, was somewhat more subtle and infinitely less enthusiastic. A daughter of Confidence, foaled in 1934, she originally had been called "New Deal" by breeder J. E. Widener—after Widener had second thoughts on the political scene, he changed the mare's name to Never Again.

Hill Prince and Middleground were more consistent than Oil Capitol in lighter campaigns. The former won six of his seven races and was second in the other to glean $46,225. His victories included the World's Playground, Cowdin Stakes and Babylon Handicap. Middleground had four wins and a third in five starts, for earnings of $54,225. The Hopeful was his only stakes.

Mrs. Emil Denemark's Curtice also was never out of the money, although he won but two of his nine outings. However, he earned more in his maiden victory than either of the two elected champions did all year when he won the Washington Park Futurity; he followed up with the Prairie State Stakes to net $87,400 for the season.

Greentree Stable's Guillotine was four for seven in his campaign, but he took the biggest prize of all, the Futurity, to wind up with a total of $94,835. Calumet's Theory, second in the Futurity, a week later won the Champagne Stakes to go along with three previous victories in overnight events, in one of which he proved sharper than Guillotine.

W. M. Peavy's Wisconsin Boy won the Arlington Futurity and Primer Stakes; Brookmeade Stable's More Sun was victorious in the Graduation, U. S. Hotel Stakes and Saratoga Special; and Palatine Stable's Quiz Show won the Eastern Shore, William Penn and Christiana Stakes.

In a year when the standings in nearly all other departments were disorganized, the two-year-old fillies presented the most orderly picture of all. Alfred G. Vanderbilt's Bed o' Roses, a daughter of Rosemont–Good Thing, by Discovery, was the clearest champion the 1949 season produced, coming within an eyelash of being unanimously acclaimed best of her division. Trained by W. C. Winfrey, she won nine races in a testing campaign of twenty-one starts extending from February through November, and topped all juveniles, regardless of sex, with earnings of $199,200. Conceived in Virginia, born in California and raised in Maryland, she competed in seven different states in her first racing season. After being un-

425

placed in her first two starts while the greenness was wearing off, she became a model of consistency, the single exception being a futile try at colts in the Futurity, and she wound up the year on a high note with four straight victories. She won seven stakes—the National Stallion, Rancocas, Colleen, Matron, Selima, Marguerite Demoiselle—and came close to exceeding Top Flight's earnings record; in the rich Arlington Lassie, on a muddy track, she did not have clear sailing, but closed gamely when free to finish third by less than a length.

Dixiana's Here's Hoping won the Princess Pat and Tomboy Stakes; George D. Widener's Rare Perfume the Fashion and Autumn Day; Calumet's Duchess Peg took the Arlington Lassie; and Ogden Phipps's Striking (a full sister to Busher and Mr. Busher) won the Schuylerville and placed in numerous other stakes.

Other leading fillies were Mrs. Connie Ring's Fleet Rings (Hollywood Lassie), Greentree's Sunday Evening (Spinaway), G. M. Crump's Tea Deb (Pollyanna) and W. G. Helis's Bridal Shower (faster division of the Polly Drummond).

CHAPTER SIXTY

THE DOWNWARD BUSINESS trend continued in 1950, but there was not so sharp a skid as had occurred in the past few seasons. Purse distribution was off, yet revenue to the states increased, and while the majority of race meetings again reported a decline, the score no longer was so overwhelming (forty-one to thirty-six). Disputes between the HBPA and track management regarding minimum purses, which had been cropping up all along during the recession, reached a crescendo in 1950; several meetings were threatened with strikes if purses were cut; at others horsemen accepted reductions.

The Preakness was cut again in value, to $50,000-added, and while the Kentucky Derby still clung to its $100,000 status, the value of the trophy was reduced from $10,000 to $5,000. However, there was no setback in quality of racing.

Veteran reporter and racing official R. E. "Lanny" Leighninger described the epic encounters between Citation and Noor in 1950 as the most thrilling series in modern turf history.

A Greek stood in the mutuel line at Santa Anita on February 25, holding in his arms a shoe box full of money. He was, he explained to a reporter, the treasurer of a Citation betting club, which had picked out the colt as a two-year-old and had wagered on him ever since according to a secret formula—part to win and part to show. Like stock in A.T. & T., the investment had not been spectacular, as such things can go, but returns had been steady. The man refused to reveal his home, other than to say he was from out of town, nor would he divulge the club's assets, other than to say the amount was "considerable." The funds had been idle for more than a year, but now the club had resumed business. "Big Cy" was back in action.

Throughout the 1949 season it had been expected that Citation would return to the races any day, but little problems kept turning up, and, besides, Coaltown was holding down the fort quite well. Late in the year the Calumet stable was shipped to California before the opening of Santa Anita, and Citation began training in earnest—the heaviest work schedule put on any horse during the meeting, according to some of the clockers.

On January 11, 1950, after an absence from competition of precisely one year and one month, he hit the comeback trail, winning a 6-furlong allowance race in 1:11⅗, while carrying 124 pounds on a sloppy track. The longest winning streak in modern racing history was thus extended to sixteen races. About two weeks later, carrying 130, Citation lost by a neck in 1:10⅘ to Mrs. John Payson Adams's Miche in an overnight handicap, while giving away 16 pounds. Watching these developments from afar, his betting club decided he now was ready to take up where he had left off, and the representative journeyed to Los Angeles to commence operations.

Citation's first stakes attempt came in the 1⅛-mile San Antonio Handicap February 11, for which he again was assigned 130 pounds. After moving up and putting away the pacesetter, Bolero, Citation took the lead, but was not unduly punished as his stablemate, Ponder, came along with one of his stretch drives to win by a length. So far as the club was concerned, this result made no difference; Citation had proved he could carry weight over a distance. He looked ripe, and any reinforcements from stablemates was just so much gravy.

Very few observers paid much attention to the horse that finished third, just half a length behind Citation, carrying only 114 pounds, yet, in a way, that was the salient feature of the San Antonio. It was the only time Citation ever finished ahead of Noor.

NOOR, 1945

(Nasrullah–Queen of Baghdad, by Bahram)

Noor was a dark horse in the classic tradition. To begin with, he was brown, and of classic mold; over 16 hands, but he looked even taller because of his legginess, he had a pronounced development of the withers (similar to Whirlaway's), a tapered barrel despite short coupling and in general a label of "cup horse" written all over him. Along with the Irish Derby winner, Nathoo, he had been purchased from the Aga Khan by C. S. Howard in a package deal for $175,000. While it is true that Nathoo was the more highly regarded of the pair, the tales that Noor merely was tossed into the deal were unfounded. Noor definitely was part of the negotiations, and the price on him alone would have been substantial (one educated guess was $75,000). There was no question as to which of the pair was more valuable on this side of the Atlantic, however. Nathoo, except for one appearance before the sale as an "international" representative in the Empire City Gold Cup, did not race in America. Noor became a champion.

Noor himself seemed a chancy proposition when he first arrived in this country; he had suspicious-looking ankles, which were fired, and the colt was turned out for months. Trained by Burley Parke, he made his American debut in the autumn of 1949, winning only one race in a brief campaign of six starts, but he startled jockey John Longden—and gave an indication of what was to come—by finishing second by a head in the San Francisco

Handicap, after propping at the start and being left at the post. He continued in training between seasons, but still was looking for his first American stakes victory on February 25, 1950, when he came out for the $100,000 Santa Anita Handicap.

Citation was considerably reinforced on this occasion, as Two Lea and Ponder also were in the field. Two Lea set a scorching pace, covering the first mile in 1:35⅕ (faster than the track record for that distance) as Citation stayed close up, waiting to move along with whatever challenge might develop, while Ponder covered the rear. It was Noor who challenged, and Citation went after him; the Irish horse took the lead in the stretch as Citation, forced around because he could not find a path on the inside, charged vainly forward when he got clear. Under 132 pounds, the heaviest burden he ever packed, he made up almost a length in the drive, but Noor, carrying only 110, went under the wire with more than a length to spare in new track record time of 2:00 for the 1¼ miles. Two Lea, whose performance was as gallant as any in her distinguished career, held on for third, and Ponder took fourth.

Thus began the most enigmatic sequence of handicap races in American turf annals. Since weights for the Santa Anita Handicap had been assigned far in advance, before Noor had emerged in his true light, they did not reflect any realistic appraisal of the horses' relative merits—actually, Noor had been assigned only 109 pounds for the race, 5 less than he had carried in the San Antonio, but Longden couldn't get down that far and was 1 pound overweight. Thereafter, however, adjustments were made.

Five pounds equals one length at a mile, says the thumb rule of handicapping, but as is true of all generalizations, this one is subject to an infinite variety of refinements. Like proud chefs, handicappers compute weights each according to his individual recipe, adding a pound here and there to account for certain factors.

428

Noor scoring his first upset over Citation in the Santa Anita Handicap.

Racing secretary Webb Everett cooked up a perfect race for the next meeting between the two, in the 1¾-mile San Juan Capistrano Handicap, closing-day feature of the Santa Anita Meeting. Citation was dropped 2 pounds to 130 and Noor raised 7 to 117, a shift of 9 pounds in Citation's favor, off his one-and-a-quarter-length defeat in their previous encounter.

These ingredients produced what 60,000 weekday witnesses were willing to certify as the most thrilling turf spectacle of modern times. There were no complicating incidents, no excuses, and none was needed. This was a horse race—Salvator and Tenny, Domino and Dobbins, Hourless and Omar Khayyam, Alsab and Whirlaway, all over again.

Citation was the hare this time, and Noor the hound. After tracking the leisurely early pace for the first mile of the marathon, run in 1:38, Steve Brooks sent "Cy" up to make his bid; at the same time, from four and a half lengths to the rear, Longden turned Noor loose.

They locked horns rounding the turn and stayed that way to the bitter end. For more than ⁵⁄₁₆-mile it was head and head, stride for stride, until the camera was required to render the verdict: Noor by a nose.

It was doubly frustrating. By that slim margin had Citation failed to exact his revenge, and that tiny thread had restrained him from wresting the financial crown from Stymie.

The time of 2:52⅘ was a new world record, and the nearest straggler was left nearly thir-teen lengths back in the leaders' churning wake. It was the final great triumph for Charles S. Howard, for the noted turfman died before Noor started again.

Citation wasn't plagued by Noor in his next two races, for the Irish horse suffered a slight training accident, and Citation also was given a respite of about two months. During the interval, the Tanforan Handicap, which had been doubled in value to $50,000 in anticipation of another duel between them, was won by Ponder.

Noor still was on the sidelines when "Big Cy" resumed action at Golden Gate Fields but that proved to be small comfort—the Calumet horse still could not escape world record competition. Citation was down to only 120 pounds for the Surprise Purse on May 17, but making a drastic adjustment in distance from his last out. Rex Ellsworth's Roman In, carrying level weight, completed the 6-furlong tour in 1:08⅖ to equal the world record and win by nearly a length. (Citation's first loss of the season had come in the La Sorpresa Handicap, and this second coincidence sent hunch players into a frenzy.)

Roman In did not win a stakes event in 1950, nor did his eminence as co-holder of a world record last long. Ten days later, at the same track, Abe Hirschberg's Bolero lowered the mark to 1:08⅕, and it was this son of Eight Thirty who provided Citation with the impetus to get in on the record-breaking spree himself.

429

In the Golden Gate Mile on June 3, Bolero (123) went even faster, as far as he went, covering the first 6 furlongs in 1:07⅗—but only the final time is official, and Citation, toting 128 pounds, moved up in the stretch to win by almost a length, drawing away, in new world record time of 1:33⅗. The winner's purse also brought Citation's earnings up to the world record sum of $924,630.

When the world's leading money winner next went to the post, for the Forty-Niners Handicap on June 17, there was Noor again. The weights—128 on Citation and 123 on Noor—represented a shift of 8 pounds in Citation's favor off the San Juan assignments, but again Noor was the victor, by a neck, and the time of 1:46⅘ was another world record. (Roman In finished third, three lengths away, under 111 pounds.)

A week later in the Golden Gate Handicap Noor had to concede the weight—carrying 127 to 126 on his rival—but regardless of the 6-pound shift, this one was the easiest victory of all. He crossed the finish three lengths clear of Citation in new world record time of 1:58⅕ for 1¼ miles. On Trust had been allowed to build up an enormous lead in this race, and after a mile in 1:34 he still was seven lengths on top. Since Noor made up that deficit in a last quarter run in :24⅕, his estimated individual time shaded 23 seconds!

The failure of these weight shifts to move up Citation, after the San Juan, has mystified turf followers ever since. One theory is that Noor for the first three races had been operating down below scale weight, where changes do not have much effect, while Citation was in the upper strata, where slight changes are magnified—a good horse scarcely notices the difference between, say, 115 and 122 pounds, but the difference between 129 and 131 can be telling. Another theory is that Noor was improving with each race while Citation was tailing off. Very likely, the explanation lies somewhere in between; Noor was unaffected by the first few weight changes, but by the time he moved up to scale weight, Citation could not take advantage of it.

In any case, the public went right along with the handicappers in evaluating the two horses. Citation was the favorite in his first four encounters with Noor, when he carried the higher weight, and Noor was the choice for the last battle, when he conceded a pound. That was the only time after his juvenile season Citation did not start as a favorite.

Ordinarily, Citation would have been retired. He was of stallion age and inclined to become gross if not heavily worked, and that put strain on the ankle. However, Warren Wright (who died before the year was out) had expressed a desire that Citation not only surpass Stymie's earnings record, but that he become the first equine millionaire in history as well. With this goal in mind, the champion was shipped to Chicago, but the ankle began to act up, so again he was sent back home. Phase two of his career had ended.

How good was he the second time around? In six successive starts Citation had bumped into a track record performance, the last five in succession having been world records. The significance of these records was subject to review, but they were records, and in most of the races concerned Citation had been conceding weight. Outside his own stable few horses beat him: Saggy, Miche, Noor and Roman In. With the exception of Miche, each of them at some time during his career had run a race faster than any horse in prior history. As for Miche, he eventually won a Santa Anita Handicap and amassed $235,185. The gray South American boasted a couple of track record performances; in one of them, before he beat Citation, he had defeated Noor.

Noor's next race following his conquests of Citation, the American Handicap at Hollywood Park July 22, resulted in another sensational performance as he carried 132 pounds to victory in 2:00⅕, while conceding 32 pounds to runner-up Dharan and 25 to third-place Frankly. He then was shipped to the East.

Easterners for some time had been sneering at the speed marks broken on the "pasteboard" Western tracks, and following the spate of new records at Golden Gate there were caustic suggestions that the surface had been specially prepared. Races were run at eight different distances during the 1950 Golden Gate meeting. At the end of forty-six racing days new records had been established for seven of these distances, from 5 furlongs to 1½ miles. The only track record which survived the onslaught was Count Speed's 1:41 for 1¹⁄₁₆ miles, and it was approached within ⅕-second.

Noor's Eastern debut was delayed when he developed a cough, and almost two months elapsed before he made his next start, in an overnight handicap at Belmont Park on September 18. Assigned 128 pounds, he lost by one and a quarter lengths to Greentree Stable's One Hitter (107), a tough little son of Shut Out, who was a menace to any horse when the weight was right. The winning time of 1:42⅘ was ⅗-second off the track record for 1¹⁄₁₆ miles. One Hitter's assignment was raised 3 pounds for the 1½-mile Manhattan Handicap four days later, while Noor's remained the same, and with the 18-pound pull the Greentree colt won again, but this time by only a neck; however, the victory was somewhat more decisive than that margin suggests, for at one point during the stretch drive Noor had reached even terms.

The aura of invincibility surrounding the dark horse from Ireland vanished on October 7 when Hill Prince beat him by four lengths in the Jockey Club Gold Cup at weight-for-age. Apparently the sandy surface at Belmont Park was not Noor's element.

When he returned to the West, however, Noor demonstrated that on his type of course he was quite a horse. There could be no sectional gibes about the brand of competition, since his two remaining conquests were scored at the expense of invaders from the East. Hollywood Park, rebuilt after the previous year's fire, held two meetings in 1950, and Noor closed out his career at the second session. On December 1 he beat the Westchester Handicap winner, Palestinian, by seven lengths in an overnight race, giving away weight and setting a new track record of 1:48 for 9 furlongs. A week later, in the Hollywood Gold Cup, sharing top weight of 130 pounds with Hill Prince (but getting 6 from the younger colt according to the scale) Noor won by a length from Palestinian as Hill Prince was three lengths farther away in third place. The time was another new track record, 1:59⅘ for 1¼

Noor arriving in Saratoga during his invasion of the East. Trainer Burley Parke is at right.

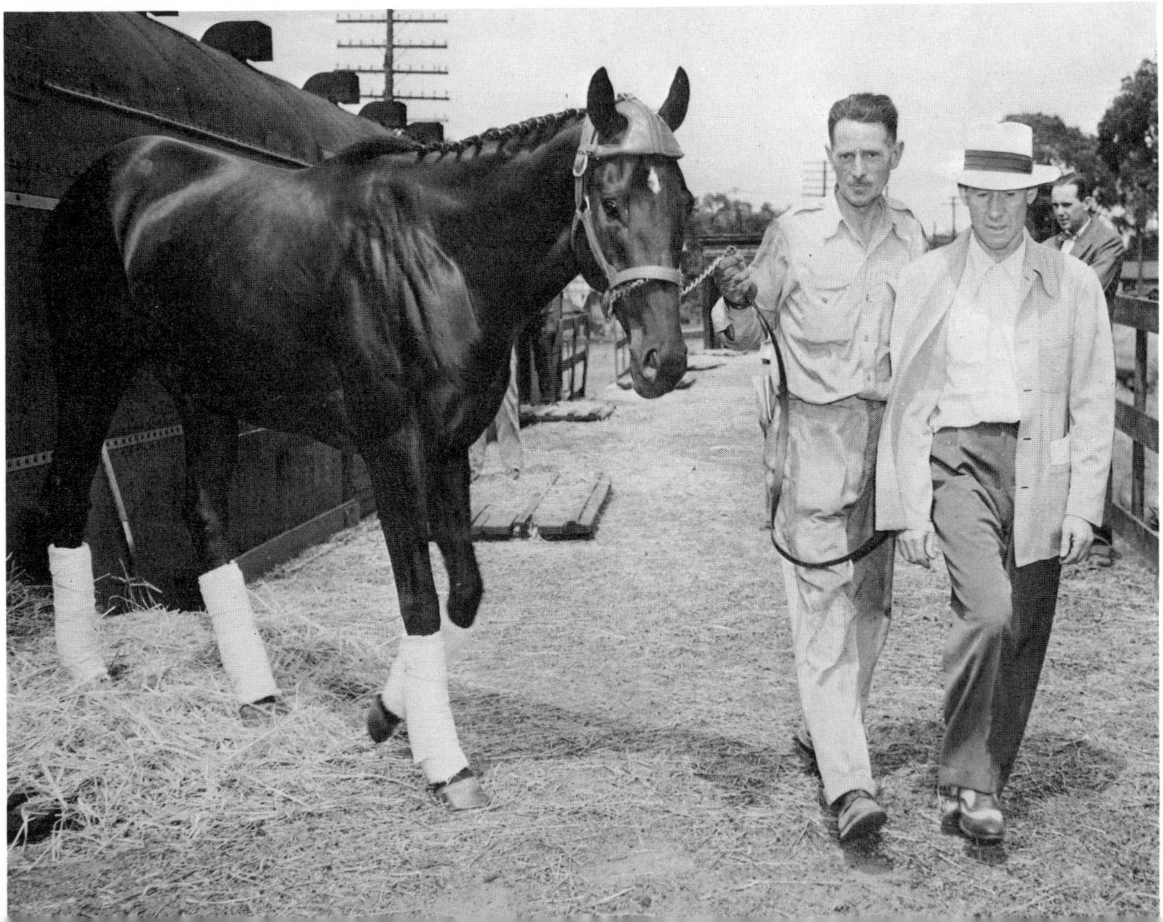

miles, and, unlike the situation that prevailed at Golden Gate, in fifty days of racing over nine distinct distances at Hollywood Park that season, just three new track records were established, two by Noor.

Moreover, Noor emerged from this victory as leading money winner of the season with $346,940, and, although it was too late to affect the championship voting (and probably would not have anyway, in view of the age-weight discrepancy) by taking the measure of Hill Prince he had conquered the Horse of the Year.

HILL PRINCE, 1947

(Princequillo–Hildene, by Bubbling Over)

Bred in Virginia at The Meadow stud of his owner, utilities tycoon Christopher T. Chenery, Hill Prince had won a watered-down version of a championship as a two-year-old. At three he was recognized across the board as best of the season in three polls, the Thoroughbred Racing Associations having begun to name champions by vote among racing secretaries at member tracks. Hill Prince was unanimously proclaimed champion of his age in the Triangle Publications voting, and barely missed similar acclamation in the balloting for over-all honors (there was one vote each for Noor and Citation).

The opposite in type to the leggy Noor, who looked taller than he actually was, Hill Prince was about the same height, but appeared shorter because of his burly physique. The powerfully muscled bay colt was built on the order of a sprinter, but his running style was more that of a stayer, and, as he demonstrated on appropriate occasions, he could do both.

By 1950 it had become customary to send horses with classic aspirations south to acquire a "winter bottom" before undertaking the spring stakes events, but Hill Prince came from right off the farm to win the 6-furlong Experimental Free Handicap No. 1 in his sophomore debut on April 5. Ten days later, in the longer, $1\frac{1}{16}$-mile No. 2, he ran into a wall of horses and finished ninth. The Wood Memorial on April 22 was his first race against King Ranch's Middleground, and Hill Prince won by two lengths. Both colts then were shipped to Louisville for the Kentucky Derby.

Middleground got in a race over the track, finishing second—for the fourth time in succession that year—to Black George in the Derby Trial. The same afternoon Hill Prince turned in an impressive public workout, but both these performances were obscured by a flash from the West.

William M. Goetz's Your Host, winner of the San Felipe Stakes and Santa Anita Derby, had arrived in Kentucky amidst great fanfare,

Hill Prince, the 1949 Horse of the Year, with owner C. T. Chenery, jockey Eddie Arcaro and trainer Casey Hayes (light suit) in the background.

Bert Morgan

reminiscent of that which featured Longfellow's trip to Monmouth Park to meet Harry Bassett in an earlier century. Your Host was owned by a movie magnate, however, and the sign on his railroad car showed the lack of restraint characteristic of certain other announcements from filmland: it described him bluntly as the 1950 Kentucky Derby winner. At that, collecting the roses seemed a mere formality after the son of Alibhai had electrified cynical hardboots with a victory at Keeneland by six and a half lengths in new track record time of 1:22⅖ for 7 furlongs, over a field that included the Flamingo Stakes winner, Oil Capitol, and Blue Grass Stakes winner, Mr. Trouble.

Your Host was a heavy favorite at Churchill Downs May 6, but faded after dueling with Mr. Trouble for a mile, and it was Middleground who finally hit the winner's circle. Ridden by fellow Texan Bill Boland, an apprentice, the King Ranch colt loomed in the stretch to win by one and a quarter lengths, as Hill Prince also closed ground to take second from Mr. Trouble. It was the second fastest Derby thus far run, timed in 2:01⅗, the third win for Max Hirsch and the second for a son of Bold Venture, who had himself been the only other horse to win with an apprentice rider.

There was an off Saturday between the Derby and Preakness that year, and Hill Prince utilized it to go one up on Middleground by defeating him in the Withers Stakes. In the Preakness a week later, Arcaro sent the Chenery colt to the front much earlier than usual, and Hill Prince drew out to win by five lengths, Middleground again second.

Hill Prince next started against older horses in the Suburban Handicap May 30, carrying 113 pounds, 5 over the scale; he finished third to the five-year-olds, Loser Weeper (115) and My Request (119)—making concessions to them of 12 and eight pounds, respectively, if the difference in age is taken into account.

When Hill Prince returned to his age group for the Belmont Stakes June 10, Middleground tilted the seesaw on him for the second and final time. Middleground hung back in this race, as Hill Prince vied for the lead, and in the stretch the son of Bold Venture—Verguenza, by Chicaro, cruised up smoothly to win by a length from Lights Up, as Mr. Trouble took third and Hill Prince faded to seventh—his only bad race of the season. Following a second to Greek Song in the Dwyer (while giving the winner 5 pounds) Hill Prince was rested for a month.

He returned to competition on August 26, beating All Blue and Your Host in the American Derby, after which he clinched leadership of his division with a brilliant performance in the Jerome Handicap. Carrying 129 pounds, he won by four lengths from Greek Ship (122)

Middleground going to the post for the 1950 Kentucky Derby, Bill Boland up.

with Navy Chief (108) third and Middleground (126) unplaced.

That was the first time in his life Middleground had finished out of the money, and the end of a most unusual career, for he later injured an ankle in training and was retired. Despite his consistency, in ten starts at three he won only two races—the Derby and Belmont—and he joined a select group, founded by his sire, of colts who won two of the three Triple Crown races, but not the sophomore championship. (The other members were Johnstown, Shut Out and Pensive.)

Having established his superiority within his own age group, Hill Prince earned his Horse of the Year title when he beat Noor in the Jockey Club Gold Cup. On his Western swing at the end of the season, under top weight of 128 pounds he was third to Your Host and Ponder, beaten a nose and a head while conceding them 4 pounds, in an overnight prep; then third in Noor's Hollywood Gold Cup. Hill Prince finished the year with a flourish, however, as he carried 128 pounds to victory in the Sunset Handicap, beating Next Move and Great Circle while conceding weight.

While Noor and Citation were dominating the West, Three Rings ran up a string of handicap races in the East: the Royal Palm, McLennan, Queens County, Edgemere and All American (dead heat with Dart By). Besides his conquest of Noor, One Hitter won the Questionnaire Handicap and Pimlico Special; and, in addition to his victory over Hill Prince, Loser Weeper won the Valley Forge and Dixie Handicaps.

Piet won the Jamaica, Toboggan, Bay Shore Handicaps and Whitney Stakes; My Request won the Brooklyn and Merchants' and Citizens' Handicaps; Brandywine Stable's Cochise won the Massachusetts, Sussex Handicaps and Saratoga Cup; Royal Governor, a sprinter, popped up to win the rich 1¼-mile Widener Handicap, and Hasty House Farm's gelding, Inseparable, was prominent in the Midwest with victories in the Stars and Stripes, Washington

Park and Lynch Memorial Handicaps. His stablemate, Seaward, won several stakes also.

Top sprinters of 1950 included Olympia (Paumonok, Camden, Roseben Handicaps), Mrs. F. Ambrose Clark's Tea-Maker (Vosburgh Handicap), Bolero (Pacific and Preview Handicaps), Addison Stable's Arise (Excelsior, American Legion, Fall Highweight Handicaps) and H. H. Hecht's The Pincher.

The distaff handicap leader was Two Lea, the only champion in the Calumet barn in 1950, a season which saw the great stable slip to second place on the list of winning owners. Lightly campaigned, but formidable in all her races, Two Lea won the Arcadia and Santa Margarita Handicaps from her sex, and raced notably against males without winning: a second to Ponder in the Maturity, and third to Noor and Citation in the Santa Anita Handicap, and a second, by half a length, to Porter's Broom in the Whopper Handicap, while conceding him 7 pounds actual weight. At the end of three seasons, Two Lea still never had finished out of the money. Her stablemate, Wistful, beat a mixed field for the Clang Handicap in teeth-chattering time of 1:22 for 7 furlongs, and placed in numerous other stakes. Bewitch won the Black Helen Handicap in 1:48 for 9 furlongs, a record for her sex, and she passed Honeymoon in earnings, finishing the season with dead aim on Gallorette's record. Nell K. defeated males in the Palm Beach, and won the Colonial and Top Flight Handicaps from her own sex; and Lithe won the Arlington Matron, Beverly and Vineland Handicaps.

Although 1¼ miles proved to be beyond his tether, Your Host came out of his upsetting adventure at Churchill Downs very well, and was a terror at medium distances the rest of the season. The speedster with the four white stockings and crooked neck, trained by H. L. Daniels, won on both coasts and in the Midwest. In addition to his two big victories at Santa Anita before the Kentucky Derby, he later won the Kent, Dick Welles Stakes

434

Your Host, the "magnificent cripple," who became a successful sire after his life insurance policy was paid off.

(7 furlongs in 1:22⅗ under 130 pounds in June) and Sheridan Handicap within his class; and the Golden State Breeders' and Thanksgiving Day Handicaps from open fields, defeating Ponder and Hill Prince in the last named-event, won in 1:41⅘, just a tick away from the Hollywood record. In the Premiere Handicap at the same track, he lost by only a nose in 1:22⅕, giving away 17 pounds to the older Star Fiddle.

Offspring of Heliopolis enjoyed a fine year in 1950. Brookmeade Stable's Greek Ship led his stable to the top of the owners' list and his sire to the head of the stallion list. He earned $140,175 with six victories, including the Louisiana Derby and Choice Stakes within his division, and the Metropolitan, Monmouth Handicaps and Empire City Gold Cup in open competition. Brandywine Stable's Greek Song won the Dwyer (from Hill Prince) and Arlington Classic.

Yolo Stable's Great Circle seemed to be everywhere up and down the Pacific Coast, and he was in the winner's circle after the Oakland, Cinema Handicaps and Del Mar Derby, setting a track record in the latter. (He was in the wrong spot in the Golden Gate Derby, however; he finished first, but was placed second for interference, and Sir Butch was declared the winner.) George Widener's Lights Up, a son of Eight Thirty, won the Peter Pan, Lamplighter Handicaps and Travers Stakes. Oil Capitol had the Everglades Handicap and Equipoise Mile to go along with his Flamingo victory; Mrs. Andy Schuttinger's Ferd won the Swift and Jersey Stakes; and Brookmeade's Sunglow did his share for the stable by winning the Chesapeake Stakes, Saranac and Discovery Handicaps, the latter in track record time.

Sophomores were making their presence felt in sprint races, too, as Mrs. Louis Lazare's Sheilas Reward won the championship of this category with wins in the Select, Fleetwing and Interborough Handicaps; and Guillotine took the historic Carter.

435

Tandem acts had become quite popular in the postwar era, and Alfred Vanderbilt had unveiled one toward the end of 1949 when his champion filly Bed o' Roses and Next Move came across the finish first and second in the Demoiselle Stakes. In 1950 the same pair finished in leapfrog order in the Gazelle Stakes as well as in the voting for the championship of the three-year-old filly division. Like her stablemate, Next Move was of peripatetic origin, having been conceived in Kentucky, foaled in California and weaned in Maryland. The big brown daughter of Bull Lea–Now What, by Chance Play, not only was voted best of her class, but received considerable mention in the handicap division balloting.

Within her classification, Next Move won the Prioress (by eight lengths), Gazelle, Cinderella Stakes, Delaware and CCA Oaks; she beat her elders in the Beldame, Ladies and Vanity Handicaps; and in her coast-to-coast raids, which netted $240,450, she battled fearlessly against colts. She failed to win in four outings among the males, but the races were won by such top ones as Hill Prince, Your Host and Sunglow, and the filly earned part of the purse in three of the races concerned.

Little Bed o' Roses defeated colts (Greek Ship and Theory) in the Lawrence Realization, and also won the Anita Chiquita Handicap from her own sex.

Apart from the Vanderbilt duo, the sophomore filly division included Cain Hoy Stable's Siama (Jasmine, Acorn, Princess Doreen Stakes, Monmouth Oaks and Comely Handicap), J. N. Crofton's speedy Special Touch (Santa Susana), Here's Hoping (Cleopatra Handicap), Ogden Phipps's Busanda (Alabama Stakes) and F. E. Dixon, Jr.'s Honey's Gal (Test Stakes).

All three polls were in agreement as to champions in every category in 1950, and Battlefield, owned by George D. Widener (the new chairman of the Jockey Club), was the selection as top two-year-old. The son of War Relic–Dark Display, by Display,—which meant that he had two close-up crosses to Fair Play in his pedigree, and three to that stallion's dam, Fairy Gold—proved to be one of the all-time bargain auction yearlings; bought for $4,500 from Jonabell Stables at the Saratoga Sales, he was never out of the money in thirteen starts in his first racing season, and he topped his generation in earnings with $198,677.

Battlefield began his campaign in February, quite early for a juvenile of stakes class, but at the time he was regarded merely as a useful prospect. Before his campaign ended on September 30, he had won the Hialeah Juvenile, Youthful, Tremont, Sapling Stakes, Saratoga Special, Hopeful Stakes and Futurity, an unusual demonstration of versatility, requiring as it does the precocity to win at 3 furlongs early in the winter, plus the stamina to hold on for 6½ furlongs over a straight course later in the year.

Runner-up in the voting, and leader on the Experimental Free Handicap, was J. J. Colando's Uncle Miltie, trained by his owner's son, Dr. Andrew Colando. An obscurely-bred son of Heather Broom–Twink-Mo, by Mokatam, named for comedian Milton Berle, the colt had not been nominated to the Futurities, but he was no joke when running. After beginning the season in claiming events, he moved right up the ladder of class, until at the end of the year he won the Champagne Stakes at a mile, and the 1$\frac{1}{16}$-mile Wakefield Stakes, while carrying 126 pounds.

Greentree Stable's Big Stretch, defeated by both Battlefield and Uncle Miltie in previous races, won the 1$\frac{1}{16}$-mile Pimlico Futurity, richest route stakes for two-year olds. Earlier in the year he had won the Sanford Stakes and Breeders' Futurity.

S. A. Mason II's To Market, swept both the rich Chicago futurities, at Arlington and Washington Parks; and Mrs. Sara Chait's speedy Lord Putnam, whose owner did not have a license in New York that year, did very well elsewhere: he won the William Penn, Narragansett Nursery and World's Playground

Stakes, plus two allowance races in both of which he set a track record for 5 furlongs. Mr. and Mrs. Fred Sharpe's Kings Hope won the Bashford Manor, Joliet, Graduation, Hyde Park Stakes and the Colorado Futurity and a division of the Silver Stakes at Centennial Park, which opened that summer near Denver. Mrs. Nat Goldstone's Gold Capitol led the Far West with victories in the Starlet and California Breeders' Champion Stakes.

Other noteworthy members of the division included Northern Star (Flash and U. S. Hotel Stakes), Nullify (East View), Rough 'n Tumble (Primer), Battle Morn (Grand Union Hotel Stakes) and Repetoire (Remsen Handicap).

Queen of the two-year-old fillies in 1950 was Aunt Jinny, bred, owned and trained by Duval Headley, who had tried to sell her but could not obtain what he considered a sufficient price. At the end of her first season the daughter of Heliopolis–Gaga, by Bull Dog, had earned $78,370, so no one was second-guessing her owner's decision. Aunt Jinny seemed unable to get rolling in the short races at the beginning of the year, and failed to win until her ninth start. However, as the distances stretched out she gained ground; she won the Demoiselle and Selima Stakes, both at 1 1/16 miles, and placed in the Marguerite at the same distance.

Flush with the success of his stand in regard to Aunt Jinny, Headley slapped a $25,000 price tag on her yearling half-brother; Greentree Stable took him up on it, and that, as shall be seen, was a windfall for the buyer.

Atalanta provided $65,190 of the $651,399 which made Brookmeade the season's top stable, with victories in the Schuylerville, Spinaway and Matron Stakes. Widener's Sungari won the filly division of the National Stallion Stakes, plus the Astoria and Colleen; and in Chicago Reverie Knoll Farm's Flyamanita won the Pollyanna and Princess Pat, while Sunningdale Farm's Shawnee Squaw won the Arlington Lassie. Clarence Hartwick's Sickle's

Louis B. Mayer, the movie magnate, whose collection of horses sold for the highest total price in history.

Image (also bred and trained by her owner) ran on both coasts, with victories in the Connors Memorial at Narragansett, and the Hollywood Lassie.

Citation and Noor, Hill Prince and Middleground, Battlefield and Big Stretch notwithstanding, one of the most exciting rivalries on the American turf in 1950 was that between jockeys Bill Shoemaker and Joe Culmone. Both 19-year-old boys were apprentices part of the season, the Texas-born Shoemaker having ridden his first winner in April of 1949, and Culmone, a native of Italy, in June. In their first full season they went at it hammer and tongs, Culmone starring in the East and Shoemaker in the West; the former, benefitting from the bug two months longer than Shoe-maker, crept ahead at one point, but the tiny Texan pulled back to even terms. On December 30, the last day of racing in the United States, each had 385 winners to his credit.

On December 31, a Sunday, Culmone went to Cuba and Shoemaker to Mexico in an effort to break the deadlock. Each rode three more winners to further complicate the picture: they had finished in what amounted to a three-way dead heat with a forty-four-year time lag. Both riders tied the record of 388 winners set by Walter Miller in 1906.

William Molter and W. Hal Bishop, who had tied for the leadership among trainers the year before, again finished in a dead heat in 1950—but this time for second place. "Red" McDaniel began his long tenure at the top.

CHAPTER SIXTY-ONE

RACING GOT BACK ON ITS FEET in 1951, as attendance approached 24-million and wagering exceeded $1½-billion. Purse distribution reached a new record gross of $55½-million, mainly because there were more races run than ever before (27,-856), but not entirely for that reason, since both average purse per race and average distribution per horse went up also. Most important, the minus signs disappeared almost completely from the summaries of race meetings: seventy-eight meetings reported gains, only three indicated losses and the latter were mild.

The Belmont Stakes was restored to $100,-000 in added value, and Chicago's two big mixed-age races, the Arlington and Washington Park Handicaps, also were raised to this level. The Preakness was boosted to $75,000, but Maryland racing suffered a sentimental blow as Havre de Grace failed to open. The old track in the upper reaches of the Chesapeake Bay, where Man o' War ran what his owner considered his greatest race, and where Citation and War Admiral won their maiden starts, had been founded in the first place with an eye to patronage from the neighboring states to the north, and as tracks in New Jersey and Delaware took over these areas, "de Grawh" bowed out of the picture.

The police action begun in Korea the previous summer had by 1951 become acknowledged as an accurate replica of an old-fashioned war, and, as had happened during the conflict a decade earlier, there was a general boom in the entertainment field, in which racing shared. However, this was not the key factor in the reversal of economic indices.

There also were two noteworthy individual cases of triumph over adversity in 1951.

Your Host immediately launched what seemed certain to be another glittering season —with a second to Bolero on New Year's Day, while conceding 5 pounds, in the San Carlos Handicap, won in new world record time of 1:21 for 7 furlongs. Five days later he won the Santa Catalina under 130 pounds, in new track record time of 1:48⅕ for 9 furlongs. But in the San Pasqual Handicap January 13, Your Host tripped over Renown's heels and fell. Jockey Eric Guerin managed to roll to safety, but Your Host fractured the ulna bone of his right foreleg in four places. The popular "Old Sidewinder's" racing days had ended, and there wasn't much hope for his life. So glum was the prospect of recovery that a $250,-000 life insurance policy was paid off—but the insurers did not destroy the colt. The son of Alibhai–Boudoir II, by Mahmoud, winner of 13 races and $384,795 in 23 starts, was saved for stud duty, thanks largely to his own courage. Twisted neck (which his owner said was the result of an injury as a weanling, but which his groom claimed was the horse's way of compensating for his eyes being set at slightly different levels), broken leg and all, Your Host became an immensely successful stallion. He never was considered seriously as a candidate for Horse of the Year, primarily because of his limited stamina, but he sired a son who won that honor more often than any horse in history, largely because of his unlimited stamina.

Having already once successfully flouted the adage that they never come back, Citation did it again in 1951; but the six-year-old stallion had his troubles. At Bay Meadows on April 18, his first start after a layoff of practically ten months, he finished third to A Lark and Pancho Supreme in a 6-furlong allowance race run in 1:09⅘, just ⅕-second off Bolero's track record. It was the first time in 39 races Citation had failed to finish among the first two, and the winner, although owned by Mr. and Mrs. N. G. Phillips, had been bred by Calumet Farm. Eight days later Citation again was third to the same pair in identical time, as Pancho Supreme won from A Lark.

The handicapper treated the veteran star gently enough for his step into stakes competition, as Citation was assigned 120 pounds for the 6-furlong Hollywood Premiere Handicap May 11. The old days, when the magic of his name was enough to shrink the field, were gone, however, and ten contestants faced the starter. After some crowding early (there frequently is in sprint races as the field goes all out from the break) Citation, next to last at the quarter pole, made up approximately three lengths in the last quarter, but nevertheless was fifth, the only time in his life he finished out of the money. His streak of remunerative races had ended at forty, and what vestige remained of his betting club presumably was dissolved. Winner of the Premiere, carrying 2 pounds more than Citation, was the fast filly, Special Touch, who covered the distance in 1:10 (she also shared with Coaltown the track record of 1:09⅕).

It was almost like old times in the Argonaut Handicap May 30 as Calumet fired a three-horse entry at the purse—Citation, Coaltown and Bewitch—but not quite: Andrew J. Crevolin's Be Fleet (118) defeated Citation (121) by three lengths, and the other Calumet runners were unplaced. That was Cy's last defeat.

He won his three remaining races with increasing ease. After defeating Be Fleet, with the aid of a 3-pound concession, in the Century Handicap, Citation won the American Handicap under 123 pounds from Bewitch and Sturdy One, with Be Fleet (112) unplaced.

In the Hollywood Gold Cup July 14, 1951,

Citation (120), ridden by Steve Brooks, romped to victory by four lengths, as Bewitch (108), ridden by Glen Lasswell, nosed out Be Fleet (123) for second money. The winner's guaranteed $100,000 purse pushed Citation well past a million dollars—and the $20,000 second money made Bewitch the world's leading money winner of her sex.

For a while, but not for long, the Calumet board of strategy toyed with the idea of probing further with the champion; however, he had reached his goal and was retired to stud after having compiled the following record: 45 starts, 32 wins, 10 seconds, two thirds, once unplaced, for earnings of $1,085,760.

Bewitch raced four more times in an effort to round off her total to half a million dollars, but added not a penny. She retired after 55 starts, 20 wins, 10 seconds and 11 thirds with record distaff earnings of $462,605. The stable had moved on to Chicago for the windup of her career, and she was loaded into a railroad car along with Citation and Coaltown to be taken back to the farm, each of them having won championships in at least two seasons. (Citation also was champion handicap horse of 1951 in one poll.)

"Do you suppose," mused trainer Jimmy Jones rhetorically, "that there ever has been a single car carrying three such horses into retirement before?"

Turf writer Joe Palmer approached it from a more provocative angle: were there ever three such horses in the same stable?

COUNTERPOINT, 1948

(Count Fleet–Jabot, by Sickle)

Despite his impressive career total, Citation was not the leading money winner of the 1951 season. That distinction was earned by C. V. Whitney's three-year-old Counterpoint, who also was named Horse of the Year by every method of selection. Such honors for the medium-sized, deceptively frail-looking chestnut

Counterpoint, the 1951 Horse of the Year, with jockey Dave Gorman and owner C. V. Whitney.

colt scarcely could have been anticipated at the beginning of the year, however, for Counterpoint won his championship as he did his races, finishing strong after a slow beginning.

The classic division as a whole was muddled early in the year, or, as Colonel Winn would have said had he still been around, the Kentucky Derby was wide open. Mrs. F. A. Genter's Rough 'n Tumble, winner of the Santa Anita Derby, was taken out of training shortly thereafter because of splint trouble, and Mrs. Walter M. Jeffords's Flamingo Stakes winner, Yildiz, was not nominated to the Churchill Downs fixture. Uncle Miltie became a favorite for the Kentucky Derby in the "futures" after he defeated Battlefield in their mutual three-year-old debut, but, along with virtually every other candidate from the East Coast, he was soundly trounced subsequently by Mrs. N. A. Mikell's Repetoire, who began the year with four straight added-money victories, in the Cherry Blossom Stakes, Experimental Free Handicap No. 1, Chesapeake and Wood Memorial Stakes.

Whitney did have a well-regarded Derby colt, but his name was Mameluke, winner of a division of the Blue Grass Stakes; Counterpoint finished third behind Arkansas Derby winner, Ruhe, and Royal Mustang in the other division.

The logical favorite for that year's Kentucky Derby would seem to have been undefeated Repetoire, but since Battle Morn had been gaining on him at the end of the Wood, and the Cain Hoy colt had the saddle services of Eddie Arcaro, it seemed even more logical to make Battle Morn favorite, which was done.

Winner of the race, by four lengths, was Count Turf, a son of Count Fleet, owned by New York restaurateur Jack Amiel (partner of former heavyweight champion Jack Dempsey) and ridden by Conn McCreary. Officially trained by Sol Rutchick, actually Count Turf had been sent to the post by George "Slim" Sulley, since his chances of victory had appeared so remote that Rutchick stayed in New York with the main part of the stable. On his own Count Turf probably would have paid an enormous price; as it was, he was lumped in the pari-mutuel "field" with four other of the least-plausible candidates at slightly under 15-to-1.

441

Royal Mustang finished second and Ruhe third, as Battle Morn, Repetoire and other logical contenders were unplaced. The Whitney colors were prominent, in a manner of speaking, for Mameluke went lame and galloped around all by himself in last place, but no one noticed the Horse of the Year tucked in the middle of the field, eleventh of the twenty runners.

A maiden in two starts as a juvenile, Counterpoint had raced only four times at three prior to the Derby. After a fourth and a win in allowance company, he was second by eight lengths to the older mare, Wistful, in the Ben Ali Handicap, following which came the Blue Grass Stakes. He actually finished fourth in this roughly contested affair, but was moved up to third upon the disqualification from first place of Sonic.

Two weeks after the Derby, Counterpoint was runner-up in the Preakness, but even so he attracted little attention. He was seven lengths behind the winner, Brookmeade Stable's Bold, and the significance of the effort was attenuated because none of the first four from the Kentucky Derby had been nominated to the Maryland classic. The future champion did even less to enhance his reputation next out, a fifth place in the Withers, which was won by Battlefield.

In the Peter Pan Handicap on June 9 Counterpoint scored a daylight victory over Battlefield in new track record time of 1:47⅘ for 1⅛ miles. The Widener colt was conceding 9 pounds on this occasion, but when they met at level weights in the Belmont Stakes a week later, Counterpoint, ridden by Dave Gorman, won by four lengths. However, in the Dwyer on July 7, Battlefield evened the score, defeating Alerted in a close race as Counterpoint finished ninth.

Later it was learned that the Whitney colt had bruised a heel, so he was put aside for a rest. It was after he returned to action—Battlefield having also been shelved by injury—that Counterpoint earned his championship.

Following a fourth under top weight in the Jerome Handicap in September, won by Alerted, Counterpoint wound up his season with four straight victories.

The first was the Lawrence Realization, which he won from Saxony by open daylight, as Alerted finished third under 12 pounds less weight. Next were the ones that did the trick.

The mighty Hill Prince was back on the scene, fresh from a victory in the New York Handicap under 128 pounds. As the Chenery colt had won his championship the previous season by defeating an older horse at weight-for-age in the Jockey Club Gold Cup, so did Counterpoint return the favor in the 1951 renewal of the same race on October 13. In one of the highlights of the year, he inched up on the heavily favored Hill Prince through the stretch and stuck his head in front at the wire. Hill Prince did not get his revenge as Noor had done to him. When he met Counterpoint again in the Empire City Gold Cup the next Saturday, it was a carbon copy of their previous race up to a point—then Counterpoint drew away to win by one and a quarter lengths, in 2:42⅖, equaling the Jamaica record for 1⅝ miles.

Assigned 130 pounds against his contemporaries in the Empire City Handicap, Counterpoint won going away from Hall of Fame (124) on a sloppy track to close out his season with seven wins in fifteen starts and $250,525.

Possibly the best testimony to the quality he demonstrated in the fall was the election in two polls of Hill Prince as champion handicap horse—he had to his credit just one stakes victory, and two seconds to Counterpoint.

In 1951 Battlefield completed his second season of racing without ever having finished out of the money, with six wins and six seconds in twelve starts as a three-year-old. He followed this same pattern in his races against Counterpoint—two wins and two seconds— but the Widener colt competed exclusively within his age division and was no menace to the champion in the voting (Counterpoint was a unanimous choice for best three-year-old in the Triangle poll). If there had been an award for entertainment, however, Battlefield and Hampton Stable's Alerted would have been difficult to overlook, for they put on quite a show. In contrast to the Noor–Citation duels of the previous season, these two were finely responsive to weight changes; with an 11-pound concession Alerted was second by a nose to Battlefield in the Shevlin; when the concession was reduced to 10 pounds for the Dwyer he dropped back to half a length; but when Alerted received 12 pounds in the Discovery Handicap he won by a head. (On the other hand, two of these races had been allowance events, so there still were grounds for the suggestion that handicappers should all be sent on a hike to the North Pole under full field pack, and horses be allowed to establish their own weights. Moreover, as became increasingly apparent as his career went on, getting a close finish out of Battlefield did not require any particular talent. Among other notions, the colt seemed to have it in his head that once he reached the front, wherever that happened to be, his job was done, and timing his run so that he reached the lead just before the finish was a ticklish matter. How much he lost as a result of this habit is anybody's guess.)

At three Battlefield won the Choice Stakes besides the Withers, Shevlin, Dwyer and Travers. Alerted, a son of Bull Lea–Hastily Yours, by John P. Grier, and about the best one that got away from his breeder, Calumet Farm, won the Laurel Stakes and Fountain of Youth Handicaps in addition to the Discovery and Jerome.

Runner-up to Counterpoint in the voting for best male sophomore was Hall of Fame, a gelded son of Shut Out, who was the principal factor in putting Greentree Stable at the top of the owners' list that year. Unplaced in the first two classics, and not eligible to the Belmont Stakes, since geldings were excluded in those days, Hall of Fame did quite well on forays away from headquarters under supervision by assistant trainer George Poole. He won the Kent and Leonard Richards Stakes in Delaware, The Arlington Classic and American Derby in Chicago, the Narragansett Special against older horses besides the Wilson Stakes at Saratoga.

The Kentucky Derby and Preakness winners met in an allowance race in June, which Count Turf won and in which Bold bucked shins; Count Turf went awry after being unplaced in the Belmont Stakes and Bold later came back to win the Saranac Handicap.

In 1951 Count Fleet (sire of Counterpoint and Count Turf) led the sire list as his get earned $1,160,847. In the handicap division the Hertz stallion was represented by Be Fleet

A well-matched pair, Battlefield (rail) and Alerted staging one of their duels in the 1951 Shevlin Stakes.

—winner of $114,900, including the Washington's Birthday, San Juan Capistrano and San Francisco Handicaps before his victory over Citation in the Argonaut—and by an even bigger money winner, County Delight. The latter colt, owned by Rokeby Stable, earned $170,985 and was ranked third to Hill Prince and Citation among the older runners of the season. Unplaced but twice in twenty starts—quite unusual in handicap company—County Delight won the Dixie, Gallant Fox, Merchants' and Citizens' and Manhattan Handicaps, finished second in three stakes and third in eight.

Within his group, he was topped in earnings only by Anita King and Gus Luellwitz's amazing gelding, Moonrush. This five-year-old son of Hunters Moon IV, already a stakes winner during three successive seasons, went on in 1951 to win $221,050, including the San Pasqual, Santa Anita, Salinas, Bay Meadows and Golden State Breeders' Handicap.

Brandywine Stable's Cochise won the Grey Lag, Arlington and Sussex Handicaps and gave the hunch players fits by running a dead heat with Post Card in the Brandywine Handicap. Arise won the Carter and Monmouth Handicaps, and in the Questionnaire ran a dead heat with Bryan G., winner of Aqueduct, Westchester Handicaps and Pimlico Special.

One Hitter did his bit for Greentree with scores in the Massachusetts, Edgemere Handicaps and Whitney Stakes; Curandero won the Washington Park Handicap and Equipoise Mile; Palestinian bridged the continent by taking the Brooklyn and Golden Gate Handicaps, and the Widener went to Sunglow.

Sheilas Reward won his second sprint championship, and among numerous others prominent in the handicap ranks were Spartan Valor, Johns Joy, Delegate, Miche, Sturdy One, Admiral Drake, Call Over and Squared Away.

The Vanderbilt filly team continued its game of leapfrog as Bed o' Roses took another turn at being champion, while Next Move lagged back. Winner of only two stakes—the Vineland Handicap under 126 pounds, and the Comely under 127—Bed o' Roses finished close up in five others under high weight. She came very near winning the richest purse in history when she took on males in her second start, the Santa Anita Maturity. Organized along futurity lines, but conditioned for four-year-olds, which allowed more time for payments to accumulate, the winner's purse in 1951 was worth $144,325 to Great Circle, who won from Lotowhite, as Bed o' Roses finished a close third, despite coming out of the race lame. Next Move's most lucrative performance was against a mixed field—a second in the Santa Anita Handicap—but she won the Las Flores from her sex.

Runner-up to Bed o' Roses in the voting for best handicap mare was Busanda, winner of the Top Flight and New Castle Handicaps in her division, and the Suburban and Saratoga Cup from open competition. Special Touch, the filly who beat Citation in the Hollywood Premiere, also won the Santa Margarita and Alameda Handicaps; and while Bewitch managed to win only the Vanity, her stablemate, Wistful, won the Ben Ali, Clark, Beverly Handicaps and Whirlaway Stakes. Other top-flight fillies older than three included Thelma Berger (Louisiana, Le Compte, and Beldame Handicaps) and Marta (Molly Pitcher and Ladies).

A daughter of Count Fleet, Walter M. Jeffords's Kiss Me Kate, trained by Oscar White, headed the three-year-old filly division. Named for a musical comedy (a practice which no longer is permissible, since copyrighted names are not acceptable for horses) she won the Acorn, Gazelle, Alabama Stakes and Delaware Oaks. The most important of the Oaks—the Coaching Club American version—was won by H. B. Delman's How, who also took the Kentucky equivalent of a filly Derby.

Runner-up to Kiss Me Kate in the voting, and leading money winner of the division, was Sickle's Image, a daughter of Sickletoy, who netted $119,775, principally through victories in the Ashland, Cleopatra Stakes, Modesty and Arlington Matron Handicaps. Among others to

444

receive mention in the voting were Belair Stud's Vulcania (Test Stakes and Diana Handicap) and Old English Rancho's Ruth Lily (Hollywood Oaks and Santa Susana Stakes).

As often happens, the crop of foals which reached racing age in 1951 included a number of flashy youngsters who promised great things for the future; as happens very infrequently, the near-unanimous choice as champion juvenile of this crop was destined to deliver much more than he promised.

Tom Fool, the second foal of Duval Headley's mare, Gaga, whose first had been the previous year's champion filly, Aunt Jinny, turned out to be something of a bargain basement purchase after all. Headley had put a price of $25,000 on the youngster, but the colt was bunged up in a run-in with a fence, and the damage, although superficial, would have militated severely against his price had he been sold in the customary manner, at auction. In his private negotiations with Greentree Stable, Headley reduced the tag to $20,000, and even at that sum there were other factors influencing the sale. Headley formerly had trained for John Hay Whitney, co-owner of the stable, and his judgment therefore was respected. For his uncle, Headley also had trained Menow, sire of Tom Fool, and sire also of Capot, who had been Greentree's first Horse of the Year.

At two, Tom Fool won five of his seven starts, was second in the other two and topped his division in earnings with $155,960. After winning his debut at Saratoga in August, followed by the Sanford Stakes, he defeated Alfred G. Vanderbilt's Cousin in the Grand Union Hotel Stakes, in which Cousin stumbled and, moreover, was required to concede 4 pounds. When Cousin defeated Tom Fool at level weights in the Hopeful next out, run over a good track, he assumed the mantle temporarily, the Vanderbilt colt having won the Great American, Flash Stakes and Saratoga Special.

After racing moved back to Belmont Park, Calumet Farm's Arlington Futurity winner, Hill Gail, beat them both, although Tom Fool

(second) and Cousin (unplaced) each had an excuse, the former having been bothered by Hitex, and Cousin (a spooky sort) having gone into the air at the break.

In the Futurity on October 6, Tom Fool scored a one-and-three-quarter-length victory over Primate, Jet's Date third, Hill Gail fourth and Cousin eighth. Starmount Stable's Primate had won the Youthful and Juvenile Stakes earlier in the season; Marlboro Stud Farm's fifth-place Jet Master had won the Hialeah Juvenile, National Stallion and U. S. Hotel Stakes; and also unplaced in Tom Fool's Futurity was the Cowdin Stakes winner, Eternal Moon.

The Greentree colt closed out his first racing season by passing his test of stamina (and courage) in the 1$\frac{1}{16}$-mile East View Stakes; although he did not like the sloppy going, he nevertheless outgamed Put Out by a neck in the stretch drive. Tom Fool skipped the Pimlico Futurity, won by Cajun.

The list of Tom Fool's conquered foes encompassed the cream of that year's crop. One notable exception was J. H. Dunn's Oh Leo, king of the Mississippi Valley, with victories in the Duncan Kenner, Hyde Park, Primer Stakes, Hawthorne Juvenile Handicap and Washington Park Futurity. The Champagne stakes winner, Armageddon, was another. In the West, the loudest challenge came from Big Noise, owned and bred by trumpet player Harry James and his wife, actress Betty Grable. The son of Khaled won the Del Mar Futurity and California Breeders' Champion Stakes; the latter event seldom was considered in voting for the championship, since it was restricted to foals bred in the state, but it carried a high purse ($30,110 to Big Noise) and often was won by youngsters who had proved themselves in open competition.

Voted best of the two-year-old fillies in 1951 was Maine Chance Farm's Rose Jet, from the first crop of foals by Jet Pilot. Trained by Bill Booth, the brown filly was unplaced but once in nine starts, despite frequent shin bucking. She won the Schuylerville and Matron Stakes, plus the testing Selima and Demoiselle, both the latter at $1\frac{1}{16}$ miles, to top her section in money as well as prestige with $132,285.

Rose Jet had to be impressive to win from Princess Lygia, a daughter of Roman, who had five wins and a second in six starts, for earnings of $86,785. Owned originally by Mrs. Harry Trotsek, wife of the trainer, the Princess won her first five starts in a row, including the Miss America, a division of the Hyde Park Stakes (beating colts), the Pollyanna and Arlington Lassie. After a layoff of nearly a month, she was sold for $100,000 to Louis B. Mayer, acting as agent for his son-in-law, William Goetz, and in her only start that year for the new ownership, the day after her sale, she ran second to Calumet Farm's A Gleam in the Princess Pat. The latter filly went east, and finished in a dead heat for third in Rose Jet's Matron.

Brae Burn Farm's Star-Enfin was another good one, winner of the Astoria and Colleen, and the division also was embellished by Blue Case (Rosedale, Spinaway), Cigar Maid (Fashion, National Stallion), Miss Nosoca (Rancocas Stakes, Margate Handicap) and others.

In 1952 new gross records were set in every category, as again more races were run, and, unlike the explosion following World War II, this trend was coming off a solid foundation. Only six of eighty-seven race meetings reported declines in business—fewer than would be expected from the normal vicissitudes from season to season—and the average purse per race reached another new high of $2,201.

The rise in average purse, however, was only a hint of the tremendous increase that was taking place in the earnings potential of stakes horses. Before World War II $100,000 had been considered an exceptional sum for career winnings—this sum was exceeded by twenty-four individual runners during the 1952 season alone, of whom ten won more than $200,-000 each. In fact, the day was fast approaching when winners of $100,000 in a single race,

while not commonplace, were no longer extraordinary.

The American Derby and Arlington Classic joined the parade of $100,000-added races in 1952, bringing the total number of such races in the nation up to ten. It was announced that the Preakness, Flamingo, Widener and Wood Memorial would be put into that category for their next renewals (which was to be true also of the Florida Derby, Westerner Stakes, Sunset and New Castle Handicaps) and Garden State Park unveiled plans for a similarly endowed futurity-type event which would top them all in gross value. Before the decade ended there were to be more than forty such events contested annually.

In Chicago the hike in values of the big races, both in 1951 and 1952, was accompanied by a reduction in distance, the more drastic changes having involved the Classic (for three-year-olds) and Washington Park Handicap (threes and up) both of which were dropped to 1 mile. This change was decried by some as a step toward jeopardizing the stamina of the native breed, and by others it was hailed as an opening wedge in what had been a disproportionate block in allocation of rich purses; as matters stood at the time, with minor variations, all $100,000 races had been clustered at the American classic distance of $1\frac{1}{4}$ miles, and the changes put the "hundred granders" within reach of a large number of horses which heretofore could not have aspired to such plums. Later, in other areas, equivalent purses were to be offered for proficiency both below and beyond the standard $1\frac{1}{4}$ miles, on dirt and grass tracks, for males and females.

In 1952, for the third time since World War II, the leading money winner was a member of the handicap division. Crafty Admiral, owned by the Charfran Stable of Charles and Frances Cohen, won nine of his sixteen starts for winnings of $277,225 during the season.

The bay four-year-old son of Fighting Fox—Admiral's Lady, by War Admiral, trained by R. B. "Bob" Odom, was a newcomer to the stakes scene for all practical purposes; he had placed in stakes as a two-year-old, but was sidelined by ankle trouble after one start at three. At four, his ankles still were noticeably large, but they did not slow him down. Only once did he fail to get part of the purse, and he was voted best handicap runner of the season.

After a win in his 1952 debut, followed by a fourth in the Hialeah Inaugural Handicap, Crafty Admiral was in light, at 107 pounds, for the Palm Beach Handicap January 23, and he scored his first stakes victory in new track record time of 1:22 for 7 furlongs. Versatility was his strong point, for Crafty Admiral then won three more races in succession, going up and down the range of distance; overnight races at 9 and 7 furlongs, followed by a conquest of Alerted, by a neck, in the 1¼-mile Gulfstream Park Handicap. After a string of seconds, and his unplaced effort in the Metropolitan Handicap, Crafty Admiral won four more in a row, demonstrating a capacity to carry weight: the Brooklyn, under 116 pounds, was followed by the Merchants' and Citizens' with 126, the Whirlaway Handicap under that same weight and the Washington Park Handicap under 128. In his final start of the year, he finished third in the 2-mile Jockey Club Gold Cup at weight-for-age.

In the Washington Park Handicap, the Charfran colt defeated To Market, second highest money winner of the handicap division; unplaced was William Helis, Jr.'s Spartan Valor, Crafty Admiral's nearest rival in the voting for the championship, who had beaten Crafty Admiral in the Hialeah Inaugural early in the season. Himself a record breaker and weight carrier, Spartan Valor also won the McLennan Handicap in new track record time of 1:47⅕ for 1⅛ miles, the Widener, Excelsior, Gallant Fox (129 pounds) and Valley Forge Handicaps, setting a Garden State Park record of 1:40⅘ for a mile and 70 yards in the last-named race, while carrying 130 pounds. To Market, sold to King Ranch during the season, won the San Carlos, Massachusetts

(new Suffolk Downs record of 2:01⅖ for 1¼ miles), Arlington Handicaps and Hawthorne Gold Cup.

Among the older runners of 1952 in the West was Brookfield Farm's Intent, winner of the Santa Anita Maturity, San Juan Capistrano, Forty-Niners and Lakes and Flowers Handicap. The son of War Relic almost affected a clean sweep of Santa Anita's rich races for his age, as he finished first in the $100,000-added Handicap, but was disqualified for interference and placed second to his victim, Miche; Intent also finished second to Phil D. in the Malibu Sequet and San Antonio Handicaps.

General Staff, owned by Leland Stanford "Larry" MacPhail, a former baseball impresario who acquired control of Bowie in 1952, was the leader in the East, outside of New York, as he won four stakes in New Jersey (Oceanport, Long Branch, Quaker City Handicaps and Salvator Mile) plus the Narragansett and Pimlico Specials.

Of the previous season's sophomore stars who had come into the handicap ranks, Battlefield won the New York and Westchester Handicaps; Counterpoint took the San Fernando and Whitney Stakes; and Alerted won the Appleton, Dixie, Healey, Questionnaire, Fort McHenry and President's Plate Handicaps and Olympic Stakes. Starting 33 times in 1952, and placing in numerous other added money events, Alerted was on his way to succeeding Display as the iron horse of American racing; before he was through, he ran in 104 races, won 20, and was in the money a further 40 times, for earnings of $440,485. The ill-starred 1951 Preakness winner, Bold, remained an equivocal quantity as he was killed by lightning after only two starts, unplaced, at four.

One Hitter won the Suburban, Monmouth and Saratoga Handicaps, and Oil Capitol won the New Orleans and Bidwill Memorial Handicaps.

The ancient Tea-Maker, nine years old in 1952, won the sprint championship with victories in four stakes and numerous placings;

other older males who rated mention in the voting were Woodchuck, Squared Away, Pet Bully, Dark Peter and Hi Billee.

In the distaff handicap division three-year-old Real Delight pushed aside her elders in the Triangle poll, but the title in the TRA poll, which was set up according to age, went to Next Move—completing the cycle with her stablemate, Bed o' Roses, each of them having won championships of one kind or another in alternating seasons for four straight years. In 1952 Next Move won the Firenze, Bay Shore Handicaps and a division of the Beldame, while Bed o' Roses took the Santa Margarita.

In her last season of racing, despite a knot on one ankle the size of a baseball, six-year-old Two Lea earned $174,550, her victories including the Vanity, San Mateo, Children's Hospital Handicaps and Hollywood Gold Cup. The latter race was a fitting highlight to a distinguished career, for she thus became the first member of her sex to win a "hundred grander," and she did it the hard way, against males. The gallant old mare left the track having started 26 times in all; she won 15, was unplaced but twice, and went into retirement with $309,250.

Sickle's Image continued to pad her bank account with victories in the Los Cerritos, F. M. Alger Memorial and Vineland Handicaps, plus numerous placings; Kiss Me Kate won the New Castle Handicap, Marta the Vagrancy and How the Ladies Handicap.

As had been the case the previous year, the three-year-old division did not jell until the last half of 1952; the champion of the division, like Counterpoint, was a late-developing son of Count Fleet, but unlike Counterpoint, he was voted Horse of the Year only in one poll.

Mrs. Walter M. Jeffords's One Count, a dark brown son of Count Fleet–Ace Card, by Case Ace, trained by Oscar White, had raced only three times as a juvenile, winning a maiden event in his last start. He began his three-year-old campaign in January, with a win, a close third, then another victory in overnight races, but he finished unplaced in his first three outings in stakes company. His first placing in stakes was a second in the Withers in May, which was followed by a third in the Preakness, and on June 7 he scored his initial stakes victory in the Belmont Stakes. Thereafter, he won the Travers, ran second in the Lawrence Realization (to Mark-Ye-Well), then, as Counterpoint had done, conquered fields that included older runners in the Jockey Club Gold Cup (beating Mark-Ye-Well and handicap champion Crafty Admiral) and Empire City Gold Cup.

The six-year-old mare Two Lea winning the 1952 Hollywood Gold Cup from male rivals for the first victory in a $100,000-*added* race by a member of her sex.

One Count, the champion three-year-old of 1952, with jockey Dave Gorman.

Mark-Ye-Well was the largest money winner of a powerful band of three-year-olds that led Calumet Farm to its fourth million-dollar season, and eighth financial title. More than that, the son of Bull Lea symbolized the awesome resources of the juggernaut stable. Calumet's Hill Gail, another son of Bull Lea, was head of the sophomore class in the early part of 1952. The first colt ever to win both the Santa Anita and Kentucky Derbies, he also had taken the San Vicente Stakes, Phoenix Handicap (defeating older rivals) and Derby Trial before an osselet forced him to the sidelines in May. While the loss of such a colt for the remainder of the season might have dismayed the ordinary stable, Calumet reached into the supply bin and brought out the unknown Mark-Ye-Well, a colt who had not raced as a two-year-old. He proved to be an able deputy —seven for eleven and never out of the money —winning both the nation's newest hundred-granders, the Arlington Classic and American Derby, as well as the Clang Handicap and Lawrence Realization, for earnings of $268,745.

Tom Fool missed the Triple Crown events because of fever and a cough, and a trip to Chicago for its rich races aborted when he turned in such an unaccountably poor per-

formance in a warm-up race that he was withdrawn from the stakes. Notwithstanding these contretemps, he was unplaced only once in thirteen starts, of which he won six, including the Wilson Stakes, Jerome, Sysonby, Grey Lag and Empire City Handicaps, the latter under 128 pounds. His duels with Battlefield in the autumn were epic, and had they continued the handicapper would have had to resort to apothecaries' weight. In the 1⅛-mile Grey Lag Handicap on October 18, carrying 119 pounds to 118 on his older rival, which amounted to a 7-pound concession on the scale of weights, Tom Fool defeated Battlefield by a nose. In the Westchester Handicap at the same distance November 1, with just 1 more pound difference in weight (125 to 123), Battlefield won by a nose; Alerted was third and Oil Capitol fourth in both these races.

A. W. Abbott's Blue Man was the nearest thing to a Triple Crown specialist that season, as he won the Preakness, ran second in the Belmont Stakes and third in the Kentucky Derby. He also won a division of the Flamingo Stakes (One Count unplaced), Experimental Free Handicap No. 2, Yankee Handicap and Dwyer Stakes to earn $259,585. Cain Hoy Stable's Armageddon, a one-eyed son of Alsab, was prominent on the scene through victories

449

in the Withers Stakes, Peter Pan, Ventnor and Benjamin Franklin Handicaps; and, although he raced only four times before injury intervened, Windy City II did very well. Head of the Free Handicaps in England, Ireland and France as a two-year-old the previous season, while owned by rodeo star Ray Bell, the colt had been sold to Mrs. Petite Luellwitz after importation to this country; in his brief three-year-old campaign Windy City II beat Hill Gail in the San Gabriel Stakes and San Felipe Handicap, and was second to the Calumet colt in the Santa Anita Derby.

Marcador and Jampol also enjoyed lucrative seasons, and three-year-olds who gained consideration among the sprinters were Hitex, Hannibal and White Skies.

The Calumet stallion, Bull Lea, was leading sire in 1952 for the fourth time, breaking his own record as his get earned $1,630,655. He was represented by no less than eleven stakes winners during the year, among them the dual champion, Real Delight, universal choice as best three-year-old filly, and also elected champion of the handicap division in one poll. Like Mark-Ye-Well (and, before him, Coaltown and Armed) she had not raced as a two-year-old, but she made up for lost time at three; winner of $236,272, her only loss in twelve starts was a close second to a male adversary.

A huge, 17-hand bay, Real Delight at times was plagued by a bad knee, but there was no evidence of it in her record. She began her career in combination races—i.e., mixed fields of claiming and allowance runners—she being classified among the latter, with good reason. After winning two such events easily, she stepped up in class to win a division of the Ashland Stakes by five, following which came her only loss. She was a fast closing second, by a head, to the excellent sprinter, White Skies, in 1:16⅘, just ⅕-second off the Keeneland record for 6½ furlongs, a distance not to the advantage of the gangling filly. That was the only time Real Delight met males, and the only time she was ridden by Donald Devine,

an apprentice who also held the dubious distinction of having lost one with Mark-Ye-Well that year.

Real Delight then won eight stakes in a row: the Kentucky Oaks, Black-Eyed Susan Stakes (ex-Pimlico Oaks), CCA Oaks—thus duplicating Wistful's achievement of the Fillies' Triple Crown—Cleopatra, Arlington Matron Stakes, Modesty, Beverly and a division of the Beldame Handicap. The Arlington Matron was changed that year into an allowance race for three-year-old fillies, but Real Delight defeated her elders in her last three starts, carrying actual top weight in each. In the Modesty, she covered a mile in 1:35⅗ while carrying 126 pounds, conceding 7 pounds actual weight to Sickle's Image; she won the Beverly in 1:34⅘ under 129 pounds, conceding 24 to her contemporary, Aesthete, and 8 to Sickle's Image. Real Delight also won her division of the 1⅛-mile Beldame in 1:51—identical to the time registered by Bed o' Roses in the other division— while carrying 126, a pound more weight. Real Delight was under more pressure to win her half, from five-year-old Marta (117).

The only member of her division mentioned in the same breath with Real Delight was her stablemate, A Gleam, a daughter of Blenheim II, out of Twilight Tear, making Bull Lea a proud grandsire. Running one-two in rich stakes is satisfying, but Calumet had enjoyed that experience often enough, and A Gleam was campaigned on the West Coast while Real Delight stayed east of the Rockies. Although she was never unplaced at other tracks, A Gleam was the proverbial "horse for the course" at Hollywood Park, undefeated winner of five stakes at the meeting. She won the Hollywood Oaks from her own division, the 7-furlong Milady Handicap from older fillies and mares in new track record time of 1:21⅗, and beat males in the Debonair Stakes, Cinema Handicap and 1¼-mile Westerner Stakes, carrying actual top weight in the last two. Possibly the most egregious display of muscle in turf history occurred at Hollywood Park on June 14, 1952, when two stakes were on the program—one open and one exclusively for females. After A Gleam had humiliated the colts in the Debonair, in the very next race her stablemates, Two Lea, Wistful and Jennie Lee, finished one-two-three in the Vanity Handicap.

Elsewhere in 1952 Jouett Shouse's Cinda won the Cherry Blossom, Betsy Ross Stakes, a division of the Colonial and the Regret Handicap; J. W. Brown's Parading Lady won the Acorn Stakes and Vosburgh Handicap; and other good three-year-old fillies included G. F. Strickland's Devilkin (owned by Mrs. J. W. Hanes later in the year), Mrs. M. W. O'Connor's La Corredora (Monmouth Oaks, etc.), Princess Lygia, and Mrs. Gerard S. Smith's Nilufer.

In 1952 the two-year-old division was in a cloud; the other members scarcely could be seen behind the overpowering presence of Native Dancer, whose career is a story in itself, which shall be related in a following chapter.

Of the others, Trio Stable's Laffango was unplaced but once in eleven starts, and netted $100,400 as a juvenile. His six victories included divisions of the Tyro and Sapling Stakes, plus the Champagne and final renewal of the old Garden State Stakes. Ben Whitaker's Tahitian King—left an orphan when his dam died, and raised on milk from a Percheron nurse mare—also was unplaced but once in a briefer schedule of eight races, of which he won the first four in succession, including the National Stallion and U. S. Hotel Stakes. Greentree Stable's Straight Face, an animal of such contentious disposition that gelding him had not subdued his spirit noticeably, won the Breeders' Futurity and Kentucky Jockey Club Stakes. The Pimlico Futurity went to Isasmoothie.

In Chicago's richest events for their age, Martin and McKinney's Mr. Good won the Arlington Futurity from Mrs. Ada Rice's Mr. Paradise, and Mr. Paradise won the Washington Park Futurity from Mr. Good. Wheatley Stable's Hilarious, after he got over his greenness, won three straight, including the Tremont Stakes, before a sickness which affected his wind ended his brief season. Allison and Prestridge's Invigorator won the Babylon Handicap and Cowdin Stakes; and, in California, Joe Palmisano's Little Request won the Haggin and Starlet Stakes, and Archie Sneed's Hour Regards took the Del Mar Futurity.

If champion colt Native Dancer was figuratively the biggest two-year-old on the scene in years, the champion filly of 1952 was literally the smallest. Mrs. E. E. Dale Shaffer's Sweet Patootie, a daughter of Alquest–Sweet Woman, by Roman, and the first foal of her dam, was so small she couldn't qualify for the select summer sales, and was so disregarded by other bidders that she was purchased by an agent for her consignor's wife in the fall sales. Described as "about" (a useful adverb) 15 hands tall, many racegoers chuckled when they saw what they believed to be the jockey going to the post on the stable pony by mistake.

What happens after they leave the post is what counts, however, and Patootie usually left it flying, her little legs churning so fast she resembled a centipede. More important, she stayed in front until the finish often enough, winning eight of her twelve starts and finishing second in all the others, to earn $61,917. Trained by H. H. "Pete" Battle, Sweet Patootie equaled the Detroit track record of :58⅗ for 5 furlongs, and won the Longport Handicap (beating colts), Jeanne d' Arc, Frizette and Alcibiades Stakes.

Despite abbreviated opportunity, Dixiana's Fulvous led the juvenile fillies in earnings with $111,375, as her three victories in four starts included both the rich filly futurities in Chicago —the Arlington Lassie and Princess Pat Stakes. Calumet's Bubbley, a full sister to Real Delight, won the Churchill Downs Debutante Stakes (the same day Hill Gail won the Derby) and Pollyanna Stakes; and Mrs. Whitaker's Grecian Queen, after winning the Schuylerville and Astarita, forecast her future Oaks quality with victories in the 1¹⁄₁₆-mile Demoiselle and a division of the Marguerite.

451

Another whose star was destined to rise even higher in subsequent seasons was E. P. Taylor's Canadiana, winner of five added money events including the important Coronation Stakes and Cup and Saucer Handicap. The daughter of Chop Chop was elected Horse of the Year in the Dominion.

Ogden Phipps' Flirtatious won the Polly Drummond and Spinaway; Mrs. Herbert Herff's Mimi Mine won the Durazna Stakes; and Mr. and Mrs. J. R. Collins's Biddy Jane won the Rancocas and Miss America, defeating Sweet Patootie in the latter.

Over a path strewn with obstacles, Anthony DeSpirito set a new riding record of 390 winners, to break the three-way deadlock that had its origin forty-six years earlier.

In an incomplete season—he rode his first winner on January 22—the 17-year-old apprentice from Lawrence, Massachusetts, was further beset by injury and suspension: he lost five days in a freak accident at Lincoln Downs in November when, after winning the race, he was thrown by Anchor Man as the horse pulled up; and in December he was suspended ten days for rough riding. Returning to the saddle on December 24, his eighteenth birthday, the New England rider picked up three winners at Tropical Park to bring his total to 376. He continued piling up his score (flying to Havana to get in three winners at Oriental Park in the process) until on December 29 he rode four winners at Tropical to tie the record of 388 shared by Miller, Shoemaker and Culmone. Another winner on each of the remaining days in the year gave him his new record.

The hell-for-leather youngster—called "DeSperado" by a few of his fellow reinsmen—used 1,482 mounts in achieving his goal, for a healthy 26 percent winning average. As Shoemaker had done out West, DeSpirito also demonstrated to several tracks in New England, where he was immensely popular, that a star attraction can be a mixed blessing. His mounts were at such short prices that a lot of customers refused to wager on them—and, on the other hand, few dared to bet against them. The result was often a lower mutuel handle.

Tony DeSpirito, the champion jockey of 1952 with 390 winners.

452

CHAPTER SIXTY-TWO

ATIVE DANCER WAS A PRO. THE son of Polynesian–Geisha, by Discovery, in his first season provided little or none of the cliff-hanging excitement customarily associated with horse racing. The feeling he inspired was the relatively calm, solid satisfaction of seeing a task accomplished with competence by an expert. Confidence that he would get the job done was a large part of his appeal—the pleasure was in observing how smoothly he did it.

Even as a two-year-old there was a professional neatness about Native Dancer's racing that belied his juvenile status—so much so that at the end of the season in two of the three polls he was elected over-all champion, an honor not accorded before or since to a horse of that age. In the dissenting poll he was runner-up in the voting for Horse of the Year, and a unanimous selection as champion two-year-old.

Bred by his owner, Alfred G. Vanderbilt, Native Dancer was foaled on March 27, 1950, at the Dan W. Scott Farm in Lexington, Kentucky, directly across the road from the Gallaher Farm, where Polynesian stood at stud. The future champion received his education at Vanderbilt's Sagamore Farm in Maryland. A handsome, muscular gray colt, standing 16 hands, except for oversized ankles, he looked every inch the part of what he was: a race horse.

In his first season of competition, Native Dancer was undefeated in nine starts, and never fully extended, since he won all his races by open daylight. Seven of them were stakes—the Youthful, Flash, Saratoga Special, Grand Union Hotel, Hopeful, Futurity and East View—and his earnings of $230,495 constituted a new record for a two-year-old. He shattered no speed marks—there was no occasion to—but in the Futurity he equaled the track (and world) record of 1:14⅗ for 6½ furlongs on a straightaway. In virtually all his starts, which ranged from 5 furlongs to 1⅟₁₆ miles, he left the impression of untapped resources; in fact, his eagerness to get going, his pulling against his jockey's restraint, was the only juvenile touch in what was otherwise the picture of a cool, veteran racing machine.

He was assigned 130 pounds on the Experimental Free Handicap, 2 pounds less than Count Fleet had rated, but Native Dancer's 7-pound margin of superiority over his nearest contemporaries, Laffango and Tahitian King, was the greatest ever given.

After his two-year-old season, Native Dancer was shipped to California, his ankles were fired and he was kept out of competition over the winter. He emerged at three a bigger, more powerfully developed horse, so heavily muscled in the manner generally associated with sprinters that not a few experts surmised that he would "step on his pedigree" at classic distances. (Although he had won the Preakness, Polynesian elsewhere had found 9 furlongs to be his limit, and while she was by Discovery, Geisha was from a sprinting female family, out of a half-sister to El Chico, the precocious undefeated two-year-old of 1938 who had faded at three.)

As a three-year-old, Native Dancer also developed into more of a professional—as a race

Native Dancer in action with jockey Eric Guerin up.

horse and as a television star. Televised coverage of major races became popular during these years, and the Dancer was a public idol; not only was he invariably the heavy favorite and a prominent factor in the result, but his distinctive coat color made him easy to follow during the action. His smiling jockey, Eric Guerin, in the cerise and white diamond Vanderbilt racing silks, became a familiar figure to millions of Americans as a result of his frequent appearances in winner's circle ceremonies.

It was as though Native Dancer's professional aplomb was increased by his status as a TV star; he provided the shows with more suspense by cutting several of his finishes fine —one of them too fine.

Trainer Bill Winfrey was unable to find an overnight race for his charge's three-year-old debut, so Native Dancer competed exclusively in stakes during 1953. After winning a division of the Gotham by two lengths, and defeating Tahitian King and Invigorator in the Wood Memorial, the "Gray Ghost of Saga-

454

more" was shipped to Louisville for the Kentucky Derby. Of all races, that had to be the one he lost.

Like the colt who put the only blemish on Man o' War's shield, the one who toppled Native Dancer from the ranks of the invincible was aptly named. Cain Hoy Stable's Dark Star, ridden by Henry Moreno, led from flagfall to finish, winning by a head in 2:02, the fifth fastest Derby on record at the time. The 7-to-10 favorite, Native Dancer, according to the official chart, was "roughed at the first turn by Money Broker, was eased back to secure racing room, raced wide during the run to the upper turn, then saved ground entering the stretch and finished strongly, but could not overtake the winner, although probably best."

At the end of a mile in 1:36⅗, Native Dancer was in fourth place, two and a half lengths behind the leader; he made up most, but not quite all of this deficit in a final quarter covered in :25⅖. In an excellent performance that was largely overlooked in the tumult which followed, Dark Star had handed the champion a tough assignment.

Technically, the 1953 result was not the biggest upset in modern Derby history (Bimelech had been 2-to-5) but practically it was,

for Mrs. Gordon Guiberson's Correspondent, regarded as the only three-year-old capable of even extending the champion, finished unplaced. This son of Khaled had won the 1⅛-mile Blue Grass Stakes so effortlessly in 1:49, breaking Coaltown's track record, that he had inspired a clique similar to the one which thought Coaltown was better than Citation before the 1948 Derby.

The disconsolate Guerin made some unfortunate remarks concerning Money Broker's jockey, Al Popara, and a number of witnesses made unflattering remarks about Guerin's ride on Native Dancer; one member of the Churchill Downs board of directors observed disgustedly, "He took that colt everywhere on the track except the ladies' room."

Dark Star had won the Derby Trial, and the larger significance of Native Dancer's defeat was that, in addition to "winter bottom," whether a candidate had a preparatory "race at the Downs" became a more pronounced factor in analyzing Kentucky Derby prospects. The unusual layout at Churchill Downs requires a horse to run through a tunnel of noise in the homestretch, and previous exposure to the nerve-shattering experience is an asset when the chips are down. Dark Star also ad-

Dark Star (inside) beating Native Dancer in the 1953 Kentucky Derby.

ministered the *coup de grâce* to the notion that saving a horse's big run for "heartbreak lane" was the best tactic in the Kentucky Derby. The romantic accounts of the winners who came from behind to snatch victory in the last strides notwithstanding, people began to notice that front runners enjoyed a definite edge in the matter of Kentucky Derby victories. A colt which grabbed the lead soon not only avoided possible jams, but was able to take the shortest path around; far more often than not, the horse in front before the Derby field turned into the homestretch has been the horse in front at the wire.

The validity of Dark Star's victory over Native Dancer was not subject to further examination. The son of Royal Gem II took three weeks off following his conquest of the champion—Native Dancer prancing to an easy, four-length victory in the Wither Stakes during the interval—and when they met again in the Preakness May 23, Dark Star bowed a tendon after leading for a mile. Native Dancer, 1-to-5 despite his Derby loss, won the race by a neck from Spring Hill Farm's Jamie K.—the first victory in which the Dancer had allowed a rival to finish lapped on him. Again misgivings arose concerning his stamina, but he quelled them in the 1½-mile Belmont Stakes two weeks later with another victory over Jamie K. in 2:28⅗, time which had been bettered only by Count Fleet and Citation in previous renewals of the Test of Champions. The margin again was only a neck, but—as had been true in the Preakness—Jamie K. (a full brother to the renowned mare, Nell K.) at one point in the stretch had been just a head behind, and the champion gradually increased his lead.

The remainder of Native Dancer's three-year-old campaign was a triumphant romp. He won the Dwyer by one and three-quarters lengths, the Arlington Classic by nine, the Travers by five and a half and the American Derby. In the latter he threw a scare into jockey Eddie Arcaro, who was substituting for the suspended Guerin, by delaying his move until he was all straightened out in the stretch; when Native Dancer finally did move, however, he drew out to win by two lengths in 1:48⅖, just ⅕-second off the track record which had been set by Colosal as a five-year-old, carrying 118 pounds, compared to 128 on the Dancer. Following this superb run on August 22, it was found that Native Dancer had a bruised heel, and the encounter with handicap champion Tom Fool, which had been eagerly anticipated for the autumn, was doomed.

The gray ghost returned to Sagamore Farm, and Tom Fool was voted Horse of the Year—an ironic turn of fate, for, immediately after a year in which there had been no clearcut champion, in 1953 there were really two.

Native Dancer did win a subsequent title as Horse of the Year as a four-year-old, by virtue of a brief but brilliant appearance on the racing scene. After winning a 6-furlong prep, he went into the 1954 Metropolitan Mile with 130 pounds, against 117 on Straight Face, who was fresh from a sparkling victory in the Dixie Handicap. The Greentree gelding sped the first 6 furlongs of the Met in 1:10⅕, while Native Dancer, after running last in the early furlongs, moved up to fifth place at the quarter pole, seven lengths behind the leader. As Straight Face continued to stride along under Atkinson's whip, the Dancer was roused by Guerin to give chase—the gap was halved by the furlong pole, and the powerful gray colt collared his rival in the closing strides to win by a neck in 1:35⅕. Jamie K., carrying 110 pounds, finished third, six lengths behind the top pair.

For the Oneonta Handicap at Saratoga, the Vanderbilt champion was assigned 137 pounds, but even at that weight, only one rival besides his own stablemate, First Glance, faced him. Native Dancer won with contemptuous ease by nine lengths in 1:24⅘ on a sloppy track; First Glance (Discovery-Bride Elect) was second, and J. W. Brown's Gigantic, winner that season of the Louisiana Derby, was another four and a half lengths away under 107 pounds. That was Native Dancer's farewell to the race track. A recurrence of his forefoot injury led to cancellation of plans for an invasion of Europe, and he was retired with the following record: 22 starts, 21 wins, one second, earnings of $785,240.

TOM FOOL, 1949

(Menow–Gaga, by Bull Dog)

While they have not been numerous, a leading two-year-old money winner who goes through a season undefeated scarcely can be classified as a rarity. Undefeated three-year-old financial leaders since World War I can be counted on one hand, and handicap horses of this caliber can be counted on one finger: his name was Tom Fool.

In ten starts as a four-year-old, the Greentree colt never lost a race, and the first six of his victories came in handicaps. They ranged in distance from 5½ furlongs to 1¼ miles, although the husky colt, like Native Dancer, in appearance and in pedigree seemed cut out more as a sprinter. In fact, in addition to his

honors as Horse of the Year in 1954, Tom Fool was elected champion sprinter as well.

An extremely muscular, handsome bay, a bit over 16 hands, Tom Fool toed out in front when standing still, but his running action was perfect. Although he was universally admired, a few observers opined that he was a trifle light behind, which trait had been noticed in other members of the Phalaris male line. In this case, however, this seems to have been a matter of relativity. Tom Fool had as powerful a set of quarters as could be found on any horse, but his development up front was so prodigious that the over-all effect was influenced thereby. (A man with shoulders 4 feet across is apt to look somewhat narrow waisted, whether he really is or not.) As his jockey, Ted Atkinson, once remarked, Tom Fool even had muscles in his eyebrows.

For his four-year-old debut in the Sation Handicap on April 25, not having raced for five and a half months, the son of Menow was assigned 128 pounds, against a field of top sprinters at 5½ furlongs. He won by two and a half lengths from Do Report (116) with the veteran speedster Tea-Maker in the beaten field. Carrying 130 pounds over 6 furlongs in

Tom Fool en route to the post with regular jockey Ted Atkinson up.

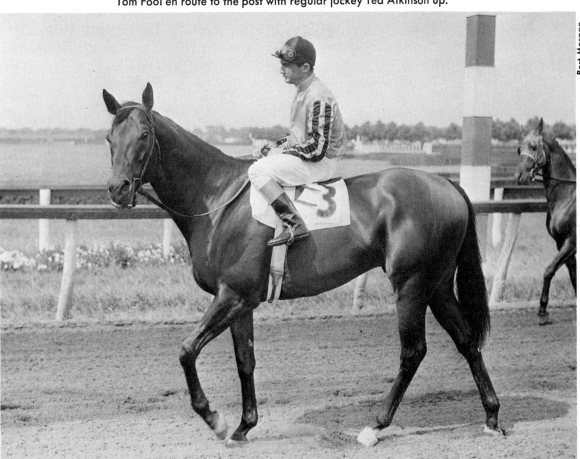

Bert Morgan

the Joe H. Palmer Handicap (named for the popular turf writer who died that year) on May 19, Tom Fool won by a length from Tea-Maker (114), Dark Peter (121) and Eatontown (115)—all specialists at the distance.

Four days later, in the Metropolitan Mile, he encountered Mrs. Esther duPont Weir's English-bred converted steeplechaser, Royal Vale, who had developed into one of the sensations of the season by winning the Miami Beach, Bowie, Gallant Fox and Dixie Handicaps, against such opponents as Crafty Admiral, One Count and Cold Command. Required to concede 3 pounds to this formidable rival, Tom Fool carried 130 over the good track in 1:35⅘ to win by half a length; Royal Vale was gaining at the end, and it augured ill for the Greentree colt should they meet again over a longer distance.

They did, the next Saturday, in the Suburban Handicap. Tom Fool, whose only previous experience at 1¼ miles had been a third in the Travers as a three-year-old, was assigned 128 pounds for the Suburban, four more than Royal Vale. Taking the lead early, the champion sprinter built up a three-length margin, which he maintained until the stretch turn, at which point Royal Vale launched his challenge. Eating into the gap with every stride, the older horse reduced it to a length at the eighth pole, and from there on in it was side by side. After a mile in 1:35⅗, Tom Fool covered the final quarter in :25 flat, holding on to win by a nose in 2:00⅗, the fastest 10 furlongs ever run at Belmont Park, with the exception of Whisk Broom II's disputed clocking in the 1913 Suburban.

On June 27, Tom Fool clicked off a double record in the 7-furlong Carter Handicap, which he won by two lengths in 1:22—tying the Aqueduct mark for that distance—under 135 pounds, the highest weight ever successfully carried in the ancient event. The field he beat included such top sprinters as Squared Away (122), Eatontown (113), Dark Peter (120), First Glance (120) and Tea-Maker (117).

As a climax to his feats of weight-carrying, he won the 1¼-mile Brooklyn Handicap on July 11 under 136 pounds, conceding a minimum of 26 pounds to the four opponents who faced him; Tom Fool thereby duplicated Whisk Broom II's sweep of the handicap Triple Crown —and became the first to accomplish the feat during a normal season.

At weight-for-age, few rival owners wanted any part of Tom Fool. In four successive stakes, not enough opposition could be mustered to warrant calling them contests, and they were run as betless exhibitions—a unique tribute in a year during which there were 24,417 horses in training.

The Greentree champion scooped up the Wilson Stakes by eight lengths, the Whitney by three and a half, the Sysonby by three and the Pimlico Special by eight, setting a new track record of 1:55⅘ for 1³⁄₁₆ miles in his final appearance on October 24.

There was some clamor to keep Tom Fool in training and try him at cup distances. He had never been tested beyond 1¼ miles, but a number of competent judges were willing to predict that, regardless of what natural talents he might have had as a router, he quite likely could have won at any distance on sheer competitive instinct and class. Quite unlike Native Dancer in his attitude toward racing, Tom Fool was the eager, peppery type; Atkinson observed that he could almost imagine him growling when another horse tried to pass.

The champion was retired to stud (he had some difficulty adjusting to his new role, but eventually became a very successful stallion) after compiling the following record on the track: 30 starts, 21 wins, seven seconds, one third, once unplaced, earnings of $570,165.

The 1953 handicap division, which Tom Fool ruled with such an iron hand, included a number of impressive performers. After his two defeats by the champion, Royal Vale won the Massachusetts Handicap, the Sussex in new track record time of 2:00⅖ for 1¼ miles at Delaware, and the Foreign Bred Stakes.

458

Tom Fool as a stallion at Greentree Stud.

Crafty Admiral never met Tom Fool, but he did well under respectable burdens himself; his fourteen starts were all in stakes, twelve were handicaps and he carried top weight in all but one of these. He won the Royal Palm, McLennan (129 pounds), Gulfstream Park (128), New York, Olympic Handicaps and Empire City Gold Cup, the latter by ten lengths at weight-for-age. At one time or another during the season he was required to make concessions to such as Alerted, winner that year of the Saratoga Handicap and Saratoga Cup; Battlefield, winner of the Appleton in track record time of 1:48⅘ for 1⅛ miles at Gulfstream; Smoke Screen, winner of four stakes including the New Orleans and Bidwill Memorial Handicaps, and Oil Capitol, winner of the Palm Beach, Widener, Ben Ali and Arlington Handicaps, to retire as the richest former auction yearling thus far on record, with $580,756.

Mark-Ye-Well began the season at Santa Anita with victories in the San Fernando Stakes, Maturity, and Santa Anita Handicap under 130 pounds, but he developed a quarter crack and did not win again after he was returned to action later in the year. Others prominent on the Western turf were Alberta Ranches' Royal Serenade, a champion English sprinter who stretched out in this country to win the 1⅛-mile American Handicap and 1¼-mile Hollywood Gold Cup; and Calumet's Fleet Bird, winner of the Argonaut and Golden Gate Handicaps, setting a new world record of 1:52⅗ for 1³⁄₁₆ miles in the latter event. The Sunset Handicap, raised that year to $100,000, was won by C. H. Jones and Sons' Lights Up.

Voted best grass horse of 1953 was Arnold Hanger's Chilean-bred Iceberg II, winner of the Bougainvillea and United Nations Handicaps. Next to Tom Fool among the sprinters was W. M. Wickham's White Skies—destined to enjoy top ranking in this category in the future—and others were Tuscany, Squared Away, Pet Bully, Algasir and Cyclotron.

459

On the distaff side, Sickle's Image led her division both in votes and money, due largely to a notable victory over males in the Washington Park Handicap for a net purse of $108,500, at the time a record for a member of her sex. Runner-up in the voting was Atalanta (Black Helen, Mermaid, Beldame Handicaps), and other older fillies or mares to receive mention were La Corredora (Ladies and Comely Handicaps), A Gleam (Malibu Sequet Stakes and Milady Handicap), Sunshine Nell, Sunny Dale (Beverly, etc.), Spanish Cream (Santa Margarita, etc.) and Real Delight (Arlington Matron, restored that year to handicap status).

Native Dancer, the year's biggest money winner, was a unanimous choice as champion three-year-old, with the bulk of second- and third-place ballots going to Level Lea (Discovery, Edgemere Handicaps, Jockey Club Gold Cup) and Dark Star.

The Dancer also led his stable to the top of the owners' rankings ($987,306), assisted by his contemporary, Find, a gelded son of Discovery, who won the 1⅛-mile Ohio Derby in new track record time of 1:48 at ThistleDown, plus the Grey Lag and Empire City Handicaps. All in all, the 1950 crop of foals bred by Vanderbilt was remarkable, as Find eventually went on to amass more than $800,000, and the crop included another gelding named Social Outcast, destined to win $668,300. (Vanderbilt was clever at devising names for his horses that were suggestive of their ancestry: Social Outcast was by Shut Out–Pansy.)

Other star sophomores of 1953 and their principal victories were Jamie K. (Leonard Richards Stakes), Chain Reaction (eight stakes including Canadian Derby), Landlocked (Choice Stakes), Chanlea (Santa Anita Derby), Rejected (Westerner Stakes) and Royal Bay Gem, "the fourth horse," so called because he always seemed to be closing at the end but not quite soon enough, although he won the Everglades, Chesapeake, Jersey Stakes and Peabody Memorial.

Although not a feminine counterpart of Native Dancer, but a unanimous selection as best of her sex, was Mrs. Ben Whitaker's little daughter of Heliopolis, Grecian Queen, trained by J. P. Conway—and ridden frequently by Guerin. After winning the Prioress, CCA Oaks and Gazelle Stakes from her contemporaries, the filly was assigned highest weight on the scale against her elders for the New Castle Handicap, first $100,000 race conditioned for females exclusively. She won this race—later to be renamed the Delaware Handicap—and followed up with another victory within her division in the Monmouth Oaks. A courageous second by a neck under 126 pounds in the Alabama Stakes to Sabette (114), and a third to Tom Fool and Alerted in the Sysonby, brought her earnings for the season up to $229,375. Sabette, also winner of the Diana Handicap and Gallorette Stakes (and runner-up to the Queen in the CCA and Monmouth Oaks, as well as third in the Gazelle), was second in the voting for best three-year-old filly.

Canadiana became the first Canadian-bred winner of $100,000 during 1953, when she added to her juvenile total with an easy victory in mixed company in the Queen's Plate, following which she took the Test Stakes at Saratoga. Other good members of the division included Cerise Reine (Ashland Stakes, Delaware Oaks), Fleet Khal (Sea Breeze Stakes, Vanity Handicap, Hollywood Oaks), Home-Made (another from the Vanderbilt crop of 1950; winner of the Vagrancy and a division of the Comely Handicap), Arab Actress, Bubbley and My Sin.

In sharp contrast to the well-defined rankings that prevailed among their seniors in 1953, the two-year-old colts were a scrambled lot: Porterhouse was elected champion in two polls; Hasty Road won the other poll as well as the most money; and Turn-to, winner of the richest race, shared top weight with Porterhouse on the Experimental Free Handicap. It was difficult to cavil at any of the selections.

A son of Endeavour II, Porterhouse was

owned by Mrs. M. E. Person's Llangollen Farm and trained by Charles Whittingham. After finishing seventh in his debut, he finished first six times in succession, including the National Stallion, Christiana Stakes, Saratoga Special and Futurity. In the Special, however, ridden by Eric Guerin, Porterhouse bumped Turn-to and Guerin struck the rival colt with his whip on his backswing, so Porterhouse was disqualified and placed last. (New York still was operating under the old rule whereby a horse guilty of an infraction automatically was set back to last. Under the modern rule, in effect in most states at that time and adopted by New York a couple of years later, a horse which interferes with another is moved back only so far as is necessary to place him behind the injured party. Thus, Porterhouse would have been officially second to Turn-to had the race been run in 1955.) In his final outing of the season, Porterhouse actually was last in the Pimlico Futurity, in which he went into the air at the start and lost all chance, straining his back muscles in the process.

A huge, blaze-faced son of Roman, owned by Mr. and Mrs. Allie E. Reuben's Hasty House Farm and trained by Harry Trotsek, Hasty Road was a champion of the Midwest with four wins in five starts in Chicago—including both the Arlington and Washington Park Futurities—and a third to stablemate Sea O Erin in the Prairie State Stakes. Shipped east in quest of new laurels, after stumbling at the start, he was a strong fourth to Porterhouse in a prep race, but then ran an inexplicably poor tenth in the Futurity. Since his sire was noted principally for begetting precocious speed, Hasty Road was on the point of being written off as just another sprinting son of Roman when he moved west to capture the Breeders' Futurity in 1:23⅕ for 7 furlongs, and the Kentucky Jockey Club Stakes in 1:36 for a mile. The big colt—who ultimately proved to be the noblest Roman of all—piled up $277,132 in his first season, thereby erasing Native Dancer's briefly held record for earnings by a two-year-old.

An Irish-bred son of Royal Charger, Turn-to was trained by Eddie Hayward and owned by the Cain Hoy Stable of Captain Harry F. Guggenheim, former Ambassador to Cuba and a naval aviator in both world wars, who named many of his horses with nautical terms. "Turn to" means "get to work," which the colt did with enthusiasm. Never unplaced in five starts, after his brush with Porterhouse in the Saratoga Special, he bucked shins in the Hopeful but finished third to Artismo and War Piper, then came back in the fall to win the richest race in world history up until that time, the inaugural of the new Garden State Stakes. Boosted in added value to $100,000 and lengthened in distance to 1¹⁄₁₆ miles, the race was similar to a futurity, but with stiffer intervening eligibility payments—the cost to start amounted to $2,385 per horse on the conventional installment plan, or $12,000 via supplementary nominations when they later were permitted. The gross purse for the 1953 running was $269,395, of which Turn-to received

Helis Stock Farm, the historic New Jersey breeding farm that was formerly Rancocas Stud.

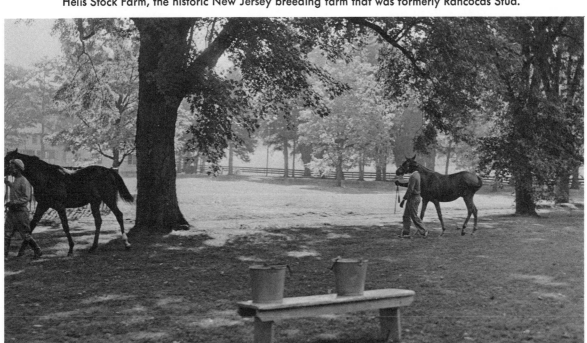

$151,282 as his winner's share, Correlation earned $53,879 second money, Goyamo received $35,409 for third and Best Years $13,470 for fourth, not counting other amounts dispensed in nominators' awards.

The Garden State was designed to attract championship aspirants from all over the nation, which it succeeded in doing to a large extent. Correlation, for example, had won the C. S. Howard Stakes in California, and among others in the field were Fisherman (Great American, Cowdin, Champagne, East View Stakes), Errard King (Longport Handicap, Tyro, World's Playground Stakes and Pimlico Futurity), Nirgal Lad (Bay State Kindergarten and Narragansett Nursery Stakes), Sea O Erin and Thither.

Elsewhere in the division, James Cox Brady's Artismo won the Sapling and Grand Union Hotel Stakes besides the Hopeful; Mrs. John D. Hertz's Double Speed was undefeated in four starts, including the Graduation Stakes and Del Mar Futurity; and Calumet's Arrogate won the Cabrillo and Starlet Stakes.

There was no confusion among the juvenile fillies of 1953, as Mrs. George D. Widener's Evening Out, trained by Bert Mulholland, was unanimously elected best in the division. The daughter of Shut Out won five straight against her sex, all stakes, before meeting her sole defeat at the hands of colts in the Futurity. Beginning with the Fashion Stakes, Evening Out also won the filly division of the National Stallion, the Schuylerville, Spinaway and Matron. Her only close call was in the National Stallion, in which Ovie Scurlock had to drive her hard to nip Fascinator by a head; in her other races, the little champion was complete mistress of the situation, so much so that the Spinaway, which she won by eight lengths from a single opponent, was run as a betless exhibition. Although she did not lead the class in earnings, in the Matron Stakes Evening Out defeated the filly who did—Hasty House Farm's Queen Hopeful. This daughter of Roman emulated her kinsman and stablemate,

Hasty Road, by taking both of the filly equivalents to Chicago's futurities, the Arlington Lassie and Princess Pat Stakes, in addition to running a dead heat with Greek Lady in the Mademoiselle, for earnings of $169,534.

W. G. Loew's Case Goods won the Astoria, Jeanne d'Arc and New Jersey Breeders' Stakes; and Maine Chance Farm had a good pair in Margate Handicap winner, Fascinator, and Incidentally, winner of the Rancocas, Polly Drummond and a section of the Colleen. Other notable members of the division were Miz Clementine (Pollyanna), Make A Play (Astarita and Marguerite), Oil Painting (Alcibiades) and Lady Cover Up, winner of the Junior Miss and Alameda Stakes, and second across the line in the Del Mar Debutante, but declared winner subsequently when it was learned that the owner of first-place Frosty Dawn had been late making an eligibility payment.

In 1953, William Lee Shoemaker re-wrote the record book, with a performance that stands out in such isolated splendor that no other jockey, before or since, has approached it.

Going after the record seasonal total of 390 winners established by Tony DeSpirito the previous year, Shoemaker passed it so fast (on October 16) that he set a new goal of 500 winners. He was clicking off winners on schedule until, on December 10, he decided he needed a rest more than another record, and took a two-week vacation. Nevertheless, by the end of the year he had ridden the amazing total of 485 winners; nor was it a "buckshot" feat, since, although he accepted an unprecedented total of 1,683 mounts (more than five a day based on a six-day week), his winning average of 29 per cent also was the highest achieved by a leading jockey since official records were instituted in 1895.

The tiny, phlegmatic rider from Fabens, Texas (near El Paso), who observed his twenty-second birthday in August, manifested a natural empathy with horses that has been seldom, if ever, equaled. Riding as though he were an integral part of his mount, he obtained responses with his hands alone that bigger boys were unable to elicit with a whip. "The Shoe" was further exceptional in that even his weight problem was different. At 4 feet 10 inches, and 100 pounds, he never had to worry about the sweat box—on the contrary because of his great skill, he frequently was given the mount on top stars who were assigned high weights, so his saddle was equipped with extra pockets to carry the necessary lead.

Although he never deliberately set his sights on records in subsequent seasons, they continued to come Shoemaker's way as a matter of course. The very next year, for example, he led the list again with 380 winners, and broke his own percentage mark with a winning average of 30 per cent.

In 1953, Shoemaker was not without competition for Pennsylvanian William John Hartack, Jr., an apprentice most of the season, rode 350 winners for an average of 28 percent, and Tony DeSpirito rode 311 for a winning average of 29 percent. (Hartack, in 1955, became the only other jockey to exceed 400 winners, when he led the list with 417.)

Earl Sande, who had set his numerous riding records before Shoemaker was born, made a brief comeback in 1953. The 55-year-old Handy Guy won with his tenth mount, Miss Weesie, at Jamaica on October 14, to receive the most enthusiastic ovation ever tendered man or beast at the "People's Track," whereupon he called it quits again.

Robert Hyatt "Red the Raider" McDaniel, in his fourth straight season as leading trainer, saddled 211 winners for a new record in his profession. The former jockey, who had accompanied Longden on that cold ride in a boxcar years before, operated a huge public stable and derived his nickname from his claiming activity. He, too, repeated his championship the

Miller

Robert H. McDaniel, leading trainer for five straight years.

next year, making it five straight, with 206, the only times a trainer has saddled as many as 200 winners in a single season. (McDaniel's reign came to an abrupt end at age 44. On May 5, 1955, about twenty minutes after he had saddled a winner at Golden Gate Fields—he didn't stay to watch the race—McDaniel stopped his car on the highest span of the San Francisco Bay Bridge, stepped out and plunged to his death.)

463

CHAPTER SIXTY-THREE

IN 1954 THERE WAS ANOTHER recession. Although gross statistics were up, they reached new heights primarily because of a further increase in the number of races run, and the majority of meetings (fifty-five of ninety-five) reported declines in daily average mutuel handle. Revenue to the states jumped almost $10½-million, but this, too, was misleading since, apart from the larger volume, some states merely had assumed a bigger percentage of the business. In New York, for example, thoroughbred racing actually produced less revenue, but the state was able to report an increase because the O'Dwyer Bite was in the process of being transferred, step by step, from the city to the state government; the "gain" was money (and less of it) that formerly had been going to municipalities. In New Jersey, the take-out was raised from 12 percent to 13 percent, all of the increase going to the state; business fell off thereafter, but the state received more revenue as a result of its larger share.

These declining economic factors did not affect the stake horses, however, and there were thirty-two individual winners of $100,000 or more during 1954 alone. While in the past some distinguished horses had come out of the yearling auctions—Man o' War, to name one—former sales yearlings were particularly prominent during the 1954 season. Nowhere was this more evident than in the three-year-old division, as each of the Triple Crown classics was won by a different alumnus of the Keeneland Sales.

Native Dancer was elected Horse of the Year in 1954 following a brief campaign. A horse of the same color, but considerably different otherwise, was Andrew J. Crevolin's Determine, the year's leading money winner with $328,700.

That the gray son of Alibhai–Koubis, by Mahmoud, came into existence in the first place was remarkable. His dam had been born with a cleft palate which her breeder, Dr. Eslie Asbury, had repaired in a unique operation with specially improvised, long-handled surgical instruments. Koubis never raced, and Determine, her first foal, was so small that after buying him for $12,000, Crevolin jokingly remarked that he must have been standing in a hole when he inspected the colt.

As noted, in 1945 Asbury had enjoyed the last laugh with Revoked, and the Cincinnati surgeon immediately offered to take this one back as well, at a profit to Crevolin, but the California automobile dealer refused. In one of several instances of prescience in regard to Determine, he observed that he might have been letting a Derby winner get away.

The big Californian ordinarily was expansive in conversation, but in this case he was restrained. After a two-year-old campaign during which Determine was a modest stakes winner, but earned back more than double his purchase price, as a three-year-old he won several Derbies, not to mention numerous other added money fixtures. In a campaign of fifteen starts, all in stakes company, the little gray colt (somewhat over 15 hands and weighing less than 900 pounds) was never out of the money. His small size and handy way of going proved to be an advantage on a couple of occasions as he nimbly picked his way through crowded situations like an expert broken field runner.

Beginning the 1954 season on January 9, with no let-up in training from the previous year, Determine was second to James Session in the San Vicente Stakes, then won the San Gabriel Stakes, San Felipe Handicap and Santa Anita Derby. In the latter he recovered from interference to traverse the 9 furlongs in 1:48⅘, and the victory encouraged Crevolin to aim him at the Kentucky Derby; trainer Bill Molter, on the other hand, was busy with other members of his large stable and somewhat reluctant to make the trip. While the project was being discussed, Determine made the decision by winning three more stakes in succession: the San Jose, Peter Clark Handicaps and Bay Meadows Derby. He thereupon was flown to Kentucky, where, in a brief period of four days, he ran two memorable races against Hasty Road.

In the Derby Trial on April 27, they ran side by side through the stretch, resembling a Great Dane and a terrier, to cross the wire with Hasty Road winner by a head in new track record time of 1:35 for the mile, although neither colt was under punishment. The third finisher, Determine's stablemate, Allied, was more than eleven lengths farther back.

In the Kentucky Derby May 1, Determine nearly lost his rider, Ray York, right after the start. Hasty Road came out somewhat from post position number 1, and the Arkansas Derby winner, Timely Tip, cut over drastically from the outside, nearly racking up the field behind him. The catlike Determine stayed on his feet, however, and York stayed in the saddle to give chase. Hasty Road set the pace, as was his custom, for the first mile, but Determine overtook him in the stretch to win by one and a half lengths in moderate time of 2:03 for the 10 furlongs. Hasseyampa was third and the well-

Determine (left) who collected several Derbies during his racing career and Gloire Fille, respectively sire and dam of the Kentucky Derby winner Decidedly.

465

backed Goyamo, previously winner of the Bahamas Handicap and Blue Grass Stakes, finished fourth.

As the Kentucky Derby frequently does, the 1954 renewal generated numerous sidelights. The first gray to win the race, Determine had succeeded where Native Dancer had failed; the first classic winner by Alibhai, and out of a Mahmoud mare, he also had succeeded where his kinsman, Your Host, had failed. On the same afternoon, Determine's older stablemate, Imbros, had won the 9-furlong William P. Kyne Handicap at Bay Meadows in new track record time of 1:48⅗ to give Crevolin victories in two $100,000 races that day. (The stable did not set a record for daily earnings, however, for, while Determine won $102,050, the purse awards in the Kyne Handicap extended all the way back to eighth place, so Imbros received but $48,800 for his victory. Their combined total did not match the $161,170 won by Calumet Farm on May 15, 1948, when Citation won the Preakness and Faultless and Fervent finished one-two in the Gallant Fox Handicap.)

It was Imbros who handed Determine his next defeat. Following a victory in the Debonair Stakes upon his return to the West Coast, the multiple Derby winner was sent against older horses for the first time, in the Californian Stakes at Hollywood Park June 12. Crevolin entered both his stars, with the observation that, at the weights, Imbros should win in record time, but Determine ought to be close. Imbros, under 118, toured the 1⅟₁₆ miles in 1:41, to equal the world record, while Determine, carrying 115—conceding 8 pounds on the scale to his stablemate—was second by a length.

After the little gray colt, under 126 pounds, blew a long lead to finish third in the Westerner Stakes to his contemporaries, Fault Free (114) and Allied (117), he was found to have an abscessed jaw and was taken out of training. (Crevolin also was out of action for a time, as the California Horse Racing Board suspended

him for six weeks because in a recorded interview, which was published, he had made some remarks considered by the board to be detrimental to racing.)

Determine returned late in the year, with a third to Imbros and Karim in the 6-furlong Pacific Handicap. In December, after voting for the seasonal championships was over, he won the Oakland Handicap from his own age, conceding 21 pounds to the runner-up, and the Golden Gate Handicap from a mixed field, conceding 21 pounds to three-year-old Poona II and 19 pounds to five-year-old Blue Trumpeter.

The little colt was at a disadvantage as a four-year-old when required to make weight concessions in handicaps. Nevertheless, he won the Malibu Sequet Stakes, Golden Gate Mile (128 pounds), Inglewood Handicaps and Santa Anita Maturity, to retire with $573,360. (In the Maturity he finished second, but was moved up when Miz Clementine was disqualified for interference—and after that incident Calumet Farm ceased racing at Santa Anita.)

Favorite for all three Triple Crown races in 1954—and winner of none—was Robert S. Lytle's Correlation, a big, sore-going son of Free America, who was taken off the work tabs by trainer Noble Threewitt early in the year and given a series of X-ray treatments. He earned his role as favorite for the Kentucky Derby by flying east from California to take two $100,000 races in a row, the Florida Derby and Wood Memorial. Although he finished sixth at Churchill Downs, he had been caught in the jam at the start, and ran well after getting back on stride, so he lost no face by the performance.

When the sophomore contingent, minus Determine, moved on to Pimlico, Correlation beat Hasty Road by a head in the Preakness Prep, and hence was made favorite for the Maryland classic. This time, however, the Hasty House colt (a $23,100 yearling purchase, from breeder Clifford Mooers) reversed the pattern he had followed at Louisville—having lost the preliminary, he won the main event. Lead-

Hasty Road (John Adams up) is greeted in the Preakness winners' circle by Mr. and Mrs. A. E. Reuben. Trainer Harry Trotsek is at left.

ing from start to finish, under a well-timed ride by John Adams, he staved off Correlation by a neck; again Hasseyampa was third and Goyamo fourth. There had been some bumping during the stretch run, which forced jockey Arnold Kirkland to take up on Hasseyampa, but his claim of foul against Correlation was not allowed.

Hasty Road abandoned the classic trail at this point, presumably because the 1½ miles of the Belmont Stakes was considered beyond his scope. Later in the season he won the Warren Wright Memorial Stakes, and as a four-year-old he overstepped his supposed pedigree limitation by taking the 1¼-mile Widener. The big speedster finally retired to stud with $541,402.

Correlation went on. In his next start after the 1954 Preakness, he was an odds-on favorite for the Jersey Stakes, but finished sixth, after participating in another bumping episode, and while conceding 15 pounds to the horses which outran him. As the sole survivor from the first two classics to make it to the post for the third one (Fisherman having run in the Derby, but not the Preakness) the Lytle colt again was favorite for the Belmont Stakes on June 12. This was the end of the line for Correlation; he finished fifth as the race was won by the champion of his generation.

HIGH GUN, 1951

(Heliopolis–Rocket Gun, by Brazado)

High Gun was a yearling purchase of an unusual sort. King Ranch had owned his dam, but sold her at auction to the partnership of K. M. and W. P. Little and Cary Boshamer. A few years later, when Max Hirsch noticed Rocket Gun's son at the yearling sales, he liked the colt's looks and bought him for $10,200. Although King Ranch made a specialty of American types, High Gun turned out to be a prototype of the European cup horse—rangy (15 hands 3 inches, but he appeared taller), long-striding, lean and hungry for distance.

Encouraging in a brief appearance at two (two wins in three starts) High Gun never failed to earn part of the purse in sixteen starts at three. Like Counterpoint and One Count, he won the championship of his division over the long routes.

His first six starts as a sophomore, none of which he won, included thirds in Correlation's Wood Memorial and Jet Action's Withers, a fourth in Brisuet's Delaware Valley Stakes and a third in the Jersey Stakes, won by War of Roses, High Gun closing promisingly at the end of the last two races. The King Ranch colt scored his first stakes victory in the Peter Pan Handicap on June 5, beating Fisherman while in receipt of five pounds.

In the Belmont Stakes a week later, High Gun met Fisherman again at level weights; he overhauled the tough little C. V. Whitney colt (who was about the same size as Determine, but stockier in physique) in the stretch to win by a neck. High Gun followed up with a rather easy victory in the Dwyer, conceding 12 pounds to his nearest pursuers, Palm Tree and Paper Tiger.

On a foray into the Midwest, along with others of the top three-year-olds, High Gun learned that there was no beating Errard King in Chicago that year. This former $7,600 yearling, owned by Boston baker, Joseph Gavegnano, and bred by John W. Galbreath, won the Arlington Classic from Helioscope and High Gun, with Jet Action fourth and Hasty Road fifth. Later, he won the American Derby from High Gun and Hasty Road, with Hasseyampa fourth.

Upon returning east, High Gun finished the season with three straight stakes victories. At weight-for-age in the Sysonby Mile, not really his best distance, he defeated such seniors as that year's Widener Handicap winner, Landlocked; Sir Mango and First Glance. He beat older runners again, conceding them actual weight, in the 1½-mile Manhattan Handicap, then set the seal on his championship claim in the 2-mile Jockey Club Gold Cup at weight-for-age.

This race had been won seven times in succession by three-year-olds, which was one of the factors that led to a decision by the Jockey Club to revise the scale of weights in 1954 so as to give younger horses less of an advantage. So, carrying 119 pounds, 2 more than his predecessors had been required to tote, High Gun was an easy winner by three lengths from another three-year-old, Fisherman.

High Gun, with $314,550, ranked second to Determine in earnings for the 1954 season; he led King Ranch to the top of the owner's standings, and Heliopolis to the top of the stallion list.

Fisherman also had his victories in 1954, including the Gotham Stakes, American Legion Handicap, Travers and Lawrence Realization within his division. His biggest score, however, came in the Washington, D. C., International. The first time in his life he raced on a turf course, the little son of Phalanx defeated a field of top runners of various ages, mostly specialists on this type of footing, over 1½ miles at weight-for-age, to become the first American winner of the big Laurel race. Errard King took the Experimental Free Handicap in addition to his two big wins in Chicago.

Of the other highly regarded sophomores in 1954, Turn-to appeared headed for an historic season after winning his first three starts, including the Flamingo Stakes, but subsequently bowed a tendon and was retired. William Helis, Jr.'s Helioscope (purchased as a yearling for $17,000 from Miss Mildred Woolwine) won a division of the Select Handicap, the Olympic Handicap in new track record time of 1:47⅗ for 1⅛ miles at Atlantic City, the Benjamin Franklin, Trenton Handicaps and Pimlico Special. Porterhouse did not win a stake; regarded hereafter as chiefly a sprinter, he still had a few surprises up his sleeve, however.

The champion three-year-old filly turned up in Foxcatcher Farm's Parlo, a diminutive daughter of Heliopolis, trained by Dick Handlen, who led her division in earnings with $135,290. After failing to win her first four starts, which included a third in the Betsy Ross Stakes, won by On Your Own, Parlo scored the first stakes victory of her career in the Delaware Oaks in June. She was unable to handle her elders in the rich New Castle Handicap, won by Gainsboro Girl, following which she ran second to Clear Dawn in the Miss Woodford Stakes (conceding nine pounds to the winner) and finished nowhere in the Monmouth Oaks, won by Evening Out.

Beginning with the Alabama Stakes on August 25, which she won while conceding 10 pounds to her two nearest pursuers, Parlo found her legs. She took on her elders again in the Beldame Handicap, carrying 116 pounds (second highest weight on the scale), and won by three lengths. In her final start, carrying 125 pounds, conceding actual weight to all but Lavender Hill (126) and making concessions to all her rivals on the scale, she won the Firenze Handicap by seven lengths from three-year-old Riverina (115) and four-year-old Spinning Top (110).

Runner-up to Parlo among the fillies her own age was Calumet Farm's Miz Clementine, who tackled all comers out West. The full sister to Two Lea won the Goose Girl, Sea Breeze Stakes, Hollywood and California Oaks within her division, and defeated males in the Cinema, Yerba Buena Handicaps and California Derby. She set new Tanforan records of 1:40⅘ and 1:49, respectively, for a mile and 70 yards and 9 furlongs in her last two victories, although her second record survived less than a month. (Ben Jones, who was smart about a lot of things besides horses, used to say that females of any kind, who ran exclusively in packs with other females, tended to become silly. For that reason he liked to run fillies against colts every now and then as a matter of course, and the practice worked well for Calumet. Miz Clementine, one in a long line of successful examples, won nine of her thirteen starts in 1954 and never failed to get a piece of the purse; she boasted $109,450 for the season's work.)

Cherokee Rose emulated her full sister, How, by winning the CCA Oaks, but the daughter of Princequillo fell victim to the bowed-tendon jinx that was plaguing Cain Hoy

Stable, and followed Dark Star and Turn-to into retirement. Queen Hopeful was quite active, winning the Orchid Stakes, Florida Oaks and Black-Eyed Susan Stakes; and others to receive mention were G. A. Cavanaugh's Blue Violin (Cleopatra, Misty Isle Handicaps) and Mrs. Louis Lazare's Sotto Voce (Jasmine Stakes, Barbara Fritchie Handicap).

Native Dancer was the champion of the handicap division, but the scramble for money among the older horses in 1954 involved runners belonging to the two leading owners, King Ranch and Andrew J. Crevolin. While Crevolin's Determine had nosed out High Gun in the sophomore financial race, King Ranch's Rejected held off Imbros in the handicap division.

Winner of $276,800 at four, including the Santa Anita, American (equaling the Hollywood track record of 1:48 for 9 furlongs) and Hawthorne Gold Cup Handicaps, Rejected was of further interest as the exemplification of the stretch-running specialist at the American classic distance. While the typical horse runs the first quarter or half-mile fastest, and slows down thereafter, Rejected literally crept through the first quarter, then accelerated during the second and third quarters. In the remainder of the race, he ran on steadily (or, sometimes at a slightly decelerated rate) devouring the tiring front runners as they came back to him. Before he retired, he boosted his earnings to $549,500, and set a Hollywood record of 1:59⅗ for his pet distance of 1¼ miles in the Gold Cup. Five of his seven stakes victories were at this distance (four of them in $100,000 races) and the other two were at only slightly shorter routes.

Imbros (purchased as a yearling for $15,100 from Woodvale Farm) earned $242,000 as a four-year-old in 1954, in a rugged campaign of twenty starts, of which he won eight and placed in nine others. Very much like his sire, Polynesian, he could get beyond 9 furlongs on pure class (he had the Santa Anita Handicap won at the sixteenth pole, but finished second to Rejected at the wire) but he was best at slightly

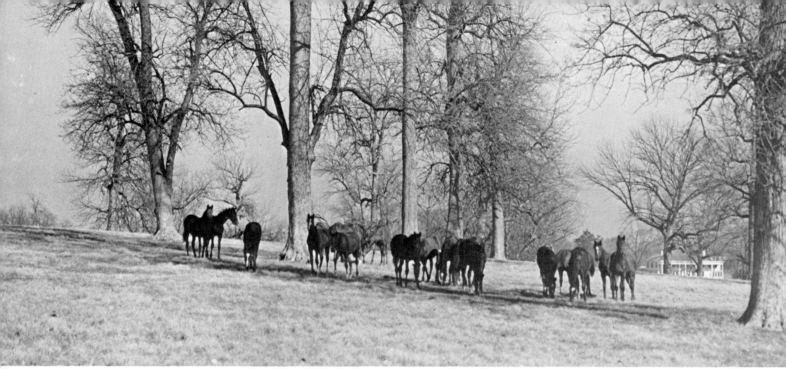

The Circle M Farm which was formerly the Idle Hour Stock Farm.

shorter distances. Besides his record-breaking wins in the Californian Stakes and Kyne Handicap, the rugged chestnut colt won the Malibu Sequet in new world record time of 1:20⅗ for 7 furlongs; the Lincoln's Birthday Handicap; the Governor Goodwin Knight Handicap in new track record time of 1:35⅖ for a mile at Bay Meadows; the Pacific and Palos Verdes Handicaps, equaling the Santa Anita record of 1:09 for 6 furlongs in the latter, carrying 128 pounds. The speed duels between Imbros and Abe Hirschberg's Berseem kept the Pacific Coast sizzling.

After ending their racing careers with joint earnings of $913,910, Imbros and his stablemate, Determine, were syndicated as a package for $900,000—quite a return on their total cost as yearlings of $27,100.

Pet Bully blossomed forth with his best season as a six-year-old in 1954, winning $240,-375, including six stakes, among them the Washington Park Handicap in 1:34⅖ for the mile, the Woodward Stakes while giving 15 pounds to Joe Jones, and the Fall Highweight Handicap under 136 pounds, conceding 19 pounds to the runner-up. Social Outcast deputized well for his sidelined stablemate, Native Dancer, by winning $192,675, including the Whitney, Gallant Fox Handicaps, Rhode Island

and Narragansett Specials. Other prominent older males of 1954, and their major achievements, were Sir Mango (Lincoln Handicap), Mark-Ye-Well (San Antonio), Stranglehold (won five stakes, placed in eight) and Straight Face (Dixie and Suburban).

Hasty House Farm's imported English-bred, Stan, was elected best grass horse, by virtue of victories in the Meadowland, Laurel Turf Cup and Arlington Handicaps, the latter race having been shifted to the infield in 1954.

White Skies (bought for $7,500 as a yearling from Hurstland Farm) was the season's champion sprinter and a fine weight carrier. He won the Paumonok with 130 pounds, the Toboggan with 132, the Roseben under 135 in 1:22⅖ for 7 furlongs, and the Carter under 133. His only loss that season was a second, while carrying 136 pounds and conceding 20 to the winner, Master Ace, in the Oceanport Handicap, won in new Monmouth Park record time of 1:09 for 6 furlongs.

Tops among the older handicap mares was Mrs. Charles Silvers's ex-claimer, Lavender Hill, winner of the Arlington Matron, Diana and Matron Handicaps. Other leaders included Alibhai Lynn (four stakes), Brazen Brat (three stakes), Cerise Reine (Santa Margarita), Sunshine Nell (Top Flight), Bubbley (Vanity),

470

Cinda (beat colts in Rumson Handicap) and Sickle's Image, who won the Modesty and closed out her elongated lifetime bank account with $413,275. Also, Gallorette's first foal, Mlle. Lorette, won the inaugural of the Gallorette Stakes.

Much of the two-year-old fireworks was provided by the first American-bred crop of Nasrullah, and foremost among these was Belair Stud's Nashua, voted champion of his age after winning six of his eight starts and finishing second in the others for earnings of $192,865.

NASHUA, 1952
(Nasrullah–Segula, by Johnstown)

Bred by his owner, and foaled at Claiborne Farm on April 14, 1952, Nashua was slated to be sent abroad with the English branch of the Belair stable, but after the death of the senior William Woodward, his son decided to keep the colt in America under the training of Jim Fitzsimmons. Ungainly as a yearling—he was growing so fast—Nashua developed into a magnificent specimen as a two-year-old, topping 16 hands at that age, and so substantial in general physique he very easily could have passed as a mature horse of handicap age. As one veteran trainer expressed it, "A man would be a fool to throw a two-year-old against that colt, unless he was hoping for something to go wrong."

Nothing serious went wrong with Nashua as a two-year-old, although he was defeated twice. After winning his debut from a field of twenty

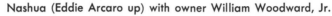

Nashua (Eddie Arcaro up) with owner William Woodward, Jr.

471

rivals in a romp down the Widener chute, he met Summer Tan for the first time in the Juvenile Stakes over the same course. The latter colt wrested the lead from him in the stretch, but Nashua came on again to win by half a length. A claim of interference filed against the winner by Summer Tan's jockey was not upheld.

For Nashua's first defeat, in the Cherry Hill Stakes at Garden State Park May 19, there were excuses, if one looked for them. It was Nashua's first race around a turn, and after running lapped on the speedy Royal Note through most of a first quarter covered in :22⅕, the Belair colt dropped back to a two-length deficit rounding the turn. Because of a tendency to bear in and run up on Royal Note's heels in the stretch, Nashua was jerked to the outside by jockey Jess Higley, but he nevertheless reduced the margin to a neck at the wire. On the other hand, no excuse was needed. Royal Note, undefeated at the time, was the favorite; he carried 3 pounds more weight, and Sam Boulmetis was as busy keeping the winner away from Nashua as he was urging him forward in the drive. The time of :58⅗ was ⅖-second off the track record.

At any rate, following this loss, Nashua was equipped with a set of blinkers, and Eddie Arcaro was put in his saddle. The new combination beat Pyrenees in the Grand Union Hotel Stakes, and Summer Tan and Pyrenees in the Hopeful, before Nashua met his second defeat.

The occasion was the Cowdin Stakes, and this time, too, there were factors that beclouded the result; Nashua, showing a trait that was to become associated with other offspring of his brilliant but temperamental sire, seemed to have a mind of his own. (As Arcaro said, "He can scare you.") There was a world of early speed in the race, and Nashua was kept under restraint as he ran with Sound Barrier, Bunny's Babe and Hartsville through a blistering quarter in :22⅗ and a half in :45⅕. Although he did reach the lead at one point, apparently resentful of the rating, he dropped back to fourth place and refused to "give" for

a few moments; however, he later responded and came on again in the last stages. He was unable to overtake Summer Tan, though, who came through on the inside to win by one and a half lengths. Whether Nashua—who was conceding 4 pounds to his principal rivals, and more to the others—could have won in any case is questionable, for Summer Tan was holding his margin at the end, and his time of 1:16 was a new track record for 6½ furlongs at Aqueduct.

Nashua equaled the Widener Chute record of 1:08⅕ for 6 furlongs in his next start, the Anticipation Purse, beating Royal Coinage, Pyrenees and Georgian; then completed his juvenile campaign with a victory over Summer Tan by a head in the Futurity, as Royal Coinage ran third and Traffic Judge fourth. (Nashua did not share his track record long, for, a couple of weeks later, with hurricane Hazel pushing on her rear, the filly Vestment covered 6 furlongs on the Belmont straightaway in 1:07⅘.)

Mrs. Russell A. Firestone's Summer Tan, a home-bred son of Heliopolis–Miss Zibby, by Omaha, also foaled at Claiborne Farm, was the leading money winner among the 1954 juveniles, with five wins in eleven starts, for $230,421. Although Mrs. Firestone sold his dam at auction for $400 after he was weaned, she kept the colt, who was turned over to the noted yearling expert, John Ward, for breaking, and to his brother, Sherrill, for subsequent training.

Besides his jousts with Nashua, Summer Tan won the Youthful, U.S. Hotel, and—the richest of them all—the Garden State Stakes. The latter race, which netted him $151,096, was nothing more than a workout, as he won by nine lengths in 1:45 for the 1¹⁄₁₆ miles on a sloppy track. There had been a melee at the start, during which Pyrenees lost his rider, but the winner handled the rest of the field with such ease the validity of the result was never questioned. Shortly after his victory, Summer Tan nearly died of a severe intestinal disorder.

472

The typical thoroughbred is under restraint of some sort from the time he is taken up as a yearling until he retires from racing, but Nashua enjoyed a brief period of freedom as a three-year-old while his owner's estate was being settled.

J. C. Meadors

Although he recovered in time to make the trek to Florida, in view of the injury to Turn-to, first winner of the race, the episode gave rise to what was known as the Garden State jinx.

The rangy bay colt, who greatly resembled his maternal grandsire, Omaha, in construction, was runner-up to Nashua in voting for the championship. However, Frank E. "Jimmy" Kilroe, who succeeded Jack Campbell as Jockey Club handicapper after the latter's death in 1954, assigned Summer Tan 128 pounds on the Experimental Free Handicap, placing him a pound above the champion.

Tilford Wilson and Carl Houston's Royal Note, a son of Spy Song, trained by Frank Gilpin, had achieved local fame before he got to the races by virtue of dazzling morning workouts. He lived up to them by winning his first six races in a row, beginning with a new track record for three furlongs at Oaklawn Park. He followed up by equaling the track record in the

Lafayette Stakes at Keeneland, and winning the 5-furlong Bashford Manor Stakes in 1:00⅕ on a slow track at Churchill Downs, ridden without a whip both times. Next came his conquest of Nashua in the Cherry Hill.

The colt had a bad knee, and sometimes went to the post looking so "ouchy" horsemen in the audience wondered whether he'd make it. He warmed out of his stiffness quickly, however, and extended his winning streak with victories in the 5½-furlong Dover Stakes in 1:04⅗, just a tick off the Delaware Park record, and the lucrative Arlington Futurity.

The streak was ended when Royal Note finished second by half a length to Royal Coinage in the Sapling Stakes, and, after running unplaced in the Washington Park Futurity, won by Georgian, Royal Note was taken out of training. Ultimately, he was sent to stud.

Clearwater Stable's Royal Coinage, by Eight Thirty and trained by Al Pupino, was never out

473

of the money in eight starts, of which he won five, including the Great American Stakes besides the Saratoga Special and previously mentioned Sapling. Ranked third best of the season's juveniles, both in the polls and on the Experimental, he bruised a foot in the Futurity, and, like Royal Note, was destined never to race.

Other two-year-old colts of 1954 in the polls were Murcain Stable's West Coast champion, Blue Ruler (Starlet Stakes and Del Mar Futurity) and Calumet Farm's Trentonian (three stakes including Golden Gate Futurity). Among the other important races, the Pimlico Futurity was won by Thinking Cap, and Flying Fury, runner-up in the Maryland fixture, won the Champagne.

Mrs. D. P. Belz's Simmy set an unusual record for non-winners of a stakes event, as he earned $94,673 in his first season of racing, thanks to seconds in the Garden State Stakes and Washington Park Futurity. He could not be classified as just lucky, though, for he came through with a win in world record time of 1:15⅗ for 6½ furlongs early the following season.

Leader of the two-year-old fillies in 1954, both at the ballot box and on the money list, was Wheatley Stable's High Voltage, a gray daughter of the French stallion, Ambiorix, and another of the top runners trained by Mr. Fitz and foaled at Claiborne. Gaining part of the purse in all twelve of her starts, High Voltage won half of them, including the Rosedale, National Stallion (beating Delta), Colleen, Matron and Selima Stakes (beating Myrtle's Jet), for earnings of $167,825. Only twice did she lose at level weights—in her first start, a maiden race, and the last race of her campaign, the Frizette Stakes—and both times she was closing ground at the end.

Delta, a daughter of Nasrullah, owned by Claiborne Farm and trained by Moody Jolley, was top filly in the Midwest with victories in the Arlington Lassie and Princess Pat Stakes, plus a second to Royal Note in the Arlington Futurity against colts.

Ranked next to this pair was Maine Chance Farm's Myrtle's Jet, a daughter of Jet Pilot, trained by I. K. Mourar. After a so-so previous record, in mid-October Myrtle's Jet won the Alcibiades Stakes at Keeneland from Lea Lane. She then swapped decisions with High Voltage in the Selima and Frizette Stakes.

After Charlton Clay's Lea Lane won her first three starts, beating males by eight lengths in a maiden race; equaling the Lincoln Fields record of :59 for 5 furlongs in the Miss America Stakes, which she won by fourteen; and winning the Pollyanna by ten lengths, horsemen in the Midwest were not considering competition from among members of her own sex. It would take a colt, at least, to outrun this big brown daughter of Nasrullah, trained by J. Price Sallee. However, when she encountered close pursuit for the first time in the Arlington Lassie, Lea Lane flinched from the whip and was nosed out by her paternal half-sister and neighbor, Delta. (Clay's Marchmont Farm was next door to Claiborne Farm, and he was the brother-in-law of Claiborne founder, A. B. Hancock.) Lea Lane lost the Mademoiselle to Alspal, was unplaced in Delta's Princess Pat, and won the Durazna from Alspal before being upset in the Alcibiades.

Among the other two-year-old fillies of 1954 to receive honorable mention were Woodlawn Farm's Blue Sparkler, Brookmeade's Gandharva, and Reginald N. Webster's Sorceress.

Racing on grass reached a peak as Santa Anita's unique Camino Real turf course, which extended outside the main track enclosure and rambled over undulating ground, proved a popular innovation. The San Juan Capistrano Handicap, won by Mrs. Edward Lasker's By Zeus, was made the showpiece of the new course. (Because portions of it were downhill, numerous grass-course records were to be set on the Camino Real. At the first meeting, By Zeus set an American record of 2:26 for 1½ miles, Thirteen of Diamonds set a record of 2:00 for 1¼ miles and Poona II set a record of 1:47⅗ for 1⅛ miles).

CHAPTER SIXTY-FOUR

HEN CITATION, AT THE AGE OF six, brought his earnings past a million dollars, it was thought that his record would be safe for at least another twenty years or so. It did not survive five years—and the colt who obliterated it was Nashua.

The big bay from Belair won $752,550 in 1955, erasing Citation's high mark for earnings during a single season. Nashua, as a three-year-old, had attained more impressive physical development: 16 hands 1 inch, 1,200 pounds and 72 inches in girth; and he added another 1½ inches in height and girth before he retired. No longer did he inspire the awe among rival trainers that he had at two, however, for the other members of his generation had had time to catch up somewhat in maturity, and there also was the distinct possibility that the magnificent colt might beat himself.

Nashua ran greenly in his sophomore debut at Hialeah, loafing as soon as he reached the lead, and Arcaro had to smack him to win by one and a half lengths from Munchausen. His blinkers were removed for the Flamingo Stakes, but the performance of the Belair colt was again less than reassuring; he swerved in the stretch and bumped Saratoga, runner-up by one and a half lengths, which led to a claim of interference that was not allowed. In the $100,000 Florida Derby, Nashua took the lead, but propped, and was all out to stave off by a neck the closing rush of Blue Lem.

No such antics were evident in his next start, the Wood Memorial on April 23, nor could Nashua have afforded them. His old rival, Summer Tan, had opened his campaign with a four-

teen-length victory earlier that month. In the Wood he took the lead immediately and Nashua gave chase. In one of the year's most exciting contests, the Belair colt made up two lengths in the last furlong—under furious whipping by Atkinson, who was substituting for Arcaro—to win by only a neck. (Summer Tan's owner, a widow, had married John W. Galbreath in February, and the colt raced under her new name at three.)

Two weeks later came the big shock, and the origin of a rivalry that dominated the American racing scene for two years—one that never has been settled to the satisfaction of everyone. In the Kentucky Derby, Nashua was first out of the gate, but was taken back to third place, ahead of Summer Tan, where he remained for 6 furlongs. Launching his drive rounding the turn for home, the favorite got his nose even with the girth of the pace-setting Swaps, but could proceed no further. The margin still was half a length in mid-stretch, but second-choice Swaps thereafter drew away to win by one and a half lengths from Nashua, with Summer Tan another six and a half lengths away. (The latter colt, who didn't care for his races too close together in any case, after his two successive hard efforts in the Wood and Derby, did not race again at three.)

The downfall of the brilliant Nashua was a source of consternation, but there should have been no cause for great surprise. Under a masterful rating job by Shoemaker, Swaps had run the 1¼ miles in 2:01⅘, among the five fastest Derbies then on record, and his :49⅖ clocking for the final half-mile was the fastest yet. Moreover, the Californian had come

475

to Louisville early enough to get in his prep race at the Downs a week before the big one—a sparkling win in 1:10⅕ for 6 furlongs, working out the mile in 1:36⅖. When the tote opened for the Derby, Swaps was virtually co-favorite from the early betting, until the Eastern money began pouring in on Nashua. Jim Fitzsimmons later suggested that his champion's defeat might have been caused by Arcaro's preoccupation with Summer Tan, but the jockey himself considerably later expressed the opinion that, at least so far as the afternoon of May 7, 1955, was concerned, Nashua had tangled with a better colt.

Like Determine, Swaps had not been nominated to the other Triple Crown events, so he took his roses and went home to California. However, Nashua was not lacking for competition in the Preakness, as he was forced to a new track record of 1:54⅗ (more than a full second faster than Tom Fool's previous mark for 1³⁄₁₆ miles) to win by a length from Saratoga.

The Belmont Stakes on June 11 was the champion's fifth hundred-grander of the season, but no one would have guessed it from the reaction of his owner. "He won off!" shouted William Woodward, Jr., ignoring the material aspects of the victory in the light of what was, to him, the deeper significance of Nashua's performance. "This is the first time he hasn't scared us," added the young sportsman. Nashua

had, indeed, eliminated the gregariousness that had characterized his earlier finishes, as he took the lead at the end of a mile and drew away to win by nine widening lengths from Blazing Count in 2:29 for the 1½ miles.

Showing a similar disregard for close companionship, Nashua next beat Saratoga by five lengths in the Dwyer. In the Arlington Classic, however, after being carried along at a merry clip by Impromptu before finally overhauling him, Nashua was under a drive to win by half a length from the late-running Traffic Judge in 1:35⅕ for the mile.

Scarcely had he returned to the East, when it was announced that the Belair colt would be back in Chicago the next month. A $100,000 match had been arranged against Swaps.

SWAPS, 1952

(Khaled–Iron Reward, by Beau Pere)

There is something about a chestnut horse, and Swaps inspired one of the most intensely loyal followings of any thoroughbred in modern history. He had a lot more than coat color going for him, too.

Foaled on March 1, 1952, at the Ontario, California, ranch of his owner and breeder, Rex C. Ellsworth, he was the most successful of a remarkable number of successful offspring by Khaled, like Alibhai and Heliopolis, an English-bred son of the famed stallion, Hyperion. At

Swaps setting a world record of 2:38⅕ for 1⅝ miles in the Sunset Handicap.

maturity, Swaps stood 16 hands 2 inches, and weighed slightly under 1,200 pounds—almost the same size as Nashua, and also magnificently muscled—although the two were not similar in general appearance. With his abnormally deep chest, Swaps looked lower to the ground, and his conformation suggested as much pure speed as staying quality. Apart from mechanical details of his physique, the Ellsworth colt's most salient attribute was a sinuous grace few horses possess. Thoroughbreds are so constructed that all of them are somewhat jerky in the movement of their hindquarters at a walk. Swaps' action was noticeably more fluid—almost like that of a greyhound. Nor did he lumber to his feet from a lying position in the manner of most large animals; he arose nimbly—for all his bulk, he was surprisingly supple and handy.

The future star attracted no particular attention at two. Starting five times at the Hollywood Park meeting, ridden by Johnny Burton, he won twice, including the June Juvenile Stakes, after which he was put aside for a rest. Returning to action at Santa Anita on December 30, under Bill Shoemaker, he won the final race of his juvenile campaign to bring his earnings for the year up to $20,950.

After Swaps won the San Vicente Stakes in January, he missed a few weeks' training because of an infection that developed on his right forefoot. Trainer Meshach Tenney improvised a pad, made of soft shoe leather, to insert between the hoof and the horseshoe, and Swaps was sent forth for the Santa Anita Derby on February 19, despite the interruption in his preparation. He won the race, but only after a three-length lead he had built up dwindled to half a length at the wire, as Jean's Joe finished second and Blue Ruler third. Swaps did not start again until his ventures in Kentucky, having been shipped there by rail, not plane.

The plain mode of transportation employed by Swaps was typical operating procedure for what was becoming the largest, and one of the most powerful, turf empires in the world.

Although in official records Rex C. Ellsworth was listed as owner of the stable, and Meshach A. Tenney as trainer, the two men were partners down the line, and had been since boyhood, with Ellsworth (one day older than his friend) in the role of senior member and owner of the majority interest. True horsemen in every sense of the word, either partner could and did perform any function connected with the vast racing–breeding organization, including routine vetting, saddlery work and horseshoeing. (The latter activity on occasion caused some unpleasantness with the blacksmiths' union.) Their lives had been centered around horses, and even after he had become a millionaire, Ellsworth disagreed with descriptions of him as an ex-cowboy. He still was a cowboy, he maintained, and intended to remain so. It was difficult to question that premise, as the cattle land in Arizona and New Mexico owned by the organization was reckoned in square miles, rather than acres.

The association between Ellsworth and Tenney began when they were eight-year-old schoolmates in Safford, Arizona, and continued thereafter with one interruption. Devout Mormons, each man served the traditional stint as a missionary—Tenney in Colorado and Ellsworth in Africa. Throughout their later success, the Mormon Church received the customary 10 percent tithe from stable earnings. Johnny Burton, who rode Swaps during most of the colt's juvenile campaign, was a Mormon and left the stable to go on his mission.

Ellsworth's entrance onto the thoroughbred scene was scarcely grand. Accompanied by a brother, Heber, he arrived in Lexington in 1933 in a rented truck and $600; the truck rattled back to Arizona with eight fillies and mares—a remarkable quantity even at Depression prices—selected strictly on the basis of looks, since the brothers could not afford to pay for pedigree.

That was the foundation of a racing–breeding complex from which emerged Arigotal, and to which was added Silver Cord, and, finally,

Khaled, Ellsworth having purchased the noted stallion from Aly Khan in 1946 for $160,000, which he had borrowed from a Denver bank. That he was able to obtain the loan probably is the most eloquent testimony to the man's reputation, as a venture of this sort is not what bankers regard as a preferred risk.

By the time Swaps came along, the Ellsworth empire was firmly entrenched with main headquarters at Chino, California, a streamlined layout of efficiency, but, to Eastern eyes, somewhat suggestive of a prison camp, with its barren paddocks and wire fences. The deficiency in grass was offset by an elaborate electronic feed mill, designed to provide all vital elements of the equine diet. A number of traditionalists were horrified by the "factory" methods of breeding, breaking and training thoroughbreds employed by the cowboy outfit —which was based on treatment of horses as outdoor animals, rather than as pets—and a widely quoted remark by Ellsworth disparaging the intelligence of horses caused quite a furor.

Few could criticize the results, however, for horses flying the black-and-red Ellsworth silks were distinguished as much by their good manners as by their speed. Ball of fire that he was in action, Swaps was gentle as a lamb otherwise, and during his invasion of Kentucky, trainer Tenney slept in the stall with the colt, another of the human-interest facets which made Swaps such a public idol.

With the money he realized from Swaps (who derived his name when the partners swapped ideas on the subject back and forth) Ellsworth was able to expand yet further, and that sum was considerable.

On his return to California after his Derby victory, Swaps was a sensation. Against his age, he won the Will Rogers Stakes in 1:35 for a mile; won the 1 1/16-mile Californian Stakes from good older horses in world record time of 1:40 2/5 while carrying 115 pounds, sharing top weight on the scale with runner-up, Determine (126); then led all the way to win the Westerner Stakes by six lengths hard held, making concessions to his contemporaries.

Swaps also had an encounter with Traffic Judge in Chicago, in the American Derby on August 20, the first start on grass for each. Under restraint practically all the way, Swaps won by a length in new American record time (for a turf course) of 1:54 3/5 for 1 3/16 miles.

Eleven days later came the return bout with Nashua, and seldom has a horse race generated such interest as this one, in which the traditional East was pitted against the informal West. Swaps went to the post a heavy favorite at 3-to-10.

Although heated discussions of the clash between Nashua and Swaps at Washington Park persisted for years afterward, the story of the race itself is simple. Nashua beat his rival out of the gate and the match was won right there. With Arcaro yelling like an Indian, and whipping furiously, the Belair colt came out flying from his inside post position. Swaps, after swerving to the outside, gave chase, but to no avail. Each time Swaps tried to thrust past, Nashua drew away a little, until eventually Shoemaker gave up and Nashua went on to win by six and a half lengths, Arcaro keeping him about his business in the stretch, even after it was apparent that no further challenge was forthcoming. Arcaro's ride was a piece of artistry. Rounding the turn for home, while Swaps still was in pursuit, Arcaro took Nashua off the rail, just enough to provide a tempting hole of questionable width on the inside, and far enough out to make it difficult to go around; it wasn't exactly "herding," which is illegal, but it presented maximum discouragement to his rival. All in all, the winning tactics were not unlike those employed by George Woolf in Seabiscuit's 1938 victory over War Admiral.

Nashua's final time of 2:04 1/5 for the 1 1/4 miles was not impressive, although the track, rated slow until the fifth race on the program, was classified only good for the match, the seventh event. The fractions were somewhat more enlightening—:23, :46, 1:10 2/5 and 1:37 3/5 for the mile, by which point Swaps was done. It was reported later that he had re-injured his foot.

478

In the froth that followed, it was maintained by his admirers that Swaps was not himself during the match. From the opposite camp came the observation that, whoever he was, it was a pretty good colt that ran with Nashua as far as he did.

Finally, there was the theory concerning the peculiar nature of match racing *per se*, which takes something extra out of a horse. While fillies and geldings might run side by side complacently, it galls the spirit of a high-class, entire male thoroughbred to be challenged in close individual combat: he is bound to prevail or knock himself out trying. According to this concept, a wide margin was to be expected in a match between two such examples as Swaps and Nashua—and, paradoxically, that the finish was not close was a compliment to the loser. He gave it everything he had, until he cracked. Swaps raced no more that year.

Returning east Nashua received a comeuppance in his first outing against older horses in the Sysonby Stakes at weight-for-age, lengthened in 1955 to 1⅛ miles.

After vying with Jet Action and Helioscope for the lead, Nashua began to fall back, and none of them could withstand the challenge of the long-striding High Gun, who rolled up in the stretch to win by a head from Jet Action, with Nashua nearly two more lengths away in third place, Helioscope fourth.

That was the final start for the brilliant High Gun, whose retirement to stud was announced a few days later. Nashua went on to an easy victory in the 2-mile Jockey Club Gold Cup on October 15, and was acclaimed Horse of the Year by a majority that was quite substantial.

Runner-up as Horse of the Year, and voted best handicap horse of 1955, was High Gun, who left the track with a total of $486,025. (Unfortunately, he proved to be a shy breeder at stud.) In addition to what amounted to a runoff for the championship of his division, his Sysonby victory had represented vengeance of a kind over his kinsman, Helioscope, who had kept High Gun from winning the handicap Triple Crown by a matter of inches. In his first start of the season, after a long layoff, High Gun won the Metropolitan Handicap on

Swaps as a stallion with owners Mr. and Mrs. John W. Galbreath.

J. C. Meadors

High Gun defeating Jet Action and Nashua in the Sysonby Stakes.

May 14 while carrying 130 pounds, following which he was assigned 133 for the Suburban, against 128 on Helioscope. In one of the spectacles of the year, the two sons of Heliopolis thundered to the wire in 2:00⅗ with Helioscope winner by a head. High Gun subsequently won the Brooklyn Handicap under 132 —finale of the series—and Helioscope subsequently beat him again in the Monmouth Handicap, with the aid of a 4-pound concession, 131 to 135.

Elsewhere in the season, Helioscope won four stakes under steadying weight in new track record time, as follows: Southern Maryland Handicap, 128 pounds, 7 furlongs in 1:22⅗; Valley Forge Handicap, 130, mile and 70 yards in 1:40⅗; Massachusetts Handicap, 126, 1¼ miles in 2:01; and Salvator Mile, 126, in 1:36⅘. He, too, retired to stud after the Sysonby, with earnings of $418,275. The Sysonby second, Jet Action, had won the Olympic Handicap and, with a 10-pound pull in the weights, had defeated Helioscope in the Washington Park Handicap, covering the mile in 1:34.

Besides those who ran in the Sysonby, the only runners of handicap age to receive men-

tion in the championship poll were the geldings Social Outcast and Alidon. "Old Sosh" set a new divisional earnings record of $390,775 in 1955, running at fifteen different tracks. He won the McLennan, J. B. Campbell Memorial (in new track record time of 1:42⅗ for 1¹⁄₁₆ miles, defeating Fisherman and Helioscope), Lincoln Special, Sunset (new track record, 1⅝ miles in 2:40⅗), Saratoga, Manhattan and Trenton Handicaps (new track record, 1¼ miles in 2:01). He also outfinished High Gun in a couple of races which neither won. Alidon was the scourge of the Pacific Coast on dirt and grass surfaces, winner of the San Luis Rey, Camino Real (new turf course record of 1:58⅘ for 1¼ miles), Golden Gate, Argonaut (main course record of 1:34⅘ for a mile) and American Handicaps (1⅛ miles at 1:46⅘, new Hollywood Park record, equaling the world record). In other categories, St. Vincent won four stakes on grass to head that group, and Berseem was voted the best sprinter.

Among the three-year-old colts that trailed Nashua and Swaps in the championship voting, Clifford Mooers's Traffic Judge, a half-brother to Hasty Road, won the Withers, Ohio Derby, Ventnor Turf Stakes, Jerome Handicap and

480

beat his elders in the Woodward Stakes. Montpelier's Saratoga, a son of Blenheim II trained by ex-steeplechase star, Frank Bonsal, was so highly nervous that he dripped gallons of perspiration in the tense atmosphere before a race. On occasion he was isolated from the regular paddock when being saddled, and special permission was granted to load him into the starting gate last. Nevertheless, he crossed the finish line first in the Chesapeake, Leonard Richards, Choice Stakes and Saranac Handicap.

Summer Tan was the only other colt to get a call in the voting, although Paul Andolino's speedy Boston Doge received some consideration in the poll for sprinters.

Nashua's unprecedented winnings notwithstanding, Belair Stud did not top the owners' standings in 1955, although it came close. On the last day of the year, Hasty House Farm took over the leadership with $832,879. The principal money winners for the stable, owned by Toledo real estate developer Allie E. Reuben and his wife, were Sea O Erin, Platan, Hasty Road, Mister Black, Queen Hopeful, Stan and Summer Solstice.

The Reubens were not the usual sort of husband-and-wife team in which the wife is a partner in name only. Mrs. Billie Reuben, a top rider in horse shows during her youth, was an expert on conformation, while her husband specialized in studying the records. The Hasty House team had first attained prominence by purchasing horses of already established reputation, in preference to the gamble of buying untried yearlings, but when they did dip into the market for young stock, the results were remarkable. Two of the three yearlings Hasty House purchased in 1952 turned out to be Hasty Road and Queen Hopeful; and Sea O Erin had been bought as a weanling.

Nashua's trainer, Jim Fitzsimmons—who had other horses in his stable besides those of Belair Stud—led the money standings for his profession in 1955, enjoying his fourth term at the top a quarter-century after his name had first headed the list. The numerical stand-

ings, however, underwent quite a change. Following the departure from the scene of Red McDaniel—and the passage of the rule which limited California trainers to a maximum of forty horses in the stable at one time—for seven successive seasons, beginning in 1955, Frank H. Merrill, Jr. and Vester R. "Tennessee" Wright exchanged the training championship back and forth.

The four-time leader, Wright, a native of Gallatin, Tennessee, operated mostly up and down the Mississippi River Valley, and the nucleus of his public stable were the horses owned by J. L. Paddock of Louisville, Kentucky, and the brothers, T. Allie and Perne Grissom, of Detroit.

Three-time leader Merrill, from Brantford, Ontario, saddled most of his winners in Canada, but he frequently made forays into the United States during the summer, and maintained headquarters in Florida during the winter.

The monopoly of these two youngsters finally was broken in 1962 by veteran owner–trainer William Hal Bishop, who had been pursuing them closely all along, and who had shared the 1949 leadership with Bill Molter. A former mule trader from Anna, Illinois, Bishop operated one of the nation's largest racing strings, with sixty horses or so in racing condition at any given time. In 1963, Howard Jacobson, a nephew of Hirsch Jacobs, took over top spot.

Although he never topped the trainers' standings, mainly because he often split his huge stable into two or three platoons and divided saddling chores accordingly, another extraordinarily successful owner–trainer was Marion H. Van Berg, of Aurora, Nebraska, who set a new numerical record for owners of 221 winners in 1960. During that year he had as many as 70 horses in training at once, and, counting runners who came and went, at one time or another during the year 111 different horses carried his colors.

Belair, which finished less than $1,500 away from Hasty House in 1955 earnings, was in the process of being dissolved during the last two months of the season. On October 30, William Woodward, Jr. was killed at his Oyster Bay, Long Island, home by a shotgun blast from his wife, who had mistaken him for a prowler during the night. Executors of the estate decided to sell the turf interests at an unusual, sealed-bid auction, and on December 15 the bids on the horses were opened at the Hanover Bank and Trust Company in New York.

Of the ultimate total of $2,237,200 received for the Belair holdings, the bulk was derived from Nashua, who was sold separately. Five bids in excess of a million dollars were made for the colt, the top one being $1,251,200, made by Leslie Combs II as leader of a syndicate, consisting also of Christopher J. Devine, John W. Hanes, P. A. B. Widener III, Harry M. Warner and Mereworth Farm.

John S. Kroese paid $205,000 for the remainder of the Belair racing stable and the coming two-year-olds; he kept two horses and sold the rest the following month for $301,300. A group composed of Miss Mildred Woolwine,

Mr. and Mrs. Harry S. Middendorf and Edward Potter, Jr., submitted the high bid of $410,000 for the mares and yearlings. Resold at public auction about three weeks later, these horses brought more than double their cost: $924,100.

The magic name of Nashua was a strong influence throughout these sales, and it also was a factor in the sale of shares Woodward had owned in syndicated stallions. Of the $371,000 the estate realized from this source, $251,000 was bid for five shares in Nasrullah, although the stallion was sixteen years old.

Swaps and Nashua, the latter racing in the name of Combs and still trained by Fitzsimmons, continued to dominate racing during their four-year-old form, and until they retired there was an unceasing clamor for a rubber match between them.

From a heated challenge, in which Ellsworth vowed to come to grips with Nashua again if he had to chase him into the Atlantic Ocean, the situation eased into one of diplomatic parrying. In mid-summer each camp published a list of regularly scheduled events in

Nasrullah, sire of modern champions

which it was anticipated that its champion would compete, and politely invited the owner of the other horse to join the proceedings. The schedules did not coincide in any particular, and as one turf writer expressed it, neither "carefully deposited gauntlet" was disturbed. There was no reason they should be, from a practical standpoint, since there were enough rich races to go around without the two titans having to fight over the same one.

As a four-year-old, Swaps displayed the most amazing exhibition of speed in history. Limited by his foot to competition on fast tracks, and limited by the handicappers to ceiling weight of 130 pounds, he won eight of ten starts, seven of them in record time and six of them under maximum load, to win $409,400, the largest sum ever earned in one season by a horse of handicap age. Virtually all of his victories were scored under restraint by his jockey —and so was one of his defeats.

Largely because of unsuitable track conditions (an operation had been performed on his foot, and if he ran on an oozing surface there was danger of seepage into the cavity) Swaps started only once at the Santa Anita meeting, winning a 1$\frac{1}{16}$-mile overnight handicap under 127 pounds from Bobby Brocato (124) by one and three-quarters lengths in 1:43. It was the only victory that year in which Swaps did not shatter a time record, but nevertheless a worthy performance in view of the interruptions to his training caused by the foot trouble, and considering that Bobby Brocato won eight stakes that year, including the $100,000 Santa Anita and San Juan Capistrano Handicaps.

Shipped to Florida, although he missed the Gulfstream Park Handicap (in which Nashua was unplaced), Swaps later won the Broward Handicap easily in world record time of 1:39$\frac{3}{5}$ for a mile and 70 yards, carrying 130 pounds. Upon his return to the West, he picked up 127 pounds for the Californian Stakes, and had a good lead in the stretch when Shoemaker began pulling him up; Porterhouse (118) roared up at the end to win by a head before Shoemaker could get Swaps going again.

The chestnut streak then won five straight races in record time. In the Argonaut Handicap, with 128 pounds, he set a new world record of 1:33$\frac{1}{5}$ for a mile. In the Inglewood Handicap, at 130, he set another new world record of 1:39 for 1$\frac{1}{16}$ miles (something of an oddity, since this was faster than the world record he had set at Gulfstream for 40 yards less distance). Assigned the same weight for the American Handicap, Swaps equaled the world record of 1:46$\frac{4}{5}$ for 1$\frac{1}{8}$ miles; and his victory in the Hollywood Gold Cup on July 14, again under 130, was a new track record of 1:58$\frac{3}{5}$ for 1$\frac{1}{4}$ miles.

In all these races, Swaps had been making large concessions to his opposition, and the point was reached at which further concessions became impossible, so long as he remained at the 130-pound ceiling. The Sunset Handicap on July 25 was a farce. No riders light enough could be found for any of his rivals, so all eight of them carried overweight—up to 5 pounds. Moreover, Swaps, who had been odds-on throughout the series (something of an anomaly in a handicap race, for which the weights, at least in theory, provide a chance of victory to all), in the Sunset went off at the legal minimum of 1-to-10. It was an overlay at that, for he won by four and a quarter lengths in new world record time of 2:38$\frac{1}{5}$ for 1$\frac{5}{8}$ miles.

Moving on to Chicago, the Ellsworth colt ran his only bad race of the year, finishing seventh in the Arch Ward Memorial Handicap (won by Hasty House Farm's Mahan) on August 25; the race was on grass, and although the surface was listed as firm, Shoemaker said it was too soft for his mount. Next time out, on the main track, Swaps carried 130 pounds to win the Washington Park Handicap by two lengths from Summer Tan (115) in 1:33$\frac{2}{5}$, a new track record and faster than any horse in the world had run the distance, except Swaps himself.

He never raced again. While Swaps was training at Atlantic City for the United Nations Handicap, a half-interest in him was sold to

John W. Galbreath in exchange for breeding stock "and other considerations" equivalent in value to a million dollars, but the colt was withdrawn from the U.N. because his foot began to trouble him. The next month, in a workout at Garden State Park, he fractured his left hind leg. After a recuperation period, part of which was spent in a sling sent down from New York by Nashua's trainer, Jim Fitzsimmons, Swaps returned to California. He entered stud with the largest collection of recognized world records (five) in history, and a lifetime performance, in summary, as follows: 25 starts, 19 wins, two seconds, two thirds, earnings of $848,900.

Among his unofficial accomplishments, Swaps more than any other horse demonstrated the impracticality of weight ceilings, and the policy later was abandoned at a number of tracks, including Hollywood Park. About a year after his retirement, Ellsworth's half-interest in Swaps was purchased for another $1,000,-000 by Mrs. Galbreath, and the horse was transferred to the Galbreaths' Darby Dan Farm in Kentucky, where he became a teammate of Summer Tan.

As a four-year-old, Nashua operated largely in an area where there was no weight ceiling, but the relationship between him and his opposition was such that there were few occasions to assign him more than 130 pounds anyway—and he lost both races in which he attempted to carry that much, although one of the losses could be classified as a moral victory.

Unable to get him a prep race, Mr. Fitz sent Nashua straight into the Widener under 127 pounds; Nashua won, but it was a hard-fought battle among four horses as the Combs colt won by only a head from Social Outcast (121), with Sailor (119) a head away third and Find (114) just a neck back of him. With this victory Nashua became the turf's second millionaire.

In the Gulfstream Park Handicap on March 17, carrying 2 pounds more, for the first time in his life Nashua was unplaced as Sailor, still at 119, won from Milleux, (110), Find

(116) and Wise Margin (113). Finishing fifth, seven lengths behind the winner, Nashua nevertheless received $2,500 for his performance; he had not put forth much effort, and it was theorized that he objected to sand being thrown in his face.

After moving north to Jamaica, Nashua won the Grey Lag Handicap with 128 pounds by a head from Find (118) and Fisherman (120), following which he carried 129 pounds to victory over Fisherman (120) in the Camden Handicap at Garden State Park May 19. Nashua thereby replaced Citation as world's leading money winner, the Camden purse having increased his total to $1,100,365.

Next came the two losses at 130 pounds. In the Metropolitan Handicap, after seemingly having surrendered, Nashua came again to make up more than two lengths in the stretch, but nevertheless was fourth—beaten less than a length for it all—behind Midafternoon (111), Switch On (113) and Find (116). The winner's time of 1:35 was only ⅕-second off the track record. In the 7-furlong Carter Handicap June 30, at the same weight, Nashua was no factor, finishing seventh, three and a half lengths behind the winner, Red Hannigan (114). That was the only time in his life he failed to add to his earnings.

The world's leading money winner then began to mend his fences. On a fast track in the Suburban Handicap, he carried 128 pounds to victory over Dedicate (111) in 2:00⅘, fastest time of the year at Belmont for 1¼ miles. On a muddy track, with 129 pounds, he scored his most decisive triumph of the season in the 1¼-mile Monmouth Handicap, winning by three and a half lengths and conceding 19 pounds to the runner-up, Mr. First, in 2:02⅘.

After all these handicaps, Nashua ran into difficulty in his first weight-for-age outing, the Woodward Stakes, which represented his return to action from an absence of more than two months caused by colic. After Nashua had put away Jet Action, Mister Gus sailed by to beat him by two and a half lengths in 2:03 over the good track. But on October 13, Nashua left the stage with a flourish, scoring his second victory in the 2-mile Jockey Club Gold Cup, in new American record time of 3:20⅖, by two and a quarter lengths from Riley; Third Brother was third, and Mister Gus was eight lengths away in fourth place.

Nashua entered stud—sound as the proverbial bell—boasting only two speed marks, but with the largest collection of money in history, up to that time, having compiled the following record: 30 starts, 22 wins, four seconds, one third, earnings of $1,288,565.

A comparison of Nashua and Swaps only leads to argument. Easterners were somewhat disdainful of Swaps's fantastic times at Hollywood Park, since new track records were established at nine of the ten distances contested during the two summers he shone there; Lucky Mel, Bold Bazooka, El Drag and Alidon also contributed world records, and several of Swaps's defeated rivals finished close enough to him to have broken the former world marks, too. Westerners in their turn brought up the question of Nashua's troubles with weight.

In the official voting, Nashua was the better at two and three. At four, Swaps was tops.

Of the Big Two's principal rivals, Summer Tan, at four won the Vosburgh and Gallant Fox Handicaps (new track record of 2:41⅗ for 1⅝ miles) and Pimlico Special; he raced briefly the next year, winning the McLennan Handicap, to bring his career total up to $542,-796. Traffic Judge (syndicated by L. P. Doherty after the death of Mooers) added the Turf Cup, Metropolitan and Suburban Handicaps to his string before retiring with $432,450.

Brookmeade Farm's Sailor, who had succeeded mainly as a sprinter at three (Toboggan and Fall Highweight Handicaps), later in 1955 had reached out to win the Roamer and Pimlico Special at 1�_3_⁄₁₆ miles. He followed up his conquest of Nashua at Gulfstream as a four-year-old, with another hundred-grander, the John B. Campbell Memorial Handicap, after which the chestnut son of Eight Thirty was retired, destined eventually to join Swaps and Summer Tan at Darby Dan Farm.

Bobby Brocato was a far more startling case of a sprinter who stretched out. Racing in the East for J. W. Brown, the son of Natchez had won the Sanford at two, Paumonok and Carter at four—nothing past 7 furlongs—but after being sold to Travis M. Kerr and turned over to trainer Bill Molter, he included among his numerous stakes victories the 1¾-mile San Juan Capistrano. Before retirement he amassed $504,510.

Llangollen Farm's Mister Gus, who spent part of the summer chasing Swaps, placed in numerous stakes at four, but won only one, the Kyne Handicap. As a five-year-old in 1956, besides his triumph over Nashua in the Woodward, he won the San Antonio and Arlington Handicaps, beating Summer Tan in the latter in 1:54⅕, new American record time for 1_3_⁄₁₆ miles on grass. A son of Nasrullah, and born in America, Mister Gus was a year older than Nashua and other members of the noted stallion's first true American crop, because he had been imported *in utero*. His stablemate, Porterhouse, besides catching Swaps in the Californian, won the 1956 San Carlos and Lakes and Flowers Handicaps, repeating victories of the previous season in each, plus the Santa Barbara and Palos Verdes Handicaps. In subsequent seasons he set a world record of 1:02⅖ for 5½ furlongs in the Hollywood Express Handicap, won the 7-furlong Los Angeles Handicap in 1:20⅘ and had collected $519,460 before he retired.

Mrs. E. E. Robbins's Midafternoon, the son of Billings who won the Metropolitan from Nashua, also took the Massachusetts and Display Handicaps, the latter in new world record time of 3:29⅗ for 2_1_⁄₁₆ miles.

Another of the four-year-olds of 1956 who created quite a stir, although he did not run against the Big Two, was Calumet Farm's Bardstown, a gelding who had not raced at either two or three. In his first season he won the Equipoise Mile, Longport, Buckeye, Quaker City and Trenton Handicaps. Not the soundest horse in the world, but tough when he was right, the son of Alibhai–Twilight Tear (hence a half-brother to A Gleam) made up for his late arrival by racing on through age seven. Among other stakes successes, he added two more renewals of the Widener Handicap to the Calumet collection, plus a Gulfstream Park Handicap, and ran his bank account up to $628,752. Along with G. S. Colella's Switch On, Bardstown was particularly effective in Florida.

Finally, the colt who finished second to Nashua in the Suburban, is of additional interest because, after his two contemporaries left the scene, in 1957 he was to be elected best handicap horse in three polls, and Horse of the Year in one.

DEDICATE, 1952

(Princequillo–Dini, by John P. Grier)

Another of the numerous stars foaled at Claiborne Farm, Dedicate was bred and owned by Mrs. Edward G. (Jan) Burke, sister of Native Dancer's trainer, Bill Winfrey; their father, Cary Winfrey, trained Dedicate. A non-winner in eight starts at two, as a three-year-old he won five in a row, including the 6-furlong Delaware Valley Stakes in 1:09⅗, tying the track record, and the 1⅛-mile Jersey Stakes in 1:48⅕, breaking the track record. However, Dedicate was eclipsed by the Swaps–Nashua coterie, and plagued by a foot problem; he subsequently lost five in a row.

As a four-year-old the small bay colt really hit stride for the first time. Although he won only three races, they were big ones—the Brooklyn Handicap, Whitney Stakes in new track record time of 1:49⅘ for 1⅛ miles and Hawthorne Gold Cup—and he was unplaced but twice in eleven starts. Dedicate beat Find in the Brooklyn, Summer Tan in the Whitney, and both of them in the Gold Cup, although Summer Tan later reversed the decision in the Gallant Fox Handicap.

At five three of Dedicate's four wins were in $100,000 events. He won the John B. Campbell Memorial and Monmouth Handicaps under top weight of 124 pounds, and beat the season's two other best horses, Gallant Man and Bold Ruler, at weight-for-age in the 1¼-mile Woodward Stakes. Dedicate also finished

Dedicate after winning the Jersey Stakes. Sam Boulmetis up.

first under top weight in another hundred-grander, the Atlantic City Handicap, but was disqualified for interference, after coming home three lengths clear under 126 pounds—shattering the track record by almost 3 full seconds, as he covered the 1³⁄₁₆ miles on turf in 1:54⅘. At retirement, he had earned $533,-200.

There was plenty of activity among the fillies and mares in 1955 and 1956. In 1955, Delaware Park instituted the Distaff Big Three series, whereby the added money of the Delaware Handicap was set at $110,000, with provisions for further increases depending upon participation by the winner in preceding races of the series, the Oaks and New Castle Stakes. There were other lagniappes, but the general air of graciousness did not extend to weight assignments. Little Parlo, previously winner of the Top Flight Handicap under 126 pounds, was rigged at 128 for the main event at Delaware—cavalier treatment for a candidate whose owner (William duPont, Jr.) had founded the track. Nonetheless, the watch charm filly won easily by three lengths, and,

along with the $99,900 purse and a $5,000 nominator's award, she became champion of her division in two of the year-end rankings. She raced on another season, winning the Bellerose Handicap of 1956, to wind up her career with a total of $309,240.

Although she was moved back to second in the rich Maturity, Miz Clementine won the 1955 Las Flores, and in 1956 she added the New Castle Stakes and Vagrancy Handicap to retire with $267,100. Delta did not win stakes at three, but she came back at four with ten victories, four of them stakes, including the Arlington Matron Handicap, to stretch her earnings to $269,215. Queen Hopeful continued to win stakes through age five, and to race through age six; she retired with $365,044.

Wheatley Stable's Misty Morn won the sophomore filly championship of 1955 at the expense of her own stablemate, High Voltage, and shared the title with Parlo as best female handicap performer. The daughter of Princequillo–Grey Flight, by Mahmoud, started twenty-two times at three, and won nine, including the Monmouth Oaks within her divi-

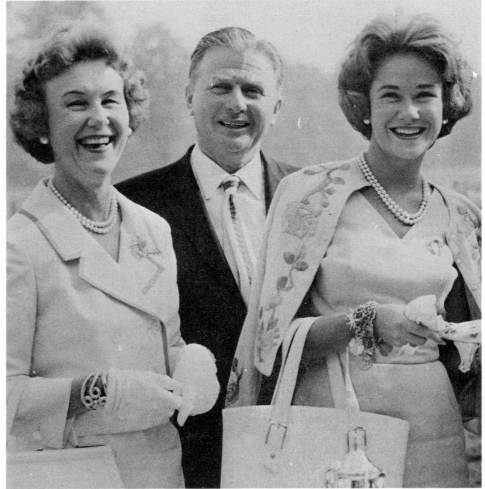

Hirsch Jacobs, leading trainer 11 times in 12 years and twice leading money-winning trainer with Mrs. Jacobs, owner of Stymie, and their daughter Patrice, owner of Hail to Reason.

Bert and Richard Morgan

sion; the Molly Pitcher and Diana Handicaps from elders of her sex; the Providence Stakes from three-year-old colts; and the Gallant Fox Handicap from a field that included older masculine rivals. In the latter event, she won by three lengths, conceding actual weight to the runner-up, in new track record time of 2:42⅖ for 1⅝ miles on a good track at Jamaica. That same season High Voltage won the Acorn, Black-Eyed Susan Stakes, CCA and Delaware Oaks and Vineland Handicap. At the end of her career she had earned $362,240.

Woodlawn Farm's Blue Sparkler, a home-bred daughter of Knave High, trained by Harry Wells, won all her stakes in her native state of New Jersey. After taking three added money events in her first two seasons of racing, she emerged as the champion of the female handicap division in 1956 with victories in the Regret, Molly Pitcher Handicaps (by eight lengths) and the $100,000 Atlantic City Handicap, defeating such formidable males as Find, Mister Gus, Bardstown, Wise Margin and Skipper Bill. Despite the affinity for her native soil, the filly, owned by Monmouth Park president Amory Haskell, did quite well elsewhere. She was a close second to Bardstown, conced-ing him actual weight, in the Buckeye Handicap, won in new track record time of 1:47⅕ for 9 furlongs at Randall Park; and finished first under top weight in the Champlain Handicap at Jamaica, but was placed second for interfering with Gandharva.

Gandharva, Rare Treat, Manotick, Oil Painting, Lalun and Searching were among the numerous other fillies prominent during the period. The latter was the heroine of one of those fascinating racetrack stories.

A daughter of War Admiral–Big Hurry, by Black Toney, Searching earned part of the purse in each of her first seven starts as a two-year-old, but she failed to win, and still was a maiden after thirteen starts at the end of the season. As a three-year-old, she resumed her frustrating pattern. Seven straight times she was in the money without winning the main part, and after she finished second five successive times owner Ogden Phipps sold her to Hirsch Jacobs for $15,000. Naturally, Searching won first out for her new owner. In the colors of Mrs. Jacobs, Searching went on and on, retiring finally with $327,381 from 25 victories in 89 starts, including numerous stakes.

PART SIX

HORIZONS UNLIMITED

CHAPTER SIXTY-FIVE

THE YEAR BEHIND NASHUA AND Swaps another crop was foaled which wasted no time earning money. Lily-Ann Stable's Getthere Jack was the leader of the spring two-year-olds by winning five straight; although he was defeated in his first start after he moved north, he completed the year never out of the money in ten starts, of which he won eight, including the Gulfstream Park Dinner and Juvenile Stakes, Tremont and Great American.

Barclay Stable's Polly's Jet, the colt who broke Getthere Jacks' undefeated string by a nose in the Belmont Juvenile Stakes, was in the process of chalking up a six-race winning streak of his own, including the Cherry Hill (new track record of :58 for 5 furlongs), National Stallion and Christiana Stakes. Although Polly's Jet later was to win the Saratoga Special, his undefeated march was halted by a colt who had lost to Getthere Jack in Florida—but who, in the long pull, was destined to top the generation.

NEEDLES, 1953

(Ponder–Noodle Soup, by Jack High)

Needles had several claims to fame. Product of a hastily arranged mating (his dam was bred to Ponder mainly because the horse had just come off the track and bookings happened to be available) he was so sickly as a foal that his name was derived from the numerous medications stuck into him. However, Needles developed into a winner of the blue ribbon at a "beauty contest" and thereupon was sold for $20,000 by breeder W. E. Leach to the D & H Stable of Oklahoma oilmen, Jack Dudley and Bonnie Heath.

The first Florida-bred classic winner, Needles was instrumental in eliminating the practice of allowing native foals a 5-pound advantage at the state's tracks. He also exploded the myth, which had been nourished by the experience of Native Dancer and Nashua, that it was necessary to have a preparatory race at the Downs in order to win the Kentucky Derby; Needles won it without even a decent workout—thus eliminating yet another jinx, attached to horses whose name began with the letter N, that formerly had applied to such favorites as Nashua, Native Dancer and Nellie Flag.

Finally, Needles underwent an unusual metamorphosis. Fast as they come as a two-year-old —and precocious enough to set a new track record of :52⅖ for 4½ furlongs in April—he defied his paternal heritage. At three, however, he emulated his sire with a vengeance; while Ponder would delay his move, it sometimes seemed that Needles was deliberately trying to outdo him on that score.

Trained by World War I aviator and former polo player, Hugh Fontaine, and ridden in his juvenile victories by John Choquette, Needles was six for ten at two, and never failed to get part of the purse. The Sapling Stakes on August 10 was his first added money victory, and in that race, with an 8-pound concession from each, he knocked two colts from the ranks of the undefeated: Decathlon (who previously had defeated Needles in the Tyro Stakes) and Polly's Jet. The D & H colt met the same pair at level weights in the 6½-furlong Hopeful, which Needles won by three

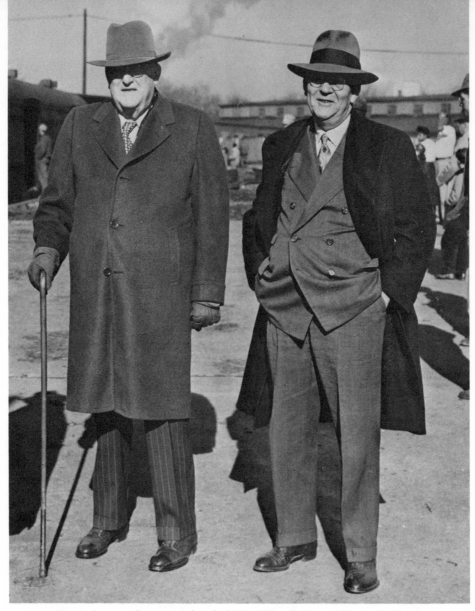

Master horse salesmen, Colonel Phil T. Chinn (left) and Henry H. Knight.

and a half lengths from Career Boy, with Polly's Jet and Decathlon unplaced.

In his remaining stakes efforts, Needles was making up ground at the end, but didn't get there. He was third, beaten a length for it all each time, in the World's Playground Stakes (won by Busher Fantasy) and Garden State Stakes, which Elmendorf's Prince John won by a nose from Career Boy. The world's richest race was the only stakes won by Prince John, whose career was ended by injury not long afterward.

In the voting for champion two-year-old, Needles shared honors with Mrs. Anson Bigelow's Nail, a gray son of Nirgal, trained by George P. "Maje" Odom. Similar in name, Nail also was similar to Needles in that his juvenile performance contradicted his pedigree, which in Nail's case was suggestive of quick speed. He waited until the 6½-furlong Futurity in October to win his first stakes event; then, after finishing unplaced in the Garden State, he won the Remsen (beating Prince John) and Pimlico Futurity, both at 1¹⁄₁₆ miles, to lead his class in juvenile earnings with $239,-930. As a three-year-old, Nail also reverted to the style of running indicated by his ancestry, in his case, sprinting, although the evidence was not conclusive because he had troubles, and never won again at any distance.

Nail, who finally retired with $250,230, was the leading money winner bred by the master

492

horse salesman of his time, Henry Hudson Knight (1889–1959). Although he certainly was to the manor born—his family owned a parcel of bluegrass land that had originated as a crown grant before America won its independence—Knight eschewed completion of his formal education to strike out on his own at the age of twenty. (By his own account, he asked his father for $100 to "go somewhere," and the senior Knight gave him $200, expressing the hope that he'd go twice as far.) After a meteoric career as a shoe salesman, Henry Knight shifted his talent to bigger game and began selling automobiles and trucks—not in units, but in wholesale lots. By the time he inherited the ancestral acreage from an uncle, he had made his own fortune, which he used to expand his inheritance. Almahurst Farm, named for Mrs. Knight, was increased to 2,100 acres, and Knight also owned several other valuable Central Kentucky farms.

Following a family tradition, he began with harness horses. He bred the champion of champions, Greyhound, holder of fourteen records including a mile in 1:55¼, plus two other Hambletonian winners, Yankee Maid and Chestertown. When he transferred his interest to thoroughbreds, Knight sold his Standardbred stock to Mr. and Mrs. Frederick Van Lennep, whose Castleton Stud continued to be eminently successful in that branch of sport.

Knight's penchant for wholesale operations was reflected in his horse activity. In 1944 he purchased the entire thoroughbred holdings of Valdina Farm, consisting of 149 horses, from the estate of Emerson Woodward; and later that same year he bought the breeding stock and young horses of Mrs. Ethel V. Mars, who had announced she was retiring from racing for the duration of the war. Among Knight's subsequent big deals was the purchase, in two stages, of huge Coldstream Stud (formerly McGrathiana), a number of mares and the successful stallion Heliopolis from E. E. Dale Shaffer; the importation of several not-so-successful stallions from France; and the purchase of 184 horses from the estate of W. G. Helis.

Knight concentrated on production of horses only. He did not race a stable, but was America's leading breeder, in volume of winners, for the 1955-1957 seasons. Nail was among the last products to emerge from his establishment, as in 1955 Knight held what amounted to a dispersal of his stock. The 123 mares and weanlings were autioned for $1,399,300.

At three, Needles took clear title to his divi-

Trainer Hugh Fointaine holding Kentucky Derby winner Needles and the traditional magnum of champagne.

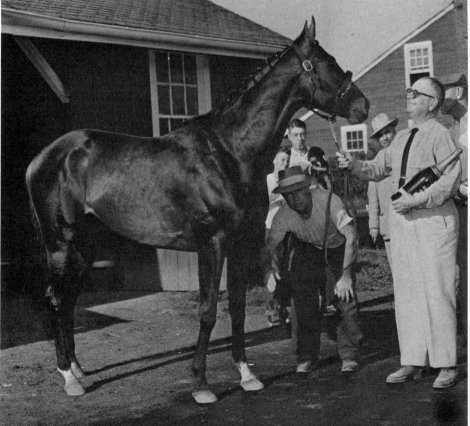

Courier-Journal and Louisville Times

sional crown. With Dave Erb as jockey, after finishing second to the aptly named Call Me Lucky in his debut, Needles won both the Flamingo Stakes and Florida Derby at 1⅛ miles, setting a new Gulfstream record of 1:48⅗ in the latter, while getting his 5-pound allowance from fields he evidently could have defeated had the advantage been the other way. Thereafter, the Florida-bred allowance was eliminated in stakes races, and eventually it was abandoned in all races.

During the six weeks between the Florida and Kentucky Derbies, Needles did not race —and it was all Fontaine could do to get him to exercise in the morning. To add to the trainer's problems, Needles drew the inside post position for the Churchill Downs classic, the worst possible spot for a horse of his late-running habit, since it meant he would have to thread his way through the entire field. When asked how he liked that post position, Fontaine shrugged and said, "I love it . . . I might as well 'cause it's the only one I'm going to get." As it turned out Needles did not have to run past the entire field—he had one horse behind him after the first 6 furlongs had been covered. From sixteenth place, and sixteen lengths off the pace, at the half-mile pole, he flowed steadily on to win going away by three-fourths of a length from Calumet Farm's Fabius, who had won the Derby Trial.

In the slightly shorter Preakness two weeks later, Needles ran last for 6 furlongs before moving up, gained about three lengths in the stretch drive, but was unable to menace Fabius, who crossed the line one and three-quarters lengths ahead, under the guidance of Bill Hartack. Three years later, the Pimlico finish line was relocated in order to make the homestretch 202 feet longer.

Needles remained on the sidelines as Fabius won the Jersey Stakes and ran second to Ricci Tavi in the Leonard Richards Stakes during the next three weeks, but the pair met again in the Belmont Stakes June 16. Needles

dawdled so in the early part he looked like a poor bet for the next race on the program, at one point dropping twenty-three lengths behind, with Erb impassive. Fabius already was heading for home as Needles was rounding the turn, seventeen lengths off the pace, and there still was an eight-length deficit remaining with only a quarter of a mile left to go.

In his usual style—he never charged forward in the stretch, but, rather, rolled on steadily and relentlessly—he moved by Fabius, although on this occasion there was a little extra chore to repel Career Boy, who also closed ground. Needles won by a neck from Career Boy, as Fabius barely saved third.

In two starts on the turf course at Washington Park, Needles never got out of last place in a 6-furlong prep, won by five-year-old Burnt Child in American record time (for grass) of 1:09⅘, and in the 1³⁄₁₆-mile American Derby he was closing at the end but still finished fifth, two and three-quarters lengths behind the winner, Swoon's Son.

That ended his sophomore campaign. Although he had won only four races, they all were hundred-granders, and he was the season's leading money winner with $440,850. The pride of the Sunshine State returned briefly at four, equaling the Gulfstream track record of 1:42 for 1¹⁄₁₆ miles in the Fort Lauderdale Handicap under 126 pounds, and ended his racing career with 11 wins in 21 starts and $600,355.

SWOON'S SON, 1953

(The Doge–Swoon, by Sweep Like)

E. Gay Drake's Swoon's Son (foaled on Friday the 13th) was the leading money winner of his crop, earning $970,605, about nine-tenths of it in Chicago. Other colts had won the big Chicago juvenile double of both futurities, and still others had won the equivalent double of the two richest races for three-year-olds, the Classic and American Derby. Swoon's Son took all four, and added several other rich plums on

494

the side. Sometimes he teamed up with his older full brother, Dogoon, himself winner of $220,360, to win both the stakes and secondary feature on the program, so Drake was kept busy counting his money.

A paragon of consistency, Swoon's Son won more than $200,000 every season he raced, and he was the first horse in history to put four such seasons together. Bred by his owner, and trained by A. G. "Lex" Wilson, the Drake colt was ridden generally by Dave Erb. Unplaced but once in thirteen starts as a two-year-old (a disqualification after finishing third in the Hawthorne Juvenile Handicap) Swoon's Son won seven races, six of them in a row. Besides the Arlington and Washington Park Futurities, beating Prince John in the latter, they included the Bashford Manor, George Woolf Memorial and Prairie State Stakes.

At three, the beautifully molded bay colt won ten of his twelve starts and was second in the other two, conceding weight in each. Within his division, in addition to his conquest of Needles in the American Derby (Erb picked the wrong mount for that one), Swoon's Son beat Fabius in the Arlington Classic, and also won the Domino, Warren Wright Memorial and Chicagoan Stakes—the latter race being the Derby counterpart at the Balmoral meeting, which had replaced Lincoln Fields on the Chicago calendar. In overnight races he set track records of 1:09⅕ for 6 furlongs at Keeneland and 1:42 for 1¹⁄₁₆ miles on turf at Washington Park. Against older horses he won twice, including the Clark Handicap at Churchill Downs under actual top weight of 128 pounds.

It was not until he himself reached handicap age that Swoon's Son was unplaced legitimately. At four and five, he won exactly half his twenty-six starts and was out of the money only seven times.

At four he won six stakes carrying 130 pounds or more, including the Equipoise Mile under 132, conceding 24 to Call Me Lucky; the Bidwill Memorial under 131, in new Hawthorne record time of 1:48⅘ for 1⅛ miles;

Swoon's Son heading for a morning workout.

and the Warren Wright Memorial Handicap with 130 in new Arlington record time of 1:21⅗ for 7 furlongs. Elsewhere in his final two seasons, Swoon's Son repeated in the Equipoise Mile (beating Bardstown, Clem and Round Table among others) and also won the Churchill Downs, La Salle, Citation, Midwest, Clang, Myrtlewood Handicaps and Michigan Sweepstakes.

The 1³⁄₁₆-mile American Derby was the

495

longest race the Drake horse won, but he twice finished second in the Hawthorne Gold Cup, at 1¼ miles, to Round Table. At retirement, when he was syndicated for $1,000,000, Swoon's Son had 30 wins, 10 seconds and three thirds from 51 starts.

DECATHLON, 1953

(Olympia–Dog Blessed, by Bull Dog)

In 1954 Fred Hooper, who had owned the stallion during his racing days, was buying up yearlings by Olympia. The tall Alabaman (who had won the Kentucky Derby with Hoop, Jr., the first yearling he ever purchased) bought five of Olympia's offspring at the Keeneland sales, but he missed the best one of the lot as Decathlon went to the River Divide Farm of R. J. Dienst on a bid of $15,500.

For sheer speed, few horses in American turf annals could match this little bay colt, and for his size he was unsurpassed as a weight-packer. Actually, Decathlon wasn't so small as he looked—he reportedly stood 15-3 and weighed 950 pounds at maturity—but he did not have the bulging muscles and blocky physique commonly associated with sprinters. Moreover, in the presence of the generously proportioned Rollie Shepp, who trained Decathlon, any horse was apt to look pony size.

Before he began his racing career, the River Divide colt stepped on a nail, and afterwards he had a peculiar way of putting down that forefoot. In action his left front leg resembled the flipper of a seal, but it did not keep him from winning twenty-five times in forty-two starts, for lifetime earnings of $269,530.

Like several other quick, handy colts, Decathlon started out with a winning streak—five straight—during which he set a new track record of :52⅗ for 4½ furlongs at Suffolk Downs, won the Bay State Kindergarten Stakes in new track record time of :58⅕ for 5 furlongs, the Narrangansett Nursery Stakes, and the Tyro Stakes in new Monmouth record time of 1:04 for 5½ furlongs (Needles unplaced).

When he ran into Needles again—and that extra sixteenth of a mile—in the 6-furlong Sapling Stakes, Decathlon was second. In his next start at 6 furlongs he was unplaced, and, as his losing streak was increased to nine successive races, it appeared that he was just another of those quick-blossoming juveniles, destined to fade from prominence as the distances got longer.

Unlike the typical nursery school sensation, however, Decathlon came back. At Tropical Park in December he added two more stakes to his collection, the De Soto and Dade County Handicaps, and thereby launched a long sequence of 28 successive races, extending over three calendar years, during which he never failed to get part of the purse. Thenceforth he never lost without conceding weight to the winner, and frequently he won while making heavy concessions. Such consistent performance is the more remarkable when it is considered that it was accomplished all at distances of 7 furlongs or less—most often less—and, while sprints are a relatively disdained form of racing so far as rich purses are concerned, it is harder to avoid upsets in that form of competition. Apart from the consideration that most sprint stakes for mature horses are handicaps, there is the tactical aspect; while a horse who happens to stumble, or get caught in a pocket, has time to regain lost ground in a race over a long distance, a sprint can be all over before he recovers. In order to put a horse in a pocket, though, it is necessary to catch him first—and with Decathlon that was seldom possible. He could rip off an initial quarter-mile in 22 seconds as casually as though he were cantering through a workout.

For two years in a row the oddly gaited colt was elected champion sprinter. (Decathlon had been acquired, incidentally, from Hurstland Farm, which also had sold champion sprinter White Skies as a yearling.) At three the son of Olympia won the Hibiscus, Hutcheson Stakes, Select, Coral Gables Handicaps, Rockingham Special, and divisions of the

Decathlon winning the Select Handicap at Monmouth Park.

Oceanport and Tropical Park Inaugural Handicaps. At Tropical he equaled the world record of 1:03⅕ for 5½ furlongs and the track record of 1:09⅗ for 6 furlongs, carrying 130 pounds in the latter race; he also equaled the Rockingham record of 1:09⅗ for 6 furlongs and the Gulfstream mark of 1:15⅘ for 6½ furlongs.

In nine starts as a four-year-old, his only loss was a second by a length to Oclirock in the Bristol Handicap, in which Decathlon carried 134 pounds and conceded 28 to the winner. The Dienst colt also dead-heated with Lord Jeep in the John Alden Handicap, while carrying 133 pounds to 111 on his rival. The champion sprinter's other stakes victories were scored in the New Year's (again equaling the 1:09⅗ track record for 6 furlongs at Tropical, this time carrying 133 pounds), Hialeah Inaugural (135), Oceanport (setting a new track record of 1:08⅗ for 6 furlongs at Monmouth, under 130 pounds), Rumson (133), Longport (his only victory at 7 furlongs, achieved under 132 pounds) and Princeton Handicaps.

Among the other notable foals of 1953, C. V. Whitney's Career Boy, winner of the U. S. and Grand Union Hotel Stakes, besides his narrow loss in the Garden State, was assigned highest weight of 126 pounds on the Experimental Free Handicap at the end of his two-year-old season. At three, misfortune and inconsistency intervened. He won the Gotham and was second in the Blue Grass Stakes (to Toby B.) but finished unplaced in the Kentucky Derby and Jersey Stakes, following which came his good second to Needles in the Belmont. In September that year, he and Fisherman delivered a classic one-two punch in the $100,000 United Nations Handicap, won by Career Boy, the only three-year-old in the field, under 116 pounds, beating such seniors as Find, Mister Gus and Dedicate. The victory gained Career Boy the title as best grass horse of 1956. Whitney sent his grass team to Paris for the Prix de l'Arc de Triomphe that fall, and Career Boy finished fourth as the Italian Ribot—hailed as Horse of the World by European experts—won his second successsive renewal. Career Boy tried the French race again as a four-year-old, but the son of Phalanx was injured in the running and retired to stud upon his return to America.

Terrang, owned originally by Rex Ellsworth and later sold to the partnership of Poltex

497

Stable and Roland Bond, was a stakes winner in each of the five seasons he raced, with total earnings of $599,285. If Swoon's Son was a horse for a city, Terrang was a horse for a track, and it would not have been amiss if Santa Anita had begun to charge him rent for tenancy of the winner's circle. The son of Khaled, trained after his sale by Carl "Slim" Roles, won no less than 10 of his 11 stakes events at the Arcadia course. He duplicated Stagehand's feat of winning the track's two most famous events —the Derby and Handicap—although it took him somewhat more time. After his Derby victory at three, Terrang sneaked upon the Handicap, finishing second in it as a five-year-old, and finally winning it at six, in his last year of competition. His other stakes were the California Breeders' Trial, Will Rogers, San Vicente, San Antonio (new track record of 1:47⅖ for 1⅛ miles), Santa Catalina twice, San Pasqual and San Bernardino (twice)—all at Santa Anita—and the Argonaut Handicap at Hollywood. Other familiar horses on the Western scene from this crop included G. C. Newell's King Ranch-bred How Now, and Elobee Farm's persistent, hard-hitting little Eddie Schmidt, who started 101 times to earn $526,-292. Robert Lehman's Count of Honor was a sensational winner of his first five races, including the 1¼-mile Westerner Stakes in 1:59⅖, then the fastest time on record by a three-year-old, before the string was snapped during an invasion of the East. In a brief career of nine starts, he had seven wins (including also a victory over the speedy Johnie Mike in 1:21⅖ for 7 furlongs), a second and third.

A well named horse was Howell E. Jackson's Tick Tock, regular as a clock, and in the money sixty times during his active career. Scarcely a stakes event was contested in which the son of Double Jay wasn't in there pitching; he had won 20 races and $386,951 through the end of his eight-year-old season.

Other males were Mrs. Wallace Gilroy's Oh Johnny, Woodley Lane Farm's Reneged, Greentree Stable's Riley, C. T. Chenery's Third

Brother (full brother to Hill Prince and Prince Hill) and Mrs. Herbert Herff's International winner, Tudor Era.

Happy Hill Farm's Kingmaker came close to achieving undying fame of a sort. He looked so good as a four-year-old (New Orleans, Grey Lag Handicaps, Whitney Stakes) that a group of wheelers and dealers were briskly lining up prospects for a stallion syndicate to purchase him, when one spoilsport called attention to the fact that the son of Princequillo was a gelding.

Five different fillies foaled in 1953 won a campaign was a subsequent effort against males their careers, foremost among whom was Claiborne Farm's Doubledogdare, who shared championships both at two and at three.

The big, strong daughter of Double Jay, trained by Moody Jolley, did not wait until autumn to tackle colts, making her debut against them at Hialeah, finishing fifth, but then defeated them in her next start, at Keeneland in April. The only other occasion she finished worse than second during her juvenile campaign was a subsequent effort against males in the Futurity. Against her sex she won five races, including the National Stallion, Colleen, Matron and Alcibiades Stakes, and was second in the other two—to Pretty Plunger in the Fashion Stakes and to Register in the Spinaway.

Although she was unplaced in Doubledogdare's Matron, the only time they met that season, Howell E. Jackson's Nasrina shared the juvenile championship with the Claiborne filly. The daughter of Nasrullah, trained by E. A. Christmas, led her category in earnings with $152,625, as her three victories in nine starts included the rich Frizette, and the even richer Gardenia. This filly equivalent to the Garden State Stakes was inaugurated in 1955. Since these events both were 1¹⁄₁₆ miles, Nasrina was counted on to improve position at three, but she was not a factor (one win in nine starts), and Doubledogdare won the championship in two polls. As a sophomore the rangy bay filly won seven races, including the Kentucky Oaks Prep (beating Princess Turia), Coronet,

498

The two-time champion filly, Doubledogdare, with Steve Brooks up.

Spinster Stakes and Falls City Handicap, defeating her elders in the last two races. Doubledogdare also had a number of near misses in 1956, losing the Kentucky Oaks by a nose and Cleopatra Handicap by a head to Princess Turia; the Misty Isle Handicap by a head to Pucker Up, while conceding 8 pounds; and finishing a close third to colts in Swoon's Son's Arlington Classic. The clincher for her title was the victory in the inaugural Spinster, a unique weight-for-age, $50,000-added event at Keeneland, for fillies and mares, three, four and five. Doubledogdare won by one and a quarter lengths from the older Queen Hopeful, as her principal rival among her contemporaries, Levee, finished unplaced.

A daughter of Hill Prince, and half-sister to

Delta, Levee had been bred by Claiborne Farm but raced for Mrs. Vernon Cardy of Quebec. A well-formed chestnut with the look of a stayer, trained by N. R. "Yorkie" McLeod, she had been good at two (Selima Stakes), but was better at three. Levee's principal victories as a sophomore were the CCA Oaks (Doubledogdare unplaced) and Monmouth Oaks against her age, and the Beldame Handicap from her seniors. She led her group in earnings with $155,800.

As the fillies entered the handicap class, the leadership passed on to Mrs. Ada L. Rice's Pucker Up, by Olympia, and trained by J. P. Conway. As a four-year-old in 1957, Pucker Up won six of her thirteen starts and was unplaced but once, her victories including the

Nineteen fillies and mares break from the modern stall gate for the 1957 Delaware Handicap, won by Princess Turia. The $110,875 winner's purse was a record for a female thoroughbred.

Arlington Matron, Washington Park (beating males in 1:34⅘ for the mile) and Beldame Handicaps. Her earnings of $229,235 were an impressive season's haul for a filly of handicap age.

J. Graham Brown's Bornastar, who beat Pucker Up in the 1957 Spinster, won that race again in 1958, and with it the championship among distaff handicap runners. The daughter of Alibhai, trained by W. G. Sparks, turned in a remarkable season as a five-year-old, as she won eight of her eleven starts. After winning two in June, including the Beverly Handicap, she suffered all three of her losses at Delaware Park, then finished the season undefeated elsewhere with six straight, including the Falls City Handicap, a victory over males in new track record time of 1:42⅗ for 1¼₆ miles at Churchill Downs, and the Vineland, besides the Spinster, which she won easily by five lengths.

Calumet Farm's Princess Turia, a half-sister to Real Delight, was a contender for the crown both at three and at four, despite a twisted foot that necessitated careful shoeing and fastidiousness as to track conditions. Besides her conquests of Doubledogdare in 1956, the daughter of Heliopolis won the Black-Eyed Susan Stakes, ran a dead heat with her stablemate, Beyond, in the Acorn (Levee third), and was just a neck behind Levee in the CCA Oaks. At four, the Princess got two-thirds of the Distaff Big Three with victories in the New Castle Stakes and Delaware Handicap, beating Pucker Up in the latter.

Honorable mention was earned by King Ranch's Dotted Line, a tough mare who sometimes ran against colts, and who beat them as a six-year-old in a division of the inaugural $100,000 Man o' War Handicap.

Other females of exceptional ability in this crop included Eugene Mori's Cosmah, Murlogg Farm's Dark Charger, Bwamazon Farm's Judy Rullah, J. Rukin Jelks's Miss Todd (four stakes at two including Cinderella Stakes which she won in the world record time of :57 for 5 furlongs), Harry La Montagne's Plotter and B. A. Dario's Venomous.

500

CHAPTER SIXTY-SIX

THE FOALS OF 1954 INCLUDED so many good ones that the crop was compared to that of 1928, whence had come Equipoise, Twenty Grand and Mate —and, although it was considerably larger than its predecessor, the 1954 group also was dominated by a trio who stood out even in that glittering company.

As is often the case, there was considerable scrambling for rankings as the crop sifted itself into order. Two sons of Olympia were among the first to appear in the national spotlight. Fred Hooper's home-bred Greek Game, trained by Ivan Parke, won his first four starts, including the Primer, Hyde Park Stakes and Arlington Futurity (defeating Jet Colonel and Round Table in both the latter events)— leading at every call in each of them. Mr. and Mrs. George Lewis's Lucky Mel, trained by Bill Molter, won seven of his first eleven starts in California, six of them in succession, and he included among his victories the San Bruno, Westchester, Haggin (in world record time of :56⅗ for 5 furlongs) and Starlet Stakes. When the Western horses made their annual invasion of Chicago after the close of Hollywood Park in the summer of 1956, this pair met in the Prairie State Stakes at Washington Park August 22. Greek Game was outrun from the gate for the first time in his life by Lucky Mel, but the eventual winner was California Kid. The latter colt, a son of Khaled owned by Ellsworth, also finished first by a head in the Washington Park Futurity, but he was disqualified for bearing out, and the verdict went to Greek Game. None of these three won another stakes that season, but Greek Game already had collected enough to top his division in earnings; later in the year, a second to Bold Ruler in the Futurity at Belmont Park increased his total to $214,805.

The eventual juvenile champion, however, was another colt, who did not show silk until some time after Greek Game's last victory. Calumet Farm's Barbizon, a son of Polynesian, won his championship in less than six weeks. Because of suspicious ankles, his debut was delayed until September 15, but he won four in a row within a month. Then, after Clifford Lussky's Federal Hill beat him in the preceding Trial, Barbizon beat Federal Hill by a desperate nose in the rich Garden State Stakes on October 27, his final start of the year. That was his only venture into added-money competition that season, but the winner's prize of $168,430 was the richest on record until then. Federal Hill's loss had cost him more than $100,000, as his award for second was a mere $63,842. There was some justice to the outcome, however, in that Barbizon's owner had paid a record sum to get him in the race. The burly dark bay had been nominated originally, but because of the uncertainty concerning his boxing glove ankles, his eligibility had been allowed to lapse, and it cost Calumet a $10,000 supplementary fee to re-nominate him. This, on top of the original fees paid, plus a subsequent $1,000 to pass the entry box and another $1,000 to start, resulted in a total ante of $12,135.

Still, it was a profitable play for Barbizon, and although a championship on the basis, essentially, of one stakes victory might appear dim on the face of it, behind him in the Garden

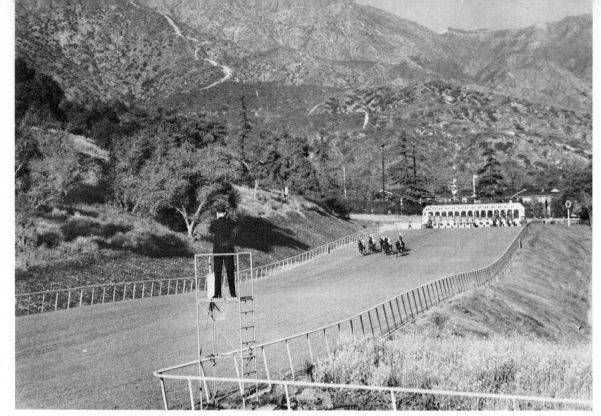

The Camino Real, hillside turf course at Santa Anita.

State ran the cream of the crop. Federal Hill won three stakes at two. The others in the defeated field included Amarullah, Ambehaving, California Kid, Prince Khaled (disqualified after having breezed home three and a half lengths clear in the earlier Del Mar Futurity in record time of 1:08⅘), Nashville, Clem, Iron Liege and the heavy favorite; Bold Ruler.

At post time for the Garden State Stakes, Bold Ruler had been regarded as the best two-year-old in the country, compared in some quarters to his elder stablemate and kinsman, Nashua. Although he finished seventeenth in the race, and dead last in his only subsequent start that year, he still had enough prestige left to rank second in the championship poll. His was an unusual case history.

There are so many factors that can affect the performance of a race horse—how he is trained, how he is ridden, who he is running against and what he has eaten, to name a few —that to evaluate a thoroughbred according to any single criterion is ridiculous. Time, the most popular basis of comparison, is a fickle jade who blows hot and cold at track to track from day to day. The significance of money

won is subject to an even wider variety of interpretation. If one particular standard must be used, the preference of the author is for weight: 132 pounds is 132 pounds, at Santa Anita or Saratoga, Woodbine or the Fair Grounds, and it was the same burden in 1910 that it will be in 1980.

Beyond the matter of pounds carried *per se,* there is the question of pounds conceded. While it obviously is more work to carry a given weight over a long distance than in a sprint, to concede weight in a sprint is more difficult, for the same reason that a heavily loaded truck —a sure bet for the cross-country haul—is at a disadavantage in city traffic.

If the foregoing ruminations be valid, then Bold Ruler was a horse of exceptional class, far beyond that indicated by a cursory summary of his record—and that record was a good one under any circumstances.

BOLD RULER, 1954

(Nasrullah–Miss Disco, by Discovery)

Bred by his owner, Wheatley Stable, and trained by Jim Fitzsimmons, Bold Ruler was foaled at Claiborne Farm on April 6. A dark

502

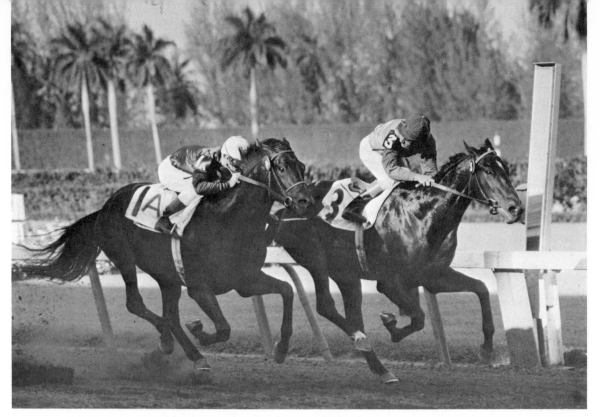

Bold Ruler winning the Flamingo Stakes from Gen. Duke.

bay, about the same size as Nashua (16 hands 1½ inches at three, 74 inches in girth), Bold Ruler was lighter, by no means delicate looking, but less robust in his lines.

Despite his legginess, Bold Ruler came out of the gate like a shot, and before he entered competition he had reeled off quarters in :22 during workouts. He won his first five races as a two-year-old, including the Youthful and Juvenile Stakes, in the process twice defeating the sensation of the winter season, Leo Edwards and H. B. Massey's King Hairan. That son of King's Stride, trained by L. H. Hunt, had succeeded Needles as winner of the Florida-bred stock show at Hialeah and, after equaling the :32⅖ track record for 3 furlongs in his first start, had been sold by breeder W. E. Leach for $35,000, topping the price realized for Needles. King Hairan then won three baby races in Florida before meeting defeat at 4½ furlongs in April, and his subsequent losses to Bold Ruler were his first attempts to get 5 furlongs.

In the second of their encounters, the Juvenile Stakes on June 6, which he won in :56 over the straightaway, Bold Ruler strained his back muscles and was kept out of competition

more than three months. With him out of the way, King Hairan won five straight stakes—the Christiana, Tremont, Great American, Sapling and 6½-furlong Hopeful—before he went awry.

Bold Ruler suffered his first defeat at the hands of Nashville (another son of Nasrullah) in his return to competition on September 24. He then won the prep for the Futurity and the big race itself, before going down again in the Garden State. The Remsen on November 6, also at 1¹⁄₁₆ miles, brought another disastrous result as Bold Ruler did not extend himself. The race was won by Ambehaving, with the Pimlico Futurity winner, Missile, second; Bold Ruler, his jockey having ceased to argue the point when his cause became hopeless, was allowed to sink to last place. The Wheatley colt was shipped to Florida after seven wins in ten juvenile starts, as something of a question mark. He emerged an exclamation point.

He came out on January 30, carrying 126 pounds in his first start at three, and conceding 12 pounds to Gen. Duke. Bold Ruler won the 7-furlong Bahamas Stakes in 1:22, tying the track record shared by Crafty Admiral (four, 107) and Trentonian (five, 114). Trailing the

503

front pair in the Bahamas were Federal Hill and Gallant Man, the latter having opened the season with a six-length trouncing of Gen. Duke in track record time of 1:09⅖ for 6 furlongs at Tropical Park, and followed up with a victory in the Hibiscus Stakes in 1:10.

Contributing further to the mythical Garden State jinx, Barbizon never won another stakes event, but contributing further to the stable's reputation for awesome resources, Gen. Duke had suddenly materialized as a Calumet replacement. Unheard of after only two starts as a juvenile, the son of Bull Lea and Wistful got better with each succeeding race at three, and backing him up was another son of Bull Lea named Iron Liege, who won his first three sophomore starts, including a victory over his stablemate in track record time of 1:42⅘ for 1 1/16 miles, before the Duke hit his stride. After that, Calumet threw both of them at Bold Ruler three times.

The resulting battles were so fierce that the Florida season, far from being just a testing ground for the main events coming up, threatened to make the remainder of the year seem anticlimactic.

Again weighted at 126, and required to concede 12 pounds to Gen. Duke and 9 to Iron Liege, Bold Ruler was bracketed by the Calumet pair in the Everglades Stakes on February 16 as Gen. Duke covered the 9 furlongs in a blistering 1:47⅖ to beat him by a head. At equal weights (122) in the $100,000 Flamingo Stakes at the same distance on March 2, after putting away Federal Hill in an intense speed duel, Bold Ruler staved off Gen. Duke to win by a neck in new track record time of 1:47. In the Florida Derby on March 30, Gen. Duke shattered the Gulfstream Park record and equalled the world record of 1:46⅘ to beat Bold Ruler by one and a half lengths. Iron Liege ran third in all three of these races (and between the two Derbies, the Calumet pair had sandwiched in a one-two act in the Fountain of Youth Stakes, which Bold Ruler skipped).

After breaking camp in Florida, Bold Ruler ranged northward to Jamaica, where he was forced to cover the Wood Memorial's 1⅛ miles in new track record time of 1:48⅘ to defeat Gallant Man by a nose. The record times notwithstanding, Eddie Arcaro was of the opinion that neither the Wood victory nor the second loss to Gen. Duke in Florida had represented what he termed Bold Ruler's "A" game; something was bothering the colt, said his jockey, but he couldn't put his finger on it. On the other hand, Gallant Man lost little time in demonstrating that his performance had been no fluke, and he did so in one of the most controversial renewals in the long history of the Kentucky Derby.

Derbytown was buzzing with excitement before the 1957 race—and seething with it afterward. First, there was the withdrawal of Gen. Duke on Derby morning; the Calumet colt, having lost an allowance race to Iron Liege and the Trial to Federal Hill, was found to be lame. (He never raced again. The lameness turned out to be a broken bone in his foot, but after that was repaired, Gen. Duke was put down as a four-year-old when he became a "wobbler," i.e., incapable of co-ordination. The condition is not rare among foals, but practically unheard of among mature horses.) In the absence of his more highly regarded stablemate, Iron Liege (who was an "uncle" of Swaps) was allowed to go off at 8.40-to-1.

Next, there was the race itself, in which Gallant Man took the lead from Iron Liege in the stretch but broke stride momentarily when his jockey, Bill Shoemaker, misjudged the finish. Thinking the race was over when he went past the infield pagoda, Shoemaker stood up in his stirrups; he realized his mistake and recovered instantly, but the lapse was enough to allow Bill Hartack to drive Iron Liege to victory by a nose. Round Table finished third and Bold Ruler—again not running his true race, according to Arcaro—was fourth.

Finally, there were the repercussions. Shoemaker, capable at the same time of brilliant feats and weird boners, had not been punished for his nap aboard Swaps in the 1956 Californian Stakes, but he was grounded fifteen days by the Kentucky officials, which led to some strain in relations between the two states. There was agitation to install targets at the finish line of American tracks, following the European practice, but while a number of other tracks adopted them, Churchill Downs did not. Shoemaker had disdained the custom among Derby jockeys of taking an orientation tour by riding in an earlier race on the program, and he had, after all, found the finish easily enough two years before.

The calmest person connected with the hectic affair was the man most injured, Gallant Man's owner, Ralph Lowe. The Midland, Texas oil millionaire reported that he had dreamed of just such an episode several nights before the race, and readily forgave Shoemaker.

Gallant Man's connections having decided that the colt did not like his races too close together, he skipped the Preakness, which Bold Ruler—bad back or not—won from Iron Liege by two lengths. It was a satisfactory performance by Bold Ruler, who had tried to bear out in the Wood and Derby, but ran fast and true at Pimlico; on the theory that pressure on his mouth had caused the tendency to go wide, Mr. Fitz had tied a piece of string on his bit to ease the pressure.

After winning the Jersey Stakes from Clem a week later, Iron Liege dropped out because of splint trouble, but there still was plenty of competition for Bold Ruler in his next start, the Belmont Stakes on June 15. Gallant Man was back in the lists, sharpened by a victory in the Peter Pan Handicap. Covering the first mile of the Belmont in an extravagant 1:35⅗, Bold Ruler still had the lead at the end of 1¼ miles in 2:01⅖, but Gallant Man took over at that point and drew out to the most impressive victory ever scored in America's oldest classic. He crossed the finish eight lengths clear of Inside Tract—Bold Ruler having faded to third, four more lengths away—in 2:26⅗, lowering the

American record for 1½ miles by a full second. As he sailed past Arcaro, the jubilant Shoemaker called out, "Hey, Eddie, look how much hold I've got on this horse!" Under that hold, Gallant Man covered the final quarter in :25⅕. (The winning time was not a world record only in a technical sense; in 1929, a horse named The Bastard had run 1½ miles in 2:23 over a virtually straight, partially downhill course at Newmarket, England.)

A combination of mild indispositions—reaction to sleeping-sickness shots, erratic pulse and just plain tiredness—led to Bold Ruler's being put on the shelf for nearly three months, and it was when he re-emerged in September that he began the march which was to take him to the top.

On September 9, carrying 128 pounds, the Wheatley colt won a 6-furlong overnight handicap from Greek Game (121) in 1:10⅕. Five days later, carrying 130 pounds, he won the Jerome Handicap in 1:35, just a tick away from the Belmont track record, defeating Bureaucracy by six lengths while conceding 17 pounds. After Bold Ruler finished third to Dedicate and Gallant Man in the 1¼-mile Woodward Stakes at weight-for-age, he was relegated to the role of sprinter. He was that— and a phenomenally good one—but he also proved he was something more.

No rival finished within daylight of Bold Ruler during the remainder of the 1957 season. On October 9 at Belmont, carrying actual top weight of 130 pounds, against older horses, in the 7-furlong Vosburgh Handicap, he won by nine lengths in 1:21⅖, lowering by ⅗-second Roseben's track record which had been standing alone for fifty-one years. The track was sloppy, but on Long Island that didn't slow down the running times; the overwhelming aspect of Bold Ruler's performance was the ease with which he beat the good four-year-olds, Tick Tock and St. Amour II, giving them 13 and 16 pounds, respectively, and 4 pounds more according to the scale. Again packing actual top weight, this time 133, the son of

Nasrullah next won the 1 1/16-mile Queens County Handicap while spotting 22 pounds to his contemporary, Promised Land (winner of $227,650 that year); 19 pounds to the older Greek Spy, who finished third; and 21 pounds to such a good older runner as Oh Johnny (unplaced). The Benjamin Franklin Handicap against his own age was a canter for Bold Ruler, as he carried 136 pounds to a twelve-length victory over Sarno and Jet Colonel, conceding them 27 and 23 pounds.

The ease of these victories at 8½ furlongs led to a revision of opinion concerning Bold Ruler's stamina, and he was entered in the $75,000-added Trenton Handicap at 1¼ miles. Through an improbable chain of circumstances, this event had developed into the race of the year.

Following his return to the West Coast, after the Kentucky Derby, Round Table went on a rampage. Racing across the continent, he compiled the longest winning streak of any colt since Citation—eleven in a row, eight of them stakes, on dirt and grass tracks, against opponents of various ages, with a couple of track records thrown in for good measure. A match between him and the heir presumptive to the three-year-old crown, Gallant Man, who had followed up his Belmont triumph with an emphatic victory in the Travers in August, was a subject of great interest. Offers for such a match were made, but refused, and Laurel went the offers one better by issuing invitations for the $100,000 Washington, D. C., International on November 11, to both these colts plus Dedicate, the handicap champion who had upset Gallant Man in the Woodward. The Laurel race was at Gallant Man's favorite distance (1½ miles) over Round Table's type of footing (grass) but in no way favorable to Dedicate, whose connections declined the invitation anyway because the colt was ailing.

Later, Round Table's owner, Oklahoma oil tycoon, Travis M. Kerr, announced that his colt probably would pass up the International in favor of the Trenton, scheduled two days be-

fore the Laurel event, and when Dedicate recovered and also was entered in the New Jersey race, suddenly there was a horse race. Gallant Man came in, too, and the $75,000-added handicap instead of the $100,000 weight-for-age event became the contest for the season's championship. Dedicate was unable to start because of a recurrence of his lameness, and—in a rare gesture of sportsmanship, since there was fourth money lying around waiting to be picked up—Sam Tufano and King Ranch withdrew the only two other entries, Wise Margin and Beam Rider, to leave the field to the three titans. Shoemaker, regular rider of both, chose Gallant Man in preference to Round Table, making it clear that his selection was not based on an opinion as to their relative merits, and Bill Harmatz took the mount on the Kerr colt.

Whoever had been trying to corner whom in all the pre-race maneuvering never was entirely clear, but it made no difference, for it was Bold Ruler—the colt ignored in the elaborate chess game and given a 2-pound concession by the handicapper—who sprung the trap. Leading every step of the way on the good track, he cruised home two and a half lengths clear in 2:01⅗, just the fractions off the Garden State record, with Arcaro showing him the whip, but never using it. Gallant Man ran gamely but futilely to finish second, and Round Table, obviously displeased with the going, came in another eight and a half lengths behind him.

Bold Ruler, eleven for sixteen during the season, earned $415,160 at three, his sole unplaced effort having been the fourth in the Derby. He was elected best of his division in all polls, and Horse of the Year in two. The other voters, apparently having decided that if the title was to be based on one race, backtracked to the Woodward and gave it to Dedicate.

Round Table, the season's leading money winner by a wide margin, with $600,258, won according to the *Thoroughbred Record's* mathematical scoring system, and was voted best grass horse in the Triangle poll.

506

Gallant Man, who came off even in his encounters with Bold Ruler (although he failed to win two of the races in which he outfinished his rival) and came home ahead of Round Table each time they met, was left with nothing but a good deal of prestige.

GALLANT MAN, 1954
(Migoli–Majideh, by Mahmoud)

Gallant Man has the unique, if dubious, distinction of having been the best horse ever to appear on the American turf without winning a championship of any kind. A bay colt, bred by the Aga Khan in partnership with his son, Aly, he was one of a group of nine yearlings purchased in Ireland for $220,000, by bloodstock agent Humphrey Finney and veterinarian Dr. D. L. Proctor, acting as agents for Ralph Lowe. By no means the most highly regarded member of the lot (among those ranked ahead of him was the colt later named Bold Nero, who finished dead last in his stablemate's Belmont) Gallant Man was quite small; at three, he stood only 15 hands 1½ inches. He was not otherwise impressive in appearance as a youngster —but his lines were perfect, and he seemed quick—and as he matured he furnished out into a handsome, compact animal.

Gallant Man was withheld from stakes competition as a two-year-old. Saddled by Gerald Bloss, he scored his maiden victory at Hollywood Park in his third start, at odds of nearly 50-to-1; when Bloss took a vacation, Gallant Man was shipped east to the stable of John Nerud, ex-jockey from Nebraska, who handled him throughout the remainder of his career. The colt won two more overnight races to complete his juvenile season with three wins in seven starts and $7,075.

It was as a three-year-old, when he opened his campaign with his track record for six furlongs at Tropical, that he emerged from obscurity. In the course of the season, the quick colt

Gallant Man is led in by owner Ralph Lowe after the colt set an American record of 2:26⅗ for 1½ miles in the Belmont Stakes. Bill Shoemaker up and trainer John Nerud (right) in striped cap.

proved also to be the finest stayer in the nation, as was attested by his record-breaking performance in the Belmont Stakes; besides the races already mentioned, there were further demonstrations of his versatility.

At the in-between distance of 1⅛ miles, in the Nassau County Handicap on September 18, his first start against older horses, Gallant Man lowered Counterpoint's Belmont record by ⅗-second to 1:47⅕, defeating the handicap champion, Dedicate, while carrying 121 pounds, equal on the scale to five-year-old Dedicate's 126. The little Lowe colt also defeated his seniors, Third Brother and Reneged, at weight-for-age in the two-mile Jockey Club Gold Cup.

He had eight wins and four seconds in fourteen starts at three, for earnings of $298,280, and, as was the case with Bold Ruler, he brought back part of the purse each time, his unplaced efforts having been fourths in the Bahamas and Swift Stakes, the latter race won by King Hairan.

The rivalry between Bold Ruler and Gallant Man was extended somewhat into their four-year-old season, but the final result remained a stalemate.

For Bold Ruler, 1958 was a phenomenal year, during which he carried 133 pounds or more in every one of his seven starts. Other horses have carried higher weights in individual races, and—in longer campaigns—carried top weight more often, but none in modern history has gone through such an uninterrupted sequence at such a high minimum load.

Delayed in his return to action by a filled ankle, Bold Ruler made his first start as a four-year-old on May 17, in the 6-furlong Toboggan Handicap under 133 pounds, which he won in 1:09 while conceding 16 pounds to Clem. At 135 for the 7-furlong Carter Handicap, Bold Ruler covered the distance in 1:22⅗ to defeat Tick Tock, who enjoyed a 22-pound pull in the weights. Gallant Man, making his first start of the season, finished third under 128 pounds.

Still at 135 for the Metropolitan Mile, Bold Ruler lost by two lengths in 1:35⅗ to Gallant Man, who carried 5 pounds less—it was their final encounter, leaving the score four-all.

With 133 pounds up, Bold Ruler gave Admiral Vee 21 pounds and a five-length licking in the 1⅛-mile Stymie Handicap. Upped to 134 for the longer Suburban, the Wheatley colt nevertheless was able to nose out Clem in 2:01 for the 1¼ miles, while conceding 25 pounds. At the same weight, he beat Sharpsburg (113) in the Monmouth Handicap, won in 2:01⅗—just ⅖-second off the track record.

Carrying 136 pounds in the Brooklyn Handicap on July 26, Bold Ruler was unplaced as the race was won by Greentree Stable's Cohoes (110). It later developed that the favorite's ankle had flared up again, and he was retired to stud, with a lifetime record of 23 wins, four seconds, two thirds and $764,204 from 33 starts.

That record was compiled by a colt who, according to his trainer's son and assistant, John Fitzsimmons, never was entirely sound. Had he been blessed with Nashua's iron constitution—or had Nashua, who often seemed to be "keeping something up his sleeve," as young Mr. Fitz expressed it, been endowed with Bold Ruler's completely generous disposition—the combination would have been enough to make Man o' War sit up and take notice.

Gallant Man's handicap career also was disappointingly brief. After exchanging decisions with Bold Ruler in New York, he went west. On neither occasion being required to menace the track record, he won the 1¼-mile Hollywood Gold Cup with top weight of 130 pounds and the 1⅝-mile Sunset Handicap with 132 pounds, as little Eddie Schmidt finished second under 110 pounds in both races.

Upon his return to the East, Gallant Man was assigned 134 pounds for the Sysonby Handicap on September 6. In a coincidental duplication of Bold Ruler's finale, this race, too, was won by Cohoes (116) as Gallant Man finished unplaced; he turned up lame the next day, and subsequently was retired to stud.

The world's leading money winner, Round Table,
with trainer Bill Molter (left), owners Mr. and Mrs.
Travis M. Kerr and groom Juan Alaniz.

With 14 wins, four seconds, one third and $510,355 from 26 starts, the runt of the litter had repaid more than double the cost of the entire batch of yearlings from which he emerged. Upon his retirement, a stallion syndicate formed by the foremost promoter of such organizations, Leslie Combs II, paid a million dollars for a 75 percent interest in Gallant Man.

Although Bold Ruler was elected best sprinter of 1958, neither he nor Gallant Man won the championship of the handicap division; that was the year for the third member of the Big Three—Round Table.

ROUND TABLE, 1954

(Princequillo–Knight's Daughter, by Sir Cosmo)

For split-second conclusions to a business transaction, there is nothing to compare with a horse sale. Although negotiations may be elaborate and tedious, the deal is consummated as concisely as possible—at the fall of an auctioneer's hammer, or the instant a claimed horse steps out of the paddock—for the good reason that the value of a race horse is subject to such abrupt changes; a $100,000 athlete can run into a fence and instantaneously become a hopeless cripple.

When two men shook hands just before the gates opened for the fifth race at Hialeah on February 9, 1957, one of the most significant horse sales in history was effected. After months of negotiations, for $175,000, Dr. John Peters, as agent for Travis M. Kerr, had purchased from Arthur B. Hancock, Jr. the colt that was to become the world's leading money winner. Making his second start as a three-year-old, Round Table finished sixth in the allowance event won by Iron Liege in track record time, but upon his return to scale, jockey Steve Brooks was reassuring in his remarks to Peters. His mount had lost more ground on the turns than the margin of his defeat, said the jockey. He would do.

Foaled at Claiborne Farm on April 6 (the

same day as Bold Ruler) Round Table grew to moderate size: 15-2 and 960 pounds at the beginning of his three-year-old form; 15-3 and 1,015 a year later, girthing 72 inches. His salient attributes were complete symmetry and absolute lack of blemish. He lived up to his appearance by becoming one of the soundest, toughest colts in history.

As a two-year-old, Round Table raced in the colors of his breeder, winning exactly half his ten starts, including the Lafayette Stakes and Breeders' Futurity, for earnings of $73,326. Inquiries concerning his sale were in progress as early as the summer of his juvenile season, and as he developed, his price tag was adjusted upward accordingly, from a reported original value of $40,000. Even when the sale was accomplished at the much higher figure many months later, Hancock was astute enough to retain a twenty percent interest in him as a stallion. His breeder noted that Round Table ran "right off his hocks," and while this trait probably would cost him some races when the surface was such that he couldn't get sufficient purchase for his powerful thrust, on the right kind of track he figured to win his share. The fact that Round Table overstepped his front hoof prints by "about a foot" when he put his hind feet down at a walk, was one of the characteristics that most attracted Dr. Peters.

In his first start after his sale, Round Table won a 7-furlong allowance race at Hialeah in 1:22⅖, following which he was shipped to California by his new owner. On an off track both times, he was third in the Santa Anita Derby (won by the Washington-bred Sir William) and fifth in Lightning Jack's San Bernardino Handicap. It was seventeen months and thirty races later before he ran out of the money again.

After winning the Bay Meadows Derby on a fast track, Round Table was shipped to Kentucky where he won the Blue Grass Stakes in new track record time of 1:47⅖ for 1⅛ miles before his third in the Derby. Upon his return to the West Coast, he was a good second

against older horses in the Californian Stakes, won by Social Climber, on May 25, and then he shot into his eleven-race winning streak; all the races were between a mile and 1¼ miles, which was Round Table's favorite operating range, and three were on the grass, which proved to be his favorite type of footing. Stakes during this skein were the Will Rogers, Westerner Stakes, El Dorado, Cinema Handicaps and American Derby within his own division; and the Hollywood Gold Cup, United Nations Handicap and Hawthorne Gold Cup against his elders. The races against his seniors were the most impressive: as the first three-year-old ever to win the Hollywood Gold Cup, Round Table equalled the track record of 1:58⅗ for 1¼ miles. Carrying 118 pounds in the UN Handicap on a turf course, sharing top weight by scale with Career Boy, the Kerr colt conceded 6 pounds actual weight to runner-up Tudor Era, a four-year-old English-bred regarded as a specialist in grass racing. In the Hawthorne Gold Cup, Round Table set a new track record of 2:00⅕ for 1¼ miles.

Twice during this winning streak it was so difficult to find opposition for Round Table that special races were carded, in which all starters received the same purse award regardless of the order of finish. In three of these races there was no betting allowed.

After his defeat in the Trenton Handicap, the widely traveled colt (he raced at ten different tracks as a three-year-old) returned to California, where, just before the year was out, he completed his sophomore campaign with a victory in the 7-furlong Malibu Sequet Stakes at Santa Anita under 130 pounds, conceding 16 to the runner-up, Seaneen. That victory, his fifteenth in twenty-two starts during 1957, was the beginning of an eight-race winning streak extending well into his four-year-old form.

The colt who couldn't win at Santa Anita during the previous meeting, couldn't lose there at the 1957-1958 session. Round Table clicked off four more stakes at the Arcadia track, by an average winning margin of nearly four lengths: the San Fernando (130 pounds), Maturity, San Antonio (equaling the world record of 1:46⅘ while carrying 130 pounds in February) and the Santa Anita Handicap, again under 130 pounds, conceding 11 to Terrang, and setting a new track record of 1:59⅘ for 1¼ miles. The champion's persistent pursuer, Neil S. McCarthy's Seaneen, gave futile chase in all five of these Santa Anita races, getting a weight concession each time (19 pounds in the Santa Anita Handicap).

As though to forestall any implication that he was of provincial quality only, Round Table flew to Gulfstream Park, where he won a prep race in new track record time of 1:41⅗ for 1¹⁄₁₆ miles, and carried 130 pounds to victory in the Gulfstream Park Handicap, equaling the track record of 1:59⅘ for 1¼ miles, and winning by four lengths from Meeting (111). At this stage of his career (Bold Ruler and Gallant Man not having put in an appearance as yet) there was not a horse in America who appeared capable of extending the Kerr Stable colt. It was seriously suggested that he be sent on a barnstorming tour around the country, like the great trotting horse of the past, Dan Patch, and run against time instead of live opponents.

At the time, the clock was his only rival— and even that could not beat him, for Round Table flew back across the continent for a special race at Caliente, which he won by nine and a quarter lengths in new track record time of 1:41⅗ for 1¹⁄₁₆ miles. It was his fifth track record performance in succession.

It was Seaneen, with the aid of a 21-pound advantage in the weights, who broke Round Table's winning streak, beating him by four and a half lengths in the Californian Stakes on May 24. From 130 pounds in that defeat, Round Table was moved up to 132 for the Argonaut Handicap two weeks later. In view of the ceiling which had prevailed during Swaps's heyday, Kerr objected to the assignment, but he accepted it, and Round Table won by a nose from How Now (116), with Seaneen

(120) third. Round Table was to accept weights in excess of 130 a dozen more times before his career ended, but he never again raced at Hollywood Park.

In the remainder of his four-year-old season, the son of Princequillo added the Arch Ward, Laurence Armour Memorial (equaling the track record of 1:48⅖ for 1⅛ miles) and Arlington Handicaps—all on the turf course— and a second Hawthorne Gold Cup to his collection.

With the Gold Cup victory on October 11, his last start of the season, Round Table increased his total to $1,336,489 and replaced Nashua as world's leading money winner. He would have arrived at his goal much sooner had it not been for Mrs. Adele Rand's Clem, a namesake of sportscaster Clem McCarthy. The son of Shannon II, trained by W. W. Stephens, blocked Round Table's progress in a frustrating series of races reminiscent of the Noor–Citation duels, and just about as inconclusive so far as weight was concerned.

Round Table beat Clem in the Armour Memorial Handicap while conceding him 20 pounds, and in the Arlington Handicap while giving 21. Then, with the aid of an identical 21-pound pull, Clem beat Round Table by three and a quarter lengths in the Washington Park Handicap. The spread was reduced to 17 pounds for the United Nations Handicap, and Clem won again, by half a length—to inflict on Round Table his first defeat over a grass course. Finally, at level weights in the Woodward Stakes, Clem again was the winner as Round Table finished unplaced.

Round Table, however, was named 1958 Horse of the Year in all methods of selection. He also won a second title as champion grass horse, and became the first thoroughbred in history to lead the over-all financial rankings in two seasons. His earnings of $662,780 as a four-year-old constituted a new record for a horse of handicap age.

This tough horse stayed on for another year, to gain his third title as best grass runner, a second handicap championship in two polls and add further to his winnings.

He also added to his stature as an honest weight carrier. Except for one exhibition event, Round Table packed 130 pounds or more (the average was 132.6) in his first eleven races as a five-year-old. He won the San Marcos (132, new American record of 1:58⅖ for 1¼ miles on turf), Citation (130, equaling track record of 1:33⅖ for a mile), Stars and Stripes (132, new American record of 1:47⅕ for 1⅛ miles on turf), Clem McCarthy (132), Arlington (132, new American record of 1:53⅖ for 1³⁄₁₆ miles on turf), Washington Park (132, new track record of 1:47⅕ for 1⅛ miles) Handicaps, and took his second renewal of the United Nations Handicap under 136 pounds, conceding 19 to Noureddin and 16 to Li'l Fella (the name meant nothing—he was one of the biggest horses in America).

Ironically, Round Table's first race at normal weight was the Woodward Stakes at weight for age, his twelfth start of the season, in which he was third to Sword Dancer and Hillsdale. Scoring his seventh victory of the season at 132 pounds or more, Round Table then won the Manhattan Handicap under that weight in new track record time of 2:42⅗ for 1⅝ miles, conceding 10 pounds to Bald Eagle.

The Manhattan had been Round Table's first attempt in his long career at a distance greater than 1¼ miles. Three weeks later, on October 31, 1959, he tried 2 miles for the first time, and Sword Dancer again beat him at weight-for-age. That was Round Table's last race. He entered stud having established or equaled one world record, three American records and twelve track records, with performance in summary as follows:

Age	Starts	Won	2nd	3rd	Unpl.	Earnings
2	10	5	1	0	4	$ 73,326
3	22	15	1	3	3	600,383
4	20	14	4	0	2	662,780
5	14	9	2	2	1	413,380
	66	43	8	5	10	$1,749,869

Note: In sixteen starts on grass, Round Table won fourteen. Total distance run in entire career: 71 miles. Total running time: 1 hour, 54 minutes and 6 seconds.

There are quantity trainers and quality trainers, and Bill Molter (1910-1960), who developed Round Table from a three-year-old into the world's leading money winner, was both. Like his Eastern counterpart, Hirsch Jacobs, after a long tenure as leading trainer from the standpoint of number of winners, Molter moved to the money list and led that. In a well-balanced career, he topped each ranking four times, saddling the most winners from 1946-1949 (tie with W. Hal Bishop the latter year) and the winners of the most money in 1954, 1956, 1958 and 1959.

A native of Fredericksburg, Texas (the home of Max Hirsch) Molter was riding in quarter-horse races while still a child; in his teens he branched out to thoroughbreds and for a time performed jockey chores for the noted trainer, Preston Burch.

Round Table winning the United Nations Handicap under 136 pounds.

Like others destined to become prominent in racing, Molter was a veteran of Caliente, and, although he did not have a mount in the big race itself, he rode in several other races on the program of March 20, 1932—Phar Lap's Day—along with such other jockeys as Longden and Arcaro. It was also at the Mexican track that Molter saddled his first winner, Holmfirth, on March 3, 1935, after weight had ended his ten-year riding career. He broke into training as assistant to L. O. Lee, conditioner of the Jack Atkin stable, taking a division of the racing string into Canada.

Molter's greatest stars came along after he had gone into business for himself as trainer of a public stable; they included Shannon II, On Trust, Bobby Brocato, Determine and Imbros, and then Round Table.

The phenomenal success of Molter, Red McDaniel, and other Western trainers of public stables created a situation in which so many of the top horses were concentrated into so few hands that the "stablemate" rule was written so as to permit horses trained by the same man—but of different ownership—to run uncoupled in the wagering in stakes races. Later, a California rule was passed limiting the number of horses in the care of one trainer to forty.

Round Table was Molter's crowning achievement, but his transformation of Bobby Brocato from a pure speedball into a stayer was quite a feat also. Patience was the key. Brisk and active as he was personally, Molter believed a horse should take his time, and he literally taught Bobby Brocato to do so, by working him at increasingly longer distances to slow him down. "When we first got Bobby we couldn't work him five furlongs in less than :58 or :59 without hampering him with too tight a hold," he said, "but later he would work in 1:04 and even slower if asked to."

At the time of his death from a heart attack in April, 1960, Molter had saddled winners of 2,158 races and $11,983,035, and he had started another big star, T. V. Lark.

A later standout in the bumper crop was Vertex, a chestnut son of The Rhymer–Kanace,

by Case Ace, bred by Frank A. Piarulli, who later took in J. J. Brunetti as partner in ownership of the colt, and trained by the breeder's son, Joe Piarulli, a former Philadelphia high school teacher. Running contrary to the usual pattern, Vertex, in a career disrupted by injury, got better as he grew older. Not a stakes winner at two, he won two added money events as a three-year-old, three such races at four and four of them at five, to emerge as one of the leading money-winning Maryland-breds in history, with $453,424.

Vertex wound up his four-year-old campaign with three stakes in a row—the Trenton, Idlewild Handicaps and Pimlico Special—then, after finishing third in his first start the next season, went undefeated through five more races, including the Gulfstream Park and Campbell Memorial Handicaps (both at $100,-000-added), Grey Lag and Camden Handicaps.

An even more pronounced case of delayed reaction was Mrs. Joe W. Brown's Tenacious, trained by J. B. Theall, who lived up to his name by winning eleven stakes after he had passed his fourth birthday. A real horse for a course, the son of Challedon–Dorothy B. Jr. took all of them at the Fair Grounds, including the Louisiana and Le Comte Handicaps three times each, and the Letellier Memorial and New Orleans Handicap twice each. About the only event of consequence in New Orleans that escaped him was the Louisiana Derby—but that already had been won by his full brother, Gigantic.

Among other members of this formidable group was E. P. Taylor's Nearctic, who replaced the same owner's Canadiana as leading money-winning Canadian foal with earnings of $152,384.

Charlton Clay's Leallah, a full sister to Lea Lane, trained by Mackenzie Miller, was the majority choice as best juvenile filly from the crop of 1954. At two the daughter of Nasrullah won seven of her eight starts, including the Colleen, Arlington Lassie, Astoria and Alcibiades Stakes; her only loss was a fourth in the Princess Pat (won by Splendored) so Leallah received a paycheck in every start to head her division in earnings with $129,240. She won the Falls City Handicap at three, but was not a contender for the championship in later years.

Reverie Knoll Farm's Romanita, a daughter of Roman, trained by Frank Sanders, was voted best two-year-old filly in the TRA poll; she won seven of seventeen in her first season, among them the Mademoiselle, Matron and Marguerite Stakes. Romanita also finished first by a nose in the Gardenia, but was disqualified and set back to third for interference. Magic Forest was declared the winner, Light 'n Lovely second. As a three-year-old Romanita won the 7-furlong Cleopatra Handicap in 1:22⅖, and the Monmouth Oaks.

William Haggin Perry's Alanesian, a daughter of Polynesian, trained by J. W. Maloney, was undefeated as a two-year-old; she started only three times and two of them were stakes, the Spinaway and Astarita. After failing to win stakes at three, she was back on stride as a four-year-old to take the New Castle Stakes and Margate Handicap.

After a modest two-year-old campaign, Claiborne Farm's Bayou (Hill Prince–Bourtai, by Stimulus) was an across-the-board choice as champion of her division at three. The fourth successive daughter of her dam to gain distinction (there were a couple of non stakes-winning males in the chain), the half-sister to Banta and Delta, and full sister to Levee, swamped her rivals in the Acorn, Gazelle Stakes, Delaware Oaks and Maskette Handicap; Bayou also was a close second to C. T. Chenery's Willamette in the Coaching Club American Oaks.

Mrs. Connie Ring's Market Basket was active, and successful, on both coasts. The daughter of Radiotherapy won the Santa Susana Handicap, Goose Girl Stakes and Hollywood Oaks in her own neighborhood at three, then crossed to Atlantic City to win the Pageant Stakes. She was prominent again at four with victories in the Santa Monica and Portola Handicaps, and placings in stakes in the East and Midwest.

Bill Beasley's Pink Velvet, by Polynesian, was the real traveler in the crop, however. As a two-year-old, she won the Shady Well Stakes at Woodbine; at three, she won five more stakes in Canada, then invaded the United States to take the Margate and Jersey Belle Stakes. As a four-year-old, Pink Velvet was down in Florida, where she won the Columbiana Handicap.

Mrs. Gerard S. Smith's Outer Space bucked her shins in her only start at two, finishing fourth, but won six in a row at the beginning of her three-year-old season, including the Mother Goose Stakes, before meeting defeat again. The daughter of Saggy added six more races as a four-year-old, including the Bed o' Roses, Liberty Belle, Vagrancy and Beldame Handicaps.

Christiana Stable's Endine, a home-bred daughter of Rico Monte, trained by Henry Clark, did not race as a two-year-old, was nothing special at three, and could have been claimed at the beginning of her four-year-old campaign. Later that year, however, the full sister to stakes winner Ricci Tavi won the big one for her division, the $110,000—plus Delaware Handicap, and the Ladies Handicap. She was back at five to become the first repeat winner of the Delaware, and she also won the Nassau County Handicap from males. Christiana Stable was owned by Mr. and Mrs. Harry Lunger, and one of Endine's younger stablemates was Tempted, who had been bred by Christiana and given to Mrs. Lunger's mother, Mrs. Philip duPont (Mooring Stable). Together these two fillies provided one of the most effective one-two punches ever seen among members of their sex.

514

CHAPTER SIXTY-SEVEN

HE NEXT TWO CROPS OF FOALS following the bumper crop of 1954 did not produce any individuals who dominated the group over a long period. With one exception in each crop, championships changed from year to year, and both exceptions were fillies; in discussing the foals of 1955, that division will be described first.

IDUN, 1955
(Royal Charger–Tige O'Myheart, by Bull Lea)

As the costliest yearling filly ever sold at auction up to her time, Idun proved that a high price was not a voodoo by winning back more than triple her cost in her first season of racing.

The filly was purchased by trainer Sherrill Ward, as agent for Mrs. Charles Ulrick Bay, widow of the former ambassador to Norway, who drew on Scandinavian mythology in naming her horses. (Idun was the guardian of the apples eaten by the gods to preserve their youth.) Ward had gone to the Keeneland sales with the intention of buying two colts and a filly, but was so struck by the beautifully balanced bay, who overreached her stride so much she seemed to be walking downhill, he determined to get her at all costs. Bred by the partnership of John W. Hanes and Leslie Combs II, she was by the sire of Turn-to and out of a full sister to Preakness winner, Faultless, second dam full sister to Kentucky Derby winner, Lawrin. Idun's price reached $63,000 before the bidding ceased, so plans to buy the colts were discarded.

In an undefeated juvenile campaign of eight starts, the filly won $220,995 to set a new record for earnings by a member of her sex, breaking Top Flight's mark ($219,000) that had been standing for twenty-six years. Not only was she a unanimous choice as champion two-year-old filly, but in the Triangle Publications' poll she was voted best of her age, regardless of sex.

Mrs. Bay, who had succeeded her husband as president of a Wall Street firm, and who held a seat on the stock exchange, apparently was in no rush to get a return on her thoroughbred investment. Idun did not make her debut until July 19. She actually finished second to Bridgework in a dash down the Widener Chute, but the latter filly's number was taken down for interference. Idun had a tendency to loaf when she reached the lead, and she beat Amorial by just a head, and Quig Flame by only a nose in overnight races.

She won her juvenile stakes races emphatically, however. It was September 21 before she was sent after the big money, in the Matron Stakes, which she took by three lengths from Poly Hi. The next month she won the Gardenia on a muddy track by three and a half from Craftiness (for a net purse of $101,750) and concluded her campaign with a one-and-a-half-length victory over Lopar in the Frizette. (As a result of her vividly demonstrated aptitude for high finance, Idun was made an honorary vice-president of her owner's Wall Street firm.)

As a three-year-old, although she was defeated as often as she won, Idun again was voted best filly in her division. She ran her winning streak to nine races with an eight-

A. B. Hancock, Jr. (left) who succeeded his father as America's leading breeder with trainer James Fitzsimmons.

at Belmont Park May 27. Idun won five of her her first loss, to A Glitter in an overnight race length victory in her sophomore debut, before ten starts in 1958, including the Mother Goose Stakes by three lengths, and the Gazelle Handicap by four and a half under top weight of 124 pounds, defeating Munch, Tempted and A Glitter. She also was impressive in some of her losses: a courageous fourth against her elders in the 1½-mile Ladies Handicap (her first outing over such a long route), a third to the good colts, Warhead and Grey Monarch, in the 1¾6-mile Roamer Handicap, and a fifth—beaten by only one and a quarter lengths for all the money —in the Beldame while conceding actual weight to her seniors, the only time during the season Idun failed to get part of the purse. A mile and a sixteenth proved to be her limit, however.

Her owner having remarried, Idun raced as a four-year-old in the name of Mrs. Josephine Bay Paul. In her final season of competition, she won the Columbiana, Colonial, Liberty Belle and Maskette Handicaps. Idun retired with $392,490. This amount of money was more than adequate substitute for the three

yearlings her trainer had intended to buy in the first place.

In all but one of her numerous stakes victories, Idun was ridden by Bill Hartack, the fiery young Pennsylvanian who developed into a worthy rival of Bill Shoemaker. In 1957, Idun's juvenile season, Hartack won his third national riding championship in a row and also led the money-winning list for the second successive year, setting a new record in the latter category as his mounts earned $3,060,501. Besides Idun, they included the Calumet aggregation (Gen. Duke, Iron Liege, Bardstown, Princess Turia) and the Garden State Stakes winner, Nadir; to crown his sensational achievements of 1957, Hartack won forty-three stakes events, thereby setting another record.

The handsome, wavy haired, blue-eyed jockey was destined to win the national championship again, thus becoming the only rider besides Shoemaker to head his profession more than three seasons. Between them, the two Bills topped the saddle standings for eight years without interruption. In sharp contrast to Shoemaker, who sat quietly on a horse, Hartack was all over his mount, scrubbing, pumping, whipping, urging him forward in every possible way.

The volatile Hartack also differed from his phlegmatic colleague in personality. Chagrined by defeat—whether in a claiming race or a stakes event—he sometimes brusquely showed his contempt for anything but the best. In his way, he was quite as much a prima donna as Tod Sloan had been, but in the case of Hartack the displays of artistic temperament were not the sort that were regarded with amusement.

He was something of a stormy petrel from the viewpoint of stewards, owners, trainers and reporters—but Hartack obviously got along very well with horses.

Mrs. S. George Zauderer's Poly Hi, ranked nearest Idun during their juvenile season, won nine of thirteen starts at two, including one string of six successive stakes. The daughter of Polynesian, trained by George Odom and ridden by Eric Guerin, won the Rosedale, Fashion, National Stallion, Colleen, Astoria and Arlington Lassie before her streak ended with an unplaced effort in the Princess Pat Stakes, won by Hasty House Farm's Hasty Doll. The latter previously had won the Miss Chicago Stakes, and finished third in Poly Hi's Lassie. Other fillies of this generation who were especially prominent at two were E. H. Lane's Margaretta (four stakes), Claiborne Farm's Sequoia (Spinaway) and Llangollen Farm's Guide Line (Selima).

As three-year-olds, the fillies of 1955 in general whipped one another back and forth. There was no more than a pound's difference between Idun and A Glitter, and just below them were clustered Big Effort, Munch and Tempted.

Calumet Farm's A Glitter, a daughter of Khaled–A Gleam, won the most money as a sophomore, with seven victories in seventeen starts, including the Betsy Ross Stakes, CCA and Monmouth Oaks for earnings of $144,645. She also won the Modesty Handicap at four to retire with a total of $196,370. Brookmeade's Big Effort, by Endeavour II, won the Acorn Stakes and Delaware Oaks at three and the Bed o' Roses and Top Flight Handicaps at four. Tartan Stable's Munch, an Irish-bred daughter of Mustang, as a three-year-old won the Cleopatra Handicap and scored a notable victory over males (Hillsdale and Li'l Fella) in the Atlantic City Handicap.

The most consistent member of the class was Mooring Stable's Tempted, a clean-limbed chestnut daughter of Half Crown–Enchanted Eve, trained by Henry Clark. A stakes winner at two, three, four and five, she won the

Bert and Richard Morgan

Idun, champion at two and three, with jockey Bill Hartack up.

Bug Brush beating Hillsdale in the San Antonio Handicap, 1⅛ miles in new world record time of 1:46⅖.

Jeanne d'Arc as a juvenile, and was not far off the pace at three with victories in the Jersey Belle, Alabama Stakes and Maskette Handicap. At four she was voted best of her sex in the handicap division, through victories in the New Castle Stakes, Diana (by five and a half lengths), Beldame (125 pounds) and Ladies Handicaps. She carried top weight of 128 in the latter event (reduced in distance to 1⁵⁄₁₆ miles when the race was moved from Belmont to Aqueduct), conceding 16 pounds to three-year-old High Bid, and 13 to her contemporary, Big Effort. She also did pace-making chores for her stablemate, Endine. At five, Tempted added repeat victories in the Diana and Maskette Handicaps to retire finally with $330,760.

Bug Brush, a daughter of Nasrullah–Bonnie Beryl (and hence a full sister to Nashville), was the first of several stars developed by C. V. Whitney's new trainer, Robert L. Wheeler, who started out with a western division of the stable. Winner of the Kentucky Oaks as a three-year-old, Bug Brush caught fire after she was shipped to California.

Ridden by Angel Valenzuela, she won four straight stakes at the outset of her four-year-old campaign: the 6-furlong Las Flores in 1:09⅖, the 7-furlong Santa Monica in 1:23, the 1⅛-mile Santa Margarita, under top weight of 126 pounds, in 1:48⅕ and, having demolished her own sex, the San Antonio against males. In one of the most phenomenal performances turned in by a filly, Bug Brush beat Hillsdale,

Terrang and Seaneen over 1⅛ miles in world record time of 1:46⅖.

Her only loss that year in California was a third, just a neck behind the winner, to Terrang and How Now in the San Bernardino Handicap. The Whitney filly then won the 6-furlong Sequoia Handicap in 1:09⅕, and beat males again in the Inglewood Handicap, winning by three lengths from Amerigo, How Now and The Searcher, and covering the 1¹⁄₁₆ miles in 1:40⅘. An invasion of the East brought disastrous results, however, for Bug Brush was unplaced in three tries: Tempted's New Castle Stakes, Diana Handicap and Endine's Delaware Handicap. Those defeats cost her dearly in the championship polls, but Bug Brush ranked second to Tempted in the voting, and tied her in mathematical performance points. Bug Brush also was back on the scene at five, but she did not regain her form; she retired with lifetime earnings of $206,392.

Conejo Ranch's Honeys Gem, a daughter of Ali's Gem–Honeymoon, as a four-year-old set a world record for her sex by winning the mile Beverly Handicap in 1:34; she also won the Milady Handicap in 1:35⅖ under 126 pounds.

Majority choice as best two-year-old colt from the 1955 crop was Maine Chance Farm's Jewel's Reward. An unwanted yearling, he went on to set a new juvenile earnings record of $349,642, a remarkable enough development in itself, made more so by the circumstance that the Garden State Stakes was his

Jewel's Reward with jockey Bill Shoemaker, Mrs. Elizabeth N. Graham and trainer Ivan Parke.

only race that year in which he failed to earn money.

Bred by his owner, the handsome bay son of Jet Jewel–Belle Jeep was of impeccable bloodlines but improbable origin. His sire had been the top-priced colt of his crop in the yearling auctions ($35,000) but never had won in six starts, although he was twice second, for earnings of $2,005. That Jet Jewel was given a chance at stud was unusual. Jewel's Reward's dam had not raced at all, so when her son went through the auction ring there was a noticeable lack of interest in the bidding for him. Again exercising her woman's intuition (prodded perhaps by the fact that Belle Jeep's first foal, Lord Jeep, was running well as a three-year-old that season) Mrs. Graham had an agent buy back Jewel's Reward for $3,500.

As a final twist, although he won money faster than any horse in history up to that time, in not one of his twelve races at two did Jewel's Reward start as favorite.

After running third in a maiden race for his debut, the Maine Chance colt competed exclusively in stakes. He was fourth in the Cherry Hill (won by Nisht Amool), second to Li'l Fella in the Juvenile and to Bolero U. in the Tyro before he won his first race—the 5½-furlong Tremont Stakes on July 10, in which his frequent rival, Li'l Fella, ran second. Jewel's Reward then was fourth in the Great American (won by Li'l Fella) and Sapling (won by Plion) before he won again. His owner provided further evidence of her faith in him by paying a $7,500 supplementary nomination fee for the Washington Park Futurity. Jewel's Re-

519

ward won the race from the hitherto invincible Alhambra. W. L. "Duke" McCue, who had been training Jewel's Reward, at this point went back to Kentucky to break the Maine Chance yearlings, and Ivan Parke took over the colt. Upon his return to the East, Jewel's Reward won the Cowdin Stakes from Nadir, Jester and Misty Flight, but had to sit out the Belmont Futurity (won by Jester) because he had not been kept eligible, and supplementary nominations were not permitted to the New York race. However, there was another, even bigger purse available a couple of weeks later.

Since its reconditioning in 1953, the Garden State Stakes had been stealing some of the thunder from the New York races, so in 1957 the Champagne Stakes, first run in 1867, was boosted to $75,000 in added value, with a system of payments which brought the gross value to more than double that sum. Supplementary nominations were permitted to the Champagne, and Mrs. Graham paid another $7,500 to get Jewel's Reward in, plus $500 to pass the entry box and $750 to start. He returned the fees with interest, as he won by a neck from Misty Flight, with Rose Trellis, Li'l Fella, Nadir and Alhambra next in line. Besides a winner's purse of $92,975 ($84,225 of which was net) the victory was an important contribution to Jewel's Reward's subsequent championship.

The Garden State Stakes, for which he was supplemented at a $10,000 fee, did not turn out so happily, as he finished seventh in the race, won by Nadir. In his final juvenile start, however, Jewel's Reward won the 1 1/16-mile Pimlico Futurity, from Nala, for his fifth victory (all stakes) and biggest purse ($115,347 net) of the season.

Claiborne Farm's Nadir, a huge son of Nasrullah, who topped 16 hands at two and was still growing, was elected champion two-year-old colt in one poll. Undefeated in three allowance races until he met Jewel's Reward in the Cowdin, Nadir later was unplaced in the Futurity and Champagne, before coming back

to dead-heat with Music Man Fox in the Garden State Trial, then winning the big one by two lengths from Terra Firma. Nadir ran greenly at times, and his undisciplined behavior, plus the fact that he had a walleye, gave him an altogether wild aspect. Like Whirlaway, he left the impression that he could do better when he settled down.

Fred W. Hooper's Alhambra, by Olympia, also had never been outrun before he encountered Jewel's Reward, although he had lost a race officially. Trained by Chuck Parke (who took over when brother Ivan went to Maine Chance) the handy, quick-stepping brown colt won his first six starts, including the Primer (by a nose from Leather Button), Hyde Park Stakes, Arlington Futurity, George Woolf Memorial and Prairie State Stakes (by a nose from Terra Firma). In the Arlington Futurity, however, Alhambra was disqualified because of a foul committed by his stablemate, Olymar. It was the *cause célèbre* of the season, since Alhambra was practically at the finish, and so far in front (four and a half lengths) it was obvious he could not be caught, when Olymar cut off Sir Ruler. Under the rule then in effect, however, neither member of the entry could finish in front of the victim, so Alhambra was set back to fourth place, behind Leather Button, Rellim S. W. and Sir Ruler. As a consequence of the affair, the rule later was changed so as to permit stewards to use discretion in incidents of this sort, and allow the result to stand if in their opinion an infraction had not really affected the outcome of a race. Alhambra won no more stakes at two, but in later years was an active and successful sprinter, retiring at age six with 23 wins and $301,464.

J. Rukin Jelks and Atholl McBean's Old Pueblo, a chestnut son of Windy City II, was undefeated in 6 juvenile starts in California. including the Cabrillo, Starlet, California Breeders' Trial Stakes and Del Mar Futurity. In the Starlet, Strong Ruler outfinished Old Pueblo by a neck, but was disqualified for coming over onto Fleet Nasrullah, so Old Pueblo inherited this victory.

Of the other members of the 1955 crop prominent as two-year-olds, Jaclyn Stable's Li'l Fella won the World's Playground besides his two victories over Jewel's Reward. He, too, knocked around for several more years, and became something of a specialist at turf course racing. George D. Widener's Jester had won the National Stallion Stakes prior to his Futurity; Wheatley Stable's Misty Flight, one of six stakes winners produced by his dam, Grey Flight, won the 1 1/16-mile Remsen; Foxcatcher Farm's Rose Trellis won the Hopeful, R. D. Prewitt's Terra Firma won the Hawthorne Juvenile Handicap and Dixiana's Fulcrum took the Breeders' Futurity.

During their three-year-old season, the rankings of the class of 1955 were almost entirely revised, with Tim Tam complete master of the scene as long as he lasted. Another Calumet Farm reserve who came off the bench, the dark bay colt from the first crop by Tom Fool, out of the famed mare, Two Lea, had started only

once at two, finishing fourth, and at the beginning of 1958 was considered an understudy to his stablemate, Kentucky Pride. When the latter colt, a full brother to Real Delight who had won both his starts at two, wrenched an ankle (he later turned out to be touched in the wind and was confined to sprints) Tim Tam was more than prepared to take over.

Beginning the year with two overnight victories, Tim Tam next finished third in a similar event won by Kentucky Pride, following which both of them were upset in their first experience in added money competition. In the 7-furlong Bahamas Stakes on February 5, Kentucky Pride was cruising on the lead when he ran out of gas after covering 6 furlongs in 1:09 1/5; Olymar rambled by to win by half a length in 1:22 4/5, as Tim Tam, closing four lengths in the drive, got up to third, just a nose behind his stablemate. That was Tim Tam's last loss until the final start of his career.

Again coming from far back, Tim Tam won the 1 1/8-mile Everglades Stakes from Kentucky Pride; their partnership was dissolved at that

Ben (left) and Jimmy Jones lead in Tim Tam (Ismael Valenzuela up), the seventh Kentucky Derby winner for Calumet Farm and the eighth for the Jones boys.

point, as the Bull Lea colt was injured in training before the Flamingo Stakes on March 1, in which Tim Tam first encountered Jewel's Reward.

The Maine Chance champion had won his sophomore debut. Ridden in the Flamingo by Manuel Ycaza, Jewel's Reward was kept under restraint close to the pace for six furlongs, and as Tim Tam made his move from farther back, Jewel's Reward went with him, racing inside his rival. They battled side by side through the stretch, with Jewel's Reward bearing out under left-handed whipping bumping the favorite. At the wire, Tim Tam was second by a head, but Hartack's claim of foul against the winner was allowed, and the decision was reversed. A winner's circle ceremony seemed out of place, so the trophy was handed to Mrs. Markey in the Hialeah directors' room.

After winning the Fountain of Youth Stakes by two lengths from Grey Monarch, Tim Tam threw a scare into his backers in the Florida Derby March 29; the 75-to-1 shot, Lincoln Road, was allowed to pile up a six-length lead during the first 6 furlongs, and still had a two-length lead in mid-stretch, but he shied as he passed the starting gate parked in the infield and Tim Tam went on to win by half a length.

The Calumet colt proceeded to Kentucky, where he defeated Nadir by a similar margin in a 7-furlong race at Keeneland in new track record time of $1:22\frac{1}{5}$, and won the Derby Trial on a slow track by a neck from Ebony Pearl, before meeting Jewel's Reward again in the Derby.

Jewel's Reward, having won the Wood Memorial from Noureddin since the Flamingo, was favorite for the Kentucky Derby, but Tim Tam's principal opposition again came from Lincoln Road. Pursuing the same tactics he had in Florida, the Sunny Blue Farm colt took the lead immediately while Tim Tam waited until he was on the backstretch to start moving. Making up almost six lengths in the final quarter on the muddy track, he was up in the final strides to win, again by half a length, Lincoln Road

holding on for second, Noureddin third and Jewel's Reward fourth.

Ismael Valenzuela rode Tim Tam in the Derby, and the same combination won the Preakness by one and a half lengths from Lincoln Road and Gone Fishin', with Jewel's Reward unplaced. The erstwhile leader of the generation was put aside for a six-month rest after that performance, and, as it turned out, the Preakness also marked the end of Tim Tam's eight-race winning streak.

In the Belmont Stakes on June 7, as the heavily favored Calumet champion began to move up at the end of a mile, Joseph E. O'Connell's Cavan moved past him and took over the lead, increasing it with every stride; to the dismay of the crowd, Tim Tam swerved repeatedly under punishment, and dropped back to finish six lengths behind Cavan, but still second, five and a half lengths ahead of his nearest pursuer, Flamingo. Immediately after crossing the finish Valenzuela dismounted, and the colt who had failed in his quest for the Triple Crown was taken back to his barn by van. X rays revealed a shattered sesamoid bone in his right foreleg, and Tim Tam was retired to stud, never having finished out of the money in thirteen starts at three, and never having failed to earn part of the purse in his life.

He was a provocative colt, who, until the Belmont, seemed to get better with each start. His performances do not look too impressive in the charts; six of his ten victories were scored by margins of less than a length, and the race at Keeneland, when Nadir forced him to top speed, was the only time Tim Tam so much as flirted with a track record. Yet, some of those performances were awesome to see, for he could run down a rival near the end of a race without any struggle having been apparent. In the Derby Trial, which he won by only a neck, Tim Tam picked his way over the sticky track like a cat; he had to thread his way past several horses, but when the time came, there was a quick scurry, and suddenly he was in front. Perhaps the best testimony to his im-

Silky Sullivan winning the Santa Anita Derby.

pressiveness lies in the fact that he left the scene before the season was halfway complete (with earnings of $467,200) yet lacked only one vote of being a unanimous choice as champion of his division. Only during Count Fleet's wartime season had a three-year-old been able to retire with his laurels after the Belmont Stakes and keep them fresh the remainder of the year.

In this matter, Tim Tam's cause was advanced shortly after his own retirement by the departure from the stage of his most logical challenger, Cavan. The Irish-bred son of Mossborough, trained by T. J. Barry, had won once in four starts at two, and was five for six at three. After two allowance wins, he had finished fifth in his first big race, the Jersey Stakes (won by Lincoln Road), then had won the Peter Pan Handicap. Following his Belmont victory, he won the Leonard Richards Stakes on June 28 by two lengths from Piano Jim, but pulled up lame and was sidelined the rest of the season.

Oddly, the "temperamental" Nadir was the only colt of his generation steady enough to receive mention in the championship voting both at two and at three. He won five of sixteen starts as a sophomore including the Select Handicap and American Derby; and a mile allowance race in 1:34⅗, defeating W. E. Britt's Westerner Stakes winner, Strong Bay.

Among numerous placings, he was second by half a length to the older Clem in the Woodward Stakes at weight for age, on the occasion Round Table was unplaced.

Mrs. Mabel C. Schlotz's Warhead won the Jerome, Discovery, Manhattan and Roamer Handicaps; Boncrist Farm's Backbone won the Chesapeake, Suffolk Downs, Kent, Providence, Choice Stakes, Hartford and Benjamin Franklin Handicaps; and Mrs. S. H. Sadacca's A Dragon Killer slew the Chicago three-year-olds in the Arlington Classic, and subsequently added the Ventnor Turf Handicap.

No mention of the 1955 crop would be complete without reference to Tom Ross and Phil Klipstein's Silky Sullivan, one of the most glamorous horses to appear in America since Man o' War. Suggestive of "Big Red" in appearance also, Silky was a gleaming chestnut of such prodigious muscular development that he seemed of a different breed, more like an artist's romantic conception of a war charger than a race horse; also, he wore steel shoes instead of aluminum. He stood a shade over 16 hands, and weighed 1,080 as a three-year-old when he was in shape (Silky consumed 12 to 15 quarts of grain a day, and his weight varied up to 1,200 pounds) but his girth was so enormous he required a custom-made surcingle, and in a field of typical thoroughbreds mincing to the post, Silky resembled a battleship under escort.

Bedecked in red leg bandages, a red shadow roll, martingale and saddlecloth, he was a sight to see under any circumstances, and in action he was spectacular. Officially, he was trained by Reggie Cornell, but the trainer freely admitted that Silky called the turns as to racing tactics.

Purchased at the Del Mar yearling sales for $10,700 from his breeders, Mrs. Nell Frances Roberts and Dr. R. H. Roberts, the son of Sullivan–Lady N Silk was of sprinting ancestry as well as conformation, but he earned his fame through his unique habit of running his races upside down. After ambling nonchalantly through the first few furlongs, the massive chestnut could throw in a quarter-mile many horses would have difficulty duplicating right out of the gate.

As a two-year-old Silky attracted considerable attention by coming from twenty-seven lengths off the pace to capture the Golden Gate Futurity at a mile. Early in his sophomore season, he electrified the audience by dropping forty lengths behind Old Pueblo during the first half-mile of the 1¹⁄₁₆-mile California Breeders' Champion Stakes, then speeding through the final quarter in less than 22 seconds—over a heavy track—to miss by only a neck. The time was unofficial, since clockings are taken only on the horse in front, but Silky made up thirty and a half lengths while the leader ran the last ⁵⁄₁₆-mile in 33 seconds. Chart-caller Al Willig had been ready to take him out of the calls, assuming Silky had been pulled up; and Old Pueblo's rider, Arcaro, stated that when he had looked over his right shoulder early in the stretch drive Silky wasn't in sight. (One wag said that Arcaro had looked over the wrong shoulder; at the time Old Pueblo was straightened out in the home lane, Silky was still over on the backstretch.) As the horses returned to scale, the winner drew a sprinkling of polite applause; Silky Sullivan was welcomed by an ovation that thundered against the distant San Gabriel Mountains.

Next time out, the golden colt came from forty-one lengths behind to win a 6½ furlong allowance race.

The idol of the public, Silky drew 61,123 fans to the 1958 Santa Anita Derby, in spite of an unfavorable weather forecast and a televised showing of the race. Possibly in deference to co-owner Ross, who had a heart condition and was not allowed by his doctor to see all of Silky's races, the big colt practically forced the pace in this one, falling only twenty-eight lengths out of it in the first 5 furlongs, according to the chart. When Shoemaker rattled his bit—the signal for Silky to get going, as the horse did not countenance such rude forms of encouragement as a whip—he flew to the front to win the 9-furlong event by three and a half lengths in 1:49⅖ from his stablemate, Harcall, owned by Mrs. Ross.

Shipped to Louisville for the Kentucky Derby, Silky Sullivan captured the imagination of Midwestern racegoers by turning on his patented surge in a 7-furlong prep race; he did not win, because he ran out of ground, but he made up a deficit of thirty lengths to finish fourth, two and a quarter lengths behind the winner. For the Derby the standard throng of 100,000 at Churchill Downs was larger than it had been in years, and there were more $2 tickets sold on Silky than on any horse in history. He went off at odds only slightly longer than those on the favored Jewel's Reward, and equal to those on the winner, Tim Tam—but it came up mud on May 3, 1958, and Silky didn't have it, finishing twelfth of fourteen starters. An eighth in the Preakness two weeks later ended his classic aspirations. After he returned to the West Coast, he lost one and won one, then was fired for suspensory trouble; he took the salt-water treatment at Del Mar, galloping over the sandy beach and swimming in the surf, and later returned to action with a victory, but he never attained his former heights.

To put a prosaic construction on this phenomenal horse, Silky was quick enough at two to work 5 furlongs in :58, and to win at 6 furlongs in 1:09⅗. Over the winter he had a bad cold, and as a three-year-old he made a noise while running. Evidently it required a few furlongs for his respiration to clear up, after which he began to run in normal fashion. His burst of extreme speed coincided with a finishing kick in races at or near a mile, but in the longer Santa Anita Derby, for example, it came well before the finish, but still in the third and fourth quarters. Presumably he would have turned it on at that same point regardless of the distance he ultimately had to travel—he merely delayed his sprint for, say, half a mile, after which he reverted to type.

Whatever he was, Silky Sullivan was a tonic for racing.

Jewel's Reward, who had finished just ahead of Silky in the Preakness and had been idle since, also turned up in California at the end of his three-year-old season. Just before the 1958 season ran out, on December 27, he finished second in the Malibu Sequet Stakes; the winner of the race was Hillsdale, the colt who took over the top spot among the foals of 1955 as a four-year-old.

Hillsdale was good at two, excellent at three and terrific at four. The son of Take Away–Johann, bred by Mrs. Helen W. Kellogg at her Murlogg Farm in Evansville, Indiana, raced in the colors of his breeder as a juvenile. He could have been claimed for $7,500 at the time of his maiden victory, but developed into a winner of six races and $21,180 in his first season; he won no stakes but maintained a good reputation in fast company on the New England circuit.

Sold for $25,000 to C. W. Smith, Detroit engineer and former Georgia Tech and Chicago Bear football player, Hillsdale was turned over to trainer Marty Fallon, a former jockey who had ridden his sire, Take Away, and had broken Hillsdale himself as a yearling. The Hoosier colt gave his new owner a fast return by winning half his fourteen starts and $123,665 as a three-year-old, including the Will Rogers Stakes, Michigan Derby, El Dorado

and Boardwalk Handicaps and the Malibu. A big (16-1, 1,150 pounds), long bodied bay, with an extraordinary sheen to his coat—he seemed to be made of highly polished wood rather than flesh—Hillsdale did not relish off tracks, and he did his best running in southern California (where it rarely rains).

He didn't relish distance beyond 9 furlongs either, but he got a furlong more as a four-year-old on pure class and courage. In thirteen starts that year, all stakes, he lost only three, finishing second in all, and never was he defeated by so much as a length, for earnings of $502,090. Except for three sprints, which he won, all his races were hotly contested struggles.

Hillsdale opened his 1958 campaign by beating Round Table (132) a head in the San Carlos Handicap, getting a 17-pound concession and covering the 7 furlongs in 1:21⅘. He defeated Jewel's Reward again in the 1¹⁄₁₆-mile San Fernando, and then chalked up his first victory at 1¼ miles in the Santa Anita Maturity, at the expense of Royal Living, who subsequently won the marathon San Juan Capistrano.

Bug Brush threw her world record at him in the San Antonio next out, to defeat Hillsdale by three-fourths of a length, the most decisive loss he was to suffer that season. A second by half a length to Terrang in the Santa Anita Handicap followed, then Hillsdale went into a winning streak of seven races.

He beat Seaneen in the Los Angeles Handicap, 7 furlongs in 1:21; he nosed out Amerigo, while conceding him 16 pounds, in the Californian Stakes; and carried 128 to victory by two and a half lengths over Fleet Nasrullah (115) in the Argonaut. Upped to 130 for the American Handicap on July 4, Hillsdale was spotting 21 pounds to Find; the Indiana colt spun 1⅛ miles in 1:47⅕ to win by half a length. When they met a week later in the longer Hollywood Gold Cup, Hillsdale (124) defeated Find (112) by a length in 1:59⅕ for 1¼ miles.

Bert and Richard Morgan

Checking the construction's progress at the new Aqueduct: Racing Commission chairman Ashley Trimble Cole (left), NYRA president John W. Hanes, trustee Alfred G. Vanderbilt and building committee chairman John W. Galbreath.

After a two-month rest at Audley Farm in Virginia, the son of Take Away returned to action at Belmont Park on September 7 with a two-and-a-half-length victory over Mystic II in the 7-furlong Sation Handicap, while carrying 129 pounds. A week later he picked up 132 for the Aqueduct Handicap at a mile, and won by three-fourths of a length from Bald Eagle (122). It was the first stakes race contested at brand-new Aqueduct, and by this time Hillsdale was an authentic candidate for Horse of the Year.

The 1¼-mile Woodward Stakes at the same track on September 26 brought together the three leading candidates for the title under weight-for-age conditions, and it was assumed that the season's crown would be added to the purse. In addition to Hillsdale, the field in-

cluded the champion three-year-old Sword Dancer; the world's leading money winner, Round Table; and Inside Tract.

Tommy Barrow—Hillsdale's jockey throughout the season—let him take the front at the start, but kept the pace throttled down to a leisurely 1:40 for the first mile, with Round Table (Shoemaker) running lapped on the leader much of the way. After Hillsdale raced Round Table into defeat, Arcaro slipped Sword Dancer through on the inside and wore down Hillsdale in the last 70 yards to win by a head in 2:04⅖.

With that costly defeat, Hillsdale ended his career.

The race for the Horse of the Year title was the highlight of the inaugural meeting at the world's largest race track, new Aqueduct—the

526

Big A—which opened on September 14, 1959. The mammoth racing plant was the culmination of a sweeping project begun five years earlier by the Jockey Club committee, headed by John W. Hanes, that had been appointed to study means of rehabilitating New York racing.

Following the committee's recommendation, all tracks in the state had been purchased by a single corporation, ultimately named the New York Racing Association, Inc., which obtained a twenty-five-year franchise to conduct racing in the metropolitan area and at Saratoga on a non-profit basis. The state, in turn, agreed to a temporary reallocation of 1 percent of the pari-mutuel handle to the new association to enable it to raise the money necessary to effect needed improvements, any possible loss in state revenue being offset by lengthening the racing season and, in 1959, increasing the daily programs from eight to nine races.

Extensive repairs were made to Belmont Park and Saratoga, and construction was begun on a completely new track on the site of Aqueduct. The largest and most modern racing plant ever conceived, among the numerous notable features of the $33-million plant were a private subway station; a grandstand 1,050 feet long and 110 feet high (the equivalent of a ten-story building) that occupied 7 of the 203 acres devoted to the layout; seats for 20,000 under cover and total accommodations for 80,000 patrons; a dining room of 1,200 capacity, two cafeterias and sixty-two bars and buffets; a twenty-five-bed hospital; 80 acres of parking space; 738 pari-mutuel windows, clustered in islands which facilitated flow of traffic; nine elevators and eighteen escalators; 300 miles of electric wiring; 700 trees; fireproof barns; a paddock in front of the stands so that spectators could watch the horses being saddled without leaving their seats; and a 1⅛-mile main track with a 7-furlong grass course inside it.

There was a touch of tradition amidst all the new fixtures, however. The eighth pole from old Aqueduct, which had been a silent sentinel at the moment of truth in the duel between Man o' War and John P. Grier during the running of the 1920 Dwyer Stakes, was installed in the garden of the new track.

The Turf and Field Club at Belmont Park.

Also, what had been a glaring gap in the ranks of American stakes races was filled by the new track. Virtually every great thoroughbred of the past was commemorated by a stakes event named in his (or her) honor—but there was no significant race named for the greatest of them all. Aqueduct instituted the Man o' War Handicap (later Stakes) at $100,000 added, and even in the age of huge purses it was unique, for the inaugural drew so many entries it had to be run in two divisions. The customary procedure when a stakes event is split is to reduce the added money of each division somewhat, but both divisions of the Man o' War—won by Dotted Line and Tudor Era—went at full steam. The total of $200,000 added was the "mostest" money with which any race ever had been endowed.

Jamaica was abandoned the year new Aqueduct appeared on the scene. From its first day of operation—William Ewing's Four Lane won the opening race—the track was a resounding success, and provided a graphic lesson in economics: the State of New York received more revenue from 10 percent of the new business than it had been getting from 11 percent of the old. Aqueduct ran only sixty-six days in the autumn of 1959, against bad weather on some of the Saturdays, but it nevertheless registered gains of 26 percent in attendance and 31 percent in mutuel handle over the preceding year's corresponding days at Belmont and Jamaica. Part of the gain in handle could be attributed to addition of the ninth race, but analysis of this factor at the other metropolitan tracks indicated that the extra race was responsible for only a 4 percent boost.

In 1960—its first full year of operation—Aqueduct set a new record of $2,698,419 in daily average mutuel handle, and revenue to the State of New York was $12½-million higher than it had been in 1958, the last year before Aqueduct entered the picture. As time went on, records continued to be shattered at the track, which registered daily averages for a complete meeting in excess of 33,000 in attendance and $3-million in wagering, with peaks of 70,992 attendance and $5,560,628 mutuel handle. (Hollywood Park continued to lead the nation's tracks in daily average attendance, but no other track approached Aqueduct in volume of wagering.)

Obviously, new Aqueduct accomplished its immediate mission of strengthening New York's position as a center of major racing. From the standpoint of American racing as a whole, the ultimate significance of the new track, and the setup which produced it, cannot be evaluated until some date in the future. The modern, efficient Aqueduct has not been without its detractors, many of whom prefer the charm and atmosphere of establishments perhaps less functional but with more flavor. On the other hand, as the newness wears off, the "gleaming monster," as it sometimes is described, might acquire a sentimental following of its own.

A number of new stars showed their wares at the inaugural meeting of new Aqueduct.

Bald Eagle was not a factor in the scramble for leadership of his generation during his first two seasons of racing, for the very good reason that he was not in America. Bred by his owner, Harry F. Guggenheim, the son of Nasrullah–Siama, by Tiger, was so growthy as a youngster it was concluded that the rodeo style of American juvenile racing would not suit him, so he was sent to England. The gangling bay, almost brown, colt, still growing (he eventually reached 16-3) and decidedly "on the leg," started just once as a two-year-old, winning the Duke of Edinburgh Stakes. Bald Eagle was somewhat a disappointment at three—he started second choice for the Epsom Derby but failed to stay the 1½ miles. He nevertheless won the 1-mile Craven Stakes and 10½-furlong Dante Stakes. There was conjecture that his three losses in England as a sophomore had been the result of temperament, for which his sire was noted and his maternal grandsire notorious, but his conduct in America was exemplary.

Bald Eagle was returned to this country in

In the winner's circle after Bald Eagle's victory in the 1960 Widener Handicap are George D. Widener (left), Harry S. Truman, jockey Manuel Ycaza, Lord Derby, owner Harry F. Guggenheim and trainer W.C. Stephens.

the summer of 1958, and ran unplaced in his only American start as a three-year-old. The next year, however, while his year older full brother, One-Eyed King, was winning other stakes, Bald Eagle won the Suburban, Saratoga, Gallant Fox Handicaps (new track record time of 2:41 for 1⅝ miles at new Aqueduct) and Washington, D. C., International for earnings of $278,357.

As a five-year-old Bald Eagle flourished. Never failing to get part of the purse in eleven starts, he won the Widener (smashing the track record by 1⅖ seconds, 1¼ miles in 1:59⅗), Gulfstream Park, Metropolitan (new track record of 1:33⅗ for a mile at Aqueduct, while carrying 128 pounds), Aqueduct Handicaps and a second renewal of the International. The stately looking stallion—he became more handsome as he grew older—earned $398,085 as a five-year-old, and was champion handicap horse of 1960 according to all methods of selection.

Another member of the same crop who underwent improvement as the result of an ocean voyage was Mrs. Tilyou Christopher's English-bred Amerigo, a son of Nasrullah's sire, Nearco, and one of the most beautiful

animals ever to grace the racing scene. The reference applies to physical appearance only, since as a youngster in England, although he won two races including the Coventry Stakes, the good-looking chestnut was classified bluntly as "an arrant rogue; a thief; a horse so temperamentally unsatisfactory as to be practically worthless for racing purposes."

The British believe that the monotony of racing can cause a horse to go sour; to offset boredom, race tracks in that country offer a wide variety of conditions—uphill and down, left- and right-hand turns, straights and so forth—and meetings at any one track are brief, usually only a few days at a time. By this concept, American racing, which entails running around and around the same old track for weeks on end, and not getting any appreciable change from track to track, is nicely calculated to drive a horse crazy.

On the other hand, horses are creatures of habit (they will run *into* a burning barn to get to the comfort of familiar surroundings) and the transformation in Amerigo after he came to this country indicates that American racing might suit them better.

By no stretch of the imagination did the

Owner R.H. Webster and trainer Lucien Laurin with Quill, Paul Bailey up.

horse sprout angel's wings during his voyage across the Atlantic. Amerigo in America still was a rogue, and an uninhibited one. He bit, kicked and fought his handlers to the extent that he often got more exercise in the saddling paddock than during the race; as trainer Harris Brown phrased it, "I don't train him, I run him." Even so, from the outset of his American racing career, Amerigo was a runner, and as he settled down he got better. In a remarkably heavy schedule for any horse, he won 12 of 42 American starts, lost a number of races by narrow margins, and was unplaced but a dozen times to earn $419,171.

Brought over in the middle of his three-year-old season, about the same time as Bald Eagle, Amerigo won four races that year, including the City of Miami Handicap in new track record time of 1:40⅗ for 1¹⁄₁₆ miles at Tropical Park. At four and five his victories included the Magic City, Ocean City, New York (new American record of 1:47 for 1⅛ miles on turf), Hialeah Turf Cup and San Juan Capistrano Handicaps.

With one exception the foals of 1956 took turns at the top; and the exception, Royal Native, did not attain prominence until her second season of racing. Among the fillies, the

first to wear the crown was Reginald N. Webster's Quill.

Bred by her owner, and trained by Lucien Laurin, the chestnut daughter of Princequillo–Quick Touch, by Count Fleet, was a reverse example of a horse for a course. The story of Quill's two-year-old campaign is easily summarized: she was invincible everywhere except Saratoga.

After two overnight wins at Jamaica, the Webster filly finished third in both her starts at Saratoga, to Rich Tradition and Lady Be Good in the Schuylerville Stakes, and to Rich Tradition and Recite in the Spinaway. Quill promptly evened the score with all hands when racing returned to Belmont Park. She won a prep race from Mommy Dear and Recite, in which Rich Tradition finished fourth; then won the Matron Stakes by three and three-quarter lengths from Rich Tradition and Levelix, with Recite fourth. Lady Be Good was unplaced in both these races.

Moving to Garden State Park, Quill won the Gardenia Trial, and concluded her campaign with an impressive victory under Paul J. Bailey in the 1¹⁄₁₆-mile Gardenia Stakes, richest race on the calendar for her division. Her margin was only half a length, but she was not under a drive, and her pursuers, in order, were Resaca, Ruwenzori, Khalita, Sybil Brand, Rich Tradition, Indian Maid and five others. With six wins and two thirds in eight starts, for earnings of $144,692, Quill was an overwhelming selection as champion of the division.

While Christopher T. Chenery's Rich Tradition, the only filly to beat the champion during the season, and who later added the Selima Stakes to her bag, might seem to have been a logical choice for runner-up, such was not the case; she was shuffled back to fourth place in the battle that took place for remaining honors.

Second in the voting was W. N. Modglin's Khalita, who won seven of her nine starts and got fourth money in both the others. The daughter of Khaled, trained by Malcolm Anderson, was undefeated in her native California, where she won the Junior League, Hollywood Lassie and Del Mar Debutante Stakes. She came east to knock off Rich Tradition in the Demoiselle, before her fourth in the Gardenia.

The widely traveled Khalita's other fourth had been in the Arlington Lassie, won by North Star Ranch's Dark Vintage, who boasted the most consistent record of all. The daughter of Wine List, trained by E. B. Carpenter, won six in a row, including the Miss Chicago, Pollyanna and Joliet Stakes before the Lassie, and her only loss was a second by a length to E. P. Metz's Battle Heart in the Princess Pat.

Mrs. Mary Keim's Indian Maid (Florida Breeders Futurity, Hawthorne Juvenile Handicap and Land of Lincoln Stakes—all against colts), Mrs. Joan Van de Maele's Merry Hill (Frizette Stakes) and King Ranch's Resaca (a maiden—but promising) also received mention.

There was an elaborate shuffling process among the fillies of 1956 during the first half of their sophomore season. Long before any of the Eastern contingent swung into action, C. V. Whitney's home-bred Silver Spoon, a big (16-1, 1,135 pounds) daughter of Citation—Silver Fog, had been a sensation at Santa Anita.

Because of an early hip injury, Silver Spoon walked with a pronounced hitch, and she had made her two-year-old debut at Belmont in an $8,000 claiming race with no takers. (She won it by six lengths.) Shipped to Santa Anita she was undefeated at the meeting, to run her winning streak up to six races. After another victory just before the end of her juvenile season, as a three-year-old she whipped through the La Centinela, Santa Ynez and Santa Susana Stakes (by ten and a half lengths) all within her own division since Bug Brush was beating the older runners (each filly won four stakes at the meeting). In the Whitney family tradition, Silver Spoon went against colts in the Santa Anita Derby on March 7, which she won with her ears pricked in 1:49 by two and a half lengths from that year's eventual Preakness winner, Royal Orbit.

In an attempt to extend the tradition a step farther, Silver Spoon was shipped to the Kentucky Derby, and although she was unable to emulate Regret, she was a creditable fifth, only three and a half lengths behind the winner; upon her return to California, she won the 1⅛-mile Cinema Handicap by four and three-quarters lengths in 1:47⅗, while conceding 9 pounds actual weight to the runner-up, with her Kentucky Derby conqueror, Tomy Lee, unplaced. She crossed the Rockies a second time, hailed as the best filly seen in America since the war.

In the East, Quill had reappeared on the scene in May. Fourth in an allowance race for her sophomore debut, she came right back to rout the fillies who had outfinished her with a six-and-a-half length victory in the Acorn Stakes, following which she won the Mother Goose by three and a half lengths. In the Coaching Club American Oaks on June 20—reduced to 1¼ miles in distance in 1959, when the Widener Chute was eliminated in the renovation of Belmont Park—Quill ran an uncharacteristic race, taking the lead much sooner than was her habit. Resaca passed her, but the Webster filly gamely came again, reducing

Royal Native, the champion handicap mare in all the polls of 1960, with jockey Bill Hartack.

the gap by one and a half lengths during the stretch drive, to miss by only half a length.

The biggest of the Oaks was the first stakes victory for Resaca, who had started the season with a win in a maiden race, a sixth in Quill's Acorn, and a victory in an overnight for non-winners of races other than maiden or claiming. When the daughter of Middleground followed up her CCA Oaks score by beating Silver Spoon two lengths in the Delaware Oaks on July 11 (Quill fifth), she assumed the mantle temporarily. In the remainder of the year, however, none of the foregoing fillies were prominent. Quill had osselet trouble and was retired for the season; Resaca, whose ankles already had been fired, tailed off and never won again; Silver Spoon, who lost a great deal of weight after being shipped east, managed to win an allowance race from Indian Maid and Royal Native at Monmouth in July, after which she, too, dwindled. A new crew moved in.

A daughter of Royal Charger–Native Gal, by Sir Gallahad III (and hence half-sister to numerous winners, including Billings) Royal Native raced for breeder R. W. McIlvain as

a two-year-old; she won a maiden event and was second in the Sorority Stakes in four outings. Following McIlvain's death, the big, racy looking chestnut filly was purchased for $40,000 by Perne Grissom, and turned over to trainer Kenneth Noe. As a three-year-old, Royal Native earned money in all her sixteen starts, of which she won half, for earnings of $127,681.

Her first seven starts that year were all at 6 furlongs; she won two—by margins of six and ten lengths—and finished second to Recite in the Miss Woodford Stakes. Following her third behind Silver Spoon and Indian Maid in a $1\frac{1}{16}$-mile allowance race, Royal Native's first start at a distance beyond 6 furlongs, the Grissom filly turned the tables in the Monmouth Oaks on August 1, which she won by three and a half lengths from Indian Maid, Silver Spoon third. (Reportedly, there was a mysterious plunger operating at Monmouth that summer who wagered tremendous sums on favorites; he went under in that race, since he had bet Silver Spoon to place.)

In her subsequent stakes races at three, Royal

Native lost by a head to Sunset Glow in the Gazelle, while conceding 13 pounds; won the Pageant Handicap by one and a quarter lengths from Sunset Glow, while conceding 9 pounds; defeated Aesthetic in the Spinster Stakes at weight for age; and was second to High Bid in the Jersey Belle Stakes.

Wheatley Stable's High Bid, a daughter of To Market, did not win a stakes event until August 26, but she finished the season strongest of all. After winning the Alabama Stakes, she was a fast-closing third in the Gazelle, and ran two creditable races against her elders, getting a third and a second in the Beldame and Ladies, both won by champion Tempted. High Bid then put three big ones together; she beat Royal Native by five lengths in the Jersey Belle, and, again tackling her seniors, won the Vineland Handicap (from Miss J. G., A Glitter and Dotted Line) and Gallorette Stakes (from Polamby, A Glitter and Equifun).

In the distribution of honors at the end of 1959, Silver Spoon was voted best three-year-old filly in one poll and had the highest score in mathematical performance points; Royal Native was voted champion in another poll, and High Bid was ranked in a tie with Silver Spoon at the top of Matthias C. "Ty" Shea's *Daily Racing Form* and *Morning Telegraph* Free Handicap. It was that close.

Royal Native was the only member of her crop to repeat her championship; as a four-year-old she won half her eighteen starts, was unplaced but twice, and earned $261,226, to be selected best handicap filly across the board. She raced from January through November, packing exceptional weight for a member of her sex.

After three wins in her first five starts, including a victory over such good male sprinters as Kentucky Pride and Talent Show in her seasonal debut at 6 furlongs, the Columbiana Handicap by four and a half lengths, and the Black Helen by three and three-quarters; Royal Native was sold for $252,500 to W. B. Mac-Donald, Jr., owner of the Miami and Tampa baseball teams. During the remainder of her career the highest-priced female thoroughbred in history was trained by Peter F. Gacicia.

In her first start for her new owner, on March 30, Royal Native won the Suwannee River Handicap by three lengths, while carrying 130 pounds and spotting 23 to the runner-up, Meadow Miss. The time of 1:42 for $1\frac{1}{16}$ miles was only $\frac{2}{5}$ second away from the Gulfstream Park record, which had been set by Round Table under 2 pounds less weight.

Under 128 pounds in the Bed o' Roses Handicap, she was second by a neck to Chistosa (106), but Royal Native came back with three straight stakes: with 126 she beat Bug Brush (123) and Tinkalero (118) in the Colonial Handicap; under the same weight she won the Top Flight from Quill (123) and Bug Brush (120); and, carrying 127 pounds in the $1\frac{1}{16}$-mile Molly Pitcher Handicap, she beat Quill again, by four lengths, while conceding her 5 pounds.

In the $1\frac{1}{4}$-mile Delaware Handicap on July 30, Quill turned the tables; Royal Native carried 129 pounds compared to 125 on the winner, but weight was not the reason. Quill won easily by nine lengths, and never in her life did Royal Native win beyond 9 furlongs.

After a trip to Chicago, where she won the Arlington Matron Handicap with 128 pounds —conceding 18 to runner-up Woodlawn and level with third-place Silver Spoon—Royal Native slipped into the longest losing streak of her career, five straight, although she was in the money in four of them. She lost twice to males on the Atlantic City turf course; ran second to Berlo in the Beldame (changed in 1960 from a handicap to a weight-for-age stakes); second to Indian Maid in an allowance race; and third to Rash Statement and Indian Maid in the Spinster. Royal Native finally got back to winning form with a win over Make Sail and Wiggle II in the Vineland Handicap.

In an attempt to overtake Bewitch as world's leading money-winning mare, Royal Native raced on at five. She failed to pass veterinary inspection at Hialeah on the morning of her first scheduled start in 1961, and was withdrawn, but she later got to the post during the Northern season. Unable to win in eleven starts, she ended her career with 18 wins in 49 starts and $422,769, less than $40,000 away from her goal.

Quill, as a four-year-old, turned in another of her brief but stunning acts, winning four of her seven starts and finishing second in the others. Besides her encounters with Royal Native, the Webster filly won the New Castle Stakes from Indian Maid and Tempted, and was second in Tempted's Diana Handicap. She also returned as a five-year-old as winner of two races—but no stakes—and left the track with 14 wins in 26 starts and $386,041.

Silver Spoon came back at four to win five more stakes in California, under formidable weights. At Santa Anita, she won the Santa Monica, Santa Maria (127) and Santa Margarita, carrying 130 in the latter and conceding 14 to Indian Maid. At Hollywood Park, the daughter of Citation won the Milady Handicap with 126 from Honeys Gem (120), and packed 130 to victory in the Vanity Handicap, defeating Tritoma (107) and Honeys Gem (118). She retired with 13 wins in 27 starts and $313,930.

Most durable of the lot was Indian Maid, who won stakes every season she raced, through age five. Besides her juvenile victories already mentioned, the Florida-bred daughter of Rinaldo–Bold Verse, won three renewals of the Falls City Handicap, two each of the Yo Tambien and Modesty Handicaps, in addition to single scores in the Beverly and Columbiana. She won 24 of 66 starts and $303,457.

Shirley Jones, owned successively by the partnership of Charles Levin, Dr. A. G. Pessin and J. S. Jones; Brae Burn Farm; and Mrs. J. O. Burgwin, was another who lasted a long time. The daughter of Double Jay won the Mermaid Stakes at two; the Test at three; two overnights but no stakes at four; the Molly Pitcher and Arlington Matron Handicaps at

five; and the Maskette and Margate Handicaps at six.

Because the crop next in line contained an extraordinary horse, the male members of the 1956 crop had only the two seasons before they entered open competition in which to display their wares to best advantage. Nevertheless, there were a large number of notable performers in this group.

FIRST LANDING, 1956
(Turn-to–Hildene, by Bubbling Over)

First Landing represented the vindication of a daring gamble. Utilities tycoon Christopher T. Chenery, of The Meadow, a farm in Doswell, Virginia, owned a broodmare named Hildene. He had purchased the daughter of Bubbling Over as a yearling for $750 at the Xalapa Farm dispersal in 1939, and the best she could do on the racetack was one third (in a maiden race) in eight starts, for career earnings of $100. At stud, however, Hildene— who later went blind—became one of the great mares in American turf annals. After producing the stakes winner Mangohick (23 wins and $115,115) to the cover of Sun Beau, and an assortment of offspring by other stallions, she had three sons by Princequillo, all of them stake winners: Hill Prince (Horse of the Year, $422,140). Prince Hill ($98,300) and Third Brother ($310,787.)

These conspicuous examples of consanguinity notwithstanding, in 1955 Chenery sent the mare to Turn-to, a young horse of brilliant racing performance, but at the time untried as a stallion. First Landing was the result. (Although the colt was foaled at Claiborne Farm, his name was suggested by the 350th anniversary of the Jamestown settlement, which was being celebrated near Doswell the year he was born.)

As a two-year-old, the burly bay son of Hildene won ten of eleven starts and was second in the other to set a new juvenile earnings record of $396,460.

First Landing was outfinished by Restless Wind in his debut, but the son of Windy City II was disqualified for swerving and First Landing moved up. That commenced a winning streak of seven races, including the Juvenile, Great American, Saratoga Special and Hopeful Stakes. Atoll, destined to become a good sprinter, forced First Landing to a hard drive to win the Great American by a neck, but the Chenery champion's victories at Saratoga were accomplished with ease. He won the Special by seven lengths and the Hopeful by five and a half, which gave Chenery clear domination of two-year-old racing at the old Spa. That was the summer his Rich Tradition monopolized the filly stakes, and E. L. Cotton's First Minister, winner of Saratoga's other two colt stakes, had finished second to First Landing in the Hopeful.

On his return to the metropolitan circuit, First Landing suffered his only official loss of the season when Intentionally beat him by a length in the 6½-furlong Futurity—the last one contested over the Widener Chute straightaway—won in 1:14⅗, just ⅕-second off the track record.

First Landing reversed this decision in the Champagne Stakes at a mile on October 11, although the result was somewhat inconclusive. Tomy Lee, who finished second by a neck, had forced Intentionally wide on the turn, and the positions of the latter two colts were interchanged by the stewards—but on the other hand, Arcaro reported that First Landing also had an excuse; his saddle had been slipping during the stretch run.

In his division of the Garden State Trial, Arcaro deliberately snugged First Landing in behind the pace-setting Crafty Skipper to accustom the colt to having a little dirt thrown at him. It was a dry-run rehearsal of the main event, for in the Garden State Stakes the track was covered with water. First Landing splashed over the sloppy track to win by a head from Tomy Lee, with Sword Dancer third, Rico Tesio fourth, Intentionally fifth and Restless

Wind also among the unplaced. The winner's award of $175,965 was the largest in history at the time, and First Landing was a unanimous selection as champion two-year-old colt of 1958.

At three, he was voted disappointment of the year by a poll, a tribute at that to the high regard in which he had been held, since the colt won five of his twelve starts and was out of the money just twice for earnings of $98,267.

In three starts in Florida he was second to Octopus in a fast 7-furlong overnighter won in 1:22⅗; won the Everglades Stakes by only a neck; and was third, behind Troilus and Open View, in the Flamingo. (How good Bayard Sharp's Troilus might have been was never established—after winning the Bahamas and Flamingo, the son of Priam II went off form, and a few months later died of colic.) First Landing looked wan and tired, and his condition was attributed to the damp, unusually hot weather in Miami that winter, a deduction which was reinforced when he won his first outing at Jamaica in a sparkling 1:10⅕ for 6 furlongs on a good track. However, he was upset by Manassa Mauler in the Wood Memorial, and, after winning the Derby Trial, was third in the Kentucky Derby itself. After the erstwhile champion finished ninth in the Preakness, it was reported that he had a kidney ailment, and he was rested for five months. On his return in the autumn, he won two overnights, was nosed out by Polylad in the Roamer (while conceding 11 pounds to the winner) and was unplaced in Greek Star's Trenton Handicap.

First Landing returned as a four-year-old to add four wins, three of them hundred-granders, to his account. As a $10,000 supplementary nominee, he won the Santa Anita Maturity from Bagdad and Linmold; he won the Laurel Maturity from On-and-On and Nimmer in new track record time of 1:49⅖ for 9 furlongs; and the Monmouth Handicap from Manassa Mauler and Talent Show. He retired to stud with 19 wins from 37 starts and $779,577—having increased the sum earned by the produce of his dam to an astounding $1,744,-654.

SWORD DANCER, 1956
(Sunglow–Highland Fling, by By Jimminy)

Bred by his owner, Mrs. Isabel Dodge Sloane, at her Brookmeade Farm in Upperville, Virginia, Sword Dancer was trained by Elliott Burch, who had taken over the racing string from his father, Preston.

The smallish chestnut colt (he eventually grew to a medium 15-3) was eligible for eight maiden races as a two-year-old and attracted no particular attention until autumn, when he won the Mayflower Stakes at Suffolk Downs on October 18, beating Atoll by four and a half lengths over a mile and 70 yards. That race—his only juvenile stakes victory—was followed by a third in First Landing's Garden State and a fourth in Atoll's Remsen, but there was something about the way the smooth-running colt handled these $1\frac{1}{16}$-mile assignments that promised better things to come. He was ranked fifth on the Experimental Free Handicap at 122 pounds, above a few colts whose records looked better than his three wins and $60,351. (Llangollen Farm's Restless Wind, for example, ranked 2 pounds below Sword Dancer, had won seven races and $281,298—including the National Stallion, Tremont, Prairie State Stakes and Arlington and Washington Park Futurities.)

Except for the fact that not much was expected of him to begin with, the experiences of Sword Dancer as a three-year-old, up to and including the Preakness, were as frustrating as those of First Landing. He was unplaced in Easy Spur's Hutcheson Stakes, won an allowance race, then was defeated by Easy Spur again in the $1\frac{1}{8}$-mile Florida Derby, which the son of Crowfoot, owned by Spring Hill Farm, won in 1:47⅕. Sword Dancer next defeated Easy Spur in the Stepping Stone Purse at Churchill Downs, covering the 7 furlongs under guidance of Bill Shoemaker in 1:22⅕—

just the fraction off the record—then lost a heartbreaker in a fantastic Kentucky Derby.

Shoemaker was on another colt this trip, having previously agreed to ride Tomy Lee in the Kentucky Derby, and that was the difference. If Shoemaker threw away a Derby on Gallant Man in 1957, he squared his account at Churchill Downs in 1959 by literally manufacturing a victory aboard Tomy Lee, whose owners, Mr. and Mrs. Fred Turner, Jr., were from Midland, Texas, home town of Gallant Man's owner, Ralph Lowe.

Having disposed of Troilus in a speed duel, Tomy Lee was in front rounding the turn for home, as Sword Dancer, ridden by Bill Boland, challenged along the outside. Although Tomy Lee carried him wide, the Brookmeade colt nevertheless drove to the front, and, as his rival went past, Shoemaker called out to Boland, "Good luck, I hope you win it."

Indeed, it did appear that Tomy Lee was ready to chuck the proceedings, as Sword Dancer entered the stretch half a length on top, but the Turner colt came again. By mid-stretch the margin had been cut to a head, and right on the wire Tomy Lee got his nose in front. During the stretch drive the colts had made contact several times as Tomy Lee, under left-handed whipping, drifted out, and Sword Dancer, under right-handed punishment, came in. However, a claim of foul lodged by Boland was not upheld, after 17 minutes of deliberation by the stewards.

First Landing was two and a quarter lengths behind the top pair in third place, and the longshot Royal Orbit, making a bold bid in the late stages, during which he gained more than five lengths, came from eighth place at the quarter pole to be fourth at the end.

Since Tomy Lee did not care for his races too close together, trainer Frank Childs announced that the colt would pass up the remaining classics, so the Preakness on May 16, raised to $150,000 in added value that year, looked to be a gift for Sword Dancer, provided he could again handle First Landing. He had no trouble

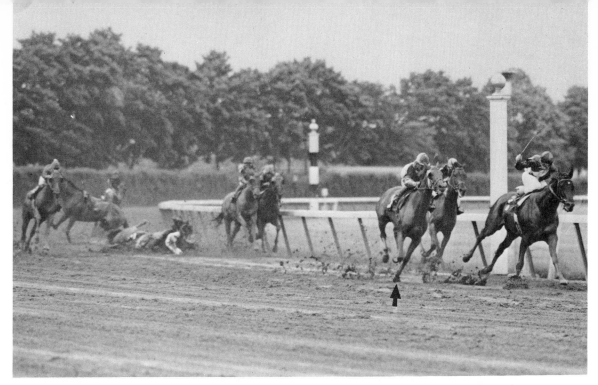

Black Hills tumbles in the 1959 Belmont Stakes as Sword Dancer (arrow) goes on to win.

on that score, but Mrs. Halina Braunstein's Royal Orbit, ridden by Bill Harmatz, roared up in the stretch to win easily by four lengths going away, with Sword Dancer a clear second, by three lengths over Dunce. The result also was a promise made good by Royal Orbit's trainer, Reggie Cornell, who had cheerfully borne the taunts that followed Silky Sullivan's Preakness loss the year before, but had vowed to come back to Pimlico someday with a winner.

Memorial Day, 1959, was a memorable occasion for Sword Dancer. The colt who up to this point had been unable to win a stakes event from his contemporaries, on May 30 easily defeated a field of older horses in the Metropolitan Handicap by three and a quarter lengths in 1:35⅕ for the mile. Under 114 pounds, the highest weight ever successfully carried by a three-year-old in this historic event, Sword Dancer was conceding from 6 to 23 pounds to his rivals according to the scale, and was giving away actual weight to most of them, including runner-up Jimmer (112). Increased to $100,-000 added value that season, the Metropolitan drew most of the Eastern handicap horses of consequence in training.

Back in his own division June 13 for the Belmont Stakes (boosted in added value to $125,000 in 1959) the Brookmeade colt en-countered unexpected opposition from H. B. Keck's Bagdad, but Sword Dancer outgamed the son of Double Jay in a long drive to win by three-fourths of a length in 2:28⅖, as Royal Orbit was twelve lengths farther back on the sloppy track. King Ranch's well-regarded Black Hills, who, following the path successfully pursued by High Gun, Gallant Man and Cavan, came up to the race off a victory in the Peter Pan Handicap, was making a good move in the Belmont, but fell after he reached third place. The colt had to be destroyed, and jockey Eddie Arcaro was grounded for six weeks by injuries. Lake Erie, the longshot in the race, stumbled over Black Hills and also fell, but neither he nor jockey Walter Blum were injured. (Arcaro was saved from more serious injury by the Caliente safety helmet, which, after being introduced at the Mexican track by President John Alessio, had been adopted as mandatory equipment at other tracks.)

Going against his seniors for the second time, Sword Dancer next won the 1¼-mile Monmouth Handicap—his third hundred-grander in a row—by two lengths in 2:05 over a slow track; the 120 pounds he carried was by far the highest weight ever packed by a three-year-old winner of that event, 4 pounds over the scale.

This amount represented a 14-pound concession to the runner-up, Amerigo (116).

An attempt at another notable feat a week later in the Brooklyn Handicap (which also had been upped to $100,000), for which Sword Dancer was assigned actual top weight of 124 pounds, resulted in a loss by three-quarters of a length to W. C. Partee's five-year-old Babu (112), who was receiving 19 pounds according to the scale of weights for 1$\frac{3}{16}$ miles in August.

Sword Dancer never conquered his fellow three-year-olds as emphatically as he did older horses, and in the Travers on August 22, Middle Brother, enjoying a 14-pound pull in the weights, finished within half a length of him, although the Brookmeade runner was going away at the finish of the 1¼ miles.

There followed the Woodward Stakes in September, in which Sword Dancer met Hillsdale and Round Table at weight-for-age with the Horse of the Year title at stake. He won it by a head from Hillsdale, and then scored another victory over Round Table at weight-for-age by seven lengths in the 2-mile Jockey Club Gold Cup on October 31.

A unanimous selection as champion three-year-old and 1959 Horse of the Year, Sword Dancer also was voted best handicap horse in the Triangle poll. His earnings of $537,004 were tops for the season.

As a four-year-old, the deep-chested little red colt carried his weight adequately, but anything above the scale for a mature horse was enough to stop him. However, he did win four of his twelve starts, and both his stakes were $100,000 events. He set a new track record at new Aqueduct of 2:01⅗ in the 1¼-mile Suburban Handicap under 125 pounds, defeating First Landing (122), Waltz (115) and Bald Eagle (133). He also became the first two-time winner of the Woodward Stakes, beating Dotted Swiss, Bald Eagle, Tompion, T. V. Lark and others at weight-for-age in the 1960 renewal, and lowering his own track record by ⅖-second in the process. Sword Dancer was second to Bald Eagle in the voting for the

handicap championship of 1960, and he retired to stud with 15 wins in 39 starts and $829,610.

TOMY LEE, 1956
(Tudor Minstrel–Auld Alliance, by Brantome)

Tomy Lee was one of the fastest-looking horses ever to appear on the American turf. Standing still, he exuded an aura of extreme speed. Sixteen hands and a bit over 1,000 pounds, he appeared taller and lighter because of his rangy, streamlined physique. His lines were refined, his bone light and his barrel so tapered as to give him the over-all aspect of a greyhound.

The beautiful bay with four white feet did not belie his appearance in action, for he was runner-up in the championship voting both as a two-year-old and at three. The English-bred colt was acquired by owner Fred Turner, Jr. as something of an afterthought. The Texan had instructed Irish bloodstock agent Bert Kerr to purchase for him at any reasonable price a weanling son of the famous Tulyar, which was done for $25,000. Solitary environment is no better for horses than it is for people, so Turner had Kerr buy a son of Tudor Minstrel primarily as a companion to his first colt; Tomy Lee cost $6,762.

The Tulyar colt, later named Tuleg, was unable to race at two because of injury, and earned $17,250 at three before a bowed tendon led to permanent retirement. Tomy Lee earned $377,117 in his first two seasons of racing. (The name had no special significance; Turner merely liked the sound of "Tommy Lee," but was afraid such a prosaic name already would have been taken, so he deleted an "m" in his application.)

The jousts with First Landing, in both of which he was closing ground at the end, were Tomy Lee's only losses as a two-year-old. Before being shipped to the East he had been undefeated in six starts in California, including the Haggin Stakes by eight lengths (beating Jungle Dancer and American Comet), the C. S.

Tomy Lee with Bill Shoemaker up leaving the paddock for the Blue Grass Stakes.

Howard, Starlet Stakes (beating Finnegan by two and three-quarters lengths) and Del Mar Futurity by three lengths in 1:09⅕ for 6 furlongs, defeating Royal Orbit and Bagdad.

As a three-year-old, Tomy Lee's pattern was just the opposite. He was second in both his early starts in California, to Ole Fols in the San Vicente and to Finnegan in the San Felipe, but was undefeated east of the Rockies. Before his memorable Derby victory he had set a new track record of 1:21⅗ for 7 furlongs in an allowance race at Keeneland, and won the Blue Grass Stakes from Dunce and Scotland.

The colt's unplaced finish in Silver Spoon's Cinema Handicap after his return to California created some unpleasantness, as Turner had entered him only with reluctance when it developed that Shoemaker could not ride because of a commitment to guide Sword Dancer in the Belmont Stakes. According to his owner, the finely tuned Tomy Lee required special handling, which Don Pierce, accomplished rider though he was, could not provide because of lack of familiarity with the colt. In anger, directed more at Shoemaker's agent, Harry Silbert, than at the jockey, Turner took Tomy Lee out of training for more than six months.

Two days before the end of the year, ridden by Johnny Longden, Tomy Lee returned to action with a sharp victory at 6 furlongs in 1:09⅕. Early during his four-year-old season he was unplaced in the San Carlos Handicap and Santa Anita Maturity, then retired to stud at L. P. Doherty's Stallion Station in Kentucky.

Tomy Lee proved to be a shy breeder—not from the usual reasons of disinterest or impotence, but through some unexplained physiological condition. His sperm was adequate in quantity, but did not survive long enough after release to be sufficiently effective to warrant his continued service as a stallion, although he did sire a few foals.

In the hope that the condition might disappear as mysteriously as it had developed, the horse was put back into training as a six-year old in 1962. That year and the next, he won four more races, none of them stakes, and Tomy Lee then returned to stud, having won a total of 14 races and $405,014.

INTENTIONALLY, 1956
(Intent–My Recipe, by Discovery)

Although there were only two seasons during which the colts of 1956 won championships, there were three such champions, since Brookfield Farm's home-bred Intentionally, trained by E. I. Kelly, was elected best sprinter of 1959, when Sword Dancer was the over-all leader.

The "Black Bullet" was of sprinting physique and staying blood—his sire had won two renewals of the marathon San Juan Capistrano Handicap, and his dam was a daughter of Discovery, which ordinarily is enough said on the score of stamina. Prior to his victory over First Landing in the 6½-furlong Futurity as a two-year-old, Intentionally had won the 5½-furlong Tyro Stakes, and he ended his juvenile campaign with a victory in the 1¹⁄₁₆-mile Pimlico Futurity, which is as far as thoroughbreds are required to travel in their first year of racing in the United States.

At three, the Brookfield colt never failed to bring back part of the purse in nine starts, of which he won five, including the 6-furlong Delaware Valley Stakes and three added money events at 1 mile: the Withers, Warren Wright Memorial Stakes and Jerome Handicap (beating Atoll by ten lengths). In the Wright Memorial at Washington Park on June 27, 1959, Intentionally carried 121 pounds to win by two and a quarter lengths from On-and-On in 1:33⅕, equaling Swaps' world record for the distance. The race was restricted to three-year-olds, so the scale of weights did not apply, technically, but Intentionally's burden was the equivalent of 132 pounds on an older horse, and this victory led to his being honored as champion sprinter of the season.

In only four starts as a four-year-old, Intentionally won the 6-furlong Toboggan under 128 pounds, conceding 6 to the formidable sprinter, Rick City, and nosed out Dunce in the Equipoise Mile, won in 1:34⅖, while carrying 126 pounds to 121 on his rival. At five, Intentionally won four of his seven starts, including the Quaker City Handicap at 1⅛ miles—his first victory at so long a distance—and the 6-furlong Sport Page Handicap under 129 pounds. He attempted 1¼ miles in the Trenton Handicap, was leading, but Carry Back caught him at the end to win by half a length.

During 1961, Intentionally had been syndicated for future stud duty, and his three starts early in 1962 were in the colors of William L. McKnight's Tartan Stable, whose trainer was John Nerud. After losing his debut over the turf course at Hialeah, Intentionally came back to win the 7-furlong Palm Beach Handicap under top weight of 126 pounds, and the 1⅛-mile Seminole Handicap (formerly McLennan) by eight lengths from Carry Back. A stakes winner during each of five successive seasons, Intentionally retired to stud with 18 wins in 34 starts, and $652,259.

Among other members of the 1956 crop, Claiborne Farm's Dunce, a son of Tom Fool, was a star on the Midwest circuit, winner of the Arlington Classic and American Derby at three and the Stars and Stripes Handicap on the turf at four. Arnold Hanger's Waltz, by Turn-to out of Harmonica, was effective on the eastern seaboard with victories in the Jersey, Leonard Richards Stakes and Dwyer Handicap at three, and the Olympic and Boardwalk Handicaps at four.

Because of his breeding, a great deal was expected of Calumet Farm's On-and-On, a son of Nasrullah and Two Lea, and although he did not quite live up to those high expectations, the half-brother to Tim Tam performed well enough to satisfy any reasonable standard. The bay colt won a dozen races and 390,718, including the Sheridan Stakes (new track record of 1:08⅗ for 6 furlongs at Washington Park) and Ohio Derby at three; and the Tropical Park (new track record of 1:46⅗ for 1⅛ miles), Orange Bowl, McLennan, Brooklyn and Arch Ward Memorial Handicaps at four.

C. V. Whitney's Dotted Swiss, a son of Counterpoint, waited until he was four years old to gain prominence, but during the 1960 season he won the Hollywood Gold Cup (by four lengths in 1:59⅖ for 1¼ miles), Sunset, Laurance Armour Memorial and Cortez Handicaps (1¼ miles in 1:59⅘). C. W. Smith's American Comet, a gelding by Free America

540

who once had run in claiming races, also came on strong when he reached handicap age, winning the Santa Catalina, San Antonio, Arch Ward Memorial, Arcadia and Michigan Mile and One-Sixteenth Handicaps among others.

The domestic foals were joined in later seasons by several good imported runners, among them Don Poggio and Wolfram. An Argentine-bred son of Los Curros, owned by Gustave Ring, Don Poggio was an excellent stayer, winner of the Gallant Fox and Merchants' and Citizens' Handicaps at 1¾ miles, the 1½-mile Manhattan Handicap and the 1¼-mile Monmouth Handicap. The French-bred Wolfram, a son of Fast Fox, imported by Major Albert Warner and then sold to Louis Wolfson's Harbor View Farm, was a specialist at grass racing. He won the New York, Hialeah Turf Cup, Bougainvillea Turf, Arcardia, Clyde Park, Edgemere and Sheepshead Bay Handicaps.

Mrs. Edith Price's Yes You Will, a son of Rough 'n Tumble, bred by his owner and raised in her backyard across the street from the Timonium, Maryland, race track, developed into a frequent stakes winner, and scored his biggest triumph in Maryland's John B. Campbell Memorial Handicap.

CHAPTER SIXTY-EIGHT

HE CROP OF THOROUGHBREDS foaled in 1957 produced the first horse since the origination of formal titles to be acknowledged champion of America for four successive seasons, but he delayed his appearance until other members of the generation made their marks.

The booming Florida breeding industry received an added boost in 1959 as Mrs. Frances Genter's My Dear Girl came out of Ocala, birthplace of Needles and King Hairan, to run off with the juvenile filly championship. Trained by ex-jockey Melvin "Sunshine" Calvert, who also had saddled her sire, Rough 'n Tumble, to win the Santa Anita Derby, the chestnut filly won five of her seven starts at two and was narrowly beaten in another, to earn $185,622 in her first season of racing.

Her introduction to competition, in a 3-furlong cavalry charge through the Hialeah stretch in February won by Niequest, was My Dear Girl's only unplaced effort. The Genter filly came back to win the Florida Breeders' Stakes, a race confined to horses foaled in the state. Then she scored one in open competition by setting a new track record of 1:03⅕ for 5½ furlongs at Washington Park. Claiborne Farm's Monarchy, a full sister to Round Table, beat her by a neck in the Arlington Lassie on July 22, following which My Dear Girl was put aside because of bucked shins.

All three of her starts after her return to competition in October were over sloppy tracks, but the speedy filly was not bothered noticeably by such conditions. She won an allowance race at Aqueduct by five lengths from Sunset Glow; took the Gardenia Stakes by a similar margin from Blue Crooner, Heavenly Body and Irish Jay; and closed out her campaign with a thrilling performance in the Frizette Stakes, during which Irish Jay wrested the lead from the Florida filly, but My Dear Girl came again to win by a nose.

Wheatley Stable's Irish Jay, runner-up in the championship polls, also won five races at two and never failed to earn part of the purse in eight starts, her fourth in the Gardenia having been the only time she was not either first or second. The lanky daughter of Double Jay, with feet that went flying in all directions, was so devastating in her debut, which she won by fifteen lengths in new track record time of :58 for 5 furlongs at Belmont Park, that she frightened away all but three opponents for her second start, the Fashion Stakes on May 27. Irish Jay won the Fashion by six lengths from the good filly, Rose of Serro, in :58⅘, which had been the track record before she broke it in her maiden race. The Wheatley speedster bucked shins in the Fashion, and was rested until Saratoga.

At the upstate New York spa, Irish Jay won a division of the Schuylerville Stakes by three-quarters of a length from Heavenly Body, then was second by the same margin to Natalma in the Spinaway, but was awarded the victory when Natalma was disqualified for having interfered with the third finisher, Warlike. After returning to Belmont Park, Irish Jay was officially defeated; beginning sluggishly in the Matron Stakes, she picked up ground for a time, but was not pushed when it became apparent she could never catch Heavenly Body, who crossed the wire eight lengths clear. In her next start, Irish Jay won the Demoiselle Stakes by a neck from Rash Statement, following which came her two losses to My Dear Girl.

Cain Hoy Stable's Heavenly Body, by Dark Star, prior to her Matron victory had invaded Chicago for its top filly events. She finished a close third in Monarchy's Lassie, and then won the Princess Pat from Pierpontella, Rash Statement, Blue Crooner, Airmans Guide and Monarchy. That was the only defeat all season administered to Hugh Grant's Airmans Guide, who won her five other starts by open daylight, including the Churchill Downs Debutante Stakes, a 6½-furlong allowance race at Keeneland in 1:16⅖, equaling the track record, and the 1¹⁄₁₆-mile Marguerite Stakes at Pimlico.

Overlooked among the stakes winners during their two-year-old season was Foxcatcher Farm's Berlo, who ran third and then won in a brief campaign of two starts, but the next year she was the sophomore leader of her crop. Like her predecessor Parlo, she was a daughter of Heliopolis, but the similarity ended there—in contrast to Parlo, Berlo was a big, rugged brown, standing 16 hands 2 inches, and girthing 74½ inches. She preserved her record of never failing to earn money by winning seven of her nine starts at three, and getting a third and fourth in the others, for winnings of $198,446.

Beginning her campaign with a pair of allowance wins at 6 furlongs, William du Pont, Jr.'s filly next won her first start in added money company, the 1⅛-mile Mother Goose Stakes, by three and a half lengths, following which she took the 1¼-mile Coaching Club American Oaks by three-quarters of a length from Sarcastic and Rash Statement. In the Delaware Oaks on July 16, the order was rearranged as Rash Statement won from Sarcastic, with Berlo third, two lengths behind the winner. A week later, the Foxcatcher filly finished fourth in the Monmouth Oaks—behind Teacation, Refute and Rash Statement—and that was her last defeat of the year.

An easy victory over her contemporaries in a division of the Gazelle Handicap (Teacation and Refute unplaced) followed by a two-length conquest of the older handicap champion, Royal Native, at weight-for-age in the Beldame Stakes, led to an assignment of 124 pounds for the 1½-mile Ladies Handicap. Conceding actual weight to all her rivals, in her first experience over such a long route, Berlo won easily from six-year-old Woodlawn (112), with Shirley Jones, Sarcastic, Geechee Lou and Tempted in the beaten field.

The field for the 1960 Washington, D.C. International breaking from the Newmarket tape.

It was a good year for big fillies, as the runner-up to Berlo in the voting for the sophomore championship was Hal Price Headley's powerfully built Rash Statement (16-1, 1,100 pounds), a daughter of Ambiorix, who won the Kentucky Oaks Prep and Spinster Stakes, besides her upset over Berlo in the Delaware Oaks. Her first stakes victory, as a two-year-old, had come in Keeneland's Alcibiades Stakes, a race named for her granddam, who also had been owned by Headley, and it represented the 100th race won by the noted horseman at the pastoral track (which he had helped to found).

Cain Hoy Stable's Make Sail, also by Ambiorix, was victorious in the Kentucky Oaks and Alabama Stakes. Besides her conquest of Berlo in the Monmouth Oaks, Fred Hooper's Teacation, by Quibu, won a division of the Margate and the Pageant Handicap; Ogden Phipps's Sarcastic, another daughter of Ambiorix, won a division of the Gazelle; and J. M. Roebling's English-bred Be Cautious won the Betsy Ross Stakes and a division of the Test.

The Corradini Brothers and George Dorney's Linita, by Indian Hemp, who had won the Cinderella Stakes as a two-year-old, continued what was to be an impressive string of stakes on the West Coast by taking the 1960 Del Mar Oaks and Las Flores Handicap. Bieber–Jacobs Stable's active Sister Antoine finished in the money 22 times in 33 starts at three, including among her nine victories the Gallorette Stakes.

Irish Jay was back on the scene with wins in the Comely and Acorn Stakes; My Dear Girl won a pair of overnight races and placed in added money events; and Airmans Guide, making only four starts before a knee injury put her out of action, won the Black-Eyed Susan and had two seconds and a third in other stakes. She took over the leadership the following season.

A huge (16-2), muscular daughter of One Count–Navigating, by Hard Tack, who looked more like a colt than a filly, Airmans Guide had not been far from the top of her division at two and three, despite sparse activity. As a four-year-old, after recovering from an unusual operation in which a bone chip was removed from her knee, she took over the leadership with a brilliant campaign of seven wins in ten starts for earnings of $239,551. She was trained by veteran B. B. "Bert" Williams, who seemed to have exceptional success with fillies, his long line of distaff stars having included Nellie Flag.

Beginning with a four-and-a-half-length win in an allowance race at Gulfstream Park in March, Airmans Guide followed with a victory over Shirley Jones and Indian Maid in new track record time of 1:22⅖ in the 7-furlong Suwannee River Handicap. After a six-week layoff, she was third, beaten a head for it all, to Staretta and Coup d'etat in the Colonial Handicap. A month later Airmans Guide came back to win the 6-furlong Regret Handicap in 1:09⅘ from Craftiness and Staretta, with Shirley Jones and Coup d'etat in the conquered field. In the Molly Pitcher Handicap July 8, won by Shirley Jones, Airmans Guide turned in one of her rare poor efforts to finish tenth, the second time in her life she failed to get part of the purse.

Howard Grant, no relation to the filly's owner, Hugh Grant, then became regular jockey for Airmans Guide, and together they won four straight. The daughter of One Count took both portions of the distaff Big Three for which she was eligible, winning the New Castle Stakes by six lengths and the Delaware Handicap (from Royal Native) by three and a half; under the system of bonuses that applied, besides a winner's purse of $104,687.50, she earned a double award of $5,000 for her nominator (in this case, her owner) and a similar award for her breeder, W. P. Little.

The big filly next won the Beldame Stakes at weight for age from Craftiness and Primonetta, and set a new track record of 1:25 for the Beard Course of 7 furlongs and 184 feet at Keeneland in a prep race for the Spinster. She finished fourth in the stakes, however, which was run on a sloppy track, as a trio of three-

544

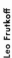

Bally Ache with Bob Ussery up going out for the Bahamas Stakes.

year-olds—Bowl of Flowers, Primonetta and Times Two—monopolized the race. Airmans Guide was sold back to her breeder after the Spinster, and she retired to stud with 13 wins from 20 starts, and $315,673.

Among Airmans Guide's contemporaries, Berlo had a frustrating experience as a four-year-old, starting only three times and finishing fourth in each; Sarcastic added the Margate and Miss America Turf Handicaps (equalling the Atlantic City record of 1:48⅗ for 1⅛ miles) to her record; Teacation won the Distaff and Maskette Handicaps; Be Cautious took the Black Helen and Sister Antoine the Santa Margarita. Linita kept going longest of all. At a four-year-old she won the Romona and Sequoia Handicaps; she was back at five to win the Milady and Vanity Handicaps; and as a six-year-old in 1963 she took the Santa Maria Handicap and another Sequoia.

Kelso, the king of the 1957 crop, did not come to public attention until his second season of racing was more than halfway gone. The colt from this crop who first attracted attention was of a different kind.

BALLY ACHE, 1957
(Ballydam–Celestial Blue, by Supremus)

Bred for sprinting and built for sprinting, Bally Ache was indeed a sprinter, but he had the classic courage that enabled him to overcome the apparent limitation of his style. His legs would scissor back and forth like high-speed clippers while his opponents seemed to take one stride to his two, but Bally Ache maintained his all-out effort every step of the way as far as he could, which was surprisingly far.

Bred by Marvin and Alan Gaines of Walton, Kentucky, Bally Ache was sold as a yearling in a package deal along with another colt for a total cost of $5,000 to a Toledo steel-mill operator, Leonard D. Fruchtman, who later assumed the stable name, Edgehill Farm. The handsome, brisk-looking bay—16 hands but seemingly taller because he was quite short-backed—was turned over to trainer H. J. "Jimmy" Pitt, who had saddled many winners in claiming company, but never a major stakes victor. Pitt was quick to recognize the windfall that had come his way. While the colt still was a yearling, he proposed that Bally Ache (the name was a tongue-in-cheek last choice on a list of several suggestions) be nominated to some of the early closing stakes. Fruchtman preferred to wait a while, a decision that cost him $60,000 in supplementary fees. However, Bally Ache more than won them back.

Bally Ache made his debut at Hialeah on February 19 in that same 3-furlong race in which My Dear Girl began her career with a tenth-place finish. Closing ground fast, Bally Ache could get up only to sixth place, although he was less than two lengths behind the winner, and never again in his career did he fail to get a purse award.

For a time, however, it appeared that he was just a sprinter, for as a two-year-old he could not win beyond 5½ furlongs.

Bally Ache's first victory was in the Hialeah Juvenile Stakes in March; in April, he set a new track record of :57⅘ for 5 furlongs at Jamaica and in May he won the Comely Stakes at the same distance. Later that month he was second to Vital Force in the Cherry Hill Stakes at Garden State Park. Bally Ache then returned to New York in June to win the Belmont Juvenile Stakes from Ouija Board in :58⅖, equaling the track record. At Suffolk Downs, he won the 5½-furlong Mayflower Stakes; at Belmont, Bally Ache was third to Vital Force and Ouija Board in the Tremont at the same distance, after running away before the start; and on July 18 he beat Vital Force in the Great American Stakes, Bally Ache's last victory of the season.

There followed the most frustrating, and expensive, sequence of races ever undergone by any thoroughbred; in four successive $100,000 races, for each of which his owner had paid a supplementary fee ranging from $5,000 to $7,500, Bally Ache was second in a photo finish. His camera costs during this skein amounted to a difference of $284,000 between first and second money, and he lost the four races by a total margin of about one length.

C R Mac Stable's T. V. Lark beat Bally

Ache by a neck in the 6-furlong Arlington Futurity; William G. Helis, Jr.'s Sky Clipper beat him a head in the Sapling Stakes at Monmouth; Sunny Blue Farm's Venetian Way defeated him by half a length in the 6½-furlong Washington Park Futurity, won in track record time of 1:15⅘; and Kennedy-Veale Stable's Vital Force (trained by the stable's attractive owner, Mrs. D. J. Kennedy) won over Bally Ache by a neck in the 7-furlong World's Playground Stakes at Atlantic City.

In 1959 tracks throughout America scheduled heavily endowed events for juveniles patterned after the Garden State Stakes. The Sapling and World's Playground Stakes, in which Bally Ache ran second, gave New Jersey a Golden Triangle of three races for two-year-olds, each at $100,000 or more in gross purse value. The two big Chicago futurities, which had been grossing more than that amount for years, were increased to $100,000 added value —i.e., contributed by the track, in addition to stakes put up by the owners—which made their gross purses hover near $200,000. Hollywood Park revamped the former Starlet Stakes into the $100,000-added Juvenile Championship, which was won by Dr. and Mrs. J. R. Smith's Noble Noor.

Since each of them had been won by a different colt, far from having served to winnow the season's two-year-olds, these enormously rich races had thrown the standings into chaos, until Warfare moved in to straighten things out.

A son of Determine–War Whisk, by War Glory, Warfare was bred by C. H. Jones & Sons, and was purchased for $12,000 early in his two-year-old season by one of the sons, Clifton Jones, at a dispersal of the ranch stock. The handsome colt, who inherited his sire's gray color but was bigger (16 hands, 1,090 pounds), raced in the name of Bellehurst Stable and was trained by Hack Ross.

In his native state he was good but not sensational, winning three races in eleven starts, including the 5½-furlong C. S. Howard Stakes. However, he showed considerably more than the statistics indicate, for, unlike Bally Ache, Warfare's difficulty was insufficient distance. He closed more than two lengths in the stretch drive of the Hollywood Juvenile Championship Stakes to finish third to Noble Noor and Tompion; he subsequently defeated Noble Noor in an allowance race; and he made up nearly seven lengths in the stretch of the 6-furlong Del Mar Futurity, to finish third to Azure's Orphan and Salatom, less than a length behind the winner. After moving east, Warfare was second to the speedy Four Lane in a 6½-furlong overnight race, and beyond that distance the Bellehurst colt was undefeated during the season.

In October, Warfare won the $50,000-added Cowdin Stakes by two and a half lengths from Vital Force, Bally Ache and Tompion in new track record time of 1:22⅗ for 7 furlongs at Aqueduct; the $100,000-added Champagne Stakes from Tompion, Bally Ache and Four Lane in new track record time of 1:35⅕ for a mile at the same track; and the richest of them all, the Garden State Stakes, from Bally Ache, Tompion and Bourbon Prince, with T. V. Lark and Azure's Orphan among the also-rans. In the latter race Bally Ache, after being replaced on the lead, gamely came again to finish only half a length behind the winner of the 1 1/16-mile event, which was run over a sloppy track.

His conquests of Bally Ache and Tompion gave Warfare clear title to the juvenile championship.

C. V. Whitney's Tompion, a son of Tom Fool, had been the standard for his generation that season, racing on both coasts. He was also the best all-around juvenile at the Saratoga meeting, which by tradition was a significant determinant of two-year-old rankings. After narrow losses at 6 furlongs to Greentree Stable's Weatherwise in the Sanford Stakes and to Pebblebrook Farm's Irish Lancer (a full brother to Idun) in the Saratoga Special, Tompion had won the 6½-furlong Hopeful Stakes

from Vital Force, with Irish Lancer and Weatherwise (later winner of the Futurity) unplaced.

Warfare also topped his division in juvenile earnings with $394,610. Both he and Bally Ache were supplementary nominees to those final three rich races (at fees ranging up to $10,000 for the Garden State Stakes) and Bally Ache, who earned about twice as much during his string of seven losses as he had during the early part of the year, when he was a frequent winner, wound up the season with $303,477.

Elsewhere in the division, Venetian Way won the Prairie State Stakes besides the Washington Park Futurity, and Windfields Farm's Victoria Park won the Clarendon, Coronation Futurity Stakes and Cup and Saucer Handicap in Canada, plus the Remsen Stakes in the United States, defeating the Pimlico Futurity winner, Progressing, in the latter.

After finishing his introductory season on an exceptionally promising note, Warfare started only twice as a three-year-old. He finished second to T. V. Lark in an allowance race and beat Francis S. in the Swift Stakes, setting another new track record at Aqueduct, 6 furlongs in 1:09⅗, before an injury led to his retirement.

Bally Ache, ridden throughout the year by Bob Ussery, opened the season with a six-length victory over Francis S. (Venetian Way unplaced) in the Hibiscus Stakes at 6 furlongs, followed by a conquest of Moslem Chief in the 7-furlong Bahamas. In his first start beyond a sprint distance, however, Victoria Park was walking away from him at the end of 1 1/16 miles covered in 1:40⅗, nearly 2 full seconds faster than the previous Hialeah record, as Bally Ache faded to a two-and-a-half-length deficit. That was in a prep race for the Flamingo Stakes—but when the big money came on the line a week later, so did Bally Ache, who won the 1⅛-mile test by three and a quarter lengths from Victoria Park. At Gulfstream Park it was the same; Bally Ache lost the 1 1/16-mile Fountain of Youth Stakes to Eagle Admiral, but won the longer and richer Florida Derby by a nose from Venetian Way. It was an exciting contest, in which Bally Ache surrendered the lead to Venetian Way in the stretch, but came again to win, in 1:47⅗ for the 1⅛ miles.

At Churchill Downs it was a different story, as Bally Ache easily defeated Venetian Way in a 7-furlong prep, but the son of Royal Coinage, saddled by Vic Sovinski and ridden by Hartack, just as easily beat Bally Ache by three and a half lengths in the Kentucky Derby, both races being run on a good track. Victoria Park was a distant third in the Derby and the favorite, Tompion, who was coming off victories in the Santa Anita Derby and Blue Grass Stakes, finished fourth.

Bally Ache ran himself out of competition in Maryland, as he won the Preakness Prep from Divine Comedy and the Preakness from Victoria Park, each by four lengths, with Celtic Ash third in both events, and Venetian Way unplaced in the Baltimore classic.

Before the Preakness, Bally Ache had been sold for $1,250,000 to Turfland, a syndicate organized by Fruchtman, Joseph L. Arnold and R. A. Alexander III. For his new owners, the colt promptly added a hard fought victory over Tompion in the 9-furlong Jersey Derby, revived in 1960 at an added value of $100,000; Celtic Ash again finished third and Venetian Way was fourth.

His easy victory in the 1 3/16-mile Preakness had graduated Bally Ache from the ranks of the sprinters. He was considered a worthy candidate for the 1½-mile Belmont Stakes until he pulled up lame from a workout the day before the race. In his absence, Green Dunes Farm's Celtic Ash, an Irish-bred son of the French stallion, Sicambre, won easily by five and a half lengths from Venetian Way, to give owner Joseph O'Connell and trainer Tom Barry the unique satisfaction of having won this race with both colts they sent after it—the other one having been Cavan. Celtic

Ash (whose owner died less than a month later) did not start after his Belmont victory; he bowed a tendon in training and was retired to stud.

Bally Ache recovered from his injury and was back in action by September. He won two allowance races and was third to T. V. Lark and the older Sword Dancer in the United Nations Handicap, then was injured again—this time permanently—in an overnight handicap at Hawthorne on October 8, finishing fourth despite a shattered ankle. Almost simultaneously, the ill-starred colt developed an intestinal infection, and he died before the month was out. During his brief but active life, the $2,500 yearling had won 16 of 31 starts with nine seconds and four thirds, for earnings of $758,522, and at the time of his syndication had been insured for a million dollars.

Tompion later in the season added victories in the Bernard Baruch, Travers and Malibu Stakes; Victoria Park won the Queen's Plate and Leonard Richards Stakes to become the most successful Canadian horse thus far, with earnings of $250,076; Venetian Way added the Warren Wright Memorial Handicap to his tally; Llangollen Farm's Divine Comedy won the Saranac and Roamer Handicaps.

But it was T. V. Lark who caught fire. The rangy son of Indian Hemp, trained by Paul Parker, had won the Tropicana Hotel Handicap at Bay Meadows before being shipped to Pimlico, where he was unplaced in the Preakness Prep and Preakness. Thereafter, he traveled widely and scored handsomely. After a win in the Argonaut Stakes and two stakes placings at Hollywood Park, he won five races in a row, four of them hundred-granders: the Arlington Classic (beating Venetian Way), American Derby (equaling Round Table's track record of 1:47⅕ for 1⅛ miles), the Washington Park Handicap in 1:34⅕ for a mile and the U. N. Handicap.

In the course of his ramblings, T. V. Lark swapped decisions with such other good three-year-olds as Merrick Stable's John William (San

T.V. Lark and jockey John Longden after their victory in the 1961 Washington, D.C. International.

Vicente, Withers, Gotham), Ralph Lowe's New Policy (San Miguel, California Breeders' Champion, Cinema), C. M. Crawford, Jr.'s Flow Line (San Felipe, Will Rogers) and Miroar Stable's Tempestuous (Hollywood Derby) to net $395,900 for the year and rank second to Bally Ache in sophomore earnings. T. V. Lark's chief claim to fame, however, was that he was the only horse of any age that season to win a race from the champion of champions.

KELSO, 1957
(Your Host–Maid of Flight, by Count Fleet)

More than any other racing country, America has had its share of great geldings, one reason being the wide base and unusually well balanced structure of the sport as a whole, which provides if not absolute, at least reasonable equality of opportunity to all horses. Most foreign countries exclude geldings from classic races, and the classics are so overwhelming in value compared to other events, that without one or more such victories few race horses can aspire to the big money. For years, geldings were barred from some American classics—but never from all—and the modern trend has been away from such restrictions; besides, there always have been other events, to which geldings were eligible, that vied with the classics in value. Moreover, the handicap, for example, which in some nations has been such a despised form of racing that a horse has little chance of adding to his stature (or finances) after his fourth birthday, traditionally has occupied an important place on the American calendar. Since geldings race on and on, without ultimate stud duty being a factor in their retirement, many of them have been able to compile remarkable records.

Throughout the history of the American

549

turf the names of famous geldings have re-sounded—from Leviathan and Walk-in-the-Water; through such famed performers as Parole, Raceland, Roseben, Roamer, Exterminator, Sarazen and Osmand; to such names of modern times as Armed, Social Outcast, Find and, the most successful gelding of them all, Kelso.

Flying the gray and yellow silks of Bohemia Stable, for four successive seasons Kelso was elected Horse of the Year, and in each of these years he took a great step toward the championship by winning the Jockey Club Gold Cup, 2 miles at weight-for-age, and one of the events from which geldings formerly were excluded.

Foaled at Claiborne Farm in Paris, Kentucky, Kelso was bred by his owner, Mrs. Richard C. duPont, who maintained Woodstock Farm in northern Maryland, near the Delaware line. Widow of a glider pilot who had been decorated for leading a night invasion of Sicily during World War II, and later was killed in a test flight. Mrs. duPont herself had been an accomplished pilot; the sports-woman also was Master of Fox Hounds of the Vicmead Hunt, and her daughter, Lana, was a champion performer in "three day event" riding. The owner of Kelso once said that the mating which produced the champion was based on one part scientific matching of blood-lines and two parts faith in the courageous stallion, Your Host, in whose syndicate she was a shareholder. (As it happened, Your Host suffered another injury the year after his son first attained prominence, and was destroyed.)

There was little about Kelso's appearance as a young horse to suggest his eventual status as a king of the turf. As a three-year-old he was a rather plain-looking dark bay or brown (as is true of a number of horses, Kelso's exact color was so difficult to pinpoint he was registered with an alternative description) with a thin neck sticking out of a none-too-copious torso. He continued to grow and develop, however, until as a five-year-old he stood a shade over 16 hands and girthed 73 inches. Ex-ceptionally wide across the hips, up front he had long, smooth muscles of a stayer, and, all in all, a hard, deer-like aspect. Although he looked resilient as a buggy whip, he had a trick stifle, and had to be campaigned carefully.

As a two-year-old the future champion put in only a brief appearance, starting three times in September at the Atlantic City meeting, when he was trained by Dr. John Lee. He won a maiden race in his debut, then finished second in his other two outings before being put aside until the next season.

In his three-year-old year, trained by ex-jockey Carl Hanford, Kelso did not come out until the Triple Crown events had been decided. He first started on June 22 at Mon-mouth, where he won a 6-furlong allowance race in 1:10 by ten lengths. He then displayed more speed at Aqueduct, winning by twelve lengths and covering a mile in 1:34⅕.

A trip to Chicago for the Arlington Classic resulted in Kelso's only defeat of the year, as he was eighth in the race won by T. V. Lark from John William and Venetian Way. Thereafter, the Bohemia gelding won six straight stakes.

Ridden by Eddie Arcaro, he won the Choice Stakes by seven lengths, the Jerome Handicap by a head and the Discovery Handicap by one and a quarter lengths in new track record time of 1:48⅖ at Aqueduct, as Louis Lee Hag-gin II's Careless John was runner-up on each occasion. Since Aqueduct still was undergoing its shakedown period, time records were broken there frequently in 1960, but in the Lawrence Realization next out, which he won by four and a half lengths from Tompion, Kelso equaled Man o' War's Belmont Park track record of 2:40⅖ for 1⅝ miles that had been standing for forty years.

He then took the Hawthorne Gold Cup by six lengths from Mrs. Mary Keim's Heroshogala with the four-year-old Calumet star, On-and-On, third and T. V. Lark among the unplaced; and next won the Jockey Club Gold Cup at Aqueduct by three and a half lengths from the good five-year-old stayer, Don Poggio, with

Kelso, champion for four successive seasons.

handicap champion Bald Eagle third, in new American record time of 3:19⅖. The track was sloppy, but Kelso's proud owner was only too happy to wade out to greet him. Mrs. du Pont was pleased to be welcoming back the Horse of the Year.

With eight wins in nine starts, for earnings of $296,690, Kelso was elected over-all champion in all polls. Kelso was the only three-year-old male since the championship polls were originated in 1936 to be voted Horse of the Year without having won at least one of the Triple Crown events for his age. However, the next year he won an even more difficult trio.

In 1961 Kelso extended the winning streak he had begun the preceding season to eleven races. Again opening his campaign relatively late, he won a 7-furlong allowance race on May 19, then picked up 130 pounds to win the Metropolitan Handicap by a neck from All Hands (117). In the Whitney Stakes on June 17, Kelso again carried 130 pounds, and although he finished a head behind Our Hope, to

whom he was conceding 19 pounds, that son of Uncle Miltie was disqualified for interference and Kelso awarded the victory. Upped to 133 pounds for the Suburban on July 4, the Bohemia Stable gelding won by five lengths from Nickel Boy, while spotting him 21 pounds. On July 22, carrying 136 pounds, he completed the sweep of New York's historic handicap races, winning the 1¼-mile Brooklyn Handicap by one and a quarter lengths from Divine Comedy (118) in 2:01⅗, only ⅖-second off the Aqueduct record set by Sword Dancer under 10 pounds less weight. Calumet Farm's Yorky, the sensation of the 1961 Florida season with victories in the Royal Palm, Mc-Lennan and Widener Handicaps, was third in Kelso's Brooklyn, carrying 122 pounds, and Our Hope (116) was unplaced.

"Kelly," as his admirers nicknamed him, had joined Whisk Broom II and Tom Fool in the most exclusive grouping of the American turf, winners of the Handicap Triple Crown. Their performances in summary are as follows:

	1913 Whisk Broom II Age 6		1953 Tom Fool Age 4		1961 Kelso Age 4	
	Weight	Time	Weight	Time	Weight	Time
Metropolitan Handicap, 1 mile inaugurated in 1891	126	1:39	130	1:35⅘	130	1:35⅗
Suburban Handicap, 1¼ miles inaugurated in 1884	139	2:00	128	2:00⅗	133	2:02
Brooklyn Handicap, 1¼ miles inaugurated in 1887	130	2:03⅖	136	2:04⅖	136	2:01⅗
Totals	395	5:42⅖	394	5:40⅘	399	5:39⅕

After resting more than a month following his great effort in the Brooklyn Handicap, Kelso made another trip to Chicago, scene of his only defeat as a three-year-old, and again he ran into difficulty. Carrying 132 pounds over a good track in the Washington Park Handicap (run at Arlington that year) and, according to the official chart, "showing a definite dislike for the going," he finished fourth to Chief of Chiefs, Talent Show and Run For Nurse, while conceding 20 pounds and up to the horses which outran him. (Kelso's conqueror of the previous season, T. V. Lark, was dead last every step of the way in this race, but the champion had not yet seen the last of him.)

Upon his return to New York, Kelso recouped with an easy, eight-length victory over Divine Comedy and the season's champion three-year-old Carry Back, in the Woodward Stakes at weight-for-age, covering the 1¼ miles in 2:00 flat, thus duplicating another of Whisk Broom II's epic feats.

While the long-disputed clocking had been supplanted as an American record, at other, faster tracks, for forty-eight years the doubt had persisted that 1¼ miles could be run that swiftly at Belmont Park. Kelso, who proved it could be done, was a great-great-great grandson of Whisk Broom II, and after his performance any number of observers were willing to throw in another couple of "greats" as descriptive, rather than genealogical adjectives.

He then scored his second victory in the Jockey Club Gold Cup, winning easily by five lengths from Hillsborough, before trying grass racing for the first time, in the Washington, D. C. International.

T. V. Lark meanwhile had come back strongly. Sold to a syndicate headed by Preston Madden, the tall (16-3) bay colt had won the Hawthorne Gold Cup and followed up with the Knickerbocker Handicap at Aqueduct in new American record time of 2:40 for 1⅝ miles on a turf course.

In the International at Laurel on November 11, Kelso and the Lark staged the most exciting duel of the season, running lapped on each other for almost the entire 1½ miles. Kelso set the pace for 1¼ miles, with T. V. Lark, ridden by Johnny Longden, in close attendance. Approaching the eighth pole, T. V. Lark drew alongside, took the lead, and slowly drew away to win by three-quarters of a length. The nearest pursuer was twelve lengths behind the American runners, and winner's time of 2:26⅕ completely shattered the former track record by 1⅘ seconds.

Kelly lost no face by his performance, and was a unanimous choice for a second term as Horse of the Year. (Oddly, he was undefeated during those two seasons except for races involving Arlington Park and/or T. V. Lark.) T. V. Lark, in his turn, was elected champion grass horse in the Triangle Publications' poll. The horse destined to replace Swaps as leading California-bred money winner of all time, with earnings of $902,194 by the time he retired the next year, won five stakes events in his native state, which was noted for its generous purses; however, none of T. V. Lark's California victories had been the big ones, yet he won seven $100,000 races elsewhere. Having been sold by his breeder, Dr. W. D. Lucas, for $10,000 at the Del Mar auctions, T. V. Lark also was the richest former sales yearling on record at the time of his retirement.

CARRY BACK, 1958
(Saggy–Joppy, by Star Blen)

Carry Back was one of the most exciting figures to appear on the American turf during the modern era, and what he lacked in verve and color—which certainly was very little—was more than adequately supplied by his gregarious, garrulous, irrepressible and witty breeder, trainer and co-owner, John A. "Jack" Price. A man of varied experience, at the age of forty-eight Price had retired from management of a family-owned machinery manufacturing company in Cleveland, Ohio, to take up

552

Carry Back (left) winning the Florida Derby from Crozier.

the race-track life. By his own statement, the stocky little man had "ruined about $200,000 worth of horses" in the process of learning his new profession. Price often spoke with tongue in cheek, and actually one of his earlier runners had been the good stakes winner, Stay Smoochie. As Carry Back became successful, Price delighted in shocking listeners by referring curtly to the colt, whose name was derived from an income-tax term, as nothing but a money-making machine. That he was, but Carry Back also blended the rough and ready, anything-goes toughness of Exterminator, with the casual confidence of Whirlaway (he, too, had a long tail that almost touched the ground) and the mysterious rapport with the public of Stymie or Silky Sullivan. The hardy "little" brown colt (he reached 15 hands 3 inchs as a three-year-old and had grown to 16-2 shortly after retirement) thrilled everyone who saw him in action, and Price was no exception.

Conceived in Maryland and foaled at Ocala Stud in Florida, Carry Back was bred for a $400 stud fee out of non-winning mare acquired by Price for $265 (part of it settlement of a past due board bill). However, there was nothing humble about the further removes of his pedigree, which included such names as Equipoise, Hyperion and Blenheim II in the third generation, and Teddy and Sir Gallahad III in the fourth. Also, while Saggy is best remembered as a lucky winner over Citation, he did boast other accomplishments, such as a world speed record, and, in any case, racing careers are one thing and stud careers another. Considering the relative quality of the mares in their books, at stud Saggy outshone Citation. (Saggy's fee, incidentally, was $750, but Price received a discount by breeding several mares to him.)

As a two-year-old, Carry Back demonstrated his amazing substance by starting twenty-one times, racing during every month of the year except December. The colt whose trademark was to be the delayed spurt was nevertheless quick enough to win a 3-furlong baby race; finish a fast-closing second to the speedster, Editorialist, in new track record time of :51⅗ for 4½ furlongs at Gulfstream Park; set a new track record of his own at the same track, going 5 furlongs in :57⅗; and finish lapped on Itsa Great Day in the Christiana Stakes at Delaware, won in new track record time of 1:04⅕ for 5½ furlongs. Carry Back was in the money in five other stakes at the more typical juvenile distances, but not until the 7-furlong Cowdin in October did he burst through to victory, defeating Globemaster (a half-brother to Nail who cost $80,000 as a Saratoga yearling and won back several times that sum) and Garwol. Subsequently, he won the Garden State Stakes at 1 1/16 miles, from Ambiopoise, and Guadalcanal and the Remsen at a mile, beating Vapor Whirl and Ambiopoise to wind up his two-year-old season with five wins and $286,299. The son of Saggy ran at times as the property of Dorchester Farm Stable (Price and his brothers) and on other occasions under the ownership of Mrs. Katherine Price, wife of the trainer. The colt's last two stakes victories were scored under the guidance of young John Sellers, a slim, handsome boy from Oklahoma, who was to be his regular pilot the following season and champion jockey of 1961.

In the 1960 championship polls, Carry Back was second to the top juvenile money winner, Hail to Reason, owned by young Patrice Jacobs, and trained by her father, Hirsch Jacobs. The son of Turn-to won nine of his eighteen starts and $328,434, including a maiden race at Aqueduct by nine lengths in new track record time of :58 1/5; the Youthful Stakes; Tremont by three lengths; Great American by two lengths, beating Bronzerullah and Carry Back; the Sanford by six lengths; the Sapling from He's a Pistol and Carry Back; the Hopeful by ten lengths in new track record time of 1:16 for 6 1/2 furlongs at Saratoga; and the World's Playground Stakes by four and a half lengths, beating Itsa Great Day, Ross Sea and Carry Back. Bob Ussery rode the champion in all the foregoing races.

In the only other encounter between the top two colts, the Tyro Stakes, won by Chinchilla, Carry Back finished third and Hail to Reason fifth. The Jacobs colt broke a sesamoid during a workout in September and was retired, to enter stud the next year as a three-year-old.

Carry Back, as a three-year-old, became the people's choice. He also was the leading money winner of 1961 with $565,349 from nine wins in sixteen starts, and a unanimous selection as champion of his age division.

His duels with Fred Hooper's Crozier (winner of the Prairie State Stakes and Washington Park Futurity at two, and the Hibiscus in his sophomore debut) during the first half of the season were the talk of the country. In Vapor Whirl's Bahamas Stakes, Crozier was second and Carry Back, facing the starter for the first time that season, was fourth; in the Everglades, Carry Back won and Crozier finished third, but was disqualified; and, in Beau Prince's Fountain of Youth, Crozier was second and Carry Back third. When the big money was at stake, however, they ran right to form. Crozier would take the lead, and Carry Back would storm from behind to nip him in the last strides. They put on their act in three $100,000 races, as Carry Back beat Crozier in the Flamingo Stakes and Florida Derby, each time by a head, and in the Kentucky Derby by three-quarters of a length.

Carry Back was hailed as another Needles following his triumph in the Kentucky Derby, which field included, besides Crozier, such other colts as Leonard P. Sasso's Globemaster, who had defeated Carry Back in the Wood Memorial, and Alberta Ranches' Santa Anita Derby winner, Four-and-Twenty. (Crozier had won the Derby Trial in new track record time of 1:34 3/5; and, later in the year, Globemaster won two other stakes, including the Arlington Classic; while "4-20," as the headline writers called him, won three more, including the Hollywood Derby.)

The comparison to Needles embraced the thought that, although Carry Back's late-running habit might cost him the Preakness, he was a sure thing for the longer 1 1/2-mile Belmont Stakes. Carry Back thereupon won the Preakness (by three-quarters of a length from Globemaster, with Crozier third) and finished seventh in the Belmont on June 3, for one of the most shocking upsets in the history of America's senior classic. Jacob Sher's Sherluck,

E. P. Taylor, colossus of the Canadian turf, accepts the 1962 Queen's Plate trophy (his seventh) from Queen Mother Elizabeth following the one hundred and third renewal of America's oldest stakes race.

Turfofsky

longest shot in the race at slightly more than 65-to-1, won by two and a quarter lengths from Globemaster, to register a record payoff of $132.10.

A son of Correspondent, trained by Harold Young, Sherluck had finished behind Carry Back in five encounters that year, and had won only one of ten starts before the Belmont. However, his earlier victory was an easy romp in the Blue Grass Stakes at Keeneland, and Belmont Park had been resurfaced by the same engineering firm which built the Keeneland track.

More important, for both the Blue Grass and the Belmont, Young had been able to borrow the services of Crozier's regular jockey, Braulio Baeza, the sphinx-like native of Panama, who, according to veteran *Daily Racing Form* chart-caller Don Fair did more for a horse than any

rider he had seen in a decade. What Baeza did for Sherluck in 1961 was win three stakes in four rides, while in thirteen starts under a miscellaneous assortment of other jockeys, the colt won just one race—the Roamer Handicap by a nose, when ridden by Bill Shoemaker.

Baeza; his fellow Panamanian, Manuel Ycaza, the fiery Cain Hoy Stable contract rider who set records in number of suspensions, but maintained a high standing despite his frequent enforced absences from competition; the Valenzuela brothers, Herberto Hinojosa, Heliodoro Gustinez, Rudolpho Campas, Sandino Hernandez and other riders of Latin American ancestry, reinforced by such veterans as Avelino Gomez, began to give the jockey standings a heavy Hispanic flavor. Lighter and, in general, "hungrier," they were winning races to the extent that the dean of trainers, Sunny Jim

555

Former President and Mrs. Dwight D. Eisenhower congratulate the Panamanian jockey Braulio Baeza after a winning race.

Fitzsimmons, at the age of eighty-eight began toying with the idea of taking Spanish lessons. (On the other hand, C. V. Whitney offered the theory that the language barrier might be responsible for the Latin jockeys' success: they were unburdened by instructions from owners and trainers.)

Carry Back was found to have a filled ankle after the 1961 Belmont, which might have been a factor during the race, although subsequent events indicated that the distance was 2 furlongs beyond his tether, for he never won a race longer than 1¼ miles. Rested until August 26, he came back with a victory over the good five-year-old sprinter, Rare Rice, in a

7-furlong allowance race. On September 2 Carry Back won the Jerome Handicap at a mile, while packing 128 pounds and conceding 17 to runner-up Garwol and 2 to third-place Beau Prince; Sherluck, getting 7 pounds, was dead last in this one. (Since his jousts with Carry Back in Florida, Calumet's Beau Prince had won the Lamplighter Handicap, American Derby and Travers.)

Carry Back then suffered three straight defeats. Under 123 pounds, top by scale and conceding actual weight to all but one of his older rivals, he was unplaced in his first race on grass, the United Nations Handicap, won by Jacnot Stable's Oink, a son of To Market who had won first money in four Chicago stakes that summer. (Oink's co-owner, Jack Hogan, was in the habit of distributing $5 mutuel tickets among his friends and employees whenever his horse ran; after the UN these cardboard tokens were worth $143 each.)

Next for Carry Back came a third in the Woodward Stakes, won by Kelso—the Florida colt's first encounter with the champion— then, back in his own division, at 1⅝ miles Carry Back again finished a distant third, to Sherluck and Ambiopoise in the Lawrence Realization at Aqueduct.

For his final start at three, Carry Back won the 1¼-mile Trenton Handicap from five-year-old Intentionally, with Robert Lehman's Ambiopoise—winner of that season's Gotham Stakes, Jersey Derby and Discovery Handicap—third.

Neither Carry Back nor Kelso began 1962 in a manner which suggested that at the end of the season they would monopolize the voting for Horse of the Year, much less that they would both be millionaires.

Continuing his activity, Carry Back was on the scene first. Although he was assigned healthy amounts of weight, it was the opposition that beat him in his first two starts, as he ran second to Intentionally in the Palm Beach and Seminole Handicaps. When Intentionally retired, Yorky, with 120 pounds, came up to win his second successive Widener (the eighth for Calumet Farm, Bull Lea and his descendants) as Carry Back ran second under 127. The New Orleans Handicap appeared to be at his mercy, but, carrying 129 pounds, Carry Back was third to George D. Widener's Yorktown and Pete Fuller's Hillsborough, conceding 16 pounds to both. Returning to Florida, at 126, Carry Back was third to Yorky (121) and Jay Fox (112) in the Gulfstream Park Handicap. (The positions of the first two were interchanged by the stewards, but Carry Back was not affected by the disqualification.)

Finally, on April 20, the relentless Price colt caught an allowance race at Aqueduct which he won by five lengths. When he returned to handicaps, however, at 125 pounds in the Grey Lag, he finished second to Ambiopoise while conceding him 10 pounds.

In May, Kelso reappeared, after another long layoff, of six and a half months. The Bohemia gelding had a filled ankle after the previous year's International and a bout with a virus at the winter training center in Aiken, South Carolina, and he had been unable to find an allowance race for a tightener; owners of other horses avoided such events that seemed likely to suit him, and the races were canceled for lack of sufficient runners. Kelly had to come in cold at 133 pounds for the Metropolitan Handicap on May 30, and New Yorkers who bet him down to 3-to-5 received another painful reminder about the basic paradox of odds-on favorites in handicap races. Ridden by Bill Shoemaker (Arcaro having retired the previous November) Kelso finished sixth as Carry Back, getting a concession of 10 pounds, roared to victory in track record time of 1:33⅗ for the mile. With that performance, Carry Back, ridden by John Rotz, became a millionaire.

On June 16, Kelso got his tightener, due to shrewd maneuvering on the part of trainer Hanford. The champion was eligible to the $25,000 Nassau County Handicap scheduled for that day, and, assuming he would go for the money, other trainers put their horses in a $7,500 allowance event earlier on the program. There was great surprise when Kelso's name showed up in the entries for the overnight race, but it was too late to back out. The race went, and Kelso won it by two and a quarter lengths, carrying only 117 pounds. (Only four runners contested the stakes, for which Kelso had been assigned 132 pounds.)

Apparently in tune, he was sent against Carry Back in the Suburban Handicap on July 4, but Hobeau Farm's Beau Purple, guided by Bill Boland, led all the way to set a new track record of 2:00⅗. Kelso (132) finished second and Carry Back (126) ran last. Another notable three-cornered rivalry was in the works.

Owned by the young Wall Street investment broker, Jack Dreyfus, and trained by H. Allen Jerkens, Beau Purple was the surprise development of the 1962 season. His sire, Beau Gar, had been undistinguished in a racing career hampered by injury, but Dreyfus had so much faith in the well-bred son of Count Fleet–Bellesoeur that he leased mares from other breeders in order to give Beau Gar a chance as a stallion. Beau Purple (along with Beau Red, Beau White, Beau Blue, etc.), was a member of the first crop.

He had won the Kentucky Derby Trial at three, but broke down in his next start and was out of action for nearly a year. After easing back into competition at four, in 1962 as a five-year-old the handsome son of Beau Gar was electrifying; regarded as essentially a sprinter at the beginning of the year, by season's end he had set four new track records and equaled two others, from 7 furlongs to 1½ miles, over dirt and grass surfaces.

However, the sparks he generated ran on alternating current. If allowed to cruise unmolested on the lead, Beau Purple was a terror, but if another horse was fast enough to hook him in the early stages, he was disinclined to pursue the issue, and faded out of contention. Ten days after the Suburban, for example, when the Big Three met again in the Monmouth Handicap, Ogden Phipps's Hitting Away, a colt not unlike Beau Purple in his front-running proclivity, was in there to burn off the early speed, and that cooked Beau Purple's goose.

Carry Back (124) was the winner, by three lengths in new track record time of 2:00⅖ for 1¼ miles, Kelso (130) was second and Beau Purple (117) third.

A week later, in the Brooklyn Handicap at the same distance, Beau Purple got the jump on the speed horses (including Hitting Away) at the start, and drew out to win by three and a half lengths, lowering his own Aqueduct record to 2:00 in the process. Under top weight of 127 pounds, conceding 11 to the winner, Carry Back finished fourth.

Kelso did not contest the Brooklyn. In fact, "King Kelly" was still looking for his first stakes victory of the season when he had another virus attack in August. In his absence, Carry Back scored an impressive victory under 130 pounds in the Whitney Stakes at Saratoga on August 4, beating his old rival Crozier by two lengths while giving him 19 pounds. After racing returned to Aqueduct, Carry Back evened his score with Beau Purple by winning a mile overnight handicap by eight lengths with 133 pounds up, as Beau Purple ran last with 127. Then, on September 3, it was Crozier's turn to achieve a measure of revenge as he took the Aqueduct Stakes, in which Carry Back was fourth, while carrying 128 pounds, 14 more than the winner, and beaten only a length for it all.

Kelso was pursuing a separate trail. Late in August he started all over, with Ismael "Milo" Valenzuela as jockey replacing Shoemaker, who had won one allowance race and lost three stakes on the champion. The new team won a 1¹⁄₁₆-mile allowance race on the Saratoga turf course from Call the Witness, but the latter horse reversed that decision in a similar event at Atlantic City September 8. As a non-winner of two races on grass, Kelso, ridden on this occasion by Don Pierce, was required to carry only 113 pounds, but he finished fourth, although less than two lengths off the winner.

Valenzuela was back aboard for Kelso's next start, and finally, on September 19, the horse destined to become 1962 champion won the Stymie Handicap under 128 pounds—his first stakes victory of the season. Ten days later the Bohemia gelding won his second renewal of the Woodward Stakes at weight for age, trouncing the three-year-old champion, Jaipur, as Beau Purple was unplaced; and at Belmont Park on October 20 Kelso won his third successive Jockey Club Gold Cup. The winning margin was ten lengths, but the time nevertheless was a new Belmont record for 2 miles, 3:19⅘, three-fifths faster than the mark previously established by Nashua.

Meanwhile, in early October Price had taken

Carry Back to France for the Prix de l'Arc de Triomphe, at weight-for-age on grass, which was won by the longshot, Soltikoff. Carry Back finished tenth of the twenty-four runners, but only five and three-quarters lengths behind the winner, and his ordinarily genial trainer was emphatically critical of the ride by European jockey Arthur "Scobie" Breasley. The jockey, who had been noticeably casual concerning his mount's chances from the time he first rode Carry Back in a preliminary workout, in turn stated merely that the colt could not stay the 1½-mile distance. Price challenged the owners of the first five finishers to a special runoff, $25,000 each and winner take all, but when only one of them indicated any interest the plan was dropped.

Upon his return to America, Carry Back met his countrymen under similar conditions on October 27 in the Man o' War Stakes, which was changed by the New York Racing Association that year to a 1½-mile event on the turf course, as a sort of companion feature to Laurel's Washington, D.C., International. Fresh from victory in the Hawthorne Gold Cup the previous week, Beau Purple spurted to the lead at once and was never caught, covering the distance in new course record time of

Kelso ("King Kelly") is greeted by his court following his third successive victory in the Woodward Stakes. Left to right: exercise boy Dick Jenkins, trainer Carl Hanford, Samuel A. Crozer, the father of Kelso's owner; Miss Lana DuPont, and owner Mrs. Richard C. DuPont. Ismael "Milo" Valenzuela is the rider.

Bob Coglianese

2:28⅗. Kelso was two lengths away second, and Carry Back fifth of the ten runners. This left the relationship among the Big Three in a turmoil (although, in their earlier encounters Carry Back had conceded weight to Beau Purple and Kelso had conceded weight to both the others, while the reverse was never true). All of them were invited to the International.

While his rivals took a brief time out, Carry Back tried the Trenton Handicap on November 3, in which he carried 129 pounds. He was nosed out by Montpelier's excellent three-year-old Mongo, under 118 pounds, an 8-pound advantage by the scale. (A half-brother to five other stakes winners, including the great steeplechase champion, Neji, Mongo won four other stakes in 1962, including the United Nations Handicap; he was the only member of his generation to defeat his elders in a $100,000 race that year.)

The Washington, D.C., International on November 12 was the last battle royal among Kelso, Carry Back and Beau Purple. As trainer Hanford later remarked, when Beau Purple was invited, Kelso was uninvited, for it was left to him to match strides with the Hobeau Farm horse in the early stages to prevent him from "stealing" the race. After racing Beau Purple into defeat, Kelso staved off a determined bid by Carry Back, but had nothing left when the French four-year-old Match II unleashed a final quarter in :24⅕ to win going away by one and a half lengths. Kelso held second by four and a half over Carry Back, as Beau Purple faded to eleventh. (Match II, as it happened, had finished fourth in the Prix de l'Arc de Triomphe the month before, and had been among the horses challenged by Price to another contest with Carry Back.)

Again, "King Kelly" had lost no stature through defeat, and he clearly dominated the American runners. He was a landslide winner in the voting for Horse of the Year. At this point, Kelso enjoyed a 3-2 edge in relative finish positions after five encounters with each of his rivals, while Carry Back and Beau Purple were 3-3 with respect to one another.

Top money winner of the 1962 handicap division, however, was Rex Ellsworth's Prove It, a son of Endeavour II, who did not contend with the Eastern candidates. Unraced at two and relatively undistinguished at three, Prove It had begun his career with the stable's second string of stakes: the Inglewood, American, As a four-year-old he won the San Fernando Stakes, Santa Anita Maturity and Santa Anita Handicap, and was back even stronger at five. In 1962, Prove It won six of thirteen starts and $348,750, all his victories in a consecutive string of stakes: the Inglewood, American, Hollywood Gold Cup, Sunset, Benjamin F. Lindheimer and Washington Park Handicaps. Both his Chicago victories were achieved under top weight in track record time.

The votes already had been counted when Kelso toted 129 pounds to victory in the Governor's Plate at Garden State Park, setting a new track record of 2:30⅕ for 1½ miles, and giving away 12 pounds to each of his nearest pursuers, Bass Clef and Polylad. Thus he became the turf's fifth millionaire, with earnings at the end of four racing seasons of $1,011,940.

Carry Back was retired to stud as the world's third-leading money winner, but after serving a book of twenty-six mares he was brought back to the races as five-year-old in 1963. In his return to competition, the Buckeye Handicap on August 17, Gushing Wind, with a 12-pound concession, beat him by five lengths, but Carry Back won his next start, an allowance race on the Atlantic City turf course. After a third in Mongo's United Nations Handicap and a fourth in Kelso's Woodward, the Price stallion finished an abysmal eleventh in Smart's Manhattan Handicap, from which he appeared to come out sore. However, on November 2, under a modest burden of 119 pounds, Carry Back came back to Garden State Park to win the Trenton Handicap a second time, beating Mongo and Smart. He was retired to stud again,

The Memorial Day crowd of 63,065 at the new Aqueduct in 1962.

after a total of 61 starts, 21 wins, 11 seconds and 11 thirds. Although his earnings had increased to $1,241,165, during his comeback Carry Back had slipped to fourth place in the financial standings, Kelso having passed him up in that department as well as having padded his score to 4-2 in their individual jousts.

Brookmeade Stable's home-bred Bowl of Flowers, trained by Elliott Burch, was champion filly of the 1958 crop both seasons she raced. The beautiful golden chestnut daughter of Sailor (although her large ankles were a source of concern) was never worse than second in eight starts, of which she won six, including the National Stallion (in new Belmont record time of 1:04⅕ for 5½ furlongs), Gardenia and Frizette Stakes. Both her seconds were in overnight races, and both the fillies which outfinished her—Shuette and De-

wali—subsequently were defeated by Bowl of Flowers in stakes. In the Gardenia and Frizette, the champion also defeated Meadowbrook Stable's Little Tumbler, who won the Futurity from colts that year, as well as the Colleen, Astoria and Alcibiades Stakes from her own sex.

As a three-year-old, Bowl of Flowers again started eight times; she won four, including the Acorn Stakes and Coaching Club American Oaks within her age, and the Spinster from her elders. She also was third, beaten only two noses, to the colts Sherluck and Hitting Away in the Roamer Handicap. Never out of the money in her life, she retired with 10 wins from 16 starts and $398,504.

Darby Dan Farm's home-bred Primonetta, the first filly by Swaps (her name in Italian means "first little one") began her career with

561

Bowl of Flowers with Eddie Arcaro up, Mrs. Isabel Dodge Sloane and trainer Elliott Burch.

Bert Morgan

a nine-race winning streak extending over two seasons. Trained by J. P. Conway, she was undefeated in four starts at two, including the Marguerite Stakes; and won her first five starts at three, including the Prioress, Miss Woodford Stakes and Delaware Oaks. She also equaled the Monmouth record of 1:08⅖ for 6 furlongs in an allowance race. A loss by a neck to My Portrait in the Monmouth Oaks, won in track record time of 1:48⅘ for 1⅛ miles, ended Primonetta's string, but she came right back to win the Alabama by five lengths from Mighty Fair and Bowl of Flowers. Later, she was runner-up to the Brookmeade filly in the Spinster, and also in the voting for the sophomore championship. As a four-year-old, Primonetta won the title as best handicap filly, with seven wins in ten starts, including the Regret, Molly Pitcher, Falls City Handicaps and Spinster Stakes. She retired with $306,690, winner of 17 races in 25 starts.

Mr. and Mrs. John W. Galbreath, the owners of Primonetta, were taking no chances. They gradually bought up land that formerly had been part of Idle Hour Stock Farm until their Darby Dan was approaching the acreage as it had comprised in the days of Colonel E. R.

Bradley. Although they boasted one of the finest collections of stallions in the world, headed by Swaps, they also booked to outside horses, and in the crop behind Primonetta, Darby Dan had a daughter of Nashua, named Bramalea, who won the Jasmine Stakes, Coaching Club American Oaks and Gazelle Handicap. (Galbreath also imported for stud duty the great undefeated European champion, Ribot, winner of successive renewals of the Prix de l'Arc de Triomphe, on a five-year lease for $1,350,000.)

Among the foals of 1959, there was a battle for the juvenile championship of the colt division, as Crimson King Farm's Crimson Satan was first in two polls, J G W Stable's Ridan was voted champion in another, and Meadow Stable's Sir Gaylord scored the highest in performance points.

A son of Spy Song, whose get were notoriously partial to sprints, but out of a staying-bred South American mare, Crimson Satan repudiated the paternal half of his pedigree by becoming the first stakes-class two-year-old in history to win five races at the maximum U.S. juvenile distance of 1 1/16 miles. Although he was quick enough to win the Lafayette Stakes

562

in the spring, the big, burly colt, trained by Gordon Potter, was no match for Ridan when it came to pure speed at conventional two-year-old distances. In the fall, however, Crimson Satan won all his starts beyond a mile, including the 1¹⁄₁₆-mile Hawthorne Juvenile (faster division), Garden State Stakes and Pimlico Futurity. He also was fourth, making up ground, in the Champagne Stakes at a flat mile, and led the male members of his division in juvenile earnings with $302,300.

As a three-year-old, the red devil—in personality as well as in name—was a disappointment in the early part of the season (leading to more talk about the Garden State jinx). Apparently unsuited to the Florida climate, and plagued by intermittent illness and unsoundness, he lost four in a row at Hialeah before winning an allowance race at Keeneland in his first start after moving north, then was unplaced in the Blue Grass Stakes, Kentucky Derby and Preakness. The son of Spy Song nosed out Jaipur and Admiral's Voyage in the Jersey Derby May 30, but was set back to third because of interference. He was then a good third to the same two colts in the Bel-

mont Stakes at 1½ miles. Crimson Satan won the Leonard Richards Stakes in late June, but the purse was taken away when chemical analysis of his urine revealed presence of the highly controversial (and prohibited) medication, phenylbutazone. Finally, on September 1, saddled by Charles Kerr (Potter having been suspended for the rest of the year), the Crimson King Farm colt won the Laurance Armour Handicap for keeps, and he added the 1⅛-mile Clark Handicap later to complete his sophomore campaign with four wins from eighteen starts, and $99,257. As a four-year-old he won the San Fernando, the Charles H. Strub stakes (formerly the Santa Anita Maturity), Massachusetts Handicap, Michigan Mile and One-Sixteenth and Washington Park Handicap. At the end of 1963, Crimson Satan's earnings stood at $785,402.

Ridan, a huge son of Nantallah, owned by the partnership of Mrs. Moody Jolley, John Greer and Ernest Woods, was undefeated in seven starts as a two-year-old, including the Hyde Park (by six lengths), Prairie State Stakes (by five and a half lengths in 1:09 for 6 furlongs), Arlington and Washington Park Fu-

Ridan, held by Henry Gervais, at the time of his retirement to stud at Claiborne Farm.

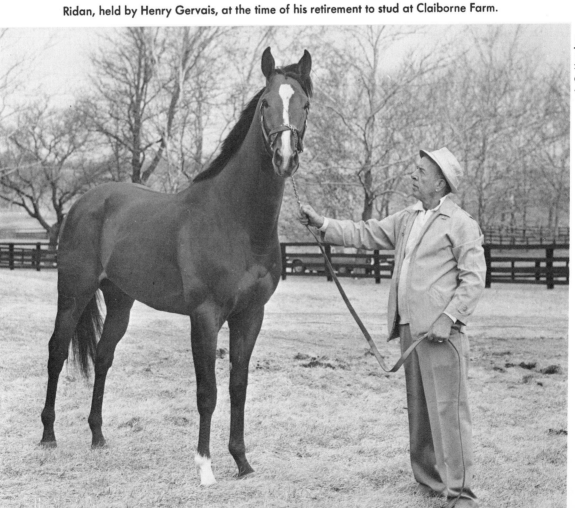

J. C. Meadors

turities, for earnings of $284,850. He also set a track record of :48⅓ for the Headley Course at Keeneland and beat Crimson Satan both times they met. Topping 16 hands and tipping 1,100 pounds in his two-year-old season, Ridan was reminiscent of one of his uncles, Nadir, in appearance, and his name was "Nadir" spelled backwards. Trained by young LeRoy Jolley, whose father, Moody, had conditioned Nadir, Ridan was smoother-looking than his predecessor. He came to be classified as a sprinter, but this was owing to his temperament rather than to any physical limitation; a racing man, given an Alladin's opportunity to specify his ideal of a perfectly constructed running horse for any distance, scarcely could have improved on Ridan. By actual measurement of his hoofprints following a 7-furlong workout as a three-year-old, at Arlington Park in 1:24⅗ (not quite top speed), he strode 28 feet, compared to the 24-foot stride of the best stayer of his era, Kelso.

Ridan, however, was headstrong and didn't take kindly to rating tactics; because of his tempestuous disposition he also was a poor shipper; it was difficult to pick racing spots.

The big colt opened his three-year-old campaign with a victory in the Hibiscus Stakes—thereby extending his winning streak to eight races—and later in the year won the Florida Derby, Blue Grass Stakes (beating subsequent Kentucky Derby winner, Decidedly, by four lengths) and Arlington Classic. His longest victory was at 9 furlongs, but he ran the season's sophomore champion, Jaipur, to a nose in the 1¼-mile Travers Stakes, the most exciting duel of the year, won in track record time of 2:01⅗ at Saratoga. Ridan also lost the Preakness by just a nose, and his jockey, Ycaza, claimed foul against the winner, Greek Money, but the stewards decided Ridan had been the culprit and suspended Ycaza for a frivolous complaint. Only in his thirteenth and final start of the 1962 season, when he came back with a cut on his leg, did Ridan miss winning a piece of the purse.

The powerful racing machine appeared only briefly at four. After winning his debut by five lengths, he took the Palm Beach Handicap by three and three-quarters lengths from Jaipur, Merry Ruler and Kelso, the latter making his first start of the 1963 season. As a measure of Ridan's stature, he was favored over Kelso in the Seminole, and required to carry 129 pounds to the older horse's 128. Kelso, however, won that 9-furlong event with Ridan second. Recurring splint trouble retired Ridan to stud, and he left the track with 13 wins, six seconds and two thirds from 23 starts, for earnings of $635,074.

Meadow Stable's Sir Gaylord, a son of Turn-to, trained by Casey Hayes, was lost in the shuffle of several 3-furlong baby races in Florida. He won his first effort at 5 furlongs after moving north, then was a fast closing fourth, beaten only a neck for it all, in Sunrise County's Juvenile Stakes. Sir Gaylord thereupon won five in a row, including the Tyro, National Stallion, Great American (covering 5½ furlongs in 1:04 for the second time that year, at two different tracks) and Sapling Stakes. He finished his juvenile campaign as a dubious prospect for longer races the next season with four successive thirds in stakes events beyond 6 furlongs.

At three, however, he was undefeated, in a brief appearance that was quite similar to his sire's sophomore season. Sir Gaylord was undisputed king in Florida, winner of three races, including the 7-furlong Bahamas Stakes by one and three-quarters lengths from Ridan and Crimson Satan in track record time of 1:22, and the 1⅛-mile Everglades Stakes by four and three-quarters lengths from Decidedly and Ridan (Crimson Satan unplaced). After he won the Stepping Stone Purse at Churchill Downs handily, the Meadow Stable colt was regarded as a favorite for the Kentucky Derby, but an injury prevented him from starting and he retired to stud with ten wins and $237,404.

George D. Widener's Jaipur, a son of Nasrullah, trained by Bert Mulholland, was a

564

Leslie Combs II, prominent syndicator of stallions, welcomes Jaipur to his Spendthrift Farm.

contender for the crown at two, and won it at three. He took four of his seven juvenile starts and was second in all the others, to net $214,-659. Among his victories were the Flash, Hopeful and Cowdin Stakes, and his seconds included narrow losses to Christiana Stable's Cyane by a neck in the Futurity and to Verne Winchell, Jr.'s Donut King by a head in the Champagne.

At three, the handsome colt opened the season with back-to-back victories in the Gotham and Withers Stakes. After an unaccountably poor showing in the Preakness (tenth) he rebounded to win the Jersey Derby upon disqualification of Crimson Satan, and followed with a victory by a nose over Admiral's Voyage in the Belmont Stakes, an event his owner had been trying to win for forty-four years. (Widener's colors first paraded to the post for the Belmont Stakes in 1918, and he had sent a total of ten candidates before Jaipur won it.

After these two successive blanket finishes, Jaipur, who had a mind of his own, for a time refused to take the track even for a gallop. He came back on August 1, though, to win the Choice Stakes from Cyane by four and a half lengths, following which was his duel with Ridan in the Travers, the third time that season the Widener colt won by a nose. Jaipur subsequently was second to Kelso in the Woodward at weight-for-age; unplaced to older horses in the Manhattan Handicap while conceding 11 pounds actual weight to the winner, Tutankhamen; and second by a length to his contemporary, Dead Ahead, in the Roamer Handicap, while conceding 9 pounds. Jaipur had won ten of seventeen races and $610,096 at the end of his second season. His second to Ridan in the Palm Beach, and a fourth in Kelso's Seminole, were his only starts as a four-year-old.

While the colts of 1959 vied for the leadership, there was no question concerning the best filly. Meadow Stable's home-bred Cicada, a daughter of Bryan G.–Satsuma, by Bossuet, and a granddaughter of the fabulous mare, Hildene, was selected champion of her generation, at two, three and four. As a juvenile she was a unanimous choice in the Triangle poll, and the next year just missed cornering all the votes, but she still polled the heaviest majority of any of that season's divisional leaders.

565

Cicada, the world's leading money-winning filly, with jockey John Rotz.

Tough and nimble, the 15½-hand bay was never out of the money in sixteen starts during her first season; she won eleven of them, including a string of six in a row at the end of her campaign. Cicada's stakes victories were the 5-furlong Blue Hen (by five and a half lengths), filly division of the National Stallion, the Schuylerville, Spinaway, Matron, Astarita, Frizette and the 1 1/16-mile Gardenia by ten lengths. Her earnings of $384,676 were a new record for one season by a member of her sex, regardless of age, and she missed by less than $12,000 the juvenile record held by her "uncle," First Landing.

In her first start at three, on February 7, Cicada took on her elders and conquered Seven Thirty (one of the top handicap mares of the season) in an allowance race at Hialeah. Cicada's winning streak was ended at seven races by the excellent older filly, Smashing Gail, a week later in the Columbiana Handicap, for which she conceded the winner 11 pounds by the scale. The Meadow Stable filly beat older fillies again in an allowance race, before losing the Florida Derby by only a nose to Ridan, after some bumping in the stretch; at that,

566

Cicada finished six lengths ahead of Admiral's Voyage, winner that season of four stakes including the Louisiana Derby and Wood Memorial, and himself loser by only a nose to champion Jaipur in both the Jersey Derby and Belmont Stakes.

Not until her fourth start was Cicada confined to her own division, and she won four straight in such company. After she won the Oaks Prep with ease, there was some talk about substituting her for her injured stablemate, Sir Gaylord, in the Kentucky Derby, but the filly instead went for the Oaks and won by three lengths. In the Acorn Stakes on May 19, Cicada came home first by one and a half lengths, and, as she survived a foul claim lodged by the rider of runner-up, Tamarona, she replaced Bewitch as the world's leading money-winning female thoroughbred.

The daughter of Bryan G. then won the Mother Goose at 1⅛ miles before meeting her first loss that year to a member of her own class, as Bramalea beat her by half a length in the 1¼-mile CCA Oaks on June 23. (Although she subsequently was a close second to Seven Thirty in the Delaware Handicap, and ran against colts in the Travers at 1¼ miles, Cicada never won beyond 9 furlongs.)

Later in the season, the world's richest filly won the Beldame Stakes at weight-for-age from six-year-old Shirley Jones and three-year-old Firm Policy (who had defeated Cicada in the Alabama) in new Aqueduct record time of 1:48⅕ for 1⅛ miles; and the Jersey Belle Stakes by five and a half lengths from her contemporaries while conceding nine pounds to the runner-up.

Having reached the point at which she set a new actual record every time she earned a penny, as a four-year-old Cicada was aimed at a more remote objective; it was attempted to make her the first female winner of a million dollars. She progressed steadily toward that goal, as far as she went.

The Chenery filly participated exclusively in handicap stakes in 1963, conceding weight to every rival in every race, repeatedly carrying more than scale for her age, and never carrying less. She began the year with a victory in the Columbiana Handicap, then pulled up sore after finishing fifth under 126 pounds in the Black Helen Handicap, won by Pocosaba (117). Again carrying 126, Cicada ran second to Old Hat (117) in the Suwannee River Handicap, and after moving north in April she won the Distaff Handicap. Assigned 128 for the Top

Flight, Cicada was third to Firm Policy (125) and Tamarona (111), but she bounced back to win two straight. Packing 127 pounds, Cicada won the Vagrancy by three and a half lengths from Bramalea (120), then followed up with a victory in the Sheepshead Bay Handicap—her first start on a grass track—carrying 128 pounds, 19 more than the runner-up.

She hauled the same weight, courageously, throughout the 1¼-mile Delaware Handicap on July 27, but was unable to catch the flying longshot, Thomas F. White's Waltz Song (116), finishing second, half a length behind the winner and just a nose ahead of the season's Western star, Table Mate.

That was Cicada's final race. Although she could have been patched up, after she injured a stifle in a work the next month it was decided to retire her rather than risk more serious damage. Not too far short of her goal at that, Cicada left the track with $783,324, having started 41 times, won 23, finished second eight times and third six times. As she was voted best handicap female of the 1963 season in two of the year-end polls, Cicada also enjoyed the distinction of having earned a divisional championship in each of the three years she raced.

Activities of other horses whose racing careers had not been completed by 1963 is beyond the scope of this work, but the group in-

Never Bend winning the 1963 Flamingo Stakes.

Owner Rex Ellsworth (left) and the trainer Meshach Tenney leading in the 1963 Preakness winner Candy Spots with Bill Shoemaker up.

cluded numerous candidates for future histories.

Cain Hoy Stable's Never Bend, from the last crop by mighty Nasrullah, set a new juvenile earnings record of $402,969 in 1962, with seven wins in ten starts, including the Futurity, Cowdin and Champagne Stakes. Oddly, the colt of unprecedented wealth for his age lost the two richest races of the season, finishing third in the Garden State and second in the Arlington-Washington Futurity, which that year replaced the New Jersey event as the world's most affluent horse race. A combination of two former futurities, each of which had been among the most valuable in the nation, the new Chicago spectacular was contested over 7 furlongs at scale weight, with $150,000 added. The purse was further swelled by various fees from owners, which amounted to a total cost of $2,500 per starter via the usual in-

stallment-payment system, or $25,000 through supplementary nomination. (For the first running, late nominees also were required to pay $2,000 to pass the entry box, but the next year this added expense was absorbed into the huge supplementary fee.)

A unique clause in the conditions provided that supplementary fees be divided equally among the first ten *original* nominees to finish, which had the effect of refunding payments to owners who had supported the race from the outset, in the event a late arrival usurped the lion's share of the purse.

As it happened, the inaugural was won by a supplementary nominee—Rex Ellsworth's Candy Spots—so all but two of the thirteen starters got their money back. Although the $357,250 gross purse was a new record, it was divided in an unusual manner, and Candy Spots' $142,250 share was not so large as the award to George Widener's Crewman for winning that year's Garden State Stakes. However, for finishing second in the Arlington-Washington Futurity, Never Bend received the record sum of $75,000, plus his $2,500 share of the winner's supplementary fee. A $10,000 nominator's award, which applied to each of the first four finishers, increased the runner-up's total take to $87,500.

A long, lean son of the South American stallion Nigromante, out of Candy Dish, by Khaled, Candy Spots was so named because of unusual white splotches scattered about his chestnut coat. He was undefeated in three starts as a two-year-old, but second in the championship voting to Never Bend.

As the two colts went into winter quarters at the end of 1962, their rivalry was whooped into another Nashua-Swaps affair, and so it appeared to be when each came out roaring at three. Never Bend was so formidable in his works that a special betless exhibition was scheduled for his first start at Hialeah, following which he won the Flamingo Stakes by five lengths, in front all the way. Across the continent, Candy Spots scored a narrow victory over Bonjour in his three-year-old debut, then won the Santa Anita Derby under somewhat ironical circumstances. A severe bump knocked him clear of a jam that was developing, and an instant later four horses went down (one mortally injured) as Candy Spots proceeded on to win. There was no second-guessing the colt's next victory, however, as he shipped cross-country to win the Florida Derby easily. Never Bend meanwhile having won two more races—one of them another betless affair, by eight lengths—the long awaited re-encounter came off in the Kentucky Derby.

Candy Spots was warmly favored, but not so much as might have been expected, because of the presence in the field of another undefeated colt, Greentree Stable's No Robbery, an insouciant son of Swaps, who had started only twice at two but had come on the next season to take three straight, including the fastest mile ever recorded by a colt of his age in New York (1:34), and the Wood Memorial while running virtually sideways.

They were all due for a surprise. In the Derby, Darby Dan Farm's Chateaugay overhauled Never Bend at the end of the mile and drew away to win by one and a quarter lengths, as Candy Spots finished third, a neck behind Never Bend, after running into a couple of pockets. (No Robbery came in fifth, and it later was learned he had bucked shins, for the fifth time in his young life.)

A chestnut son of Swaps, and full brother to Primonetta, Chateaugay had been a steady but unsensational two-year-old, and although the Derby was his fourth victory in as many starts at three, he had not attracted any particular attention until he won his first added-money purse, the Blue Grass Stakes, just nine days earlier. The impression held by many that he had been a lucky winner of the Derby (the Darby Dan colt ran with a chicken bone tied to his bridle for luck) was fortified two weeks later when Candy Spots, again favorite despite his loss at Louisville, whipped him soundly, by three and a half lengths, in the Preakness. Never Bend, slated not to win a race longer than 9 furlongs, finished third, four and a half more lengths away. His two principal rivals abstaining, Candy Spots next won the Jersey Derby handily, his fourth $100,000 event within less than three months. The Ellsworth colt was 1-to-2 for the 1½-mile Belmont stakes (at Aqueduct) on June 8. However, it was Chateaugay who proved best in the test, and this time there were no excuses, for Candy Spots had been on the lead at the end of 1¼ miles, but faded to a two-and-a-half length deficit at the wire.

The remainder of the year's racing did nothing to clarify the blurred picture in the classic division. Never Bend ran well against older horses in the Woodward Stakes and United Nations Handicap, but the only other stakes event he won was the 1⅛-mile Yankee Handicap, in which Chateaugay was fourth.

Chateaugay added the Jerome Handicap, and a victory in an overnight race while carrying 130 pounds, to his score card, but he also finished third in Outing Class's Dwyer, Crewman's Travers and fourth in Dean Carl's Lawrence Realization. (Outing Class and Crewman finished behind Chateaugay in the Jerome, and in all his losses he was conceding weight to the winner.

In a Midwestern campaign, Candy Spots, also giving away weight, was upset by B. Major in the Chicagoan Stakes, but snapped back to take the two big ones, the American Derby and Arlington Classic. B. Major was second in the Derby and third in the Classic, in which the runner-up was Sunny Blue Farm's Admiral Vic, who later developed into a star of that area, winner of three stakes, including the Hawthorne Gold Cup.

Upon his return to the East, however, Candy Spots finished fourth in the Travers, behind third-place Chateaugay. Never Bend was last in that race, the final encounter among the three colts who had dominated the 1963 Triple Crown events. After another fourth, to older horses in Kelso's Aqueduct Stakes on Labor Day, Candy Spots was taken out of training and sent home, never having failed to get at least a piece of the purse, and leading money winner of the season with $604,481. In the championship voting, the dual classic winner, Chateaugay, got the nod, with Candy Spots second and Never Bend third.

Among the fillies from this crop, honors at two were split between Mrs. Russell Reineman's Smart Deb and Mrs. Ethel Jacobs' Affectionately. A daughter of Dedicate, Smart Deb began with a sensational string of seven straight wins, including the Miss Chicago, Mademoiselle, Princess Pat, Arlington Lassie and Matron Stakes. She came home three lengths on top in her eighth start, too, the 7-furlong Astarita Stakes, but was disqualified for interference and placed last. In five starts thereafter, at a mile and beyond, she did not win again, although she took second in Main

Swaps's Gardenia, third in Fool's Play's Selima and Wise Nurse's Marguerite Stakes.

Affectionately, by Swaps out of the hardy mare Searching, ran up six victories in a row, including the Fashion, Polly Drummond and National Stallion Stakes, before her streak was snapped with a second in the Colleen Stakes to No Resisting, a filly she had defeated before and was to do so again. Thereafter Affectionately won the Astoria, Sorority and Spinaway Stakes in succession, but Smart Deb beat her off in a speed duel for the Matron Stakes, in which the Jacobs filly faded to third. She finished her campaign with two more thirds, at a mile in the Frizette, won by Pam's Ego, and Gardenia Trial, won by Wise Nurse with Smart Deb second.

At three, Smart Deb won the Beaugay and Arlington Matron Handicaps, and Affectionately won the Interborough (Smart Deb third) but they both were overshadowed during their second season by other members of the crop.

Miss Eleanora Sears' Spicy Living, by Gallant Man, seemed to have established a clear leadership when, after finishing second to Lamb Chop in a division of the Comely Stakes, she won the Betsy Ross, Acorn and Mother Goose Stakes in quick order, with Lamb Chop third in the latter two.

William Haggin Perry's Lamb Chop had won the La Centinela and Santa Susana Stakes at Santa Anita, and placed in the Santa Ynez, before crossing the continent for her series with Spicy Living, and the daughter of Bold Ruler–Sheepsfoot, by Count Fleet, quickly avenged her defeats. Lamb Chop, Spicy Living and Smart Deb ran one-two-three in both the Coaching Club American and Monmouth Oaks; since Smart Deb had been second in the Mother Goose, Lamb Chop also had evened the score with her.

Spicy Living won just once more as a three-year-old, a six-and-a-half-length victory in the Delaware Oaks, in which Lamb Chop did not participate, but the Perry filly went on to pile up a thoroughly remarkable season. Giving

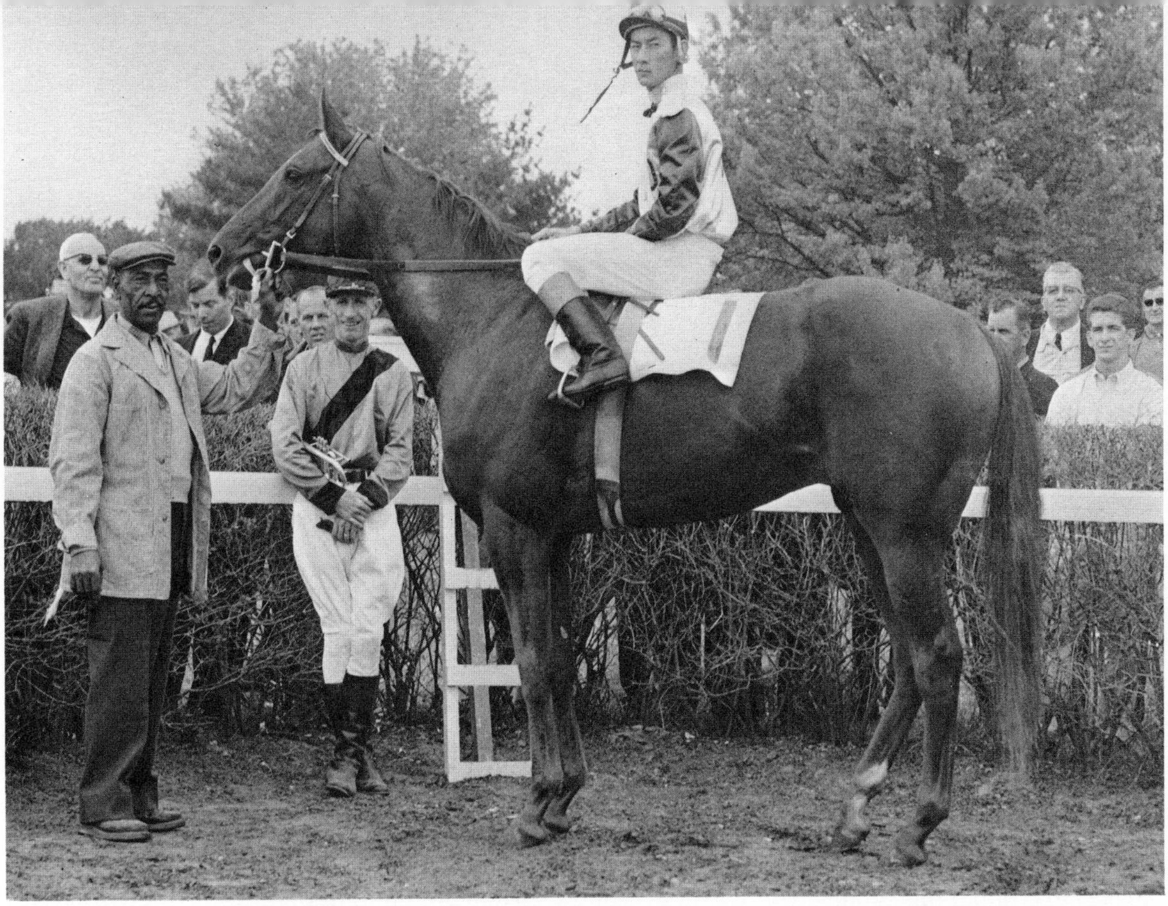

Chateaugay with Braulio Baeza up after winning the Blue Grass Stakes.

away weight on each occasion, she was second by a length to Barbwolf in a division of the Test Stakes, and nosed out by Tona in the Alabama Stakes. Lamb Chop then came back to win the Gazelle Handicap within her division, and lost the Beldame Stakes by only a nose to five-year-old Oil Royalty. Older fillies also were eligible to the weight-for-age Spinster Stakes on October 17, but only one was sent to oppose Lamp Chop after she had sizzled through a prep race in 1:24⅗, a new record for Keeneland's Beard Course of 7 furlongs plus 184 feet. Because of the dearth of competition, the $50,000-added Spinster was declared a betless exhibition, and, true to the billing, Lamb Chop made a show of her four rivals, winning by eleven lengths. On November 5 she followed up with a twelve-length victory in the Jersey Belle Stakes, while carrying top weight of 123 pounds 1 1/16 miles in new track record time of 1:41⅗. After sweeping the board in all the championship polls, Lamb Chop took a curtain call. Carrying 126 pounds, 3 above scale, for the Firenze November 28, she won by two lengths from Waltz Song (123).

The two-year-olds of 1963 offered sparse material for relative evaluation in their first season of racing. Harbor View Farm's Raise a Native appeared to be the best offspring of Native Dancer yet to come to the races (in America—the Dancer's get did well in Europe, too) as he sauntered through his only four races without defeat. He set a track record of :57⅘ for five furlongs at Aqueduct, equaled it in winning the Juvenile Stakes and set another track record of 1:02⅗ in winning the Great American Stakes at 5½ furlongs, but that was as far as he went. An injury led to his retirement early in August, but he was elected champion two-year-old in one poll.

The richer races for this division were thoroughly scattered, as no colt managed to win more than one. Miss Mary Fisher's Golden Ruler won his first four races, including the Arlington-Washington Futurity, but then was unplaced in the Breeders' Futurity, won by Duel. Harbor View Farm's Roman Brother also won his first four starts, including the Champagne Stakes, but thereafter ran second to Hurry to Market in a division of the Trial and in the Garden State Stakes itself. The New York Futurity went to Bupers; the Hopeful

The stallion barn at Claiborne Farm.

Stakes to Traffic; the Sapling to Mr. Brick; the Del Mar Futurity to Perris; the Hollywood Juvenile Championship was run in two divisions, won by Malicious and Nevada Bin; and the two sections of the Cowdin were won by Chieftain and Dunfee. Both Chieftain and Dunfee won two other stakes of lesser value during the year, and other winners of as many as three added money events included Amastar, Big Pete and Northern Dancer, the latter a standout in Canada, where his victories included the Coronation Futurity at 1⅛ miles, who later crossed the border to win the Remsen.

Although it was exceeded in gross value by the new Arlington-Washington Futurity, by adhering to more conventional methods of dividing the purse the Garden State Stakes continued to offer the largest award to the winner, and Hurry to Market's share in 1963 was $190,374, biggest in history. Because of his inordinate size (16 hands 3 inches, and 1,100 pounds) the huge son of To Market, owned by Roger Wilson and Mrs. T. P. Hull, Jr., had not entered competition until September 10. The Garden State on November 9 represented his third victory in six starts, during which he never had finished out of the money, and, since most of the other prominent two-year-olds fin-

ished behind him in that race, Hurry to Market was the majority choice as champion of his age.

The juvenile fillies also presented a kaleidoscopic aspect. Although Wheatley Stable's Castle Forbes did win two of the major events, the Sorority and Gardenia, they were her only two stakes victories in fourteen starts. The Arlington-Washington Lassie (inaugurated in 1963 and patterned as a companion feature to the rich Chicago futurity) was won by J. Kel Houssels's Sari's Song, also winner of the Hollywood Lassie and Princess Pat. Briardale Farm's Tosmah won seven in a row, including the Mermaid, faster division of the Astarita, and the Fritzette Stakes, before running unplaced in the Gardenia. Jacques D. Wimpfheimer's Petite Rouge won the Adirondack, Spinaway and other Astarita; Houssels's Leisurely Kin won a division of the Paradise Valley Stakes in world record time of :50⅗ for 4½ furlongs, a division of the Arizona Futurity from colts, the Cinderella Stakes and Del Mar Debutante; the Matron Stakes went to Mrs. George P. Greenhalgh's Hasty Matelda, and the Selima to Mrs. W. M. Jeffords' My Card, a half-sister to Post Card, Yildiz and One Count, foaled when her dam was nineteen years old. In the championship tabulations, honors among the fillies were divided between Tosmah, and Castle Forbes.

Unlike the unsettled situation that prevailed among younger horses, the 1963 handicap division was well under control. "King Kelly" was back on the scene, ruling with a firm, if not iron, hand.

Despite the tardy beginning to his career, missing out on the profitable purses available to two-year-olds, and the improbable progress thereafter, when he was limited for all practical purposes to half a season's activity for four years, the Bohemia gelding (who never had attained a seasonal financial championship) emerged from his fifth campaign as the second-richest thoroughbred in history. He also embellished an already unique distinction by earning his fourth title as Horse of the Year.

In 1963, for the first time, he followed a conventional program that included winter racing. After his previously described exchanges with Ridan in the Palm Beach and Seminole Handicaps, the champion was assigned 131 pounds for the Widener on February 23. Beau Purple (125), after stumbling at the start, recovered immediately to grab the lead, and under beautiful rating by Bill Boland he bade farewell to the turf with one of his patented performances, cruising in front all the way. Although he closed some ground toward the end, and was easily best of the others, Kelso still lacked two and a quarter lengths of catching the winner. That was Beau Purple's only 1963 race. Having emulated Nashua by taking Florida's biggest handicap first out, and having evened the score 3-3 in his account with Kelso, he was retired to stud, winner of 12 races and $445,785.

Kelso took off on the longest seasonal streak of his career—eight straight stakes. He won the Gulfstream Park Handicap with 130 pounds, the John B. Campbell with 131, the Nassau County with 132 (changed to an allowance stake but still Kelso conceded 18 pounds to the runner-up) and the Suburban— his second renewal—with 133, conceding 22 pounds to the second-finisher. Following these four contests at steadily increasing assignments, Kelso got a breather, such as it was, in a pair of allowance stakes, for which the weights were fixed by the conditions instead of by the handicapper. He won the Whitney Stakes under 130 pounds, and the Aqueduct under 134, conceding 5 pounds to runner-up Crimson Satan in the latter. His next two victories, at weight-for-age, were romps for the perennial champion. He won the Woodward for the third year in succession, by three and a half lengths, from Never Bend and Crimson Satan, and—proving definitely that he was best in the long run—Kelso gained his fourth straight victory in the 2-mile Jockey Club Gold Cup, by four lengths. No other horse ever had won either of these races more than twice.

However, the king, whose domain evidently did not include grass, achieved distinction of another sort in his next start, the Washington, D. C., International on November 11. Kelso's streak came to an end as, for the third year in a row, he finished second. The winner by half a length was Mongo, who covered the 1½ miles in 2:27⅖, the fastest clocking ever recorded in the race except for T.V. Lark's record-breaking run two years earlier, when he had upset Kelso.

Whether turf course racing should be considered the champion's Achilles heel is questionable. While he had not won any of the four stakes he contested on grass, he never had finished worse than second, and Beau Purple also had thrown a track record at him in the 1962 Man o' War Stakes. Finally, Match II, as a French horse, was thoroughly trained on that kind of running surface, and in this country Mongo was unmistakably a grass-track expert.

As had been true in previous years, the International loss was more than offset by Kelso's previous accomplishments, and again he was elected Horse of the Year by an overwhelming majority, having won nine of twelve starts to top the handicap division in earnings with

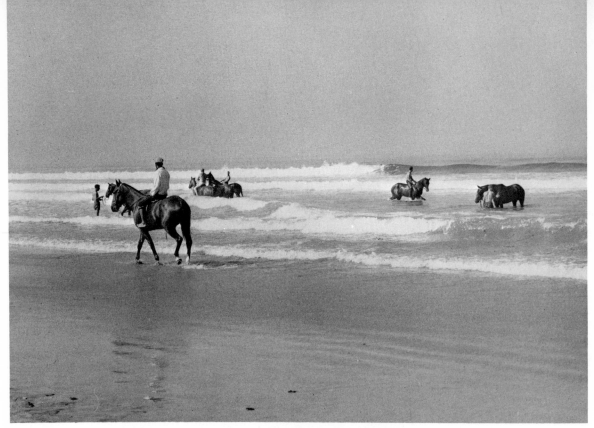

Horses taking the surf treatment at Del Mar.

$569,762. Over all, his record at the end of 1963 showed 45 starts, 31 wins, nine seconds and $1,581,702.

At the age of six, Kelso was better-looking than ever, and he ran to his looks. As this history closed he appeared poised for yet another campaign, with the world's financial leadership dead in his sights.

On Tuesday, November 5, 1963, voters of New York City approved a referendum, sponsored by Mayor Robert F. Wagner, that authorized a study of ways and means to implement off-track betting as an additional source of municipal revenue.

Thus occurred the first stirrings of what could develop into yet another new era of American thoroughbred racing, and a radically different one.

Just a few weeks before Election Day, at the annual testimonial dinner of the Thoroughbred Club of America on October 17, guest of honor John Hay Whitney had delivered an almost eerily prophetic State of the Union message on American racing, as it stood at the end of 1963:

I am here tonight on the premise that I have done something for racing, and because the Thoroughbred Club [of America] is a group that cares about the quality of racing.

It's a 31-year-old tradition of this dinner that the guest of honor is given a license to sound off—and that all his sounds are to be forgiven immediately—whether or not to forgive is to forget. It's something like Congressional immunity.

I know something about that tradition because I was here in 1938. I wasn't the guest of honor, but I was the pick-up rider for one: my mother.

I don't mean to spoil the pyrotechnics of the finest party known to American racing. But I propose to sound off rather quietly.

I was not angry by proxy twenty-five years ago, not really exploding, and I am not angry in person tonight But we were anxious then and I am anxious now.

This is what my mother then asked me to say: "It is most urgent that you, who know what I mean by the spirit of racing, should see clearly this conflict of interest between commercialism and sport. We cannot allow the spirit of racing to be bought."

And this is what I think we still have to guard, more jealously than we have been doing: The Spirit of Racing.

574

What goes on eight or nine or, God forbid, ten times every afternoon at Aqueduct or Arlington, or Santa Anita, or even here at your charming Keeneland, is horse races, and I enjoy these as much as anyone. But the Thoroughbred Club represents the very fiber of horse racing. To preserve the spirit—and the sport—of racing, we have to remember that racing and races are not the same thing.

I don't say that we should try to go back to the racing of years ago, even if we could, which we can't. Racing has become a mammoth industry. It takes money to support such an industry, and it takes a considerable degree of commercialization to provide that money.

Nobody, for example, says Aqueduct is pretty. It looks, as a lady described it after her first view, "like a supermarket". It is a supermarket, which is what it was designed to be. It is not functionally perfect, but it is functional. It is big enough to meet the competition of other states, and to market our product—horse races—on the super-scale so characteristic of America today.

Right now there are nearly 2,000 horses stabled at Aqueduct and Belmont. Again, there must be. You all understand the hazards of racing, and you know that to put on nine races a day with an average of nine horses—nine hopefully sound horses—in each race, over a period of months, 2,000 horses is not an excessive stock.

You, also, readily see through the popular myth which has it that there is easy money in horse racing, and at the same time realize that the owners of those 2,000 horses cannot subsist strictly *pour le sport*. They would like, at least, to break even—many of them need to—and preferably to make a little money.

This means that there must be purses commensurate with the cost of breeding, feeding, training and just plain worrying a horse to the races. And this can only come from large-scale betting.

But money, if not exactly the root of all evil—and, having some, I have reason to think it's the root of quite a lot of good—is undeniably the source of a great deal of temptation. Especially the large quantities of loose money which pari-mutuel betting attracts.

So, granting that we must be commercial, where do we draw the line that keeps commercialism within safe bounds? We draw it, I would submit, at that point at which the horse begins serving the ends of commercialism, rather than commercialism serving the needs of the horse. And we are getting dangerously close to that line, if indeed it hasn't already been breached.

It may be necessary to provide gimmicked-up betting combinations that become more a test of the numbers-player's luck than of the handicapper's skill. These certainly increase the pari-mutuel take, and though they divert attention from the horse, they do the horse no harm—at least directly. The danger is simply that they increase the temptation to treat horse racing as a giant lottery rather than a sport.

There are other trends I find more directly disturbing.

The spirit of racing is in jeopardy wherever and whenever sportsmen lose control.

Nearly all of our tracks are now owned, operated and controlled by businessmen, in racing as a business.

We find state governments greedy for ever more and more track revenue—not to advance the interests of racing, but simply to fatten the state treasury. At the same time, we find racing commissionerships being passed out as political plums, not to the men best qualified, but to men in line for political rewards—and too often to men who will run racing as a business, not as a sport. To the states, it too often is a business. And which side will these patronage appointees see their bread buttered on—the horse's side, or the governor's?

In my own city of New York, where we are fortunate in our state commission chairman, we find the mayor trying to set up municipal horse parlors of his own—an off-track betting scheme designed not to help racing, but to exploit racing.

At some tracks, we find it mandatory that there be an eight-horse field in each race, or else no race. Quantity, not quality, is the watchword. In order to increase racing profits, we find racing seasons lengthened into northern winters, night racing inaugurated; now a ninth race, sometimes even followed by a tenth.

There are well founded suspicions that at some tracks the management is more concerned with the publicity value of fast times and track records than with the soundness and well-being of the horses. While the times set on fast, hard tracks may please the crowds and seize the headlines, they bring no pleasure to the owners and trainers of the sore and lame horses that have been thus sacrificed to showmanship.

"Getting and spending", Wordsworth wrote, "we lay waste our powers."

Getting and spending, we lay waste our horses. And we especially are laying waste our two-year-olds. In the first eighteen two-year-old stakes of any consequence in America this year, there were 14 different winners. One of these winners made more money—$75,000—for finishing second in one race than he had made for winning any of several other races. Race tracks can and should do what they can to attract the best horses, and virtue should be rewarded. But I submit that $75,000 is a rather spectacular premium for failure.

I must admit at this point that perhaps the most spectacular reward for failure this season was received by Greentree. The prize wasn't gaudy, but the failure was. Our trainer, John Gaver, received a package the other day. It contained a very attractive silver bowl. John naturally assumed it was a trophy for one of our horses that had won a stakes. He couldn't remember winning any stakes recently, so he put on his glasses and read the inscription.

It was for Malicious our two-year-old colt that ran—if I may use the term loosely—for the opulent rewards in the Arlington-Washington Futurity. Of 15 starters, Malicious finished 14th, 17 lengths up the track. And the 15th horse hadn't finished. He'd jumped the rail and gone cavorting off into a parking lot. For this they gave us a silver bowl, and we shall treasure it. I don't know whether the fence-jumper got a trophy, too.

The rewards, whether for winning or for losing, offer almost irresistible temptations to race a two-year-old more times than are good for him. This year two-year-olds came to Aqueduct in September with as many as 14 races behind them. Some of them had their futures behind them, too. More had been asked of

their bones, muscles and tendons—and their hearts—than they were ready to give. The result of this kind of gold rush was races, some of them rather good races. But this was not racing, which is the name of our game. In racing, there is a greater purpose than a purse.

The tremendous overlay of stakes money for two-year-olds, so incongruous with their abilities and so destructive to their potential, is a direct result of treating racing too much as a business and not enough as a sport. It's a trend which needs watching, lest racing devour its young. And you are the people to watch it.

There are other things we can do—and should do—to check the slide of racing toward the level of professional wrestling. We can, and should, simply in our capacity as citizens, demand that racing commissioners be racing men. We are not a lobby, nor do we want to be, but we do have a voice and we can make that voice heard. Men qualified to administer the business of racing are not necessarily qualified to administer the sport of racing. We have got to get that message across.

Each state legislature has lawmakers in it who look on racing as a golden goose, the sole function of which is to provide golden eggs for the state treasurer's chronically unfilled basket. But if we let them squeeze too hard for extra eggs, they're going to cook our goose—feathers and all.

So what do we do? For one thing, we see to it that these legislators are as alert to the sporting aspects of racing as they are to its easy-money possibilities. I don't mean that we should form a "horse party" to elect our own people, or even that we should act at a political force. But we should consider it our duty to educate legislators to the damage greed can do to our sports, and to the need for preserving the sporting spirit.

As for ourselves, we've got to keep our eye on that spirit. We've got to promote the return of the horse.

Kelso has been the monumental exception this year, and for several years, to an overall mediocrity in all age divisions of thoroughbred racing (Lamb Chop certainly cannot be called mediocre either). This mediocrity has been so spectacular that it can no longer be ignored. And if we ask ourselves why, I think we'll find at least part of the answer in our having, too often, let the horse be lost in the horse-race business.

Let me repeat that I'm not pleading for a return to the Good Old Days. I enjoyed the old days as much as any of you, and wouldn't mind going back for a while, if possible. But only for a while. And it isn't possible. We have a glimpse of the old days each year at Saratoga, and that is insufficiently sufficient. Like a single brandy after dinner. We used to have a touch of the Good Old Days at Belmont, and—legislature willing—we shall again. Which reminds me of the return to Belmont after the first meeting at the Big A. One of the office girls, walking under those trees on the way to her typewriter, was heard to remark: "Isn't it nice to be back at the Little B."

There are things we can't have again, and things we possibly shouldn't have again. I remember we had a trainer once who came to me and asked if I could get him some Benedictine. I thought then it was odd, for I knew him as a Bourbon man. It was not until much later that I realized that *that* Benedictine was not for the man, but for the horses! That, of course, was a part of the old days we would not want again.

People often ask me why I still race in England. I race in England because I have had fun there, and because I still do. I am realist enough to know that English racing is not, in this age, a substitute for ours. It really sets no helpful example for American racing, except one. But that one is fundamental.

Compared with ours, English racing is what the country corner store is to the supermarket. On a big day at Newmarket, 10,000 is a big crowd. And very few of these get to sit down. But sitting or standing, they appreciate the horse. Not merely as a gambling device that happens to breathe, but as a horse—as a creature of flesh and blood and heart and spirit. If their horse is beaten, they are likely to understand that he was cut off and had no chance—even if the horse and his trainer know better.

What they have, and what we seem to be losing, is the personal interest in the animal. And this concern for the horse is central to the spirit of racing. This, and the fun of racing, are the spirit of racing. Lose this spirit, and there will be no racing—only races. This was what my mother meant when she said we "cannot allow the spirit of racing to be bought."

It will not be bought if we keep commercialism within bounds. Uncontrolled, commercialism can be our enemy. Contained, it can be our friend. But only we can contain it. Only we can bring about the return of the horse, and put the horse back in racing.

It's up to us, who know the spirit of racing, and who care about it, to preserve as, in the words of your—and may I say my—late, great Joe Palmer, an "athletic contest among horses."

As long as men like John Hay Whitney continue to influence the sport, the future of thoroughbred racing in America is assured.

CHARTS

LEADING MONEY WINNERS BY SEASONS

Year	Two-Year-Olds Horse	Earnings	Three-Year-Olds Horse	Earnings	Handicap Division Horse	Earnings
1900	Commando	$ 40,862				
1901	Blue Girl	64,105				
1902	Savable	46,100	Major Daingerfield	$ 57,685	Waterboy	$ 50,775
1903	Hamburg Belle	47,125	Africander	70,810	Colonial Girl	49,635
1904	Artful	57,805	Delhi	75,225	Beldame	26,850
1905	Burgomaster	39,500	Sysonby	144,380	Go Between	38,255
1906	Electioneer	53,701	Accountant	83,750	Nealon	44,890
1907	Colin	131,705	Peter Pan	86,790	Ballot	55,915
1908	Sir Martin	78,590	Fair Play	70,215	King James	38,253
1909	Sweep	41,323	Joe Madden	44,905	Olambala	22,815
1910	Novelty	72,630	Sweep	22,625	Plate Glass	13,165
1911	Worth	16,645	Governor Gray	15,051	Star Charter	14,655
1912	Helios	12,524	The Manager	12,270	Donald McDonald	16,080
1913	Old Rosebud	19,057	Ten Point	12,840	Buckhorn	11,175
1914	Regret	17,390	Roamer	29,105	Borrow	20,195
1915	Dominant	18,945	The Finn	17,985	Short Grass	16,395
1916	Campfire	49,735	Dodge	26,410	Old Rosebud	31,720
1917	Sun Briar	59,505	Omar Khayyam	49,070	Cudgel	33,826
1918	Eternal	56,137	Johren	49,156	Exterminator	26,402
1919	Man o' War	83,325	Sir Barton	88,250	Exterminator	52,405
1920	Tryster	49,925	Man o' War	166,140	Exterminator	56,827
1921	Morvich	115,234	Grey Lag	62,596	Exterminator	71,075
1922	Sally's Alley	94,847	Pillory	95,654	Chacolet	73,970
1923	St. James	89,385	Zev	272,008	Spot Cash	46,420
1924	Master Charlie	95,525	Sarazen	95,640	Princess Doreen	69,220
1925	Pompey	121,630	American Flag	68,350	Sarazen	42,970
1926	Fair Star	88,960	Crusader	166,033	Chance Play	86,800
1927	Anita Peabody	111,905	Sir Harry	86,842	Crystal Pennant	97,200
1928	High Strung	153,590	Victorian	126,750	Golden Prince	121,600
1929	Whichone	135,455	Blue Larkspur	153,450	Sun Beau	105,005
1930	Equipoise	156,835	Gallant Fox	308,275	Mike Hall	112,975
1931	Top Flight	219,000	Twenty Grand	218,545	Equipoise	107,375
1932	Ladysman	111,435	Gusto	145,940		

LEADING MONEY WINNERS BY SEASONS (cont'd.)

Year	Two-Year-Olds Horse	Earnings	Three-Year-Olds Horse	Earnings	Handicap Division Horse	Earnings
1933	Singing Wood	$ 88,050	Inlander	$ 57,430	Equipoise	$ 55,760
1934	Chance Sun	83,985	Cavalcade	111,235	Faireno	27,160
1935	Tintagel	75,100	Omaha	142,255	Azucar	117,950
1936	Pompoon	82,260	Granville	110,295	Top Row	106,600
1937	Menow	65,825	War Admiral	166,500	Seabiscuit	168,580
1938	El Chico	84,100	Stagehand	189,710	Seabiscuit	130,395
1939	Bimelech	135,090	Challedon	184,535	Kayak II	170,875
1940	Whirlaway	77,275	Bimelech	110,005	Seabiscuit	96,850
1941	Alsab	110,600	Whirlaway	272,386	Big Pebble	159,437
1942	Occupation	192,355	Shut Out	238,972	Whirlaway	211,250
1943	Occupy	112,949	Count Fleet	174,055	Thumbs Up	97,100
1944	Pavot	179,040	Twilight Tear	165,555	First Fiddle	124,105
1945	Star Pilot	165,385	Busher	273,735	Stymie	225,375
1946	Education	164,473	Assault	424,195	Armed	288,725
1947	Bewitch	213,675	Phalanx	269,250	Armed	376,325
1948	Blue Peter	189,185	Citation	709,470	Shannon II	211,610
1949	Bed o' Roses	199,200	Ponder	321,825	Coaltown	276,125
1950	Battlefield	198,677	Hill Prince	314,265	Noor	346,940
1951	Tom Fool	155,960	Counterpoint	250,525	Moonrush	221,050
1952	Native Dancer	230,495	Mark-Ye-Well	268,745	Crafty Admiral	277,225
1953	Hasty Road	277,132	Native Dancer	513,425	Tom Fool	256,355
1954	Summer Tan	230,421	Determine	328,700	Rejected	276,800
1955	Nail	239,930	Nashua	752,550	Social Outcast	390,775
1956	Greek Game	214,805	Needles	440,850	Swaps	409,400
1957	Jewel's Reward	349,642	Round Table	600,383	Dedicate	259,500
1958	First Landing	396,460	Tim Tam	467,200	Round Table	662,780
1959	Warfare	394,610	Sword Dancer	537,004	Hillsdale	502,090
1960	Hail to Reason	328,434	Bally Ache	455,045	Bald Eagle	398,085
1961	Cicada	384,676	Carry Back	565,349	Kelso	425,965
1962	Never Bend	402,969	Jaipur	395,437	Prove It	348,750
1963	Castle Forbes	237,690	Candy Spots	604,481	Kelso	569,762

Name in italics indicates top money winner of the year concerned, regardless of age.

Year	Reg. Foals	Days of Racing	No. Races	No. Horses Racing	Purse Distribution	Average Purse per Race	Average Dist. per Horse
1900	3,476	—	7,226	—	—	—	—
1901	3,784	—	8,391	5,127	—	—	—
1902	3,600	—	7,483	5,271	—	—	—
1903	3,440	—	—	5,525	—	—	—
1904	3,990	—	8,594	5,962	—	—	—
1905	3,800	—	8,473	6,232	—	—	—
1906	3,840	—	6,957	5,962	5,420,381	$ 779.12	$ 909.15
1907	3,780	1,004	6,252	5,662	5,375,554	859.81	949.40
1908	3,080	921	5,699	5,405	4,351,691	763.58	805.12
1909	2,340	724	4,510	4,890	3,146,695	697.71	643.49
1910	1,950	1,063	6,501	4,180	2,942,333	452.59	703.90
1911	2,040	1,037	6,289	4,038	2,337,957	371.75	578.98
1912	1,900	926	5,806	3,553	2,391,625	411.92	673.12
1913	1,722	969	6,136	3,541	2,920,963	476.03	824.89
1914	1,702	906	5,849	3,632	2,994,525	511.97	824.48
1915	2,120	839	5,454	3,700	2,853,037	523.10	771.09
1916	2,128	1,035	6,098	3,754	3,842,471	630.11	1,023.56
1917	1,680	902	5,899	4,200	4,066,253	689.31	968.15
1918	1,950	610	3,968	3,575	3,425,347	863.24	958.13
1919	1,665	686	4,408	3,531	4,642,865	1,053.28	1,314.88
1920	1,833	1,022	6,897	4,032	7,773,407	1,127.07	1,927.92
1921	2,035	1,074	7,250	4,623	8,435,083	1,163.45	1,824.59
1922	2,352	1,182	8,045	5,049	9,096,215	1,130.66	1,801.58
1923	2,763	1,319	8,991	5,437	9,675,811	1,076.16	1,779.62
1924	2,921	1,456	10,007	5,906	10,825,446	1,081.78	1,741.52
1925	3,272	1,656	11,579	6,438	12,577,270	1,086.21	1,953.59
1926	3,632	1,713	12,065	7,218	13,884,820	1,150.83	1,923.63
1927	4,182	1,680	11,832	7,794	13,935,610	1,177.78	1,787.99
1928	4,503	1,613	11,465	8,171	13,332,361	1,162.87	1,631.66
1929	4,903	1,599	11,133	8,332	13,417,817	1,205.22	1,610.39
1930	5,137	1,653	11,477	8,791	13,674,160	1,191.44	1,555.47
1931	5,266	1,660	11,690	9,128	13,084,154	1,119.26	1,433.40
1932	5,256	1,518	10,835	9,017	10,082,757	930.57	1,118.19
1933	5,158	1,746	12,680	9,176	8,516,325	671.63	928.10

LEADING MONEY WINNERS BY SEASONS (cont'd.)

Year	Reg. Foals	Days of Racing	No. Races	No. Horses Racing	Purse Distribution	Average Purse per Race	Average Dist. per Horse
1934	4,924	1,959	14,261	9,470	10,443,495	$ 732.31	$1,102.79
1935	5,038	2,133	15,830	10,544	12,794,418	808.23	1,213.43
1936	5,042	2,033	15,344	10,757	12,994,605	846.88	1,208.01
1937	5,535	2,140	16,250	11,515	14,363,562	883.91	1,247.37
1938	5,696	2,140	16,243	12,185	14,946,609	920.18	1,226.64
1939	6,316	2,199	16,967	12,804	15,312,839	902.50	1,195.94
1940	6,003	2,096	16,401	13,257	15,911,167	970.13	1,200.20
1941	6,805	2,162	16,912	13,683	17,987,225	1,063.57	1,314.56
1942	6,427	2,228	17,593	12,614	18,136,118	1,030.87	1,437.77
1943	5,923	2,052	16,094	11,258	18,555,680	1,152.95	1,648.22
1944	5,650	2,396	19,228	12,959	29,159,099	1,516.49	2,250.10
1945	5,819	2,480	19,587	14,307	32,300,060	1,649.05	2,257.64
1946	6,579	3,020	23,940	17,601	49,291,024	2,058.94	2,800.46
1947	7,705	3,134	24,884	19,063	53,932,141	2,167.34	2,829.15
1948	8,434	3,183	25,388	20,254	54,436,063	2,144.16	2,687.66
1949	8,770	3,309	26,832	21,616	52,317,078	1,949.80	2,420.29
1950	9,095	3,290	26,932	22,554	50,102,099	1,860.31	2,221.42
1951	8,944	3,394	27,856	22,819	55,551,124	1,994.22	2,434.42
1952	8,759	3,515	29,051	23,813	63,950,236	2,201.30	2,685.51
1953	9,062	3,635	30,069	24,417	72,870,819	2,423.45	2,984.42
1954	9,031	3,685	30,467	25,294	74,255,611	2,437.24	2,935.70
1955	9,195	3,827	31,757	26,056	76,643,696	2,413.44	2,941.49
1956	9,791	3,979	33,445	26,507	81,311,581	2,431.20	3,067.55
1957	10,757	4,120	34,982	27,355	85,300,966	2,438.42	3,118.29
1958	11,159	3,910	33,325	28,099	85,467,082	2,564.65	3,041.64
1959	12,039	4,218	36,579	28,623	92,848,541	2,538.30	3,243.84
1960	12,644	4,304	37,661	29,773	93,741,552	2,489.08	3,148.54
1961	13,531	4,641	40,744	30,381	98,846,843	2,426.04	3,253.57
1962	14,475	4,772	41,766	33,579	103,525,712	2,478.71	3,083.05
1963	Incomplete						

584

YEAR	Leading Jockeys (races won)	Leading Jockeys (money won)	Leading Trainers (races won)	Leading Trainers (money won)	Leading Owners (amount won)	Leading Breeders (races won) (money won)	Leading Sires (amt. won by get)
1900	C. Mitchell, 195				J. R. & F. P. Keene $111,357		Kingston $116,368
1901	W. O'Connor, 253				William C. Whitney $108,440		Sir Dixon $165,682
1902	J. Ranch, 276				Green B. Morris $98,350		Hastings $113,865
1903	G. C. Fuller, 229				William C. Whitney $102,569		Ben Strome $106,965
1904	E. Hildebrand, 297				H. B. Duryea, $200,107		Meddler, $222,555
1905	D. Nicol, 221				James R. Keene, $228,724		Hamburg, $153,160
1906	W. Miller, 388				James R. Keene, $155,519		Meddler, $151,243
1907	W. Miller, 334		James Rowe, 70		James R. Keene, $397,342		Commando, $270,345
1908	V. Powers, 324	J. Notter, $464,322	A. J. Joyner, 71	James Rowe, $284,335	James R. Keene, $282,342		Hastings $154,061
1909	V. Powers, 173	E. Dugan, $166,355	H. Guy Bedwell, 122	S. C. Hildreth, $123,942	Samuel C. Hildreth, $159,112		Ben Brush $75,143
1910	G. Garner, 200	C. H. Shilling, $176,030	F. Ernest, 105	S. C. Hildreth, $148,010	Samuel C. Hildreth $152,645		Kingston $85,220
1911	T. Koerner, 162	T. Koerner, $88,308	W. B. Carson, 72	S. C. Hildreth, $49,418	Samuel C. Hildreth $47,473		Star Shoot $53,895
1912	P. Hill, 168	J. Butwell, $79,843	H. Guy Bedwell, 84	J. F. Schorr, $58,110	John W. Schorr $58,225		Star Shoot $79,973
1913	M. Buxton, 146	M. Buxton, $82,552	H. Guy Bedwell, 87	James Rowe, $45,936	Harry Payne Whitney $55,056		Broomstick $76,009
1914	J. McTaggart, 157	J. McCahey, $121,845	H. Guy Bedwell, 84	R. C. Benson, $59,315	John W. Schorr $85,326		Broomstick $99,043
1915	M. Garner, 151	M. Garner, $96,628	H. Guy Bedwell, 97	James Rowe, $75,596	L. S. Thompson $104,106		Broomstick $94,387
1916	F. Robinson, 178	J. McTaggart, $155,055	H. Guy Bedwell, 123	S. C. Hildreth, $70,950	H. Guy Bedwell $71,100		Star Shoot $138,163
1917	W. Crump, 151	F. Robinson, $148,057	H. Guy Bedwell, 66	S. C. Hildrith, $61,698	A. K. Macomber $68,578	John E. Madden, 213	Star Shoot $131,674
1918	F. Robinson, 185	L. Luke, $201,864	Kay Spence, 58	H. Guy Bedwell, $80,296	J. K. L. Ross $99,179		Sweep $139,057

YEAR	Leading Jockeys (races won) (money won)	Leading Trainers (money won)	Leading Owners (amount won)	Leading Breeders (races won) (money won)	Leading Sires (amt. won by get)
1919	C. Robinson, 190	Kay Spence, 96	J. K. L. Ross	John E. Madden, 311	Star Shoot
	J. Loftus, $252,707	H. Guy Bedwell, $208,728	$209,303		$197,233
1920	J. Butwell, 152	Kay Spence, 74	Harry Payne Whitney	John E. Madden, 313	Fair Play
	C. Kummer, $292,376	S. A. Clopton, 74	$270,675		$269,102
		L. Feustel, $186,087			
1921	C. Lang, 135	S. C. Hildreth, 85	Rancocas Stable, $263,500	J. E. Madden, 424	Celt
	E. Sande, $263,043	S. C. Hildreth, $262,768	(Harry F. Sinclair)		$206,167
1922	M. Fator, 188	Henry McDaniel, 78	Rancocas Stbl, $239,503	J. E. Madden, 366	McGee
	A. Johnson, $345,054	J. A. Parsons, 78	(Harry F. Sinclair)	J. E. Madden, $568,785	$222,491
		S. C. Hildreth, $247,014			
1923	I. Parke, 173	C. B. Irwin, 147	Rancocas Stbl, $438,849	J. E. Madden, 419	The Finn
	E. Sande, $569,394	S. C. Hildreth, $392,124	(Harry F. Sinclair)	J. E. Madden, $623,630	$285,759
1924	I. Parke, 205	J. A. Parsons, 93	Harry Payne Whitney	J. E. Madden, 318	Fair Play
	I. Parke, $290,395	S. C. Hildreth, $225,608	$240,193	H. P. Whitney, $482,865	$296,204
1925	A. Mortensen, 187	J. J. Duggan, 70	Glen Riddle Farm	J. E. Madden, 383	Sweep
	L. Fator, $305,775	G. R. Tompkins, $199,245	(S. D. Riddle), $199,143	J. E. Madden, $535,790	$237,564
1926	R. Jones, 190	W. Perkins, 82	Harry Payne Whitney	J. E. Madden, 368	Man o' War
	L. Fator, $361,435	S. P. Harlan, $205,681	$407,139	H. P. Whitney, $715,158	$408,137
1927	L. Hardy, 207	S. C. Hildreth, 72	Harry Payne Whitney	John E. Madden, 362	Fair Play
	E. Sande, $277,877	W. H. Bringloe, $216,563	$328,769	H. P. Whitney, $718,144	$361,518
1928	J. Inzelone, 155	J. F. Schorr, 65	Edward B. McLean	Himyar Stud, 331	High Time
	L. McAtee, $301,295	J. Reed, 65	$234,640	H. P. Whitney, $514,832	$307,631
		J. F. Schorr, $258,425			
1929	M. Knight, 149	L. Gentry, 74	Harry Payne Whitney	Himyar Stud, 335	Chicle
	M. Garner, $314,975	J. Rowe, Jr., $314,881	$362,305	H. P. Whitney, $825,374	$289,123
1930	H. R. Riley, 177	C. B. Irwin, 92	C. V. Whitney	Audley Farm, 318	Sir Gallahad III
	R. Workman, $420,438	J. Fitzsimmons, $397,355	$385,972	H. P. Whitney, $690,280	$422,200
1931	H. Roble, 173	J. D. Mikel, 72	C. V. Whitney	Audley Farm, 359	St. Germans
	C. Kurtsinger, $392,095	J. W. Healy, $297,300	$422,923	H. P. Whitney, $582,970	$315,585
1932	J. Gilbert, 212	G. Alexandra, 76	C. V. Whitney	Himyar Stud, 267	Chatterton
	R. Workman, $385,070	J. Fitzsimmons, $266,650	$403,681	H. P. Whitney Estate, $560,803	$210,040

YEAR	Leading Jockeys (races won) (money won)		Leading Trainers (races won) (money won)		Leading Owners (amount won)	Leading Breeders (races won) (money won)		Leading Sires (amt. won by get)
1933	J. Westrope, 301	R. Jones, $226,285	Hirsch Jacobs, 116	R. A. Smith, $135,720	C. V. Whitney $241,292	Harry Payne & C. V. Whitney, 282	Harry Payne & C. V. Whitney, $342,866	Sir Gallahad III $136,428
1934	M. Peters, 221	W. D. Wright, $287,185	Hirsch Jacobs, 127	R. A. Smith, $249,938	Brookmeade Stable (Mrs. Dodge Sloane) $251,138	Harry Payne & C. V. Whitney, 310	Harry Payne & C. V. Whitney, $320,955	Sir Gallahad III $180,165
1935	C. Stevenson, 206	S. Coucci, $319,760	Hirsch Jacobs, 114	J. H. Stotler, $303,005	A. G. Vanderbilt $303,605	Arthur B. Hancock, 292	Arthur B. Hancock, $359,218	Chance Play $191,465
1936	B. James, 245	W. D. Wright, $264,000	Hirsch Jacobs, 177	J. Fitzsimmons, $193,415	Milky Way Farm Stable (Mrs. Ethel V. Mars) $206,450	Arthur B. Hancock, 314	Arthur B. Hancock, $362,762	Sickle $209,800
1937	J. Adams, 260	C. Kurtsinger, $384,202	Hirsch Jacobs, 134	R. McGarvey, $209,925	Mrs. Chas. S. Howard $214,559	Arthur B. Hancock, 279	Arthur B. Hancock, $416,558	The Porter $292,262
1938	J. Longden, 236	N. Wall, $385,161	Hirsch Jacobs, 109	E. H. Sande, $226,495	H. Maxwell Howard $226,495	Arthur B. Hancock, 300	H. P. & C. V. Whitney, $374,049	Sickle, $327,822
1939	D. Meade, 255	B. James, $353,333	Hirsch Jacobs, 106	J. Fitzsimmons, $266,205	Belair Stud (Wm. Woodward) $284,250	Willis Sharpe Kilmer, 269	Arthur B. Hancock, $345,503	Challenger II $316,281
1940	E. Dew, 287	E. Arcaro, $343,661	D. Womeldorff, 108	T. Smith, $269,200	Charles S. Howard $334,120	Arthur B. Hancock, 302	J. E. Widener, $317,961	Sir Gallahad III $305,610
1941	D. Meade, 210	D. Meade, $398,627	Hirsch Jacobs, 123	B. A. Jones, $475,316	Calumet Farm (Warren Wright), $475,091	W. S. Kilmer, 256	Warren Wright (Calumet Farm), $528,211	Blenheim II $378,981
1942	J. Adams, 245	E. Arcaro, $481,949	Hirsch Jacobs, 133	J. M. Gaver, $406,547	Greentree Stable (Mrs. Payne Whitney, $414,432	Arthur B. Hancock, 333	Mrs. Payne Whitney, (Greentree Stable), $536,173	Equipoise $437,141
1943	J. Adams, 228	J. Longden, $573,276	Hirsch Jacobs, 128	B. A. Jones, $267,915	Calumet Farm (Warren Wright), $267,915	Arthur B. Hancock, 346	Arthur B. Hancock, $619,049	Bull Dog $372,706
1944	T. Atkinson, 287	T. Atkinson, $899,101	Hirsch Jacobs, 117	B. A. Jones, $601,660	Calumet Farm (Warren Wright), $601,660	Arthur B. Hancock, 322	Warren Wright (Calumet Farm), $990,612	Chance Play $431,100
1945	J. D. Jessop, 290	J. Longden, $981,977	S. Lipiec, 127	T. Smith, $510,655	Maine Chance Farm (Mrs. Eliz. N. Graham), $589,170	Mereworth Farm, 307	E. E. Dale Shaffer, (Coldstream Stud), $791,477	War Admiral $591,352

YEAR	Leading Jockeys (races won) (money won)	Leading Trainers (races won) (money won)	Leading Owners (amount won)	Leading Breeders (races won) (money won)	Leading Sires (amt. won by get)
1946	T. Atkinson, 233 T. Atkinson, $1,036,825	W. Molter, 122 Hirsch Jacobs, $560,077	Calumet Farm (Warren Wright), $564,095	Arthur B. Hancock, 350 Mereworth Farm, $962,677	Mahmoud $638,025
1947	J. Longden, 316 D. Dodson, $1,429,949	W. Molter, 155 H. A. Jones, $1,334,805	Calumet Farm (Warren Wright), $1,402,436	Mereworth Farm, 358 Warren Wright (Calumet Farm), $1,807,432	Bull Lea $1,259,718
1948	J. Longden, 319 E. Arcaro, $1,686,230	W. Molter, 184 H. A. Jones, $1,118,670	Calumet Farm (Warren Wright), $1,269,710	Mereworth Farm, 330 Warren Wright (Calumet Farm), $1,559,850	Bull Lea $1,334,027
1949	G. Glisson, 270 S. Brooks, $1,316,817	W. Molter, 129 W. H. Bishop, 129 H. A. Jones, $978,587	Calumet Farm (Warren Wright), $1,128,942	Mereworth Farm, 347 Warren Wright (Calumet Farm), $1,515,181	Bull Lea $991,842
1950	J. Culmone, 388 W. Shoemaker, 388 E. Arcaro, $1,410,160	R. H. McDaniel, 156 P. M. Burch, $637,754	Brookmeade Stable (Mrs. Dodge Sloane), $651,399	Mereworth Farm, 313 Warren Wright (Calumet Farm), $1,090,286	Heliopolis $852,292
1951	C. Burr, 310 W. Shoemaker, $1,329,890	R. H. McDaniel, 164 J. M. Gaver, $616,392	Greentree Stable (Mrs. C. S. Payson & J. H. Whitney), $637,242	Mereworth Farm, 299 Warren Wright (Calumet Farm), $1,198,107	Count Fleet, $1,160,847
1952	A. DeSpirito, 390 E. Arcaro, $1,859,591	R. H. McDaniel, 168 B. A. Jones, $662,137	Calumet Farm (Mrs. Gene Markey), $1,283,197	Mereworth Farm, 270 Mrs. Gene Markey (Calumet Farm), $2,060,590	Bull Lea $1,630,655
1953	W. Shoemaker, 485 W. Shoemaker, $1,784,187	R. H. McDaniel, 211 H. Trotsek, $1,028,873	A. G. Vanderbilt $987,306	Mereworth Farm, 246 Mrs. Gene Markey (Calumet Farm), $1,573,803	Bull Lea $1,155,846
1954	W. Shoemaker, 380 W. Shoemaker, $1,876,760	R. H. McDaniel, 206 W. Molter, $1,107,860	King Ranch, (Robert J. Kleberg, Jr.) $837,615	Calumet Farm, 201 Mrs. Gene Markey (Calumet Farm), $1,139,609	Heliopolis $1,406,638
1955	W. Hartack, 417 E. Arcaro, $1,864,796	F. H. Merrill, Jr., 154 J. Fitzsimmons, $1,270,055	Hasty House Farm (Mr. & Mrs. A. E. Reuben) $832,879	Henry H. Knight, 223 Mrs. Gene Markey (Calumet Farm), $999,737	Nasrullah $1,433,660
1956	W. Hartack, 347 W. Hartack, $2,343,955	V. R. Wright, 177 W. Molter, $1,227,402	Calumet Farm (Mrs. Gene Markey), $1,057,383	Henry H. Knight, 293 Mrs. Gene Markey (Calumet Farm), $1,528,727	Nasrullah $1,462,413
1957	W. Hartack, 341 W. Hartack, $3,060,501	V. R. Wright, 192 H. A. Jones, $1,150,910	Calumet Farm (Mrs. Gene Markey), $1,150,910	Henry H. Knight, 284 Mrs. Gene Markey (Calumet Farm), $1,469,473	Princequillo $1,698,427

YEAR	Leading Jockeys (races won) (money won)	Leading Trainers (races won) (money won)	Leading Owners (amount won)	Leading Breeders (races won) (money won)	Leading Sires (amt. won by get)
1958	W. Shoemaker, 300	F. H. Merrill, Jr., 171	Calumet Farm (Mrs.	Henry H. Knight, 260	Princequillo
	W. Shoemaker, $2,961,693	W. Molter, $1,116,544	Gene Markey), $946,262	Claiborne Farm, $1,414,355 (A. B. Hancock, Jr. & Sr.)	$1,394,540
1959	W. Shoemaker, 347	V. R. Wright, 172	Cain Hoy Stable (H. F.	King Ranch, 227	Nasrullah
	W. Shoemaker, $2,843,133	W. Molter, $847,290	Guggenheim), $742,081	Claiborne Farm, $1,322,595 (A. B. Hancock, Jr.)	$1,394,540
1960	W. Hartack, 307	F. H. Merrill, Jr., 143	C. V. Whitney	E. P. Taylor, 267	Nasrullah
	W. Shoemaker, $2,123,961	Hirsch Jacobs, $748,349	$1,039,091	C. V. Whitney, $1,193,181	$1,419,683
1961	J. Sellers, 328	V. R. Wright, 178	Calumet Farm (Mrs.	E. P. Taylor, 265	Ambiorix
	W. Shoemaker, $2,690,819	H. A. Jones, $759,856	Gene Markey), $759,856	Mrs. Gene Markey (Calumet Farm), $1,078,894	$936,976
1962	R. Ferraro, 352	W. H. Bishop, 162	Rex C. Ellsworth	E. P. Taylor, 263	Nasrullah
	W. Shoemaker, $2,916,844	M. A. Tenney, $1,099,474	$1,154,454	R. C. Ellsworth, $1,678,769	$1,474,831
1963	W. Blum, 360	H. Jacobson, 140	Rex C. Ellsworth	E. P. Taylor, 300	Bold Ruler
	W. Shoemaker, $2,526,925	M. A. Tenny, $860,703	$1,096,863	R. C. Ellsworth, $1,465,069	$917,531

Year	Yearlings Sold	Average Price	Revenue to States
1900			
1901			
1902			
1903			
1904			
1905			
1906			
1907			
1908			
1909			
1910	550	$ 325.00	
1911	390	230.00	
1912	243	517.29	
1913	316	371.66	
1914	398	653.97	
1915	375	695.40	
1916	426	931.87	
1917	643	1,030.00	
1918	509	827.53	
1919	335	2,139.78	
1920	400	1,727.22	
1921	395	2,273.72	
1922	534	2,199.94	
1923	640	2,015.88	
1924	600	2,230.39	
1925	582	3,207.53	
1926	751	2,639.81	
1927	703	2,758.78	
1928	852	2,269.00	
1929	855	2,538.68	
1930	1,030	1,966.15	
1931	1,070	980.18	
1932	952	569.95	
1933	813	695.89	
1934	746	824.65	$ 6,024,193.31
1935	831	1,192.31	8,386,255.00
1936	892	1,576.29	8,611,537.90
1937	877	1,675.96	8,434,792.00
1938	985	1,563.90	9,576,334.75
1939	1,150	1,459.00	10,369,807.00
1940	1,258	1,185.95	16,145,182.00
1941	1,072	1,215.00	21,128,173.00
1942	1,061	637.75	22,005,278.00
1943	873	1,865.99	38,194,726.56
1944	818	3,916.93	55,971,232.87
1945	986	5,146.37	65,265,405.48
1946	1,287	5,909.24	94,035,859.47
1947	1,465	4,184.42	97,926,984.16
1948	1,629	3,624.64	95,803,363.95
1949	1,818	2,834.96	95,327,052.96
1950	1,739	2,920.82	98,366,166.67

Year	Yearlings Sold	Average Price	Revenue to States
1951	1,695	4,038.68	117,250,564.00
1952	1,640	$4,320.91	$142,489,696.00
1953	1,637	4,470.05	167,426,465.00
1954	1,625	4,972.66	178,015,828.00
1955	1,583	5,451.64	186,989,588.00
1956	1,672	5,298.96	207,456,272.00
1957	1,638	5,426.65	216,750,621.00
1958	1,783	5,021.62	222,049,651.00
1959	1,716	5,747.20	243,388,655.00
1960	1,911	5,262.65	257,510,069.00
1961	2,021	5,529.14	264,858,077.00
1962	2,279	5,527.60	287,930,030.00
1963	2,324	5,611.12	316,570,791.00

EVOLUTION OF AMERICAN TIME RECORDS SINCE 1900

FIVE FURLONGS

Time	Horse, Age, Weight	Track and Year
:59	George F. Smith, 4, 100	San Francisco, 1895
:58 ⅗	Jack Nunnally, 3, 108	Oakland, 1907
	Silver Stocking, 4, 102	Seattle, 1908
:58	Tern's Trick, 3, 97	Oakland, 1910
:57 ⅕	Pan Zareta, 5, 120	Juarez, 1915
:57	Encantadora, 3, 115	Centennial, 1951
	Miss Todd, 2, 119	Hollywood, 1955
:56 ⅗	Lucky Mel, 2, 122	Hollywood, 1956
	Bettyanbull, 4, 118	Turf Paradise, 1958
:56 ⅖	Bettyanbull, 5, 120	Turf Paradise, 1959

SIX FURLONGS

Time	Horse, Age, Weight	Track and Year
1:12	Bummer, 4, 80	Kinloch, 1900
	Lux Casta, 3, 111	Brighton Beach, 1902
1:11 ⅘	Dick Welles, 3, 109	Washington Park, 1903
	Ivan the Terrible, 2, 92	Worth, 1904
1:11 ⅗	Roseben, 4, 147	Belmont, 1905
	Col. Bob, 2, 92	Santa Anita, 1907
1:11	Chapultepec, 3, 112	Santa Anita, 1908
	Prince Ahmed, 5, 117	Empire City, 1909
	Priscillian, 6, 113	Hamilton, 1911
1:10 ⅘	Iron Mask, 5, 127	Douglas Park, 1913
	Leochares, 3, 109	Douglas Park, 1913
	Orb, 2, 90	Juarez, 1913
1:09 ⅗	Iron Mask, 6, 115	Juarez, 1914
1:09 ⅕	Clang, 3, 110	Coney Island (O.), 1935
	Mafosta, 4, 116	Longacres, 1946
	Polynesian, 4, 126	Atlantic City, 1946
1:08 ⅖	Fair Truckle, 4, 119	Golden Gate, 1947
1:08 ⅕	Bolero, 4, 122	Golden Gate, 1950
1:08	Dumpty Humpty, 4, 115	Golden Gate, 1957
1:07 ⅘	Crazy Kid, 4, 118	Del Mar, 1962

SEVEN FURLONGS

Time	Horse, Age, Weight	Track and Year
1:25 ⅖	Clifford, 4, 127	Sheepshead Bay, 1894
1:25	The Musketeer, 4, 108	Saratoga, 1902
1:22	Roseben, 5, 126	Belmont, 1906
	Clang, 3, 105	Arlington Park, 1935
	High Resolve, 4, 126	Hollywood, 1945
1:21 ⅘	Honeymoon, 4, 114	Hollywood, 1947
	Buzfuz, 5, 120	Hollywood, 1947
1.21 ⅖	Ky. Colonel, 3, 116	Washington Park, 1949
1:21	Bolero, 5, 121	Santa Anita, 1951
1:20 ⅗	Imbros, 4, 118	Santa Anita, 1954
1:20	El Drag, 4, 115	Hollywood, 1955

ONE MILE

Time	Horse, Age, Weight	Track and Year
†1:35½	Salvator, 4, 110	#Monmouth, 1890
1:38	Voter, 6, 122	Brighton Beach, 1900
	Orimar, 6, 109	Washington Park, 1900
1:37 ⅘	Brigadier, 4, 112	Sheepshead Bay, 1901
1:37 ⅖	Dick Welles, 3, 112	Harlem, 1903
	Kiamesha, 3, 104	Belmont, 1905
1:37 ⅕	Centre Shot, 3, 105	Santa Anita, 1908
	Manasseh, 4, 93	Juarez, 1913
	Vested Rights, 3, 105	Juarez, 1913
1:36 ¼	Amalfi, 6, 107	Syracuse, 1914
1:36 ⅕	Sun Briar, 3, 113	Saratoga, 1918
†1:34⅘	Roamer, 7, 110	Saratoga, 1918
1:36 ⅕	Fairy Wand, 5, 107	Saratoga, 1919
1:35 ⅘	Man o' War, 3, 118	Belmont, 1920
1:35⅗	Audacious 5, 118	Belmont, 1921
1:35 ⅖	Cherry Pie, 3, 113	Belmont, 1923
1:35	Jack High, 4, 110	Belmont, 1930
1:34 ⅖	Equipoise, 4, 128	Arlington, 1932
	Prevaricator, 5, 118	Golden Gate, 1948
1:34	Coaltown, 4, 130	Washington Park, 1949
1:33 ⅗	Citation, 5, 128	Golden Gate, 1950
1:33 ⅕	Swaps, 4, 128	Hollywood, 1956
	Intentionally, 3, 121	Washington Park, 1959

† Run against time.
# Old Monmouth Park—straight course.

A MILE AND ONE-SIXTEENTH

Time	Horse, Age, Weight	Track and Year
1:45	Carnero, 5, 107	Hawthorne, 1899
1:44 ⅘	Hyphen, 3, 102	Brighton Beach, 1902
1:44 ⅗	Glassful, 3, 101	Washington Park, 1903
	Israelite, 4, 101	Brighton Beach, 1905
1:44 ⅕	Royal Tourist, 3, 104	Oakland, 1908
1:43 ⅗	Gretna Green, 5, 100	Fort Erie, 1909
	Trap Rock, 3, 112	Fort Erie, 1911
1:42¾	Celesta, 4, 108	Syracuse, 1914
1:42 ⅕	Dot, 3, 100	Belmont, 1923
1:42	Top Row, 3, 109	Bay Meadows, 1934
	Bull Reigh, 5, 121	Bay Meadows, 1943
1:41 ⅗	Snow Boots, 4, 117	Santa Anita, 1946
1:41	Count Speed, 4, 122	Golden Gate, 1947
	Imbros, 4, 118	Hollywood, 1954
1:40 ⅖	Swaps, 3, 115	Hollywood, 1955
1:39	Swaps, 4, 130	Hollywood, 1956

A MILE AND ONE-EIGHTH

Time	Horse, Age, Weight	Track and Year
1:51 ⅕	Watercure, 3, 100	Brighton Beach, 1900
	Roechampton, 3, 94	Brighton Beach, 1901
1:51	Bonnibert, 4, 120	Brighton Beach, 1902
1:50 ⅗	Charles Edward, 3, 126	Brighton Beach, 1907
1:50	Vox Populi, 4, 110	Santa Anita, 1908
1:49 ⅗	Roamer, 3, 124	Laurel, 1914
1:49 ⅖	Borrow, 9, 117	Aqueduct, 1917
	Boots, 6, 127	Aqueduct, 1917
1:49 ⅕	Man o' War, 3, 126	Aqueduct, 1920
1:49	Goaler, 5, 94½	Belmont, 1921
	Grey Lag, 3, 123	Aqueduct, 1921
1:48 ⅘	Chilhowee, 3, 115	Latonia, 1924
1:48 ⅗	Peanuts, 4, 114	Aqueduct, 1926
1:48 ⅖	Hot Toddy, 4, 110	Belmont, 1929
	Blessed Event, 4, 111	Hialeah, 1934
1:48 ⅕	Discovery, 4, 123	Aqueduct, 1935
1:47 ⅗	Indian Broom, 3, 94	Tanforan, 1936
	Shannon II, 7, 124	Golden Gate, 1948
	Coaltown, 4, 114	Hialeah, 1949
1:46 ⅘	Noor, 5, 123	Golden Gate, 1950
	Alidon, 4, 116	Hollywood, 1955
	Swaps, 4, 130	Hollywood, 1956
	Gen. Duke, 3, 122	Gulfstream, 1957
	Round Table, 4, 130	Santa Anita, 1958
1:46 ⅖	Bug Brush, 4, 113	Santa Anita, 1959

A MILE AND ONE QUARTER

Time	Horse, Age, Weight	Track and Year
2:03 ¾	Banquet, 3, 108	†Monmouth, 1890
2:04	Charentus, 6, 106	Yonkers, 1900
2:03 ⅘	Gold Heels, 4, 126	Brighton Beach, 1902
2:03 ⅕	Waterboy, 4, 124	Brighton Beach, 1903
2:02 ⅘	Broomstick, 3, 104	Brighton Beach, 1904
	Olambala, 4, 122	Sheepshead Bay, 1910
2:00	Whisk Broom II, 6, 139	Belmont, 1913
	Cover Up, 4, 117	Hollywood, 1947
1:59 ⅘	Shannon II, 7, 124	Golden Gate, 1948
	Coaltown, 4, 128	Gulfstream, 1949
1:58 ⅕	Noor, 5, 127	Golden Gate, 1950

† Old Monmouth Park—straight course.

A MILE AND ONE-HALF

Time	Horse, Age, Weight	Track and Year
2:30 ¼	Goodrich, 3, 102	Washington, 1898
2:29 ⅗	Thunderclap, 3, 108	Laurel, 1919
2:28 ⅘	Man o' War, 3, 118	Belmont, 1920
2:28 ⅗	Handy Mandy, 3, 109	Latonia, 1927
	War Admiral, 3, 126	Belmont, 1937
2:28 ⅖	Sorteado, 4, 112	Belmont, 1939
2:27 ⅗	Bolingbroke, 5, 115	Belmont, 1942
2:26 ⅗	Gallant Man, 3, 126	Belmont, 1957

TWO MILES

Time	Horse, Age, Weight	Track and Year
3:26 ½	Judge Denny, 5, 105	Oakland, 1898
3:25 ⅘	Fitz Herbert, 3, 106	Pimlico, 1909
3:25 ⅗	Everett, 3, 107	Pimlico, 1910
3:21 ⅘	Exterminator, 5, 128	Belmont, 1920
3:20 ⅘	Market Wise, 3, 114	Belmont, 1941
3:20 ⅖	Nashua, 4, 124	Belmont, 1956
3:19 ⅖	Kelso, 3, 119	Aqueduct, 1960

Note: Where a record was broken more than once during the same year, only the fastest time is listed.

COMPARATIVE MEASUREMENTS OF THREE FAMOUS HORSES

	Man o' War	Gallant Fox	Equipoise
Height at withers	16.2 ¼	16.1 ¼	15.3 ¾
Height at rump	16.2 ⅛	16 ¼	15.3 ¾
Length of body	16.2 ⅛	16 ½	15.2
Girth at heart	76 ½	73	72
Girth at waist	74 ¾	67 ¼	71
Circumference of throatlatch	36	32	31
Length of neck	31 ¼	30	33
Length of shoulder	28	24 ½	22 ⅞
Width between forelegs	5 ½	5	4 ⅜
Circumference of forearm at swell	22	18 ½	18 ½
Circumference of front cannon, midway	8 ⅝	8 ¼	7 ½
Circumference of stifle at swell	46	37 ¼	35
Circumference of hind cannon, midway	9 ⅛	8 ½	8 ¼
Circumference of gaskin at swell	19	17 ¼	18

AMERICA'S TEN GREATEST RACE MARES

(As determined by a poll conducted by Delaware Park among members of the American Trainers Association)

	Mares	Starts	1st	2nd	3rd	Unpl.	Earnings	Score in Voting
1.	Gallorette, 1942	72	21	20	13	18	$445,535	548
2.	Twilight Tear, 1941	24	18	2	2	2	202,165	426
3.	Regret, 1912	11	9	1	0	1	35,093	412
4.	Top Flight, 1929	16	12	0	0	4	275,900	382
5.	Miss Woodford, 1880	48	37	7	2	2	118,270	371
6.	Busher, 1942	21	15	3	1	2	334,035	287
7.	Beldame, 1901	31	17	6	4	4	102,570	268
8.	Princess Doreen, 1921	94	34	15	17	28	174,745	219
9.	Bewitch, 1945	55	20	10	11	14	462,605	203
10.	Imp, 1894	171	62	35	29	45	70,119	166

PARADE OF FINANCIAL CHAMPIONS

+Year	Leading American Money Winner	* Owner (Breeder)	Starts	1st	2nd	3rd	Unpl.	Earnings	Average per start
1823	AMERICAN ECLIPSE, ch.h., 1814, by Duroc	C. Van Ranst (Nathaniel Coles)	8	8	—	—	—	$ 56,700	$ 7,088
1845	PEYTONA, ch.m., 1839, by Glencoe	Thomas Kirkman (James Jackson)	7	6	1	—	—	66,000	9,429
1861	PLANET, ch.h., 1855, by Revenue	T. W. Doswell (same)	31	27	4	—	—	69,700	2,248
1881	PAROLE, b.g., 1873, by Leamington	G. Lorillard (A. Welch)	127	59	24	15	29	82,184	647
1885	MISS WOODFORD, br.m., 1880, by Billet	Dwyer Bros. (Geo. W. Bowen & Co.)	48	37	7	2	2	118,270	2,464
1889	HANOVER, ch.h., 1884, by Hindoo	Dwyer Bros. (Clay & Woodford)	50	32	13	3	2	118,872	2,377
1892	KINGSTON, br.h., 1884, by Spendthrift	Dwyer Bros. (James R. Keene)	138	89	33	12	4	138,891	1,006
1893	DOMINO, br.c., 1891, by Himyar	J. R. & F. P. Keene (B. G. Thomas)	25	19	2	1	3	193,550	7,742
1920	MAN o' WAR, ch.c., 1917, by Fair Play	Glen Riddle Farm (August Belmont)	21	20	1	—	—	249,465	11,879
1923	ZEV, br.c., 1920, by The Finn	Rancocas Stable (J. E. Madden)	43	23	8	5	7	313,639	7,294
1930	GALLANT FOX, b.c., 1927, by Sir Gallahad III	Belair Stud (same)	17	11	3	2	1	328,165	19,304
1931	SUN BEAU, b.h., 1925, by Sun Briar	W. S. Kilmer (same)	74	33	12	10	19	376,744	5,091
1940	SEABISCUIT, b.h., 1933, by Hard Tack	C. S. Howard (Wheatley Stable)	89	33	15	13	28	437,730	4,918
1942	WHIRLAWAY, ch.c., 1938, by Blenheim II	Calumet Farm (same)	60	32	15	9	4	561,161	9,353
1947	ASSAULT, ch.c., 1943, by Bold Venture	King Ranch (same)	42	18	6	7	11	675,470	16,083
	ARMED, br.g., 1941, by Bull Lea	Calumet Farm (same)	81	41	20	10	10	817,475	10,092
	STYMIE, ch.h., 1941, by Equestrian	Mrs. E. D. Jacobs (Max Hirsch)	131	35	33	28	35	918,485	7,011
1950	CITATION, b.h., 1945, by Bull Lea	Calumet Farm (same)	45	32	10	2	1	1,085,760	24,128
1956	NASHUA, b.c., 1952, by Nasrullah	Leslie Combs II (Belair Stud)	30	22	4	1	3	1,288,565	42,952
1958	ROUND TABLE, b.c., 1954, by Princequillo	Kerr Stable (Claiborne Farm)	66	43	8	5	10	1,749,869	26,513

+ Year indicated is the year in which the horse concerned became leading money winner, but records reflect complete racing careers.

* Owner indicated is owner of record at the time the horse became leading money winner.

American Eclipse actually raced only 8 times, but received prize money in a livestock exhibition also.

MAN O' WAR'S COMPLETE RACING RECORD

As a two-year old, 1919

Date	Track	Event	Weight	Distance	Track Condition	Time	Finish	Earnings
June 6	Belmont Park	Purse race	115	5 fur. (s)	Fast	:59	Won by 6	$ 500
" 9	" "	Keene Memorial Stakes	115	5½ fur. (s)	Slow	1:05⅗	" " 3	4,200
" 21	Jamaica	Youthful Stakes	120	5½ fur.	Good	1:06⅗	" " 2½	3,850
" 23	Aqueduct	Hudson Stakes	130	5 fur.	Fast	1:01⅗	" " 1½	2,825
July 5	"	Tremont Stakes	130	6 fur.	"	1:13	" " 1	4,800
Aug. 2	Saratoga	U.S. Hotel Stakes	130	6 fur.	"	1:12⅖	" " 2	7,600
" 13	"	Sanford Memorial Stakes	130	6 fur.	"	1:11⅕	2nd by ½	700
" 23	"	Grand Union Hotel Stakes	130	6 fur.	"	1:12	Won by 1	7,600
" 30	"	Hopeful Stakes	130	6 fur.	Slow	1:13	" " 4	24,600
Sep. 13	Belmont	Futurity Stakes	127	6 fur. (s)	Fast	1:11⅗	" " 2½	26,650
								($ 83,325)

As a three-year-old, 1920

Date	Track	Event	Weight	Distance	Track Condition	Time	Finish	Earnings
May 18	Pimlico	Preakness Stakes	126	1⅛ mi.	Fast	1:51⅗	Won by 1½	$ 23,000
" 29	Belmont Park	Withers Stakes	118	1 mi.	"	#1:35⅘	" " 2	4,825
June 12	" "	Belmont Stakes	126	1⅜ mi.	"	#2:14⅕	" " 20	7,950
" 22	Jamaica	Stuyvesant Handicap	135	1 mi.	Good	1:41⅗	" " 8	3,850
July 10	Aqueduct	Dwyer Stakes	126	1⅛ mi.	Fast	#1:49⅕	" " 1½	4,850
Aug. 7	Saratoga	Miller Stakes	131	1 3/16 mi.	"	1:56⅗	" " 6	4,700
" 21	"	Travers Stakes	129	1¼ mi.	"	#2:01⅘	" " 2½	9,275
Sep. 4	Belmont Park	Lawrence Realization Stakes	126	1⅝ mi.	"	#2:40⅘	" " 100	15,040
" 11	" "	Jockey Club Stakes	118	1½ mi.	"	#2:28⅘	" " 15	5,850
" 18	Havre de Grace	Potomac Handicap	138	1 1/16 mi.	"	#1:44⅘	" " 1½	6,800
Oct. 12	Kenilworth Park	Kenilworth Park Gold Cup	120	1¼ mi.	"	#2:03	" " 7	80,000
								(166,140)
								$249,465

Time Records, as follows:

Equaled track record, Travers Stakes, 1¼ miles.
New track record, Potomac Handicap, 1 1/16 miles.
New track record, Kenilworth Cup, 1¼ miles.
New (competitive) American record, Withers Stakes, 1 mile.
New (competitive) American record, Jockey Club Stakes, 1½ miles.
New World Record, Dwyer Stakes, 1⅛ miles.
New World Record, Belmont Stakes, 1⅜ miles.
New World Record, Lawrence Realization, 1⅝ miles.

In all his starts as a two-year-old, Man o' War was ridden by John Loftus; Clarence Kummer was his jockey in all his starts at three, except the Miller Stakes (Earl Sande) and Travers Stakes (Andy Schuttinger).

JOCKEY CLUB SCALE OF WEIGHTS FOR AGE

Distance	Age	Jan.	Feb.	March	April	May	June	July	Aug.	Sept.	Oct.	Nov.	Dec.
½-mile	2	x	x	x	x	x	x	x	105	108	111	114	114
	3	117	117	119	119	121	123	125	126	127	128	129	129
	4	130	130	130	130	130	130	130	130	130	130	130	130
	5 & up	130	130	130	130	130	130	130	130	130	130	130	130
6 furlongs	2	x	x	x	x	x	x	x	102	105	108	111	111
	3	114	114	117	117	119	121	123	125	126	127	128	128
	4	129	129	130	130	130	130	130	130	130	130	130	130
	5 & up	130	130	130	130	130	130	130	130	130	130	130	130
1 mile	2	x	x	x	x	x	x	x	x	96	99	102	102
	3	107	107	111	111	113	115	117	119	121	122	123	123
	4	127	127	128	128	127	126	126	126	126	126	126	126
	5 & up	128	128	128	128	127	126	126	126	126	126	126	126
1¼ miles	2	x	x	x	x	x	x	x	x	x	x	x	x
	3	101	101	107	107	111	113	116	118	120	121	122	122
	4	125	125	127	127	127	126	126	126	126	126	126	126
	5	127	127	127	127	127	126	126	126	126	126	126	126
1½ miles	2	x	x	x	x	x	x	x	x	x	x	x	x
	3	98	98	104	104	108	111	114	117	119	121	122	122
	4	124	124	126	126	126	126	126	126	126	126	126	126
	5 & up	126	126	126	126	126	126	126	126	126	126	126	126
2 miles	2	x	x	x	x	x	x	x	x	x	x	x	x
	3	96	96	102	102	106	109	112	114	117	119	120	120
	4	124	124	126	126	126	126	126	125	125	124	124	124
	5 & up	126	126	126	126	126	126	126	125	125	124	124	124

CHAMPIONS BY SEASONS, CLASSIFIED AS TO CATEGORY

Year	Two-year-old Male	Two-year-old Female	Three-year-old Male	Three-year-old Female	Handicap Division Male
1936	Pompoon (1,2)	Apogee (2)	Granville (1,2)		Discovery (1)
1937	Menow (1,2)	Jacola (2)	War Admiral (1,2)		Seabiscuit (1)
1938	El Chico (1,2)	Inscoelda (1,2)	Stagehand (1,2)		Seabiscuit (1,2)
1939	Bimelech (1,2)	Now What (1,2)	Challedon (1,2)	Unerring (1)	Kayak II (1,2)
1940	Our Boots (1) Whirlaway (2)	Level Best (1,2)	Bimelech (1,2)		Challedon (1,2)
1941	Alsab (1,2)	Petrify (1,2)	Whirlaway (1,2)	Painted Veil (1)	Mioland (1) Big Pebble (2)
1942	Count Fleet (1,2)	Askmenow (1,2)	Alsab (1,2)	Vagrancy (1)	Whirlaway (1-tie, 2)
1943	Platter (1) Occupy (2)	Durazna (1) Twilight Tear (2)	Count Fleet (1,2)	Stefanita (1)	Market Wise (1,2) Devil Diver (1-tie)
1944	Pavot (1,2)	Busher (1,2)	By Jimminy (1)	Twilight Tear (1,2)	Devil Diver (1,2)
1945	Star Pilot (1,2)	Beaugay (1,2)	Fighting Step (1)	Busher (1,2)	Stymie (1,2)
1946	Double Jay (1) Education (2)	First Flight (1,2)	Assault (1,2)	Bridal Flower (1)	Armed (1,2)
1947	Citation (1,2)	Bewitch (1,2)	Phalanx (1,2)	But Why Not (1)	Armed (1,2)
1948	Blue Peter (1,2)	Myrtle Charm (1,2)	Citation (1,2)	Miss Request (1)	Citation (1) Shannon II (2)
1949	Hill Prince (1) Oil Capitol (2)	Bed o' Roses (1,2)	Capot (1,2)	Two Lea (1-tie)* Wistful (1-tie)	Coaltown (1,2)
1950	Battlefield (1,2,3)	Aunt Jinny (1,2,3)	Hill Prince (1,2,3)	Next Move (1,3)	Noor (1,2,3)
1951	Tom Fool (1,2,3)	Rose Jet (1,2,3)	Counterpoint (1,2,3)	Kiss Me Kate (1,3)	Hill Prince (1,3) Citation (2)
1952	Native Dancer (1,2,3)	Sweet Patootie (1,2,3)	One Count (1,2,3)	Real Delight (1,3)	Crafty Admiral (1,2,3)
1953	Porterhouse (1,3) Hasty Road (2)	Evening Out (1,2,3)	Native Dancer (1,2,3)	Grecian Queen (1,3)	Tom Fool (1,2,3)
1954	Nashua (1,2,3,4)	High Voltage (1,2,3,4)	High Gun (1,2,3) Determine (4)	Parlo (1,3,4)	Native Dancer (1,2,3) Social Outcast (4)
1955	Needles (1,3) Nail (2,4)	Doubledogdare (1,2) Nasrina (3,4)	Nashua (1,2,3,4)	Misty Morn (1,3) High Voltage (4)	High Gun (1,2,3) Social Outcast (4)
1956	Barbizon (1,2,3) Greek Game (4)	Leallah (1,2,4) Romanita (3)	Needles (1,2,3,4)	Doubledogdare (1,3) Levee (4)	Swaps (1,2,3,4)
1957	Jewel's Reward (2,3,4) Nadir (1)	Idun (1,2,3,4)	Bold Ruler (1,2,3) Round Table (4)	Bayou (1,3,4)	Dedicate (1,2,3) Swoon's Son (4)
1958	First Landing (1,2,3,4)	Quill (1,2,3,4)	Tim Tam (1,2,3,4)	Idun (1,3) A Glitter (4)	Round Table (1,2,3,4)
1959	Warfare (1,2,3,4)	My Dear Girl (1,2,3,4)	Sword Dancer (1,2,3,4)	Silver Spoon (3,4) Royal Native (1)	Round Table (2,3) Sword Dancer (1) Hillsdale (4)
1960	Hail to Reason (1,2,3,4)	Bowl of Flowers (1,2,3,4)	Kelso (1,2,3) Bally Ache (4)	Berlo (1,2,3,4)	Bald Eagle (1,2,3,4)
1961	Crimson Satan (1,3) Ridan (2) Sir Gaylord (4)	Cicada (1,2,3,4)	Carry Back (1,2,3,4)	Bowl of Flowers (1,3,4)	Kelso (1,2,3,4)
1962	Never Bend (1,2,3,4)	Smart Deb (1,3) Affectionately (2,4)	Jaipur (1,2,3,4)	Cicada (1,2,3,4)	Kelso (1,2,3) Prove It (4)
1963	Hurry to Market (1,3) Raise a Native (2) Malicious (4)	Tosmah (1,2) Castle Forbes (3,4)	Chateaugay (1,2,3) Candy Spots (4)	Lamb Chop (1,2,3,4)	Kelso (1,2,3,4)

Key: 1—Triangle Publications, Inc., by poll among staff of *Daily Racing Form* and *Morning Telegraph*.

2—*Turf and Sports Digest*, by poll among selected sports writers and sportscasters. Fillies and mares, 3-year-olds and up, included in 1 category; added in 1960.

3—Thoroughbred Racing Associations, Inc., by poll among racing secretaries at member tracks.

4—*Thoroughbred Record*, by a mathematical scoring system in which points are awarded for stakes victories only.

Female	Sprinter	Grass Horse	Steeplechaser	Horse of the Year
	Myrtlewood (1)		Bushranger (1)	Granville (1,2)
			Jungle King (1)	War Admiral (1,2)
Marica (1)				Seabiscuit (1,2)
Lady Maryland (1)				Challedon (1,2)
War Plumage (1)				Challedon (1,2)
Fairy Chant (1)			Speculate (1)	Whirlaway (1,2)
Vagrancy (1)			Elkridge (1)	Whirlaway (1,2)
Mar-Kell (1)			Brother Jones (1)	Count Fleet (1,2)
Twilight Tear (1)			Rouge Dragon (1)	Twilight Tear (1,2)
Busher (1)			Mercator (1)	Busher (1,2)
Gallorette (1)			Elkridge (1)	Assault (1,2)
But Why Not (1)	Polynesian (1)		War Battle (1)	Armed (1,2)
Conniver (1)	Coaltown (1)		American Way (1)	Citation (1,2)
Bewitch (1)	Delegate (1-tie)*		Trough Hill (1)	Capot (1)
	Royal Governor (1,tie)			Coaltown (2)
Two Lea (1,3)	Sheilas Reward (1)		Oedipus (1,3)	Hill Prince (1,2,3)
Bed o' Roses (1,3)	Sheilas Reward (1)		Oedipus (1,3)	Counterpoint (1,2,3)
Real Delight (1)	Tea-Maker (1)		Jam (1)	Native Dancer (2,3)
Next Move (3)			Oedipus (3)	One Count (1)
Sickle's Image (1,3)	Tom Fool (1)	Iceberg II (1)	The Mast (1,3)	Tom Fool (1,2,3)
Lavender Hill (3,4)	White Skies (1)	Stan (1)	King Commander (1,3)	Native Dancer (1,2,3)
Parlo (1)				Determine (4)
Parlo (3,4)	Berseem (1)	St. Vincent (1)	Neji (1,3)	Nashua (1,2,3,4)
Misty Morn (1)				
Blue Sparkler (1,3,4)	Decathlon (1)	Career Boy (1)	Shipboard (1,3)	Swaps (1,2,3,4)
Pucker Up (1,3,4)	Decathlon (1)	Round Table (1)	Neji (1,3)	Bold Ruler (1,2)
				Dedicate (3)
				Round Table (4)
Bornastar (1,3,4)	Bold Ruler (1)	Round Table (1)	Neji (1,3)	Round Table (1,2,3,4)
Tempted (1,3,4-tie)	Intentionally (1)	Round Table (1)	Ancestor (1,3)	Sword Dancer (1,2,3)
Bug Brush (4-tie)				Hillsdale (4)
Royal Native (1,3,4)			Benguala (1,3)	Kelso (1,2,3)
				Bally Ache (4)
Airmans Guide (1,2,3,4)		T.V. Lark (1)	Peal (1,3)	Kelso (1,2,3,4)
Primonetta (1,3)			Barnabys Bluff (1,3)	Kelso (1,2,3)
Seven Thirty (4)				Prove It (4)
Cicada (1,3)				
Oil Royalty (4)		Mongo (1)	Amber Diver (1,3)	Kelso (1,2,3,4)

Notes: *Note tie in Poll No. 1.

In 1943, Market Wise and Devil tied for best handicap male in Poll No. 1 and Market Wise also was voted champion (by himself) in Poll No. 2.

In 1944, Devil Diver won both polls.

In 1949, Two Lea and Wistful tied for best three-year-old filly in Poll No. 1.

In 1949, Royal Governor and Delegate tied for best sprinter in Poll No. 1.

In 1957, Bold Ruler was Horse of the Year in Polls Nos. 1 and 2; Dedicate was Horse of the Year only in Poll No. 3.

INDEX

Numbers in parentheses denote the page on which the horse's breeding is listed.
Names of horses are set in italics.

604

610

612

616

618

620